W9-AOM-117

"COMPREHENSIVE . . . covers most of the common problems which concern parents. Its encyclopedic nature and the specific practical advice it gives will make it helpful to many."
—Dr. Louise Bates Ames, Associate Director, Gesell Institute of Human Development

"AN IMMENSELY PRACTICAL MANUAL."
—*Psychotherapy and Social Science Review*

"COMPASSIONATE, EASY-TO-READ, WELL ORGANIZED . . . PACKED WITH IMPORTANT, USEFUL INFORMATION FOR PARENTS."
—Jean Hall, Science/Medical Editor, *Gannet Westchester Newspapers*

CHARLES E. SCHAEFER, Ph.D, has written fourteen books, including *Teach Your Baby to Sleep Through the Night,* and is Director of the Crying Baby Clinic at Fairleigh Dickinson University.

HOWARD L. MILLMAN, Ph.D, is director of psychological services at the Children's Village in Dobbs Ferry, New York. He has written three books.

Ø **SIGNET** (0451)

PARENTING WISDOM

☐ **CHILDRENS MEDICINE: A PARENT'S GUIDE TO PRESCRIPTION AND OVER-THE-COUNTER DRUGS by Ann and James Kepler with Ira Salafsky, M.D.** A clear, concise guide for today's parents faced with a confusing array of prescriptions and over-the-counter drugs for children. With drug profiles, a listing of side effects, cautions and restrictions, and interactions with other drugs, this guide will help you make an informed decision about any trade or generic drug you give your child.
(146549—$3.95)

☐ **COPING WITH TEENAGE DEPRESSION, A Parents' Guide by Kathleen McCoy.** Shows parents how to prevent the depression that commonly underlies so-called normal teenage rebellion. There is practical advice on communicating and listening carefully, and on sending out messages of respect and support to troubled young adults. (136632—$4.50)*

☐ **HOW TO HELP CHILDREN WITH COMMON PROBLEMS by Charles E. Schaefer, Ph.D. and Howard L. Millman, Ph.D.** A practical guide to child care, from toddlerhood to adolescence, which gives the widest possible range of strategies for dealing with your child. "Down-to-earth advice for effectively coping with everyday problems"—American Orthopsychiatric Association (152247—$4.95)

☐ **SOLO PARENTING: YOUR ESSENTIAL GUIDE *How to Find the Balance Between Parenthood & Personhood* by Kathleen McCoy.** In this comprehensive sourcebook, the author talks with over one hundred solo parents, as well as dozens of professionals, and offers ideas for coping with the tough issues facing single parents. Listings of counseling services, hotline and support organizations. (259002—$8.95)

*Prices slightly higher in Canada

Buy them at your local bookstore or use this convenient coupon for ordering.

NEW AMERICAN LIBRARY
P.O. Box 999, Bergenfield, New Jersey 07621

Please send me the books I have checked above. I am enclosing $_____
(please add $1.00 to this order to cover postage and handling). Send check or money order—no cash or C.O.D.'s. Prices and numbers are subject to change without notice.

Name_____

Address_____

City _____ State _____ Zip Code _____
Allow 4-6 weeks for delivery.
This offer is subject to withdrawal without notice.

HOW TO HELP CHILDREN WITH COMMON PROBLEMS

Charles E. Schaefer, Ph.D. and Howard L. Millman, Ph.D.

A SIGNET BOOK

NEW AMERICAN LIBRARY

*To the alleviation of problem behaviors in children
and the promotion of satisfying family living.*

Publisher's Note

The ideas, procedures, and suggestions contained in this book are not intended as a substitute for consulting with your physician. All matters regarding your health require medical supervision.

NAL BOOKS ARE AVAILABLE AT QUANTITY DISCOUNTS WHEN USED TO PROMOTE PRODUCTS OR SERVICES. FOR INFORMATION PLEASE WRITE TO PREMIUM MARKETING DIVISION, NEW AMERICAN LIBRARY, 1633 BROADWAY, NEW YORK, NEW YORK 10019.

Copyright © 1981 by Litton Educational Publishing, Inc.

All rights reserved. No part of this work covered by the copyright hereon may be reproduced or used in any form or by any means—graphic, electronic, or mechanical, including photocopying, recording, taping, or information storage and retrieval system—without permission of the publisher. For information address Van Nostrand Reinhold Company, 135 West 50th Street, New York, New York 10020.

This is an authorized reprint of a hardcover edition published by Van Nostrand Reinhold Company. The hardcover edition was published simultaneously in Canada by Van Nostrand Reinhold Ltd.

How to Help Children with Common Problems previously appeared in a Plume edition published by New American Library.

SIGNET TRADEMARK REG U.S. PAT OFF AND FOREIGN COUNTRIES
REGISTERED TRADEMARK—MARCA REGISTRADA
HECHO EN CHICAGO, U.S.A.

SIGNET, SIGNET CLASSIC, MENTOR, ONYX, PLUME, MERIDIAN and NAL BOOKS are published by NAL PENGUIN INC., 1633 Broadway, New York, New York 10019.

First Signet Printing, March, 1988

1 2 3 4 5 6 7 8 9

PRINTED IN THE UNITED STATES OF AMERICA

Acknowledgments

We are indebted to our wives, Anne Schaefer and Judith Millman, for their support and helpful suggestions throughout all phases of this book. Special thanks go to Phyllis Saccone for her clerical and administrative assistance with the manuscript. The interest, encouragement, and advice of Eugene Falken, Vice President, Van Nostrand Reinhold Co., were also much appreciated.

A Word about Pronouns

The English language does not make it easy for us to talk about a child without indicating whether it's a "him" or a "her." To solve this difficulty, we decided to arbitrarily alternate, using *he* one time and *she* another time when what we had to say applied to children of either sex. Please consider that the child mentioned is the one you have in mind, even though the sex reference doesn't always agree.

Contents

Preface

It's tough to be a parent. At times all parents feel harassed, worried, confused, and bewildered. It is little wonder, then, that studies have shown that parents want professional advice and support in bringing up their children and are delighted when such assistance is provided. The purpose of this book is to provide parents and other adults with useful information and strategies for dealing with the everyday problems of normal children from early childhood through adolesence. We have attempted to present practical methods for resolving a wide variety of specific behavior problems such as lying, stealing, shyness, overactivity, and bedwetting. Beyond the scope of this volume are extremely abnormal or bizarre behaviors, and behaviors associated with mental retardation or other physical problems. The behavior problems in this book are grouped into six general categories: Immature Behaviors; Insecure Behaviors; Habit Disorders; Peer and Sibling Problems; Antisocial Behaviors; and Other Behaviors (sex, drug, and school difficulties).

Surveys of parents concerning the raising of children have revealed that they want a book with three main features: (1) a professionally sound book written in nontechnical language, (2) a book that gives practical answers to practical questions, and (3) a book where answers would be found without a lengthy search. In writing this book we have tried to meet these criteria while combining good science with good common sense. We also endeavored to make the book comprehensive (covering a wide variety of problems), up-to-date (incorporating the latest research findings), and non-doctrinaire (open to many useful approaches).

We were motivated to write a book for parents after we completed a book for professionals—*Therapies for Chil-*

dren: A Handbook of Effective Treatments for Problem Behaviors. We realized that the many effective ways of changing children's behavior could be translated into concrete action that parents might take. This book is our way of making the most effective, scientifically-based methods available to parents.

Other unique features of this practical reference book include sections describing the common causes of childhood problems as well as ways to prevent problems from occurring, illustrative case reports, and recommended readings for parents and children.

Apart from parents and parents-to-be, this book should be of interest to a wide range of professionals who work with children, including teachers, child care counselors, psychologists, psychiatrists, social workers, recreation specialists, and nurses. It would also be appropriate for courses on childrearing, child therapy, and management of childhood behavior problems.

CHARLES E. SCHAEFER, PH.D.
HOWARD L. MILLMAN, PH.D.

Dobbs Ferry, N.Y.

Introduction—
Behavior Problems of Children

It is generally recognized that all children go through periods of emotional and behavior difficulty. Indeed, data from the California Growth Study[1] show that both boys and girls average five to six problems at any given time during the preschool and elementary-school years. The prevalence of these behavior difficulties declines with age for school-age children. Thus, younger children, ages 6 through 8, by far exceed older children, ages 9 through 12, in the number of behavior deviations. Moreover, boys have a higher incidence of behavior problems than do girls. Also noteworthy is the finding that there seems to be very little difference in the amount of problem behaviors exhibited by only children and children with siblings.

Although common, the problems of normal children should not be considered unimportant by parents and therefore left to self-resolution. These problems need to be confronted and effectively resolved since neglect or mismanagement can lead to more serious difficulties. Parents tend to find rationalizations for avoiding taking any action when their child has a behavior problem.

The most common rationalizations are:

1. The problem is being exaggerated and is actually much milder than the person who is pressuring the parents to seek help believes it to be.
2. It will go away with time.
3. Taking action might in some way damage the child's sensitive nature or paradoxically make matters worse by "making the child think about it more."
4. The child "by nature" is destined to have the problem and nothing can be done.

NORMAL vs. ABNORMAL BEHAVIOR

When is a child's behavior problem so severe or abnormal that professional help is needed? Anna Freud, who is carrying on the work of her father, Sigmund Freud, once wrote that "the demarcation line between mental health and illness is even more difficult to draw in childhood than in later stages." The difference between normal and abnormal behaviors is one of *degree,* that is, how often and how frequently does the behavior cause a problem for the child, the parents, and/or the community. If the discomfort to the child and/or others is quite frequent or very severe in nature then professional counseling or therapy for the child and family may be warranted.

The more misbehaviors the child exhibits, the less age-appropriate the behavior, the longer the duration of the problem, and the more resistant the child has been to efforts to help him, the more likely it is that professional assistance is required to solve the problem.

Apart from the severity, persistence, and resistance to change of a problem, there are certain signs to look for which indicate that a child is experiencing serious psychological difficulties:

1. Prolonged, constant anxiety, apprehension, or fear which is not proportionate to reality.
2. Signs of depression, such as a growing apathy and withdrawal from people.
3. An abrupt change in a child's mood or behavior so that he just does not seem to be himself anymore. For example, a very considerate and reliable child suddenly acts irresponsibly, self-preoccupied, and hostile to others.
4. Sleep disturbances, such as sleeping too much, not being able to sleep enough, restless or nightmarish sleep, not being able to get to sleep, or waking up early.
5. Appetite disturbances, including loss of appetite, gain of weight due to excessive eating, or eating bizarre substances such as dirt or garbage.
6. Disturbances in sexual functioning, such as promiscuity, exposing oneself, or excessive masturbation.

The research[2] indicates that when parents are concerned about a serious behavior problem in their children, they are most likely to turn to their extended family for advice and assistance. The second most frequent source of help they look to is local mental health professionals, school counselors, family doctors, and the clergy. These highly trained professionals are available locally, and parents should feel free to seek their services when problems arise or to answer questions. To obtain a therapist for their child, parents might want to ask the family doctor for a referral, or call the local mental health or family service association.

PARENTS AS HELPERS

There is a growing body of evidence indicating that parents, with a little guidance from professionals, can successfully resolve a number of problem behaviors in their children.[3] Unfortunately, a great deal of useful information, whether from the scientific literature or from the experience of other parents, is not received by parents. Some child-rearing techniques for specific problems are potentially more effective than others, although much more research is needed. Among the more promising techniques for helping children with their problems are:[4]

1. Rearranging the child's schedule.
2. Rewarding desired behaviors.
3. Reassuring the child by being supportive.
4. Ignoring misbehavior by paying absolutely no attention to it.

Since all children are individuals, there is no universal or simple formula for resolving their complex behavior problems. It seems wise, then, for parents to become skilled in a number of the more effective ways of helping children. In this way they are likely to increase the probability of their finding the approach that works best for their particular child. In light of the above, the authors of this book have followed a pragmatic rather than dogmatic orientation and present several different ways to solve each childhood problem. Einstein once replied when he was asked how he worked, "I grope." Hopefully, this guidebook will help parents grope in the right direction.

REFERENCES

1. Mac Farlane, J. *et al.*: *A Developmental Study of the Behavior Problems of Normal Children Between Twenty-one Months and Fourteen Years*. University of California Press, Berkeley (1954).

2. Fandetti, D.V. and Gelfand, D.E.: "Attitudes towards symptoms and services in the ethnic family and neighborhood." *American Journal of Orthopsychiatry* 48: (1978), pp. 477–486.

3. Reisinger, J.J. *et al.*: "Parents as change agents for their children: A review." *Journal of Community Psychology* 4:(1976), pp. 103–123.

4. Mesibov, G.B.: "Effectiveness of several intervention strategies with some common child rearing problems." Paper presented at the meeting of the American Psychological Association, San Francisco (August 1977).

HOW TO
HELP CHILDREN
WITH COMMON
PROBLEMS

1

Immature Behaviors

The immature child has not developed behaviorally, psychologically, intellectually, or socially according to some accepted standard. Most usual is the criterion of "average" as defined by peers and adults. Therefore, if a child shows a lag in any area of development, he or she may be labeled as "immature." The behavior is viewed as being more characteristic of the behavior of a younger child. Many children develop unevenly. They may be very mature in one area and very immature in another. For example, a child might be very neat, organized, and show great self-control in school. Yet at home she might be overly dependent, messy, and complaining. A frequent problem is that parents may label children as immature, when in fact they are as mature as other children of that age but do not meet the parents' personal expectations. Also, children may be relatively mature and occasionally regress under some form of stress to more childish behavior. A significant point is that the more infantile behavior such as whining or complaining usually ceases when the stress is over. Criticism of the immature reaction usually serves to intensify the problem. Emotional support and encouragement enables the child to weather the storm, give up the babyish behavior, and resume her usual relatively more effective way of coping.

This chapter covers the most typical immature behaviors. A global behavior such as general immaturity is not covered. Following the plan of this book, specific problem behaviors are described, and specific approaches are offered. Therefore, a parent complaining that a child is immature has to say *how* that child behaves. If a child clowns, daydreams, and uses time poorly, then those three immature behaviors may be dealt with. Otherwise, parents wind up using general approaches which are often ineffective in changing behavior. The behaviors covered are hyperactive, impulsive, short-attention-span-distracted, silly-clowning, daydreaming, messy-sloppy, time-used-poorly, selfish-self-centered, overdependent, and whining-complaining. These behaviors are often seen as indicators of an inability of the child to cope with the demands of a variety of situations. The demands or expectations of peers and adults for a child to act maturely or age-appropriately are often not met by a large number of children. This chapter will describe typical instances of immature behavior and suggest methods to prevent or promote more mature behavior. Coping more adequately leads others to be more satisfied with a child's behavior and leads to the child feeling more self-satisfied or having a better "self-image." Overcoming specific problems paves the way for achieving more self-confidence, independence, and satisfying social relationships.

It is worth noting some general ideas about emotional maturity. Mature children are relatively flexible and respond to some degree, rather than all or none. They are able to delay their reaction rather than have to act immediately. Their ability to tolerate tension should gradually increase. By school age, they should be able to tolerate and handle minor everyday stress without exploding or falling to pieces. Promoting maturity and preventing immature behavior may be accomplished by the following (see the individual sections for specific details). Teach children how to focus their attention, solve problems, delay gratification, effectively use their time, accept responsibility, and give and get attention. Socially, you model and encourage concern, consideration, and sensitivity to others. Each day, children should feel relatively competent, self-accepting, and have a sense of personal satisfaction.

HYPERACTIVE

Excessive physical movement (beyond a normal or acceptable limit) is termed hyperactivity. Reasonably objective parents can recognize when the amount and degree of activity (constant and involuntary) is different than that of peers of the same sex. When in doubt, a visit to a classroom or recreational setting for children of the same age can be illuminating. Requesting a friend to observe and provide objective information regarding comparative activity levels is especially helpful. A very useful concept is that hyper-activity is indicated by the inappropriateness and undirect-ness of the activity, as compared to the very active but purposeful and productive child. Practical indicators to par-ents are the frequent reports of the child "being all over the place" and "climbing the walls" in various settings and the frequent failure to complete tasks in spite of much activity. They rarely sit still and their "motor is always running."

Studies have shown there to be far more hyperactivity among boys and among children from "economically dis-advantaged" groups. It must be noted that high activity lev-els are typical in children who are normal 2 and 3 year olds, mentally aged 2 or 3, highly exploratory and very intelli-gent, overly nagged by adults, and environmentally de-prived.[1] Most studies have found that 5 to 10 percent of all children are hyperactive. Approximately 40 percent of chil-dren referred to mental health clinics are hyperactive.[2] Maturation often brings some reduction in activity by the teen-age years, but some hyperactivity and poor concentra-tion can persist throughout adulthood.

Reasons Why

Constitutional temperament is an important concept, since some children appear very active from birth. Genetic factors are considered to be highly significant in producing hyper-activity. Hyperactivity often accompanies epilepsy and au-tism, but a large number of hyperactive children are thought to have a subtle brain dysfunction that causes the purpose-less excessive movement. Blows to the head and poisoning can cause hyperactivity. In addition, environmental influ-ences serve to reinforce or reduce hyperactive behaviors. As discussed in the following section, adult responses can both cause or exaggerate hyperactivity in children and be used to promote purposeful activity. Parents can obtain in-formation on possible causes of hyperactivity (as well as names of diagnostic centers that evaluate children) from the Association for Children with Learning Disabilities, 4156 Library Road, Pittsburgh, PA 15234.

It is essential to evaluate the specific cause of hyperac-tivity in a child. Pediatric and psychological testing are crucial, and the ideal evaluation may be obtained at a multi-disciplinary diagnostic center. On one hand, awareness of the neurological basis for hyperactivity often leads to a more understanding and tolerant attitude by adults. Rather than blaming the child for purposefully bothering everyone, the focus can be on aiding the child in slowing down and effectively coping with an organically caused problem. Secondly, there are relatively rare instances where electrical brain malfunctioning, endocrine disturbances, and tumors are causing excessive activity. In those rare instances, it is essential that the correct diagnosis is made and that the best medical treatment be carried out. There is much recent controversy over nutritional and allergic causes of hyperactivity. Many allergists claim that specific substances can cause a hyperactive reaction in children. The controversial Feingold diet[3] eliminates foods with artificial flavoring, aspirin, and salicylate (a type of salt). Most parents find it extremely difficult to keep their child from eating ice cream, soft drinks, bakery products, and a variety of fruits and vegetables. At this writing scientific evidence has not demonstrated the effectiveness of these claims.

How to Prevent

Promote a Healthy Environment. Numerous studies have clearly demonstrated that the physical and mental condition of the pregnant mother affects activity level and concentration of her child. During pregnancy, various diseases, drugs, and prolonged and intense stress have been associated with later hyperactivity in the toddler. Adequate maternal nutrition and drug (alcohol, cigarettes, tranquilizers, marijuana, etc.) abstention is the best assurance of a normal prenatal environment. Recently, there is growing evidence of a link between hyperactivity (and other learning and behavior problems) and method of delivery. Use of forceps and heavy doses of drugs have been implicated in causing the combination of hyperactivity, impulsivity, and distractedness in some children. There is a growing belief that the "natural" childbirth methods are the best means of avoiding physical insults to the newborn's central nervous system. Similarly, adequate nutrition, protection, and sensory stimulation of the infant assure maximum development. Even in the crib, infant studies demonstrate the positive effects on maturation of mobiles and toys of different textures. As the child matures, excessive stimulation (noise level, constant arguing, messy and disorganized environment) or inadequate stimulation (deprivation of play materials and other normal experiences) is to be avoided. Normal and purposeful activity is maximized by a normal and relatively organized environment. Since there is a strong relationship between nagging and hyperactivity, nagging of the child is to be avoided. A typical problem is the nagging of a child who is temperamentally different than the parents. Some acceptance and accommodation to the child's natural tempo will prevent problems.

Teach Purposeful Activity. Parents underestimate the powerful effect of their consistent teaching of purposeful behavior. From infancy on, parents can *positively reinforce* (see following section) purposeful activity. Attention and praise for any accomplishment of the infant and toddler strengthen effective behavior. In the same vein, parents and siblings serve as *models* of the ability to focus upon, and complete, tasks. Early observational learning sets the tone for focused behavior. Throughout childhood, the parents' level of (and effectiveness of) activity serves as a model to be imitated by the developing child. Similarly, parents can demonstrate the use of language as a guide for purposeful behavior ("I must finish this and then I'll rest"). Language also serves as a self-monitoring device ("This isn't finished properly, so I'll fix it").

What to Do

Verbal Reinforcement of Appropriate Behavior. The opposite of hyperactivity is an appropriate level of activity, especially purposeful or productive activity. Parents should strive to point out any productive behavior and try to *catch* the child doing well ("Terrific, you are carefully finishing the job"). When a child sits still, pays attention, and completes a task, the parent could say, "How nice that you sat still and finished it." Daily goals can be specified, and the child's efforts to reach these goals should be praised ("You really tried harder to sit still during dinner"). At the end of a day, the child may be told about his improved efforts at calmer, more purposeful activity. At times, it may be necessary for the parent to *demonstrate* (or model) appropriate, purposeful activity. When the child then imitates the parents' behavior, positive statements (or concrete rewards) should follow immediately. The modeling and praising may have to be frequently *repeated*. With younger children, immediate praise and short-term rewards work best. With older children and teenagers, long-term rewards and written contracts[4] work very well.

Contracts. Homme[5] lists basic rules for contingency contracting (an agreement to give rewards in return for desirable behavior). If the child does what you want him to, *then* he gets to do something that he wants. The reward should be frequent, small, and immediate and for actual accomplishments rather than for "obedience." Initial contracts should approximate the final behavior desired. The contract should be clear, fair, and attainable. Contracts must be adhered to, and the unwanted behaviors should never be reinforced.

A contract may specify that better behavior or completion of specific tasks will result in rewards or privileges. The sample contract below uses a chart to illustrate the process of counting behaviors so the child or teenager sees the process as clear and fair. Many contracts can be written without charts. For example, a teenager might sign: "I agree to be calmer in school and complete all homework assignments. If my teacher gives a positive report after 2 months from today, you will buy the phonograph for me that we agreed upon." The parent and teacher discuss the degree of improvement necessary for a positive report. Noticeably less excessive movement and completion of all assignments would be appropriate improvement.

SAMPLE CONTRACT

I agree that I will earn 10¢ extra allowance each day and a surprise event during the weekend if I sit more quietly during dinner and finish my chores.

Signed _____

Parent _____

	Mon	Tues	Wed	Thurs	Fri
1) Make bed and be ready on time in morning					
2) Take out all garbage before dinner					
3) Sit still at dinner					

One check mark is earned for each task. Sitting still is earned by parental assessment of improvement, while items 1 and 2 are checked at the appropriate time. More than 10 checks during the week result in a surprise weekend event (bowling, movies, visiting relatives, etc.). Arguments about checks are not allowed. A check mark might also be deducted as a penalty (arguing might cost one check mark).

Point System. Similar to using contracts, many parents find that a system of just placing check marks on a chart or giving poker chips is useful in showing children when their activity is appropriate.[6] These earned check marks or chips might be traded in for small toys, extra privileges, going on special trips, etc. Check marks are earned for set, realistic intervals of time at home when the child does not exhibit hyperactivity. A powerful method is to have the teacher use the same system in class. Since behavior is often specific to given situations, this type of method may also be used while the child is in a public place with the parents. It is very useful for parents to carry a notebook and record earned checks. The checks or rewards should immediately follow appropriate behavior, and no consequences (ignoring) should follow hyperactive behavior. If necessary, unusual hyperactivity might result in some loss of earned points.

Points, tokens, or checks are useful since they immediately follow behavior and the child does not stop an activity to consume or look at the tokens. Most significantly, points can be used for different kinds of behavior, and the payoff rate is changed as the child's behavior improves. Also, the kinds of rewards earned by token accumulation may be changed and tailored to the parents ' philosophy. Some parents believe that allowances should be earned by accumulating tokens, while others are adamantly against using money. Special events, extra privileges, more independence, etc., may be used as earned rewards. A point system may be essential for those children who are not responsive to praise. The system must be consistent and points given only for the specified behaviors. Children must be able to immediately earn a minimum amount of tokens. And, great effort and achievement must result in more tokens and a more valuable reward. It is essential to appropriately tailor rewards to the age and interests of the child.

SAMPLE POINT SYSTEM PROGRAM

Behavior	*Earn*
Not leaving seat without permission	One token every 10 minutes
Completing tasks	Two tokens for each assignment or chore completed without help or reminders

The program is designed for both home and school. For every 10 minutes when the child does not leave his seat (at school or during mealtime at home or in a restaurant), one token is given to him. With progress, the length of time is increased. Independent completion of a task or chore results in two tokens. The child collects the tokens and can purchase small toys and extra privileges that are tailored to his interests. Some examples would be small toy cars costing ten tokens, staying up a half-hour later for 15 tokens, treated to a movie or bowling for 25 tokens, etc. The principle is that the child's improved behavior should result in earning rewards at a reasonable rate. Too many or not enough rewards indicates that the system was not designed properly, and adjustments in expectations and/or costs should be made. When the child is relatively able to remain in his seat and able to complete assignments independently, the system is discontinued. Many parents then use other behaviors so that the child can still earn rewards by improving different problem behaviors. However, a useful method is a "success party" where the tokens are put away because the child has succeeded and the method is no longer necessary. It is essential that the same types of rewards and privileges are still available through natural means such as allowance or presents.

Provide Structure. The child must know clearly what is *expected.* Without anger, the parent should state very clearly and descriptively what behavior is appropriate: "Jumping from one thing to another stops you from finishing that lovely picture." "Sticking to that drawing until it's finished would be terrific." "When you feel wound up, you can calm down by breathing deeply and looking out the window." Positive reinforcement, previously discussed, is a concrete way of showing the child what behavior is expected. When parents are relatively *consistent* and *predictable*, the hyperactive child feels safer and calmer. Both parents must basically agree to respond to the child in a similar fashion. Therefore, the child learns that positive responses from both parents follow less random, more purposeful activity.

Preparing a child before an event takes place may be very helpful. Before entering a department store the parent might state: "There will be a lot of noise and many people; you can stay with me and feel calm. Children are not allowed to touch things. You can hold this toy." When the parent is in a department, the child might sit and complete a dot-to-dot book or read a new and interesting book. The key is the use of good strategies which prepare the child to focus on an activity and which structures time for him until he learns to do so independently.

At home, distractions can be minimized by aiding the child to *organize* his room. Desks should be cleared of tempting, unnecessary objects. Places for possessions should be designated and labeled (for young children). The initial task of organizing should be a family activity, where everyone helps in a positive, relaxed atmosphere. Very useful is the procedure of telling the young child to carefully observe a sibling or peer who is a *good model.* Watching a constructive, efficient sister can teach a valuable lesson. Children often do well at this type of observational learning.

The idea is that vicarious learning (by observing others) is very powerful. Comparing the child to the "better" sibling is definitely to be avoided. Observational learning is facilitated by a positive atmosphere, where watching a good model is seen as fun. Do not use this method if the child is generally angry or resentful. If the child is receptive and likes the idea of learning to calm down and be more effective, then watching others may be a very useful tool.

At home, there should be planned periods of exercise.

Gymnasium equipment (including a punching bag) in a cleared basement or room with a mat may be a lifesaver for both the child and the parents. Good strategy might be for 15 minutes of exercise while dinner is being prepared. When the child is "hyped up," a controlled release of energy is a good strategy. The child learns to focus his energy in a nonharmful way. Additionally he should be told about the beneficial aspect of building his strength and endurance. Household tasks requiring energy (shoveling snow, cleaning an attic, stacking wood, etc.) should be assigned, and some form of payment may be helpful. Planned periods of relaxation are also useful. Again, the key is to provide structure by specific suggestions such as listening to favorite music while relaxing for 15 minutes. Kitchen timers are invaluable for helping the child to keep track of time.

Promote Self-control. Of the many methods possible, *self-talk* is one of the most powerful. The child is taught to talk to himself in order to guide his own behavior. Rather than moving purposelessly, he is taught to tell himself (first aloud and then silently) what to do. ("I want to finish this. So, I'll pay attention and play later.") He can be reminded to say to himself, "Stop and think." When parents observe hyperactivity, a pleasant reminder can be made to say a key phrase in the child's own language ("Calm down," "What should I be doing?", etc.). It is crucial for the parent to note the child's actual ability to calm down and engage in purposeful activity. Verbal praise ("That was great, you calmed yourself down") should follow, in addition to check marks when necessary. (See section on Impulsivity for further details.)

Any *self-monitoring* activity is helpful. A pedometer could be strapped on a leg and the child asked to reduce his daily mileage. With some children who love attention, praise for accomplishment suffices. For others, the previously discussed method of positive reinforcement should be employed. The child can be taught to record how many problems he can solve or how many blocks he can place in a box in a short time period. This serves to focus his attention and he learns the important concept of self-monitoring as compared to adult monitoring. Then he can evaluate his own accomplishments. For improvement over past performance, he can be taught to administer *self-rewards*. Completing tasks or doing more problems results in *his* deciding to reward himself by playing or reading a comic book for 10 minutes. The previously discussed kitchen timer is an excellent tool for self-monitoring.

In some instances, striking results are achieved through *excessive movement*. The parents get the child to consciously overdo the excessive involuntary behavior. When a child moves his arms or feet excessively, he can be asked immediately to perform exercises (like raising his arms up and down) for a few minutes. For unusual periods of restlessness, a child may be asked to run back and forth for 2 minutes. The basic idea is to interrupt the uncontrolled movement and gradually accomplish more voluntary control of activity. Essential for success is the positive attitude of the parents, who view this method as helpful (not as a punishment). Another means of achieving slower and more voluntary control is the practice of *motor inhibition*. The child is shown how to draw, place objects in a box, string beads, check off words, etc., in a *very slow, careful manner*. Success is measured by slowness and accuracy.

Professional Methods. Mental health professionals are now employing methods that may be sought when parental methods are not successful. Medically supervised drugs or dietary modification may be appropriate. Muscular relaxation, desensitization to stress, and various biofeedback methods (breathing, brain waves, muscle training) are promising treatments that have specific application with hyperactive children.

Case Report

An 8-year-old boy was hyperactive and rarely completed tasks. Results of psychological testing and neurological examination suggested a combination of some anxiety and constitutionally-based hyperactivity. The parents had tried various approaches, such as rewards for a good week, spankings for wildness, and traditional psychotherapy at a mental health clinic for 1 year.

Although he felt somewhat happier, he was still destructively hyperactive both at home and in school. Two parent interviews were held to set up a sophisticated method of positively reinforcing appropriate (purposeful and productive) behavior. A crucial step was to have the parents genuinely praise productive behavior and ignore hyperactivity. The parents' pattern of anger, scolding, and sarcasm had to be broken. Checks were entered in a notebook for purposeful behavior; extremely wild behavior resulted in a loss of two checks. Checks were not to be debated or discussed in any manner. More than five checks per day resulted in going to bed 15 minutes later. At least 25 checks per week resulted in a special event (bowling, movies, fishing, etc.) alone with his father. More structure was provided, especially by helping the boy organize his room and by the parents demonstrating how to finish various activities. A simple form of verbal self-instruction was successfully employed. Whenever he said, "I'll finish this and play later," his parents praised him. After 5 weeks a dramatic reduction in hyperactive behavior at home occurred.

More difficult was the classroom behavior. A meeting was required with one of the authors, the parents, the teacher, and the school psychologist. A plan was agreed upon for the school psychologist's secretary to let the mother know by telephone the daily number of checks earned. Gradually, more checks were earned, and notable improvement occurred after 2 months. The boy appeared less anxious, less hyperactive, and more able to complete tasks.

Books About Hyperactivity For Parents

Adler, Sidney J.: *Your Overactive Child—Normal or Not?* Medcom, New York (1972).

Cautela, Joseph R. and Groden, June: *Relaxation: A Comprehensive Manual for Adults, Children, and Children with Special Needs.* Research Press, Champaign, IL (1978).

Minde, Klaus: *A Parent's Guide to Hyperactivity in Children.* Quebec Association for Children with Learning Disabilities, Montreal (1971).

Reistroffer, Mary and McVey, Helen Z.: *Parental Survival and the Hyperactive Child.* University of Wisconsin, Madison, WI (1972).

Renshaw, Domeena C.: *The Hyperactive Child.* Nelson-Hall, Chicago (1974).

Safer, Daniel J. and Allen, Richard, P.: *Hyperactive Children: Diagnosis and Management.* University Park Press, Baltimore (1976).

Stewart, Mark A. and Olds, Sally W.: *Raising a Hyperactive Child*. Harper and Row, New York (1973).

Wender, Paul H.: *The Hyperactive Child: A Handbook for Parents*. Crown, New York (1973).

References

1. Cruickshank, W. P. and Hallahan, D. P. (eds.): *Perceptual and Learning Disabilities in Children, Vol. 2: Research and Theory*. Syracuse University Press, Syracuse (1975).

2. Wender, P. H.: *Minimal Brain Dysfunction in Children*. Wiley, New York (1971).

3. Feingold, Ben F.: *Why Your Child is Hyperactive*. Random House, New York (1975).

4. Dardig, Jill and Heward, William: *Sign Here: A Contracting Book for Children and Their Parents*. Behaviordelia, Kalamazoo, Michigan (1976).

5. Homme, Lloyd: *How to Use Contingency Contracting in the Classroom*. Research Press, Champaign, IL (1973).

6. Alvord, J.R.: *Home Token Economy: An Incentive Program for Children and Their Parents*. Research Press, Champaign, IL (1977).

IMPULSIVE

Impulsive children spontaneously act in a sudden, forceful, compelling and unpremeditated manner. Consequences are not considered, in spite of the fact that many of these children when questioned are able to describe negative consequences which they do not like. At the moment they respond quickly and without thinking, appearing to be at the mercy of their impulses. They are usually unable to tolerate any delay in gratifying their desires, and they often do not plan ahead. Frequently, their first reaction to a situation is an inappropriate one.

It is difficult to accurately specify the incidence of impulsivity, but it is clear that children under 8 are relatively more impulsive than children from 9 through 18. Generally, 5 to 10 percent of children are extremely impulsive (similar to the incidence of hyperactivity). Another 10 percent are moderately impulsive, causing fairly frequent and continuing problems for themselves and others. Impulsivity often underlies aggression and what adults consider to be immaturity or inadequate moral development. These children are often seen fighting and arguing and are often described by peers as "spoiled brats" who always want their own way. The ability to delay gratification is crucial both to adequate individual personality development and as an essential ingredient of appropriate and satisfying social interaction.

Reasons Why

Extreme impulsivity is believed to often be organically caused, where the brain mechanism relating to inhibition is thought to function inadequately. The organic cause could be genetic, a particular constitutional disposition, a developmental lag, or a neurological dysfunction. Constitutionally, some children appear to be born with an "impulsive cognitive tempo," causing instantaneous reactions to most situations.

Other frequent causes of impulsivity are anxiety and cultural influences. Anxious, tense children (with various psychological conflicts) frequently act as if they were in a paniclike state. They act on their first thought, rather than being able to calmly consider alternatives. Similarly, sad, pessimistic children often choose smaller, immediate rewards, whereas happy children frequently select the larger but delayed reward. The sad child acts on immediate need and does not examine alternatives. Some children learn or model impulsive behavior from their subculture or from their immediate family. They learn to act impulsively and are often rewarded by adults for behaving spontaneously without considering alternatives and for choosing instantaneous rewards.

How to Prevent

Teach Delay of Gratification. Very young children normally learn that getting what they want immediately is frequently impossible. Learning to wait (delay immediate gratification) is one of the most important lessons of early childhood. The goal is for the child to be capable of waiting for a reward with a minimum of tension or anger. Waiting is taught by parents who take a firm stand that the child can not have what he wants when he wants it. By not giving in, the parents teach children that they have the capacity to wait for longer and longer periods of time. The parents' attitude during this "lesson" is crucial. The angry, tense parent would inadvertently teach children that waiting is a difficult, negative experience. The firm parent who exhibits a positive or neutral mood teaches children that waiting is a necessary, acceptable part of growing up.

Language provides the child with a tool for learning delay (see "Teach Self-Talk" in the "What to Do" section). The young child is taught how to say, "I can wait" for whatever he or she desires. Up to kindergarten, most children tend to give themselves instructions out loud. By first grade, most children should have learned to be able to think thoughts such as "I won't eat all the candy now or I'll get sick." With young children it is essential to praise or reward them when their overt self-talk and actual self-control behavior *match*. Prevention of impulsivity is therefore achieved by teaching young children *how* to delay by using language.

Children can also be taught to delay by using fantasy.[1] For example, a child can be told how to think of a picture of the toy that he wants right now. Waiting is made possible by picturing this pleasant image. A child might also use his imagination to create a movie of himself engaging in an activity while waiting for the real activity to start. A number of children respond very well to this procedure of imagining pleasant objects or events which *distract* them from focusing on their immediate desires.

Child's play[2] also teaches a child how to behave more appropriately. Through play, parents can encourage a child to act out a role which involves patience and consideration for others. At first it may be necessary for parents to be the puppet or the animal who waits and takes turns while saying, "I can wait while the others having fun." By telling stories, role playing, and drawing with the child, parents can model numerous self-control behaviors.

Another teaching goal is to make young children realize that their actions have consequences for others. The earlier and clearer this concept is, the more likely that children will learn to delay their responses. It is explained that their impatience and need to have things immediately causes problems or annoyance to others. Although it must be handled sensitively, group rewards based upon a child's behavior is a very powerful teaching device. If their sibling (especially the youngest) can wait patiently and without complaining, then they all get a special treat. Therefore, the children learn that their ability to wait has a positive effect and rewarding consequences.

Teach Problem Solving. In the next section, problem solving is described in detail as a means of helping impulsive children become less impulsive. Briefly, we will outline the teaching of problem solving as a means of *preventing* the development of impulsivity. Spivack and his colleagues[3] discuss problem solving methods for both preventing and lessening impulsive behavior. Problem solving is enhanced when parents ask children to evaluate their thinking ("Was that a good idea?"). Preschoolers should be specifically taught that there are *alternative* solutions to problems. If a child wants a friend to play a game with her and the friend refuses, the child might become angry, sad, or try to force the friend to play. A simple discussion of other alternatives serves to develop the child's problem solving abilities. For example, the child could be taught to say, "If you play this game with me, then I'll play your favorite game." She might be told that she could say to herself that "I really want to play it now, but I'll wait until she's ready to play later." Another alternative is for the parent to ask if there could be a substitute activity that might be fun for both children. In these social situations, the parents should act as a model and guide for the child to develop solutions to problems. Parents can suggest possible solutions and discuss probable causes for the reactions of others. When children demonstrate alternative thinking and good decision making, parents should be immediately praising and encouraging. Children who lack basic problem solving skills often act in a helpless or impulsive manner. The child must become aware of problems, develop alternative solutions, learn how to proceed and what to do about obstacles, consider the consequences of actions, and be keenly aware of the actions and feelings of others. We present this here as a specific means of preventing impulsivity, but we also view these skills as facilitating general adjustment and preventing the development of personal and social difficulties.

Young adolescents can be shown how to apply problem solving techniques in real situations. The preventive aspect is very clear since many adolescents are "hot headed" and act impulsively on their first thought or feeling. This often leads to conflicts with peers and adults. During dinner or in private conversations, parents can discuss basic problem solving approaches and ask the child to think of examples. In analyzing a problem, the facts (description of what is) must be differentiated from the person's interpretation of the facts. Rather than jumping to conclusions, the process of thinking of alternative interpretations or explanations is demonstrated: "That girl might be teasing you because she likes you or she wants to see how you'll handle her remarks about you." Many adolescents find that talking out loud to parents or to themselves is a useful way of considering alternatives or anticipating consequences. "If I ask her to go to the dance, she might laugh at me or she might say yes. If I don't ask her to go, she won't have the chance of accepting. Should I take the chance of being rejected? I think I can take being refused and not feel like a jerk." The adolescent will then be prepared and ready to solve problems when they arise.

What to Do

Teach Problem Solving. Parents see impulsive reactions and often do not realize that the child may *not know* the steps required in order to be reflective and then take purposeful action. Usual comments such as "Work out the argument yourselves" do not work. Similarly, just having a child delay his responses does not lead to more effective responses. These children often feel helpless and extremely frustrated that their efforts are not successful. Anger and sadness are frequent reactions. Parents can actively teach their child how to think. Parents must demonstrate *cause and effect* ("If you hit children, *then* they will be annoyed") and *probability* ("What is likely to happen if you always interrupt people when they are speaking?"). *Consequences* of actions should be considered. A key concept is that there are *alternative* solutions to a problem ("If no one is home, you can call me at work; go to a neighbor; play outside until I get home"). Whenever possible, children should first be asked what things they think should be done. The goal is for the child to be able to think up and evaluate the results of several possible solutions.

Whatever the age of the child, the parent can teach the application of problem solving to situations as they arise.

Fifteen minutes of conversation reviewing a situation that happened is a worthwhile investment of time. A key is the child's perception that the parent is not blaming or criticizing but is truly interested in helping the child become more reflective and effective. After reviewing other approaches to an incident, the child should be asked if he could anticipate when such a situation might arise again. The impulsive child is then being prepared to act more thoughtfully and responsibly. Some impulsive children require a type of conditioning, so that they *automatically* switch to a calm, problem solving approach in the heat of the moment.

Teach Self-talk. Self-talk as a means of *delaying gratification* is a very powerful method in counteracting impulsivity. The child must learn to postpone pleasure. Waiting their turn in a game, not eating candy before dinner, not interrupting a conversation, not blurting out ideas—all may have to be taught. Recent research [4,5] highlights the effectiveness of having children say, "I can wait my turn" to themselves. By teaching them how this self-talk helps them to be patient, children gradually learn to apply it in various situations. "It's good to learn how to wait" stresses the positive aspect of being able to wait and not act instantly.

Parents should model the effective use of self-talk in solving their own daily problems. For instance a parent might verbalize in front of a child, "I'd better stop and think before I do this." It is also very effective when siblings and peers model appropriate self-talk, e.g., "I know I'm late, but there's nothing I can do about it. I'll hurry but I'll stay calm." The behavior corresponding to these thoughts is then demonstrated.

A parent might also use pretend play to show a child how to think and act in certain problem situations. If a child is having difficulty, for example, handling teasing from a peer, the parent might pretend to be the child in the situation and role play appropriate thoughts and behaviors: "I won't hit her even if I'm angry. I will tell her how angry I am and that she shouldn't say that anymore." Then the parent acts out, saying to the peer, "I'm angry at being called names; you cut that out." Pretending that the peer does not stop, the parent might then say, "I'll just walk away and ignore her" (and act this out). This type of role playing can be very educational.

Self-talk may be tremendously enhanced by using reminder cards[6] or pictures drawn by the child or the parent. The pictures serve to remind the child how to act more appropriately. The child who does not listen to others might draw a face with huge ears and write underneath LISTEN TO WHAT PEOPLE ARE SAYING. A large card might be displayed, stating THINK BEFORE I TALK. The *key ingredient* is for the child to learn to think of the image on the card during the actual situation. Therefore, when the teacher or person is speaking, the child thinks to himself, "Listen to what she is saying" or "Think before I talk."

Reward Reflective Behavior and Penalize Impulsive Acts. Children should be taught *self-reinforcement,* where they compliment themselves for waiting or for thinking of a better approach to a situation. Also, any instance of calm, reflective behavior should be rewarded by adults. Whenever impulsive children delay a response and consider consequences, the parent should specifically compliment them. Parents must catch the child tolerating frustration and immediately reinforce this rare event. ("That was terrific. You lost that game and you still kept playing.") When the child acts impulsively, have the child demonstrate how to consider alternatives and then *reward* him with praise or accumulated points to earn a reward. (See section on hyperactivity for examples of setting up a reward system.) Many children respond to the continuous reinforcement of reflective behavior with a rapid decrease in impulsivity.

For those children who are less responsive, research has demonstrated the effectiveness of "response cost" and "time-out" procedures. When a child constantly talks out impulsively or immediately wants his way, a brief "time out" in his room can be effective, if calmly and consistently employed. Similarly, when using points or tokens, a loss of these earned symbols can be used for very unacceptable behavior. For example, for impulsive complaining about food and rules, a child can lose five points. For patience and not complaining during a meal or before bedtime, ten points is recorded. Extra play, allowance, or television viewing time may be useful daily rewards. Firm limits and expectations are clearly spelled out by these sanctions.

Prompts and Cues. Very impulsive children may have to be shown a concrete cue such as making a *C* with their left thumb and index finger, which stands for "control." Under stress, they can look at this *C*, calm down, relax, and not impulsively lash out or speak out. They therefore learn to cue themselves to calm down and be more self-controlled. Learning to praise themselves for this better behavior is essential.

Professional Methods. Similar to hyperactivity, there are methods used by professionals that are particularly effective with impulsive children. Many means are used to promote a psychologically and physically calm feeling. Muscular relaxation and various biofeedback procedures have been successful. Controversial, but frequently effective, is the use of psychotropic drugs for very impulsive children who have been *unresponsive* to other approaches. Most impulsive children can respond to some combination of the preceding methods if used consistently in a positive manner. Even those children who require medication can soon be withdrawn from medication if appropriate parental methods are used with the child who is in a more receptive state.[7]

Case Report

An 8-year-old boy had a history of impulsive behavior which caused many problems. He spoke out in class, constantly interrupted others, could not stick to rules in a game, and could not wait (had to have what he wanted when he wanted). Professional intervention consisted of four sessions to teach him muscular relaxation and alleviate his pessimistic and negative feelings about himself. The parents were shown how to teach problem solving and self-talk.

A joint meeting with the teacher led to her very beneficial use of 10-minute problem solving sessions with him two times per week. She was able to show him how to consider alternative courses of action to the specific problems that arose in the classroom. Instead of blurting out and interrupting, he learned to write his thoughts down and say them when it was his turn to speak. He was shown how to consider what to do rather than doing whatever came to his mind. The parents used a similar approach at home, but primarily focused on modeling and teaching him self-talk. Instead of helping him with specific homework, they helped him learn to follow rules and wait by saying helpful phrases to himself. His father played a major role by encouraging the development of self-talk, such as "People like it when I don't interrupt," "I can wait until tomorrow to play with Daddy." The parents felt they had a specific means of helping their son, and they did not feel helpless. This was the major factor in changing the family atmosphere of tension and anger to a more positive and optimistic tone. There was an immediate change in the boy's feeling that his parents were on his side, and a dramatic reduction in his negative and pessimistic comments occurred. Although still relatively more impulsive than his peers, within 2 months he was noticeably improved. Many adults and children spontaneously complimented him on being able to wait and follow rules. A key to permanent change is the child's development of better self-control skills in an environment that is consistently encouraging and rewarding each improved step.

Books for Parents About Impulsivity

Shure, Myrna B. and Spivack, George: *Problem Solving Techniques in Childrearing.* Jossey-Bass, San Francisco (1978).

Staub, E.: *The Development of Prosocial Behavior in Children.* General Learning Press, Morristown, NJ (1975).

Thoresen, C. E. and Mahoney, M. J.: *Behavioral Self-Control.* Holt, Rinehart & Winston, New York (1974).

Books for Children About Impulsivity

Lexau, Joan M.: *Benjie on His Own.* Dial Press, New York (1970). Ages 6 to 9.

Effective problem solving is shown in an urban setting. Instead of waiting for an older friend to walk him home, Benjie impulsively goes on his own. Patience and persistence is shown by young Benjie as he walks through scary city streets. Responsible, effective behavior is demonstrated as Benjie seeks help for his sick grandmother.

Clearly, Beverly Bunn: *Henry and the Clubhouse.* William Morrow, West Caldwell, NJ (1962). Ages 8 to 10.

Confronting obstacles and solving problems are demonstrated

by Henry as he delivers newspapers. With much humor, Henry faces challenges and learns lessons about responsibility. Persistence and frustration tolerance are illustrated.

Schwarzrock, Shirley and Wrenn, C. Gilbert: *Understanding the Law of Our Land.* American Guidance Service, Circle Pines, MN (1973). Ages 11 and up.

Making and changing laws are used to illustrate the rights and responsibilities of older children, and impulsive breaking of laws by adolescents is depicted. Anecdotes are used to illustrate why laws are made and how they operate. Throughout, problem solving methods are discussed. Effective ways of changing laws are suggested.

References

1. Saltz, Eli: "Stimulating Imaginative Play: Some Cognitive Effects on Pre-Schoolers." Paper presented at the meeting of the American Psychological Association, Toronto, Canada (August 1978).
2. Schaefer, Charles: *The Therapeutic Use of Child's Play.* Jason Aronson, New York (1976).
3. Spivack, George, Platt, Jerome J., and Shure, Myrna B.: *The Problem-Solving Approach to Adjustment.* Jossey-Bass, San Francisco (1976).
4. Meichenbaum, Donald: *Cognitive-Behavior Modification.* Plenum, New York (1977).
5. Mischel, Walter: "How Children Postpone Pleasure." *Human Nature:* (December 1978), pp. 51–55.
6. Palkes, Helen *et al.:* "Porteus Maze Performance of Hyperactive Boys After Training in Self-Directed Verbal Commands." *Child Development* 39: (1968), pp. 817–826.
7. Schaefer, C. E. and Millman, H.L.: *Therapies for Children: A Handbook of Effective Treatments for Problem Behaviors.* Jossey-Bass, San Francisco (1977).

SHORT ATTENTION SPAN—DISTRACTIBLE

Attention span is the length of time an activity is pursued. Attention is interfered with by distractibility, where the individual is uncontrollably drawn to some other activity or sensation. The child's focused, on-going behavior is interfered with by the distracting noise, sight, or personal feeling. Only a short time is spent on an activity, and a task is not stuck to. This type of child shifts from one activity to another and is easily sidetracked. Persistence is the ability to continue an activity. A persistent distractible child will come back to an activity and complete it. The nonpersistent distractible child does not complete tasks. Also, attention requires the ability to focus and screen out unessential material. A poor screening or filtering mechanism results in difficulty in efficiently attending to relevant information or events.

Even infants vary in distractibility. When an infant is reaching for something or gazing at an object, sounds or new sights may or may not easily distract that infant. Distractible infants may stop drinking a bottle when their attention is drawn away. As children develop, they learn to attend selectively and not pay attention (both looking and hearing) to irrelevant matters. Selective attention increases as mental age increases. Average length of attention span is approximately 7 minutes for 2 year olds, 9 minutes for 3 year olds, 12 minutes for 4 year olds, and 14 minutes for 5 year olds. If a 2 year old plays with a toy for a half-hour, her attention span is long. If she can usually only play for a few minutes, a short attention span is indicated. The distractible toddler continuously moves from one activity or toy to another. In a school setting, the distractible young child loses belongings, misplaces items, doesn't finish tasks, and is continually drawn away by any new event. The most confusing aspect of attention span to parents is that length of attention depends upon the type of stimulus. If a toy is interesting enough, even very young distractible children may play with that toy for a very long time.

Distractibility may be a basic cause for hyperactivity in some children. Attention span can easily be measured by timing how long an activity is pursued. However, looking *and* thinking is required, and real attention is measured by the *appropriateness* of the response. Some children can stare at material without thinking. Approximately 5 to 10 percent of children have a seriously short attention span. While attention span increases with age, many of these children remain relatively inattentive throughout adolescence.

Reasons Why

Short attention span (similar to hyperactivity and impulsivity) is often caused by a lag in neurological development. Either slow maturation or an organic brain malfunction can result in short attention span. Aside from developmental lag or central nervous system dysfunction, short attention span is also an inherited, constitutional trait.[1] "Temperamental" differences may be observed from infancy on. Some children are very active, distractible, and move from one activity to another. Other children may be very persistent and virtually nondistractible. It is a brain mechanism that enables efficient focusing and appropriate screening of irrelevant stimulation to occur. Additionally, perceptual skills must be adequate. Visual and auditory perception is the ability to receive sights and sounds, understand the meaning, and respond appropriately. If the child has a weakness in being able to distinguish figure-background relationships, poor attention results. When the teacher is speaking and other noises are present, this child is not able to focus on the teacher's voice as the essential sound and the other noises as being irrelevant background. Similarly, a child may be visually confused and not able to focus on the significant visual part of his environment.

The child who doesn't understand "sequencing" will similarly become confused and not appear to pay attention. The sequence of events (first, second, third, etc.) requires that the child listen, understand, remember, and take appropriate action. Young, distractible children cannot "knock once on that door, then open the window, and then bring me that pencil."

Environmental and psychological factors also play a large role in causing a short attention span. Children who feel anxious and insecure may remain dependent upon external guidance and instructions. They are not able to stick to tasks themselves, needing support and encouragement. The immature and impatient child often feels that task completion is unimportant, saying, "I want to do something else." They have not developed patience or persistence, which are necessary in sticking to tasks. With limited persistence, children become discouraged, stop trying, and do not finish what they started. Insecurity and lack of confidence lead to an inability to pay attention and resist distractions. Additionally, children who live in a private fantasy world have limited attention for their environment. Problems in sustaining attention are also seen in a variety of children with learning disabilities, retardation, and emotional disturbance.

How to Prevent

Promote Adequacy and Success. From an early age, children will not stick to a task if they are criticized or frequently unsuccessful. Continuous stress by parents on what is wrong and how it should be done better often leads to a child giving up. The child avoids unpleasant feelings by moving from one activity to another and does not face the possible failure of not completing a task. Anxiety is avoided by the child not paying attention and constantly moving on to the next situation. Therefore to prevent this type of limited attention, you carefully select tasks that assure success and then praise task completion. "Nothing succeeds like success" is an appropriate saying in the promotion of selective attention and the ability to withstand distractions. The child who feels inadequate will quickly stop paying attention at the first mildly frustrating situation. Adequacy is enhanced by a combination of parental praise and encouragement and the successful completion of tasks. The sensitive parent makes sure that the first 5 years of life are filled with many instances of success geared to the child's ability level. Too difficult or too easy tasks do not promote feelings of adequacy and competency. Solving mildly and moderately challenging problems does lead to feelings of mastery in the child. The child, who feels that "I can do it," pays attention and withstands distractions.

Teach and Reinforce Focused Attention. From infancy, focusing can be taught and reinforced. Parental attention and praise for the young child's increasing ability to focus are keys to preventing the development of poor attending skills. The very young child should be praised for playing with a toy (in an enjoyable manner) for long intervals. A 3-year-old child can be complimented for building two houses with blocks.

Many skills are based upon adequate recognition of sameness and difference between objects. The child must pay attention to the salient features of objects in order to recognize similarities or differences. "That's great. You put all the small blocks here and all the large blocks there." Focused attention also implies persistence. Praise and rewards should be given for persisting in the face of distractions or frustrations. "Wow! You kept trying even though you kept missing the target." The child can be taught how to avoid distractions. A parent may model by continuing to do a task while the child acts like a disruptive classmate.

When a child goes from one incomplete task to another, the parent can ignore or mildly discourage this behavior. The key is always to avoid reinforcing distractibility. When the child is distracted, attention (positive or negative) to that behavior is to be avoided. By 4 years of age, most children should have learned how to differentially control their attention. They are able to discriminate when to pay attention (when someone is speaking, reading, etc.) and when not to (free play, resting, etc.). Efficient academic learning depends upon the development of focused attention and control over distractibility.

Adequate Maternal Prenatal Care. Short attention span may result from an inadequate uterine environment. Maternal physical and mental health is the best insurance for preventing poor attention based upon any insult to embryonic brain development. Most parents are now familiar with the negative effects on the fetus from maternal drug consumption (tobacco, marijuana, alcohol, and various pills). However, serious psychological trauma in the pregnant mother can also adversely influence the fetus. Poor attention and learning problems in children have been seen as resulting from prolonged maternal tension during pregnancy.

What to Do

Provide Structure and Reduce Distractions. Distractible children respond best when adults structure the environment to *minimize distractions* and maximize the attractiveness of the stimuli to be attended to. As the child attends more efficiently, the amount of structure should be reduced. There is considerable evidence that reducing stimuli[2] is quite effective for many distractible children. Carpeting and drapes reduce extraneous sound. Materials can be out of sight by the use of cabinets and closed shelves. Desks should be organized and uncluttered. When a task or game is completed, materials should be put away immediately. Some children respond very well to using a cardboard with a space cut out. The opening is used to expose only that problem, paragraph, or picture that is relevant. Children who are distracted by sound are sometimes elated by their use of ear plugs or cotton. Studying in a noisy environment or taking a test can become easier by literally blocking out any noise. A helpful rule is always to try to gradually expose the child to normal conditions. Less and less effective ear plugs can be used as the child learns to withstand auditory distractions.

Structure is also provided by *careful task planning*. At first, children can respond better to material that they like, and then less desirable material should be introduced. Tasks, chores, and school assignments should be specific not general. The child needs the experience of very frequent successful completion of short, specific tasks. To assure this, time spent on tasks should be short with planned rest or play periods. Task time is gradually increased as the child demonstrates the ability to pay attention for longer periods. A kitchen timer is useful as a means for signaling the end of work or play periods. Many children enjoy the responsibility of setting the timer and feeling more independent by planning the intervals and monitoring themselves.

Rather than letting things happen naturally, structuring requires strategy. All instructions should be given clearly and specifically. It is crucial that you make sure that your child is looking at you before giving any instructions. Very important is the avoidance of unnecessary talk. Overly verbal parents are detrimental to children with short attention spans. Similarly, clear instructions are given regarding only the relevant aspects of a task. Parents who are themselves models of "reflectivity" teach children to pause, think, and listen rather than act impulsively. Minimally, parents must understand that children must learn to reflect upon conversation rather than jumping to conclusions quickly. Being reflective enables the child to have a framework for then focusing upon speech or written words. Expectations should be spelled out clearly and adhered to. Routines should be generally *predictable*. Distractible children find it hard to tolerate disorganization and continuous changes in routine. Similarly, consistent consequences provide a safe, knowable structure. Children learn that certain behavior is followed by specific consequences. Children who usually know what to expect and feel safe are less prone to feel confused and be easily distracted.

Reward Attending and Resisting Distractions. Attention span, like any behavior, can be increased by rewarding longer and longer intervals of focused attention. Positive consequences, such as praise or rewards, should follow periods of attending and instances of continuing an activity in the presence of distractions. Parents, teachers, and others must *pay attention* to the child when the child is *paying attention* [for specific reward methods (contracts, use of tokens, etc.) see the section on hyperactivity]. All too often distractible children receive attention when they are distracted, rather than for those (perhaps rare) intervals of focused attention. Extrinsic rewards (such as checks used to purchase toys) are very effective means of building up weak attending skills. For example, a parent might give a child one check for looking at the task material. Three checks can be given for working on a task, while five checks result from satisfactory task completion. This graduated approach has been very successful in homes and schools.[3] By giving some reward (one check, a smile) even for the minimum response of looking at material, some success is assured. Some children have been pleasantly shocked when an adult provides some type of reinforcing response for an incorrect response and an even greater reward for a correct response. This is in contrast to previously negative or neutral responses to incorrect answers, often resulting in children's anger and eventual giving up. Therefore, the child should be frequently *rewarded for trying!* Paying attention even for 15 seconds should be consistently rewarded. Even consistent looking at others (eye contact) may have to be rewarded. Parents frequently say, "How can I be positive when he can only pay attention for 5 seconds?" The answer is that you must be consistently positive after the good 5 seconds, keep at it, and 2 weeks later there might be 10 consistent seconds of attending. Strengthening attention span requires adult patience, repetition, and endurance. A kit for training attention in very young children has been developed (see "Additional Readings for Parents"). The basic format is similar to the ideas presented above. Focal attention is trained and efficiency is gradually achieved. For these children, the normally developed ability to selectively and accurately attend and concentrate must be taught.

In group situations, group rewards for paying attention (consistent on-task behavior) have been successfully used. The one or two distractible children in a class may concentrate better in an atmosphere that consistently rewards focused attention. At home, all siblings can be praised or rewarded when they all are quiet and pay attention to someone speaking or entertaining. Interestingly, research[4] has shown that even rewarding one child for paying attention often has the effect of improving other children's attention skills.

Professional Methods. Specialized tutoring (often by a special education or learning disability teacher) may be done by the school or obtained privately. The key concept is the teaching of the basic skills that underlie the ability to concentrate. Children must often be taught to focus on the *critical aspects* of a situation or problem. Word games are often used (parents can also employ them) to illustrate discrimination skills. The child must be able to listen and become aware of the critical element. "I put salt on my cereal to make it sweet." Which word is wrong, why, and what would be correct? Another related issue is training in *figure-ground perception.* Exercises are given, both visual and hearing, illustrating the important "figure" from the less important "background." The teacher's voice in class is the figure and the other material is the background at that moment. Some children require intensive work in learning *sequential thinking.* They become confused and do not understand what goes first, second, and third. Therefore, training this skill enables them to pay attention and understand sequences of events.

In psychotherapy, many of the self-control techniques are appropriate. Children learn to use self-talk to guide their behavior: "Stop, look, and listen"—can be thought by the child and practiced in various situations. Very young children often need a method of resisting distraction[5] by practicing saying to themselves, "I'll keep working even if someone asks me to stop." Other appropriate techniques include relaxation, breathing training, and possible use of biofeedback. The basic idea is to teach the child how to physically and psychologically relax, so the attending process becomes more natural and efficient. Muscle relaxation training has been particularly effective for overly active, distractible children. For anxious, tense, insecure children (where the problem is emotional), more traditional play or psychotherapy is appropriate. Here, the conflicts may then be understood and resolved. The more secure child will be more able to attend and resist distractions.

Case Report

An 11-year-old girl had a long history of poor attention and distractibility. Play therapy for 6 months when she was 5 years old had been completely unsuccessful. Therefore, the parents had not sought other professional help. A detailed psychological evaluation revealed a combination of short attention span, distractibility, and impulsivity. Intelligence was above average, personality development was somewhat immature, and academic achievement was 1 year below grade level. A neurological examination indicated "soft signs" of neurological involvement. The implication was that the attentional weakness was a long standing constitutional weakness.

Professional intervention consisted of several parent counseling sessions and 5 months of individual psychotherapy. The parents were counseled as to appropriate ways to reward attending. They began to praise better attention and her increasing ability to not be distracted. A key aid was the mother's playing the game of making noises while the child was working. When the child kept doing her homework, the mother praised her ability to keep concentrating. The mother also helped her daughter organize her room and plan her activities. The father took her on special weekend outings, when the teacher reported improved attention to school work. Psychotherapy focused on her understanding that this weakness was not her fault, but she could learn to overcome it. A combination of muscle relaxation and self-talk was used. She learned to relax and then ask herself helpful questions. "What does the teacher want us to know," "I must listen and remember the important things," "What am I supposed to do now," "I can keep working even when some children are talking," etc. Additionally, as with many older children, she had developed many negative, guilty feelings and had a very poor opinion of herself. Open talk regarding her strengths and past frustrations was helpful. However, the crucial aspect of therapy was her growing awareness of her better attending skills. She felt more competent. The positive feedback from parents, teachers, and peers was a thrilling experience for her.

Books for Parents About Distractibility

Fagen, S.A., Long, N.J., and Stevens, D.J.: *Teaching Children Self-Control.* Charles E. Merrill, Columbus, OH (1975).

Santostefano, S.: *Training in Attention and Concentration (Kit).* Educational Research Associates, Philadelphia.

References

1. Thomas, Alexander *et al.: Temperament and Behavior Disorders in Children.* New York University Press, New York (1968).
2. Cruickshank, W.M. and Hallahan, D.P. (eds.): *Perceptual and Learning Disabilities in Children. Vol. 1: Psycholeducational Practices.* Syracuse University Press, Syracuse (1975).
3. Statts, A.W.: *Child Learning, Intelligence and Personality: Principles of a Behavioral Interaction Approach.* Harper & Row, New York (1971).
4. Okovita, H.W. and Bucher, B.: "Attending Behavior of Children near a Child who is Reinforced for Attending." *Psychology in the Schools* 13 (1976), pp. 205–211.
5. Patterson, C.J. and Mischel, W.: "Plan to Resist Distraction." *Developmental Psychology* 11 (1975), pp. 369–378.

SILLY–CLOWNING

"Don't be such a clown. You always act so silly." These statements are frequently made by adults to children who appear to be foolish and lacking in common sense. These children often act like jokesters or, at the extreme, like buffoons. Some children act silly, regardless of the social context or the consequences. They often appear foolish to peers, relatives, and teachers. The negative responses of others do not diminish the frequency of the silly behavior. Other children appear to go into their act, which seems like a purposeful attempt to behave like a clown. Silliness decreases as the child gets older. However, silliness can become a habit and then appear to be "part of a child's personality." Even as a teenager and adult, the individual may retain his jokester or clown image. For some, it may be their main way of relating to others.

There are no statistics as to the number of children who act relatively silly at various ages. Also, there are no estimates as to what percentage of time a child must act foolishly before such action is considered a problem. Additionally, silliness must be differentiated from general immaturity. Immature children usually lag behind their peers in a variety of behaviors, often appearing physically immature. Here we are considering specific social behaviors that make these children appear foolish and clownlike. Even more than with other behaviors, parental tolerance is a key factor. Some parents do not view frequent giggling, face making, noises, and joking as inappropriate in children under 10 years. Other parents have very little tolerance and label minimum amounts of these behaviors as silly and unacceptable. The concern about silliness therefore becomes a combination of the amount of the child's behavior and the parents' attitude and tolerance. A helpful indicator is peer and teacher reaction. A silly reputation with peers, who then tease or ostracize the child, indicates a problem. Teachers' judgments of relative silliness and unpopularity is another sign of difficulty.

Reasons Why

Seek Attention. Being silly or acting like a clown results in attention from others. Many children feel negatively about themselves but feel worthwhile when they obtain attention. For many children positive or negative attention is rewarding. Some parents enjoy clownlike behavior and actively praise, smile, or in other ways reward that behavior. Reinforced behavior is repeated and can become habitual. Some parents overreact and show very strong negative or punitive reaction to clowning. Unfortunately, negative attention can serve to reinforce the behavior. And some children clown more to gain revenge against the punitive parent. However, children who seek and crave attention repeat the behavior that gains attention and causes a strong parental reaction. Also, peer influence is very powerful. Frequently, peers encourage or even provoke a child to act foolishly. Positive *or* very negative peer reaction can reinforce clowning in the lonely child who is desperate for attention.

Habitual Silliness or Never Learned Appropriate Humor. Silliness is typical in young children and is contagious when peers act silly. For some children silliness can continue as a habit which is not given up for more appropriate humor. Appropriate attention-getting methods and more acceptable humor may literally never have been learned. These children may believe that the only way to be noticed is to be laughed at. Similarly, they may feel that the only way to be humorous is to be a clown.

Divert Attention. Some children act foolishly to divert attention away from their own problems. Therefore, people won't notice their perceived inadequacies but will only see the clowning. Other children may be diverting attention away from a sibling or even be defusing a tense parental relationship. The clowning brother may be protecting his vulnerable sister by focusing attention on himself. The child who (accurately or inaccurately) thinks his parents might hurt each other psychologically or physically may offer himself as comic relief. Instead of the parents interacting, they become involved in laughing at the child or trying various ways to stop him from behaving so foolishly.

How to Prevent

Model and Teach Appropriate Humor. Most effective in preventing children from frequent clowning is a positive lesson that children learn from observing the family. Children who see parents who are humorous without clowning learn to imitate that type of humor. Parents can literally teach a child how to be funny without the child having to make faces or shrieking. You can say to a child, "It's very funny to me when I read about the man who was selling hot dogs. The sign said—'Hot Dogs $5.' There was a line of hungry people who came to the store and only found a lot of dogs with their tongues hanging out." The story demonstrates to the child how words can have different meanings. The humor is in seeing that hot dogs can mean frankfurters or dogs that are too warm. Some children understand the humor immediately. It is extremely helpful for parents to explain various types of humor early. Their children therefore develop a variety of ways of being funny, not just by clowning.

Parental teaching of humor can be guided by some basic research findings concerning the development of humor in children.[1] For example, 5 year olds laugh at "Why can't you starve in the desert? Because of the sand-witches there." Ten year olds laugh at "Why can you jump higher than the Empire State Building? Because it can't jump at all." The second joke requires understanding of grammar and a type of abstract thinking. The child understands that the humor is in the implication that—Why can you jump higher than the Empire State Building *can jump?* The younger child understands the play on the words sandwich and sand-witch, and can visualize a witch flying over the desert. In both cases, parents can both demonstrate this type of humor and teach and explain it to the child. In both cases *incongruity* is humorous, and laughter increases with age. Combining two things or ideas that usually don't go together can be funny. "Why did the silly child throw the clock out of the window? He wanted to see time fly." This joke depends on the knowledge of the expression "time fly" meaning time going by quickly, and that throwing the clock causes the clock (time) to fly through the air.

Another important aspect of humor is the violation of expectations. Some children have to be shown how an expectation is violated and why it is funny. If children do not develop this capacity, they feel different because they do not find funny what their peers frequently laugh at. A typical type of joke is a picture of a skier going down a slope leaving two ski tracks. You see two tracks leading to a tree, the tracks separate around the tree, and then come together. There are no words and you see the skier continuing down the hill. The humor is in understanding that the realistic expectation is that the skier would either hit the tree or go around it on one side or the other. It is impossible for the action depicted to have taken place. Most children laugh when they "get it." As children mature they develop better and better abstract thinking. They are able to understand the type of absurdity presented above in a more sophisticated fashion. Many theories of personality development contain references to the importance of individuals being able to see humor in life's absurdities (ridiculously unreasonable situations). As children mature they learn to appreciate satire and parody, both being more sophisticated than slapstick or clowning humor. With these alternatives, older children do not have to obtain laughs only by clowning. They can imitate in a comical manner (parody) or they can use wit or sarcasm to both be funny and to comment on social foibles (satire).

Laughing at oneself is a powerful lesson. By not taking oneself so seriously, there is less of a need to be defensive. The child would be less prone to use silliness to gain attention or to feel worthwhile. Overseriousness can therefore be diminished by seeing the humor in one's own behavior. You can say to a child, "Wasn't that funny how I tried too hard and knocked things over. Next time I'll take it easy and watch more carefully." Humor therefore serves to relieve tension. The moral that can then be added will usually be more acceptable to the child. Instead of a deadly serious lecture concerning the need to be careful and pay attention, these messages are given in a mildly humorous context.

Demonstrate Attention Giving and Getting. Children can be shown from a very early age how giving to and receiving attention from others can be a positive experience. Paying attention when a person is speaking and frequently expressing appreciation are essential. Children then grow up in a relatively open, appreciative atmosphere where attention seeking does not become a desperate, often unsatisfied desire. You can say, "That was really nice how you helped by being quiet while we were working." Any comment regarding a child's unique contributions goes a long way in reducing the development of attention seeking silly behavior. "You really tried hard to build that clubhouse even though you didn't have the right wood." When receiving positive attention, the parent can graciously say, "Thanks for noticing what I did; I enjoyed doing it." Attention seeking diminishes as positive attention increases! Giving appropriate attention not only prevents the silliness pattern, but it promotes a general *feeling of adequacy* in the child. Children who feel adequate do not have to act like buffoons.

A very valuable preventive lesson is how to seek attention in a positive manner. Occasional clowning may result in positive attention, but clowning should not be a main source of attention. Asking for feedback may lead to positive responses. The child can learn to say, "How does this drawing look?" Adults or peers may be uncommunicative or not naturally responsive. In this case, asking for feedback may be very effective in obtaining attention. With generally angry or sarcastic people, asking for feedback may or may not work. Parents must be ready and willing to communicate appreciation, or children may feel frustrated and continue to clown. If parents show children how to request feedback, it may lead to more feedback even from those parents who do not spontaneously show appreciation.

What to do

Analyze Cause and Take Action. Parents can sit back and calmly ask, ''Why does my child so frequently act so silly?'' This analysis may lead to immediate, effective action. It may be as straightforward as realizing that a child desperately craves attention. Two courses of action may work dramatically. (1) Give the child more attention. Some parents have tremendous difficulty in paying attention to their children and in expressing appreciation. By setting the goal of attention giving, parents can begin to provide what has been missing. Attention takes many forms. You can spend time with a child, play games, have long talks, share your own feelings, show your own work or hobbies, be more enthusiastic, etc. The key is to sensitively observe the child's responses and provide more of the attention that *she likes.* (2) Arrange situations that will result in more attention being given to a child. Some parents underestimate the power of their child being in the limelight in some way. Children enjoy giving a music recital, participating in team sports, belonging to clubs, having a special hobby, etc. The key is that the activity should result in the ''deprived'' child receiving positive attention. Again, the rule is to make suggestions, try various activities, and sensitively observe the child. Even one arranged activity may do the trick of promoting good feelings and decrease the need to seek attention.

The child who just hasn't learned various styles of humor must be shown and taught. It should be clear at this point that parents who look with an open mind can understand cause and effect. ''My daughter just doesn't seem to know how to be funny except by clowning.'' This insight should be immediately followed by the positive step of showing that child how to be appropriately humorous. Similarly, parents can spot the child that clowns to divert attention from other problems. In this case, the "other problems" must be addressed. Parents must be open-minded enough to consider that a child may be clowning because the family atmosphere is too tense or belligerent. Once recognized, the parents can directly affect the cause by working together to create a more positive psychological climate. Parents' use of laughter and niceness can have the apparently surprising result of less silliness in their children. The most useful indicator is to look for patterns and timing of clowning. It may then be quite apparent that certain events (arguing, criticism, etc.) are followed by foolish behavior.

Reinforce Humor and a Child's Strengths and Ignore Silliness. Behavior that is truly ignored will diminish. Parents often underestimate the effectiveness of ignoring silliness. By not responding, silly behavior will lessen. In order to maximize the child's social development, ignoring should be combined with reinforcing of positives. All incidents of appropriate humor should be focused upon and praised. Very important here is the purposeful attempt to build the child's self-esteem by also reinforcing some of the child's unique strengths. The key is to praise specific behavior: "Your willingness to help around the house is terrific." "It's a pleasure to hear you practicing the piano." "I'm really glad you do your homework without having to be told." The child who begins to feel more appreciated will be less inclined to act like a buffoon.

Case Report

Two girls, ages 9 and 13, were always giggling, pushing each other, and making foolish faces at home. In school and with peers, they had a reputation of clowning and frequently acting in a silly manner. The parents communicated to the girls that their behavior was annoying and immature and was leading to a bad reputation and social isolation. The parents had frequently tried punishing silliness with no success. One family interview clearly revealed a tense marital relationship and many differences of opinion between the parents as to handling the girls. The girls appeared desperate for attention and frequently clowned just when the parents were expressing sadness or anger. Two counseling sessions were held only with the parents. The girls' behavior was explained in terms of diverting attention away from the parents' negative interaction, as well as their seeking positive attention. A plan was agreed upon for the parents to express more positive feelings in general and to argue less with each other. Additionally, they were specifically to provide more attention and praise to the girls together and also to spend some time with each of them alone.

The combined approach was immediately successful in lessening silly behavior at home. However, it was several months before clowning in school and with peers diminished noticeably. A follow-up interview was held 6 months later. The parents reported that the girls were more receptive to discussing their behavior at home. It was a slow process of their realizing the negative consequences of clowning and the more appropriate ways of gaining attention and making friends. A key ingredient was the improved communication between parents and children, brought about by the diminished parental strife and increase in their positive attention to the children.

Books for Children About Silly Clowning Behavior

Front, Sheila: *The Three Sillies*. Addison-Wesley, Reading, MA (1975). Ages 5 to 9.

A handsome young man wants to marry a farmer's pretty daughter. Her behavior is silly, and he decides to marry her only if he can find three people sillier than she. Silly behavior is vividly and humorously depicted, with appropriate illustrations.

Wells, Rosemary: *Noisy Nora*. Dial Press, New York (1973). Ages 4 to 7.

Nora, the middle child in a mouse family, acts foolishly in order to gain attention from her busy parents. Disappointed, Nora runs away and then returns. Written in rhyme, the tale illustrates the extremes that children use to seek attention.

References

1. McGhee, Paul E.: "Development of the humor response: A review of the literature." *Psychological Bulletin* 76: (1971), pp. 328–348.

DAYDREAMING

Pleasant, wishful, imaginative thoughts called daydreams are frequent in normal children. Daydreaming has come to mean the indulging in reveries at *inappropriate times*. It also carries the implication of difficulty in paying attention. Most typical are daydreams about being heroes, winners, and world famous. Television, comic books, and movies often serve to exaggerate this tendency in children. After being exposed to super heroes, many children daydream (and often dream at night) about having super powers themselves. Destructive and conquering daydreams also occur. Daydreams persist throughout childhood and adolescence. With the onset of puberty, many adolescents show an increase in the time spent daydreaming.

The main indicator of difficulty is daydreams interfering with appropriate functioning. When a child daydreams *instead* of paying attention, completing tasks, interacting with peers, etc., then problematic daydreaming is indicated. Additionally, a negative sign is more and more time spent in daydreaming. Fleeting daydreams are typical, but prolonged fantasies are not. When an 8 to 10 year old frequently spends more than 10 minutes in reveries, this is not a typical reaction. Problematic daydreaming is evident when children of any age describe their fantasies as fabulous and their everyday life as being boring or too difficult.

Reasons Why

Daydreams Perceived as More Satisfying than Reality. When a child *feels* that real life is too difficult or unusually unsatisfying, daydreaming becomes a pleasant escape. Wishes are fulfilled by imagination. Fantasies provide a strong feeling of satisfaction in comparison to the boredom of everyday activities. Daydreaming is seen by the child as being an easier task than solving social or academic problems. Children may become more and more preoccupied with fantasies and less involved in coping with their real surroundings. They become absorbed in their own thoughts and spend more time in their private world. Some children develop imaginary companions who provide them with a satisfying relationship. This is especially true for children who feel excluded or who have no friends. In daydreams, they are heroes, winners, or famous and are immune from criticism or negative feelings. These children have the capacity to function effectively in their environment. However, their talents are diverted from gaining praise from others and recognition for completing tasks.

Compensation for Real Handicaps. Children with physical handicaps often daydream about being normal and famous. As discussed in the introduction, when daydreaming becomes an interference with other activities or becomes excessive, it is a cause for concern. More subtle is the daydreaming of children with an "invisible handicap." Children with learning disabilities, who appear normal, have the real handicap of being unable to cope with the usual educational environment. Their continued failure and difficulties often lead to daydreaming as an escape. These children often have great difficulty understanding complex instructions or abstract ideas. Many children are very frustrated by their inability to read as well as they should (according to their intelligence) or to express themselves either verbally or in writing. Whatever the specific handicap is, the real frustrations can easily lead to problematic daydreaming. The satisfaction or feeling of power not attainable in the real world is sought in fantasies.

Daydreaming as a Habit. Daydreaming is frequent in young children, and a small percentage of children do not outgrow this pleasurable habit. Some children are quite prone to developing habits (such as nailbiting, scratching, etc.), and the habit then continues as a familiar and accustomed way of behaving. Even when a child's everyday activities are relatively satisfying, excessive daydreaming still occurs. Some children develop specific times to daydream. A frequent, and unfortunate, habit is fantasizing while a teacher (or parent) is speaking or lecturing. Other children daydream at certain times when there is nothing to do. In a ritualistic manner, some children may prepare themselves to daydream for a half-hour before or after dinner.

Daydreams of Shy Children. Vivid daydreaming is especially prevalent in shy children. Children who felt unprotected by their mother or psychologically separated prematurely from parents, often develop shyness and feelings of inability to cope.[1] They experience awkwardness and embarrassment in social interactions. In comparison, fantasies provide great pleasure and no negative feelings. Shy children can be seen to spend time in pleasant reveries with a smile on their faces. Of great concern is that they often become more anxious in social situations and participate less and less with others. Proportionately, their daydreams become more reinforcing and occur more frequently.

How to Prevent

Promote Early Competency. Since excessive daydreaming most frequently represents a reaction to perceived inadequate coping, assuring adequacy is the best preventative. Basic feelings of competency are set before age 5. Children must feel both *adequate and safe* in order to effectively deal with their environment. Instilling a feeling of competency prevents the child's need to develop satisfaction from daydreaming. The parent finds the line between providing adequate protection and permitting independence. Appropriate independence is indicated by a child's being able to accomplish tasks that result both in praise from others and in his own recognition of task completion. Real, necessary *chores* are the best tools available throughout childhood. The 3 and 4 year old should be given tasks that he can carry out yet that are sufficiently challenging. Parents who are overprotective delay feelings of competency in their children. These children often develop the unfortunate combination of feeling powerful and superior yet helpless and inadequate at the same time. Only their grandiose daydreams support their unrealistic perception of themselves. As the child matures, feelings of competency must keep pace. You must avoid the "Achilles heel" syndrome, where children are protected from life's problems. The other extreme of psychological abandonment must also be avoided. The best way to prepare children is to gradually expose them to real difficulties. One excellent means, not used enough by parents, is to *talk* about "problems that kids have to face." These talks serve the purpose of mentally preparing children for the many unexpected situations that must, and can, be coped with. Additionally, parents can role play difficult situations. The parent can pretend to be a teasing child while the child handles the situation calmly. Whenever a child does not know what to do, the parent switches roles and demonstrates calm and effective behavior. "I don't like being teased; please stop it." "When you stop teasing, I'll play with you" (then walks away).

The beginning of school is a real test of the child's ability to cope with academic and social demands. Children with an unrealistic or shaky self-concept are often shocked by the difficulties they face in school. These children are prone to resorting to daydreaming as a source of satisfaction and confirmation of themselves as being adequate. You should therefore do everything possible to prepare the child, including discussions with the teacher before school starts or very early in the year. Preparation might take the form of discussing the child's strengths and weaknesses with the teacher in order for the teacher to specifically help the child, if necessary.

Stress Daily Satisfaction. Some children are quite competent, yet they do not feel satisfied with their performance. Usually feelings of satisfaction accompany the competent handling of tasks. By being aware of the possible need to discuss and reinforce feelings of satisfaction, you can prevent many later difficulties, especially daydreaming. The relatively satisfied child does not need to develop substitute means of satisfaction. Effective means of stressing the daily attainment of satisfaction are modeling, discussion, and reinforcement. The parent models feeling satisfied by actually being pleased (and demonstrating this pleasure) with daily activities. When you enjoy preparing dinner, getting ready to leave the house, talking on the telephone, talking about business activities, etc., your child learns that style of living. If you find and demonstrate little satisfaction from daily activities, your child will learn by imitation and he may well become a daydreamer in order to feel pleasure. Discussion is simple. Talk about feeling satisfied with your own behavior and actual accomplishments. "I really enjoyed finishing my report." "It was nice to hear my boss compliment me on my work." "It wasn't perfect but I did my best and I feel great." Reinforcement is the praise you give the child for carrying out daily activities. Don't underestimate the power of a smile when children talk about feeling pleased. Smiling and verbal praise for feeling good are very effective means of increasing a child's feeling of personal satisfaction and worth.

Special Plans for Handicapped Children. Many children have some handicap: Some otherwise normal children have terrible handwriting, poor coordination, move slowly, etc. These subtle handicaps, along with any obvious handicaps, require special strategies. You should do anything possible to assure that the handicap is not preventing active participation with peers. Also, some children who do participate retain their feelings of inferiority because they are aware of their being different in some area. It may take good strategy and planning, but these children may need to be involved in recreational programs after school or on weekends. Children with poor coordination should be involved in noncompetitive activities where they can gradually improve. Physically handicapped children should engage in activities that do not require skills in their weak area. Similarly, slow or uncompetitive children should not be exposed to neighborhood games requiring these attributes. The handicapped or awkward child should be involved in a club where talk or appropriate activities are provided. These children often do well in hobby clubs (photography, stamp or coin collecting, model building, etc.), guided sightseeing tours, religious discussion groups, and so forth.

What to Do

Plan Activities. Daydreamers must not be bored or isolated, which frequently occurs. Real life must become more interesting, challenging, and pleasurable than fantasies. Whenever possible, activities involving peers should be arranged. When not possible, their energy should be channelled constructively. With young children, time limits for task completion may be very effective in discouraging daydreaming. *Short tasks* can be completed with no fatigue or boredom. Tasks could require attention, speed, memory, and note taking. Children should be encouraged, and rewarded if necessary, for writing creative stories, poems, paintings, reports about people they admire, etc. However, the stress should be on *active* participation. Solitary activities such as reading or working alone may encourage daydreaming. Also, it is not possible to assess when daydreaming is occurring, since no overt response is called for. In comparison, group discussion, drama, working on projects with peers, etc., do require interaction. An understanding group leader can be asked to watch for blank expressions, inappropriate smiles, or wandering eyes which might indicate daydreaming. The leader should immediately take action to assure involvement in on-going activities. Participation and attention may also be checked by asking the child questions about what has occurred. It is essential that you discuss specific plans with the teacher in order to make certain that the quiet nondisruptive child is not permitted to continue daydreaming.

Whenever possible the child should join structured clubs. It is worth the money and travel arrangements for the chronic daydreamer to participate in a productive club. The child's preferences may clearly indicate the type of club to seek out. If preferences are not clear, the child may have to earn rewards and privileges by attending (and actively participating in) an available club. After-school clubs include photography, arts and crafts, cooking, science, language, nature, art, etc. These activities may be provided by the school, museums, libraries, religious groups, or parent organizations such as associations for children with learning disabilities. Parents must themselves become assertive and determined enough to locate appropriate group activities for their child. When formal groups are not available, you can arrange activities with one or two other children. Even arranging three meetings with a specific purpose (like building a gocart) may be very effective. Don't be bashful in approaching other parents and suggesting activities. Another option is having a sibling actively interest the child in activities. We have had great success with parents hiring "companions" to interest youngsters in various events and hobbies.

Reward Attentiveness and Productivity. Ignore daydreaming and reward the opposite behavior—paying attention and being productive. This method follows the learning theory principle that inappropriate behavior should be ignored and appropriate behavior should be reinforced. When parents or teachers observe substantial productive periods, they should praise the child and use tangible rewards if necessary (see previous discussion of tokens). A very powerful method is for the parents to grant extra privileges or rewards when the teacher reports less daydreaming in school. There should be a conscious effort to provide more praise and positive reactions in order to make a child's real life more rewarding than her imaginary world. With very young children and with extremely excessive daydreamers, *interrupting* the fantasies may be necessary. In a pleasant manner, the adult should call the child's name, ask a question, or touch or shake him. This is an effective way of diminishing the duration of fantasizing, and whenever possible the child should then be engaged in conversation or some activity. *Scolding* should always be *avoided*. Criticism and punishment lead to counter-anger and may sometimes even reinforce daydreaming.

With relatively cooperative children, you might ask them to voluntarily limit their daydreaming and gradually reduce the time spent per daydream. The child can use a timer for these planned fantasy periods. Planning behavior can have the effect of bringing it more under the child's voluntary control. This is especially true if you reward the child for his increasing voluntary control of daydreaming.

Assess Theme of Daydreaming. Valuable clues can be gained through an open discussion of the daydream content. This does require a relatively free and trusting relationship. If the child is frequently criticized by parents, an honest discussion of details may not occur. If children do discuss the content, it may be clear as to what preoccupies them and why. With some children, it may be a straightforward series of heroes and fame fantasies. The child fantasizes being the best at various activities and receiving prizes and adulation from others. This type requires the action discussed previously. However, it may be that the content demonstrates specific concerns that can be addressed or remedied. For example, the child might daydream that he lives in a peaceful castle where everything is calm. The parents might see the clue that the home atmosphere may be too chaotic and disturbing for the child. More organization and calmness at home could diminish or eliminate the daydreaming.

Seek Professional Help. When the child or adolescent has difficulty in telling the difference between daydreaming and reality, professional help should be immediately sought. Professional intervention is also indicated when specific approaches are consistently employed for several months with little success. Short-term psychotherapy or counseling may be quite effective in reducing daydreaming and promoting more satisfying functioning. There are a variety of "growth experiences" that may help the generally dissatisfied child who resorts to fantasizing. Many adolescents have benefited from yoga, sensitivity, and assertiveness training. Professionally led groups can be quite effective in aiding adolescents to gain more satisfaction from relating to their peers. Children who learn to feel good about themselves and to meaningfully relate to others daydream less.

Case Report

A 14-year-old girl was frequently daydreaming at home and at school. Her schoolwork was not up to par, and her teacher reported that "her daydreaming was interfering with her concentration and her performance." At home, she spent a great deal of time in her room and was apparently daydreaming even when she listened to music or while doing homework. She had few friends and frequently expressed boredom. Two family therapy sessions and eight psychotherapy sessions with the girl resulted in a reduction in time spent on daydreaming and more productive involvement with her environment.

Key ingredients were the development of active plans for the girl and the teacher's communication with the parents. Plans were made for increased social participation. It was agreed that she would join an after school photography club, which met twice a week. On Saturday morning, she would attend the local recreation center. The teacher's daily phone call regarding less daydreaming and improved class participation resulted in extra allowance and a special weekend event (if there were at least three positive calls). In psychotherapy, her perception of her life as both scary and dull were discussed. After 2 months, the girl's analysis of her progress was that she was doing more, felt happier, and didn't only look forward to daydreaming. Schoolwork and homework were completed satisfactorily.

Books for Children about Daydreaming

Asch, Frank: *Rebecka*. Harper & Row, New York (1972). Ages 3 to 6.

A young boy is overly dependent upon his dog and daydreams about being married to her. He would not play house with a new girl next door because he said he was already married. At the end he plays with the girl and decides that it is better for a dog to be a dog and a person to be a person.

Cone, Molly Lamken: *The Real Dream.* Houghton Mifflin, Boston (1964). Ages 12 and up.

A 15-year-old girl never sees things realistically. She daydreams and rationalizes but finally learns to resolve real problems appropriately. Her refusal to see her boyfriend's faults is vividly portrayed. Emotions had led her to lose sight of the importance of realistically dealing with everyday demands.

Little, Jean: *Spring Begins in March.* Little, Brown, Boston (1966). Ages 10 to 12.

A 10-year-old girl doesn't complete school assignments because she always daydreams and is disorganized. She learns to appreciate her grandmother by reading her old diary. A rebellious and frustrated girl learns to cope with school problems with the aid of her family.

Mazer, Harry: *The Dollar Man.* Delacorte Press, New York (1974). Ages 12 and up.

A 13-year-old boy is overweight, lonely, and fatherless. He daydreams of being thin and having a heroic father. After many difficulties, he meets his father who does not want to have anything to do with him. He is very disappointed but learns to stop daydreaming and to deal with reality.

Viorst, Judith: *I'll Fix Anthony.* Harper & Row, New York (1969). Ages 3 to 6.

A 5-year-old is very angry with his older brother who won't play with him. He frequently daydreams about getting even with Anthony. The young boy relieves his frustration about his unkind brother by daydreaming. Parents can discuss frustrations and daydreaming with their child since the story purposely has an open ending.

Willard, Mildred Wilds: *The Luck of Harry Weaver.* Franklin Watts, New York (1971). Ages 8 to 10.

Harry has no friends, is teased, and spends most of his time daydreaming and wishing for better luck. He becomes interested in helping a boy with many problems. After believing his increased popularity was due to a good luck cricket, he realizes that he was responsible for his good luck through his own effort.

Reference

1. Zimbardo, Philip G.: *Shyness: What It is, What to Do About It.* Addison-Wesley, Reading, MA (1977).

MESSY–SLOPPY

Some people think of *messiness* as meaning dirty or untidy and *sloppiness* as meaning careless. However, dictionaries, as well as other sources, list *messy* and *sloppy* as synonyms. Messy/sloppy means being careless, slovenly, confused, disordered, dirty, untidy, and lacking neatness or precision. For example, on a widely used scale[1] to rate children's behavior, one of the areas measured is called "Messiness, Sloppiness." Children with high scores are unconcerned about adult standards of cleanliness. The three questions rated are to what degree is the child messy or sloppy in his or her eating habits, careless about appearance and belongings, and prone to get dirty and untidy quickly.

Young children are normally messy, so once again we have a situation where problematic messiness is messiness "to a greater degree than normal." Parents who expect perfection or more than the child is capable of are often disappointed and angry. Realistic expectations and awareness of child development and the behavior of peers are helpful. However, it is often readily apparent when children are unusually untidy and careless concerning clothes, toys, school materials, or appearance. Also, dirty habits are obvious when the child will not wash, enjoys being dirty, or frequently gets very dirty. Further indicators of problematic sloppiness are when situations become unhealthy or unsafe, and when the child or parent cannot find things.

A great deal of conflict occurs between parents and young teen-agers. Teenagers are constantly telling their parents that most teen-agers are sloppy and that their parents should leave them alone. Arguments over personal appearance and messy rooms are one of the most typical aspects of a "generation gap." Parents are very frequently told by their children that they are old fashioned and uptight. There are very few parents who haven't heard, "I'll dress the way I want and keep my room the way I like it, and I don't care what anyone thinks." For many teen-agers, messiness has become a sign of independence, a badge of honor, or a means of identifying with a peer group.

Reasons Why

Demonstrating Independence or Anger. "Looking the way I want" is a familiar phrase heard from early childhood through adolescence. Personal appearance is one of the most basic areas of self-expression. Since tidiness is often stressed by most parents, many children develop messiness as a means of asserting independence. The more parents insist on cleanliness and orderliness, the more determined many children are to do things in their own sloppy way. When parents are strict in many areas of children's lives, these children often look for some means of demonstrating their uniqueness. Sloppiness in personal appearance is a more obvious indicator of "this is how I want to dress." Less obvious is the development of a disorganized and careless approach to a variety of tasks as a sign of independence.

Most adults recognize the rebellious aspect of sloppy and dirty clothing and habits. Anger can be expressed by the flaunting of conventional rules. Children who feel generally angry or bitter, "get even" with the world by not conforming. They often appear proud of their dirty appearance and describe cleanliness as being unnecessary or stupid. Frequently, adolescent messiness is a result of the combination of a sign of independence and an expression of anger as a type of revenge for real or imagined unfairness.

Refusal to Be Responsible. More specific than a general expression of independence or anger is a child's refusal to accept the responsibility that accompanies "growing up." Since children are not born with an urge for neatness, the value of tidiness must be learned. There are a variety of reasons for children to not want to accept their own role in achieving self-care. The most clear cut is the toddlers's refusal to give up his lack of responsibility. Infants and toddlers enjoy messy play and dirtiness. There is a transition from the infantile pleasure of messiness to a more mature satisfaction with cleanliness and neatness. Children who lack sufficient satisfaction in their lives are reluctant to give up the gratification of sloppiness.

Lack of Organizational Skills. There are many reasons why some children lack the skills necessary to be neat and organized. Some have never learned how to be neat. They may have grown up in a messy, disorganized home or even in a sub-culture that does not value neatness. Their parents did not model this type of organized behavior. More typical is the case of concerned parents who themselves are relatively neat, but who have messy children. These disorganized children may have been "overprotected" and never learned independent, organizational skills. Their parents took care of things and never really expected them to function independently. Most difficult are the subtle situations where parents say that they expect their children to take care of their rooms yet communicate the feeling that the children are not capable. These "double messages" are quite destructive and lead to much tension and disharmony. The net result is a child who does not develop the skills necessary to prepare and organize her room, personal possessions, and clothing. Finally, there are children who are not motivated to learn organizational skills. The lack of motivation may stem from different sources, but the children appear lazy and uncaring. Typically, there has never been sufficient reason for them to develop neat habits. Most usual is the lack of parental positive reinforcement for the learning and carrying out of neat behavior.

Emotional factors play a role in the development of what most adults assume are perceptual skills not really affected by emotional status. In a widely used psychological test of copying designs,[2] two important "emotional indicators" of poor performance are "confused order" and "careless overwork." Children are not organized in the placement of their drawings or are careless and have to erase over and over again. The implication is clear that children's emotional problems lead to impairment in a task as basic as copying designs.

Deserving of special mention are the children with subtle handicaps that interfere with the ability to organize their environment. Indeed, some children may even lack the physical coordination necessary for the continued maintenance of a neat and organized appearance. Children with cerebral palsy are easy to recognize and understand. Children with relatively poor coordination are called clumsy and are frequently unmercifully criticized for years. Even more difficult to recognize are children with subtle perceptual deficits. On psychological testing, psychologists are able to pinpoint perceptual weaknesses where the child cannot recognize shapes and forms in different positions. These children literally cannot see the sock in the middle of the room, let alone in a drawer with other clothing. Special help and arrangements are necessary to help this child be organized enough to be able to find and store various objects. Arranging compartments in drawers and closets can avoid endless scolding and nagging. Similarly, these children misbutton clothing, put belts on improperly, wear different colored socks, do not tuck clothing in, and often look "discombobulated."

Organizational deficits are even more difficult to recognize. Some children have a weakness in *sequencing*, causing great difficulty in remembering what comes first, second, third, etc. For them, organizing becomes a hopeless task if it involves following steps in sequence. Similarly, organization can be torture for children who have trouble in *consequential* thinking. They have great difficulty in understanding and/or remembering the consequences of actions. These children, although often bright in other areas, do not understand that certain responses *follow* certain actions. "Cause and effect" are often unclear to them. What is obvious to adults is often not at all obvious to these children. On the most basic level, they do not understand that being able to find objects requires that they be kept in specific places. The consequence of lack of organization is being made to find needed objects. The consequence of being sloppy is that many peers and adults will have a negative impression of the child and therefore reject him. Some parents find it very difficult to understand that their child may not really comprehend these social consequences.

How to Prevent

Early and Continuing Training. Preschoolers can be taught to keep a relatively neat room. From 2 years on, simple rules of neatness should be encouraged. The very young child can participate in putting toys back in a box. Three year olds should not live for days in a room with piles of objects interfering with walking. Simple organization of certain types of toys in one place will lead to a habit of placing things in the same place. This procedure will avoid the endless searching for things and promote early organizational habits. Parents should also teach the basics of planning ahead, keeping a check list when necessary, and doing tasks in order. Never underestimate the power of *modeling* neatness both in personal appearance and taking care of objects at home.

Regular chores. Children should have appropriate chores throughout childhood and adolescence. Parents have the continuing responsibility to carefully consider and plan age-appropriate jobs. The toddler should put dirty clothes in a hamper and toys in a closet, box, or cabinet. From 5 years, a child should make her bed and aid in some aspect of cleaning. Children can sweep, vacuum, or dust. They can empty waste cans, take garbage outside, set the table, wash or dry the dishes, etc. The key is the expectation that children participate in the everyday process of maintaining a relatively clean and orderly home.

Self-grooming. The toddler can be taught to avoid excessive dirtiness. A helpful principle is that young children are capable of *discriminating*. Toddlers in play clothes can roll in the dirt and get paint and clay on themselves. When dressed to visit relatives, they can avoid getting dirty. By school age, children should be aware of personal grooming. They should already have the awareness and skill to comb their hair, tuck their clothing in, and look in a mirror to assess whether they need to wash their faces. At home, parents can make grooming a reasonably enjoyable activity. Children should be given a choice as to the type and color of comb or brush they prefer. Similarly, they can go to the store and choose toothpaste and toothbrush that they would like to use. *Active participation* is much better than passively receiving things that parents have selected.

In training children to be neat and organized, activities should be performed *together*. The more interaction the better. A family shopping trip to choose deodorants, combs, etc., can be a natural and valuable experience for children. In all self-care tasks, *parental praise* and *acknowledgment* of children's performance are absolutely essential.

Teach Concern for Others. Parents often wish that their children would want to be neat in order to please themselves. However, as mentioned previously, neatness is not an inborn instinct. Children become neat in order to please others. Therefore, instilling concern for others is a preventive measure against the development of excessive messiness. The child learns that pleasing others is important and can become personally satisfying. Having a neat room and a clean body pleases parents, and *later* becomes a personally satisfying habit. Similarly, a child can learn to discriminate by pleasing parents by having an especially clean room when visitors are expected. Her room may be sloppy at times and then cleaned and neatened when it *matters* to her parents or herself.

Modeling concern for others is crucial. The parents should *demonstrate* their concern for each other's wishes plus their genuine concern for their children. Only in this manner does true concern for others develop at an early age. The parent who takes time to fix a child's toy or talk to a child about his favorite games demonstrates caring. It is then natural for the child to care about pleasing parents by being neater and more organized. A *cooperative* atmosphere is developed, where people care about each other and cooperate by demonstrating helpful and sensitive behavior. Concern for children is demonstrated by friendly but firm instructions to "please remove your things from the living room before you go outside." Angry, dictatorial statements are not helpful ("Clean the living room this minute. I want to see a spotless floor!").

What to Do

Teach and Reward Neatness. There are a variety of formal and informal ways of rewarding neatness. Prior discussions of use of tokens and contracts are quite applicable here. Neatness in any form by a messy child should be rewarded and praised. The child should be taught that being neat is convenient, helpful, and considerate of others and is not just for looks or showing off. We will review some specific approaches to promoting neatness.

Demonstrate and reward steps to neatness. This approach is essential for older children who literally do not *know how* to be neat. It is also the most direct approach with young children who have not learned neatness skills or who only have a weak undestanding of what to do. Therefore, a sloppy room, forgotten or poorly done chores, or poor or disorganized homework may indicate a lack of knowledge rather than a negative attitude. The goals must be explained simply and broken down into steps. Some children respond well to the use of a chart to show *where* things belong and *when* a chore should be done. Children must be *shown how* the task should be carried out. Finally *improvement*, not perfection should always be praised. Many children respond very well to praise when they have learned to be neat and a formal reward system may not become necessary.

Using these principles, parents can sensitively assess the child's deficiencies and teach the necessary skills. For example, many young children are not aware of the steps involved in keeping a room neat and organized. You can start by showing them *where* toys belong. Often it is necessary to decide with a child where things should go. A toy box, a book case, and especially a large metal cabinet with shelves are possible storage places. When they should put things away should be made clear. In some households, before bedtime works. However, many children are too tired, and bedtime arrives with no time for cleaning. Therefore, a set time after dinner (say 7:45 to 8 P.M.) may be more workable. You demonstrate by having the child watch you do it. Next time, the child puts things away while you praise his efforts.

When you are sure that the child knows what is expected and how to do it, the following methods may be used to demonstrate your conviction to follow through on your teaching.

Open or closed door: This method is applicable to one or more children in a bedroom. You inspect the room at an agreed upon time. If the room is satisfactory, you leave the door open. If not, you close the door. The closed door indicates that the room needs work. One practical method would be for the child to go out to play only when the door is left open. If shut, the room must be cleaned by the children before going out or before watching television, etc. This type of structure avoids verbal criticism and defensive arguments.

Locked cabinet: An inspection can be made periodically (perhaps before bedtime). The child or teen-ager has been told that any toys, games, or clothing not in their proper place will be locked in a cabinet for 2 days. Longer intervals may be necessary in some cases. The items are tagged with the date that they will be returned. Some parents like a library card method, where the return date is specified on a card. This also teaches organization, where the cards are kept in a box. Another variation is some cost for the child to redeem the object. Possible costs are a money fine or a deduction from a weekly allowance, deprivation of some pleasure, or performance of a task chore. As with all methods, parental attitude must be matter of fact or humorous rather than tense and punitive.

Charts. Listing the target behaviors is a concrete and effective tool. The basic task of grooming can be placed on a chart and checked off by the child or a star posted by a parent. The specific task should be listed next to the time of day. Morning—brush teeth, wash hands and face, brush hair, tuck clothing in properly. After school—change clothes, wash. Before bedtime—wash, brush teeth. A straightforward system of points earned for personal appearance and room neatness may be very effective. Points can earn privileges such as television viewing, extra allowance, etc. For those parents who do not use a formal system, an effective penalty could be washing windows in their room for failing to keep objects in their place. A dramatic offer by parents would be to ask children if there are parental habits that they would like changed. Constructing a parent chart would be an example of "practicing what you preach."

A variation of parents constructing a chart is having children make a chart of their messy habits and which ones are important or unimportant to them. Similarly, they can list what they consider to be important or unimportant chores. The child should be asked to agree to change one messy habit. An effective penalty is to perform an unimportant chore if he does not change the messy behavior. This method is particularly effective for children who do not respond to the use of money as a reward or penalty.

Provide Outlets for Independence and Responsibility. From age 6, parents should not pick up after children.

Taking care of their things is *their* job. You might say that you will not go into a dirty room to talk or change the sheets or pick up clothes. Therefore, young children may learn to keep a clean neat room that adults would like to be in. Minimally the child has the responsibility of having a neat room at times when parents expect it (weekends, visitors, showing a house for sale, etc.). At other times, parents might communicate that children have the right to keep a room the way they want to.

Since major causes of messiness are a desire for independence and a refusal to be responsible, outlets have to be developed. The child can learn independence and responsibility by being given appropriate chores with allowance geared to successful completion. The key is to give children and adolescents more and more independent responsibility at a rate they can handle. There are many instances of 12 year olds who are not allowed to visit a friend's house or go on a train without an adult. Many heated arguments occur between children who want more responsibility and parents who say they are not ready. Achieving the correct degree of independence is crucial. You may be guided to some extent by what your child's friends are permitted to do. A useful rule of thumb is to gradually increase the level of responsibility and assess the child's ability to handle it. The messy child who expresses dissatisfaction frequently may well need more opportunities to obtain satisfaction. The relatively satisfied child will have less of a need to flaunt a "messy, who cares" attitude.

Special Approaches for Special Problems. Children who are awkward, clumsy, slow, sloppy, and unable to find things need special help, not criticism. Just trying harder does not make them neater and more organized. They need even more of the types of methods previously described under "Demonstrate and Reward Steps to Neatness." However, these children need more concrete demonstrations, more encouragement, more praise, and most of all more understanding of their weaknesses. Blaming them for their real inabilities not only doesn't help, it invariably leads to more arguments and a poor self-concept by the children. These children think of themselves as "bad" and often act in a manner that confirms that image. It is difficult for some parents who have an awkward, messy child to praise the small positive steps that they do take. "Congratulations, you look neater today" should be said to the child who looks *relatively* better because he tied his shoelaces. Children feel much better when you say, ''I know how hard it is for you to keep your room neat, but I'll help.'' This is in contrast to—''How can you still be such a slob when I've shown you a million times how to straighten your room?'' The child with subtle perceptual problems can't find what he's looking for. This takes very special planning and organizing, so he will learn where to put things and how to find them.

Case Report

A 13-year-old girl was extremely messy in personal appearance and in the care of her room. Additionally, she was disorganized both in the care of her personal belongings and in her schoolwork. When interviewed, the parents believed strongly that their daughter was bright, quite aware of how things should be done, and had always been exposed to a relatively neat and organized home situation. Her 15-year-old brother, although not fastidious, was relatively neat in his personal appearance and schoolwork. The parents were very responsive to two sessions of counseling, and they subsequently successfully employed the following strategy.

Initially, they used a straightforward reward system for both neater appearance and schoolwork. For each day of ''improved'' neatness (judged by the mother), the girl was given an extra $.25 in allowance. Analysis of the family situation led to the parents' acceptance of the need to provide greater independence. She was allowed to go to bed 1 half-hour later on nights before school and 1 hour later before non-school days. Additionally, she was permitted more freedom in choosing her own clothing and in how she would spend her additional allowance. The messy and disorganized room was quickly eliminated by both parents helping her organize her room and by building additional shelves in her closet for specific articles of clothing.

The parents later reported that they were very satisfied with the results and offered the following analysis. They felt that both of them helping their daughter in her room and giving her more independence greatly improved their relationship and changed the tense atmosphere. The reward system, combined with a later bedtime, worked immediately in an improved personal appearance with a neater room.

They believed that schoolwork initially improved as a means of earning more allowance. However, her general attitude appeared more positive, and she showed a more genuine interest in doing better schoolwork.

Books for Parents About Messy-Sloppy Behavior

Sloane, Howard N.: *Not 'Til Your Room's Clean*. Telesis, Fountain Valley, California (1976).

Books for Children About Messy-Sloppy Behavior

Raymond, Charles: *Jud*. Houghton Mifflin, Boston (1968). Ages 9 to 12.

Jud refused to help his father with household chores. The family moves from the city to a rural area and Jud hates it. Gradually, he learns to love and respect nature. He also comes to accept the necessity of hard work.

Gilbert, Nan: *Champions Don't Cry*. Harper & Row, New York (1960). Ages 10 to 13.

A 13-year-old girl lacks the self-discipline to become a tennis champion. Gradually, she learns to have patience, practice, and control her temper. Her progress and eventually winning a tennis tournament were due to developing self-discipline.

Little, Jean: *Spring Begins in March*. Little, Brown, Boston (1966). Ages 10 to 12.

A 10-year-old girl doesn't complete school assignments because she is careless and disorganzied. Her sister tutors and helps her take care of a new puppy. Gradually, the girl becomes more concerned, organized, and does better in school.

Ness, Evaline M.: *Do You Have the Time, Lydia?* E.P. Dutton, New York (1971). Ages 5 to 8.

A young girl is always busy but never finishes what she starts. She never sets priorities, and she is extremely disorganized. Her little brother loses a race because she did not finish what she said she would. Through misfortune, she learns to be organized and take the time to do things properly.

References

1. Spivack, George and Spotts, Jules: *Devereux Child Behavior Rating Scale: Manual*. Devereux Foundation, Devon, PA (1966).
2. Koppitz, Elizabeth M.: *The Bender Gestalt Test for Young Children*. Grune & Stratton, New York (1975).

TIME USED POORLY

Many children use time poorly. The most frequent complaints of parents are that their children dawdle, procrastinate, or are just lazy. We have grouped these problems together since they overlap somewhat, and all relate to inefficient use of time. Time is used slowly or not at all (lazy), wasted (dawdle), or put off until some future time (procrastinate). More specifically, *lazy* means inactive, not energetic, sluggish, and disinclined to action. *Dawdle* is to spend time idly, fruitlessly, or lackadaisically. *Procrastinate* is to intentionally and habitually put something off that should be done. A common element is that poor use of time often leads to a lack of being on time (not punctual or prompt).

In American homes, "hurry" is the most common word used at 8 A.M. Many children and adolescents find it very difficult to plan their time wisely, especially during the mornings. Therefore, most children could learn to use time more efficiently, and parents can aid them by using some of the approaches described in this chapter. All children occasionally dawdle, procrastinate, or act in a lazy manner. There are no statistics on the number of children in whom these characteristics are a frequent problem. However, a great number of children develop patterns of behavior where they are often described by others as lazy, or a dawdler, or a procrastinator.

Developmentally, children gradually learn about the concept of time. Typically, 3 year olds know their age, 4 year olds know when their next birthday will be and what day of the week it is, and 5 year olds know months and year. By 4 years, children can realize that their birthdays are one of a series and understand the concept of growth and change. Parents are often unaware that many children do not really understand time concepts until the age of 10 years. After age 10, children can be expected to be punctual most of the time, since they can understand the passage of time and how to plan ahead. However, there are very wide differences in children's awareness of time concepts. Much anger and resentment may be avoided by parental awareness of their children's awareness. Some parents expect 6, 7, or 8 year olds to be able to use time wisely and be punctual on their own, whereas it is typical for children this age to require guidance and aid in planning, in order to be ready, have assignments in on time, or do chores within a specific time period.

Reasons Why

Expression of Psychological Conflict. Time frequently is used as a tool in psychological battles between parents and children or within a child.

Power struggle. The more adults push, the more the child pulls. Parents try to hurry the child, and the child appears to slow down or dawdle. Children express their desire for independence and power in a variety of ways. Here, they assert themselves by using time in a manner that puts them in a position of control and their parents in a position of frustration and helplessness. This reaction is quite frequent when parents nag or make time a heated issue by their aroused (and often ineffectual) attempts to push an apparently resisting child. Children who feel bossed and that they have no control often misuse time in the morning as a means of asserting their own power. The result of this pattern is that children receive *attention* (even in the form of anger) for using time poorly. This attention inadvertently reinforces the problem, and the result is a prolonged power struggle over time, which the child usually wins by not being on time. The child's feeling of success makes the pattern even stronger. If these children are on time, they experience a sense of failure and are therefore locked in a rigid pattern of inefficient use of time. Overcontrolling or frantic parents can produce or exaggerate this form of power struggle.

Passive-aggressive expression of anger. Children become angry at their parents for a variety of reasons. Not getting what they want typically results in anger at parents. However, it is the exaggeration of this normal anger that can result in a child using time to get even. *Frequent punishment* and nagging are a major cause of slowness and dawdling as a type of rebellion (rather than open defiance). Behind this behavior is the feeling that "no one tells me what to do or when to do it." These children often appear *selfish* and *inconsiderate*. Their difficulties are blamed on others, and they see their poor use of time as the responsibililty or the problem of others. They come across as self-centered, seeing only their own interests. Any confrontation results in their anger towards adults and their stubbornness being aroused. They often become careless regarding schedules or appointments, perfunctorily do assignments or chores, and often neglect the essential aspects of what they are doing.

Avoid unpleasant situations. Procrastination or lateness is a means of avoiding disliked people or situations. Children and many adolescents therefore express their anger by using time to avoid disliked (or feared) situations. Laziness can become the means by which children avoid any type of situation which they believe will make them anxious or uncomfortable. Anxiety about starting the day can result in ineffective time use. Children anxious about school days do not dawdle on weekend mornings! Additionally, anxious children often perceive time as passing too slowly (a smaller percentage feel time passing too quickly). Time is perceived as an enemy to be coped with rather than a commodity to be used wisely. Very frequent also is poor use of time to *avoid failure*. Children then do not commit themselves to using time appropriately for fear of risking failure or feelings of psychological rejection. *Daydreaming* is a typical means of avoiding pain and engaging in pleasant fantasies. Children who frequently daydream do not use time well. Rather than purposeful stalling, they spend time "lost in thought." Another means of avoidance is *perfectionism*. The child who views anything short of perfection as unacceptable winds up accomplishing very little. Overly compulsive children who strive to be perfect waste enormous amounts of time. Even dressing can become an elaborate, time-consuming ritual. Effective preparation of any kind is therefore interfered with. What starts out as perfectionism which serves to avoid confrontation or anxiety winds up being a self-defeating habit.

Time Doesn't Matter. There are sub-cultures or families where time does not matter. Children learn that, in a sense, time has little value. Therefore, time is not used in a realistic, considerate, or productive manner. Time is wasted, put off, or used haphazardly. In these situations, parents are often not displeased with their children until others express dissatisfaction. Most typically, the school complains that the child is late, does not hand in assignments, wastes time, etc. Parents then see the discrepancy between their time values and society's demands on their children.

Children who are not used to routines do not develop the habit of establishing set patterns and accomplishing what has to be done within a time limit. Often, these children have not learned the consequences of not following rules and of using time poorly. Since the adults in their lives do not value time, there have been no real positive or negative consequences (rewards or punishments) regarding time usage. They have not heard statements such as "you can go out and play only when your room is clean." They have not learned that how time is used does very much matter. These children typically cannot *delay gratification.* They want their desires fulfilled immediately and cannot work now and enjoy later. Frequently heard is their comment that "everything will work out and get better later." This is especially true of children who procrastinate.

Unrealistic Parental Expectations. Many parents have no idea of the development of *time concept* with age. They expect 5 year olds to be ready on time or be punctual without concrete guidance and reminders. Therefore, many problems can arise from the clash between parent and child over use of time. On the other hand, parents can understand and be tolerant of the child's level of time awareness. Unrealistic time expectations lead to problems about time and also heighten the general level of family tension. *Patience* is required of parents to accept that a child's pace is not as rapid as an adult's. The impatient adult yells and nags rather than allowing extra time. Children are naturally less coordinated and more careless, impulsive, and distractible than are adults.

Similarly, *temperamental differences* cause difficulties. In one family, there may be one child who has always been slow moving and easy going. And there may be another child who moves quickly, accomplishing many tasks. If the slow-moving child is constantly criticized, time becomes more and more of a source of anguish. Even more striking is the situation of two energetic, punctual parents having a relatively lethargic child. Acceptance of constitutional physiological differences is often very difficult for parents. A helpful reminder is that slowness is a natural rhythm for some children, and great pressure should not be used to change them.

Some parents cannot accept the notion of actual intellectual *deficits* regarding *time* in their child. Some children literally cannot estimate the passage of time. Some are disoriented and forget how much time has passed. Others have the specific problem of not being able to remember the sequence of events or steps in a task. People are aware of these problems existing in retarded children. However, many "normal" children have these specific weaknesses in time concepts. Some grow out of it quickly while others do not. Today, psychological and educational testing can accurately pinpoint these difficulties. Many children can learn time concepts if taught properly. One example is that a time perspective is necessary for the ability to delay immediate gratification. The young child may see next week as being extremely remote. Basic understanding of time concepts is the underpinning for the efficient actual use of time.

How to Prevent

Teach and Model Effective Use of Time. From earliest infancy, children experience time as set by their family. Infants are conditioned to be gratified immediately or to wait for gradually increasing periods. In our society, by age 3, many children see the world as totally revolving around them and are unable to wait. They have not learned that time can be used in many ways, and that they must learn that you can't always get what you want when you want. Very young children enjoy finishing a task within a time limit. They feel successful by accomplishing setting the table, stringing beads, etc.

The toddler can learn to follow *routines* and *reasonable time limits*. Routines establish a feeling of regularity. A time for play, rest, schoolwork, or chores can be set at age 3. Reasonable time limits can be set and reinforced. Meals, dressing, washing, etc., should be accomplished within age-appropriate time limits. By asking a simple question, most parents know what reasonable means at different ages. A 7 year old does not require an hour to consume a meal. A 9 year old does not need 40 minutes to get dressed in the morning. By establishing limits at an early age, poor use of time can be prevented.

Punctuality should be modeled by parents, who should expect and reinforce punctuality in their children. You should *remind* young children about the passage of time and expect and reward gradual progress. The use of a kitchen timer or alarm clock is an excellent training device. It is an impersonal reminder of time passing and the end of a time interval. For example, young children procrastinate about going to bed. A timer should be set for 15 minutes with the agreement that the child shuts the light and gets into bed. There are no arguments when the buzzer goes off. Children who learn to accomplish objectives on time do not develop problems with time.

"Don't pull off 'till tomorrow what you can do today." You should live and teach this valuable proverb. The *procrastinator* puts things off and typically criticizes and blames others. An appropriate proverb here is—"It's not what you say, it's what you do." Tedious or difficult tasks should not be put off. What must be learned by children is "do it now" not "I'll do it tomorrow." *Excuses* must be carefully avoided. The following statements are all too familiar in a great number of families: "I'm too tired to do it now," "I don't have the time to do it," "I'll start dieting and exercising tomorrow." Behind these statements are the wish and expectation that things will work out by themselves. Prevention of difficulties is best accomplished by feeling and projecting the attitude that "I'll make it happen" not "I hope it happens." You should communicate to children that it is important to get things done now. Put simply, you show interest in your children's activities, check on progress, help them when necessary, and praise their efforts.

One important key to effective time use is the teaching of *organizational skills*. You teach that tasks, especially if they appear overwhelming, should be broken down into steps. Then—*get started!* The child should be helped to lay out clothes or objects as an aid to being efficient and reasonably fast. Don't nag and do show that you want to be helpful. Positive thinking is demonstrated by modeling and saying aloud statements such as—"It feels great getting things done," "If I don't do it, it won't get done and I'll feel terrible." This style naturally leads to the teaching of self-control and self-reward. The goal is the independent setting of a time to work and then consistently working in that place. This conditions the child to set regular times and work, not play, in that selected work setting (a corner of a room or at a desk). Self-reward is accomplished by self-praise: "I'm really glad I finished. It was hard but I did a good job." Additionally, children can make a list of enjoyable activities and do those activities *only* after completing a chore or assignment (self-reward).

At times, it may be helpful to let the child suffer the natural consequences of wasting time. The child might then miss breakfast, be late for school or a movie, or be scolded by friends for not being on time or fulfilling a promise to accomplish something. Many parents fall into the "Achilles heel" syndrome, where they want to protect their children from harm. By constantly protecting the child from the natural consequences of poor time use, the child does not learn the importance of using time wisely. Using time wisely can be bolstered by doing a simple form of leisure counseling. When the family atmosphere is pleasant, the ways of spending time should be discussed openly and specifically. The time for fun should be set aside and planned. Some families always wait until the last minute to make arrangements. Planning a trip or participation in an event is an invaluable lesson for children. By participating in the preparation for an event, children experience the appropriate use of time for planning, doing what is necessary, and finally enjoying the fruits of prior labor.

Promote Consideration and Sensitivity to Others. Real caring about the feelings of others is a strong antidote to time wasting that affects others. Procrastination and irresponsibility about time can be prevented by the practicing and teaching of consideration of others. Being late inconveniences others. If a child is late, it is not helpful to nag, scold, or punish. It is helpful to say, "Please don't be late again; our friends expect us on time. Now, let's hurry." Being slow when others are all working quickly results in being seen as a nonhelpful slowpoke. "Trying your best" is as applicable to working quickly and efficiently as it is to doing the best you are capable of doing.

Sensitivity to others' feelings should be demonstrated by

the usual psychological atmosphere you create. In the morning, you can project warmth and tenderness (emotional closeness), or irritability, tension, and anger. Your awareness of your own moods can lead to your promotion of a climate of caring for others. In a similar fashion, you can be pleasant, encouraging, and alert, or troubled, moody, lethargic, or impatient. One example is the mood set at bedtime. Some parents are tired and irritable and set a negative tone, which is exaggerated by a child's dawdling while preparing for bed. You could tell interesting stories at bedtime, making it a pleasant experience. Stories about the past and the exploits of family members are interesting to all aged children. When the story is over, children go to sleep. In this atmosphere, complaining and procrastination do not develop.

Avoid Linking Conflicts with Time. Personal achievement is a worthwhile end in itself. When achievement is used as a competitive weapon, problems can develop. If doing something correctly is valued, then correctness will be less likely to be used as a means of demonstrating superiority or making someone feel inferior. Quite frequently not achieving is used as a means of revenge. In essence, we are saying that time usage should not be linked with negative feelings. You should avoid using time as a punishment. For example, it is not wise to punish children by 20 minutes of inactivity. This is not only boring but demonstrates the use of time as a weapon.

Similarly, avoid developing a pattern where time is part of a power struggle. By nagging and yelling about children moving too slowly, use of time becomes part of a struggle between parent and child. Being effective in accomplishing your goal avoids the repetitive, ineffective nagging and scolding. The use of consistent rewards for being on time results in children being on time. Also, be very aware when children appear to be stalling due to fear of trying or as a means of expressing anger. Encourage and accept their direct expressions of feeling. Do not allow poor use of time to become a means of expressing a psychological conflict. Therefore, dawdling will not develop as a means of expressing anger or fear or for controlling adults.

What to Do

Lazy. There are a variety of approaches for the sluggish child who at times will not even attempt tasks. Mutual *problem solving* is a good start. An open discussion is held as to the specific problems and what *we* (the family) can do. A solution is sought together. Topics discussed include what causes the slowness, what are the consequences, and what could be done differently. Suggestions are requested from the child, and suggestions are made for the child's consideration. Some slow children have responded well to the following ideas.

Morning slowness. The child should set an alarm clock to an agreed upon time. A radio-alarm may set a pleasant mood by waking the child to a preferred type of music. A morning shower or a cold, wet cloth on the face is a good awakener. An open window provides a cool room conducive to awakening. Some children respond very well to a brief exercise period. Any method should avoid the trap of parental nagging. You can pleasantly say to your child, "I don't like being a nagging alarm clock—you can get up and be quicker on your own."

Perfectionistic slowness. Some children check and double check their actions and think for a long time before acting. Some perfectionistic children can take 1 half-hour to wash or get dressed. This type of compulsive slowness has been subjected to a "time and motion" study.[1] Basically, the child carries out slow rituals with increasing speed until achieving tasks within a more reasonable time limit. You analyze which tasks can be eliminated or sped up (time and motion analysis). In a positive emotional atmosphere, the child can then try the suggestions and use a stop watch to measure improvement. For example, the child who takes 1 hour to get ready for breakfast can reduce the time to 40 minutes. For some children, clothes selection the night before leads to greater efficiency in the morning.

Tasks not attempted. Some children appear so lazy that they do not want to do much of anything. For these children, a very strong incentive system may be necessary. The contracts and token economy approaches discussed in the chapter on hyperactivity are quite applicable. It may be necessary to make the attempts at doing tasks concretely worthwhile for the inactive child. In order to earn television watching, extra allowance, special trips, etc., the child would have to become active and do what is deemed necessary. At first, it is often helpful to reward small steps and trying tasks. After the child progresses, then satisfactory task completion should be rewarded.

Dawdle. The dawdler wastes time and fools around. Several games can be played with young children in order to reduce dawdling. "Beat the clock" is used to get the child to focus on a task and complete it. One example is "eat your vegetables before the timer goes off." The child should be asked how much time is necessary, and the timer is set to that figure. Praise or some reward may be used for beating the clock. Nagging is never employed. With some children, deprivation is successful. "No dessert if you can't beat the clock." Similarly, young children enjoy parental counting to see how fast they can go. "How many seconds does it take to put on your socks and shoes?" Reducing the length of time results in praise and/or rewards. Some children respond well to three announcements—10 minutes to go, 5 minutes left, and then only 1 minute left. Others respond to fast marching music which leads them to dress and do tasks in a quicker fashion. Music also serves to promote a cheerful morning mood. A metronome may also be helpful to encourage a quicker pace. In a controlled study,[2] foreign coins were earned by a 5-year-old girl by successfully reducing dawdling and better preparation for school. Specific time intervals were set for the girl to accomplish the following tasks (which were checked off as she did them)— wake up, make bed, get dressed, straighten room, comb hair, no whining, eat breakfast, leave house. At bedtime, dawdling may be drastically reduced by playing fun games. Young children can march around to music, and when the music ends they immediately go to bed.

In the morning, dawdlers can receive a reward for awakening on time. Morning tasks should be specified and checked. With some children, going to bed 1 hour earlier and waking 1 hour earlier quickly reduces dawdling, and they quickly prefer usual bed times. The child learns that being on time is a better option. In extreme cases, a child's clothing can be put in a car, and he dresses while being driven to school. This usually leads to dressing on time from that point on. There should be a clear expectation for children to be ready on time. At times, consistent negative consequences quickly solve the problem. If children miss the bus, they pay for a taxi with their own money. If, for any reason, dawdlers do not get to school, they should receive no attention (conversation, game playing, etc.) from adults. Boredom and loneliness can make school activities appear more desirable.

"Self-talk" may be suggested (and modeled) by the parent. You can show a child how saying things to yourself can speed things up and help promote a cheerful mood. "Well, it's time to get up. I'm going to have fun today. I'll start by quickly getting ready for school." The self-talk should be tailored to the child's problems. For example, some children can productively say, "Don't do something else, finish getting ready first," "Don't waste time, it's good to finish what you're doing," or "It feels good to be working faster and accomplishing something."

Procrastinate. Procrastinators express many reasons why they should not do something now. Somehow, things will work out or they will do it later. In order to counteract this self-defeating cycle, you must take effective, focused action. You should insist on a set time for children to accomplish something, make sure they do it, and praise or reward their efforts. Some parents report success by providing a special treat in the lunch box for those children who stop procrastinating and are on time. Point systems work very well when behavior is monitored and points given for gradual reduction of procrastination. It takes effort for parents to be aware of their child's postponing homework, not answering letters, not cleaning their room, or any procrastinating behavior. Awareness and an informal reward system can greatly reduce procrastination. Some parents are not aware of their child's self-defeating pattern of behavior or have never praised children for not putting off unpleasant chores. It is essential to praise or reward any efforts on the child's part to change the pattern, and negative comments must be avoided. It is not helpful to say: "You're a real loser. You always put off doing anything you don't like. When are you going to grow up?" Similarly, you must avoid being a poor model who puts tasks off until some vague time in the future.

The following guidelines are helpful for a variety of forms

of procrastination, especially for doing tasks that require writing or reading. Distraction should be reduced, and a specific place always used for the activity. A specific quota of number of pages or items should be set. After completing the quota, a predetermined self-reward should be engaged in. Rewards can be listening to a record, having a snack, playing a game, etc.

One direct and effective approach to procrastination is to attack the irrational beliefs that often cause the problem. For example, overcoming inertia and self discipline are often necessary antidotes to procrastination. Ellis and Harper[3] discuss two irrational ideas—"that you can more easily avoid facing many life difficulties and self-responsibilities than undertake more rewarding forms of self-discipline" and "that you can achieve maximum human happiness by inertia and inaction or by passively and uncommittedly enjoying yourself." Focused family discussions can reveal these beliefs and provide a forum for changing the behavioral pattern. Children, especially teen-agers, may be very responsive to a calm discussion of the need to overcome inertia and develop self-discipline. Similarly, the perfectionist who puts off completing the job because it's never good enough may respond to a discussion of this pattern. You can suggest that "I don't have to be perfect all the time; it's okay to fail or not to do the best job at times."

Another irrational belief is, "If I don't think about it, it will somehow disappear." This is similar to, "I don't have to do it now; it will get done tomorrow." It should be pointed out that things do not get done by themselves and wishing does not make something happen. Once the child understands the illogical nature of these beliefs, a practical plan can follow. Most direct is setting schedules for accomplishing objectives. This can be done in a written contract. "I'll read 20 pages a day before watching television." "I will straighten my room before going out to play." Parental praise or rewards can soon be stopped since the child will learn the good feelings that accompany doing what has to be done *now*.

Case Report

A 14-year-old girl dawdled frequently. She was almost always late for school and other appointments and took large amounts of time to accomplish easy tasks. Analysis of the family pattern revealed a great many power struggles between parents and daughter. The more the parents tried to hurry her, the more she dawdled. Her older brother was a "star" who did everything well. She resented him, felt inadequate, and dawdling became an excuse for not doing well. Committing herself to a task could expose her to risking failure. Two counseling sessions with the parents and two psychotherapy sessions with the girl successfully altered the pattern.

The parents agreed to stop nagging and yelling, and falling into situations that resembled battles. They used a simple reward system of extra privileges (the girl requested staying up a half-hour later) on any day when she was ready on time. After 3 weeks of very little dawdling, the later bedtime became permanent as an indication of her acting in a more grown-up manner. Additionally, a special event was planned for the weekend if she showed a dramatic reduction in time spent on everyday tasks. Bathroom time went from an average of about 40 minutes to a more typical 15 minutes. Psychotherapy consisted of an open discussion of her anger and struggles with her parents, resentment towards her brother, and fear of failure. This insight helped her understand how she wound up in a self-defeating pattern of wasting time. She was receptive to using "self-talk." When she started dawdling, she would say, "Stop wasting time, do what you're supposed to do." When she became more purposeful and quicker, she would say, "That's better, now we're getting somewhere." Many people naturally congratulated her for being on time and for doing things more quickly. A 1 year follow-up revealed virtually no dawdling, a happier girl, and much fewer heated family arguments.

Books for Parents about Time Used Poorly

Ellis, Albert and Knaus, William J.: *Overcoming Procrastination.* Institute for Rational-Emotive Therapy, New York (1978).

Books for Children About Time Used Poorly

Raymond, Charles: *Jud.* Houghton Mifflin, Boston (1968). Ages 9 to 12.

Jud's father can't get him to help with household chores. After moving to a rural area, Jud learns to accept the necessity of hard work.

Holman, Felice: *Professor Diggins' Dragons*. Macmillan, New York (1966). Ages 9 to 11.

A professor uses dragons as a symbol of peoples' faults and problems. During a summer, he helps five children cope with their problems. Lazy Lydia learns that work can be fun.

References

1. Marks, I.M.: *Living with Fear*. McGraw-Hill New York (1978).
2. Gickling, Edward E.: "From a Dawdling to a Doing Daughter." *Education 95* (1975): pp. 381–385.
3. Ellis, Albert and Harper, Robert A.: *A New Guide to Rational Living*. Wilshire Book Co., North Hollywood (1977).

SELFISH/SELF-CENTERED

Selfish people are overly or exclusively concerned with themselves. They concentrate on their own well-being or pleasure *without regard for others*. Several words are used to describe selfishness, such as self-centered, egocentric, and narcissistic. Self-centered people are concerned with their individual desires rather than the interests of society, and they appear to be relatively independent of outside influence. Their outlook or perspective is limited to concern with their own activities or needs. However, very intelligent and creative people can be independent, often ignore others' opinions, and be quite self-centered. One key difference is that these creative people are extremely productive in contrast to unproductive, narcissistic individuals.

It is very important to recognize that children are naturally egocentric. The toddler's universe is centered on himself. It is as if "I and the rest of the universe are one." Young children have a single viewpoint—their own. With time and experience, they learn to see things from someone else's point of view. Taking another's perspective is necessary before a child can understand how a situation appears to others and why and how others react. Young children have egocentric speech. They talk to themselves while acting, with some of the content being very idiosyncratic. With development, egocentric speech disappears. Inner speech develops which is essential for thinking (perceiving, abstracting, and generalizing). By 4 or 5 years of age, adequate communication skills have developed. There are only rare occurrences of egocentric speech or behavior indicating total self preoccupation. Preschoolers become more aware both of themselves and of others' view of them. By ages 6 through 9 years, children become much less egocentric, and they learn about the attitudes and opinions of others. However, they still feel very intensely and absolutely about their viewpoints and do not easily assume an impartial stance.

During the early school years, children learn to criticize themselves and to view their behavior by others' standards. The process develops from a concrete and literal approach to a more detached and impartial viewpoint. Children are then able to learn vicariously, not only by direct experience. They learn and gain experience through sympathizing with or imagining the experiences of others. What is natural for the preschooler is a sign of difficulties for the older children. By 5 or 6 the child should be relatively aware of having an impact on others. Children learn to project themselves into another's place ("walk in someone else's shoes"). Concern for others (people or animals) requires the realization of what it might feel like to be in their place. They can imagine what it feels like to be hurt or tortured. Children try to experience what things feel like by acting. They assume various roles, acting like animals or people they see in their lives or on television. By dressing up and acting like someone other than themselves they learn to understand others.

There are several indicators of problematic self-centeredness. Being so concerned with one's feelings can result in unproductive interaction with the world. Therefore, low productivity is one clue. This is similar to "spoiled" children who get everything they want without having to put forth any real effort. Often the selfish individual at times reveals a poor self-concept and a negative view of others. Also, few moral values are typical in selfish youngsters. Lack of group belongings is another indicator. Self-centered children often have difficulty relating to peers. They do not view their participation as "we" do things together, but rather as what "I" want. From a positive point of view, a feeling of belonging and identifying with others is seen by children experiencing a cohesive group feeling. The "we" feeling is seen when individuals in a group are open in expressing feelings and frequently communicating with each other.

Reasons Why

Fearful. Children can develop and maintain a predominantly selfish attitude because of a variety of fears. Fears of closeness to others, rejection, abandonment, and change may be interrelated and part of a generally fearful approach to life. The result of fearfulness can be a pulling back into oneself. Therefore, individuals who become frightened of involvement with others often become solely concerned with their own safety. Quite typical is the pattern of children being abandoned (physically and/or psychologically) or rejected and feeling scared and angry. They then can become self-centered and concerned with personal safety and happiness regardless of the feelings or concerns of others. Similarly, children who have frequently felt hurt by others develop a fear of becoming close or attached to others. By not psychologically exposing themselves through personal involvement and caring about or for others, they cannot be hurt again. The net result is a child who appears selfish and self-centered.

Generally fearful children often view any type of change in their lives as anxiety provoking. They see things only through their eyes and an understanding of others' viewpoints can be viewed as a scary change. Therefore, fear of change can both cause and/or exaggerate self-centeredness. Further complicating the picture is that selfish children often worry about possible negative consequences of their behavior. Therefore, they do not *share* their feelings or ideas which keeps them stuck in a pattern of self-preoccupation. A final cause of selfishness is the fearfulness engendered by parents who are teasing, capricious, or inconsistent in their child-rearing approach. The uncertainty and unpredictability can also cause the pattern of fear, turning inward, and selfishness.

Spoiled. Parents "spoil" children by being overprotective and all-giving. These parents try to prevent any discomfort and act immediately to eliminate any discomfort to the child. It is often guilt that drives parents to gratify all of their child's needs. Parents might react to their own deprived childhood and want their children to have everything that they missed. Parents who did not really want children or who dislike having children may overreact by being too concerned and too nice to their offspring. Therefore, children do not develop tolerance or coping capacity and remain stuck in an infantile, egocentric way of interacting. They clearly appear to others as only concerned with themselves and having little patience or tolerance for others. Being spoiled often leads to a combination of being selfish, shy, and having secret recurring fantasies of being great and the center of attention.

Parents sometimes teach their children to be selfish by their overly solicitous behavior. They try to protect their children from any type of frustration. The parents are incensed when anyone appears to be unfair to their children. They are quick to agree with their children's perceptions that others are taking advantage of them. Children are frequently lectured to stand up for their rights and not let themselves be stepped on by others. They become (in a sense as their parents taught them to be) selfish individuals who are not concerned with fairness to others.

The "only child" has a greater chance of being spoiled by parents. The child can easily be adored and overprotected. He does little of the mature activities that could lead to the assuming of responsibilities. This is combined with having no sibling to share things or ideas with. Therefore, the result can be a very self-centered child who expects to be the center of attention and only sees things from his or her point of view.

Immature. In order to give up selfishness, a certain level of maturity must be reached. For example, children must learn to control their impulses before they are able to keep agreements. Children who cannot tolerate frustration and must have what they want when they want it cannot keep their word. They feel justified in not keeping an agreement because they just *had* to have or do something else. Therefore, they appear selfish and do whatever they please in spite of discussions held and agreements reached. They cannot handle responsibility, and adults frequently describe them as "never having grown up." Similarly, immature children have not developed the type of judgment necessary to be sensitive to others and act accordingly. If intellectual judgment is not adequate, concern for others will not develop. This can be seen by behavior which always seems either inappropriate or insensitive. The child appears to be doing the wrong thing at the wrong time. This generally poor judgment makes it appear that the child is selfish and doesn't care about others, when these attitudes have not developed because of immaturity in the development of accurate social perception and the accompanying appropriate behavior.

At the simplest level, some children have *not learned* more mature behavior. This can occur for numerous reasons. Obvious causes are retardation, language disturbances, and other forms of developmental learning disorders. The point is that some children remain selfish because they have not learned caring or other directed behavior. They may literally not have been taught or more likely may never have been *motivated enough* to learn or care how things look or feel to others. These children respond best to a planned series of educational lessons designed to teach the value of concern for others, accompanied by a "how to do it" approach. At the present time there are still disagreements about whether schools should or should not teach these kinds of moral values.

How to Prevent

Promote Self-Acceptance. The most direct way of preventing selfishness is to help the child feel worthwhile, adequate, and secure. Children who accept themselves as worthwhile individuals and feel safe can naturally care about others' welfare. They are not preoccupied with their own self-doubts. Therefore, there is no need to develop a self-centered manner of living. Since a person's self-concept is derived from the behavior of significant others, there is no substitute for consistent demonstrative acceptance. Children who are accepted and loved feel good about themselves. You show acceptance by having empathy and respect for the child's strengths and weaknesses. There are other possibly negative influences (peers, school, authority figures, relatives, etc.), but "loved" children continue to feel worthwhile even under considerable pressures outside the home. Children who do not feel accepted by their parents are much more vulnerable to negative or stressful messages from others.

Loving a child can be broken down into unconditional positive regard, cherishing, and caring.[1] Parents should communicate to their children that they are intrinsically worthwhile, and not that they are loved only when they behave properly. This unconditional positive attitude results in a "safe" feeling of security and acceptance. Cherishing is the appreciation of a child's uniqueness and special qualities. Practically, parents demonstrate this by encouraging individuality and psychological separation as an autonomous person. Caring means interest in children's thoughts, feelings, and activities and being generally concerned about them. Some physical affection by both parents clearly demonstrates caring in a nonverbal way. Even warmly shaking hands or an arm around a shoulder is an effective illustration of caring.

Constant criticism does not promote self-acceptance. A family atmosphere filled with frequent tension, anger, and irritability leads to generally lower feelings of self-worth. Competition, as a crucial or frequently stressed issue, can also lead to a shaky feeling of adequacy. Intense competition leads to children having to prove their worthwhileness and feeling insecure and uncertain about themselves. Selfishness is prevented by accepting and loving children and avoiding or diminishing criticism, intense competition, and negative family interactions.

Model and Teach Concern for Others. Self-centered parents should not expect to have children who have high regard for the feelings of others. There is no way of minimizing the powerful influence of the parents as models for their children. Showing real interest in your children, and in others, is a basic model for caring about others. Feeling responsible for the welfare of others and sharing your time, energy, or money with others are clear illustrations of a nonselfish approach. "Giving of yourself" is mentioned over and over again in the psychology literature as an essential ingredient of any meaningful relationship. "Love" has often been defined as caring about someone else's well being more than your own.

Similarly, concern for others is demonstrated by displaying and discussing unhappiness about the suffering of others. In some families, display of any type of emotion is seen as inappropriate. By being demonstrative and expressing feelings about others, children learn to feel concern themselves. Conversations only about things or self-centered interests do not promote concern for others. Following this reasoning, if happiness is attained at the expense of others, then concern for others is not demonstrated. Some forms of humor are based on the foibles or inadequacies of others. By stressing sarcastic humor, a noncaring attitude can be promoted. Therefore, other forms of humor should be stressed.

Happiness should be lived and discussed as attained, in part, by *giving* of oneself. Most important is the *reception* by the other person of your positive intent. Some people say how they mean well, yet others do not perceive them as well meaning. The skill required is to assess the motives of others and help them to reach their goals. Many psychologists and authors have warned parents about the dangers of a possessive or selfish attitude towards their children. Parents can respect their children (and others) as worthwhile individuals. This is demonstrated by real concern for their wishes and a purposeful attempt to bring out the best in others.

Empathy is the understanding of others from their point of view.[1] You should try to see things from your child's perspective. *Communication* of your understanding is the key ingredient. You can say to a very upset child, "It must feel really bad not to be invited to that party." This communicates understanding of the child's feeling. Discussion and helpful suggestions can come later. Parents model concern for others by being empathic both with their children and with others. Empathy can be directly taught by discussing how different situations result in certain feelings in people. Bullying leads weaker children to feel hurt, sad, frustrated, and angry. Very instructive are dinner conversations where feelings of people are discussed. You can show an empathic, caring quality in your description of the importance of the feelings of others.

Give Responsibility. Responsibility for others is a natural method of experiencing and learning concern for others. The person who has been helped usually expresses gratitude which leads to the helper feeling good about the process. Responsibility for the care of a pet is an excellent experience from early childhood on. The level of responsibility is geared to the child's competency. Four and five year olds can put food in a dog's or cat's dish. Brushing, walking, and throwing a ball to the pet are all appropriate activities. Helping younger children is an age-old natural task. Overburdening a child with responsibilities is not appropriate. Specific helpful tasks with younger children can be an excellent source of gratification gained by helping others. Many people continue a lifelong sense of dedication and concern about others by helping or taking care of a handicapped or weaker sibling.

Performing chores is another significant area of responsibility. Children learn that they are responsible for, and capable of, performing tasks that are important for group welfare. Sweeping, taking out garbage, setting the table, etc., are contributions to household functioning. Chores should always be age-appropriate and within the child's capabilities. Chores should never be meaningless busy work. Many children will accept performing chores as a natural part of family life. For those children who do not, their own privileges can depend upon their living up to their responsibilities to others. A generally helpful guideline is to involve children in discussing and defining the responsibilities of all family members. It can be constructive and fun to list everyone's responsibilities. For some children, it can be a real eye-opener to see the list of Mom's and Dad's responsibilities. These lists should contain not only tasks (earning money, buying food, cleaning the house, etc.) but also attitudes and feelings (being cheerful, helping others, etc.). Children should always be encouraged to participate in the reasoning and decision-making process of assigning responsibilities.

What to Do

Teach Empathy by Role Playing. Role playing [2,3] is by far the most frequent method used by professionals to reduce selfishness in people of all ages. Acting the role of another is to behave and speak *as if* you were that character. Research[4] has shown that costumes and masks lead to children expressing usually inhibited behavior. Old clothes can be used to dress up and act out plays. Children can plan or improvise various themes. Actual family events or fantasies can be expressed. Puppets are excellent devices to express feelings; children can do puppet shows for family and friends. Even more effective are adults acting the role of a puppet and then *switching roles*. This role reversal enables children to see and hear another role and then act that role themselves. For example, an adult can act in an exaggerated manner like a selfish child who only thinks of himself and wants everything. The child can also act that role, thereby focusing on the issue of selfishness. Acting out behavior can lead to that behavior becoming more under voluntary control. Most effective is the modeling that you can do by then acting the part of a caring, genuine, nonselfish individual. The potential is excellent for adults and children to act out various roles and actually *experience* the positive feelings involved in assuming a different, if exaggerated, role. Expressing oneself through another role is a direct way of reducing self-preoccupation. Embarrassing or sentimental feelings about others becomes more permissible in this playful "make believe" approach.

"Role reversal," mentioned above, specifically promotes the understanding and acting out of another's viewpoint. By reversing roles, children directly learn about the concept and frame of reference of others.[5,6,7] Extremely effective is the learning and switching of points of view. Children can act like parents, teachers, or other authority figures, and parents can act like children. It is the experience of the feelings of others that leads to *empathy* for others. Children will see what it is like to deal with a child (as depicted by a parent) who does not listen, constantly interrupts, wants his own way all the time, is impatient, does not care about anyone else's point of view, etc.

A novel approach is to make tape recordings of voices and then listen.[8] Children or adults may be surprised to hear the selfish, whining, complaining, or harsh tones of their voices. Role playing may then be used to act in a tolerant and empathic manner. This may well reverse the cycle of being selfish, being actually rejected by others, and behaving even more selfishly. A key is to intervene in the selfish pattern and assure that nonselfish behavior is practiced and then used in real life situations. In role playing, the goal is to achieve a feeling of interest in, and satisfaction from, helping others.

A variation of role playing especially appropriate for young children is "mutual story telling."[9] Parents can readily adapt this method used by many psychotherapists. A story can be told by the child, and then a similar story told by a parent with clear values and appropriate (caring and nonselfish) behavior illustrated. You use the child's characters, but your story demonstrates concern for others and better solutions to problems. You ask your child to tell a story with a moral. Each story has a beginning, a middle, and an end. After the child tells the story, you tell your own version. It can be instructive and fun for you to make up a story first and then have the child tell another version. Again, the point is to focus upon the verbalizing, and experiencing, of empathic behavior.

Demonstrate, Discuss, and Reinforce Positive Results of Caring. Caring is to feel interest or concern about something or somebody. There is an implication that you share (give and enjoy with others) when you care. You can show and teach children how to care and share. Encouragement and praise should be used to promote caring in children. Any instance of caring should be positively reinforced in some manner. You should involve children in projects which require cooperation and helping others. Typical examples are collecting money for charities, teaching less able students, reading for blind people, and volunteer work in a hospital. *Group experiences* are invaluable for learning to help others. Activity or psychotherapy groups for children are designed for group members to help each other. Good classroom teachers also promote positive group interaction rather than only using student-to-teacher interaction.

When attempting to change attitudes, such as selfishness, some general principles apply. Positive attitudes, such as caring, develop in a context of trust, which is promoted by expressing warmth, accurate understanding, and personal disclosures of feelings and attitudes. Defensiveness does not promote an atmosphere conducive to attitude change. Feelings of being part of a unit (family, neighborhood, religion, etc.) should be stressed. Positive group feelings should be sought and emphasized. Discussions can focus on how things could be better at home, and behaviors can be discussed which would help other family members be more content. Some examples are not yelling, being neat, volunteering to help before being asked, doing things immediately and not putting them off, etc. It is the commonality of concerns that should be stressed, not the differences. The outcome of these approaches is to change the attitude of selfishness to one of caring and group belongingness.

Demonstrate and Discuss Negative Effects of Selfishness. It is not helpful to discuss selfishness while, or directly after, a child is being selfish. Discussions should always take place under pleasant circumstances. When the child is being selfish, a quick gentle reminder is in order. Selfish situations should be discussed in order to show children the negative consequences of their behavior. Not giving others a turn, always wanting to be first, not listening when others are speaking, are good examples. Egocentric behavior is often disruptive to others and leads to poor peer relations. The consequences are that peers will not like self-centered children. A key concept is to help children see that selfish behavior often leads to *their not getting what they want*. Popularity, friends to play with, a good reputation, etc., are outcomes that children often want.

Self-centered children often feel justified and self-righteous. It is necessary to discuss and clarify their misunderstandings and misconceptions which may be causing their egocentric points of view. Seeing everyone as evil or potentially dangerous sets the tone for preoccupation with one's own safety. Discussing perceptions of children, based upon their past experiences, can reveal their overgeneralizing from one experience. They can learn to be more open-minded and less rigid about their expectations and perceptions. A rational *problem solving* approach can help a child see the negative effects of his perceptions and behavior. Solving problems requires an understanding of *all sides* of an issue. This is a natural and effective means of discussing and learning about the perspectives of others.

Case Report

A somewhat fearful 15-year-old girl was seen by most people as being extremely selfish and self-centered. Her parents were particularly concerned that she apparently did not care about the welfare of others and was known as being extremely insensitive to others. Several sessions were held with the girl, parents, and younger brother and sister. The first two sessions consisted of family members' complaints about each other, and a very strong feeling on the girl's part that nobody liked her and that she could only rely on herself. Two approaches (discussing negative effects of selfishness and role playing) led to an improved family atmosphere and a more caring attitude by the girl.

Discussions took place concerning the frequently critical and complaining interactions at home. All agreed to try to be more sensitive and to express more interest and concern about each other. Everyone participated in a general discussion about the negative effects of self-centeredness. It became clear that the girl's total preoccupation with her own welfare was a result of her general fearfulness, need to feel safe, and feelings of rejection and isolation. She appeared to feel relieved that the family members shared her concerns and that she was not "different" or "strange." Role playing was performed during the sessions and at home. This process resulted in experiencing and discussing what situations looked like from others' points of view. Very striking was the girl's experience of seeing the parents play her role of being selfish, insensitive, and aloof. She understood the vicious cycle of her behavior actually putting people off, their rejecting her, and her feeling lonely and mistrustful. Her lessened defensiveness and more interest in others led to more positive involvement with peers. A 6 month follow-up revealed that she was much happier and more caring. Family relationships remained more positive and less complaining.

Books for Children about Selfish Self-centered Behavior

Barrett, John M.: *Oscar the Selfish Octopus*. Human Sciences Press, New York (1978). Ages 4 to 8.

Oscar believes that everyone should please and serve him. When other sea creatures are turned off by his selfishness, he blames them for not appreciating his greatness. The turning point comes when he is helped by two starfish to escape being eaten by a shark. Children will enjoy the illustrations and the progress from lonely, self-centeredness to friendship.

Norris, Gunilla Brodde.: *A Time for Watching*. Knopf, Westminster, MD (1969). Ages 8 to 10.

A lonely Swedish boy gets into trouble by being too curious.

He does anything to discover how things (watches, machines, etc.) work. He has no concern for others when he takes things apart. Finally, his father understands his curiosity and helps channel his son's interest.

Tunis, John Roberts: *Highpockets*. Morrow, West Caldwell, NJ (1948). Ages 10 and up.

"Highpockets" is a new member of the Brooklyn Dodgers. Instead of teamwork, he only plays for his own glory. Through helping a boy injured in a car accident, he learns about helping and sharing. Descriptions of baseball games will interest young readers. The athlete changes from self-centered to caring about others and feels much more personal satisfaction.

Burch, Robert Joseph: *Renfroe's Christmas*. Viking, New York (1968). Ages 8 to 11.

Nine-year-old Renfroe hangs the old family Christmas tree over their shed. He thinks that the angel tells him to be less selfish than he has been. Contrary to what he is told, he strongly believes that it is better to receive than to give gifts. Giving his watch to a retarded boy results in happiness and his thinking that the Christmas angel waved at him.

Taylor, Mark: *A Time for Flowers*. Children's Press, Chicago (1967). Ages 4 to 7.

A Japanese boy and girl demonstrate unselfishness by trying to help their grandfather. They get into trouble by trying to earn money to buy glasses to replace their grandfather's broken ones. The story also depicts children's impatience in growing up and not liking to be "too little" to do things.

Watson, Nancy Dingman: *Tommy's Mommy's Fish*. Viking Press, New York (1971). Ages 5 to 8.

This realistic story describes a young boy who very much wants to give something special to his mother. Through much difficulty, he persists in his goal to get a present which would be from him alone without assistance of others. He fishes all day until he finally catches a bass as a birthday gift for his mother.

Zolotow, Charlotte Shapiro: *My Friend John*. Harper & Row, New York (1968). Ages 4 to 6.

Caring about others in a mutual friendship is clearly depicted. Two boys know and respect each other's strengths and weaknesses. They have fun together and cooperate whenever possible.

De Gering, Etta Fowler: *Seeing Fingers: The Story of Louis Braille*. David McKay, New York (1962). Ages 10 to 12.

A moving story of a blind man who helps others. He demonstrates his concern for others and shares whatever he has. The invention of Braille (a system of reading and writing using raised dots) is told in an interesting and educational manner. Mr. Braille generously devotes his life to other blind people.

References

1. Schaefer, Charles: *How to Influence Children*. Van Nostrand Reinhold, New York (1978).
2. Chesler, M. and Fox, R.: *Role-Playing Methods in the Classroom*. Science Research Associates, Chicago (1966).
3. Corsini, R.J.: *Roleplaying in Psychotherapy: A Manual*. Aldine, Chicago (1966).
4. Zimbardo, Philip G.: *Shyness: What it Is and What to Do About It*. Addison-Wesley, Reading, MA (1977).
5. Johnson, D.W.: "Role reversal: A summary and review of the research." *International Journal of Group Tensions* 1:(1971), pp. 318–334.
6. Johnson, D.W. and Johnson, F.P.: *Learning Together and Alone: Cooperation, Competition, and Individualization*. Prentice-Hall, Englewood Cliffs, NJ (1975).
7. Johnson, D.W. and Johnson, R.T.: *Joining Together: Group Theory and Group Skills*. Prentice-Hall, Englewood Cliffs, NJ (1975).
8. Wahlroos, Sven: *Family Communication: A Guide to Emotional Health*. Macmillan, New York (1974).
9. Gardner, Richard A.: *Therapeutic Communication with Children: The Mutual Storytelling Technique*. Jason Aronson, New York (1971).

OVERDEPENDENT

Dependent behavior involves the seeking of excessive help, affection or attention from another. The overdependent child shows many signs of immaturity such as whining, crying, and dependency behaviors. The child often interrupts conversations being held by his parents. He frequently demands that they do things for him that he could do for himself, *e.g.*, a 16 year old asking his mother to comb his hair. Rather than showing initiative, the child keeps going to an adult for assistance. Physical proximity—the need to stay close to an adult—is yet another behavior of the dependent child, as is attention seeking or wanting the parent to frequently watch him, talk to him, or look at something he has made. After age 4, another sign of overdependency is crying when separated from the mother even for a short period of time.

Whining is a particularly prevalent form of immature, dependent behavior. Children tend to whine the most in the preschool and early school years. Over and over they complain, "Why can't I stay up a little longer?" "There's nothing to do." "Why can't I invite Mary over to play?" Although the requests are natural, the whining child just won't take no for an answer. Nor will the child on her own initiative take steps to satisfy her wants or needs.

Strangely enough, many parents who have overdependent children do not seem concerned about such behavior even if the child is 12 years old. Although they find the immature behaviors discomforting, the parents believe they are normal behaviors or that the child will outgrow him. Girls in particular are not likely to outgrow passive dependent behaviors.

Reasons Why

Parental Reinforcement. Some children learn to manipulate adults and get their way by playing the baby role. The child may cling, ingratiate, be cute, hide, and run. Some adults find such babyish behavior extremely winsome. Other parents do not want their child to grow up and thus reinforce immature acts. They want their child to remain infantile and dependent upon them. Another group of parents overprotect their children with "smother" love. They won't let their child out of the yard because of the "rough" neighborhood kids.

Guilt. Some parents seem to give in to a whining child out of some unconscious guilt, like not loving the child enough or being away from the child too much, or because the child is sickly or handicapped.

Parental Permissiveness. If a parent has difficulty setting limits, a child is likely to whine and manipulate until the parent gives in. Such parents are often fearful that their child will not like them if they are tough, or they are uncertain of their position so they easily back down and give in to a child's unreasonable demands.

Attention or Power. Some children will whine or cry as a way of gaining their parents' attention. Others, feeling overly controlled by their parents, will use it as a way of fighting back and gaining some power over their parents.

Self-centered. A narcissistic child sees others only in terms of how they can be of use to him. Imbued with self-importance, the narcissistic child often seems to collect injustices and to become upset over minor unfair practices.

Feeling Deprived. The child who feels neglected or deprived may live in a continuous state of envy over the privileges or favoritism shown to others. Such a child may complain, whine, and show poor frustration tolerance. The antidote for this child is lots of special attention from the parents. Each day the child needs time *alone* with her parents.

How To Prevent

Encourage Decision Making. From an early age encourage the child to make choices such as what cereal to eat, what clothes to wear, and what games to play.

Provide Early Support. Children can become independent only after they have learned that they can depend on their parents' acceptance, approval, and support. If a young child's basic dependency needs are not met by responsive parents, he may lack sufficient support and nurturance to progress successfully to higher levels of independence. Parents who are very responsive to a 1 year old's cries and need to cling are likely to find a more independent and self-confident child at age 3.

Be Undomineering. Parents who tend to dominate their children by imposing many rules and by nagging generally produce obedient but dependent children.

Be Responsive. Give immediate and friendly attention to any request the child makes. Do not procrastinate or be vague in your response ("We'll see," "Maybe") without a good reason; do not automatically say "No" without having a good reason. If a "No" seems indicated, state it firmly and explain the reason. Then stick to your guns.

Do Not Pamper. Pampering involves two practices:
1. Giving the child things he does not need and frequently does not even want.
2. Doing things for the child that she is able to do for herself.

What To Do

Be Firm. Once you make a reasonable demand on a child or take a fair position, resist all efforts by the child to get you to give in. In a firm, prompt, and matter-of-fact way, let the child know that you mean business and will not tolerate further argument or whining. Don't be cranky or angry; be *firm* and definite.

To illustrate, if you are tired and your child asks to be read just one more story, say definitely, "I'm tired now and I want to read my paper. You can look at your picture books." Once she realizes you mean what you say, your child will understand the futility of whining or nagging. If a child is constantly complaining that she has "nothing to do," reply that you have both a lot of work and pleasant things to do but have difficulty finding time to do them all. Convey to the child the idea that she must take responsibility for occupying her own time.

To circumvent whining, make a rule to cover the usual pleas, and stick to the rules with great determination. For example, bedtimes and mealtimes are always to be at certain hours no matter what the child wishes. No special food, drink, or toys will be bought for the child during ordinary trips to the supermarket.

Under no circumstances change your mind to stop a child

from whining or crying. Change your mind only if someone comes up with a reasonable fact which had not occurred to you and which throws a new light on the problem.

Correction. Whenever your child engages in dependent behavior, correct her in a friendly, matter-of-fact way, encouraging her to feel that she can act maturely, and reminding her of how good she will feel by acting like a big girl.

In correcting a child be sure to identify the unacceptable behavior ("You just interrupted me"), state your feelings about the behavior ("I feel like leaving the room when you cry"), and point out an acceptable alternative ("When you talk to me without whining I'll listen to what you have to say"). In correcting a child do not engage in name calling ("What a baby you are!") or threats ("You're really going to get it if you keep that up!").

Ignoring. If a child persists in crying or whining after you have explained the unacceptable nature of this behavior and have suggested a more appropriate alternative, systematically ignore further repetitions of the child's behavior. This means paying absolutely no attention to a child's whining or crying and seeing to it that such behavior does not pay off for the child. After first getting worse (child will increase the behavior to get you to back down), the whining or crying is likely to gradually disappear. The child will discard it once he realizes it's no longer effective in getting his way, getting your attention, or getting your goat.

To further illustrate the ignoring technique, if you know your child can do something, arrange not to hear the child's request for help. Be occupied with an important task of your own. Acknowledge the child's request with a simple word or phrase of encouragement such as "I'm sure you can do that." Sometimes you may have to leave the room until the child finishes the task. Quiet, steady ignoring of a child's pleas together with simple encouragement will promote independence and self-reliance.

Reward System. Teach your child that it pays to act in a more mature way. This involves careful observation and recording of the dependent behavior.

Pinpoint. First specify clearly the exact behaviors you want to change, such as "asks for help when she can do it herself," "baby talk," "clinging," or "whining."

Reward. Post a list of these dependent behaviors (*e.g.*, crying, whining), and tally the number of times they occur each day. Give the child a concrete reward for reducing the occurrence of the behaviors to a predetermined level. For example, you might state, "If you whine less than five times today, you can watch your favorite T.V. show tonight." Praise the child for showing more mature behavior ("Great, waiting for me to finish talking was being a Big Boy.").

Penalize. Select one dependent behavior you want to eliminate, such as whining, crying, or interrupting, and every time the child engages in it, send the child for 2–5 minutes of "time out" in her own room or in the corner of a room. For example, if your child starts whining about having to do something, say "Jane, go to your room and sit on your bed until you're ready to talk about your chore without whining." Check the child after a few minutes to see if she is ready to talk without whining. If still upset, the child may have to sit by herself for awhile longer.

Praise. Be sure to give the child attention and praise when the child is acting in an independent, mature way. Give the child a smile, pat on the shoulder, and verbal praise.

Give More Freedom. Decide on one specific area of growth for the child and promote it, such as the child going out of the yard on his own. Insist that the child engage in this independent behavior on a regular basis. This will get you in the habit of gradually placing more and more demands on the child. Don't make your demands too high which will discourage the child or too low which leads to underachievement.

Indulge. For the clinging child, give extra love and hugging. Overindulge the child for awhile by giving much more affection than asked for to ensure that the child gets enough.

For the child who cries, instruct the child to go to his room and have a really good cry and to cry as long and loud as he wants since he is hurting. This change in your approach may have the paradoxical effect of reducing the crying.

Case Reports

Case #1. A 4-year-old girl was experiencing difficulty adjusting to nursery school.[1] She would cry, scream, and throw temper tantrums when her mother left the classroom, and these behaviors continued until the mother returned. The child would occasionally show this separation anxiety on other occasions, outside the classroom. The girl's parents were separated and the mother worked. With professional advice the following strategy was instituted to deal with the problem.

The mother was counseled to remain in the vicinity of the preschool for a while. Once the child exhibited nonanxious behavior, the mother was called into the class to reinforce the child for acting this way. The length of time the child had to display nonanxious behavior was gradually increased, from a few seconds to several hours. Also, the length of time the mother remained to reinforce the child was gradually decreased from 7 minutes. This plan resulted in almost immediate cessation of the anxious behavior. After 17 days it was no longer necessary for the mother to reappear.

Case #2. To control the whining behavior of a 5-year-old boy the parents instituted a point system.[2] Each time the boy whined, he lost ten points. Whining was defined as "a verbal complaint conducted in a sing-song (wavering) manner in a pitch above that of the normal speaking voice." The boy earned points each day by completing various household tasks such as emptying the trash. A total of 50–60 points accumulated at the end of each day earned the boy privileges or treats, such as watching T.V. or going on a picnic. The points earned and lost were recorded on a 5-by-7-inch note card.

After the point system was initiated, the boy's whining was immediately reduced to a low level.

Case #3. The parents of a 4-year-old boy reported that he whined and shouted a great deal at home.[3] Observations revealed he engaged in such behaviors about ten times a day. Typically the parents would attend to their son's whining and shouting by either comforting him or ordering him to stop. With professional advice the parents began a new procedure of ignoring him when he whined or shouted. They would turn away from him and engage in other activities. Whenever possible, they left the area entirely. This strategy reduced the inappropriate verbalizations to an average of only two a day.

Books for Parents About Over-dependent Behavior in Children

Sloane, H.N.: *No More Whining*. Telesis, LTD, P.O. Box 8020, Fountain Valley, CA 92708.

References

1. Neisworth, J.T. *et al.:* "Errorless elimination of separation anxiety: A case study." *Journal of Behavior Therapy and Experimental Psychiatry* 6:(1975), pp. 1–4.
2. Christophersen, E.R. *et al.:* "The home point system: Token reinforcement procedures of application by parents of children with behavior problems." *Journal of Applied Behavior Analysis* 5:(1972), pp. 485–497.
3. Hall, R.V. *et al.:* "Modification of behavior problems in the home with a parent as observer and experimenter." *Journal of Applied Behavior Analysis* 5:(1972), pp. 53 –64.

2

Insecure Behaviors

Most of the problem behaviors covered here have often been called "neurotic" types of behavior by professionals and by the public. We use the more common term *insecure*, which accurately describes children basically lacking in confidence and frequently feeling fearful and anxious. In the United States, approximately 10 percent of children have serious feelings of insecurity that interfere with their functioning.[1] Behaviors covered are anxious-worrier, fearful, low self-esteem, depressed-self-injurious, hypersensitive to criticism, shy-withdrawn, and compulsive-perfectionistic. Some children are described as cowardly or being a sissy. The cowardly child is fearful, timid, lacks courage, and has little self-confidence. These problem behaviors are covered in the sections concerning low self-esteem, fearfulness, and hypersensitivity. There is a growing interest in preventing the development of insecurity. Early exposure and education helps familiarize children with potentially fearful situations.[2] Children can be shown and taught how to cope with new situations in an assertive, effective manner.

Insecurity may be prevented by raising children in a manner that promotes self-confidence, adaptability, and optimism. However, since all children experience some form of insecurity, the basic issue is the effectiveness of helping children cope with their feelings. Almost all children become fearful, depressed, and hypersensitive at times. When this occurs, parents try to help but are often seen by children as being unhelpful and critical. The key is to communicate understanding and that you are truly on the children's side, not against them. You create a psychological atmosphere of relative calmness and clarity of purpose. Within this positive atmosphere, you provide children with the specific suggestions and guidance set forth in each section dealing with the specific problem. The aim is to quickly and efficiently help children cope with the expected feelings of anxiety, fear, and oversensitivity. By reviewing the following sections you learn how to teach children to cope with stress, relax, focus their thinking, solve problems, be assertive, and think and behave in an optimistic and positive manner.

References

1. Joint Commission on Mental Health of Children: *Mental Health: Infancy Through Adolescence*. Harper & Row, New York (1973).
2. Poser, E.G.: "Toward a theory of behavioral prophylaxis." *Journal of Behavior Therapy and Experimental Psychiatry* 1: (1970), pp. 39–43.

ANXIOUS–WORRIER

Some people think of anxiety as a general feeling of present uneasiness, and worry as a concern about future events. Dictionaries list anxiety and worry as synonyms, and we will use these words interchangeably. Anxious/worry means distress, brooding, apprehensiveness, and uneasiness about impending or anticipated problems or pain. The infant's feeling of security is very tenuous. Sudden noise or events scares him. By age 3, children show anxiety about physical harm, loss of parental love, being different, or not being able to cope with events. In early childhood, anxieties about imaginary dangers are very common. The height of anxiety occurs between 2 and 6 years of age. Anxious feelings occur when real or imaginary danger is thought about. The negative, agitated sensations feel the same to the child whether they worry about realistic or imaginary possibilities. Symptoms of anxiety include agitation, crying, screaming, pacing, obsessive thinking, insomnia, nightmares, poor eating, sweating, butterflies in the stomach, nausea, breathing difficulties, and tics.

Anxious children are often easily frightened and appear to look for things to worry about. They often feel ill at ease, apprehensive, and overtly anxious about everyday situations that others are unconcerned about. Highly anxious children are often less popular, creative, and flexible than others. They are more suggestible, indecisive, cautious, and rigid. Their self-concept is relatively poor, and they often feel more dependent on adults. Anger at others is usually not expressed openly. Strikingly, highly anxious elementary and secondary school children score lower on intelligence and achievement tests. The implication is that anxiety interferes with their ability to function efficiently. Worry often leads to a vicious cycle. Tension is increased and unpleasant facts are often denied. Instead of seeking alternative solutions, the individual becomes paralyzed by worry.

Young children view parents as providing security and protection from danger. The developing ability to cope with and tolerate anxiety is set during these early experiences. Great anxiety is caused by early separation from parents. Loss of parental love is a continuing possible source of anxiety in children. In adolescence, identity problems cause great anxiety. Early adolescence often brings a number of anxiety symptoms such as nervousness, headaches, loss of appetite, upset stomach, and trouble sleeping.

Reasons Why

Insecurity. The chief cause of anxiety is a lack of an inner secure feeling. A pattern of chronic worry is set up because the child feels a general lack of safety and is filled with self-doubts. Worry can be projected on and connected with anything. The main contributors to childhood insecurity are listed below.

Inconsistency. Parent or teacher inconsistency promotes confusion and anxiety in children. Life becomes an unpredictable and scary series of events. More vulnerable children are most likely to become very anxious when treated inconsistently. Children who are constitutionally more easy going and placid are more able to tolerate a lack of consistency. Typically, one parent expects one thing and the other expects the opposite. Children literally become caught in the middle. When there are several children, one child may be the target and become extremely anxious. High anxiety can also occur because of the school environment. A teacher can add still another element of inconsistency. In fact, any significant adult may alone give strong inconsistent and confusing messages to children.

Perfectionism. Adult expectations of perfection directly lead to anxious reactions in a significant number of children. Very high achieving, uncaring, or easy-going children may escape the anxiety of not fulfilling the adult's expectations. Others develop tension and worry about not doing well enough. The standards are too high and adults never seem satisfied.

Permissiveness or Neglect. Children often feel insecure when there are no clearly defined limits. Lacking a reservoir of confidence and experience, many children feel lost and abandoned. They lack guidelines of behavior that will please others and themselves. Often, these children appear to be seeking limits from adults. Some act as if they desire to be punished as a means of finding some clear reaction from adults.

Criticism. A diet of intense criticism from adults or peers leads to tension and worry. Children feel self-doubts and begin to anticipate criticism. Any type of self-exposure may bring on serious anxiety, especially if children know that they are being evaluated or judged in some way. Speaking or performing before others, taking tests, or playing a game can trigger off anxiety.

Adult Confidant. Some adults confide in children as if they were adults. The premature burdening of children is likely to produce anxiety. Most children (whatever their age) do not have the maturity to keep problems in perspective. When children are told about parental financial, sexual, or social problems, they often begin to worry about the future. They inappropriately feel burdened, as if they should be doing something to help. A particularly vulnerable situation exists in one-parent families, where that parent does not have an adult friend or relative to confide in. That single parent may share all these feelings with a child and inadvertently burden the child with unnecessary concerns. Even very bright children can feel emotionally overwhelmed and confused by adult problems.

Guilt. Children feel very anxious when they believe they have behaved badly. Particularly destructive is a pattern where they feel a general sense of not doing the right thing. From age 2 to 6 years, imagination is strong but distinguishing reality from fantasy is weak. This period is likely to produce worried children who anticipate punishment for being bad or for thinking bad thoughts. Some children become intensely anxious because they fantasize killing or torturing others. They have not learned the normalcy of negative thoughts and the difference between thinking and doing.

A pattern develops where children worry, become less active, and then feel guilty about their inactivity. This is the procrastinating child, who worries instead of doing. They get no place, and their energy is drained by worry. Other children react to guilt by becoming overly active. They feel ill at ease unless they're doing something.

Parent Modeling. Anxious parents very frequently have anxious children. Children learn how to worry and look for danger around every corner. They observe parents who handle most situations with much tension and concern. Adults are seen becoming tense when planning trips, preparing for events, discussing the future, etc. The atmosphere is filled with concern about what might happen as compared to a relatively relaxed and optimistic outlook. Defensive or emotionally guarded parents can produce a similar reaction. Children easily imagine the worst when they see their parents' protective approach. If parents can't be openly emotionally responsive, children imagine that there must be a serious reason for their guardedness.

Excessive Frustration. Too much frustration causes anger and anxiety. Children are frequently unable to express anger because of their dependency upon adults and therefore experience heightened anxiety. Frustration stems from many sources. Children feel unable to reach a variety of goals. They may perceive themselves as not doing well enough in school, with friends, with siblings, or with adults. It may be that the goals are too high or that anxious children do not apply themselves well enough. The continued feeling of not doing well enough lays the groundwork for a great deal of anxiety. A vicious cycle develops: frustration—anxiety—indecisiveness—hopelessness—worry. The chronic worrier has a habit of worrying, and problems do not get solved. "When my problem is over, I'll stop worrying." Instead of taking action, the child thinks too much. Frustration and tension increase, and the child feels helpless.

How To Prevent

Foster Understanding and Problem Solving. Understanding oneself, others, and things is an excellent preventer of anxiety. Knowing "what causes what" also helps. Parents should strive to *explain* things to children in language that they comprehend. From an early age, they should learn how things work. Especially important is understanding the functioning of the human body. Many children develop worries about their body because it is a total mystery to them. One hears young children worrying that their heart might stop or that they won't be able to breathe if they fall asleep. Parents should be excellent sources of how to solve problems. You teach children how to pose a question and then think of several possible alternative approaches. Based upon their growing knowledge of cause and effect, they can learn to select the approaches that have the greatest likelihood of succeeding. Then, they are able to decide upon a course of action and do it. They learn how to take risks based upon their best thinking. Action is better than indecisiveness and worry. You teach them that not succeeding is much better than not trying! Failure and stress can be tolerated when people feel like they are doing their best. Self-confidence comes from understanding *how* to approach and solve problems. Handling stress is a type of problem. Children should be shown how to analyze a stressful situation and aided in figuring out *what to do*. Some situations require a relaxed and patient approach. Others require quick decision making and trial and error methods. Parents help children to *discriminate* between situations and to take appropriate action.

Children of all ages are very responsive to "what if" games. Asking them what they would do under various circumstances prepares them to cope adequately. "What if a bully said he'd beat you up after school?" Children could give possible courses of action. You then add possibilities that were not mentioned. They could ignore him, tell the teacher, avoid the situation, talk openly to the bully, face up to him, etc. Preparation is an antidote to worry! You reinforce feelings of competency by coping with problems yourself and aiding children to do the same. Problems are to be faced, not avoided. Tranquilizers, food, or any form of escape are not solutions to problems. When children express worry, you accept their concerns and help them to feel relieved and to cope with pressures.

Promote Security and Self-Confidence. From infancy, parents must be especially sensitive to building a foundation of secure feelings. The game of "peek-a-boo" is a natural, time-honored way of helping infants understand and tolerate the temporary disappearance of a parent. This is a pretend game that gives infants experience in coping with mild, playful anxiety. They learn to enjoy the disappearance and reappearance of people. It is essential to not sneak out on a toddler to avoid a scene. Temporary crying will be prevented, but separation anxiety and mistrust will be promoted. The general rule is to *gradually* introduce children to anxiety-provoking situations. Do not force children to do something that frightens them. Children should gradually spend more and more time away from home. Sending a child, who has never been away from home for more than a few days, to summer camp for 2 months is not a good idea.

Self-confidence is gradually strengthened by repeated experiences of success. Make sure that tasks and chores are properly designed so that children succeed. A reservoir of good experiences enables children to tolerate lack of success. It is then natural for them to think, "It's okay, I usually do quite well." You can enhance this ability by suggesting this type of positive self-talk when things are not going well for a child.

Accept All Fantasies. Young children are frequently frightened by their fantasies about death, monsters, and strange events. Teenagers have fantasies about hurting others, death, and sex. A relatively frequent occurrence is that children feel guilty, frightened, and worried about their thoughts. They then imagine that there must be something wrong with them or that their thoughts might come true. To prevent the development of anxiety, parents should communicate total acceptance about the naturalness of all fantasies. Many children are so ashamed that they will not tell parents or their friends. If parents talk about thoughts and fantasies as natural, children will be likely to not feel worried and will talk to others about their strange or scary thoughts.

Young children should be taught the difference between thinking and doing. Wishing to bash your brother's head is okay; doing it is forbidden. Dreams or daydreams about anything are normal. In fact young children should be encouraged to use their imagination productively. Fantasizing can be a form of mastery. Thinking about being a hero, a sports star, a scientist, etc., promotes the consideration of options and motivation to achieve. Therefore, fostering positive fantasies and accepting all prevents anxiety and aids self-acceptance.

What To Do

Accept and Reassure. Very anxious children need reassurance from calm, firm adults. Staying calm yourself is necessary if children scream, cry, pace, or panic in any way. You show an acceptance of their anxiety by not criticizing or blaming them for being so foolish or upset. Instead, you provide an atmosphere of safety and optimism that whatever they feel will be handled and will pass. Parent and teacher should strive to provide a secure, nonthreatening context. Reassurance can be fostered by the following types of statements. "You're very important to me. I love you for yourself, not only for what you do." "Many people feel very upset and get through it." "Sometimes it seems that nothing will help, but the feeling passes and things are fine again." When you spend time with children, you do not give them partial attention or give the feeling that there are more important things that you should be doing. You communicate that it is more important and enjoyable to be with children than to be doing anything else. This is even more reassuring than words.

Arguing with children is to be avoided. If you try to reason and they yell or say that you don't understand them, back off. The important thing is to be sensitive and not to prove anything other than that you care at that moment. You may feel helpless, but do not underestimate the power of just "being there" for your child.

Reassurance is also demonstrated by the priority you assign to minor stressful events. There are plenty of major difficulties to be upset about. You assure your child that many problems in life are to be expected, handled, and forgotten. This type of perspective is extremely reassuring to children, who often tend to see every event as a major crisis. Rather than feeling overwhelmed and powerless, you take whatever steps are possible in coping with problems and feelings, and then move on. Getting stuck or having to be perfect is a dead end.

Teach Relaxation. Anxiety and relaxation are mutually exclusive. One can't do two contradictory activities at the same time. Simply put, children can be shown to take a few deep breaths, let go of all muscles, and relax completely. They are told to feel limper and limper. A textbook about child counseling[1] states that the antidote for anxiety in children is relaxation training. You can use and adapt parts of a comprehensive book[2] that details every phase of learning to relax all of the muscle groups of the body. The child learns to relax deeply by slowly tensing parts of the body—jaw, neck, forehead, arms, or legs, etc. You help the child become aware of tension and how to relax that tense area. Repetition is essential! The child should practice at least twice a day: Morning and night are usually convenient. It also helps tense children feel relaxed before going to school and before going to sleep. It is very important to make relaxation an enjoyable experience and not overly serious or difficult.

After children have learned and practiced relaxation, a very powerful method is "cue controlled relaxation."[3] You teach children to say a word or phrase to themselves that will help them relax. They can choose one of the alternatives you offer, such as "calm down," "relax," "cool it," or "take it easy." Once they choose, they say the cue word and relax completely. After many repetitions, they just think the phrase and totally relax. A helpful intermediate step is to have them imagine, or listen to you describe, an anxiety provoking situation. They then immediately think of the phrase and relax, which counters the usual reaction of anxiety. It might help for you and your child to write down an inventory of causes of worry and stress. The inventory can then be used as a source of anxiety producing concerns to imagine while relaxed. Anxiety about seeing a physician or dentist can be diminished. In very intense cases, the dentist can help by soothingly describing a pleasant scene while the child relaxes. The final step is to use the method by themselves under any stressful condition. The method is not only effective for reducing anxiety, it also leads children to feel less helpless and more independent and competent.

Use Various Strategies to Counter Anxiety. The relaxation discussed above is very effective and may be combined with other strategies. While relaxing, the child can think of pleasant, calm scenes (''positive imagery''). Children respond very well to images of vacations, beaches, swimming, boating, etc. This is particularly useful in the practice stage of relaxation, since it helps children to let go of muscular tension.

Slow, deep breathing is another useful strategy. You show the child how to rhythmically breathe deep through the nose. Many teen-agers find it helpful to count their breaths from one to ten and focus on the numbers. Parents might find a book concerning Japanese meditation[4] to be quite valuable. That style of meditation is a combination of breathing and counting. This method leads to an experience of less anxiety and often to a slower pulse rate. Tension control may also be enhanced by isometric exercises. There are many books available describing the pushing of muscles against each other. A child can push against a wall for 15 seconds, expend much energy, and naturally relax the muscles afterwards.

A variety of strategies can be used to combat anxiety. When tension starts, children might read a good book, listen to music, look at artistic works, or do some creative activity such as drawing, painting, cooking, or pottery. Exercise or any new or enjoyable activity can be engaged in. Pleasurable activities counteract tension. Noncompetitive play with parents or siblings can be quite satisfying to children. Sometimes, a warm bath does wonders. Another method is to suggest that children ''let go'' of their worries. You can describe a natural process of riding along with things and not getting stuck in worry. Finally, total focus on one problem may be effective. The child picks one initial area of concern and tries to solve it if possible. The idea is to *do* whatever is possible about that problem so you feel that you've done your best. Further worry or concern does not help and is unnecessary. Problems (poor school work, no friends, etc.) should be faced one at a time. After taking constructive action, you choose the next problem and begin to think about it and work on it.

Positive Self-Talk. Whenever possible you can combine methods to make them more powerful. This is especially important if one method (such as relaxation) is not effective enough. Positive self-talk may be used alone or while relaxing. Many children have not learned to stop saying negative or anxiety producing comments to themselves. The first step is to stop self-statements such as, "I'll never fall asleep. I'm always more upset than anyone else. I know something terrible is going to happen." The next step is to ask for, and suggest, positive self-comments. Children can practice out loud and then say it to themselves. "I'm upset, but things will get better. When I start to worry, I'll relax and feel better. Nobody's perfect; I'll do the best I can. When you try your best, that's all anyone can ask for. Worry doesn't help, action does."

The goal is to help children learn to say things to themselves, so that they are independently able to analyze a situation and react accordingly. They can say, "Be calm and relax," and then use a method that they like to counter anxiety. When panicked by a problem or test, they can say, "Calm down and relax," think of a pleasant scene for a few seconds, and then go back to the problem.

Encourage Expression of Feelings. Open expression of one's feelings often counteracts unspoken worries. Family discussions may be held where everyone shares their thoughts and concerns. This is a real live example of the acceptability and normalcy of all feelings. Private conversations can be held where total freedom of expression is encouraged. Catharsis, where everything is said, is helpful to many children. You might consider letting children express anger and frustration in whatever language they choose behind closed doors. This often lessens the intensity of children's worries. Games can be played with children that encourage expression of feelings.[5] Inhibited, anxious children find game playing an acceptable way to express a variety of emotions. You can select games where open-ended questions are asked, such as "How do children feel when teachers are too strict?" or "What could you do if someone sneaks in line in front of you?"

Story telling is very effective in putting feelings into

words. Mutual story telling,[6] which is used by many psychotherapists, is readily adaptable by parents. Children tell a scary or strange story, and then parents tell another version. The basic idea is to tell stories where the heroes openly express their feelings, take effective action, and feel good about themselves. Children learn to tell similar stories, and it is a valuable learning experience. Modeling by adults enhances the effectiveness. Adults demonstrate that it is acceptable to describe feelings of helplessness, rage, love, hate, etc.

Professional Methods. When anxiety is very intense and prolonged, professional help should be sought. This is especially important if parental methods do not diminish children's anxiety. Many professional methods may be partially adapted by parents. For example, *systematic desensitization* is used by many therapists. This is a sophisticated version of gradual exposure to anxiety-producing thoughts or situations. While relaxed, increasingly worrisome images are described. *Biofeedback* consists of allowing children to see or hear their own bodily functioning. Heart rate, muscle tension, sweat on the palms, temperature, etc., are depicted by sounds or electronic waves on a screen. The child's task is to slow down or make the sounds quieter. Considerable success has been achieved in reducing bodily tension with this method. Hypnosis has been effectively used to decrease anxiety. Professionals use hypnosis to induce relaxation and calm feelings, and positive suggestions are made while children are under a hypnotic trance. However, children have frequently responded to positive suggestions made repetitively while not hypnotized. The suggestions take the following forms: ''By practicing relaxing, you'll be able to get rid of your worries.'' ''Each day you'll feel better and better and less worried about the future.'' ''Children are supposed to have fun and learn, not worry.''

Case Report

A 5-year-old girl suddenly developed intense anxiety and worries without apparent cause. She was concerned that her parents would leave or die, that robbers would invade her house, and that no one would be her friend. She cried easily and appeared generally tense. Two methods were suggested to the parents. One was to encourage open expression of feelings through play and talk. This proved to be quite effective as the girl had puppets express all kinds of imagined catastrophes. After several play sessions, the intensity of anxiety during the stories and at other times was much less. The other method was to use any strategy to counter instances of high anxiety. When she became agitated, the parents would play a game with her and tell her pleasant stories. According to plan, the parents carefully played more with her when she was not anxious in order to prevent the reinforcement of her anxiety. The combination of more free expression and quickly interrupting worry was successful. Within 2 weeks her behavior was back to normal.

Books For Parents About Anxiety and Worrying

Benson, Herbert: *The Relaxation Response*. Morrow, New York (1975).

Bernstein, D.A. and Borkovec, T.C.: *Progressive Relaxation Training*. Research Press, Champaign, IL (1973).

Lupin, Mini: *Peace, Harmony, Awareness: A Relaxation Program For Children*. Learning Concepts, Austin, TX (1977).

Books for Children About Anxiety and Worrying

Blume, Judy Sussman: *It's Not The End Of the World*. Bradbury, Scarsdale, NY (1972). Ages 10 to 12.

An 11-year-old girl learns to cope with her parents' separation. She worries about impending changes—selling their home and moving with their mother to a different city.

Blume, Judy Sussman: *Then Again, Maybe I Won't*. Bradbury, Scarsdale, NY (1971). Ages 12 and over.

A 13-year-old boy moves to a wealthy suburb. He becomes very anxious, develops a "nervous stomach," and worries about his emerging sexual feelings. Gradually he becomes calmer and more understanding about his feelings.

Fassler, Joan: *The Boy With A Problem*. Behavioral Publications, New York (1971). Ages 4 to 8.

A boy worries about a secret problem. He can't concentrate on school work, sleeps and eats poorly, and never smiles. Medicine and maternal advice don't help. He feels better when a friend seriously listens to him in a nonjudgmental way.

Fassler, Joan: *Don't Worry Dear.* Behavioral Publications, New York (1971). Ages 4 to 6.

Understanding parents help an anxious young girl to overcome bed-wetting, thumb sucking, and stuttering. Rather than panicking or becoming punitive, they are calm and praise progress.

Hall, Lynn: *Sticks and Stones.* Follett, Chicago (1972). Adolescents.

A 16-year-old boy is ostracized because of his friendship with a homosexual boy. Town gossip causes him intense worry, shame, and self-doubt. He learns to resolve his worries and accept his friend.

Jacobson, Jane: *City, Sing For Me.* Human Sciences Press, New York (1978). Ages 6 to 10.

A young girl is very anxious about moving from her rural home to a big city. Traffic, crowds, and noise scare her. After much difficulty, she meets a girl, develops a friendship, and feels good about her new home.

References

1. Keat, Donald B.: *Fundamentals of Child Counseling.* Houghton-Mifflin, Boston (1974).
2. Bernstein, D.A. and Borkovec, T.D.: *Progressive Relaxation Training.* Research Press, Champaign, IL (1973).
3. Russell, R.K., Wise, F., and Stratoudakis, J.P.: "Treatment of test anxiety by cue-controlled relaxation and systematic desensitization." *Journal of Counseling Psychology* 23:(1976), pp. 563–566.
4. Huber, Jack: *Through An Eastern Window.* St. Martin's Press, New York (1965).
5. Gardner, Richard A.: *The Talking, Feeling, and Doing Game.* Creative Therapeutics, Creskill, NJ (1973).
6. Gardner, Richard A.: *Therapeutic Communication With Children: The Mutual Story Telling Technique.* Aronson, New York (1971).

FEARFUL

Fear is an unpleasant strong emotion caused by awareness or anticipation of danger. Fears are *learned*, but there are the instinctual fears of loud sounds, loss of balance, and sudden motion. Children experience terror or fright over a large number of things or situations. Unreasoning and over-powering fear results in a *panic state*, while aversion or reluctance to face situations is called *dread*. When an irrational fear persists, the term used is a *phobia*. Typical childhood fears include dark, abandonment, mutilation, loud noises, illness, monsters, animals, heights, transportation, storms, strangers, and unfamiliar situations.

Three factors have been identified in childhood fears.[1] (1) Physical injury—poisons, operations, war, being kidnapped. (2) Natural events—storms, riots, dark, death (these fears decrease significantly with age). (3) Psychic stress—tests, mistakes, social events, school, being criticized. Some children appear to be generally timid and fearful, while others have one or two specific fears. Boys and girls, in most studies, have been equally fearful.

At least half of all children have the common fears of dogs, dark, thunder, and ghosts, with 10 percent having two or more serious fears. Fears are most common between 2 and 6 years. Between 2 and 4, fear of animals, storms, darkness, and strangers are frequent. These fears diminish by 5 years and disappear by 9 years. From 4 to 6, imaginary fears like ghosts and monsters predominate, peak by age 6, and disappear by age 10. As many as 90 percent of children under 6 develop some specific fear which leaves naturally. Supernatural fears (ghosts, Dracula, Frankenstein) still concern 20 percent of children age 5 through 11. Physical dangers are typical from age 10 and up. An important statistic concerning school is that 20 percent of children fear tests and do poorly due to those fears. From a positive point of view, fear enhances survival by alerting us to danger and preparing us to protect ourselves. Adrenalin flow prepares the body to take action for fight or flight. Physical and psychological mobilization is helpful in meeting and warding off danger. For example, we want children to be afraid of cars so they should be careful, but not mortally frightened.

Dreams very frequently reflect fears. If children discuss their dreams, parents can often understand what is frightening their children. As children mature, their feelings in general become more specific and intense. Most children outgrow fears if their environment is secure and irrational fears are discouraged. Intense fears do not naturally go away and punishment or ignoring are not effective. Specific fears may lead to general feelings of apprehension, insecurity, foreboding, or free-floating anxiety. Intense or prolonged fears should be taken seriously. Not wanting parents to leave is much different than extreme overreactions and fear of abandonment. Indicators of a need for professional help are fear of all objects in any category and debilitating, intense fear. Strikingly, children and teen-agers who watch a great deal of movie or television violence are relatively more fearful than those who do not.

Reasons Why

Traumatic Experiences. Traumas occur when mental stress or physical injury result in more than momentary fear. Children feel helpless and not prepared to cope with events. The result is residual fear that may become more intense and last for some period of time. There are many situations that can trigger off this type of fear. Some are obvious and well known while others are relatively subtle. For example, being bitten or menaced by an animal may cause specific fear of that animal, fear of all animals, or even a heightened fearful approach to any situation. How far a fear broadens from the original feared object is called *generalization.* Fears often generalize in children to whole categories. In young children, a traumatic experience with a sheepdog could lead to a fear of all dogs, all animals, or all wooly or fuzzy objects. Other potentially traumatic experiences are hospitalizations, operations, fire, water, thunder, crashes, falling, etc. Bathing can be scary in terms of slipping into the water or stinging soap getting in their eyes.

More subtle traumas are the constant bombardment of bad news and disastrous events that are depicted in media. Even if your own town is safe and friendly, murders, robberies, and physical injuries of all kinds are shown on news stories. Children may develop a view of the world as a mean, scary place! Television, movies, and comic books frequently contain violence of every description. The negative effects of more fear and aggression in violence watchers has been amply documented.[2] For example, television viewers between

7 and 11 years of age are scared more frequently than children not viewing the programs usually seen by that age group.

Projected Anger. A typical reaction of childhood is to become angry at maltreatment, feel rage, and wish to harm the adults. The wish is a taboo or unacceptable feeling which then is projected onto adults. "I hate you and want to hurt you—(unacceptable)—you hate me and will hurt or kill me." This pattern is especially strong between the ages of 2 and 6 years. Similarly, impulses to engage in any kind of unacceptable behavior may lead to guilt and fear of punishment. Children have all kinds of aggressive, sexual, or strange thoughts and fantasies that can scare them directly or lead to projection. *Fear* of punishment gets projected onto people being furious at them or fantasies of being punished by monsters, criminals, or supernatural beings. Projecting anger is normal, but intense or prolonged projection is not. Some children and teen-agers have not learned to accept or handle their own anger.

Control Others. Fears may become a means of influencing or manipulating others. At times, being fearful may be the only (or very powerful) means of getting attention. This pattern directly reinforces the child for having fears. It becomes more gratifying to be frightened, and the feelings may be intensified. The problem is that fear then becomes both very rewarding yet painful at the same time. It is particularly strong when fear is the only, or main, way for children to influence or control their parents. The struggle by parents to calm the child becomes a pattern, with parents experiencing failure in accomplishing their goal. One outstanding example is a school phobia. Children show extreme fear of going to school, and the result is that parents allow them to stay home. Children get their wish of avoiding school and remaining home. This is strengthened if the parent is ambivalent about sending the child to school or inadvertently makes staying home a fun or rewarding experience. The net result of these types of situations is that fear becomes a means of influencing others. As with other childhood problems, the original reason for the fear developing may lose its effectiveness, but the fear has become a habit.

Constitutionally Highly Reactive. Parents frequently describe some children as always having been overly sensitive, high strung, timid, or fearful. They describe a pattern almost from birth or during the first or second year of overreactivity. These children react very strongly to sound, sudden motion, changes in the environment, etc. The implication is clear. These children's central nervous systems appear to be constitutionally more sensitive than others. It takes less to set them off, and they often take a longer time to recover their equilibrium. The cause is some combination of heredity, conditions during pregnancy, and delivery. In popular terms, these children seem to be built that way. The child who cries wildly at a sudden, moderately loud sound may be more susceptible to developing intense fears. This "high strung" child later appears to overreact to many diverse situations. Usual surprises and unfamiliar people and situations may not at all phase a more placid child. The overly sensitive child may easily develop fears, which quickly generalize to other situations.

At 4 or 5 years, imagination becomes well developed. These children are very prone to imagining all kinds of frightening events. When the intensity or duration of fears dramatically increases, the fears are called phobias. Phobias can strongly influence children's lives, often interfering with everyday functioning. One example is the fear of falling asleep. These overly sensitive children may imagine that they won't wake up or that they're completely helpless. Anything might happen to them or some unimaginably horrible dream may occur.

Psychologically or Physically Weakened. When children are fatigued or sick, they are often more prone to developing fears. This is especially true if the physically weakened state is prolonged. Malnourishment and low blood sugar are not rare. The state of debilitation leads to a helpless vulnerable feeling. The usual psychologically protective mechanisms are not adequately functioning. Similarly, if a child's self-esteem is generally low, she is more susceptible to fear development. She feels sad, isolated, helpless, and less able to cope with scary thoughts and feelings. Overly permissive parents contribute to this pattern by not fostering feelings of competency in meeting demands and limits. Children with low self-esteem or who are weakened physically feel unable to cope with real *or* imagined danger.

Reaction to Family Atmosphere.

Criticism and scolding. Excessive criticism may well lead to children becoming fearful. Children feel that they can do nothing right and anticipate negative reactions. They appear to expect criticism and frequently look timid and cringing. Frequent threat of negative evaluation can have the same effect. A specific example is the child who is scolded for getting dirty. Fear of dirt is an obvious result, but a more general fear of being messy or disorganized may occur. The form of a fear depends upon the area of frequent criticism. Children who are criticized for being too active or intrusive may become timid and shy.

Strict and overly demanding. An atmosphere of excessive strictness can produce generally fearful children or children especially fearful of authority. These kids may be terrified by teachers or policemen, who represent authority. Overly demanding parents often do not understand that there are fears expected at different ages. They have little tolerance for the temporary fears that children exhibit. By not accepting these occurrences and by expecting "smooth sailing," they criticize their children for being normal. Parental overexpectations are powerful causes of fear of failure in children. Similarly, perfectionistic parents often have fearful children, who cannot meet parental demands and become afraid to try.

Family conflicts. Intense or prolonged battles between parents, between siblings, or between parents and children create tense atmospheres. Continuous heated arguments promote feelings of insecurity. Insecure children feel less able to handle usual childhood fears. Even discussion of everyday financial and social problems may frighten children. Sensitive children often feel burdened by family problems which they cannot understand or misinterpret as being hopeless situations. These feelings are magnified if parents are perceived as incapable of dealing with problems.

Fears modeled. Witnessing fears in adults, siblings, or peers is very influential. Children learn to be afraid by imitation. It is very usual for very fearful children to have at least one fearful parent. Fears are accepted as a natural way of life. Demonstrating or frequently discussing fears can have a similar effect. A mother who is frightened of insects and heights may have a similarly frightened child. However, because fear generalizes it is possible that a child could develop a fear of almost anything. Parents who are afraid of not being able to cope with everyday stress promote a generally fearful view of the world in a child. It should be kept in mind that some children are more susceptible than others due to their general temperament. It is very usual for one child of timid parents to be extremely fearful while other siblings may not be at all fearful.

How to Prevent

Prepare for Coping with Stress. Childhood should be a time of continuous preparation for coping with any type of problem, particularly stress. There should be ample amounts of explanation, reassurance, and forewarning of possible difficulties. Sexual maturation (body hair, menstruation, nocturnal emission) should be discussed openly and in advance. Play is used by children to practice how to handle both feelings and events; it is a natural means of learning how to handle fear. Acting out fears is often a relieving experience. Water games lead to more familiarity with water, and any aroused fear can be handled in the play situation. Pretend games help children of all ages act out satisfying and constructive means of handling new feelings and the accompanying stress. It is very effective when traumas are anticipated and children are prepared properly. Discussions can take place, or young children can play act what the traumatic event might be like. Children's books are available which describe positive handling by children of operations, death of a relative or pet, divorce, etc. With temporary professional help, a child can be prepared for operations.[3] The family receives brief counseling to insure maximum emotional support of the child and to resolve current conflicts, and the child is given specific methods for handling the operation.

A general rule is to promote assertive and effective means of dealing with the environment. Overprotection should be studiously avoided. Active dealing with the feared object is encouraged. It is not effective to only ignore, remove the feared object, or force children into fearful situations. Children are taught *mastery* and *caution*, not fear. A good example is to discuss handling of dogs. "Strange dogs could bite. Do not pet or approach stray dogs. Sudden movements that could scare dogs are to be avoided. If a strange dog approaches, be calm and prepared. If a dog attacks yours, drop the leash. Do not get between fighting animals; it doesn't help your pet and you can get very hurt. If a dog attacks, you can try very loudly yelling 'sit' or 'stop.' Don't forget to climb on top of anything possible to get away. Don't lose your head. Run or fight, don't just stand still." This is the type of calm explanation and advice that could make a big difference in an actual emergency. Additionally, the child feels prepared and more competent.

Be Empathic and Supportive. When parents are perceived as relatively understanding and helpful, children feel more able to cope with fearful situations. Reasonably secure children handle things better and feel that their parents are there to fall back on. Love and respect enhance security, whereas frequent threats or criticism do not. Empathy is demonstrated by understanding and participating in a child's thoughts and feelings. A nonjudgmental and respectful attitude towards fear is communicated. The most direct means of illustrating empathy is by promoting and accepting the freedom to think and feel *anything.* Behavior is good or bad while all feelings and fantasies are fine! When children express confused or scary feelings, parents should be accepting and helpful. Children often need help in understanding and interpreting stressful reactions. You might say, "Kids often have strange or scary thoughts; it's the way you grow and learn how to handle different ways of feeling." Any thought or event that scares children should be discussed with them as soon as possible. Discussion should correct a child's tendency to exaggerate or distort his understanding of the cause and meaning of fear. His understanding and growing ability to handle fears should be praised.

The fear response should never be used for discipline or punishment. Unfortunately, there are still many parents who say things like, "If you keep doing that a monster will get you" or "Children who masturbate go crazy." Even more unfortunate is the use of these types of statements to tease or for amusement. Children's fears are not amusing to them, and even if they don't look it, they often feel insecure when hearing outlandish threats. This is especially true for children under 6 years old who may have a blurred distinction between real and imaginary. You help children learn to distinguish between realistic concerns and unrealistic fears. It is not helpful and is belittling to say, "Don't be crazy; your fears aren't real." Since fears are real to children, they cannot be shamed out of them. Fears should be expressed and not ignored or ridiculed. For example, children need reassurance about concerns such as death and not a detailed explanation.

You know you're on the right track if children describe your reaction to their fears in positive terms. *Overdoing* concern is not helpful. Being overprotective doesn't give them a chance to be and feel more and more competent. Similarly, you do not burden children by frequently discussing adult problems (money, sex, business, etc.) with them or within hearing distance. Telling children how good they are is similarly not helpful. Children know they are not always good and often become scared or guilty about their badness and anger while parents are praising them in this overly global manner.

Early and Gradual Exposure to Feared Situations. New and potentially fearful events or ideas should be gradually experienced. The process of discontinuing use of a night light should be positive. The game is to have a dimmer and dimmer light each night or the door closed more and more until the child feels comfortable sleeping in the dark. Dentists' and physicians' offices should be visited before examinations or treatment takes place. They should be shown what things look like and what will take place. Information should be made available in any form that the child finds interesting. It is very effective to have them observe a happy, nonfearful child being treated. Children who demonstrate mild fear should have experiences designed to prevent deeper fear. They can look at books about the feared situation (dentists, hospitals, dog, subways, etc.). Since children are active and have much energy, they may be encouraged to play with, and throw around, toy animals. Some children feel good by punching a bag with a picture of the feared object on it.

Bedtime should be a pleasant, relaxed time and not a hurried or tense situation. It is calming to spend a few minutes discussing positive things, telling stories, or reading to them. Partially open doors, a dim light near the bed with a convenient switch, or a flashlight may be comforting to chil-

dren. A natural *counter-conditioning* process is the preventative for fearfulness. Gradual exposure, while children
feel okay, serves to slowly condition them to handle mild
fear and to take more risks. Walking down a long dim cor-
ridor gives children practice in not being afraid. The first
time it could be with an adult or with the use of a flashlight.
Each time, less and less support will be necessary.

Express and Share Concerns Openly. By living in an atmosphere where feelings are shared, children learn that concerns and fears are acceptable. We are not talking about
overdoing it by sharing all feelings or sharing thoughts that
are only adult concerns. It is appropriate to talk about realistic concerns or fears that we all have. Children see adult
courage to admit fears, which defuses any sinister or mys-
terious quality. "Wow, that program was scary. It seemed
so real that I feel concerned about spaceships on our lawn.
I bet I'll feel funny for awhile." This puts fear in perspective. Children hear that it's okay to be frightened and that
fear passes. Children then do not feel alone or that they are
weird or cowardly. Their feelings should be listened to respectfully. They want and deserve some sympathy for their
fears. It is comforting to hear, "Fears are natural, everybody is afraid at times."

If parents deny danger or fear, this can be especially
frightening. Children feel fear and see cues of fear in adults,
who pretend not to feel fear. Children tend to imagine that
something is so scary or horrible that adults can't even face
it. Then, children may well develop a specific fear of that
situation or become generally fearful.

Model Calmness, Adequacy, and Optimism. Parental discomfort and fears directly scare children. For example, if
parents have not resolved their own fear of death, children
quickly learn to fear death also. It is comforting if children
hear something like, "It's important to do your best and
have a good time so when death comes, you're ready for
it." Similarly, "Everyone dies; it's as much part of living
as being born" or "We're all part of nature and we return
to nature after death." Of course, many adults discuss religious concepts as a means of understanding death and other
events.

Fears should not be discussed continuously or overem-
phasized. Acknowledgment of fears and a reasonably brave

approach are good examples for children. It is necessary to avoid frequently emphasizing negative "what if" situations. In some families, there are frequent mentions of bad things that may happen to people. This is an atmosphere of "behind every silver cloud, there's a dark lining." This promotes a worried, fearful approach. Pessimism is catching. If you feel that things are okay, the feeling is projected. A relatively optimistic, calm approach leads to handling fears well and to no overreactions. You work out your own problems and speak acceptingly of the risks and dangers we all face.

If you are showing fear in children's presence, you should take immediate action to reduce it. You might discuss your fears with a relative, friend, religious counselor, or mental health professional. Children are greatly influenced by your approach. If you show interest in electrical storms or high winds, your child learns to be interested, not terrified. If you matter-of-factly go to a dentist and report feeling pleased that your teeth are now in good shape, your children usually develop the same approach.

What to Do

Desensitize and Counter-Condition. The goal is to help overly sensitive, fearful children be less sensitive or non-reactive to their areas of sensitivity. A general rule is that children become desensitized to fear when the feared object or thought is paired with anything pleasurable (counter-conditioning). It is very effective to have children play a favorite game or any fun activity while fearful. All kinds of specific fears have been eliminated by this method. A child might dress in a Batman costume and play out scenes in a dim room as a first step in overcoming fear of the dark. Hide and seek might be played in a darkened room. First the parent hides and the child looks; then the child hides and the parent tries to find him. Densensitization naturally occurs when children are enabled to watch (from a distance) a feared event. Children should not be forced to pet a dog. The best approach is to let children watch dogs being fed behind a window, then watch in the same room, and then feed a biscuit to the dog. The gradual progression permits more and more bravery. Dog stories should be read and puppies should be played with. Rather than parental persuasion, a "natural" loss of fear results.

Fear can be turned to active enjoyment. Family togetherness helps desensitization, since children feel safer in a group. A neighborhood teen-ager may be used to engage in feared activities (swimming, sports, etc.) with a child. Children admire teen-agers, and the activity might soon become enjoyable. Some children panic at the sound of thunder. Parents might imitate the sound and have children do the same. Storms should be discussed and explained. Watching rain and lightning should be made into a game. How many lightning flashes occur in a minute? How much rain collects in a cup in 15 minutes? *Self-desensitization* should be encouraged. Children can independently learn to use this method with any fear. They might look at scary animals or monsters in a book, draw, take photographs, write a story, discuss fears with siblings, etc. This changes the helpless feeling into one of actively doing something constructive. Repeated exposure desensitizes, while avoidance of feared situations prolongs or increases fear.

Observing models is a natural form of desensitization. Children learn how nonafraid individuals handle situations. Actual observation or watching films both work. The observed child progressively deals fearlessly with more and more fearful situations. "Average" models are best, or children may see the model as having special qualities that enable them to be brave. The observations convince some children that what they fear is really safe. One example[4] is the use of videotaped peer models overcoming test anxiety. The models were gradually exposed to more and more fearful test situations. The observing children became less fearful of academic tests. Another example is the successful use of watching children successfully undergoing hospitalization and surgery.[5] Parents should take every opportunity to prepare children for potentially traumatic situations. By being aware of the types of preparation methods available (such as films), you can seek them out and aid your fearful child.

Some children are quickly desensitized by a simple method called paradoxical intention. You tell children that they can pretend being more frightened than they've ever been. "Show me just how frightened a child can be when she's standing on a cliff." The girl would then act out being scared to death of the high place. At times, the effect is that children begin to feel that their fear is foolish and unnecessary. Similarly, fears can be overcome by overdoing exposure. You can desensitize children to sudden loud noises by having them pop a roomful of balloons with a needle.

Rehearsal. Practice enables children to feel comfortable while repeating mildly fearful events. In young children play is a natural form of rehearsal. Puppets and acting permit children to express a variety of feelings and fears. Praise by adults reinforces children for rehearsing dealing with feared objects. A chart indicating progress is rewarding to some children. *Behavioral rehearsal* is the performing of behavior which deals assertively with situations. Anger may be felt, acted out, and transformed into action such as hitting dolls or yelling at pretend monsters. Some children respond very well to *cognitive rehearsal,* which is the mental practicing of going through various activities. It is similar to an adult reviewing alternative behaviors mentally in order to prepare for some situation.

Positive Imagery. A special use of imagination to reduce fears is the purposeful employment and practice of visualizing pleasant scenes. Young children find this especially useful. Their heroes are visualized helping them deal with fearful situations. You demonstrate how it's done, and then your child makes up a similar story. ''Wonderwoman and you are at home when suddenly all the lights go out. You're afraid but the two of you find candles and go to the basement to change the fuse. You feel great that you were able to fix the problem. Wonderwoman congratulates you and flies away in her invisible plane.'' Another variation is to have children visualize their favorite activity such as baseball, driving a car, being on a beach, etc. While enjoying the scene they imagine a mildly fearful event occurring. For example, while driving a sports car, the child sees a large dog along the road. The dog chases the car as the child drives quickly away. Then he slows up and the dog comes to the window. The boys pets the dog and drives away. Imagination is used as a means of seeing oneself being more and more able to tolerate fear and eventually being relatively fearless.

Older children should be told how their imagination can be used to overcome fears. While they're comfortable, you both can describe humorous stories about the feared object.

Each story should progressively approach real life events. If children become anxious, you sensitively back off and defuse the fearful part of the story with humor or by changing the subject.

Reward Bravery. You should be sensitive to children's readiness to change, grow up, and be braver. Praise for each step and concrete rewards are very useful. Cause, time, and place of fears can be pinpointed. Being able to tolerate a very small amount of that situation should be rewarded. Many children enjoy earning rewards by showing how brave they can be. For example, if they say hello to a stranger they can earn 5 points. Answering the telephone can earn 10 points, and talking to different people can then gradually progress by earning points, which are used to purchase privileges or toys.

School phobia is another good example. You must react immediately by insisting that children attend school.[6] Even if they complain about intense fear or physical pain, they must go. A medical examination should be scheduled during nonschool hours. Most parents know the pattern of psychosomatic stomach aches—once school is avoided, the somatic complaints almost always disappear. But a negative medical evaluation is a clear indicator of the psychological nature of the fear of school. The child is sent, or taken, to school and praised for attending. With young children, a party can be held to celebrate the overcoming of their fear of going. With this, and other fears, progress is rewarded, and any form of reinforcement of fear is carefully avoided. Often, children who stay home from school are reinforced for this behavior by parental attention, playing games, watching television, etc.

Self-talk. Learning to talk differently to oneself is a very powerful antidote to fear. The helpless, fearful feeling is replaced by an independent feeling of competency. It is quite straightforward to suggest to children that they silently talk to themselves in order to feel better. You explain that thinking scary thoughts make things seem scarier. Thinking positive thoughts leads to calmer feelings and braver behavior. "I can take it; I'm getting braver. It'll soon be over; everything's fine. I'm okay; it's just my imagination. Monsters are just in movies; nothing will happen. Thunder can't hurt me; I'll just enjoy the storm." It is essential to show children how they can stop their scary thoughts. They can think "stop" and immediately say a positive comment to themselves. The "I can't help it" feeling must be replaced by a positive course of action.

Relaxation. Muscular relaxation is very helpful with physically tense children and teen-agers. They learn to relax tension and fear away. Relaxing your muscles counteracts fear build-up. Similar to self-talk described above, relaxation gives children a positive focus. Fear of the dark can be counteracted by learning to relax completely. This is particularly effective if children have practiced repeatedly in their own bed. They will have learned to relax on cue to a simple word like "relax." Some children can effectively practice relaxing in a warm bath. This gives them good practice, and they can use their imagination to recapture the warm, relaxed feeling. Therefore, when they go to sleep, they have a method to overcome fear. They relax their muscles and can imagine being in a warm bath.

Relaxation may also be effectively combined with desensitization described previously. It is very effective to describe more and more fearful scenes while the child is relaxed. Fear becomes less and less intense as the child is exposed (in imagination or in real situations) repeatedly to feared situations without becoming anxious. The fear becomes deconditioned. There are a variety of simple relaxation methods[7] that lead to a calmer feeling and general lowering of fearful states.

Meditation. A variety of meditation techniques have been used by individuals of all ages to feel calmer and less fearful. The simplest forms, and most usable with children, are breathing rhythmically and/or counting slowly. Breathing rhythmically[8] has been used to reduce children's fear of school tests. Not only is anxiety lowered, but attention is sharpened, and distraction can be more adequately resisted. You show children how to breathe slowly and evenly, and monitor their practice. The key is even, natural breathing with no pauses. There should be a continuous, rhythmical up and down movement of the abdomen. It is important to be sensitive to what works best for your child. Some children are helped by focusing their attention on a bright object in their room. It is quite effective to teach meditation after a child has mastered muscular relaxation, described above.

A helpful guideline is the child's self-report about what works and what feels good.

Case Report

A 5-year-old girl was extremely frightened of the dark, loud noises, and separation from her parents. Her parents had not left her with anyone since her intense fear began at age 4. Consultation with the parents consisted of developing strategies to reduce fears, from least to most intense. Her fear of loud noises was approached by a simple desensitization procedure where she was given various objects to make more and more noise herself. All methods were tailored to increase self-reliance and decrease the intense attachment to her parents. After she was able to make loud noises, she was gradually introduced to louder and louder sounds with accompanying praise and rewards for "growing up." Her father made a tape recording of noises that scared her and she adjusted the volume. Fear of the dark was approached with positive imagery and rehearsal. She imagined herself in dim rooms with her favorite television personality, "Mr. Rogers." The parents were told to imitate Mr. Rogers's soothing voice to tell her that she was brave and darkness was okay. She then pictured herself and him in dark rooms together. Rehearsal consisted of her walking in dim rooms and then staying in a darkened room for increasing intervals. All progress resulted in matter-of-fact praise for her acting like a big girl.

Finally, separation from parents was accomplished more easily than the parents expected. Since the girl was very pleased and proud of overcoming her fear of loud noise and the dark, she was looking forward to being like other children who stayed with babysitters. Her favorite local teenage girl was hired. The parents left for 5, 15, 30, and then 60 minutes on successive nights. They stuck to this even though the girl wanted them to stay out longer. By the weekend, they went out for 4 hours and returned to their daughter sleeping in her darkened room. The babysitter reported no problems and said that the girl enjoyed playing games and proudly went to bed.

Books for Children about Fear

Arundel, Honor: *The Girl in the Opposite Bed.* Nelson, Nashville, TN (1971).

A 14-year-old girl is fearful of having an appendectomy and afraid of dying. She copes with her fears and takes interest in others' problems.

Byars, Betsy Cromer: *The 18th Emergency.* Viking, New York (1972). Ages 9 to 11.

An 11-year-old boy overcomes his fear of being hurt, when he finally faces the school bully. He learns to face difficulties and vows to stop doing things that antagonize others.

Carpelan, Bo Gustaf Bertelsson: *Bow Island: The Story of a Summer that was Different.* Delacorte, New York (1971). Ages 11 to 14.

An 11-year-old boy befriends a fearful retarded young man. The boy's friendship helps the man overcome intense fear of storms.

Eckert, Allan W.: *Incident at Hawk's Hill.* Little, Brown, Boston (1971). Ages 11 and over.

A 6-year-old boy overcomes his fear of being lost and develops self-confidence by surviving in the wilderness. A female badger protects and feeds him for several weeks.

Fassler, Joan: *My Grandpa Died Today.* Human Sciences Press, New York (1977). Ages 4 to 8.

A young boy reacts to his grandfather's death. Happy memories and the positive relationship are stressed. Grandpa had taught the boy many things and had prepared him for the death.

I and the Others (Writer's Collective): *It's Scary Sometimes.* Human Sciences Press, New York (1978). Ages 4 to 8.

This book helps children feel less different or ashamed about being fearful. It aids children in distinguishing between useful and unnecessary fears. Descriptions of real fears by children are revealing and entertaining.

Membling, Carl: *What's in the Dark?* Parents' Magazine Press, New York (1971). Ages 4 to 7.

A little boy's thoughts and fear of the dark are vividly portrayed. He thinks about the silence and the activities that are going on outside his room. Policemen, firemen, truckers, etc., are awake to protect others and deliver goods.

Moskin, Marietta D.: *Toto*. Coward, McCann and Geoghegan, New York (1971). Ages 5 to 8.

A father sensitively supports his 7-year-old fearful son, who learns to overcome his fear of danger. The boy saves a baby elephant who lives in a game preserve.

Southall, Ivan: *Benson Boy*. Macmillan, New York (1972). Ages 9 to 11.

An 11-year-old boy overcomes his fears in order to help his mother who is having a baby. He has to ask a mean, scary, and isolated man for help.

Viorst, Judith: *My Mama Says They're Aren't Any Zombies, Ghosts, Vampires, Creatures, Demons, Monsters, Fiends, Goblins, or Things*. Atheneum, New York (1977). Ages 4 to 7.

This book vividly describes children's fears. By children reading about fears, their own fears are seen as more acceptable. A young boy learns to accept his mother's comments that monsters are not real.

Wallace, Art: *Toby*. Doubleday, Garden City, NY (1971). Ages 9 to 11.

Vividly depicted is a 9-year-old boy's fear of making new friends and fear of heights. He becomes friendly with a boy who helps him get down a rope and become less fearful of high places.

Welber, Robert: *The Train*. Pantheon, Westminster, MD (1972). Ages 7 to 9.

An 8-year-old girl overcomes her fear of the unknown with help from her understanding family. Her family each relates his or her own fear, which helps the girl cross the scary meadow in order to watch the trains go by.

Books for Parents about Fears

Grollman, E.A.: *Explaining Death to Children*. Beacon, Boston (1967).
Kent, Fraser: *Nothing to Fear: Coping with Phobias*. Doubleday, Garden City, NY (1977).

Ross, Helen: *Fears of Children*. Science Research Associates, Chicago (1970).

Walker, C.E.: *Learn to Relax*. Prentice-Hall, Englewood Cliffs, NJ (1975).

Wolman, Benjamin: *Children's Fears*. Grosset & Dunlap, New York (1978).

References

1. Miller, Lovick C., Barrett, Curtis L., Hampe, Edward, and Noble, Helen: "Factor structure of childhood fears." *Journal of Consulting and Clinical Psychology* 39:(1972), pp. 264–268.

2. *Television and Growing Up: The Impact of Televised Violence*. Government Printing Office, Washington, D.C. (1972).

3. Cline, F.W. and Rothenberg, M.B.: "Preparation of a child for major surgery: A case report." *Journal of the American Academy of Child Psychiatry* 13:(1974), pp. 78–94.

4. Mann, J.: "Vicarious desensitization of test anxiety through observation of videotaped treatment." *Journal of Counseling Psychology* 19:(1972), pp. 1–7.

5. Melamed, Barbara G. and Siegel, Lawrence J.: "Reduction of anxiety in children facing hospitalization and surgery by use of filmed modeling." *Journal of Consulting and Clinical Psychology* 43:(1975), pp. 511–521.

6. Kennedy, Wallace A.: "School phobia: Rapid treatment of fifty cases." *Journal of Abnormal Psychology* 70:(1965), pp. 285–289.

7. Benson, H.: *The Relaxation Response*. William Morrow, New York (1975).

8. Linden, W.: "Practicing of meditation by school children and their levels of field dependence—independence, test anxiety, and reading achievement." *Journal of Consulting and Clinical Psychology* 41:(1973), pp. 139–143.

LOW SELF-ESTEEM

Underlying many childhood problems is a basic feeling of low self-esteem. An extremely important determinant of behavior is how children feel about themselves. Feeling basically worthless and lacking self-respect influences their motives, attitudes, and behavior. Everything is seen from a pessimistic point of view. Parents are justifiably concerned when they see indications of low self-regard. Children should feel good about themselves, that is, they should have a basically good self-concept.

Adequacy of self-image may be assessed by answering three questions: "Who am I?" "How am I doing?" "How am I doing compared to others?" Self-worth usually is measured by performance in school, on the job, and in social relations. In an achievement oriented society, competence and relative productivity are used as an indicator of a person's value. The importance of the way children feel about themselves is reflected in a term used to refer to adults who work with children professionally—*Self-Esteem Specialists*. It is important to note that self-esteem naturally fluctuates widely. Feeling good stems from achievement, praise, and belonging to a group. Therefore, very negative and very positive feelings towards oneself vary according to specific outcomes.

Children who lack self-confidence are not optimistic about the outcome of their efforts. They feel incapable, inferior, pessimistic, and easily discouraged. Things always seem to go wrong; these children give up easily and frequently feel intimidated. "Bad" and "helpless" are adjectives used for self-description. Frustration and anger are handled poorly and often turn into vengeful behavior against others or themselves. Unfortunately, their behavior typically leads others to view them as negatively as they see themselves. Children who feel like failures often perceive rewards given to them as due to luck or chance, not as a result of their own action. Reward is effective if children believe that it is obtained because of their characteristics and behavior. This is called "internal locus of control." Children perceive a casual relationship between their behavior and rewards.[1] Feelings of internal control usually increase with age and achievement. Children gradually develop more self-confidence and feel more independent and free.

Reasons Why

Faulty Child Rearing Practices

Overprotective. Children who are overprotected do not learn to cope for themselves, feel independent, or respect their own judgment. They often become timid and afraid of making mistakes. Parents "spoil" them by giving too much and not allowing the child to handle normal stress. These children feel very vulnerable, easily hurt, and incapable of fending for themselves. At times, some children may appear overly confident and grandiose, but under this facade is a basic lack of self-confidence.

Neglectful. When parents disregard children, they are left to their own devices. Although some may become independent and gain self-respect through approval of others, many children respond by accepting the message that they are not worth bothering about. They are physically and psychologically not cared for, and the usual direct result is a worthless feeling. This is particularly true since the more adults know and understand children's problems, the better the children feel about themselves.

Perfectionistic. Many parents fall into a pattern of overly high and perfectionistic expectations. They expect their children to display increasing strengths and not any weaknesses. The predictable result is a child who feels inadequate and incapable of measuring up. These children are negatively compared, and compare themselves to outstanding success. Frequently, they overreact to failure and exaggerate the negative aspects of situations. Feeling unable to really succeed, they give up, procrastinate, or don't really apply themselves.

Autocratic and Punishing. Some parents communicate an aura of total power and despotic rule. Their methods are most frequently authoritarian, and punishment is employed excessively. Positive interaction and mutual respect are lacking. Children perceive themselves not worthy of high regard. The most destructive combination is when the father is demanding and authoritarian with his son. This pattern is the opposite of the use of rewards and incentives which promote high self-esteem.

Critical and Disapproving. Parental acceptance, affection, approval, understanding, and praise result in high self-regard and high striving for achievement. Rejection and criticism result in feelings of worthlessness and a "what's the use of trying" attitude. Adult blame leads to the "naughty" child self-image, which then is often acted out. "Naughty" children act badly, confirming their image of themselves and proving to the parents that the bad label was correct. Similarly, children who are constantly told how awkward and clumsy they are often feel and act awkwardly. Their failings are always pointed out, while positive feedback is rare or nonexistent. When a parent is highly critical of his spouse's childrearing methods, this also fosters low self-esteem in children (as well as in the spouse). Another very powerful influence is the approval style of teachers. Students who feel that their teachers disapprove of them are low in self-regard and academic achievement and often behave badly.

Modeling. Parents who feel relatively poor self-esteem are models whom children frequently emulate. They treat children with the same lack of respect they feel for themselves. Children feel that not thinking much of yourself is natural. They imitate their parents' comments about others being more successful. The children are not growing up in an atmosphere where positive things are felt about oneself. Parents who do not strive to do their best frequently have children who behave similarly. Peers and siblings are also influenced by the way adults treat a child. The more parents or teachers express approval of a child, the more accepted he is by peers (and ultimately, by himself). Therefore, adults are literal models who display or do not display accepting behavior.

Differentness or Handicapped. Children who appear much different than others usually feel low self-esteem. They feel too ugly, short, tall, stupid, or different in some way. What often develops is anger towards oneself for being different and hatred of others for seeing them or for pointing out their differentness. Another negative experience results when total acceptance and admiration from others are unsuccessfully sought for. The same pattern occurs with handicapped children, often in a more intense manner. The physical proof of being different or not normal is always present. Feeling worthless is a direct experience that unfortunately gets reinforced by negative stares or cruel comments.

Learned Irrational Beliefs. The most significant source of irrational beliefs is at home as compared to school or community. These beliefs then cause a variety of self-defeating behaviors. Irrationality is listed separately because of its self-sustaining power. The beliefs themselves develop from the previously described faulty child-rearing practices, modeling, and feeling very different from others. Children think to themselves statements such as, "I can't do anything right," "Nothing works out for me," "I must be retarded if I can't do that," etc. They believe that they are incapable of handling new situations. When changes occur (a new baby, a geographical move, a divorce), they feel that their self-worth is threatened, are filled with self-doubt, or are paralyzed into inaction. In the early years of life, significant adult behaviors determine an individual's self-concept. Being treated very badly sets the stage for low self-esteem. "Feeling inferior" is a negative, irrational belief that may be a significant factor in the rest of a person's life.

Young children do not have the judgment and perspective that maltreatment is the adult's problem and not theirs. They have not learned to use self-talk to understand events. They cannot say, "I'm not always bad; it's my father who sees everybody as bad." Therefore, negative comments and behavior are seen by them as total indictments of their personalities.

How to Prevent

Foster Rationality and Self-Understanding. Children should grow up in a relatively rational atmosphere where they are taught rational thinking themselves as soon as they are capable. Any false or overly generalized belief should be dispelled early. "I failed once, so I'll never try again," is a typical example of childish illogic. Similarly, being yelled at does not mean that you are worthless or a "bad" person. It should be explained that sometimes their behavior is inappropriate or that adults are sometimes in irritable moods which get inappropriately taken out on others. They should be taught that self-esteem fluctuates and that good and bad feelings are normal and to be expected. If you pay attention to fostering rationality, you realize that we frequently underestimate children's capacity to understand. It is very helpful for children to know that standards *vary* and that there are no universal measures of goodness. "Beauty is in the eye of the beholder" may be clearly and concretely explained. This is especially crucial for children who look different and begin to feel that no one (other than their parents) will ever love them. The well-known proverbs and fairy tales can be a source of help and should be read to children. "There are plenty of fish in the sea" who find a particular fish attractive and fun. Even young children understand the concept of a person with a weakness developing other areas of strength. Those strong areas (skill, sensitivity, knowledge, humor, etc.) are very much sought after by others.

Family discussions can take place about self-worth *not* depending upon how well one does at one particular thing. People can happily live with meaningful, limited goals and not feel worthless for not reaching great heights. "I'm okay" is a terrific feeling that can be achieved by living in a daily, decent manner and accomplishing small steps. Winning must be avoided as the *only* measure of success! You may have to counteract a system that is geared to honoring only a few winners and treating most individuals as losers. Children grow up feeling that winning is the only way of pleasing adults and themselves. You *can* teach family values that truly "doing your best" is a real definition of success. Any type of perfectionism is by definition illogical. You can admit to children your concerns and failures, that "nobody's perfect," and that all people have different strengths and weaknesses. Understanding and accepting oneself and really trying hard leads to a natural feeling of success.

Encourage Competency, Independence, and Enjoyment. There are many ways of preparing children for coping effectively with their environment. Real competency at an age-appropriate level means that children are exercising their skills, learning, growing, and feeling relatively secure in the process. Over- or underprotecting is harmful. You teach children to be flexible so that they can assess a situation and apply their skills in a focused, non-self-conscious manner. When your child is faced with a problem or stress, you encourage her to use her head and you provide help only as needed. Sibling fights and arguments should be used as a basis for discussions of *better* ways of dealing with each other. The children should be asked to contribute alternative solutions to the problem. Better ideas and behavior are praised, and punishment is avoided whenever possible. Children learn to enjoy their growing competence in independently handling situations.

Whenever possible, children should be given *choices*. Ask them to describe and evaluate situations and listen carefully. Their opinions should be respected, encouraged, and expanded. Rather than giving a solution if needed, you should give two possible solutions and ask which one suits them better. A focus on their growing interests and desires is crucial. Children feel better about themselves when they *accomplish their goals!* Your role as a guidance counselor (not an admonisher) is truly helpful. You can help them to anticipate problems, avoid mistakes, not get discouraged, and think clearly. Hopefully, in a positive family atmosphere, many of the children's goals will be the same as yours. Children learn to want to succeed, to please others, to have fun, and to be self-reliant. These goals should be openly discussed and purposely encouraged.

Like prepared childbirth, children should be prepared to cope with stress. You can anticipate the stresses of childhood and help children to understand their responsibilities. Their morale is increased when they are clear as to what is expected of them. Throughout childhood, they should have appropriate assignments and chores. It is essential that they are capable of completing these tasks, and that they receive meaningful praise and rewards. Children feel more accepted when their mistakes are not always pointed out. Praise the part of their behavior that is right and don't expect perfection! Global praise is not helpful. Specific praise for specific behavior is effective. This fosters their obtaining personal satisfaction in doing a competent, honest amount of work. From a positive point of view, don't forget that there is no substitute for happy, enjoyable activities. Many happy family times promote general happy, competent feelings in children.

Provide Warmth and Acceptance. High self-esteem is directly promoted when children feel "accepted." Clearly defined and reinforced limits are necessary. Permissiveness is not equivalent to warmth. Children feel worthwhile when they are loved within a secure, clearly defined context; they thrive on trust and encouragement and not blame. If a child receives poor grades or fails, your attitude is crucial. Emotional support is necessary, because they need the feeling that you're on their side rather than another source of rejection. Many parents underestimate the negative effect of their children overhearing criticism of others. Criticizing or downgrading certain occupations, races, or religions promotes negative feelings. Speaking positively of others enhances a general feeling of acceptance of self and others.

Spontaneous affection should be displayed frequently. Some parents find it very difficult to express positive feelings. Open expressions of love are very powerful enhancers of self-esteem. Do not only express affection when children are behaving well or achieving. Similarly, it is very beneficial to openly express *optimism.* You can look at the good side of things both for yourself and for your children. They learn to be optimistic (rather than pessimistic) by living in an atmosphere that focuses on strengths and not weaknesses.

Acceptance of self is enhanced by family pride. Families can maintain scrapbooks and pictures of various events. There are always good things to collect and discuss. Diaries could be kept and mementoes saved. Time spent together should be planned to be maximally enjoyable. Family get-togethers could involve singing, game playing, and discussion of local happenings. You can be very influential by keeping the tone as warm and optimistic as possible. One negative parent can put a damper on the feeling of warmth discussed here. Everyone benefits when parents help each other in feeling happy and providing an accepting atmosphere. All family members should feel that they are basically in the same boat, working towards the common goal of mutual support.

What To Do

Focus on Positives. Changing low self-esteem requires an intense focusing on the child's attributes. As the old song says, "accentuate the positives." Any strengths and accomplishments should be recognized and encouraged. A good start is to ask children to make an *inventory of assets.* This can be explained to be helpful in the same way that a business does an inventory count to see what types of goods are available and what constructive steps need to be taken. Children can list their good points, their skills, and their efforts. This is a concrete demonstration of focusing on positives, rather than dwelling on negatives. When discussing these lists or in speaking to a child, his strengths should be elaborated upon. Inquiring about his feelings and listening carefully communicates that he really is *special*. Talking about your feelings concerning him communicates a message that he is special to you. The positive focus leads to a feeling of *closeness* to parents. This feeling is an antidote to feeling worthless and alone.

Approval, attention, appreciation, and praise should be plentiful. *Positive feedback,* at every opportunity, fosters good self-feelings. Put downs should be avoided at all costs. Ridicule and sarcasm have no place in promoting self-esteem. The following comments are some examples of positive feedback. "I appreciate seeing your smiles." "You were really patient while I was busy (shopping, fixing the car, preparing food, etc.)." "Thanks for helping your brother." "I appreciated your telling the truth." "I admire how hard you work on your assignments." "It was great how you waited your turn." "I liked the way you helped without being asked." "Your consideration of your friend's feelings was really nice to see." "Your sense of humor was particularly good this evening." "It's fun building this model with you." *False praise* should be avoided. Children feel worse if they believe you are lying to make them feel better. There are plenty of real positive behaviors that can be observed and highlighted.

When children are discouraged, don't expect too much at that time. That may be a time for patience and low-key encouragement. Expecting too much is counterproductive. Expecting small, positive steps is supportive. Children who feel inferior can gradually learn to *compensate* for their weaknesses by developing their strengths. "Doing what you think is right" can be a positive first step. Rather than being overwhelmed and seeing tasks as too big to tackle, they should be encouraged to do what is right for now. They can be explicitly told to "do the right thing at the right time" and derive satisfaction from those moments.

Positive self-talk is very powerful. Children can be shown how to think, "I'm okay; I can do it" rather than, "I'm no good; I'll never do it right." Self-hate mechanisms must be blocked and eliminated. Discover (observe, ask) what negatives children dwell on, and suggest that they stop themselves from engaging in that *bad habit*. Your suggestions should be concrete and clear. You can communicate the following types of thoughts that children should begin to think to themselves. *"Trying your best* is what counts, not doing better than others." "Each day we try to become more self-confident and feel better and better about ourselves." "Try to become involved and satisfied in what you're doing, not self-conscious." "Slowly, we learn to be more confident and independent." The above are forms of suggestions that children can use to encourage themselves. They can begin to see themselves as more courageous and competent. They can learn to discriminate more. There are situations where they cannot do well and they can let others lead. When their strengths permit, they can be more dominant.

Provide Constructive Experiences. When children have developed low self-esteem, it is necessary to become a master strategist in providing reconstructive experiences. You must find various activities and use powerful means to insure the child's participation. At first, it may be necessary to use meaningful rewards since the child may not want to participate in anything. Scouting, music, hobby clubs, sports, etc., are all potentially morale boosting activities. It may take careful planning to assure successful experiences, but it is worth it. Children must feel adequate and competent while mastering the activity. A helpful guideline is to make sure that the group leader is sensitive and includes everyone at his level. Leaders who stress winning and only encourage the already competent children are inappropriate. The leader must stress cooperation, sharing leadership with many, and group participation by all. If your child is so below others in skill development, that group may not be a good one in spite of adequate leadership. It may be necessary to find, or create, a group that does not seem overwhelming to your child. For example, parents have been very successful in developing noncompetitive coordination training programs for several awkward children. Well-planned recreation activities can do wonders for children with low self-esteem.

Constructive experiences must be realistic; goals set must be achievable. Tasks and chores should be designed to be productive, moderately challenging, and necessary. Children should feel that they are *contributing* to the family's welfare. *Helping others* is morale boosting. At home, children should assist others in accomplishing tasks. Helping younger children is quite worthwhile. You should be creative in seeking community activities where children or teenagers can help others. Specific jobs, hospital volunteer work, reading to the blind, shopping for the handicapped, and entertaining or visiting shut-ins are all possible.

At home, some strategic moves may have positive consequences. You might consider having your child room with a more optimistic and encouraging sibling. Spending time with and emulating a good model can be effective in changing the vicious cycle of low self-esteem. Either the sibling or the parents should take every opportunity to discuss daily events. Some specific suggestions regarding social skills may be necessary. Children with poor self-regard often communicate a negative attitude about themselves and towards others. They may be responsive to suggestions to show more interest and be more considerate of others. Another technique at home is having VIP (very important people) days, where one person is the center of attention. Family members should be more attentive, considerate, and try to specially please that individual. Favorite activities and food should be provided. Some families have had positive results with a role reversal day. Children become parents for a day and have their wishes followed by others.

A powerful means of enhancing self-esteem is through some form of dramatic acting. This could be role playing at home or being members of a formal play in school. Research[2] has demonstrated that increased self-esteem in 7 year olds resulted from participation in creative drama and by video feedback. Children viewed themselves on television in a variety of activities. You can be creative by enlisting community or school support to donate or fund the necessary equipment and personnel. Many schools already have teachers and television or film equipment. Therefore, it might be relatively easy to arrange to record children's activities or dramas and show it to groups of parents and children. Being the center of positive attention is invaluable.

Use Rewards and Contracts. Analyze what a particular child finds rewarding so that your efforts to change negative feelings can be more efficient. Once you know what children find reinforcing, you then set goals with them and reward efforts accordingly. At the beginning of this book, contracts are discussed at length. The basic idea is that fulfilling obligations is an important and rewarding experience. Reaching agreed-upon goals leads both to obtaining valued rewards and to the desperately needed feeling of personal worthiness. Contracts may range from cleaning a room to doing homework for a specific amount of time each day. Creative parents can sign contracts with children which include the requirement for children to not make negative self-comments.

More and more, children should learn to help themselves and be more self-reliant. Once understanding contracts, they can write their own and reward themselves. It is morale boosting to feel self-control. They can develop their own nonwritten contracts. "I'll watch television after doing 1 hour of homework and taking the garbage out." Feeling satisfied inside is a natural and direct result of fulfilling one's own contracts (long-term or short-term goals).

Case Report

A parent used some of the techniques discussed in a child development course with her own child. She later told the instructor how she helped her 10-year-old boy to feel better about himself. He had been making many negative comments about himself and appeared very discouraged. She involved him in a Saturday recreation program with a sensitive, charismatic leader. At home, she taught him to stop putting himself down with negative comments. Instead, she showed him how to think positively and to focus and think about his good qualities. The mother reported a noticeable change in his attitude. The boy proudly told his mother of the recreation leader's interest in his progress. He looked less discouraged, anticipated participating in the recreation program, and made very few negative comments.

Books for Parents About Low Self-Esteem

Samuels, Shirley: *Enhancing Self-Concept in Early Childhood.* Human Sciences Press, New York (1977).

Coopersmith, S.: *The Antecedents of Self-Esteem.* Freeman, San Francisco (1967).

Neisser, Edith G.: *The Roots of Self-Confidence.* Science Research Associates, Chicago (1970).

Books For Children About Low Self-Esteem

Barrett, John M.: *No Time for Me*. Human Sciences Press, New York (1978). Ages 4 to 8.

Jimmy's parents love him, but they work and are too busy to spend time with him. He feels very hurt, angry, and abandoned. His self-concept is strongly affected by his perception of being separated and abandoned by his parents.

Behrens, June York: *Who Am I?* Children's Press, Chicago (1968). Ages 3 to 6.

Six-year-old children are shown (through photographs) accepting differences and similarities of various races and nationalities. All proudly say who they are and what they like. The book stresses pride in being Americans and coming from different heritages.

DePaola, Thomas Anthony: *Andy (That's My Name)*. Prentice-Hall, Englewood Cliffs, NJ (1973). Ages 3 to 5.

Self-respect and courage are shown by a little boy. He stands up to older children who tease him.

Ets, Marie Hall: *Bad Boy, Good Boy*. Crowell, New York (1967). Ages 6 to 10.

A 5-year-old Mexican American has very low self-esteem. He engages in all kinds of bad behavior, but begins to feel good about himself through positive school experiences.

Garcia, Edward and Pellagrini, Nina: *Homer the Homely Hound*. Institute for Rational Living, New York (1974). Ages 7 to 11.

This book is designed to help children learn to cope with feelings of low self-esteem and fear of failure. The irrational ideas associated with failure and fear of rejection are explored by using the ugly duckling theme.

Green, Phyllis: *The Fastest Quitter in Town*. Addison-Wesley, Reading MA (1972). Ages 6 to 9.

A young boy thinks very little of himself. Through a relationship with his great-grandfather, he learns not to give up on himself.

Greene, Bette: *Philip Hall Likes Me, I Reckon Maybe*. Dial, New York (1974). Ages 10 to 13.

A 12-year-old rural girl does everything well. Philip, whom she likes, has no use for girls. She succeeds and gains Philip's friendship through self-confidence and a belief in herself.

Hall, Lynn: *Troublemaker.* Follett, Chicago (1974). Ages 11 to 14.

A 13-year-old boy feels worthless and has frequent temper outbursts. The story depicts a boy who lives up to his bad reputation. The events are quite sad. The only positive relationship is with his dog.

Limbacher, Walter J.: *Becoming Myself.* Pflaum, Dayton, OH (1970). Ages 10 to 11 years.

Through reading, activities, and discussion, children explore their feelings. It helps children understand themselves and their relationships with others. Self-discovery and feeling comfortable about oneself are the stated goals.

Schwarzrock, Shirley and Wrenn, C. Gilbert: *Do I Know the "Me" Others See?* American Guidance Service, Circle Press, Minnesota (1973). Adolescents.

Practical suggestions are given for adolescents to know themselves better. Being aware of others' reactions and developing a good self-concept are stressed.

Van Iterson, Siny Rose: *Pulga.* Morrow, West Caldwell, NJ (1971). Adolescents.

A 15-year-old boy lives in poverty and hunger. He takes advantage of an opportunity to better himself by becoming a truck driver's helper. He learns to overcome his fears, makes decisions, and begins to feel worthwhile.

Waber, Bernard: *You Look Ridiculous, Said the Rhinocerous to the Hippopotamus.* Houghton Mifflin, Boston (1966). Ages 5 to 8.*

A hippopotamus learns to accept herself, after being teased for not having a horn. The story humorously makes the point of the negative effects of wishing to be what you're not.

Wolcott, Patty: *Super Sam and the Salad Garden.* Addison-Wesley, Reading, MA (1975). Ages 3 to 7.

In 10 words, a story is told of a heroic boy growing a garden in the alley of an apartment building. Colorful illustrations appeal to young children.

Wolcott, Patty: *My Shadow and I.* Addison-Wesley, Reading, MA (1975). Ages 3 to 7.

A young boy and his shadow run, dance, and fight together. The boy and his shadow bravely fight a scary tree.

References

1. Nowicki, Stephen and Strickland, Bonnie R.: "A locus of control scale for children." *Journal of Consulting and Clinical Psychology* 40:(1973), pp. 148–154.
2. Noble, Grant. Egan, Paul and McDowell, Sandra: "Changing the self-concepts of 7 year old deprived urban children by creative drama or videofeedback." *Social Behavior and Personality* 5:(1977), pp. 55–64.

DEPRESSED/SELF-INJURIOUS

Depression is a feeling of sadness and gloom, often with reduced activity. Self-injurious behavior occurs when people damage or hurt themselves. Suicide is an extreme form of self-injurious behavior that often occurs in depressed individuals. We will deal with both problems in one section since the causes and ways of handling the problems are so similar. Only recently has there been a growing awareness of the increasing number of depressed children under 12 years. Currently, it is estimated that one in five children has some form of depression.[1] Strikingly, 58 percent of parents of depressed children are also depressed. Sad, helpless reactions are common among the 1,000,000 children who are battered and abused each year in the United States. To make the situation even more serious, there is a widespread professional opinion that depression at times underlies a variety of children's behavior problems such as bedwetting, tantrums, truancy, fatigue, school failure, delinquent acts, hyperactivity, and psychosomatic problems. Delinquency often covers up feelings of loneliness and despair. Approximately half of the adolescents in trouble with the law are depressed. This situation is called a "masked depression."

Because of their dependency upon adults, children often feel despondent and helpless. Depressed children rarely show joy or pleasure, often have a soft monotonous voice, lack a sense of humor, and rarely laugh. There may be mood swings and disturbed sleep patterns. They may be tearful, irritable, miserable, and cling for support. Some become detached and aloof, while others appear overtly anxious. Rather than complaining of sadness, children may have physical complaints (headaches, stomach aches). They may not feel like doing anything, lose interest in playing sports or games, and suddenly do poorly in school. It may be hard to arouse their interest in anything. They may feel rejected and unloved and not be easily comforted. Often, they prefer isolated, self-comforting activities to interacting with others. To others, they may seem too serious, solemn, and grown up. They underestimate themselves, seeing themselves and the world through "dark glasses."

When very angry, many children from 8 to 12 threaten to hurt or kill themselves. After their anger subsides, they usually apologize and say that they didn't mean it. Children who do hurt themselves are often extremely self-critical, which is an important early warning sign. Self-injurious behavior, including suicide, is relatively frequent and on the rise.[2] In a 10-year-period, suicide among 15- to 19-year-olds went from 6.3 per 100,000 to 11.0. In this age group, suicide is actually the second leading cause of death. Adolescents most frequently commit suicide after school failure, or because of the death of a parent or relative, parental divorce, continued family conflict, poverty, and poor peer relations. Suicide is the eighth leading cause of death in 5- to 14-year-old boys. By 7 or 8 years, children usually understand the concept of death and suicide.

Some children are self-assaultive. They threaten or actually hurt themselves. Many "accident prone" children would fall into this category. Some acts are quite self-destructive, for example, not taking absolute essential medicine, such as insulin. Similarly, extreme risk taking often turns out to be self-destructive. These individuals may jump over a long drop, cross a street in heavy traffic, or drive at extremely high speeds. Self-injurious behavior includes scratching, cutting, slapping, and punching oneself. Some children chew or pick their skin or swallow objects or poisons. Rhythmic movements like head banging are relatively common in infancy, but usually subside by 3 or 4 years. Body rocking is common and may indicate a need for more physical activity. Severe or prolonged head banging (even into a pillow) may cause stress at home, teasing, and feelings of worthlessness. Hair pulling is not too common, but does occur more frequently in girls under 12. While normal children are self-injurious at times, seriously emotionally disturbed and retarded children frequently brutally injure themselves.[3]

Reasons Why

Guilt. Children who believe that they are basically rotten or bad want to be punished. They think that they deserve to be hurt because of their bad thoughts and/or behaviors. Guilt feelings come from having committed a breach of conduct, from feeling responsible for imagined offenses, or from a general sense of inadequacy. "I am so bad no one could possibly love me." With this feeling, expressions of love and acceptance are not believed. The situation becomes more serious when others actually like these children less because their behavior is such that they appear to ask for rejection. Others say, "How can you like him when he acts as if he didn't deserve to be liked?" Children who feel guilty blame themselves for any problems or failure and often talk to themselves in very negative terms. "I'm such a jerk, no wonder my parents can't stand me." Typically, when others are upset, angry, or irritable, these children feel responsible. "If only I hadn't acted that way, my mother wouldn't cry all the time." When children are told that something isn't their fault, they don't believe it. They feel that others are just trying to be nice. Since they already feel guilty, words don't affect their negative self-concept.

Childhood, and even lifelong, guilt may result from *early deprivation.* Many children do not receive sufficient nurturance (affectionate care and attention). These children have not received the basic care that enables them to feel wanted and psychologically safe and secure, and they develop a feeling of unworthiness. Therefore, they fall into a pattern of punishing themselves for being bad and unlovable. They also feel that they don't deserve to be happy, and depression becomes a natural way of life.

Anger Turned Inward. The children described above who feel guilty may well become angry at themselves and become depressed or hurt themselves in some way. This is a straightforward way of punishing yourself for being bad. Even more typical is the situation where children become very angry at the unfairness of others. They see their parents, teachers, peers, or siblings as unfair, mean, and insensitive to them. Usually, there is some combination of truth and imagination or exaggeration to their feelings. Normal events become blown up, and more than usual and temporary anger may result. Because of their dependence upon adults for physical support and psychological approval, direct expression of anger is unlikely. Additionally, most adults disapprove of direct expression of anger by children. It is not rare to hear, "Don't ever let me hear you speak like that again or I'll wash your mouth with soap, not speak to you, punish you, etc."

In frustration, some children turn their anger, which was originally directed towards others, against themselves. It is as if the anger has to be expressed somehow. Some children do express anger through physical activity, cursing to themselves, telling friends, etc. But those who don't, become self-demeaning and wind up hurting themselves in some way. Hurting yourself while feeling depressed is not an unusual combination.

Feeling Helpless. Depression usually follows a conviction that one just cannot cope with everyday problems. Prolonged helplessness and despair may lead to suicidal thoughts as a means of escaping a hopeless situation. At times, helplessness is combated by some form of self-stimulation such as rocking, head banging, or some types of self-injurious behavior. It is as if causing self-stimulation or pain means that one is not totally helpless.

A recent theory that has received a great deal of research support and widespread discussion is "learned helplessness."[4] Children may come to believe that they have no real choices and that their behavior has no effect on their environment. They feel that they cannot control situations, obtain gratification, or relieve their own suffering. This pattern is most frequently caused by an inconsistent, unpredictable, uncontrollable environment. The parents may be extremely inconsistent, and their children cannot predict what kind of reaction will result from their behavior at any given time. Overprotection may also contribute to a child's feeling relatively helpless. Well-meaning adults may frequently make work too easy and not challenging enough for children. As a result, children feel helpless, unproductive, and inadequate. Helplessness is reinforced by repeated failure or by what the child sees as too easy or unwarranted success.

Reaction to Deep Loss. Children are vulnerable if their feelings of self-esteem all depend upon one external source. If that source is no longer available, depression is very likely. Young children are more vulnerable to loss of parents, while older children then feel devastated if that all important supply of acceptance vanishes. Some children are more sensitive and vulnerable than others. Even if there are several sources of acceptance, the death or departure of an important individual or pet may precipitate very strong emotional reactions. Children experience the loss as a major trauma (a disordered mental or behavioral state caused by emotional stress). They may become unable to carry on daily activities, dependent, disinterested, pessimistic, or suicidal.

Children under 6 years are especially vulnerable to separation from parents. The high divorce rate often causes young children to feel abandoned and deserted by the departing parent. Some young children feel similarly abandoned by friends or relatives leaving. There is a significant loss of positive reinforcement that was very important to the child. Some children also react very strongly to the loss of a pet or material possession. Loss of parental love may be experienced due to continual marital disharmony between parents. The general feeling of personal loss may well lead to self-destructive behavior.[2] Any continuing social difficulty may lead to a loss of self-esteem and self-confidence. This is especially true when children had been doing relatively well in school and then perceive a loss of academic adequacy.

Gain Attention, Love, Sympathy, or Revenge. Quite frequently children will hurt themselves or express feelings of sadness as a means of obtaining love and sympathy from others. This is especially true when attention cannot be gained by other means. The gaining of attention becomes complicated because love and revenge may be sought at the same time. Children become very angry because they are not loved, yet still desperately want to be loved and valued by parents and others. Those who don't love them will be taught a lesson. Those adults will feel very badly when they see the child in trouble, hurt, or dead. Suicide will make others feel sorry for the martyred child. Revenge for being hurt or rejected will be achieved by this impulsive act. Suicide might also be considered as a way of not having to face people who are causes of pain, rejection, disgrace, or humiliation. Revenge may be obtained by self-destructive acts such as delinquency, drug consumption, or poor school grades. Passive children may pull their hair, eyebrows, or eyelashes out to express anger towards their parents. This is especially effective when parents feel embarrassed by their child's bald spots.

Some children may inadvertently be reinforced for hurting themselves. Parents show concern and pay attention to children who hurt themselves. This may set a pattern, especially when parents do not pay much attention to children at other times. Young children may pick or scratch their skin before mealtime. If food frequently follows this act, the scratching may become habitual. A child may be sitting on a potty and not liking it so he bangs his head. If head banging frequently results in being removed from an unpleasant situation, it may become habitual. What confuses parents is that behavior generalizes, and the child bangs his head when any situation becomes unpleasant.

Reaction to Tension. Tension may be defined as opposition or hostility between individuals and an inner feeling of unrest, often accompanied by physical indications of emotions (sweating, muscle tightness, and increased pulse). Children who frequently experience negative feelings in interaction with others develop a need to relieve tension. During stress or fatigue, older children may pull their hair or scratch themselves. This apparently self-destructive behavior therefore may actually be positive to the individual who feels better when engaging in that behavior. These children try to develop some means of coping with intense and prolonged stress. Depression often results when children cannot master stress in some satisfactory manner. Suicidal thoughts stem from the searching for a means of ending unavoidable, continuous tension.

Family Context. More than half the parents of depressed children are depressed people. It is always difficult to assess how much of a disposition is inherited and how much is learned from living with people who are often depressed. There is evidence that suggests that proneness to depression is an inherited characteristic. This proneness would certainly be brought out by living with a parent who is a model for a depressed approach to life. Even without any genetic predisposition, parental depressed models certainly lead to children imitating various aspects of depression. Children learn to be pessimistic, sad, worried, and not easily aroused to joy or pleasure. Depressed or withdrawn parents do not communicate well with their children. The lack of communication directly contributes to isolated, helpless, and depressed feelings.

Intense or very frequent family conflicts may lead to depressed feelings in children, especially in the more sensitive ones. Young children are particularly vulnerable since they do not understand that adults often need to hash out problems. They may see parents as locked in mortal combat when in actuality they are having relatively normal arguments. Parents who actually are engaged in serious unresolved marital conflicts are very likely to have one or more depressed children. Intense and continued sibling rivalry may also lead to great sadness in a particular child. That child may feel constantly picked upon and unable to get away from hostile brothers and sisters.

Some parents have extremely strong strivings for achievement for themselves and their children. Expressions of failure, frustration, and unhappiness by their children are not acceptable. These parents don't want to hear about problems and *do not listen* to their children. Children are spoken at or to rather than with and often give up attempts to communicate. Rather than listening, talking, and solving problems, they become depressed. Prolongation of this pattern may lead to suicidal thoughts or acts.

Physiological. Possible physical causes of depression must be considered. When children have been well adjusted and depressed reactions occur (suddenly or gradually), medical causes must be ruled out. This is especially important when the other causes of depression described previously do not appear to exist. Hormonal imbalance might exist, especially in girls at puberty. Other causes of depression are iron deficiency, anemia, thyroid dysfunction, viruses (especially mononucleosis in teen-agers), food allergies, and blood sugar irregularities.

How to Prevent

Open Communication and Expression of Feelings. Basic warmth and acceptance are promoted by respecting and listening to children. It is crucial that children feel that adults take them seriously and can be turned to for support and guidance. An essential aspect is that adults allow open expression of all genuine feelings, especially anger. In this atmosphere, anger does not have to be expressed in other ways such as gaining revenge by self-destructive acts. All feelings can be accepted and discussed. There is no substitute for children being able to discuss angry, jealous, hopeless, sexual, etc., feelings with parents or some adult. You anticipate problems and prepare children to cope with typical occurrences. Discussion of the naturalness of death is a good example. From 4 years on, death should be periodically discussed at the child's level of comprehension. Death is natural and life goes on. Parents must come to terms with their own feelings towards death and think about the most helpful way of discussing it with children. Some parents use religious concepts. Others talk of the naturalness of becoming part of the universe. The important concept is that death or any loss is discussed matter of factly and openly. When children have no preparation, they often react with intense anger and depression when they experience death or loss of a relative, friend, or pet.

Communication has been defined as any behavior, verbal or nonverbal, that carries a message which is perceived by someone else.[5] Several helpful rules of communication have been spelled out. Some are adapted and selectively listed here: (1) Action speaks louder than words. It's what you do rather than what you say you do that counts. (2) Be clear, specific, and positive when communicating. (3) The meaning of a communication depends upon the experiences and perception of each person. (4) Be honest, fair, considerate, and tactful. (5) Don't lecture, nag, or make excuses. Sensitive and constructive communication fosters a caring and optimistic family setting.

Promote Adequacy and Effectiveness. Individuals who do not feel a general sense of helplessness do not lapse into hopelessness and depression. It is essential to promote feelings of adequacy and independence. Active problem solving and gaining personal satisfaction prevents helplessness.

Children should be given choices and their sense of having good judgment continuously reinforced. This is accomplished by setting challenging but reachable goals and expecting children to master most tasks. You encourage children to try and take the initiative, rather than use a passive approach to situations. Their problem-solving ability should always be strengthened. Cause and effect relationships should be clearly discussed. Young children can learn to be aware of cause and effect both in nature and in their efforts, *e.g.*, thunder is caused by lightning moving through the air. Problems are solved by asking questions and coming up with possible solutions. The idea is to promote an active approach to facing everyday or unusual problems.

The above efforts are intended to immunize children against easily falling into a helpless depression when things go wrong. Additionally, you attempt to provide a relatively predictable and controllable environment. This means that children should feel influential in affecting what happens at home. Their suggestions should be listened to and followed when possible. You should avoid being inconsistent or whimsical in your child-rearing approach. Some well-meaning parents attempt to be open and flexible, and instead cause feelings of chaos or confusion in children's minds. Children under 8 years are especially vulnerable to feeling helpless when parents' behavior is not predictable. Also, some children who feel helpless hurt themselves as a way of feeling and demonstrating that they have some power. Promoting real adequacy and independence prevents this self-injurious pattern.

Promote Many Sources of Self-Esteem. ''Having all your eggs in one basket'' is not a good idea. Children are especially vulnerable to depression if their self-worth basically depends upon one or two sources. This is similar to people whose main attraction is good looks. Any blemish or signs of age triggers depressed feelings. People who basically only relate emotionally to their spouses are likely candidates for depression, and, unfortunately, suicide is not rare in those situations. Some children become extremely attached to one parent, almost to the emotional exclusion of anyone else. You should encourage children to feel close to other adults, as well as to peers. Loss of approval is much less threatening when there are several sources of approval and acceptance.

A child's interests and skills should be broadly developed. Good, solid self-concepts are promoted by competency in diverse areas, not by being a specialist in one. This also gives her a good base for later deciding which skill to develop more fully. Additionally, children receive positive feedback from others in each area of interest and competence. Therefore, children become less fragile and vulnerable to loss of one skill (or one person).

Model Optimism and Flexibility. By imitating parents, children can learn to count their blessings, not their misfortunes. You must be aware of your direct influences in promoting optimism or pessimism by your own example. Parents who focus on the problems and tragedies in life usually have children who do the same. The best indicator is to be aware of the amount of time spent on positive vs. negative topics. If much of the conversation is dominated by worry and concern about the future, a negative atmosphere is generated. Instead, the future should be viewed with interest and excited anticipation. An optimistic attitude can be worked at and developed. Rather than worry, take action! Rather than getting stuck on problems or grudges, move on. Resentment and other forms of anger should be brief and not emphasized. Good feelings should not be kept to yourself. Let children know your accomplishments, pride, successes, and happiness. Too many people are free with negatives and stingy with good feelings. Children are beneficially influenced by hearing positive statements and witnessing an adaptive, flexible approach to problems. In this atmosphere, psychologically or physically hurting oneself is extremely unlikely.

Be Alert to Warning Signs. There is no substitute to being sensitive to children's feelings and behaviors. Be aware of any signs of continuing feelings of helplessness or depression. Take children's complaints seriously and with respect. Pay attention to their comments and nonverbal behavior. Making light of children's complaints may lead to depression or self-injurious acts as a means of gaining attention or respect. A good warning and indicator of a need for professional evaluation and intervention is any *sudden change in behavior.* Personality change (happy-go-lucky to serious, dependable to undependable, reasonable to irrational, etc.), withdrawal, inefficiency, poor schoolwork, and loss of interest should be immediately taken seriously. Any disruption of the usual routines of eating, sleeping, and studying may indicate depression. Loss of weight, irritability, and fatigue are significant. Be alert to the presence of any possible self-destructive objects in a child's room such as a rope, pills, or a knife.[2] Some children become isolated or may suddenly give away their most valued possessions. Any talk about suicide or hurting oneself, no matter how casual, should be taken seriously. In teen-agers, alcohol or any drug use may be early signs of depression. The tip off is the need for drugs to feel good, especially in order to enjoy themselves or face social events.

What To Do

Openly Discuss Sadness and Hurting Oneself. Many adults avoid confronting children for fear of intensifying their negative feelings or precipitating self-destructive behavior. Instead, taking children seriously and listening empathically has a beneficial effect. Telling children that anger and depression are temporary is often a reassuring experience for children. They feel that adults can face strong feelings and that things will turn out all right. Very sad children should be asked directly if they have thought of hurting or killing themselves. Individuals are frequently glad that someone asked since they may be hesitant to bring it up themselves. The question does not put ideas in children's minds. Rather, it demonstrates concern and willingness to face and discuss any feelings. However, we are not suggesting belaboring the issue or asking questions if you would communicate fear and uncertainty about your own ability to cope with the issue.

All feelings are legitimate to express and discuss. Grief should not be hidden or covered up as quickly as possible. Feelings of grief for any reason should be ventilated and sympathetically discussed. Help children express all feelings, including guilt. It is very helpful to clarify what actually happened and what the child imagined. However, it is crucial to communicate that we all have some guilt feelings after a loss. It is perfectly normal to think about what we should have done or what we shouldn't have done. We all learn the lesson to be nicer to each other while alive or while we are together. Do not expect a "stiff upper lip" or "boys don't cry." Instead, encourage expression of all feelings. Crying, laughing, sadness, anger, and remembering many details are all appropriate. Separation from departed or dead close ones should be a topic for discussion. Individuals say good-bye in their own unique ways, which should be encouraged and accepted. Open discussion of feelings takes place in an accepting and supportive atmosphere provided by friends and family.

Assure Perception of Goal Achievement. Depressed children must be able to feel that they can currently set and achieve some goal. They should be helped to think about what they might want to accomplish, no matter how insignificant it appears. Some children want to finish a collection they have started, while others want to feel helpful by doing extra chores. The key is to make sure that children perceive their own behavior as leading to external or internal rewards. This directly counteracts the helpless feeling that nothing they do matters. It also leads to some positive feeling of accomplishment as well as providing a focus for attention and an outlet for energy.

Plan and Do Enjoyable Activities. Do not allow children to vegetate or wallow in sadness or helplessness. Be active in planning enjoyable activities, even if children say that they want to be left alone. Children who do not want to do anything should be helped to participate in activities even in a minimal way. It is crucial to avoid isolation and to *involve* the child with others. Other children or adults should be told that children may not participate, but that they should be treated normally and that they will eventually come around. The optimistic attitude that children will come out of it should be expressed directly. Another helpful aspect is the planning of *future* activities. This is a clear demonstration of the expectation that children will participate by the time the event takes place. It also gives children the opportunity to possibly look forward to something. During activities, adults serve as models of becoming involved and enjoying activities. Children's interests should be kept in mind. Possible events include picnics, boat rides, watching or participating in sporting events, visiting friends or relatives, dining out, special trips to new places, etc.

Positive Self-Talk. In a straightforward manner, children should be told that negative self-statements make things worse. You do not focus on negatives or say things such as "Things will never get better," "I don't deserve to be happy," or "Hurting myself will make things better." Children can learn to monitor their own thoughts. You should say to kids that they will feel better by learning to say positive things to themselves. By being sensitive to children's feelings, you custom tailor positive self-comments for them. Helpful comments include, "Things will work out," "Soon, I'll feel happy again," "My friends and relatives will help me feel good," "Stop feeling sorry for yourself and do something," and "Helping others makes you feel good." You analyze a child's negative approach and suggest some positive self-comments to counteract pessimistic or guilty feelings. Thinking positively leads to acting positively!

Eliminate Self-Injurious Behavior

Use overcorrection. Overcorrection[6,7] is a mild form of punishment which has been very effective with many types of children. The misbehavior leads to children having to perform other behavior which serves to correct or "overcorrect" the misbehavior. The corrective behavior should be related in some way to the misbehavior, follow immediately, and be actively performed for a relatively long period of time. One frequently used method is called *restitutional overcorrection.* This type has become increasingly popular in the courts as an effective and beneficial form of punishment for crimes. The individual apologizes and then makes things better in some way. If the individual broke or destroyed objects, his task is to fix those objects. Or, the individual may perform work in order to pay for the destruction. There are many ways of creatively using this method. The idea is to correct a situation and work towards improving it. For example, a chronic head banger is made to wash her hair, dry and brush it, and hold an ice pack on her head for 5 minutes after every episode of head banging. After several repetitions, head banging is diminished greatly and usually eliminated. A child who bites his hand could be made to wash his mouth with an antiseptic solution, brush his teeth, and rub cream on his hand. Very young aggressive children may hit themselves out of frustration and anger. They might be made to pat the hit area for 2 minutes. Put simply, children do not like to perform this type of behavior and most often decide to eliminate the misbehavior. The beauty of the process is that parents can be firm and effective immediately without becoming angry, insulting, or critical towards children.

Another form is *positive practice overcorrection.* A behavior is practiced which is physically incompatible with the inappropriate behavior. Children may use their hands to hurt themselves in some way such as scratching, picking, or hitting. One effective approach is to enforce relaxation for some period of time depending upon age. A 4 year old might be made to relax for 15 minutes, while a 10 year old might relax for a half-hour. Relaxing is incompatible with hurting oneself. Another variation is having children do something constructive with their hands for some time period. That could vary from building or fixing something to performing exercises, like squeezing a rubber ball 50 times. In some instances, overcorrection may work even if the practiced behavior is not related to the misbehavior. Head bangers might have to do some tedious activity for 10 minutes after each instance of head banging. With uncooperative children some other means may have to be employed to assure their performing the required behavior. A good method is that they must cooperate in order to earn privileges such as television watching, allowance, use of the telephone, etc. Therefore, they do the "overcorrection" behavior in order to earn desired privileges.

Use rewards and time outs. After any self-injurious behavior, a "time out" may be enforced. This could mean going to a spare, relatively barren room for 10 minutes. Sending children to their room usually doesn't work since they do enjoyable activities there. When inappropriate behavior leads to boring isolation, the behavior decreases. To maximize effectiveness, you positively reward appropriate behavior at other times. This means that if children who hurt themselves go for an hour without doing so, you praise or reward them in some manner. You could employ the earning of points for appropriate behavior with the points then used to earn extra privileges or toys. A point to remember is that forcible restraint is rarely effective. For example, holding a head banger is only a temporary solution and often leads to much anger and physical struggling.

Medication. This method is listed here for situations where the above methods have not been effective or could not be employed for some reason (such as lack of time or the unavailability of adults for a period of time). Antidepressant drugs have been prescribed successfully by pediatricians and child psychiatrists. We believe that drugs are not the treatment of choice and certainly not the first course of action. However, if drugs are used, they should be given in the context of specific action to change the conditions that caused a depressive reaction. Children taking medication may be more amenable to open talk, setting and achieving goals, and enjoying activities. Once they become involved, the drugs should be quickly tapered off and eliminated. Long-term use of antidepressants is definitely inappropriate.

Case Study

A 14-year-old girl had gradually become apathetic, began doing poorly in school, cried frequently, and had several careless accidents where she hurt herself. Her parents reported that she expressed no concern of being hurt and said that her doing poorly didn't really matter. Discussion with the parents revealed a relatively distant parent-child relationship. The situation took a positive turn due to two courses of action. The first was an awkward and gradual attempt by the parents to openly discuss the girl's feelings. They had to set up a half-hour after dinner to assure a conversation, since everyone going their own way was the custom. The first few attempts were almost unbearably awkward for all concerned. However, they began to discuss her feeling unhappy, lonely, and hopeless. As she expressed herself, they also spoke more of their feelings. The second planned action seemed to smoothly follow the opening of communication. That was to plan and do enjoyable activities. In the past, they only went to movies, bowling, or to visit relatives. Parents and child did not communicate much during these activities. They began to go to more events that allowed for family interaction. They went on boat rides, picnics, and amusement parks where they enjoyed themselves and interacted.

Books For Parents About Depression

French, Alfred and Berlin, Irving: *Depression in Children and Adolescents*. Human Sciences Press, New York (1979).

Grollman, E.A.: *Explaining Death to Children*. Beacon, Boston (1972).

Books For Children About Depression

Green, Phyllis: *A New Mother for Martha*. Human Sciences Press, New York (1978). Ages 4 to 8.

A young girl learns how to cope with the death of her mother and remarriage of her father. She learns to accept the permanency of death from her father and new mother.

Green, Phyllis: *Ice River*. Addison-Wesley, Reading, MA (1975). Ages 8 to 12.

A sad boy struggles with his parents' divorce and mother's remarriage. His sadness changes through exciting adventures with his friends.

Smith, Doris B.: *A Taste of Blackberries*. Crowell, New York (1973). Ages 8 to 10.

A 10-year-old boy copes with his friend's sudden death. This powerful realistic story aids children in accepting their feelings and mourning appropriately.

Stolz, Mary: *By the Highway Home*. Harper & Row, New York (1971). Ages 9 to 12.

The death of a brother in Viet Nam is faced by a 13-year-old girl. Her emotional outbursts led her parents to become more sensitive to her grief.

References

1. National Institute of Mental Health: *Causes, Detection and Treatment of Childhood Depression*. NIMH, Washington, D.C. (1979).
2. Frederick, Calvin J.: *Self-Destructive Behavior Among Younger Age Groups*. Department of Health, Education and Welfare, Rockville, MD (1977 ADM 77–365).

3. Kauffman, James M.: *Characteristics of Children's Behavior Disorders.* Merrill, Columbus, OH (1977).
4. Seligman, M.E.: *Helplessness: On Depression, Development, and Death.* Freeman, San Francisco (1975).
5. Wahlroos, Sven: *Family Communication: A Guide to Emotional Health.* Macmillan, New York (1974).
6. Ollendick, Thomas H. and Matson, Johnny L.: "An initial investigation into the parameters of overcorrection." *Psychological Reports* 39:(1976), pp. 1139–1142.
7. Ollendick, Thomas H. and Matson, Johnny L.: "Overcorrection: An overview." *Behavior Therapy* 9:(1978), pp. 830–842.

HYPERSENSITIVITY TO CRITICISM

"She's so overly sensitive; you can't say anything to her." "He's impossible. He takes everything the wrong way." These types of statements about children are very common. Being overly sensitive is to be highly responsive and easily hurt emotionally. There is an overresponse to the attitudes and feelings of others. When others make any type of judgment or evaluative comment (criticism), overly sensitive children cannot accept the comment without feeling hurt. They may react to the hurt in a variety of ways, such as withdrawal, shyness, anger, sadness, etc. Actual mild teasing or imagined slights lead to strong negative feelings. They are often keenly aware of the imperfections of others who are seen as bad and hurtful.

A usual period of oversensitivity is from 5 to 8 years. However, there is an important difference between a child who is fairly overly sensitive at times and gets over it quickly and a child who is frequently quite overly sensitive and takes a long time to get over it. Many children seem to have intense reactions to almost every event. When most others see a teacher as good, they describe the teacher as bad. They complain about the teacher's tone of voice, facial expressions, and unfair practices.

While this section covers hypersensitivity, it is also directly applicable to problems of moodiness. Overly sensitive children are often quite temperamental and subject to periods of gloominess. The causes of moodiness are quite similar to the causes discussed for hypersensitivity. In fact, sudden mood changes (happy or sad) without apparent reason may be constitutional, similar to overreactivity from birth. Small events often trigger large emotional reactions.

Reasons Why

Feelings of Inadequacy. When individuals basically feel inadequate, they are highly vulnerable to any type of criticism—even the most benign comment may be taken as a personal attack. They come across as overly sensitive and very defensive, as if they have to continually protect themselves. Often, they cannot even accept compliments. They are either suspicious of the motives of the complimentor or feel that they do not really deserve praise because of their inadequacy. Their low self-esteem makes them overly vigilant to any type of evaluation by others. Evaluation is expected to confirm their inadequacy, and therefore should be avoided at all costs. However, any type of feedback from others is, by definition, an evaluation or judgment. Therefore, they are overly sensitive to feedback, are prepared for the worst, and often misperceive comments as being more negative than was intended.

Feeling "different" than others is a typical cause of seeing oneself as inadequate. Children see themselves as not as smart, attractive, desirable, athletic, humorous, etc., as others. They overreact to any comment made about their sensitive area. However it is quite common for the awkward, uncoordinated child to become overly sensitive in general, not just to comments about clumsiness. Children with identifiable differences are most vulnerable. They look different than average, and are subject to teasing. Characteristics that are pointed out include being short, tall, fat, thin, large features (nose, ears, teeth), missing limbs, etc. Inadequate feelings are also often aroused by the arrival of a new baby or by sibling rivalry in general. When attention is taken away, children take it personally and feel that it is their fault. New babies are often resented, and a period of oversensitivity may occur. Well-functioning older brothers and sisters are another frequent source of negative comparison. The young child feels less adequate and very sensitive to comparisons between siblings made by others. Extreme sensitivity is often shown at home to sibling or parental teasing. Even matter-of-fact comments are often taken badly by children who feel inferior to their siblings.

Unrealistic Expectations. When children expect too much of others, they are continually disappointed. An oversensitivity develops since children often want *total* acceptance as indicated by positive feedback from others. Any sign of disapproval is taken very badly. These children have the perfectionistic expectations that others will be nice and always sensitive to their needs. The result is children who never feel satisfied and who are hypersensitive and hypervigilant to criticism. Very frequent is their complaint that parents are always unfair and picking on them. The parents are surprised and state that they go out of their way to be fair to that child. Ironically, they often think that they favor the child who is so sensitive and complaining.

The unrealistic expectations can be exaggerated by a variety of factors. Most typical are overly protective or indulgent parents. Their children grow up expecting to be pampered and catered to. The normal stresses of childhood are exaggerated in the eyes of children who expect special treatment. These "spoiled" children come across to others as always wanting their own way and as incapable of accepting criticism or any type of feedback other than praise. Perfectionistic parents often have perfectionistic children who expect too much. These parents are often surprised at their children's oversensitivity and criticize them for "not being able to take it." They miss the obvious connection that their children have imitated perfectionism and therefore expect others, especially their parents, to be perfectly sensitive to them.

Control Others. Some children develop oversensitivity as a means of controlling others. Most adults feel guilty when children react strongly. Children learn that oversensitivity can be used as a means of subtly expressing anger and getting back at others for real or imagined wrongs. The patterns becomes stronger and stronger since hypersensitivity "works" in achieving attention and strong reactions in others, especially in parents. In addition, the child is described and labeled by others as overly sensitive, and the child literally lives up to this reputation.

Similarly, there is a self-fulfilling prophecy that occurs when children see others as being too critical of them. Others are seen as bad and hurtful, and children act badly and hurtful in return. Their negative behavior results in actual criticism from others, which is seen as proof that others really are hurtful. The result is a general oversensitivity and a need to get back at others in some effective way. Hypersensitivity has by then become a characteristic way of relating to others.

Constitutional Hypersensitivity. After extensive research,[1] a type of children who were "difficult" practically from birth was identified. Their characteristics included irregularity in physiological functions, negative or withdrawal responses to new situations, poor adaptability to change, frequent negative moods, and a high degree of intense reactions. These children are constitutionally overly sensitive. They are built that way! Their nervous systems are more highly reactive than those of average or very easy-going children. Parents, in the research cited, used similar child-rearing practices compared with parents of normally sensitive children. This supports the notion that the hypersensitivity was constitutional, rather than a result of some parental behavior. From birth, some children are much more reactive than others to noise, pain, light, temperature, motion, etc. They are more sensitive and more easily aroused than other infants. In many cases, it is as if they have an "all or none" reaction. Once set off, almost all of their reactions appear very strong. This is in contrast to children who react differentially according to the strength of a particular event. The implication is that they inherited their highly sensitive nervous systems.

Another cause of overreactivity is some type of negative influence on the developing brain. From conception on, the brain can be influenced by environmental conditions. Neurological or biochemical problems[2] frequently underlie hypersensitivity. Maternal illness or excessive tension during pregnancy may affect the developing brain and result in later overreactivity. Some trauma during birth may subtly damage some portions of the brain. Childhood diseases, especially high fevers and convulsions, can influence brain development. This area is still controversial since brain dysfunction cannot be observed in the same procedures. A brain that does not function efficiently and is often overreactive cannot be identified with precision. It is *inferred* that there is a subtle malfunction of the brain rather than actual damage. It is as if information goes into a faulty "switchboard" in the brain and the response that is made by the child appears to be unnecessarily strong or intense.

How To Prevent

Build Up Tolerance. It is relatively easy to understand that children who are overprotected can't take criticism. They have not gotten used to the usual stresses and criticisms that one encounters. To prevent hypersensitivity you should not overprotect children, but you should literally "toughen them up." You build children's tolerance to criticism by a gradual and sensitive exposure to feedback of all types. We are not talking about intense or frequent criticism, similar to throwing children in the water so they learn to sink or swim. We are talking about the gradual process of helping children learn to "take it." Young children soon learn that "you can't always get what you want." This basic understanding is necessary for children to be able to tolerate frustration and be able to accept negative as well as positive responses from others. Some children are devastated by their first experience of being teased by peers or adults. This may be prevented by mild, playful teasing at home. Children learn that teasing will not destroy you and that you can still feel worthwhile even when someone makes fun of you. You can help children grow up emotionally by playful teasing. "It's too bad you're too weak to throw that ball." The child learns to accept the teasing, throw the ball, and feel proud. The teasing should not be in areas of any oversensitivity and should be in areas where the child can succeed with some effort. Similarly, you might say, "I guess you're not smart enough to figure out how that toy works." Children learn that your comment does not mean that they're stupid, but that it is a style of speaking that can be taken in good spirits as a means of getting someone to try harder.

Gentle teasing builds up tolerance, and children quickly learn to accept teasing or criticism without feeling crushed. Role playing may be used constructively. Young children can play with puppets who criticize each other. You can demonstrate realistic criticism and appropriate ways of responding. Children over 5 years can play the part of another child and engage with you in make-believe situations. When another child says, "I can't stand your yelling," inappro-

priate responses are rage, withdrawal, or sadness. Appropriate responses are, "Thanks for telling me; I'll try to
speak more softly," "I didn't realize I was yelling; I'll try
not to," or "Let me know if you think I'm yelling so I'll
realize when I'm doing it." Practice in being tolerant prepares the child to be able to accept anything less than positive feedback from peers and teachers.

Teach Relative Reasoning. Hypersensitive children act as
if all criticisms were devastating and were indications of
their total inadequacy. A means of preventing this overreaction is to teach children at an early age to think more logically. One criticism does not mean you're bad. You can be
good at some things and bad at others. You can do the same
thing well at times and not at other times. This is the idea
of relative, rather than absolute, reasoning. Preschool children think in absolute terms—good or bad, black or white.
As early as possible, children can be taught that there are
middle grounds to ideas and situations, not just extremes.
Rather than there being "truths," there are opinions of various individuals and groups. It is very important for older
children to really understand that criticism is one person's
opinion and not a total indictment of their personality. Criticisms do not mean that you are totally or permanently a
certain way. A criticism is an opinion about you at a particular time under certain circumstances. Criticism may then
be seen as a potentially helpful response to be considered,
rather than a cause for mobilizing all defenses.

Model Openness to Feedback. If children observe a parent violently reacting to criticism, they learn to act similarly. Parents who accept criticism gracefully and attempt
to modify their behavior to please others provide a positive
example of responding. The general idea is to be open to
and request feedback from others. Asking someone their
opinion about your behavior is an excellent means of demonstrating willingness to expose yourself to potentially constructive comments. You become more aware of your impact
on others and then are able to modify your behavior in a
direction that will please yourself and others. A significant
example is your asking for children's opinions. Some parents are reluctant to ask what children think for fear of
somehow weakening their parental authority. Actually, this
process increases the child's respect for you since it directly

demonstrates your respect for the child's views. If children tell you that you're too mean, rigid, nasty, unfair, stupid, insensitive, etc., you can thank them for their opinion and ask for illustrations. You might tell them that you will think about their comments and perhaps try to be less unfair or whatever. Scolding or punishing children for sharing their perceptions is a mistake! Listening does not mean agreeing with what is said.

Your own oversensitivity should be kept in line. Many parents inadvertently serve as models for being on guard against likely attacks from others. Children overhear parents discussing work or social situations. When others are frequently described as nasty, backbiting, or mean, children learn to expect people to be like that, and therefore over-react to any slight indication of negativeness in others. This sets the tone for hypersensitivity to comments from people, whom you basically mistrust.

Strengthen Feelings of Adequacy. From infancy on, you encourage and praise children's coping abilities. There is no substitute for feeling adequate, which is a direct preventative of hypersensitivity to criticism. Individuals who feel relatively adequate most of the time are much less vulnerable to criticism. They are naturally able to say things to themselves such as, "Some people think I'm terrible, but I know that I'm good at most things." Your saying statements like this about yourself serves as a good model for children. When we feel good about ourselves, the negative comments of others can be shrugged off. If we have serious self-doubts, it takes only a minor criticism to provoke upset and anger. The most direct way of fostering adequacy is to make sure that children have the skills to cope with most aspects of their environment. If children lack an essential skill, you teach it or make arrangements for them to learn it some-where. The very awkward child should learn and practice basic coordination skills. Socially inept children should practice being aware of others and acting appropriately. Children who are weak in solving problems should frequently review problem situations and figure out (or be helped at first to figure out) alternative solutions. This directly prevents the most extreme form of teasing for being inferior to peers. Also, children know when they cannot do tasks as well as others. They feel much better when they have at least a minimal amount of knowledge and skill in areas significant in their peer group.

Do not underestimate the power of building up a child's strength. All children can do something well. By being sensitive you can encourage and provide opportunities for a child to excel in something. The socially awkward child who does poorly in school might be an excellent swimmer. Being an outstanding swimmer gives this child a feeling that, ''I'm really good at something; I'm not a total failure.'' A traditionally helpful route for unattractive or handicapped children is to develop their personality. By being sensitive, friendly, helpful, and outgoing, they gain acceptance from others and do not become socially isolated.

What To Do

Confront Illogical Ideas. It is illogical to believe that criticism from peers or adults means that a child is worthless. However, many hypersensitive children experience criticism *as if* it were both proof of their inadequacy and a major attack on their personality. Both ideas may be confronted directly, discussed, and disproved. Discussions may be very effective if they take place in a supportive, noncritical atmosphere. It may take considerable effort to show children that you all can discuss a sensitive topic without becoming angry or defensive. Criticism should be seen as potentially valuable information. Children can learn to differentiate between valid criticism and criticism that is due to the other person being generally angry or upset. An open-minded, considered approach is needed as compared to a defensive ''leave me alone, I don't want to hear'' one. Teen-agers in particular may desperately need constructive, open discussions regarding their hypersensitivity and self-consciousness. Children can, and should, learn that their expectations of others are unrealistic. It is necessary to sensitively yet firmly confront children who expect total consideration and acceptance from others. They are deeply hurt by very mild, constructive criticism, *as if* it meant that they were under attack and completely rejected by the other person.

Children are prone to having many assumptions that turn out to be quite illogical when examined.[3] It is very helpful to say to them that we all have mistaken assumptions and that a necessary and positive step is to discover and change our illogical beliefs. For example, many children have come to believe that the world is a threatening place where people are likely to hurt and embarrass them. Therefore, they are continually on guard, expect people to do hurtful things, and see many examples of this. Discussing assumptions may reveal that their original perception was based upon one or two bad experiences, which convinced them that you have to expect the worst. You can show them the danger of "seeing what you expect to see." Personal examples by all are very helpful. Success is reached when children see that they are disregarding the 90% good experiences and are crushed by the 10% bad experiences. In a similar vein, children may feel like a failure or reject because they are not good at one activity or because they are excluded from a desirable peer group. They must be shown that it is illogical to believe that one is a failure because of one or several disappointments. "You are still a nice, decent, worthwhile person even though you are rejected." Not doing well in school does not mean that children are failures. It may mean that they have specific learning problems, inadequate preparation, or poor study habits. The logical approach is to understand the situation and take appropriate action. Illogical beliefs strengthen the vicious cycle of hypersensitive feelings and the engaging in behavior which turns others off.

Teach Problem Solving. Some children who see the illogical nature of their hypersensitivity already have the problem-solving skills to proceed on their own. Other children are very weak in their ability to analyze everyday problems and decide what to do.[4] They may have to be specifically taught how to think of alternative courses of action and consider the consequences of each action. Without this skill they are likely to remain overly sensitive. They perceive their inability to handle situations and are understandably touchy when others point it out in a friendly or in a teasing manner.

For example, a 10-year-old girl became extremely upset any time her peers told her that she was too bossy and stuck up. She thought that they picked on her unfairly ("others act the same way and they don't get criticized"), and she felt helpless about changing the situation. A few of her good friends had stopped playing with her. When analyzed, it became clear that she was unable to clearly think about this or similar problems. All she saw was a hopeless situation. Her parents showed her how to pose the problem and consider different solutions. The problem was that her behavior antagonized peers who then rejected her. She wanted their friendship, but could not figure out what to do. Conversation quickly led to an awareness that she could act differently and predict what would happen. Her "stuck up" reputation was based upon her overenthusiasm about her belongings. The other children felt that she bragged and flaunted her possessions, which made them feel less fortunate and angry towards her. The "bossiness" was a combination of overtalkativeness and always wanting to be first or having to decide what activity should take place. She proudly arrived at possible solutions that she would (and did) try. She stopped talking about her new clothes, many photograph records, and fabulous collection of dolls from all over the world. In games, she let others go first and tried to be a follower and give others the chance to lead. Her prediction, which came true, was that she would be more accepted by others.

In the above situation, it was essential that the parents recognized her weakness in solving problems. They expressed amazement that their girl who was so advanced in school could not understand such an apparently simple situation. Many bright children lack social problem-solving skills! Additionally, once the girl began her plan to behave differently, she did not fall to pieces when children continued to tease her. She felt clear about the situation and her plan, so she was less vulnerable.

Self-Talk. Some hypersensitive children find that self-statements help them feel much better when criticized. When a teacher tells children that their answer is wrong, instead of becoming upset, they can say, "Wrong answers don't mean I'm a terrible student." Many self-statements naturally follow the previous discussion of illogical ideas. Once illogical beliefs are identified, corrective self-comments should be employed. Another example would be, "Being called dumb doesn't mean I'm retarded; I'm pretty good at learning." Regarding name calling, it may be very useful for children to think, "My mother isn't what they say; she's really very nice." Self-talk serves the useful purpose of reducing the helpless feeling that children have. They feel that they can only suffer and be continually hurt. Parental suggestions that self-talk helps many people can set up a positive expectation that children will be able to feel less hypersensitive.

Once children begin to think differently, there is a natural progression to feel and act differently. They can be encouraged to think of helpful phrases when being criticized. "I'm becoming much more able to take comments," "Be tolerant," "Keep cool," "Just listen to what they're saying," "Maybe I should be nicer," etc. Self-talk is therefore used to reverse the expectation that children have about being "overly sensitive." You set up an expectation that your child can take comments from others in a matter-of-fact way. "I can listen to what others think without always feeling upset."

Compensate for Constitutional Oversensitivity. Children should be told that they have always reacted very strongly to situations. However, they can learn to make up for this tendency by developing counteracting strategies. Analyzing and recording types of events and time of day of overreactions sometimes reveals clear patterns. Some children are particularly hypersensitive for an hour after awakening or at the end of the day. By planning pleasing activities and avoiding stress at those times, these periods may be handled quite successfully with a minimum of effort. A helpful guideline is that many adults are slow risers and have to learn to compensate. It is quite usual to hear, "Don't talk to me until I've had two cups of coffee." The compensation is that others learn to not talk to the person at certain times, and the person temporarily avoids others. Children with early morning sensitivity can relax for 10 minutes by reading, watching television, jogging, or doing whatever feels good to them. Similarly, children who fatigue or become overly sensitive in the evenings should plan accordingly. School work, chores, or serious discussions should take place before dinner. Pleasurable activities should be planned for the difficult emotional periods.

Children who show no pattern, but are continually too sensitive, must learn to cope with this weakness. If all family members accept the problem and do not blame the child for purposely acting terribly, change is easier. The atmosphere becomes supportive rather than disapproving. Children should be taught how to relax their muscles on cue. They practice tensing and letting go of all parts of their body. Therefore, they can counteract their physical tension at moments of oversensitivity. When criticized, speaking in front of a group, meeting strangers, etc., children can purposely relax. This is especially helpful to those children who have local areas of strong tension. Many have a tense neck, forehead, jaw, or stomach. This relaxing prevents tension build-up. Additionally, they can learn to think of pleasant images to counteract upset feelings. For example, in school, while worried about being called upon, children can quickly image themselves lying on a beach and feeling calm or playing a favorite sports activity. The idea is to intervene in their natural tendency to overreact by substituting any form of interfering activity.

Case Report

A 14-year-old boy was very defensive about comments made concerning him by peers, teachers, and parents. He took many comments the wrong way and became very upset when criticized in any manner. This pattern had become stronger and stronger for the past year. His parents believed that he felt socially inadequate and extremely self-conscious since puberty. An open discussion was suggested and carried out in a 3-hour conversation behind locked doors on a Sunday afternoon. The boy and the parents agreed to try to solve the problem, since his oversensitivity was causing continuous tension. The 3-hour minimum is a valuable way of communicating the importance of the problem and the willingness of all to devote the time necessary to work on it. His illogical beliefs quickly emerged. In an embarrassed way, he revealed to his parents for the first time that he felt like a "loser" since his friends went out with girls and he didn't. He felt self-conscious and not mature enough to relate to the girls in his class. The discussion centered around his physically being somewhat less mature than his peers and the naturalness of his lack of readiness to socialize with girls. He was visibly relieved at his parents' acceptance of his normalcy. When asked about his friends, he revealed that he couldn't talk to anyone about his concerns that he wasn't normal.

The result of the discussion was a feeling of freedom to develop at his own pace. He had the strong belief that he should be interested in, and spend time with, girls. The pressure was removed, and his conviction that there was something wrong with him was greatly diminished. His parents reported a drastic reduction in his general oversensitivity to both peers and adults.

Books For Children About Hypersensitivity To Criticism

Berger, Terry: *I Have Feelings.* Human Sciences Press, New York (1970). Ages 4 to 8.

Many different feelings are portrayed through photographs and simple descriptions. Children are helped identify, understand, and accept feelings of anger, jealousy, love, hate, loneliness, and shame.

Burch, Robert J.: *Queenie Peavy.* Viking, New York (1966). Ages 11 to 13.

A 13-year-old girl is overly sensitive and thinks that everyone is against her. Gradually, she becomes more understanding and self-accepting and gives up delinquency.

Carlson, Natalie Savage: *School Bell In The Valley.* Harcourt Brace Jovanovich, New York (1963). Ages 8 to 11.

A 10-year-old rural girl is teased for not knowing how to read. Embarrassed and afraid, she quits school. When she has enough money, she returns to obtain a good education.

Waters, Virginia: *Color Us Rational.* Institute for Rational Living, New York (1979). Ages 4 to 8.

Children learn the difference between rational and irrational thinking and behavior by coloring pictures of people and animals. This book may help counteract oversensitivity due to irrational beliefs.

Wise, William: *The Cowboy Surprise.* Putnam, New York (1961). Ages 5 to 8.

A boy and girl are overly sensitive to being teased for wearing glasses. This "beginning reader" book describes how a famous cowboy wears his glasses to school to show that even cowboys wear glasses.

References

1. Thomas, Alexander, Chess, Stella, and Birch, Herbert G.: *Temperament and Behavior Disorders In Children.* New York University Press, New York (1968).
2. Schaefer, Charles E. and Millman, Howard L.: *Therapies For Children.* Jossey-Bass, San Francisco (1977).
3. Ellis, Albert and Grieger, Russell: *Handbook of Rational-Emotive Therapy.* Institute of Rational Living, New York (1978).
4. Shure, Myrna B. and Spivack, George: *Problem Solving Techniques in Childrearing.* Jossey-Bass, San Francisco (1978).

SHY

Shy children frequently avoid others and are usually timid, easily frightened, distrustful, bashful, modest, reserved, and hesitant to commit themselves to most things. They shrink from familiarity or contact with others. In social situations, they do not take the initiative or volunteer, are often silent, speak softly, and avoid eye contact. Others usually see them as dull, boring, and to be avoided which leads to increased shyness. Since shy children are rarely disruptive or cause trouble, they often go unnoticed (especially in school). Additionally, many adults value and reinforce shyness, thinking that "children should be seen and not heard." In situations that appear difficult, shy children withdraw and often leave the scene. Shy preschoolers and school-age children have great difficulty in participating with others. Periods of normal shyness occur at 5 or 6 months and again at 2 years. The incidence of shyness is very high. Approximately 40% of teen-agers and adults describe themselves as shy and unable to make satisfying contact with others.[1,2]

Some children are just less outgoing and less talkative than others, while other children derive pleasure from solitary activities. This is different than timid children who feel unworthy and are seen that way by others because they do not assert or defend themselves. Assertive children express their opinions and rights without denying the rights of others and act in their own best interests. Shy children are often self-conscious, communicate poorly, and do not present themselves well. They feel internal discomfort, often have symptoms of anxiety, become restless, and want to leave social situations. They often feel different and inferior, believing that others think badly of them and that social contact will turn out to be a very negative experience. This fear of negative evaluation is often accompanied by the awkward social behavior of being clumsy and inarticulate. Many shy children do not participate in school or in the community, but act differently at home. The situation is even more serious when children are shy at home also.

Shy children frequently lack social skills. They do not show interest in others, do not give and receive communication, or do not show sympathy and consideration of others. This prevents others from seeing their good qualities. They have a hard time both meeting new people or enjoying new experiences. Therefore, they receive little social praise and are not sought by teachers or peers. Unstructured groups or parties are especially difficult situations for shy children.

Reasons Why

Feelings of Insecurity. Children who feel insecure do not feel safe enough to venture forth and expose themselves to others. They lack self-confidence and self-reliance. Growing up, getting hurt, or taking social risks are quite frightening to them. They are preoccupied with feeling safe and avoiding embarrassment. Their self-preoccupation often leads them to be less aware of what's happening around them. Because of their fearful attitude, they do not practice social skills. There is a vicious cycle of becoming shyer and shyer due to lack of practice and lack of positive feedback from others. They might have one or two shy friends.

Overprotection. Children who are overprotected by their parents are frequently inactive and dependent. Because of their limited opportunities to be adventurous, they become quiet, passive, and shy. This child-rearing approach most frequently leads to timidity and babyishness. The children have not learned to trust themselves in dealing effectively with the environment or with others. Some parents overprotect children out of ignorance. They believe that children cannot take care of themselves and need continuous protection from all dangers and risks. Generally, fearful parents become overly concerned that their offspring must be protected from a frightening and harsh world. Guilt leads some parents to feel overly responsible for their children. These parents may feel guilty because of their lack of interest in, or not really wanting to care for, their children. Overprotected children may shy away from others because they only like it when things go their way. Therefore, they can't compromise or give and take with others.

Disinterest. Some parents openly display a lack of interest or caring for their children. This could be a general lack of concern for children or a belief that a disinterested parental attitude promotes independence in children. Rather than independence, parental disinterest often leads to a timid, shy personality. These children feel unworthy of others' interest and do not have the inner confidence necessary to venture forth socially.

Criticism. Parents who frequently openly or subtly criticize their children often promote the development of timidity. Since these children frequently receive negative responses from adults, they become hesitant, uncertain, and shy. Parents may be critical because "that's the way I was brought up and it feels natural." Or, parents may believe that criticism is a good and necessary technique by which children learn how to behave. The result of excessive criticism is often a fearful and shy child.

Teasing. Children who are teased and ridiculed may well become shy. Parents and siblings may habitually poke fun at vulnerable children who respond by withdrawal from others. To avoid ridicule, the children avoid social contact. They fear and are overly sensitive to being judged, rejected, or embarrassed. Children who are younger than all or most of their siblings are prone to being mistreated and teased by their brothers and sisters. The result is an easily embarrassed and shy child. Particularly destructive is the ridiculing of children's awkward attempts to relate to others.

Inconsistent. A very inconsistent approach to child rearing can produce shyness. Parents may be too strict and then too lenient, or very caring and then unconcerned. The result is that children become insecure and do not know what to expect. They may become shy *both* at home and at school. It is possible for some children to be shy only at home and not with others. These children may spend a great deal of time searching for people who are totally consistent towards them.

Threatening. Parents may only threaten children with punishment and not follow through. Or parents may threaten frequently and follow through at times. Also, withdrawal of love and acceptance may frequently be threatened. Children may react to continuous threats with fear and timidity. They withdraw as a means of avoiding the possibility of threats being carried out. Their posture towards people becomes defensive and nonassertive.

Teacher's Pet. This category is added here because of the prevalence of shy children becoming dependent on the teacher. A vicious cycle is set in motion since the teacher's pet is teased and shunned by others. Teachers often reinforce the pattern by feeling sorry for and liking the sweet, shy children. These children often become more dependent upon adults and shyer with their peers.

Self-Label as Shy. A self-perpetuating pattern is set when children accept themselves as shy. Situations are perceived through their timid, self-critical eyes. It is as if they were committed to proving that they really are shy and unassertive. Any information or events to the contrary are warded off. They do not believe that any compliments given to them could possibly be true. Their belief is "I'm just shy—that's my personality." Since they feel inferior, they avoid contacts with others so that their inferiority is not discovered. The inferior belief prevents their taking assertive action which could lead to getting what they want and could counteract their feelings of inferiority. Negative self-talk is quite typical. "I just can't talk to anyone. I know they'll hate me. I had better not say anything because I'll sound like an idiot."

Temperament or Physical Handicap. Some children appear to be shy almost from birth. There is evidence to support the notion of constitutional or hereditary shyness. Some babies are noisy and outgoing, while others are quiet and appear content to be by themselves. This pattern may continue throughout their lives. If constitutionally shy children are treated in any of the ways listed under "Feelings of Insecurity," intense shyness is very likely. Problems can also result when parents or foster parents are very outgoing and children are shy. This could lead to constant conflict where parents are pushing their resistant, embarrassed children to be more sociable.

Physical handicaps frequently cause shyness. Obvious handicaps and differentness can lead children to become self-conscious and overly sensitive. They avoid others so as not to be stared at or talked about. Subtle handicaps like learning disabilities or expressive language problems may also lead to social withdrawal.

Parental Modeling. Shy, quiet parents often produce shy children. A very strong combination is an hereditary shy disposition and living with shy adult models. Children are prone to fall into a shy lifestyle as led by these parents. Social contacts are minimal, and other people are often discussed in fearful or mistrustful terms. At times, nonshy parents may model fear of others by frequently discussing people in negative ways. The parents may relate well to people but instill a fear of others in their children who hear others frequently being ridiculed by their parents. People are discussed as if they should be avoided or mistrusted.

How to Prevent

Encourage and Reward Socializing. From an early age provide as many pleasant, happy experiences with peers as possible. Visiting people with similarly aged children is very helpful. Special trips with one or more children can be great fun. If a child is particularly shy, one or two easygoing children should be sought as possible play- or tripmates. It is very effective to reward socializing. When children are playing or talking nicely, you should smile and comment about how nice it is for everyone to be having a good time. You can bring treats and give them to children only while they are interacting well. Do not give treats during awkward or silent periods. Well-meaning adults often inadvertently reinforce shy behavior by doing nice things in an effort to make bad situations better. Any attempt by children to be sociable should be rewarded by a smile, good word, or positive gesture (hand on shoulder, holding hands, etc.). Children should not be permitted to remain isolated from others for long periods. Solitary television viewing for several hours a day should be avoided.

It is beneficial to help children understand social events. You can explain how others feel, think, and behave. The meaning of others' behavior can then be better understood and not misinterpreted. For example, children often take the appearance of social cliques as a personal rejection. It can be explained that children who know each other often stick together and do not easily accept newcomers. "It does not mean that they don't like you or that you are a terrible kid." Children should be shown *how* to act in a socially age-appropriate manner. Some children need this more than others, but all could benefit from some friendly guidance and suggestions. "Children like it when you give them a turn." "It's nice when you let others choose a game." "You don't have to be the leader all the time; you can just relax and enjoy yourself."

Encourage Self-Confidence and Naturalness. Children should be encouraged and praised for being self-reliant and acting in a natural way. It is not necessary to pretend to be different or perfect. You can be yourself and express your opinions openly. When children feel, talk, and play freely, they should be complimented for having a good time. They can be taught that it is not necessary to get along with everyone. It is natural to not be liked by some and to only like certain people. At home children should be taught how to take kidding and teasing and not overreact. Stress and conflicts are to be met and dealt with, not run away from. Adults underestimate the power of preventing problems by anticipating difficulties and preparing children to cope.

It is important to not inadvertently reinforce shyness by anger, overattention, or saying how cute and coy the behavior is. Children should not be overprotected and told "no" or "stop" frequently. Self-confidence is not built by making all decisions for children, being too strict, having overly high expectations, or teasing and belittling them. Strengths and achievements should be frequently pointed out with pride.

Encourage Mastery and Skill Development. Very young children should be helped to feel adequate, capable, and important. Their self-esteem is enhanced by being able to effectively master the environment. They should be given

tasks that are mildly challenging so that they can frequently
feel successful. Rather than waiting for good things to happen, children should be encouraged to try and be active in
achieving what they desire. The teaching of skills that peers
value is invaluable. Excellent athletes, musicians, dancers,
etc., feel confident and are frequently sought out by others.
If children are not well coordinated, it can be very beneficial to provide early training individually or in a small noncompetitive group. Not used enough are hobby clubs where
children can both learn better skills and naturally meet and
interact with others while centered on an activity.

Provide a Warm and Accepting Atmosphere. Love and attention do not spoil babies. The more warmth and acceptance, the better. Children should be allowed to say "no"
to situations where they can exercise choice. Therefore, their
autonomy can be respected, and they can feel accepted even
if they do not agree with you. Statements like "don't ever
talk to your father that way" and "children should be seen
and not heard" should be avoided. Children feel loved and
wanted and secure when they experience "unconditional
positive regard." You communicate basic acceptance of
them as people even if you don't like certain behavior. They
should feel that they "belong" in the family and can come
for support, whenever necessary, without embarrassment.
Help and suggestions should be given sensitively and freely.

What To Do

Teach and Reward Social Skills. Any effort to relate to
people should be praised or rewarded in some way. Points
can be earned by children for engaging in any social approach behavior. The point system should be designed so
that more difficult behavior (such as going to a party and
speaking to several children) earns more points. The points
can be used to purchase rewards and privileges. It is often
necessary to reward small steps, such as moving closer and
closer to others or accompanying you to the door to welcome visitors (without the child speaking). After a while
the child may be able to welcome people alone. While rewarding progress, do not criticize! Children who want to be
less shy should participate in the process. For example, they
can be given a counter and asked to count the number of

times during the day when they *initiated* interaction with others.

Some children respond very well to praise and rewards for less shyness and more social contact. However, many children need to be taught social skills. If children feel that you are on their side, are not critical, and want to be helpful, you can be effective in changing the shyness pattern. You teach and *coach* the child's steps in learning and *applying* social skills. Children can keep diaries which periodically should be discussed with them. You should be empathic regarding their difficulties and then make specific suggestions concerning other ways of handling the situation.

Social skills training may be broken down into the following steps—instruction, feedback, behavioral rehearsal, and modeling.[3] The most effective aspect of teaching is the actual rehearsal of different ways of behaving. *Instruction* consists of any specific ways of relating to people. Time should be spent on introductions. Saying "hello" first is sometimes a big step for children. Other skills are giving and accepting compliments, smiling, nodding, and eye contact. Children should prepare for conversations by learning things that interest others and realize that sharing ideas and information is necessary. Conversations are kept going by two people sensitively participating. *Active listening* is a key ingredient. Children must learn that they can communicate to others that their comments are important and worthwhile. This is demonstrated by paying attention, saying things that illustrate understanding, and asking questions and making statements that further the conversation. Being profound or entertaining is not essential; being a good and appreciative listener is. *Feedback,* in a matter-of-fact way, helps children to understand and then improve their skills. They must be told how they came across to parents and others in a descriptive, nonjudgmental manner. *Modeling* takes place by showing children *how to act.* You demonstrate good skills and show them how to do it.

Behavior rehearsal occurs when children rehearse the better social behavior learned by instruction, feedback, and modeling. *Role playing* is the major approach. Children are natural actors and often enjoy acting problems out. Children are asked, "What would you say or do if. . . . ?" Different situations are then acted out in a dramatic fashion. It is easier to see how we come across socially in this make-believe play. The situations seem real, but they are safer than real situations. Spontaneity can be encouraged, and new and better ways of interacting are directly experienced. Children often enjoy role playing a king or queen who is able to do or say anything. Another powerful method is to have shy children act like the most popular child. *Role reversal* is most effective. You switch roles with children, and alternative ways of behaving are acted out. A child can be the shy, silent person at a party, and you can be the host. After a few minutes, the child then becomes the host and tries out some of the type of behavior you just illustrated. If children get stuck, you can coach them by whispering suggestions. Children under 9 often love to use puppets. This accomplishes the same purpose but makes the situations more distant and less threatening for young children. The puppets talk and interact.

Desensitize Shyness. Children can learn that social situations need not be scary. They can ease into situations and become more sociable by gradual steps. Their *imagination* should be constructively used. They can be taught to relax all their muscles and feel completely limp. Relaxation is a direct antidote to anxiety. While relaxed in their room, they can imagine small steps that they have been unable to take. They can visualize saying hello to one person at a party. Gradually, they can think about themselves doing previously feared social behavior. It is crucial that they then engage in these behaviors *a little at a time* in real situations. They can gradually be desensitized to the negative feelings associated with social interaction. You can help by making new situations as pleasant as possible. One friend and then more can be invited to visit the child. When attending a party, the child can be paired with one friend so the situation does not seem overwhelming. At parties constructive jobs can be great aids to overcoming awkwardness. Children can be given something constructive to do, such as helping serve or cleaning up. It is important to avoid putting shy children in the spotlight. You should not make a fuss over them in front of others.

Shy younger children should *gradually* be introduced to rougher play and to larger groups. In the spirit of desensitization, uncommunicative children can be encouraged to communicate less directly through drawings. It is often more acceptable for them to discuss the drawings with you. Various exercises can be used such as looking in a mirror and describing oneself or practicing conversational skills by talking about a topic while alone. Another method is to hire a teen-age companion who can gradually and naturally introduce the child into different situations. The companion communicates respect and positive regard for the child. This goes a long way in helping children feel good about themselves and secure enough to take more social risks. Once a child feels comfortable with the companion, it makes visiting places and interacting with others easier. Some children are aided by a technique called "paradoxical intention." They are asked to show everyone just how shy they really are. They are not to talk to anyone no matter what. After awhile, the effect is that children *relax* and want to communicate with others.

Encouraging Assertiveness. Children should be taught to openly ask for what they want. They must learn to overcome their timidity, fear, and embarrassment about expressing themselves. Equally important is saying "no" when one doesn't want to do something. Many children are unable to refuse to do things, so they do them and then feel resentment toward others, as well as personal weakness. In the same vein, they can learn to tell their reactions to others. When someone's behavior causes strong positive or negative feelings in the child, he can express this openly to them. Part of this process is preparing children to be able to take possible negative reactions from others. Self-assertion should be discussed as a basic right. It is not necessary to become incapacitated because of the behavior of others. In fact, children can be shown how to be more assertive by helping others. A good start is to have them help younger or less adequate children in learning, doing a chore, or playing games.

Fourth-grade girls have been effectively taught how to be assertive.[4] Parents can follow the model of giving information to children as to *how* to be appropriately assertive. Role playing is performed, and assertive behavior is pointed out and replayed in an improved manner. Children learn to analyze situations themselves and respond to feedback. You can then discuss being more forthright and effective in everyday, real-life situations. If another child talks constantly, your child can learn to say, "That's very interesting, but have you thought of looking at it differently?" Your child can then go on to express his opinion in a manner that has been rehearsed at home. Similarly, if children want to play a certain game or change the type of activity, they can *politely* and *effectively* voice their opinions.

Enrole Child in Supervised Play or Group Skill Training. When shy children engage in group activities, some talk and interaction occur naturally. A sensitive group leader is essential. Parents should be assertive enough to talk to the leader about their child and make suggestions. The non-talking game of "charades" may open some children up to expressing themselves in front of others. Names of movies, books, or events may be acted out and guessed by the group. Group leaders should feel free to reinforce children for talking by praise and by earning points. Parents can provide things children like most if they earn points in these structured group activities. Some children can communicate by drawing and then learn to discuss their drawing with others.

Children may respond well to supervised play with younger, less shy children. At times, playing with younger relatives is the first step to being able to communicate with peers. Shy children become drawn into games naturally. The leader must involve children in *interactive* group games. Games should be selected where children have to help each other and communicate. Cards, checkers, chess, baseball, etc., are not appropriate. Monopoly, hiking, catching butterflies, three-legged races, dramatic play, etc., may be used to encourage cooperation and talk.

Hobby groups with sensitive leaders should be made mandatory. This is a direct method of developing skills in a context conducive to communication about the activity. Music, athletics, crafts, and electronics may be areas of interest that children can develop, thereby leading to a natural acceptance by peers. Others show interest and admiration when a child develops competence and skill in some area.

Teach Positive Self-Talk. One of the most destructive aspects of shyness is the individual's belief that she has a "shy personality." Events are seen and interpreted through a shy perception, continually confirming a self-concept as a shy person who cannot relate to others. You can teach children that shy behavior is what people do and not what they are. This can interrupt the irrational belief and negative self-talk that perpetuates shyness. By experimenting with new behaviors, exciting possibilities emerge. "Shyness" can diminish or disappear as behavior changes! Children can discover the thrill of being adventurous and taking risks. You explain how risks can be taken in small steps. At a party, children might try first saying ''hello'' to everyone there. During the next party, the child might engage in a 2-minute conversation with the friendliest and most accepting child. You help children by pointing out their strengths and by focusing their attention on such. A shy, 14-year-old girl should be told about her outstanding knowledge of photography which should be used to interest others. Instead of her putting herself down for not being popular, she should think to herself how terrific it is to have an exciting and productive hobby.

''Self-talk'' should be demonstrated in a natural way. ''When I'm with important people, I think about my achievements rather than how much better everyone is than I.'' You then analyze your child's problem and make specific suggestions as to negative self-statements to avoid and positive self-talk to use. They must stop saying statements like the following. ''I'm no good; everyone's smarter than I am.'' ''It's no use; I'm too shy to talk to anyone.'' ''I'm so nervous; I'll never change.'' ''Who would be interested in a boring, dull person like me?'' ''If I say anything, they'll see how foolish I am, and everyone will laugh at me,'' etc. You show them that positive statements are both true and very helpful in feeling better and acting differently. ''I'm really okay; I know as much as anyone else.'' ''Even if people might not like me, I'm going to say what I think.'' ''I can take it if people think I'm silly.'' ''The world won't end if people laugh at what I say.'' Parents underestimate the power of this type of positive thinking, and its ability to diminish the number and intensity of negative thoughts. Recently, psychotherapists have frequently employed techniques like ''cognitive restructuring'' or rational-emotive therapy, which are sophisticated versions of positive self-talk. The basic idea is to change the way individuals think about themselves. ''It's not my fault that kids tease so much.'' ''I can still feel good about myself even if some kids think I'm weird.'' Parents may directly challenge the child's irrational beliefs of having to be perfect, wanting total acceptance from others, or being unable to tolerate any criticism or aggression. By practicing positive thinking and experimenting with new behaviors, there is the probability of an increasing positive attitude and a gradually improved way of relating to others.

Case Report

A 9-year-old had always been very shy. He often felt lonely but was frightened of playing with peers and only reluctantly responded to adult interest. The parents had unsuccesfully tried to interest him in group activities. A pattern of avoiding others had developed, with some awkward attempts on his part to relate to peers. Two consultative meetings with the parents changed the increasing shyness. The most important concept was convincing the parents to play a direct role in teaching (and role playing) social skills to their son. They underestimated both his lack of knowledge of social skills and their own ability to directly and specifically teach him better ways of relating. Since he felt lonely and wanted friends, he was eager to learn once the parents made their interest clear. They convinced him that they did not blame or criticize him but were on his side to help him learn to be more sociable. Most effective was both parents demonstrating how to have a conversation, be an active listener, and share opinions. They had fun with positively coaching the boy in rehearsing ways of relating better.

An additional method was a very simple version of positive self-talk. They told him to stop the negative thoughts he was having and showed him how to think positively. In the school playground, he would stand on the side thinking, "No one will play with me; I can't do anything right." He practiced saying to himself, "I'll take a chance and join in. I can take a little teasing." Parents and child were pleased with the increasing amount of positive time spent with other children.

Books For Parents About Shyness

Alberti, R.E. and Emmons, M.L.: *Your Perfect Right: A Guide to Assertive Behavior.* Impact, San Luis Obispo, CA (1970).

Cartledge, Gwendolyn and Milburn, Joanne F.: *Teaching Social Skills to Children.* Pergamon, Elmsford, NY (1979).

Zimbardo, Philip: *Shyness: What It Is, What To Do About It.* Addison-Wesley, Reading, MA (1977).

Books For Children About Shyness

Cohen, Barbara: *Thank You, Jackie Robinson*. Lothrop, Lee and Shepard, New York (1974). Ages 10 to 13.

A very shy boy and an old man both love baseball. The boy overcomes his shyness and manages to get a signed baseball from Jackie Robinson for his terminally sick friend.

Hooker, Ruth: *Gertrude Kloppenberg (Private)*. Abingdon, Nashville, TN (1970). Ages 8 to 12.

Bashfully shy, 11-year-old Gertrude can't make friends. She expresses loneliness and her search for a friend in her diary. She develops an interest in gardening and slowly overcomes shyness and develops many friends.

Krasilovsky, Phyllis: *The Shy Little Girl*. Houghton Mifflin, Boston (1970). Ages 11 to 14.

Shyness and unhappiness are sensitively described and illustrated. A little girl is very timid and self-critical. Her attitude towards herself changes, and she becomes more self-confident as she relates to a new girl in school.

Schwarzrock, Shirley and Wrenn, C. Gilbert: *Easing The Scene*. American Guidance Service, Circle Pines, MN (1970). Ages 11 and over.

Overcoming feelings of inadequacy is described as necessary in order to socialize well with others. Friendliness and consideration of others are urged. Appropriate social behavior is described and illustrative examples are given. Throughout, practical suggestions are clearly presented.

Schwarzrock, Shirley and Wrenn, C. Gilbert: *To Like and Be Liked*. American Guidance Service, Circle Pines, MN (1970). Adolescents.

Practical suggestions are given to improve skills in making friends. Liking oneself and enjoying being with others are discussed. Relationships are influenced by the degree of sincerity, individual differences and values, and style of communication. Also discussed are the need for acceptance and approval, best friends, and the forming of cliques.

Skorpen, Liesel Moak: *Plenty for Three*. Coward, McCann and Geoghegan, New York (1971). Ages 4 to 8.

A boy and girl (two) play happily while a shy girl (one) is lonely and sad. The story is colorfully illustrated and written in verse. At the end, all three play well together in a treehouse.

Snyder, Zilpha Keatley: *The Changeling*. Atheneum, New York (1970). Ages 11 to 14.

A shy girl becomes self-confident because of a friendship with another girl. They play imaginary games about villains and secret rituals. Slowly, the girl feels more able to make friends and assert herself.

Wrenn, C. Gilbert and Schwarzrock, Shirley: *Can You Talk With Someone Else?* American Guidance Service, Circle Pines, MN (1970). Ages 11 and over.

This book offers encouragement for shy adolescents to develop conversational skills. Often teen-agers think that they have nothing worthwhile to say. Friendliness and a desire to communicate are stressed. Effective communication depends upon an open exchange of ideas, attentive listening, empathy, and possessing relevant information.

References

1. Zimbardo, Philip: *Shyness: What It Is, What To Do About It*. Addison-Wesley, Reading, MA (1977).
2. Wassmer, Arthur C.: "Seeing through shyness." *Family Health*:(March 1979), pp. 32–34.
3. Bornstein, Michell R., Bellack, Alan S., and Hepen, Michael: "Social-skills training for unassertive children." *Journal of Applied Behavior Analysis* 10:(1977), pp. 183–195.
4. Bower, Sally, Amatea, Ellen, and Anderson, Ronald: "Assertiveness training with children." *Elementary School Guidance and Counseling* 10:(1976), pp. 236–245.

COMPULSIVE-PERFECTIONISTIC

Compulsivity is an irresistible impulse to act in an often irrational manner. Perfection exists when there are no flaws or faults. A perfectionist regards anything short of perfection as unacceptable. In this section we are concerned with children who feel compelled to act in some perfectionistic manner. Young children often feel that they must do some stereotyped repetitive act. At the extreme, the ritualistic "magic" counteracts bad luck or wards off threats. Doors are open and closed or locked and unlocked several times, steps are walked up and down, hands are washed very frequently, and objects lined up meticulously. Objects (steps, lines, lamp posts) are often repetitiously counted. From age 2 to 7 years, many children play games, recite sayings, and perform rituals rigidly. By age 12, absolutism gradually becomes relativism. Depending upon learning experiences and intelligence, children become more flexible and understand that rules are not absolutes but are agreed upon standards. Young children, on the other hand, see nonconformists as wrong and inferior if they do not follow the rules.

Compulsions are common from age 8 to 10 years. If the behavior interferes with ordinary activities or takes excessive time, a serious problem is indicated. Individuals who have developed a compulsive personality are typically described as orderly, fussy, punctual, overly conscientious, overly attentive to details, hating dirt, disorder, or messiness, and seeing these traits as virtues. Cleanliness, safety, and superstitions (not stepping on cracks, walking under ladders, etc.) or personal superstitions (touch doorknob several times, walk on certain paths, etc.) are believed to be necessary in order to avoid bad luck. Compulsive or perfectionistic children believe that things must be done "just so" or they become worried or upset. Bedding, clothing, homework, etc., must be arranged in a specific, acceptable way to them.

Mild compulsivity or perfectionism, if handled well, may be a definite asset. Children may accomplish a great deal and be rewarded by others. Many parents and teachers view perfectionism and orderliness as virtues and do not try to modify these traits. These children accumulate things, organize, collect, and are frugal with money. They may be tense and hardworking but may also be too meticulous and become lost in details. Therefore, it becomes a matter of adult judgment as to the proper balance in childhood between striving for excellence or perfection and being flexible and easy-going enough to adapt to realistic failure and difficulties.

Reasons Why

Feel Safe and Good. Perfectionism and rituals are attempts by children to feel good by seeking pleasure. They are trying to *master the environment* by engaging in behavior that they hope will work. Faulty learning could have led to their not knowing the usual or correct response to situations. Instead of focusing on problems and doing their best, they wind up using rigid or mechanical approaches that do not work. Yet, they keep striving for what look like positive goals to them. If they conform to certain rituals, this might lead to *acceptance* by their peer group. Since they feel positively motivated, they resist adult help even if they admit that their behavior is inappropriate or irrational. Rituals or perfectionism make them feel good and help them feel safe and secure, even though others judge their behavior as incorrect. Others see these children as focusing on minor or irrelevant aspects of situations.

Relieve Tension and Reduce Fear. Avoiding pain is a strong motive. Perfectionistic behavior is an attempt to avoid the anxiety or fear that accompanies less than perfect performance. Insecurity and uncertainty are handled by engaging in the "right" behavior. The correct behavior may be a result of *accidental pairing* of events. While feeling very tense, a child ate a new enjoyable food which led to a reduction in tension. The radio happened to be playing at that time. That child may develop the ritual of having the radio on as a means of relieving tension. This pattern is also the potential beginning of overeating as a tension-relieving device. "Right" behavior may also stem from the *illogical* equating of objects with negative feelings. For example, dirt may be equated with badness or evil. The usual procedure is to wash dirt to be clean and avoid germs. Children overreact and wash compulsively to avoid the symbolic fearful meaning of dirt.

Fear is reduced by engaging in behavior that *postpones* some undesirable event. By counting or arranging objects, children delay some imagined or realistically tense situation. Children may fear being hurt outside and therefore spend considerable time doing some repetitive activity before leaving home. Very powerful is postponing contacts with others that have been fearful in the past. Children therefore try to delay that situation for as long as possible.

Critical adults may be avoided by the child having to make a drawing or model absolutely perfect in every detail.

Compulsiveness is self-perpetuating since only *temporary* relief from tension occurs. Rituals and perfectionism must be repeated each time anxiety mounts again. Unfortunately, *self-doubts* dominate the children's feelings about themselves. Children who repeat behavior doubt that they performed the behavior correctly, become anxious, and have to repeat the act again. Other children perform symmetrical behavior because of self-doubts. They can't choose or take sides so they have to balance every act or line objects up so they are exactly the same. These insecure, indecisive children experience a great need for orderliness and organization in order to reduce tension.

Cope with Guilt. Compulsivity may be a counteraction to the desire to be messy, sloppy, and disorganized. Children may then feel upset if they are not extremely neat and clean. Instead of being the slob that they wanted to be, they became the model of orderliness. Because of adult reactions or the child's own beliefs, feelings of guilt result from having "forbidden" wishes. Guilt is discharged by engaging in ritualistic or perfectionistic behavior. The forbidden feelings might also be aggressive, sexual, or bizarre. Some children have strong antisocial impulses. They may want to steal, lie, bully, and cheat. Instead, they feel guilty and become models of virtue who are horrified by this behavior in others. Children feel less guilty by engaging in the "proper" behavior of only getting 100's on school tests, having a perfectly neat room, or counting every tree on a street.

These guilt-ridden children feel that they have to work very hard in order to justify their existence. They are overly scrupulous and feel guilt over minor misdeeds or not fulfilling any obligation. Leisure time makes them feel guilty and tense. They seek purposeful and constructive activities.

Strict Parental Expectations. Children learn that things must be done in a specific and exact manner because parents expect it. Overly strict parents are themselves rigid and perfectionistic, with little tolerance for a child's deficiencies and inconsistencies. The parents often discourage open expression of feelings and may be socially isolated. The home atmosphere emphasizes etiquette and cleanliness.

These parents frequently tell their children that they can and should do better. Often heard is, ''I know you can do it so don't give me any excuses.'' These parents lack *empathy,* and are unable to see things from a child's perspective. They feel quite virtuous and see other parents as lax and overly permissive. They both model and reinforce compulsive behavior! The parent-child relationship is typically neutral, cold, or hostile. The parents are often models of meticulous perfectionism, who may have begun a hostile tense struggle with their child soon after birth. Toilet training is typically begun too early and accomplished with much anger and tension.

As a reaction to strict parents, some children comply directly by exhibiting the expected perfectionistic behavior. Other children become hostile or anguished, and react by becoming overly conscientious. However, once the pattern of compulsive behavior is set, it most usually becomes self-perpetuating.

Avoids Confronting Real Problems. Perfectionism and compulsivity may become a diversionary tactic. The real source of discomfort is avoided, and ''safe'' behavior is performed. Real difficulties or conflicts are not faced or resolved. Rather than trying to obtain warmth and support from cold parents, ritualistic behaviors are performed. Problems with peers or school may be similarly avoided by becoming involved with minute details of situations. Emerging sexual feelings may similarly be avoided by compulsive activity. In fact, any strong feeling may remain unexpressed and transformed into a ritual act of a compelling need to perform perfectly. The pattern becomes one of avoiding problems, not resolving conflicts, and not expressing feelings openly. Therefore, the children appear to have a mechanical quality. Obligations may be fulfilled, but there is little warmth or easy give and take with others.

How to Prevent

Be Tolerant. Tolerance means to allow behavior that deviates from some standard. In this sense, a tolerant parent behaves in a manner opposite to that of a perfectionistic one. Children's deficiencies and inconsistencies should be tolerated, rather than judged and criticized. We are not talking about extreme permissiveness, which implies a tolerance for all kinds of inappropriate behavior. Rather, tolerance should be exercised for the normal and expected inconsistencies and fluctuations in compliance, effort, and politeness. You do not have to approve of rudeness, but it can be tolerated at times and not exaggerated out of proportion. When children behave badly, you can *empathize, not criticize.* "I guess it's hard to be polite all the time, but you've been nice most of the time." The positive statement is added to the understanding comment, increasing the accepting tone. Therefore, children feel that they are basically accepted and do not have to develop a perfectionistic approach in order to be approved of by their parents.

Tolerance means avoiding the use of extreme threats or guilt to motivate children. "If you ever curse again, you'll be severely punished" is an ineffective and unnecessary threat. It guarantees failure and could easily lead to a child who becomes emotionally constricted and perfectionistic in his use of language. Guilt is a powerful cause of compulsivity. Statements such as "you'd never do that if you really loved me" or "you could leave me all alone if you really want to" make children feel guilty. Children build up feelings of being blameworthy and bad and may react by becoming compulsively neat, careful, clean, etc. A relatively tolerant attitude in the absence of guilt-provoking comments is an excellent preventative of debilitating perfectionism in children.

Promote Adequacy and Competency. Children who feel adequate do not have to be perfectionists. They feel worthwhile and do not have to work very hard in order to justify their existence. You promote adequacy by complimenting children for their achievements and carefully encouraging signs of maturation. Growing up means being able to effectively master the demands of the environment. You help children to independently perform tasks at their level and to tackle challenges. Frequently doing tasks for children undermines self-confidence. It takes patience to wait while a young child fumbles at a task, but it's worth it. Children learn to say to themselves, "That's great, I did it by myself," and adult praise becomes less necessary. Any indication of appropriate independence and decision making should be encouraged. If children's choices are frequently criticized, children feel inadequate. If children are not ready to make decisions in a particular area, they should be given two acceptable alternatives and then praised for their choice.

Competency means that children are able to respond appropriately and face and solve problems. Therefore, they should be encouraged to face tasks and not procrastinate or avoid work. This is accomplished by being a good model yourself and by direct teaching in real-life situations. When the child says, "I don't feel like doing it now," you respond with some version of "Don't put off 'till tomorrow what you can do today." You should not underestimate your own problem-solving skills and the benefits of helping children learn to solve problems. You say to them, "What has to be done and how can you start?" Rather than doing it for them or telling them how to do it, you ask them leading questions. The result is children who are, and feel, competent and who do not need perfectionism as a means of coping or avoidance.

Being adequate also means being an effective communicator. Make sure your children are able to express themselves clearly and make their wishes known. Some children become tongue tied, especially with peers. You can help them practice good communication at home. They can pretend that you're a friend and tell you something that is hard for them to express. If they get stuck, you can help by showing them how a sensitive topic might be phrased. For example, constructive criticism of friends is difficult to express. They can be shown how to express positive feelings and then make a possible suggestion that some other behavior might work even better for their friends.

Encourage Expression of Feelings. Open expression of feelings prevents the development of compulsive rituals which serve the purpose of indirectly expressing something. Children who can't express anger may develop a need to repeatedly touch an object rather than scream or punch. This would not develop if children were permitted to talk openly about their extreme anger towards siblings, parents, etc. You might also encourage physical activity along with expressions of anger. Saying, "I hate you," and punching an inflated punching toy is an excellent relief valve. Parents who are relatively open usually have children who behave similarly. Parents who bottle up anger have to go out of their way to help their children avoid that pattern. You can admit to children that "I still haven't learned to say how I feel, but I hope you can do it.'' You can explain that saying how you feel helps you feel better and that ''we can all try to be more open with each other.''

Avoid Superstition and Ritual. Superstition promotes compulsive behavior to ward off bad luck. If parents don't walk under ladders, don't leave home on Friday the 13th, always knock on wood for luck, etc., children learn that ritualistic behaviors are necessary. Not being superstitious is easy to say, but some people cannot stop life-long superstitious habits. It is still possible to encourage children not to imitate or develop these habits. Children might well be told that they are not duplicates of their parents, and they can be independent about their choices and beliefs. Another means of preventing compulsivity is to purposely vary behaviors. You might experiment with sitting in different seats at dinner, or varying the order in which things are done at home. Rather than customarily repeated acts (rituals), flexibility and creativity might be tried.

What to Do

Use Reconditioning. Compulsive behavior is associated with feeling safe (or avoiding anxiety). It is necessary to recondition the child so that compulsive behavior is no longer necessary to avoid anxiety. Strategies are used to condition the child to be able to behave without rituals or perfectionism and still feel good. Many children have to learn how to *relax* on cue. You teach them how to tense and then relax all their muscles. Some children can simply relax before a task and prevent the rise of anxiety which leads to compulsive behavior.

A more powerful method is to teach relaxation and then *desensitize* children so they do not have to engage in repetitive behavior in order to avoid anxiety. While relaxed, you have children imagine themselves not doing their usual rituals. Each time they imagine that scene, they become less and less anxious. Therefore, they become desensitized to that ritual and will gradually be able to behave freely. For example, many children have to arrange objects exactly or they become upset and worried. While they relax, you tell them to imagine leaving their room without arranging the objects. They visualize leaving the room, and they learn that they can experience mild anxiety without being over-whelmed or destroyed. Each day, they visualize the same scene until they can imagine it with no anxiety. Then, they leave their room without arranging and are congratulated for this progress.

Another form of desensitization is to simply present more and more anxiety-provoking scenes each time. The first scene would be very mild in that the arrangement would be only slightly different. Each day, the arrangement is less and less orderly until they can visualize leaving the room without touching the objects (such as shoes, pencils, etc.). Then they actually leave the room each day in an increasingly less perfect manner (without lining up or repetitively touching things). Another form of desensitization is to have children imagine their compulsive behavior in a very unpleasant situation. For example, they can imagine lining up shoes and feeling sick, being teased viciously by friends, or an earthquake taking place. This method pairs the compulsive behavior with a negative image, thereby weakening the pleasurable effect of the compulsion. This approach is applicable to any type of compulsion or perfectionism, such as only handing in school papers with no marks or erasures, touching doorknobs six times, checking doorlocks four times, whistling in corridors, etc. The use of visual imagery helps the child to use his imagination constructively. It also serves the beneficial psychological purpose of increasing his feelings of self-control and decreasing his helpless attitude.

Some motivated children respond to the simple reconditioning process of interrupting compulsive rituals immediately. In discussion, they have to agree to the desirability of being less compulsive. At first, you may have to help by physically restraining them from continued touching, washing, lining up, etc. You do this with her permission and with a noncritical attitude. Distraction also works well. The child might be interested in a game or activity that interferes with the continuation of the habitual behavior. The goal is for children to use self-control by interrupting rituals by themselves. Instead of continuing their usual behavior, they stop and congratulate themselves. Soon, they can anticipate when they will act and not engage in any compulsive behavior.

Finally, overcorrection is another form of reconditioning. Some children respond very well to a simple procedure of overdoing a problem behavior. In order to overcome the unnecessary habit, the child is asked to voluntarily overdo the compulsion or perfectionism. At times, reward or punishment may be used to insure compliance. When children begin lining up, touching, erasing, etc., they stop and do some exercises with their arms and hands for 5 minutes. For example, they may raise arms over head and then touch shoulders, waist, shoulders, over head, etc. After several repetitions, the compulsive habits often begin to weaken.

Substitute Constructive Behavior. An important point is that compulsive or perfectionistic behavior is unnecessary and inefficient. Instead of wasting time, you show children how they can use their good intentions constructively. There can be a gradual process of substituting less and less extensive rituals, which result in the spontaneous giving up of all rituals. For example, a 12-year-old girl took 1 hour in the bathroom in order to wash a certain way, arrange the toothbrush, and hang the towels perfectly. Washing took 1 halfhour since each finger had to be soaped and rinsed three times. She was told to wash and rinse two times, fold the towel twice, and leave. Seeing her success, she gradually reduced the process to 15 minutes and felt proud of herself.

A teen-age boy[1] replaced his compulsive rituals with constructive behavior. He was checking numerous times to make sure all locks were locked. Instead of being criticized, he was praised for his concern and asked to check the locks once and record the process. Self-talk was used, where he said, "I've checked it; it's locked." The idea is to identify some positive value in the behavior, keep the positive aspects, and eliminate the unnecessary repetitive parts. It is helpful to say that failures and relapses are okay. You keep trying until you're successful.

Reward Noncompulsiveness. When compulsive children are not being compulsive, they should be congratulated and rewarded. Don't underestimate the effectiveness of having children earn privileges, toys, phonograph records, etc., by giving up perfectionism. A 5-year-old boy[2] was fascinated with electrical devices, plugged and unplugged them, and switched them on and off repeatedly. After several approaches were employed unsuccessfully, a simple reward system worked. Poker chips were earned for noncompulsive behavior and traded in for toys. Compulsive behavior resulted in a deduction of chips. Very successful is the use of a time out from the ability to earn chips (e.g., nothing can be earned for 30 minutes). Rather than only eliminating compulsions at home, it is important to generalize the better behavior to other areas. Friends, relatives, and teachers should participate. The parents could be notified of compulsive behavior, and chips could be deducted.

While compulsive behavior is diminishing, open expression of feelings and a free direct approach should be encouraged and rewarded. Some parents find it hard to encourage and accept open expression of anxiety, worry, and anger. It is as if they feel personally threatened or worried that open expression is harmful. Bottled-up feelings are harmful, while saying what you feel defuses the anxiety and the fear behind perfectionism. Similarly, you encourage children to *do*, not think. Compulsive children often need help in facing situations and taking direct action. The key is to praise or reward direct, effective action and to discourage various rituals.

Any indication of better self-control and reduction of perfectionism should be praised. Children often require specific "how to" suggestions. For example, stop watches can be given to children with the suggestion that they will be able to reduce the unnecessary time spent compulsively doing an activity. For example, they might time washing, stop in 2 minutes, and earn a reward. Older children should be taught to administer self-rewards for improvement. They might read a favorite book or play their phonograph when reaching the desired goal of a specific amount of time. Similarly, adolescents may not hand in schoolpapers because they're not perfect enough. An amount of time can be set and rewards administered for handing in whatever has been accomplished. Perfectionistic teen-agers soon learn that their efforts are still good within a time limit, and that it is much better to hand things in on time. Parental rewards can be suspended since the natural consequences of punctuality are rewarding.

Case Report

A very bright 15-year-old girl was excessively orderly and overly concerned with minor details. She was resistant to various attempts by her parents to "loosen her up." Her room was absolutely neat, and she became quite upset and angry if anyone touched or changed her arrangements. In schoolwork and in conversation, she often became caught up in details and often missed the main point. She responded very well to a combination of desensitizing and reward. Her parents asked her to imagine that her room was left slightly messy. Since she was aware of the interfering nature of her perfectionism, she agreed to imagine a messy room each night. After 1 week, she spontaneously left her desk slightly messy.

Special week-end events were planned as a reward for progress. She agreed to try to not pick up on every detail of a conversation and to focus on the main points. The parents took her to a new movie in a neighboring city as her reward for not pursuing details. At first she needed to have those times pointed out to her. She soon stopped herself, saying, "There I go again," and laughing. Similarly, her school reports were reviewed by parents, and unnecessary details were checked off. Her eliminating the details was praised, and she was soon able to check papers herself. Reportedly helpful was her imagining handing in imperfect papers and receiving a B grade. This upset her, but repeated imagining enabled her to accept the prospect of receiving less than A with no emotional arousal.

References

1. Weiner, Irving B.: "Behavior therapy in obsessive-compulsive neurosis: Treatment of an adolescent boy." *Psychotherapy: Theory, Research and Practice* 4:(1967), pp. 27 –29.
2. Ayllon, Teodoro, Garber, Stephen W., and Allison, Mary G.: "Behavioral treatment of childhood neurosis." *Psychiatry* 40: (1977), pp. 315–322.

3 ———

Habit Disorders

INTRODUCTION

The term *habit disorders* or *nervous habits* refers to persistent, largely involuntary patterns of dyscontrol of motor functions in children. They include bedwetting, soiling, nailbiting, thumbsucking, overeating, sleepwalking, tics, and stuttering. Since habits have been repeated so often in the past, and are so overlearned, they are notoriously resistant to change. They tend to be automatic reactions that the child has little control over. Sigmund Freud once observed, "Many of us are unconscious about our habits." Often we perform habits without realizing that we are doing them.

Why do "nervous" habits develop in children? Some investigators have suggested that they offer a release of nervous tension and are pleasant or satisfying to some instinctual impulse. Others maintain that habits are learned and can be unlearned in a systematic way. Still others assert that habits are often a symptom of an underlying conflict which must be treated before the habit will disappear. To this date no one has conclusively discovered "the" cause of maladaptive habits. Most likely they are due to a combination of factors.

Typically, parents do not recognize the seriousness of a child's undesirable habits. Parents tend to believe they do not have to face up to a problem with forethought, honesty, and a definite plan of action for overcoming it. As a matter of fact, children do not usually outgrow habits. The tendency is to grow into them until the habit becomes an ingrained part of the child. Even if a child does eventually outgrow a bad habit, the process often involves years of unnecessary suffering and conflict for the child and family.

Apart from ignoring bad habits, parents often repeatedly prod their child about the habit. They criticize, nag, or severely punish the child which tend not only to be ineffective but to create an unpleasant negative climate in the home. Alternate ways of responding to these problems will be the focus of this chapter.

How does one stop a long-term habit? Is it simply a matter of "will power" as some people have suggested? The latest scientific research indicates that there are methods that parents can apply to enable a child to cut down or eliminate undesirable habits. Among the methods that have proven effectual in controlling habits are changing the consequences of a habit, altering the antecedents, increasing the child's awareness of the habit, suggestion, substitution of alternative behavior, and teaching the child ways to reduce nervous tension and solve underlying problems. No single method has been found to be universally effective in reducing children's habits. The best approach seems to be an intensive one which combines several strategies for optimum effectiveness.

In addition to offering parents practical advice on how to handle children's habits, we have attempted to provide complete information about each disorder, including its prevalence, its seriousness, its developmental nature, its usual outcome, its medical aspects, and the most likely reasons why the disorder occurs.

THUMBSUCKING

When a child inserts his thumb into his mouth, his lips form a seal around the thumb, and sucking movements of the lips, cheeks, and tongue result. The palmar surface of the thumb is usually facing upward. Often the child's other hand rubs a body part such as the ear or hair, or a comfort object such as a stuffed animal or blanket. Linus, for example, in the "Peanuts" cartoon, sucks his thumb earnestly while holding his blanket to his cheek.

Although quite common in the first and second years of life, the incidence of thumbsucking has been found to gradually decline with advancing age in children. More specifically, about 40 percent of 1 year olds, 20 percent of 5 year olds, and 5 percent of 10 year olds actively suck their thumbs in our society.[1,2] Thus, most children just naturally outgrow the habit, but a few continue it into adolescence and adulthood. Of those children who frequently suck their thumbs in the first few years of life, about 50 percent will terminate the habit by age 5, 75 percent by age 8, and 90 percent by the age of 10. Most children who later suck their thumbs will begin the habit by 9 months of age. More girls than boys are chronic thumbsuckers.

Reasons Why

Sucking for its own sake is a powerful drive in the young. There is evidence now that even *in utero* some infants suck their thumbs. Infants suck not only because it is needed for nourishment, but because it is pleasurable. It gives the child pleasant, warm, full, and comfortable feelings inside. It is also a restful, relaxing experience for the child. The use of pacifiers is a well-known example of the calming effect of sucking on young children. Children turn to thumbsucking when they are afraid, when hungry, when sleepy, or when in need of pleasurable experiences. Gradually this sucking stops of its own accord as the child matures and develops alternate sources of security and pleasure.

It is clear from numerous studies conducted to date that children who suck their thumbs are no more emotionally disturbed than other children. There is also lack of support for the theory that bottle-fed babies are more likely to be thumbsuckers than breast-fed babies.

Effects of Thumbsucking

Dentists have been warning us for over a century of the ill effects produced by thumbsucking on the jawbone development, *i.e.*, tooth deformity, difficulties in chewing and breathing, and facial disfigurement.[3] Research has clearly established the fact that thumbsucking does indeed increase the risks of dental and facial malformations.[6,7,8,9]

The age of the child, intensity and duration of sucking, and condition of the mouth will influence the likelihood of dental problems.

Thumbsucking typically exerts pressure upward on the palate, outward on the upper front teeth, and inward on the lower front teeth. This tends to make the upper teeth protrude out, the lower front teeth to protrude in, and the palate too narrow. These three effects, termed malocclusion, are also referred to as buck teeth and open bite.[4,5]

The effects are usually trivial if thumbsucking is terminated before the eruption of the permanent teeth. When the habit is broken by the age of 5, before the permanent teeth erupt, the malocclusion tends to correct itself.[5] The longer the child persists in the habit beyond about age 6, the greater the risk of permanent malocclusion. If it continues after a child begins losing his primary teeth, it "can not only deform the bones of a child's young jaws but can also act like a crowbar to permanently unbalance the jaw muscles. Once unbalanced, these jaw muscles may keep distorting the jaws even more as he grows."[10]

It is estimated that the thumbsucker increases the risk of developing malocclusion by about 20 percent.

Apart from the dental difficulties, it has been noted that the thumbsucker tends to be less responsive to others when sucking so that he or she is less likely to respond when called by name.[11] When sucking, the thumbsucker tends to shut out the outside world and become dreamy and preoccupied. The use of spontaneous speech by the thumbsucker is also curtailed. The problems of an older thumbsucker are further increased when other children make fun of him and he becomes aware of acting like a baby.

How to Prevent

What can parents do to forestall chronic thumbsucking by their children?

Substitute a Pacifier. Recent research supports the use of pacifiers as an advantageous substitute for thumbsucking. As opposed to the thumbsucking habit, the use of a pacifier is almost always spontaneously given up by the child by about 3 years of age. Moreover, children who suck a pacifier during the first year of life show a markedly lower incidence of thumbsucking in later childhood. However, if you let a thumbsucking habit become entrenched, the child will usually refuse a pacifier as a substitute.

Although the chances of a malocclusion may be slightly raised by sucking a pacifier, the incidence of malocclusion among pacifier suckers had been found to be substantially less frequent than among thumbsuckers.[8]

Also noteworthy is the fact that the newer pacifiers are flatter and more inclined than the older cylindrical-shaped ones. This means that the newer ones conform more to the roof of the mouth and approximate the shape of the mother's breast in the infant's mouth. Since the sucking action of the infant tends to pull this new pacifier as opposed to pushing it up and outward, some claim that it will tend to correct malocclusion in young children.[1]

Tolerance. A substantial number of preschool children will suck their thumbs at bedtime, or when they are tired, ill, shy, or upset. Most of these children will outgrow the habit by age 4. Thus, parents should avoid making an issue about it when the child is young.

Provide Security. The more secure the child, the less need to seek comfort from the thumb. If the child is experiencing any strong sources of stress, such as school difficulty, or sibling rivalry, try to reduce the pressure as much as possible. Be sure the home atmosphere is one of ease, security, calm, and happiness, as well as there being friendship between parents and between parents and children.

Increase Sucking Time. If your baby seems to be searching for his or her thumb immediately after finishing nursing, or at frequent intervals between feedings, try to find a way to increase sucking time and thereby head off thumbsucking. Some of the steps you might consider are: a nipple that flows more slowly; a longer, more relaxed feeding time; not hurrying to change the baby from a 3-hour schedule to a 4-hour schedule. Also, a little later is a good idea for weaning the baby from the breast or bottle to a cup.

What To Do

Ignoring. With young children (age 6 or below, before permanent teeth start to emerge), the weight of professional opinion and common sense is to generally ignore the thumbsucking habit. The main reasons for this tolerant approach are threefold: First, most children stop the habit of their own accord by age 5 or 6 and usually before the permanent teeth start coming through. Second, making an issue of sucking can cause the problem to get worse; it can magnify the issue out of proportion and create a power struggle between parent and child. Finally, when the thumbsucking child exhibits emotional problems in addition to the thumbsucking (such as fearfulness or aggressiveness), stopping the sucking may well precipitate other behavior problems or nervous habits such as tics, nail biting, or tantrums. On the other hand, studies show that the well-adjusted child is not any more likely to exhibit new behavior problems than other children.[1]

It seems best, then, to adopt a tolerant attitude and generally look the other way with young thumbsuckers. Be relaxed and don't let the habit embarrass or upset you. Show the child by your words and actions that you do not consider the sucking to be an important matter. Rather, concentrate your energies on promoting the child's general happiness and feelings of being loved, understood, and accepted. Work to eliminate any strong sources of stress that may be on the child since this often stops the thumbsucking. Consider if the child's emotional needs are being overlooked because of such factors as the arrival of a new baby, too much criticism, or too difficult an adjustment to day care or nursery school. If any of these conditions exist, do what you can to relieve the strains while trying to open up better channels of communication so the child feels understood and supported.

While ignoring the thumbsucking, you can strive to keep the child busy with constructive alternate activities that keep his or her hands occupied. Be sure the child is often played with by adults and peers. Provide a variety of play materials that stimulate active use of the hands, such as modeling clay and crayons.

Above all, ignoring the thumbsucking means not using any of the following aversive measures: nagging, shaming, threatening, ridiculing, yelling, or punishing. Do not use any mechanical restraining devices or foul tasting applications. Ignoring means not giving any attention—including applying unpleasant consequences to the habit. Noteworthy is the fact that many parents find it very difficult to overlook this habit since they consider it so distasteful and unsanitary. In the old days various brutal practices were employed to stop the habit, including tying a child's hands to his side at night. One German pediatrician would actually cut off the thumbs of children who were obstinate in their sucking. Hopefully, the modern day parent will find it easier to take a casual attitude towards the habit in the young child.

Guidance. With older children who carry the habit into school years, there is a real danger of dental deformities. It seems wise then, for the parent to try to motivate the child to want to stop the habit at this stage. Give the child guidance as to the negative effects of thumbsucking and try to enlist the child's cooperation in the application of corrective measures. Describe some of the procedures (see following sections) that have helped other children stop the habit. State your own mild disapproval of the habit as well as your confidence in the child's ability to eliminate it. If these motivational efforts fail, it seems best not to force an unwilling child into corrective efforts. By taking a firm or punitive stance, you may create tension between you and the child or stimulate emotional problems in the child that are more difficult to overcome than dental malocclusions. The following is a list of some active steps you can take to stop the habit if the child wishes to cease.

Rewards and Penalties. Rewards, including social praise and tangible objects such as food and toys, have been used successfully by parents to help children control their thumbsucking. Edible reinforcers provide substitute "oral gratification" and thus a kind of weaning or fading process. The first step in setting up a reward procedure is to *limit* a child's thumbsucking to a particular place (own room only) and time (nap and bedtime only). Once the child agrees to these limits, the parents in turn agree to observe the child at other specific times during the day—such as TV watching time in the evening. If the child does not have the thumb in his or her mouth when observed, and if the thumb is not wet and soggy, the child and/or the parents post a star on a prominently displayed chart. Five stars earn the child a concrete reward or prize. After the first prize is earned, ten stars are needed for the next reward. Praise is combined with the giving of stars and material rewards. After a period of time, only the praise is given the child for periods of no thumbsucking.

Once the child has been successful in not sucking at set times during the day, a reward system for dry thumb nights can be established. Before they retire at night, the parents check the child and if the thumb is out and dry, the parents say, "Good," and place a star on the chart. If the child is observed sucking the thumb at night, the thumb is gently removed by the parents.

Some parents have found that in addition to giving rewards, imposing a mild penalty for each incidence of observed thumbsucking helps the child weaken the habit very quickly. The usual penalty is the withdrawal of a positive reinforcer. For example, at bedtime a parent might initiate the routine of reading to a child, but the story reading would be stopped every time the child is observed to be thumbsucking while listening.[12] Other parents have penalized a child by turning the TV off for 5 minutes whenever the child is observed thumbsucking in front of it. If the child is agreeable, you might also coat the thumb with a bitter tasting substance (available at drugstores) so as to ensure an immediate unpleasant consequence to the thumbsucking.

Other Techniques. It is usually best to combine a reward-penalty procedure with several of the following adjunct methods.

Reminders. Remind the child to stop thumbsucking whenever you observe this behavior during the day. You might use such verbal cues as "Thumb" or "Don't." At night, just remove the thumb from the child's mouth after the child is asleep.

Removal. Taking away a child's preferred comfort object may reduce the child's enjoyment of thumbsucking and lead to its demise. Thus, if a child always sucks while holding a certain stuffed animal, you might establish the rule that from now on the stuffed animal must remain in the child's room—with a view towards limiting the thumbsucking to this room.

Competing response. Once thumbsucking has become a long-standing habit, it is very difficult to stop unless you have something else to do with your hands. Teach your child, then, a competing physical response when he or she feels the urge to suck the thumb. Clenching the fist, *i.e.*, making a fist by putting the thumb under the other four fingers, is typically prescribed as a substitute response. The family should praise the child for incidents of fist clenching behavior. Other forms of competing responses include chewing gum and sucking on lollypops.

Restrictive measures. A wide variety of ways to prevent a child from inserting a thumb in the mouth have been tried, including mitts, thumb guards, hand and elbow splints, adhesives over the thumb, binding the arm to the side, and sewing the sleeping garment over the hand. In general, the value of such methods has not been proved, and the unmotivated child will usually find a way to circumvent them. For the older child who is willing, however, some form of restriction may be used as an adjunct technique. For example, the child might wear mitts while watching TV.

Social pressure. Some parents have instructed siblings to prompt the child when thumbsucking occurs and to report any instance of continued thumbsucking to the parents. If the parents observe the child sucking while watching TV with the siblings, everyone loses TV privileges for a while. Grandparents and relatives can be enlisted to give encouragement and to praise the child for instances of no thumbsucking. Furthermore, you might solicit the teacher's help. If the child is still sucking the thumb in kindergarten, you can ask the teacher to inform the class that they are expected to give up such a habit at this stage.

Awareness training. Thumbsucking tends to be an unconscious habit that is difficult to stop since you are not aware you are doing it. You can help the child become more aware of the thumbsucking by having the child consciously suck the thumb in front of a mirror for 5 to 10 minutes—once or twice a day at set times. Such practice helps bring the habit under more conscious, voluntary control. The child tends to be more aware of when the thumbsucking occurs—what it feels like and what he or she looks like when doing it.

This repetitive practice also tends to make the thumbsucking more like work than pleasure. Vigorous sucking of a thumb for a period of time tends to be boring, and the pleasure soon pales.

Suck your own thumb. Dr. Rudolf Driekurs has suggested this practice as a way of deliberately encroaching on an area the child considers special to him or her. In disgust and/or resentment, the child may give up the habit. However, this method may, at least temporarily, interfere with your relationship with the child.

Dental Appliances. Research to date has shown that the most successful and certain way to stop thumbsucking habits is by an oral appliance inserted in the child's mouth by a dentist.[1] Usually in a little over a week the habit is eliminated, and once stopped, the habit tends not to reappear. Dentists will usually not install these devices until the child is at least 6 years old and the habit has persisted for an extended period. The first type of appliance consists of a bar or fence stretching across the palate. This device prevents the thumb from contacting the palate and thus breaks the suction and reduces the pleasure of thumbsucking. A second device is a larger grate designed to prevent the thumb from easily entering the mouth. A third type of appliance has sharp spurs which can be directed toward the tongue or the palate; thumbsucking then results in either painful contact with the thumb, or a pushing of the spurs into the palate.

Studies have found the spurs to be the most effective of the three devices, and this procedure is successful in 90 to 100 percent of the cases.[6] Unfortunately, the dental devices are quite unpleasant for the child to wear so that most parents are reluctant to use them. Also, some children show the following side effects from wearing the appliances: speech difficulties, irritability, and sleep and eating problems. These adverse effects, however, tend to be temporary in duration.

Suggestion. Most children are very suggestible, especially when very young. Thus, while rocking your preschool child, who is obviously relaxed and perhaps a little sleepy, you might say the following in a soft, lulling almost hypnotic manner:

"You are really getting bigger and bigger, and smarter and smarter every day. Pretty soon you'll be going to school just like the big kids . . . and pretty soon you'll be so very big that you will not suck your thumb anymore. Of course lots of little kids suck their thumbs; perhaps I sucked my thumb when I was a very little boy. But if I did, as I grew bigger and bigger, like lots of little boys and girls, I stopped sucking my thumb because I grew up, and I'll bet pretty soon you are going to get so very big that you will not suck your thumb anymore. Maybe it will be next month, perhaps you will be so big by tomorrow, or maybe the next day, that when your thumb goes in your mouth you will say, 'No thumb, I'm not going to suck you anymore, because I'm a big girl now. You just stay out of my mouth. Big girls don't suck thumbs. That is just what little people do. I am getting to be a big girl. You, Mr. Thumb, stay out of my mouth.' Yes, darling, you are getting big and pretty and soon you will not be sucking your thumb anymore, not anymore.''

Case Reports

Case #1. Charlie, age 9, sucked his thumb at home during an average of 2 hours of daily television viewing and while asleep.[13] Orthodontia for a conspicuous malocclusion of the front teeth could not begin until the thumbsucking was stopped. Moreover, speech was marked by a severe lisp which may have been indirectly related to thumbsucking. Frequent reminders by the parents and the application of medication to the hand before bedtime had failed to reduce the habit. With professional advice, the parents then implemented the following procedure.

Charlie and his two sisters, who usually watched TV with him, were told that the TV would be turned off for 5 minutes each time he was seen thumbsucking. The siblings were asked to help by reminding Charlie to stop whenever they saw him thumbsucking. In this way, they were made culpable if he was caught by his mother, thus justifying their loss of TV time too. In addition, the following sleeptime procedure was started. After Charlie had gone to bed, his mother made three observations: the first a half-hour after he fell asleep, the second midway between the first and third observations, and the third just before the mother went to bed. If the thumb was in his mouth during any of these observations, it was removed. The father, who arose early in the morning, checked Charlie's thumb at that time. Also, Charlie's hand was coated twice with medication (*Don't,* Commerce Drug Co., Farmingdale, New York) soon after he had fallen asleep and just prior to the mother's retiring. After about 2 weeks of this treatment, the thumbsucking was virtually eliminated during TV viewing and markedly reduced at night.

Case #2. Hilary, age 4, began sucking her thumb at the age of 3 months, at which time she was given a pacifier.[14] She refrained from thumbsucking until age 2, and the pacifier was withdrawn. Thumbsucking resumed immediately, and neither constant reminders nor the application of medication to the thumb at night before bedtime was successful in controlling the habit. To reduce the sucking the parents proceeded in the following manner. First they recorded the presence or absence of thumbsucking every 15 minutes from 2 hours before bedtime until 2 hours after bedtime. Praise ("Very good," "That's great") and candy (Lifesavers and other assorted hard candies) were given only if the child had not sucked during each prebedtime observation interval. This reinforcement was continued for 6 weeks, and the following method was used to determine if the child had sucked her thumb during any 15-minute interval. A "behavioral seal" was constructed by taping a piece of litmus paper to the child's thumb. When contacted by saliva the litmus turns grey; prolonged sucking, such as at night, turns the paper white. Results revealed that the prebedtime thumbsucking was markedly reduced by this method. Although not directly treated, the postbedtime thumbsucking fell off in rough equivalence to prebedtime thumbsucking. In lieu of the litmus paper, it should be noted that the parents could have inspected the child's thumb during each observation interval to see if it was wet or soggy. Although not as accurate, the visual inspection might have worked just as well.

Books About Thumbsucking For Children

Ernst, K.: *Danny and His Thumb.* Prentice-Hall, New York (1973). Ages 3 to 7.

Danny, age 6, has sucked his thumb for a long time. He likes the taste of his thumb and enjoys sucking it. Danny eventually becomes less fond of thumbsucking and discovers when he is active in tasks such as feeding his fish, riding his bike, and household chores, he is too busy to suck his thumb.

Fassler, J.: *Don't Worry Dear.* Behavior Publications, New York (1971). Ages 4 to 6.

With the support and understanding of her parents, Jenny outgrows her thumbsucking, bedwetting, and stuttering during her preschool years.

Klunowicz, B.: *The Strawberry Thumb*. Obingdon Press, New York (1968). Ages 3 to 6.

Anna-May, age 3, loves to suck her "strawberry thumb, her munchable, lunchable, sucking-good thumb." All efforts by her parents to discourage the habit fail, until her grandmother teaches the girl how to dress up and make a puppet out of the thumb.

References

1. Lichstein, K.L.: "Thumbsucking: A review of dental and psychological variables and their implications for treatment. *JSAS Catalog of Selected Documents in Psychology* 8(1): (1978), p. 13.

2. Roberts, J. and Baird, J.T.: *Parent Ratings of Behavioral Patterns of Children*. DHEW Publication No. (HSM) 72-1010, Washington, D.C.

3. Chandler, T.H.: "Thumbsucking in childhood as a cause of subsequent irregularity of the teeth." *The Dental Cosmos* 2: (1978), pp. 565–569.

4. Brenner, J.E.: "Thumbsucking, dental and psychological aspects." *New York State Dental Journal* 40: (1974), pp. 78–80.

5. Hellman, M.: "Open-Bite." *International Journal of Orthodontics* 17: (1931), pp. 421–444.

6. Haryette, R.D. *et al.:* "Chronic thumbsucking: A second report on treatment and its psychological effects." *American Journal of Orthodontics* 57: (1970), pp. 164–178.

7. Lewis, S.J.: "The effect of thumb and finger sucking on the primary teeth and dental arches." *Child Development* 8: (1937), pp. 93–98.

8. Humphreys, H.F. and Leighton, C.B.: "A survey of antero-posterior abnormalities of the jaws in children between the ages of two and five-and-a-half years of age." *British Dental Journal* 88:(1950), pp. 3–15.

9. Swinehart, E.W.: "Structural and nervous effects of thumbsucking." *Journal of the American Dental Association* 25:(1938), pp. 736–747.

10. Berland, T. and Seyler, A.E.: *Your Children's Teeth*. Meredith Press, New York (1968).

11. Cattell, R.: *Raising Children with Love and Limits*. Nelson Hall Co., Chicago (1972), pp. 120–121.
12. Knight, M.F. and McKenzie, H.S.: "Elimination of bedtime thumbsucking in home setting through contingent reading." *Journal of Applied Behavioral Analysis* 7:(1974), pp. 33–38.
13. Ross, J.A.: "Parents modify thumbsucking: A case study." *Journal of Behavior Therapy and Experimental Psychiatry* 6: (1975), pp. 248–249.
14. Hughes H. *et al.* "A behavioral seal: An apparatus alternative to behavioral observation of thumbsucking." *Behavior Research Methods and Instrumentation* 10:(1978), pp. 460 –461.

NAILBITING

Surveys show that a large number of children bite their nails from time to time. A substantial number of children continue to bite their nails so frequently that the nails become unsightly, and soreness or bleeding often occurs. Many children do not just outgrow this habit, since even among college students nailbiting is a problem of considerable magnitude, affecting 25 to 36 percent of this population.[1] The fingernail biting habit has been found to be more common among women than among men.[2] Nailbiters often feel ashamed to display their nails in public and may appear anxious and uneasy in social situations.

Although quite common, nailbiting is one of the most difficult habits to modify, possibly because nailbiters appear to be sensitive to social disapproval and thus bite their nails in solitude under reinforcing conditions. This tends to reduce the motivation to change. Since the sooner the habit is dealt with, the easier it is to change, it would seem most helpful for a child with a persistent nailbiting habit if the parents offer assistance in stopping the habit before it becomes well entrenched.

Reasons Why

Many people appear to bite their nails as a way of releasing tension, nervous energy, or anxiety.[3] It may also serve to satisfy a libidinal or aggressive drive. Some children may start because they observe others doing it. Still others may begin nibbling nails after breaking one or because they can't stand the sight of a jagged nail edge. Whatever the original source, the habit may remain long after the original cause has disappeared.

How To Prevent

Keep your child's nails trimmed and filed so that there are no rough edges. As mentioned above, some children begin nailbiting habits simply as a substitute for appropriate nail maintenance procedures. With smooth nails, a child will have no reason to trim a rough edge with his or her teeth.

A child who is physically active and whose hands are kept occupied with constructive activities will also be less likely to begin the habit.

What To Do

Nagging, shaming, or scolding the child about a nailbiting habit is more likely to aggravate the habit than to help it. Rather, a parent should discuss with the child the disadvantages of the habit (scarred, unsightly fingers; social disapproval; people associate it with an emotional problem) and thus try to increase a child's motivation to overcome it. A child who is motivated to stop can combine several of the following strategies.

Record Keeping. Most children over the age of 8, and some younger, are capable of observing and recording the incidents of their nailbiting. On a notecard she can make a tally mark each time she bites her nails or puts a finger in her mouth; she should also jot down what she was doing just before she started nailbiting. In this way she can learn to look for those situations that come just before nailbiting, such as TV watching, and make efforts to avoid these triggering events until she has gained some control over the nailbiting. Studies have shown that just recording the frequency of a problem behavior is often effective in reducing it. Such recording seems to lead to an increased awareness and evaluation of how one uses one's time and energy.

If the child is too young or immature to keep a record, the parents should do it for him or her by making a periodic observation of the child; you might set a kitchen timer at varying time intervals to remind you to make an observation.

Rewards. Once the record sheets reveal the average number of times a child is nailbiting during a day, the parents can set a goal for improvement (say five times less a day) and give a small daily reward for meeting this goal. In addition the child might earn a big, once-a-week payoff such as a trip to the zoo or a movie. You might use a point system wherein if a child bites five times less a day, he or she earns five points. A total of 25 points earns a concrete reward or special privilege. Set the goals small, and don't expect the child to take giant steps forward . . . or to go "cold turkey" and not bite anymore. Also remember to frequently maintain interest and ask the child what rewards he or she would like to add to the list.

Apart from tangible rewards, do not overlook the power of adult praise and attention in reinforcing less nailbiting. Many parents have a tendency to pay attention to the negative aspects of their children's behavior while overlooking what they do right. Be sure the family notices and comments favorably on the record sheet when it indicates a successful day in regard to less frequent biting.

Penalties. If the child is willing, a penalty for biting can be combined with a reward for nonbiting so as to eliminate the habit more quickly. One form of self-punishment is for the child to wear a ¼″ rubber band around his wrist and to snap the band hard against the inside of his wrist immediately after he bites his nails. He should also snap himself (hard enough to hurt) whenever he feels the urge to bite. Research shows that punishment delivered while one is in the act of biting is more effective than punishment that comes after one has already bitten one's nails.

Another form of punishment is the removal of a positive reward, such as the loss of TV time or the loss of money through a fine (child pays 25¢ whenever he or she is observed to nailbite by a parent).

Awareness Training. Since nailbiting tends to be an automatic, unconscious occurrence, you can help your child become more aware of the act by the following procedure.[4] Ask your child to set aside 5 minutes each morning and evening to sit in a quiet place in front of a mirror. The child is to slowly go through the motions of biting his or her nails as though really doing it. While playing the role, the child is to say out loud. "This is what I am not going to do." You might set a kitchen timer so the child knows how much practice time remains. This procedure should give the child more awareness and thus more voluntary control over the nailbiting habit.

Competing Response. In view of the fact that you can't bite your nails while you are doing something else, teach your child a competing activity to perform whenever the urge to nailbite occurs. An effective competing response is to put your hands down by your side and clench your fist real hard until you feel tension in your hand and arm. The child should engage in a competing response for 2–3 minutes following the temptation to bite or actual nailbiting.[4] Other competing responses include tapping your fingernails on a hard surface, rubbing worry beads, knitting a sweater, and shuffling cards. The child should reward himself or herself for engaging in the competing response by immediately having a sip of soda or a piece of candy which will tend to strengthen the occurrence of competing activities.

Engaging in competing responses seems to be a better way of inhibiting the nailbiting habit than such strategies as coating the nails with a bitter substance such as iodine or valerian, or use of restraints such as mitts or artificial nails. In some cases, however applying artificial nails to the top of bitten nails will give the nails a chance to grow.

Teach Relaxation. Assuming that nailbiting is primarily the result of excessive tension or anxiety, you might help the child learn an alternate coping mechanism for anxiety-provoking situations. Cue-controlled relaxation is one such mechanism.[6] The aim of cue-controlled relaxation is to teach the child to achieve a state of relaxation in response to a self-produced cue-word, such as *calm* or *control.* The procedure has two steps: (1) training in deep muscle relaxation,[7] and (2) pairing the cue-word with the relaxed state. The cue-word association is established by having the child attend to his/her breathing while subvocally repeating the cue-word with each exhalation. For the first five pairings, a parent repeats aloud the cue-word in synchrony with the child's exhalations; the child then continues this procedure for 15 more pairings. A 60-second period is then allowed for the child to attend to the general feelings associated with relaxation. Then the cue-word is repeated another 20 times. The child is encouraged to practice both the relaxation exercises and the cue-word association procedure on a daily basis. Once skilled in the technique, the child is instructed to recognize the increases in anxiety associated with nailbiting and then apply the cue-controlled procedure, *i.e.*, exhaling and subvocalizing the cue-word *calm*.

Case Report

Perkins and Perkins[5] report the case of a 19-year-old female college student with a long-standing habit of biting the nails on her right hand. By observing and recording the incident of each nailbiting, she became more aware of the places and times she was prone to nailbite. She discovered that she bit her nails the most whenever her hands were idle, such as while watching TV or a movie, or listening to a lecture in class. She found that by engaging in a competing activity in these situations, such as scribbling or tearing and folding paper, she was able to keep her hands busy and out of her mouth. She also bit quite often when nervous or upset about something; in these situations she engaged in the competing activity of clenching her fist or clasping her hands in her lap. At other times the only thing that worked was to keep a rubberband around her wrist and to pop herself everytime she had the desire to bite her nails.

The girl also used a point system to reward herself for success in reducing the habit. Since she usually bit her nails 20 times a day, she decided to give herself five points a day for every day she bit her nails less than 15 times. If she bit more than 15 times a day, she subtracted ten points from the possible 35 for the week. Each week she rewarded herself for a 25-or-higher point total by buying herself a record or something comparable that she had been wanting but did not think she deserved. As she progressed in her program, she rewarded herself only if she met more stringent goals, such as a maximum of 12 nailbitings a week, then 9, then 5, etc. Furthermore, her boyfriend agreed to take her out to a dinner and play if she collected at least 180 of the possible 210 points for a 7-week period. If she failed to reach this total, she agreed to pay her boyfriend $15 to go out with the guys on a Saturday night. Even though she failed to earn enough points to win this special reward, she felt the point system was the most helpful aspect of the program. This program was effective in eliminating the nailbiting after 5 weeks of effort.

Books for Parents About Nailbiting

Perkins, D.G. and Perkins, F.M.: *Nailbiting and Cuticlebiting: Kicking the Habit.* Self-Control Press, Box R-B, Suite 1217, Keystone Park, 13773 N. Central Expressway, Dallas, TX 75243 (1976).

This book attempts to share the latest information about nailbiting with the public. The book can be used by adolescents and adults to control their nailbiting habit, or by parents who wish to assist their children.

References

1. Adesso, V.J. and Vargas, J.M.: "A survey of nailbiting behavior among college students." Unpublished manuscript, University of Wisconsin-Milwaukee (1973).
2. Williams, D.G.: "So-called 'nervous habits.' " *Journal of Psychology* 83: (1973), pp. 103–109.
3. Koch, H.L.: "An analysis of certain forms of so-called 'nervous habits' in young children." *Journal of Genetic Psychology* 46: (1935), pp. 139–169.
4. Azrin, N.H. and Nunn, R.G.: "Habit-reversal: A method of eliminating nervous habits and tics." *Behavior Research and Therapy* 11: (1973), pp. 619–628.
5. Perkins, D.G. and Perkins, F.M.: *Nailbiting and Cuticlebiting: Kicking the Habit.* Self-Control Press, Dallas, TX (1976).
6. Barrios, B.A.: "Cue-controlled relaxation in reduction of chronic nervous habits." *Psychological Reports* 41: (1977), pp. 703–706.
7. Self-management tapes. *Relaxation Exercises for Children.* 1534 Oakstream, Houston, TX 77043 (1974).

BEDWETTING

Bedwetting or enuresis can be defined as the repeated, involuntary discharge of urine into the bed by a child age 4 or older. An occasional wet bed is not considered a problem; most bedwetters wet several nights a week or every night. Two types of bedwetters have been identified in the literature: the "continuous" bedwetter who has been wetting since birth, and the "discontinuous" wetter who had achieved a significant period of nighttime dryness (at least 3 months) and then resumed bedwetting. Most children (80 percent) display the continuous type of bedwetting.

Bedwetting is a common childhood problem. The data indicate that as many as one out of every four children between the ages of 4 and 16 have this problem at one time or another. At any one time about 12 percent of children ages 6 to 8 wet the bed, 5 percent at age 10–12, and 2 percent in young adulthood.[1] More boys than girls have a bedwetting problem. Rather than wetting at night, some children wet themselves during the day (diurnal wetting), usually when excited or busy at play. When children wet during play, they should go to the toilet before going out to play and perhaps be made to play near home for a few days so they can reach a toilet quickly. The parents might also call the child in at regular but gradually lengthened intervals to go to the toilet until the playtime wetting ceases.

Reasons Why

There are many theories as to the underlying causes of bedwetting, but none have been conclusively proven. For the discontinuous type of bedwetter who starts nighttime wetting again after a substantial period of dryness, the cause often appears to be some external stress or emotional crisis that makes the child anxious, such as the birth of a new sibling, physical illness, or a family move. The most plausible explanation for bedwetting in the continuous type of child who never achieved nighttime dryness is a maturational lag, *i.e.*, slow physiological maturation of bladder control mechanisms.[2] This seems to be inherited since the parents of enuretic children have a history of being enuretic themselves as children about three times as often as the parents of nonenuretic children. Others suggest that bedwetting is the result of a developmental lag interacting with maladaptive toilet training practices.

Estimates of an organic cause for bedwetting, such as a urinary tract infection, range from 1–10 percent, with 1 percent being the more likely figure. If the child has both day and nighttime wetting, painful urination, or possibly a seizure pattern, a thorough physical exam seems appropriate. Unfortunately, when a medical problem relating to bedwetting is discovered and treated, such as a mild urinary infection, it does not usually result in a decline of the bedwetting.

How to Prevent

In toilet training a child, avoid the extremes of being lax and indifferent about bladder control and being overly punitive, *i.e.*, severely punishing, scolding, or shaming the child for wetting the bed. Punitive methods tend to make the child feel guilty, inadequate, and/or anxious. When a child is markedly anxious or fearful, it is hard for him to learn new behaviors, such as nighttime control. It is also wise to delay bladder training until the child is uncomfortable about daytime wetting, has bowel control, and is able to hold urine for several hours at a time. Such readiness signs usually occur around 18 to 24 months.

It has been suggested that if parents pressure a child to achieve nighttime control before the child is mature enough, the child may lose confidence and have greater difficulty in bladder control. Some investigators[3] feel that if parents were to completely ignore the slow development of bladder control in the child, this would lead to spontaneous cure by the time the child reaches 7 or 8 years. Unfortunately most parents become quite upset about the bedwetting so that the child becomes anxious and discouraged which makes the problem worse.

What to Do

Some parents mistakenly make a direct attack on the bedwetting by criticizing, shaming, or severely punishing the enuretic child. Some become emotionally cold and distant to the child, while others try to reason with bedwetters to get them to "try harder." In general, these tactics are not only ineffective but may actually make the problem worse. Above all, parents are best advised to respond to the bedwetting in a calm, matter-of-fact manner and show confidence in the child's ability to eventually control this behavior. When the child becomes anxious, ashamed, or discouraged about the wetting, it becomes more difficult to extinguish.

Some limited success has been achieved by limiting the amount of fluid a child can drink after 6 P.M. and by requiring the child to urinate before going to bed. The use of drugs, such as tricyclic antidepressants (Imipramine), has been found to alleviate the bedwetting in one out of every three bedwetters, but when the medication is withdrawn, a resumption of wetting is the general rule. The following techniques seem to hold the most promise for effectively eliminating the problem. In using any procedure, it is important to obtain the child's cooperation and make it a joint effort to overcome the problem, rather than attempting to force a method on a child.

Star Chart. Ask the child to keep a record of wet and dry nights. Dry nights are highlighted on the chart with gold stars, and a reward, such as extra time alone with a parent, is given for each stage of improvement. While ignoring wet nights, the parents praise the child for each dry night. Such a reward system helps motivate the child by giving him an incentive, a specific goal to achieve, and a picture of his progress in reducing the habit. Star charts have been found to be particularly effective with young bedwetters.

Reduce Stress. If the child had been dry at night and then started wetting again, check to see if some stress occurred just prior to the resumption of bedwetting, such as the birth of a new sibling, a move to a new neighborhood, a family quarrel, or the extended absence of a parent for any reason. If an uncontrollable external stress seems to be triggering the bedwetting, do what you can to reduce the child's anxiety by giving extra attention, support, and understanding to the child.

At bedtime sit with the child for 10–15 minutes of comforting talk so the child goes to sleep relaxed, feeling sure of your interest and support. You might also spend extra time during the day interacting on a one-to-one basis with the child in pleasant activities. Use this time to observe the child and to try to uncover any areas of conflict or unresolved anxiety.

Impose a Penalty. Some parents require the school-age bedwetter to change the bed sheets after wetting and to see that the bed clothes get washed. This seems to be a logical consequence to the act of wetting.[4] Do not scold or lecture when establishing this procedure.

Another parent imposed the following penalty. The child was required to sign a chart on the refrigerator each morning to indicate if the bed was wet the night before. If the child forgot to sign in, it cost 10¢ and 50¢ if the child did not tell the truth (as verified by spot checks). The child was not allowed liquids after 6 P.M. until 14 consecutive dry nights were achieved. This procedure soon eliminated the problem since liquids with dinner were very motivating to the child.

Retain Urine. Studies have shown that a number of bedwetters are not able to retain a normal amount of urine in the bladder.[5] Thus, training the child to tolerate greater and greater quantities of urine in the bladder can often produce a greater bladder capacity. One form of "retention training" is as follows: Teach the child to control his bladder during the day by making a game out of it wherein the child keeps trying to break his own record. He is told to hold off going to the bathroom to urinate as long as possible and is then asked to urinate in a measuring cup. The amount he is able to hold is written down. When the child is able to hold 12–14 ounces, the likelihood of his overcoming bedwetting is often increased.

Another form of retention training is to instruct the child to "stop and start" the flow of urine while urinating during the day. First explain to the child that urine is stored in a small "balloonlike" container inside the body. There is a doughnut-shaped muscle at the end of the balloon which, when tightly closed, holds the urine in. The child's bedwetting problem is due to the fact that the doughnut muscle is weak and opens up at night to let urine out (demonstrate by letting air out of a balloon). The solution is to strengthen the muscle by exercising it. If the child is interested in stopping the bedwetting, explain that you can teach an exercise program that has helped many children with such a problem. This is the program: Each morning when you get up and it is not a school morning, drink as much water as you can. Pretty soon you will have to urinate. When you go to the toilet let some urine out and then stop it. Then let some more out and clamp it off again. Do this over and over as you urinate. Pretty soon your doughnut muscle will become strong and the bedwetting will stop.

Nighttime Awakening. The first step in this procedure is to determine what time the child usually wets the bed each night. If, for example, you find that the child usually wets 2 hours after retiring, set an alarm clock to go off in the child's room just before this time. When the alarm goes off, the child arises, urinates in the toilet, and sleeps through until morning. After 7 consecutive dry nights this way, set an alarm for 1½ hours after bedtime. Seven consecutive dry nights is the criterion for further gradual reductions in time, to 60 minutes after bedtime, to 45 minutes, and finally to 30 minutes. The child is then to go to the toilet every other night without the alarm clock to fade out its use. When this procedure was used with a 13-year-old girl, who also cleaned her bedsheets when wet, the bedwetting was soon eliminated.[6]

Bell and Pad Method. If a schoolage child continues to wet the bed despite your efforts to help, you should probably seek professional assistance. The ''bell and pad'' conditioning apparatus has been the most successful of reported professional treatments. With 2–3 months of use, it succeeds in about 70 percent of the cases. About 30 percent of these successes will relapse, but a second application of the device usually overcomes the relapse or resumption of wetting.

The apparatus consists of a special training pad which is placed on the bed under the child. The pad, when moistened with urine during the night, closes an electrical circuit which rings a bell and turns on a light. This awakens the child and stops the urination. Once the child learns to inhibit urination during sleep, the bell and pad apparatus is removed.

Best results with this device are obtained by contacting a professional psychologist who will not only provide the equipment but the needed supervision as well.

Books for Parents on Bedwetting

Baller, W.R.: *Bedwetting: Origins and Treatment*. Pergamon, New York (1975).

Schaefer, C.E.: *Childhood Encopresis and Enuresis: Causes and Therapy*. Van Nostrand Reinhold, New York (1979).

References

1. Hallgren, B.: "Enuresis: A clinical and genetic study." *Acta Psychiatrica n32*: (1957), p. 123.
2. Esman, A.H.: "Nocturnal enuresis." *Journal of Child Psychiatry* 16: (1977), pp. 150–158.
3. White, M.: "A thousand consecutive cases of enuresis: Results of treatment." *Child and Family* 10* (1971), pp. 198–209.
4. Dische, S.: "Management of enuresis." *British Medical Journal* 3: (1971), p 33.
5. Esperanca, M. and Gerrard, J.W.: "Nocturnal enuresis: Studies in bladder function in normal children and enuretics." *Canadian Medical Association Journal* 101: (1969), p. 324.
6. Singh, R., Phillips, D., and Fischer, S.C.: "The treatment of enuresis by progressively earlier waking." *Journal of Behavior Therapy and Experimental Psychiatry* 7: (1976), pp. 277–278.

SOILING

Soiling or encopresis can be defined as persistent passing of stools into one's clothing after the age of 3 years. Its onset is most common from ages 3 to 8. While less common than bedwetting, encopresis is not rare; its prevalence among 8-year-olds has been found to be 2.3 percent for boys and 0.7 percent for girls—roughly one-third the corresponding rate for enuresis.[1] The incidence of soiling declines spontaneously at a rate of 28 percent a year, and it virtually disappears by age 16. Thus, the long-term prognosis for soiling is good, although it may last 2 or 3 years before it disappears. With treatment it often improves within a few weeks and disappears by 2–3 months. It is rare in adolescents and young adults except in severely retarded or psychotic persons.

Most encopretic children soil after returning home from school in the afternoon, particularly during periods of stress or excitement. Soiling is seldom caused by children who deliberately expel feces; most often it results from retention of stools. Prolonged retention or constipation produces an impacted and distended bowel. Bowel movements become infrequent, with large, dry stools which are painful to pass. As a rule encopretic children are not aware of the normal urge to move their bowels because of the severe constipation. Many parents do not know that the child is constipated, and a surprising number of these children are treated for diarrhea because they are so impacted with feces that there is a leakage of mucus and stools.

"Continuous" encopresis means that the child never achieved control of his bowel for any significant period of time. "Discontinuous" means that the child had control but subsequently lost it and resumed soiling. External stresses such as starting school can cause regression in bowel control.

Soiling can have a profound impact on those it afflicts. A child who begins soiling is likely to have an increasingly impaired self-concept. He or she may defend against the loss of self-regard by taking an "I-don't-care attitude." The social relationships of an encopretic child are often drastically affected. A child may be ridiculed by peers and be removed from the classroom. Thus, soiling is not a behavior that should be overlooked by parents.

Reasons Why

It has been common to blame coercive toilet training for a child's encopresis, but the evidence for this position is weak. As previously mentioned, some children will lose bowel control under periods of intense stress or emotional upset.

Studies[1] have found that a substantial number of parents of encopretic children had been encopretic themselves which suggests, at least in part, a hereditary component. About one-fourth of children with encopresis have regular problems with constipation.

The typical case of encopresis does not have a physical or organic cause. It begins during the preschool years when the child begins to retain feces for a variety of reasons (*e.g.*, tendency towards constipation, improper diet, faulty bowel training, family crisis). In about half the cases, a precipitating event can be identified. As retention occurs, the child's bowel becomes distended and, eventually, impacted. The anus then becomes partially open, and seepage occurs even though a large fecal mass is retained. Once a child's bowel is chronically distended with feces, even if the psychological factors that initially may have caused the retention abate, the physical condition will continue because the lower colon has become nonfunctional. It has lost its shape and muscle tone and does not respond to fecal matter with an urge to defecate.

How to Prevent

Since some encopretic children have been reported to have problems with their aggressive impulses, it may be helpful for parents to teach children how to be appropriately assertive when they are angry. Children who are constantly angry or tense need to be taught how to control their reactions to daily events so these emotions do not become chronic.

Children who tend to ignore the "call to stool" or urge to defecate should be helped to establish regular toileting times during the day. Just after breakfast is a good time, but it may mean awakening the child a little earlier in the morning so as to allow enough time to get ready for school.

Poor eating habits may be contributing to a child's constipation. Meal times should occur at regular intervals. They should be periods of relaxation and pleasant conversation rather than occasions of tension or quarrels. Generally a normal diet with foods selected from the four basic food groups (meat, fish, and eggs; breads and cereals; milk and milk products; fruits and vegetables) and a caloric intake suited to the child's energy output helps in constipation prevention. A variety of fresh vegetables and most fresh or dried fruits are particularly helpful in supplying needed residue. Plenty of fluids is also recommended.

Avoid strict toilet training and an attitude that feces are "disgusting." Your child may react to strict, punitive toilet training by fearful submission or open rebellion—both of which can lead to soiling and constipation.

What to Do

A comprehensive treatment plan seems best, which helps relieve the child's physiological and psychological difficulties.[2] Treatment is most effective when supervised by a mental and/or physical health professional.

Physiological. Since four out of five encopretic children have been found to be constipated, it is essential that the fecal impaction be cleaned out so that normal "call to stool" sensations are restored. The child should be given one or two *Fleet* enemas (available from a drugstore) to thoroughly empty the colon.

Because of its binding effect, milk in the child's diet is limited to 1 pint a day, and the diet may be adjusted to include larger amounts of roughage and citrus and dried fruits. Bread, pastries, and sweets are kept to a minimum.

Toilet Training. The child's toileting habits often need to be retrained. The parents should insist on a routine of two 10-minute sessions on the toilet each day, the sessions occurring at set times and monitored by a kitchen timer. The toilet sessions should be scheduled just after a meal, especially after the morning meal.

Rewards and Penalties. With younger children it is helpful to maintain a star chart which records the completion of each toileting attempt (an extra star is given for a successful elimination, and for a period of no soiling). Stars are traded in for special privileges or material rewards. An effective reward is 30 minutes alone with a parent wherein the child chooses the activity. A penalty for each soiling incident may be imposed such as washing out the soiled garment or taking a bath. Hiding of soiled underwear is handled by numbering each pair and replacing missing underwear with money from the child's savings or allowance.

Support and Encouragement. It is comforting for the child to know that the problem is not unique and to have the physiology of the problem explained. The parents should not blame the child or themselves for the difficulty but work cooperatively with the child to correct it. The emphasis should be on parental praise for appropriate defecation and a matter-of-fact attitude to soiling (no scolding, shaming, ridiculing, or yelling).

Care should be taken not to place one child in the "baby" role in the family wherein regressed behavior like soiling would be expected. The parents should try to identify and minimize any strong sources of stress on the child, such as marital quarrels or sibling rivalry.

Case Reports

A 3-year-old boy was severely constipated and often needed medication to move his bowels. The father decided to intervene as follows: The child was told that the goal was more regular bowel movements. When the child defecated in the toilet, he was told he could play in the tub with toy boats. He was also given a gold star each day he used the toilet appropriately. Three stars earned the boy a new toy boat. If the child did not have a bowel movement at the set toilet time, he was asked to repeat the rules before leaving the room. The boy immediately began using the toilet after this procedure was initiated, and the constipation disappeared.[3]

An 8-year-old girl had not had a normal bowel movement for 5 years.[4] Her stools were sporadic, usually soft and watery, and came at any time of the day. The child's colon was found to be impacted with feces, and it was thoroughly evacuated by means of enemas at the beginning of the program. Then the parents instructed the child to go to the bathroom immediately upon awakening each morning. If a reasonable amount of fecal material was produced, the child was praised and given a reward. If not, a glycerin suppository was administered, which was usually successful by the time the child had to leave for school. In these cases she received half a reward.

If the child had not defecated just before it was time to leave for school, a small volume *Fleet* enema was administered. In this case the child was given support and encouragement but no reward. When the child's clothing was inspected after supper, she received praise and a reward if there was no soiling. If soiling was found, she was deprived of television for the evening. Thus, the program involved two rewards (one for defecating and one for not soiling) and one punishment (for soiling). After 2 weeks of no soiling the suppositories and enemas were discontinued for 1 day a week. For each additional week of no soiling, an additional day without these cathartics was added the following week. The 2 days were spaced apart, *i.e.*, Wednesdays and Sundays. Additional (off-cathartics) days were added to the program for each successive week without soiling. This process continued until the child was completely free of soiling and off cathartics for 2 weeks. Then the reward and punishment procedure was terminated.

Although the child had soiled daily prior to treatment, she soiled three times during the first 2 weeks of the program and only five times throughout its duration. On only 15 occasions during the 75 days of treatment did she fail to defecate on her own.

Finally, a 9-year-old boy had been soiling himself daily for 2 years and wetting the bed nightly. He usually soiled when preoccupied with other activities, such as playing in school or with neighborhood children. His parents blamed the soiling on his laziness and punished him severely for the soiling (shaming, sending to bed with no dinner). With professional counseling, the parents tried a new method which involved no punishment. The parents agreed to ignore or treat matter-of-factly the soiling and to praise and reward all nonsoiling incidents. The father rewarded the son by spending 30 minutes each day with him on an activity of the son's choice, such as playing ball, watching a sports activity, or just walking through the woods together. In addition the parents worked out a contract with the boy wherein the boy would come in each half-hour when not in school and attempt to defecate. He was given a nickel each time he attempted to defecate for at least 5 minutes. Each evening he was allowed to go to an ice cream store to spend the money he earned from these attempts. In school his teacher agreed to prompt the boy every half-hour to go to the rest room. She sent home a daily checklist with the times marked when he had gone to the rest room. At first the parents had difficulty ignoring the soiling episodes since they had a deep-seated belief that the boy should be punished for such behavior. With counseling they were able to eliminate their hostile outbursts and concentrate on rewarding appropriate behaviors. After 2 months of this program, the soiling ceased completely and the bedwetting—although not directly treated—declined substantially. The relationship between the boy and his parents also became much more positive.

Books for Parents on Soiling

Schaefer, C.E.: *Child Encopresis and Enuresis: Causes and Therapy.* Van Nostrand Reinhold, New York (1979).

References

1. Bellman, M.: "Studies on encopresis." *Acta Paediatrica,* Scandinavia Supplement 170: (1966), p. 121.
2. Levine, M.D. and Bakow, H.: "Children with encopresis: A study of treatment outcome." *Pediatrics* 58: (1976), p. 845.
3. Graubard, P.S.: *Positive Parenthood.* New American Library, New York (1977).
4. Wright, L.: "Psychogenic encopresis." *Ross Timesaver* 20: (1978), pp. 11–16.

SLEEP DISTURBANCES

The value of adequate sleep to children is important not only for the proper functioning of the various bodily systems, but also for the psychological well-being of the child. Apart from their adverse effects on the child, sleep disturbances can be especially trying and irritating to parents. These difficulties interfere with the parents' own immediate and often pressing needs for restful sleep.

Mild sleep disturbances are very common in childhood especially in 2 year olds, and in children ages 3 to 5. They are normal reactions and expressions of the insecurities involved in growing up. Most parents will have to deal with a child whose sleep is disturbed in one way or another. Disturbing dreams and restlessness in sleep are the two most common disorders. For about one-third of children ages 3 to 10 years, disturbing dreams will be present.[1] At age 10 the peak incidence of disturbing dreams occurs (almost half of all girls this age experience them), and then the incidence of such dreams declines rapidly for both sexes.

Although mild and temporary sleep disturbances are common occurrences in childhood, severe and/or persistent sleep difficulties are the earliest signs of emotional upset in children.[2] The difference between normal and pathological sleep disturbances is a matter of degree rather than kind. If the problem is severe and chronic, as, for example, many successive nights of prolonged wakefulness or almost nightly nightmares over an extended period, then there may be a serious emotional disturbance present that requires professional counseling.

Reasons Why

The underlying causes of sleep disturbances are multiple, including anxieties, internal conflicts, physical disorders, overstimulation, situational stress, fear of the dark, and fear of losing voluntary control when going to sleep.

For very young children sleep is like a separation from parents, and many sleep disturbances are linked with separation anxiety. The child might be afraid something may happen to her parents while asleep. The child feels in special danger because conscious control is lost during sleep. Older children, ages 4 to 6 years, often have specific fears of what might happen while asleep, such as their parents may be harmed by robbers, or a fire may break out in the house.

Recent sleep research has established the fact that sleep is cyclical in nature, characterized by the child going in and out of four or five periods of really deep sleep. After emerging from the deepest sleep stage, rapid eye movements (REM) usually occur which are associated with vivid dream activity. Studies of sleep-walking, sleep talking, night terrors, and bedwetting show that these disorders occur during sudden, intense arousal from the deep sleep stages and are unrelated to REM sleep.[3] These are called disorders of *arousal*. Narcolepsy or excessive sleepiness, on the other hand, is associated with the abnormal occurrence of REM sleep and is thus regarded as a disorder of sleep. It is becoming increasingly clear that disorders of arousal are most often associated with signs of neurological immaturity, especially upon their initial occurrence in younger children. There is often a family history of these arousal disorders. Before research with sleep polygraphy, these disturbances were commonly considered to be caused by "bad dreams." It is evident now that bad dreams are not the cause of these difficulties.[3] Although the underlying causes of these arousal disorders are still poorly understood, they seem related to individual physiologic differences and possible genetic factors. Anxiety and environmental stress are also frequently evident, particularly when these problems persist into late childhood and early adulthood, suggesting multiple interacting etiologies.

The major sleep disorders of youth will be discussed in the following sections. Childhood sleep disturbances fall into six major categories: reluctance to sleep; restless sleep; nightmares; arousal disorders, such as sleepwalking and night terrors; insomnia; and excessive sleep.

Resistance to Going to Sleep

Almost all young children go through a period when they will resist going to sleep. If the parents show excessive concern, distress, or inability to follow through firmly in managing the situation, the child's sleep resistance may get worse. Some children resist going to sleep because of anxieties or overstimulation, while others get quite lonely off by themselves and still crave the reassuring feeling they get from their parents' company.

Resistance by Very Young Children. Children below the age of 3 years are often disinterested in going to bed and will often awaken at night and demand to be held and attended to. The strategies children develop to postpone bedtime are familiar to every parent, and bedtime rituals can take hours if parents are unwary. Children will ask for just one more drink of water, just one more story, or another trip to the bathroom.

Prevention is the key to handling these resistances so as to forestall a power struggle.

How to Prevent

Establish a regular routine: A consistent bedtime routine is important for the establishment of a regular sleep-awake cycle. A regular schedule allows the child to be physiologically ready for sleep at the same hour each evening. Be sure to establish a regular hour for both going to bed and for waking up. These times should be changed only for special occasions. The hour just before bed should be a quiet, relaxing time for the child. Thus it is not a time for roughhousing with the child or for watching scary TV programs. A bedtime snack or warm bath can help prepare a child for sleep. If the child's father comes home relatively late from work, it may be necessary to push back the child's bedtime to 7:00, 7:30, or 8:00 P.M. so there is time to play with the father after dinner. An extra nap in the morning or an especially long nap in the afternoon may be required to make up for the missed sleep in the evening.

Advanced notice: Children will go to bed more readily when they receive advanced notice from their parents that bedtime is approaching. To suddenly say to a child, "Go to bed," is to invite resistance. Give an advance warning 5 or 10 minutes ahead of bedtime so the child can get ready for it.

Be supportive: Try to associate going to sleep with as much pleasure, affection, and relaxation as possible. For example, you might read or tell a child a bedtime story, say an evening prayer, sing a goodnight song, or have a close, intimate talk with the child after she is in bed. These bedtime rituals should be calm and relaxing. Rituals, to young children, have a kind of magic effect in protecting them from the dangers of sleep.

Be firm: Make it clear to the child when you give the goodnight kiss that this is the end of your interaction for the night. Leave the room without hesitation or uncertainty and, if necessary, state that you are not coming back. If the child whines or cries after you leave, ignore these protestations, and they will probably disappear in a few minutes. The key is to expect your child to go to bed at the same time each night and to firmly and confidently enforce the time for bed. If the child states that she is not sleepy, convey the message that you expect her to rest or play quietly in bed until sleep comes. Do not insist that the child fall asleep immediately since children usually take up to a half-hour to go to sleep.

Security objects: A blanket or cuddly stuffed animal in the crib can give the child much security as he makes the transition from wakefulness to sleep.

Affection: One of the best ways to prevent sleep disorders in the very young is to be sure the child is getting plenty of affection from both parents. Do not give constant or intense criticism which will make the child feel uncertain of your love.

No early-to-bed penalty: Do not send your child to bed early as a punishment. This tends to associate going to bed with punishment in the child's mind.

What to Do

Nighttime crying: Reluctance to go to sleep and night wakenings are the most common difficulties in children before the age of 13. Thus it is quite common for young children to cry a bit before falling asleep, or to wake up crying during the night and want to be held by their parents. In severe cases, wakefulness may persist for hours or for most of the night. Severe cases of nocturnal wakefulness have drastic effects on the physical and psychological well-being of the parents.

Many parents, particularly with the first child, tend to overrespond to the child's nighttime crying and reinforce its occurrence. Look for the following signs that the child is spoiled and is crying primarily to gain your attention. Does the child progressively want you to hold her for longer and longer periods each night? Does the crying suddenly stop when you pick the child up? If both these conditions are present, the child is probably spoiled, and you should try the following procedure which involves "planned ignoring" of the crying. After briefly checking the child's first outcry to be certain he is not ill, wet, or hurting, it seems best to leave the room and let the child cry it out. Unless the child is obviously panicky and needs to be held briefly, you should just return to cribside every 20 to 30 minutes to wipe the child's face. Typically, the child with a well-established habit of waking up and crying at night will cry an hour or 2 the first night, 30 to 60 minutes the second night, and then for increasingly shorter intervals over the next several nights until he no longer wakes up at night. It is important for you to completely ignore the crying except to quickly wipe the child's nose at reasonable intervals.

Child is not sleepy: If, despite all your efforts at prevention, you find your child still resists going to sleep at night, you should consider if the child is being put to bed when she is not sleepy. If this seems to be the case, you might try reducing or eliminating the child's daytime nap or postponing bedtime a bit and see if this solves the problem. Like adults, children vary in their sleep needs.

Fear of the dark: Some children are reluctant to go to bed because of a fear of the dark. If this seems to be bothering your child, you might try one or more of the following steps.

Be understanding: Do not be impatient or ridicule this fear by calling it silly or ridiculous. It is very real to the child. Treat it sympathetically and respectfully. Encourage the child to talk about it with you and show that you not only want to understand but that you are sure nothing will happen to him in the dark. Give the child plenty of affection and assure him that you are nearby and will not let anything bad occur. Of course, you should never punish a child by threatening that the "bogeyman" will get him if he's bad. It is also a good idea to avoid scary movies or TV shows and cruel fairy tales for a while.

Provide a light: Leave a dim light on in the hall and open the child's door so he will not be in complete darkness. Or you might allow the child to keep a flashlight under his pillow so he can turn it on when he needs it.

You might want to tell a story when you give a child a night light, such as: "A long, long time ago, when people lived in the forest, there really were wild animals to be afraid of in the dark. Since the people knew the animals would not go near a fire, they kept a fire burning all night so they would be safe and warm. How would you like to have a little light at night, like a pretend fire, so you can sleep safe without worrying about those make-believe wild animals?"

Rearrange the room: If dark shadows in the room seem to be disturbing the child, you might place a heavy curtain over the window, or rearrange the position of the bed so the child is less apt to notice them.

Tell a story: Margaret Wise Brown's book, *Night and Day,* describing a white cat who liked the day and a black cat who liked the night, has helped some preschoolers get over a fear of the dark.

Company: It sometimes solves the problem to have a sibling in the room until the fear subsides. If you have a pet, consider letting the animal sleep in the same room with the child. You might tell the animal, in front of the child, to protect the child from whatever imaginary fears the child has.

Hopping out of bed: A favorite trick of young children is the habit of popping out of bed soon after being put to bed. In most cases parents need to be firm about this and *promptly* return the child to bed. It may be necessary to lower the mattress in the child's crib to prevent climbing out.

Some children refuse to stay in bed because they fear separation from a parent or are worried that one or more parents will go out during the night. These children need positive reassurance that the parents will be home at night. If their fear is realistic, the parents may have to remain at home more at night for a time. Above all, do not tell your child you will be nearby and then slip out of the house once the child is asleep. Other children repeatedly get up to spend time alone with a parent who has been too busy to interact during the day. More time alone before bedtime is the solution here. Still other children get out of bed because they are bored, not sleepy, and are looking for something to do. Allowing quiet play in the bedroom is one solution to this problem. You may find, however, that the best cure for this is to reduce nap time during the day or allow a later bedtime.

Resistance by Older Children. Apart from ages 1 to 2½, sleep resistances peak again in incidence at ages 4 to 6.[6] While the toddler frequently resists sleep for fear of separation from the parents, older school-age children report[5] that they are afraid of going to bed primarily because of noises and shadows in the room, and for fear of being alone. Furthermore, school-age children state that the most common reasons they have trouble falling asleep are: not being tired, noises, worries, and physical pain.[5] Once asleep, the children say that nightmares and physical pain are most likely to wake them up.

The previously mentioned strategies for preventing sleep resistances in younger children are equally applicable with older children. Some specific measures for handling sleep resistances in older children follow.

What to Do

Later bedtime: Putting a 5 or 6 year old to bed at too early an hour—8 o'clock or even 9 in some cases—may cause sleep resistance in the child. So consider if a later bedtime or the elimination of the daytime nap will help resolve the problem. If you do give a later bedtime, make a deal that there will be no stalling or complaining if this is granted. Be sure the hour of retiring is part of a consistent sleep routine which includes a regular hour to wake up. If the child's bedtime is postponed a half-hour observe the child when waking up in the morning over a 2-week interval; if the child is difficult to awaken and obviously needs more sleep, the later bedtime may have to be canceled.

Fear of the dark: As children grow older, their fear of the dark may increase as they develop a greater imagination and awareness of potential dangers. The darkness may become filled with robbers, monsters, or bogeymen. Some children who fear the dark can be comforted and reassured easily and they will quickly fall asleep. Others may require more prolonged comforting from you. Be sure to reassure the child that such fears are normal and that he will soon overcome them. Leaving the door open with a light on in the hall can help dispel a fear of the darkness. Some children prefer to keep a flashlight under their pillow.

Reward a decrease in resistance: Set up a star chart and reward the child for each night that she goes to sleep readily and stays asleep without fuss or strife.

Quiet time: A short period of no physical activity or excitement just before bedtime can help an active child slow down and get ready for sleep. During this time, quiet activities should be scheduled, such as reading a book, listening to stories, or watching a relaxing, nonviolent TV show.

Much later bedtime: Some parents have tried a rather drastic strategy which involves keeping the child up much later than the parents' usual bedtime and then waking the child at the usual time. This procedure is repeated until the child learns that it is unpleasant (and very tiring) to stay up late at night.

Night prowler: Around age 3 some children go to bed easily but get up in the middle of the night and begin activities like wandering around the house, getting food out of the refrigerator, or even going outside to play. These children are awake and aware of what they are doing.

To prevent such a wandering habit from occurring, it seems best to have children sleep in a crib until at least 2½ years of age. You should also keep the crib mattress at its lowest level and the crib side all the way up after about 6 months of age. Thirdly, don't leave large stuffed animals in the crib for the child to climb on. Be sure the child grows up with the firm conviction that he is not permitted to leave his crib or bed without permission until morning.

What can you do if you have a habitual night prowler? Often a positive reward, combined with firmness and a mild punishment for prowling, works well. For example, you might place a star on a conspicuously displayed chart for each night the child stays in bed. Several stars earn the child a treat or special privilege. Whenever the child roams at night, promptly escort him back to bed, while expressing your displeasure and reminding the child of the rule.

Nighttime prowling probably does very little harm if you ensure that the outer doors are securely locked and dangerous or valuable things inside the house are locked up. Tying some bells loosely to the child's door will alert you to the fact that the child is up. Many of these children settle down to sleep quickly after a brief excursion to satisfy their desire for food or play. This period of night prowling often disappears spontaneously when the child is about 4 years of age.

Some parents have put a stop to nighttime prowling by the rather drastic method of tying a crib net (a section of tennis or badminton netting) over the top of the crib or placing extensions on the crib so the child cannot climb out. The child may cry when this is done, but the crying usually disappears by the third night. With older prowlers, parents have placed a gate across the doorway or have used a hotel-type of door chair, out of the child's reach, but with enough slack to see out the door. Typically, the child soon accepts such gadgetry as proof that you mean business about no more prowling.

Sleeping in the parents' bed: Don't let your child develop the habit of coming in and sleeping in your bed at night. Parents deserve privacy, and children need to learn to be independent of their parents at night. Be strict about this from the start, and escort the child back to his room and talk to or comfort the child there. The following cases illustrate what to do if your child has developed this habit.

Case reports. A manipulative 11-year-old boy was brought to the pediatrician by the mother because he couldn't go to sleep at night.[6] He continually got up at night and went into his parents' bedroom complaining about something. The child was observed to domineer the mother in the pediatrician's office. Counseling revealed that the boy was very hostile towards his father but was a "very good boy" for his mother. The parents were instructed to become a closer team, to exclude the boy from some of their activities, and to involve him in more outside activities. The mother withdrew somewhat from the boy and backed the father in needed discipline. The boy was told by both parents to stay away from their bedroom after the lights were out or he would be grounded and not allowed out of the house after school. This warning was followed by rapid improvement in his behavior and mood.

In another case,[7] a 5-year-old boy refused to go to bed, and it often took the parents several hours to get him to sleep. Then he continually got up throughout the night. Once or twice a night, he would climb into his parents' bed and lie down between them. His mother was willing to have him stay but his father would take him back to his own bed. Despite the father's efforts to stop this habit, the boy would be asleep in their bed when the parents woke in the morning. To correct this problem, a counselor advised the parents to meet all requests for refreshments and play *prior* to bedtime. A night light, a glass of milk, and a cookie were placed on his night table. The boy was told he would receive eight tokens (poker chips) if he stayed in bed through the night (excluding trips to the bathroom). These tokens were exchangeable on a daily basis for a variety of pleasurable activities, such as watching TV, visiting friends, or going to a movie, and for edible treats such as cookies, candy, and pies. Once the child was in bed and the door to his room closed, the parents were instructed to ignore all communications from him. If the boy got up, the parents gently ushered him back to bed without discussing or reasoning with him. Whenever the boy got into bed with them, they pretended they were asleep and made it uncomfortable for him by tossing and turning and rolling over so he had little or no room to move his body. Initially, this tactic resulted in the boy's accidentally falling off the bed without the parents giving any signs of having been awakened. If the boy did not return to bed of his own accord, his mother escorted him back in a matter-of-fact way without scolding or reasoning with him. Within 2 weeks the boy did not attempt to sleep with the parents again, and he slept peacefully through the night in his own bed.

In another situation, Anne, age 3, started coming into her parents' bed at 2:30 each night. The parents returned her to her own bed three times the first night but finally gave in. The second night they were so tired they didn't bother to return her to her own bed. For the next week Anne crawled into bed with them at the same time each night.

To encourage the child to sleep in her own bed, the parents initiated the following three-step procedure. First, they bought her a doll to keep her company in bed. Anne was told she could play with the doll the following day only if she stayed in her crib the night before. The child's nap was also eliminated to ensure she was quite tired at night. Finally, whenever Anne came into their bed at night, the parents put her back with a sharp reprimand. Within a week this procedure solved the problem.

Restlessness

Restlessness or physical or mental unrest at night is common in children. It has a variety of manifestations, including tossing and turning, drawing up the legs or waving the arms in a purposeless manner, kicking off the covers, grinding the teeth, head banging, and waking at a light noise. Brief restlessness is exhibited from time to time by all children, but in many cases it is so pronounced or persistent that parents consider it a problem. Macfarlane[2] and her associates found restless at night at age 21 months to be regarded as a problem for 38 percent of boys and 27 percent of girls; the corresponding frequencies for age 11 declined to 22 percent and 16 percent. At age 14, 11 percent of boys still show restlessness at night while it has practically disappeared in girls.

Restless movements seem to be a tension release for children. Most of the children who display nighttime restlessness also exhibit daytime restlessness, overactivity, and excitability. The nighttime fidgetiness seems to be an extension of daytime tendencies. Sometimes the child is overtired and needs 8 to 12 hours more sleep a week than he gets. A child who is engaged in many activities such as work, play, athletics, study, scouts, music lessons, and so on can be encouraged to sleep later on weekends, and to use afterschool naps to prevent fatigue from building up.

Teeth grinding or bruxism is another common sleep disorder in children. A study of children ages 6 to 12[8] revealed that 14 percent of normal children grind their teeth. Occasionally it is done so noisily that parents hear it in another room. Severe grinding can erode teeth enamel, and cause the child to wake up in the morning with tired jaws. One strategy for overcoming bruxism is to teach the child how to become more relaxed and how to relieve tension just before bedtime. In addition to a quiet, nonexciting time just before bed, you might teach the child a relaxation procedure to perform before bed which stresses the tensing and relaxing of the musculature. The manual by Cautela and Groden[9] describes the elements of muscle relaxation and tension reduction.

Head bangings, head rolling, and bed rocking are rhythmic motor habits of children which also appear to release stored up tension. About 15 to 20 percent of children will exhibit these habits, which often appear between 2 and 3 months of age. In most children the habits are transitory, although in about 5 percent of the cases they remain for months or years, usually disappearing between the ages of 2½ and 3 years. Head banging, if not too vigorous or protracted, is not a cause for alarm. It is suggested that the time before bed be spent quietly so the child does not go to bed overexcited. Some parents have reported success with providing a child with a pleasurable substitute to distract the child from head banging. Substitute activities include music, hobby horses, swings, and a metronome set to synchronize with the child's rhythmic movements.

Nightmares

A nightmare is a nocturnal fear or fright reaction occurring during sleep. It is generally precipitated by a frightening dream. Mildly disturbing dreams often begin to be reported by 3 year olds, but as a rule they are not particularly disturbing and the child simply cries out and is easily quieted. By 4½ to 5 years, the bad dreams increase in frequency and severity. The classic nightmare is a more severe fright reaction than the mildly disturbing dream. It involves a sudden loud scream while sleeping which is accompanied by signs of intense anxiety: sweating, dilated pupils, fixed facial expression, and difficulty breathing. The child feels like she is suffocating, as if a heavy weight were on her chest, finds it difficult to breathe, and becomes panicky. The child can usually wake up fairly quickly after a nightmare and can be quieted rather easily. The child of 5 is often able to describe, in vivid detail, the frightening dream content. Sometimes the children are afraid to talk about their nightmare for fear it may come true. Frightening as they are, nightmares are less severe reactions than night terrors which will be described in a later section.

The causes of nightmares may vary, including transient or deep-seated anxieties or conflicts or fear of punishment due to angry feelings towards a parent. Such feelings and concerns may be repressed during waking hours, but they emerge when the child's defenses are lowered during sleep. Usually, disturbing dreams are not the result of parental failure to give enough security or love. However, if these are lacking, the anxieties will be worse. Physical causes, such as febrile illness or gastric indigestion, may also trigger off disturbing dreams.

Almost all children are occasionally troubled with mildly unpleasant dreams during early childhood (ages 1 to 4). Nightmares, however, tend to reach a peak incidence between ages 4 and 6, and even about 28 percent of children ages 6 to 12 still have nightmares.[8] The 5- or 6-year-old girl, in particular, seems prone to be disturbed by nightmares.[11] The content of the nightmare tends to vary in accord with the age of the child. Children ages 1 to 4 typically have unpleasant dreams of wild animals chasing them, while school-age children (ages 5 to 12) most often have had dreams concerning personal difficulties, or strange, bad people threatening them.

Occasional bad dreams or even nightmares need not be the cause of parental alarm, despite the fact that they may signal the presence of at least temporary insecurity in the child. If the disturbing dreams are frequent or recurrent, unusually severe, or quite upsetting to the child, however, they may well reflect a serious emotional disturbance in the child that requires immediate parental, and possibly professional assistance. Measures that parents can take to deal with disturbing dreams follow.

How to Prevent. Nightmares seem less likely to occur if the child avoids overly stressful and overly exciting activities during the day, if parents do not scold or punish the child just before bedtime, and if the period just before bed is a quiet, pleasant time with warm interactions between parents and child. Parents are also advised not to use severe threats to gain obedience. For instance, never threaten to abandon the child if she misbehaves, or say that the bogey-man will get her if she is bad. Help the child feel safe and loved during the day since this forms the basis for resting comfortably at night. Be sure the child is cared for at times by caretakers other than parents so the child does not become so dependent on you that her dreams are disturbed by fears for your safety.

What to Do

Parental support. The most immediate need for a child who has had a nightmare is for parental support. While remaining calm and confident yourself, go quickly to the child and hold and cuddle her. Turn on the light to show the familiar room and to help the child awaken fully. Talk soothingly and reassuringly. Explain that she had a bad dream, that dreams are not real, and that they are a kind of make-believe during sleep. Let the child know that everyone has scary dreams at times but that dreams can't hurt us if we know they are only make-believe. (You may have to repeat this discussion the following day when the child is fully awake.) Reassure the child that you are nearby and will not let anything bad happen to her. The younger child may need considerable comforting until able to go back to sleep.

Sometimes the child wants to have a small light left on in the room or in the hall, or to have the door left open. It seems wise to grant such requests. It is usually best, however, to discourage the child's coming into the parents' room for the rest of the night; stay with the child in her own room until she is ready to fall asleep again. If you take the child to your room, she is likely to want to do it every time. If the child remains fearful, aspirin has a mild sedative effect.

Investigate possible causes. Seek to uncover the cause of *recurrent* nighttime fears. Is the child under any tension that can be avoided, such as school problems or difficulties with peers or siblings? If so, try to help the child think of solutions to the problem. Be sure you are not placing too many demands on the child, or making the child overdependent on you. Are there any marital conflicts that the child may be aware of? Does the child watch violent TV shows or movies prior to experiencing the nightmares?

The content of the nightmare may give you a clue to the underlying causes of the dream. If a parent suffers a violent death in the dream, consider if that parent has been overly strict with the child or if hostilities due to Oedipal feelings may be present. You may want to help the child connect the scary dream with the actual events which may have stimulated the dream. For example, if you suspect that a visit to a doctor precipitated a bad dream, you should encourage the child to talk about it. To begin a discussion you might speculate, "Could it be that your going to the doctor yesterday upset you a lot and maybe led to your having a scary dream last night?" A good talk with you and your expression of concern may help alleviate any such fear. You can also encourage the child to "act out" the bottled up fear: You and the child might, for example, play "doctor" wherein the child plays the role of the doctor who gives the feared shot. In this way the child should feel more in control of things and less fearful.

Confronting scary dreams. It is often wise to help the child face up to and overcome the frightening object in his dreams. This reduces the fear by providing a sense of mastery and self-control. For instance, you might have the child draw a picture of the black spider which attacked him in the nightmare. When the child completes the drawing, encourage the child to attack the picture, yell at it, pound it with his fists, and finally rip it up and destroy the spider. You might also play the role of the spider and have the child jump on you and beat on you until you run away in mock fear. The child might want to play the role of the spider first while you model how to fearlessly attack it.

In a similar vein, parents might want to follow the practice of the Senoi tribe in Malaysia[13] who teach their children that when they have a scary dream they should always picture themselves in the dream advancing and attacking in the teeth of danger. In the dream the child should feel free to call for assistance from his fellow tribe members, when necessary, but should fight on by himself until help arrives. The Senoi feel that dream characters and events are bad only as long as one is afraid and retreats from them. They will continue to seem bad and fearful as long as one refuses to come to grips and master them. You can teach your children to reshape their dreams to have better endings by imagining themselves actively and courageously overcoming the previously feared objects or events. In this way the dream can help children work through problems and stresses experienced during the day.

Case Report. John, an 11-year-old boy, had been experiencing nightmares for a year and a half.[14] He would awaken in a panic and come to his parents' bed. Most nights he insisted on sleeping with his room light on. Since the boy was in therapy at the time for other difficulties, his therapist helped the boy overcome the nightmares by the techniques of "supportive confrontation." While holding the boy on his knees, the therapist asked him to close his eyes and imagine that the dream monster was present in the room. The therapist added that he was right there and would protect the boy and help him get rid of the monster. When the boy reported he saw the monster, the therapist held the boy firmly, pounded loudly on the desk, and shouted several times, "Get out of here, you lousy monster, leave my friend John alone!" This incantation and pounding was repeated by the therapist who added, "Get away and stay away— don't you ever come back or I'm going to get you! You leave my friend John alone!" Although the boy stated that the monster was no longer present, the therapist repeated this procedure once more, alternately demanding, "Get away and leave me alone!'' The therapist then asked the boy to join him in this process, and the boy was soon actively pounding and shouting also. The procedure was repeated a final time with the room completely darkened. The child was then given explicit directions to "chase" the monster with this procedure whenever he saw the creature. The boy was able to successfully use this technique during the week, although the monster did not go away immediately. After the boy practiced the procedure with the therapist again during the next week, the nightmare problem greatly diminished thereafter.

Arousal Disorders

As previously mentioned, studies of sleepwalking, sleep talking, night terrors, and bedwetting disclose that these sleep disturbances occur during sudden, intense arousal from the deep sleep stages and are not related to normal dream activity. Rather than being caused by "bad dreams," these disorders seem to primarily be the result of a delayed central nervous system development which may be genetic in origin. When the problems continue into late childhood, one often finds external stress or anxieties contributing to the problem. The various disorders of arousal often appear in the same person at different times, and there is often a family history of such disorders.[3] They are similar in that they all have a sudden onset at which time the child is not responsive to the environment. Children have no memory of these disturbances the following morning. One researcher[15] observed that the type of arousal disorder a child exhibits is related to the child's proclivity for imagery: Sleepwalkers were found to be more prone to motor activities such as athletics, while children with night terrors were prone to visual imagery.

Sleepwalking. Sleepwalking or somnambulism usually occurs 1 to 3 hours after the child falls asleep. Low levels of awareness and responsiveness to the environment are evident in the sleepwalker who is difficult to arouse. Although the child has an unsteady gait and may stumble, he is able to avoid objects and usually not injure himself. The eyes are glassy but open. The child may walk around his room, other parts of the house, or outdoors. The following morning the child remembers little or nothing of these actions which last from a few minutes to a half hour. Considerable parental concern about this disturbance is typical, but the children themselves usually show little concern. The walking generally ends with the child returning on his own to bed to sleep.

Despite popular opinion the sleepwalker is usually not acting out a dream. Rather, there is increasing evidence that sleepwalking is associated with a maturational delay in the central nervous system. One can usually induce sleepwalking in a child by standing her on her feet while the child is in a deep sleep state (about an hour or 2 after falling asleep). About 10 to 15 percent of all people exhibit sleepwalking at some time in their lives prior to adolescence. Most often, child somnambulists show a decrease in incidents as they grow older.

What to do. The child who is found sleepwalking should be led back to bed. By tying bells to the child's bedroom door, you will be alerted to the sleepwalking incident. With a highly suggestible child, you might keep giving a direct suggestion that he will fully awaken as soon as he feels his feet touch the floor at night (arousal cue). Some parents have confined the sleepwalking to the bedroom by securely fashioning a screen door or unscalable gate to the child's bedroom door. If nightmares usually precede the sleepwalking, you can interrupt this chain of events by fully awakening the child (cold water on the face and back of the neck) when you hear the child moaning and tossing in her sleep.

In cases of severe sleepwalking (one to four times a week over an extended period), medication (Imipramine, 10 to 50 mg. at bedtime) has been used successfully.[17]

Sleep Talking. Somniloquy or talking in sleep is experienced by most children at one time or another. It may be limited to a few mumbled words or may include clearly recognizable phrases reflecting thoughts and activities of the previous day. The words may indicate preoccupation with an anxiety provoking situation, such as failing a subject in school. During an illness when fever is present, sleep talking and other sleep disturbances often occur.

By listening to the sleep talking, you may be able to find out what is troubling the child so that you can have a good talk about the topic the following day. Some children may just be overexcited before bed which carries over, so try to make the time just before bed as quiet and relaxing as possible and see if this reduces the talking or crying out in sleep.

Night Terrors. Pavor nocturnus or night terror refers to severe panic reactions accompanied by frantic motor activity and sleep talking in a child arousing from deep sleep. In a night terror there is more extreme anxiety and loss of reality than in a nightmare. Typically the child suddenly sits upright in bed and screams. He appears to be hallucinating or staring wide-eyed at an imaginary object, breathes heavily, often perspires, and is in obvious distress. The frightening content of the night terror does not build up gradually in a dream but occurs instantaneously.[18] The child is not fully awake, does not recognize people, and is disoriented in time and space. He will, however, reply to questions and gradually responds to soothing and reassurance. In the morning he has no recollection of this nocturnal event. The attacks tend to resemble each other and to show a periodicity.[17]

Young children with night terrors tend to be highstrung, physically active youngsters who go to bed exhausted and tense. The terrors usually occur during the first few hours of sleep. Though seen in older children and adults, night terrors are most common in the preschool-age group.

How to prevent. The hour before bedtime should be a quiet one, avoiding TV, exciting stories, and roughhousing. A warm bath before bed can also help. Be sure no sudden loud noises disturb the child's sleep since these can trigger an attack.

If a preschool child is very active physically and then goes to bed exhausted, give a nap (or rest period) in the afternoon on a regular basis.

What to do

Parental support: Hold the child comfortingly, help orient her to reality, and give reassurance. Tell who you are, where the child is, and that everything is all right. "It's O.K. honey. Mommy is here. You just got frightened in your sleep but you're safe in your bed. Everything is going to be fine. Mommy won't let anything bad happen to you."

Stay with the child until the episode is over (a few minutes to a half-hour). A restful sleep usually occurs thereafter.

Medication: The drugs Imipramine[16] and Diazipam[3] have been used successfully to stop night-terror attacks from occurring.

Adenoids: One study[19] found that adenoidectomy in children seems to free the air passages and encourage brain oxygenation. Of 23 children operated on, 22 recovered from the night terrors immediately after the operation.

Play release: Children often experience relief from fears when they are given the opportunity to give expression to these anxieties in the medium of play.[20] Help the child work through the nighttime fears by encouraging the child to confront the feared objects in dramatic or puppet play and to overcome the scary creatures or things by outwitting them, using magic, or superfriends to help, or calling on family or friends for assistance after fighting courageously by oneself until help arrives.

Increased Sleep

A subtle, rare, and disturbing problem in children is oversleeping. Oversleeping refers to sleeping much more than the individual's usual sleep patterns. The reasons for increased sleep are many, and the remedies will depend on the basic cause of the disorder.

Reasons Why

Psychological. Psychologically, sleep can sometimes be a retreat from the stresses of living. We have all experienced the kinds of stresses which we are tempted to avoid by remaining peacefully asleep. So if you observe a sudden, excessively long sleep period by your child, try to talk to the child and encourage her to express (and effectively solve) any underlying problem or psychic trauma.

Excessive sleepiness or hypersomnia can also result from boredom. A small number of dull, disinterested children will indulge in much daytime sleep as a means of passing the time. The solution for boredom is to involve the child in more daytime activities such as scouts, sports, and hobbies.

For some children, oversleep may signal a depressed mood. The child wishes to withdraw from a world which has given him so much pain, and his body cooperates through sleep—lots of sleep. Here again you need to uncover the reason for the depressed feeling and give the child hope, reassurance, and effective ways to solve the problem.

Physical. In some instances, the cause of increased sleep will be physical in nature.

Physical exhaustion: Your child may be sleeping a great deal because of an exhausted, run-down physical state. This may result from too much activity during the day and/or too little sleep at night. The remedy is to reduce the child's schedule of daytime activities and to ensure that she retires at a set, reasonable time each night. Occasionally a teenager will oversleep when withdrawing from a period of taking amphetamines or "uppers" to stay awake during an examination period. Two or three days of extended sleep will usually cure this problem. However, if the child has consumed high doses of amphetamines for an extended period, serious depression may occur or withdrawal which may require medical treatment with antidepressant drugs.

Narcolepsy: Narcolepsy is a physical disorder characterized by *recurrent* episodes of drowsiness and sleep during the daytime. The child is not lazy or emotionally disturbed but has an irresistible feeling of drowsiness followed by sleep occurring from a few to many times a day. Many people afflicted do not actually fall asleep but fight a day-long battle against drowsiness. In about two-thirds of the adult cases, cataplexy is also present (the sudden loss of muscle tone resulting in falling to the ground while consciousness is maintained). Some adults with narcolepsy also have sleep paralysis (the sudden awareness while falling asleep that one cannot move or cry out) and hypnagogic hallucinations (vivid visual or auditory imagery occurring at sleep onset). Early diagnosis of this disorder is important since the symptoms can be relieved by your physician with stimulant drugs (*i.e.*, methylphenidate). The cause of this disorder seems to be genetic, at least in part, since it has a higher familial incidence.[21] Since the early signs of narcolepsy are often present in childhood and adolescence (but go unnoticed), it is important to arrange a medical exam for a child who exhibits recurring episodes of daytime drowsiness or fatigue such as falling asleep in the classroom, while riding in automobiles, or while watching TV.

Other physical disorders: Excessive sleep is associated with hypothroidism, viral encephalitis, hypoglycemia, sleep apnea hypersomnia, and other diseases. A thorough medical exam is needed to make a differential diagnosis in these cases.

Insomnia

Insomnia is the inability to obtain adequate sleep, and it may take any or all of three forms: difficulty in falling asleep, difficulty remaining asleep, and premature final morning awakening. What constitutes adequate sleep for a child will vary, of course, depending on the child's age and individual requirements. The average amount of sleep required at different ages declines from 13 hours each night at age 2, to 11 hours at ages 6–8 years, 10 hours at ages 10–12, and 8 or 9 hours from 16 to 18 years. Most children go to bed between 7–9 P.M. (only 10 percent go to bed later). As a general rule, an individual has had enough sleep if she has had no daytime sleepiness, irritability, fatigue, or impaired performance. The child who is healthy, happy, and rested is probably getting enough sleep.

Insomnia is not a rare disorder in childhood, especially among teen-agers. A recent survey[22] of high school students found that 12 percent complained of chronic and severe sleep difficulties, while 37 percent reported occasional and mild sleep disturbances. These figures are similar to those reported by other surveys of adolescents and young adults. With older adults, between 15 and 30 percent complain of chronic insomnia.

Reasons Why. When a child complains of insomnia and associated daytime sleepiness, one should first rule out any physical disorders which may be causing the problem. In addition, parents need to be sure that the child is not taking drugs of any sort, and that the problem is not due to diseases which produce periods of oversleeping or sleep apnea (temporary cessation of breathing). Young children may resist going to sleep because of a specific trauma, such as anxiety about having been put to sleep for a tonsillectomy, or the death of a loved one who has "gone to sleep." Similarly, most cases of insomnia in adolescence are not due to physiological causes but to psychological factors such as worry or tension because of an inability to cope with personal, family, or school problems.[22] These adolescents also tend to experience low self-esteem, mild depression, and daytime fatigue. Adult insomniacs show these same tendencies to be anxious, obsessive, and to lack self-esteem. Some children with unusually high daytime activity levels have difficulty going to sleep at night because it is hard for them to "rev down" their motors.

How to Prevent

Schedule. Be sure your child maintains a regular sleep schedule which means going to bed at the same time each night and getting up at the same time each morning (use an alarm clock). The schedule for weekdays should be the same, or closely approximate the schedule for weekends in order to preserve the child's circadian rhythm. Naps by older children during the day should be avoided.

Self-calming routine. The hour before bedtime should involve quiet, relaxing activities such as reading or watching TV. Do not let your child get overly stimulated by rough-and-tumble play or scary movies. A hot bath just before bed can help relax the child.

Moderate eating. Eating should be moderate and sensible. Avoid heavy meals late at night. One should also avoid caffeinated foods 5 to 7 hours before bed, such as coffee, cola, chocolate, or cocoa. Avoid alcohol—a drink before bed may help you get to sleep but may cause restlessness later in the night. A light snack before bed may aid sleep, especially if it is rich in L-tryptophan—a natural and essential amino acid which apparently has sleep-inducing properties. Common foods high in L-tryptophan are: milk (cold or hot), beans, cheese, chicken, eggs, hamburger, peanut butter, peanuts, pork chops, steak, and tuna.

Exercise. Encourage your child to get plenty of exercise during the day to ensure that a mild degree of physical exhaustion is present at bedtime. Regular and vigorous exercise, like playing tennis, tends to induce longer sleep and more sleep in the deeper stages.

Sleep environment. When a child's bedroom is kept too warm and with no fresh air, sleep tends to be of poor quality as well as quantity. Keep the bedroom cool and use a humidifier so the child's throat does not become dry. A noisy, overcrowded sleeping area is also undesirable. Noise from a sibling's record player or a loud TV can prevent a child from sleeping soundly. Try to prevent or screen out extraneous noise if at all possible.

Bed restriction. Do not let the child use the bed for reading, watching TV, or relaxing. The child should only use the bed for *sleeping*.

What To Do

Getting up. Advise your child to lie down to sleep only when sleepy. If she doesn't nod off in 15–20 minutes, she should get out of bed and do something else. Monotonous physical activity such as push-ups or washing the kitchen floor might promote sleep. Reading a dull book or watching a TV talk show may also help induce sleep.

Mental relaxation. A child cannot worry or think anxiety-arousing thoughts in bed if he is counting sheep or imagining pleasant scenes. Teach your child to attend to mental or pleasant images so as to relax his mind after going to bed. First the child should select a calm, relaxing image such as a beach scene, a skiing scene, or a scene from a summer vacation.

If the child has difficulty visualizing a pleasant scene, you might have to guide his fantasy by saying in a soft, monotonous tone of voice something like:

> Now Jim, when you go to bed at night you may want to relax by turning on that make-believe TV set in your mind. As you watch behind your closed eyes, the screen will brighten and soon you will be able to see your favorite TV show. As you let your body go loose, the picture will get clearer and clearer. You can watch your favorite cartoon, if you like, or you might just imagine you are sailing on the boat with your father. You can smell the fresh

sea air and feel the warm sun shining down on your body. The air smells so good and the sun feels so warm as you go drifting along in the boat. Pretty soon you will feel yourself drift off into a nice deep, pleasant sleep. Your body feels so warm, comfortable, and loose. You feel so drowsy, so contented, so good.

You might play this "pretend game" several times during the day with your child until he can clearly picture the scene in his mind and feel relaxed. Then you would repeat the above verbalization just after the child goes to bed at night to help him go to sleep. Be sure to talk in a soft, slow, almost hypnotic tone of voice.

Another form of the guided fantasy technique is to have your child listen to a tape-recorded story created from the child's favorite fantasy characters and everyday likes and dislikes. You play the tape as a bedtime story. The child is encouraged to feel that she has a controlling influence in putting a favorite figure to sleep within the story and is gently led to accept sleep by choice.[31]

Muscle relaxation. Teach your child how to release tension from muscles by tensing and relaxing specific muscle groups in a systematic manner.[23] Have the child concentrate on a single muscle group such as the arm. Ask him to flex his biceps and make a muscle like "Popeye the Sailor," hold it for a few seconds, and then let go of the tension by relaxing and pretending that the arm is a "wet noodle." Then ask the child to tense and relax his legs, his stomach muscles, his mouth and forehead muscles, and his shoulders. An older adolescent might benefit from biofeedback training in which an electromyogram (EMG) machine gives specific information as to muscle tension. Also, show him how to take a deep breath, hold it a few seconds, and then let it all the way out. Ask him to breathe in and out in a monotonous way while imagining a pleasant scene. Or while exhaling, the child might say quietly, "Ommmmm" or "Mmmmmm," and at the same time empty his mind of mental pictures.

If the child has difficulty relaxing his muscles, you might gently massage his forehead and rub his shoulder muscles to release tension at bedtime.

Problem-solving skills. Adolescents experiencing severe insomnia over an extended period may need to learn how to cope better with personal problems.

Problem-solving: Skills for coping with personal problems can be learned by studying a guidebook.[24] The problem-solving procedure involves identifying a personal problem, specifying the controlling conditions, generating and evaluating possible solutions, selecting one, putting it into practice, and evaluating its efficacy. For example, an adolescent identified worry about homework as often interfering with her sleep.[26] Using the problem-solving strategy, she pinpointed the source of the worry (procrastination) and developed a plan to change her behavior (a homework schedule and contract with her mother to help her carry it through).

Irrational beliefs: Sometimes an adolescent needs to change faulty beliefs about sleep or about chronic sources of worry. The faulty belief must be pinpointed (*e.g.*, I must achieve all A's in courses), and its self-defeating, illogical nature analyzed. Self-study guides for undermining erroneous beliefs and developing more adaptive ones are available.[27, 28]

Paradoxical strategy. Instead of training oneself to relax in bed, the opposite approach can be as effective. Instruct the child to keep her eyes wide open and fight going to sleep. She should stare intensely at a spot on the ceiling for as long as she can. This paradoxical procedure has made many children sleepy rather than keeping them awake.

Positive thinking. Counter worries and negative thoughts by suggesting that your child think of 5–10 nice things about himself and to repeat this list softly to himself a number of times.

Change bedtime. Your child should select a bedtime when she can fall asleep most naturally, one best suited to her individual characteristics and sleep requirements. Some adolescents are "late-night" people and/or function quite well on just 5 hours of sleep.

Don't reinforce. Do not reinforce insomnia by allowing your child to come to talk with you or sleep in your room. Be firm if this happens, and every time your child comes into your room when she should be in bed, tell her to go back to her room and return the child physically if necessary. Carry out this procedure with a minimum of talking to the child.

To illustrate, a 17-year-old boy would repeatedly enter his mother's bedroom prior to bedtime and talk about his worries.[32] Visiting his mother's bedroom occurred every night and ranged from 4 to 20 times an hour. If the boy was not allowed to talk with his mother, he had difficulty falling asleep; sleep was typically delayed about 3 hours. With professional advice the mother no longer would listen to his worries prior to bedtime in her bedroom. Rather, she provided him with a special time earlier in the evening to talk about his worries with her in their living room. If the boy visited her bedroom in an evening, the following evening's special time was canceled. This procedure quickly brought the insomnia under control.

Reassurance. Tell your child that a lot of children have difficulty falling asleep at times. Tension due to worrying about some problem is usually the cause, and this tension, if it persists, can be controlled by various relaxation or problem-solving procedures. Advise the child not to worry about not getting enough sleep since she's probably getting more rest than she realizes. It is important to let the child know that there is no known physical harm that comes from poor sleeping. Worry over lack of sleep only compounds the problem.

Medication. Sleep-producing drugs such as Flurazepam should be used only as the last resort, after other alternatives have been exhausted. Since a large number of purported insomniacs really do sleep surprisingly well, no chronic medication for insomnia should be prescribed without an all-night recording of actual sleep time at a sleep laboratory. When used regularly for over a 2-week period, most sleep medications lose their effectiveness and are prone to result in both psychological and physiological dependence.

When a drug is necessary, sleep laboratory studies indicate that Flurazepam (15 to 30 mg.) at bedtime is effective in both inducing and maintaining sleep in young adult insomniacs.[30]

Case Report. Susan, 11 years old, was constantly fatigued at school because of a long standing difficulty in falling asleep.[33] Although she went to bed at 9 P.M., it took her about 2 hours to fall asleep. Apart from ruminating about various events of the previous day, Susan's sensitivity to external sounds interfered with her efforts to fall asleep.

A professional therapist helped her with this problem by first giving her instructions for relaxation as she was lying in bed. The relaxation procedure consisted of the alternate tensing and relaxing of various muscle groups. Susan responded well to the relaxation, and fell asleep 1 hour afterwards. A 30-minute tape recording was made of the relaxation instructions which Susan used by herself for the next 2 weeks. During this time, she fell asleep either halfway through or immediately after the tape was completed. A new tape was made eliminating the tension phase and giving instructions for only muscle relaxation. After 1 week she was provided with a 15-minute version of this tape, and after another 2-week interval, with a final recording. This tape was only 5 minutes in duration, consisting of instructions for self-relaxation. After 1 week she did not need this tape and simply reminded herself on going to bed to shut out all external noises and ruminations, and concentrate only on self-relaxation. She was now able to fall asleep almost immediately.

Books for Parents about Insomnia

Rubinstein, H.: *Insomniacs of the World, Goodnight.* Random House, New York (1974).

Colligan, D.: *Great Insomnia.* Watts (1978).

Books for Children about Sleep Disorders

Beckman, K.: *Lisa Cannot Sleep.* Franklin Watts (1969).

Book about counteracting bedtime fears.

Mayer, Mercer: *There's a Nightmare in my Closet.* Dial Press (1968). Ages 3–7.

A little boy learns to overcome his fear of the dark and of the nightmares hovering there.

References

1. Sperling, M.: "Etiology and treatment of sleep disturbances in children." *Psychoanalytic Quarterly* 24: (1955), pp. 358–368.
2. Macfarlane, J.W. *et al.*: "A developmental study of the behavior problems of normal children between twenty-one months and fourteen years." University of California Press, Berkeley (1954).
3. Anders, T.F. and Weinstein, P.: "Sleep and its disorders in infants and children: A review." *Pediatrics* 50: (1972), pp. 312–323.
4. Ames, L.B.: "Sleep and dreams in childhood." In *Problems of Sleep and Dreams in Children*. E. Hams, ed. MacMillan, New York (1964).
5. Csikszentmikalyi, M. and Graef, R.: "Socialization into sleep: Exploratory findings," *Merrill-Palmer Quarterly* 21:(1975), pp. 3–18.
6. Austin, G.: *The Parents' Guide to Child Raising*. Prentice-Hall, Englewood Cliffs, NJ (1978).
7. Ayllon, T. *et al.*: "Behavioral treatment of childhood neurosis." *Psychiatry* 40: (1977), pp. 315–322.
8. Lapouse, R. and Monk, M.: "Fears and worries in a representative sample of children." *American Journal of Orthopsychiatry* 29: (1959), pp. 803–818.
9. Cautela, J.R. and Groden, J.: *Relaxation: A comprehensive Manual for Adults, Older Children, Younger Children, and Children with Special Problems*. Arthur P. Little, Cambridge, MA (1978).
10. Kessler, J.W.: *Psychopathology of Childhood*. Prentice Hall, Englewood Cliffs, NJ (1966).
11. Ilg, F.L. and Ames, L.B.: *Child Behavior*. Harper and Row, New York (1955).
12. Foster, J.C. and Anderson, J.E.: "Unpleasant dreams in childhood." *Child Development* 7: (1936), pp. 77–84.
13. Stewart, K.: "Dream theory in Malaysia." In *Altered States of Consciousness*. C. Tart, ed. Wiley, New York (1969), Chapter 9.
14. Handler, L.: "The amelioration of nightmares in children."

Psychotherapy: Theory Research & Practice 9: (1968), pp. 54–56.

15. Anthony, E.J.: "An experimental approach to the psychopathology of childhood: Sleep disturbances." *British Journal of Medical Psychology* 32: (1959), pp. 19–37.

16. Pesikoff, R.B. and Davis, P.C.: "Treatment of Pavor Nocturnus and somnambulism in children." *American Journal of Psychiatry* 128:: (1971), pp. 778–781.

17. Anthony, E.J.: "An experimental approach to the psychopathology of childhood: Sleep." *British Journal of Medical Psychology* 32: (1959), pp. 19–37.

18. Fisher, C. *et al.*: "A psychophysiological study of nightmares and night terrors." *Journal of Nervous and Mental Disease* 158: (1974), pp. 174–188.

19. Agrell, I. and Ahelsson, A.: "The relationship between pavor nocturnus and adenoids." *Acta Paedopsychiatrica* 39: (1972), pp. 46–53.

20. Irwin, E.C. and Shapiro, M.I.: "Puppetry as a diagnostic and therapeutic technique." *Psychiatry and Art* 4: (1975), pp. 86–94.

21. Yoss, R.E. and Daly, D.D.: "Narcolepsy in children." *Pediatrics* 25: (1960), pp. 1025–1033.

22. Price, V.A.: "The prevalence and correlates of poor sleep among adolescents." *American Journal of Diseases of Children* (1979), in press.

23. Bernstein, D.A. and Borkovic, I.D.: *Progressive Relaxation Training.* Research Press, Champaign, IL (1973).

24. Coates, T.J. and Thoresen, C.E.: *How to Sleep Better: A Non-drug Program for Overcoming Insomnia.* Prentice-Hall, Englewood Cliffs, NJ (1977).

25. Bootzin, R.R.: *Behavioral Treatment of Insomnia: A Clinician's Guide.* Biomonitoring Application, New York (1976).

26. Kirmil-Gray *et al.*: *Treating Insomnia in Adolescents. Pediatrics* (1979).

27. Meichenbaum, D.: *Cognitive Behavior Modification.* Plenum, New York (1977).

28. Goodman, D.S.:*Emotional Well-being Through Rational Behavior Training.* Charles C. Thomas, Springfield, IL (1978).

29. Rosen, G.: *Relaxation.* Prentice-Hall, Englewood Cliffs, NJ (1976).

30. Kales, A. and Kales, J.D.: "Sleep disorders." *New England Journal of Medicine* 290: (1974), pp. 487–499.

31. Porter, J.: "Guided fantasy as a treatment for childhood in-

somnia." *Australian and New Zealand Journal of Psychiatry* 9: (1965), pp. 169–172.

32. Yen, S.: "Extinction of inappropriate sleeping behavior: Multiple assessment." *Psychological Reports* 30: (1972), pp. 375–378.

33. Weil, G. and Goldfried, M.: "Treatment of insomnia in an eleven-year-old child through self-relaxation." *Behavior Therapy* 4 (1973), pp. 282–284.

EATING PROBLEMS

The eating problem most commonly encountered is consumption of the amount and type of food leading to obesity. Eating too little is less common, but still a serious problem, the extreme form of which is self-starvation, called anorexia. More usual are special food likes and dislikes, fussiness, and dawdling (the section on "Poor Use of Time" also covers dawdling).

Obesity

Obesity is the presence of excess bodily fat. One straightforward definition is that children who look fat are fat. Physicians use charts with average weights for age, sex, and height. According to this approach, obesity is defined as being 20 percent or more above the average weight. Almost one-third of children under 18 years are considered overweight. Most striking is the fact that 60 to 85 percent of fat children remain fat throughout their lives. And the longer children remain fat, the more probable it is that they will be fat adults. Also striking is that fatness runs in families. When neither parent is obese, there is only a 7 percent chance of a child becoming an obese adult. With one obese parent, there is a 40 to 50 percent chance of becoming an obese adult. With two obese parents, there is an 80 percent chance of becoming an obese adult.[1] There are compelling reasons why obesity must be *prevented*, rather than coped with by lifelong dieting. In general, there are fairly good short-term results with dieting, counseling, exercise programs, and behavior therapy, but significant and maintained weight loss is still disappointingly rare. Most people gain their weight back, and their "crash diets" are often harmful to their body systems.

Parental habits directly influence the weight of children. Parents are most often quite similar in fatness or leanness due to their similar attitudes towards eating, calorie intake, and calorie expenditure.

It is important to note that boys and girls differ in their weight patterns.[2] Boys during years 1 through 10 are leaner. At adolescence, girls normally gain more fat while boys lose fat. Therefore, it is even more important for girls not to be obese since they do not "naturally" lose their baby fat at adolescence. By 17 years, children of obese parents are *three times* as fat as children of lean parents. With three siblings, if one is fat, there is an 80 percent chance of at least one other sibling being obese. The implications are clear. Children with two lean parents are the leanest. If either parent is fat, the children are likely to be fat. And if both parents are obese, the children have the most body fat. Additionally, socioeconomic status affects the pattern of overweight development. Both boys and girls who come from poor families are leaner than affluent children. However, poor females become fatter by middle adolescence, while affluent girls become leaner.

Many people believe that obesity is inherited, that is, that obesity is genetically determined. Therefore, they reason that obese children and adults should relax and enjoy it. The evidence clearly refutes this idea. It is very rare that children are obese because of genetic or glandular problems. Being overweight is caused by excessive calorie intake and/or insufficient activity. The effects of caloric intake are clear—certain calories are stored (fats and carbohydrates), and other forms of calories are not stored (proteins). By increasing protein intake and decreasing fats and carbohydrates, a more "balanced diet" results, and weight will not be gained. Drugs have side effects, result in temporary weight loss, and are not recommended for children. Along with a regular medical evaluation, a thyroid and glucose tolerance test can be used to demonstrate that there are no organic causes of obesity.

By 1 year, the obese pattern may be set. Certainly by 3 years of age, many children have specific food likes and dislikes (especially for vegetables). Lifetime eating habits are heavily influenced by these early childhood experiences. Fat parents prefer a norm of fatness. Having a thin child often makes them feel uncomfortable. Being fed is the earliest satisfaction, while being hungry is the earliest frustration. These basic feelings occur in a continuing interaction within the feeding person. However, adults very frequently underestimate a child's self-regulation skills. From a very early age, children are quite good at how much and what to eat. Strikingly, 58 percent of children resent their parents forcing them to eat food they don't like.

Obesity is clearly a negative condition in our society. Obese children are often rejected by peers, are clumsy and poor athletes, and have more diseases, bone problems, and accidents. They overeat, are underactive, have a poor body image, and are very influenced by external eating cues (rather than internal hunger sensations). Similarly, obese adults are less healthy, have more heart disease and accidents, and die earlier than nonobese people. Additionally, there is considerable prejudice against fat people, who statistically earn less money. Being overweight is more frequent with increasing age, lower socioeconomic status, and in females. Approximately half of the American adult population who suffer from ordinary obesity, have had it since childhood.

Eating Too Little

The most severe problem is eating so little as to approach (and sometimes die of) starvation. This extreme form called anorexia nervosa, will be briefly described here to alert parents to the need for *immediate* professional help if this condition develops. Anorexia[3] is a fanatic desire to be thin, with females, at or just past puberty, far outnumbering males in incidence of occurrence. At least a 20 percent weight loss is necessary for a child to be called anorectic. Characteristic features of anorexia are "the pursuit of thinness as an indication of independence, delusional denial of thinness, hyperactivity, preoccupation with food, and perfectionistic attitude."

There are few statistics available regarding children who are too thin, dawdle, or who are very finicky eaters. Except for the rare cases of malnutrition, these problems are not injurious but are sources of concern or aggravation to parents. Lean parents usually serve as models and have lean children. Problem undereating develops as a *reaction* to the environment and can occur with obese, average, or lean parents.

Pica

We will very briefly discuss the eating of unusual objects (pica) in order to alert parents to this specific eating problem. Pica occurs primarily between the ages of 1 and 3 years. Children may eat clay, dirt, paint, plaster, etc. Causes include stress, inadequate mothering, nutritional deficiencies, and hookworm anemia. Parents are often immature and impulsive. Treatment includes moving into new housing, reducing stress, and increasing nurturance. Medical evaluation and follow-up are essential, especially because of lead (and other metal) poisoning.

Nutritional Goals

After 1 year, (the age in years $\times$ 100 + 1000) = required calories. Ideal calorie consumption should be 8 to 15 percent protein, 35 to 45 percent fat, and 35 to 45 percent carbohydrates, plus daily vitamins. For growing teen-agers, a minimum of 1200 calories is necessary. Children should (1) eat nutritional foods, (2) enjoy eating, (3) eat in a socially acceptable manner, and (4) eat a variety of foods. Foods should include fish, meat, eggs, milk, green and yellow vegetables, raw leafy vegetables, whole grain cereals, citrus fruits, and a vitamin D source. Eating problems are prevented by the very early training of appropriate food consumption and adequate physical activity.

Obesity

Reasons Why

Overeating as a source of psychological satisfaction. Eating should be enjoyed and should provide a balanced nutritional intake for a healthy and well-functioning body. Instead, many children overeat considerably because it causes a good psychological feeling. Infants put food or objects in their mouth as a direct way of obtaining satisfaction from sucking and a full feeling. Symbolically, this early comfort is achieved by oral satisfaction throughout childhood (and often throughout life). When life is unrewarding or upsetting, the individual consumes food to "fill an empty feeling." Eating a lot makes up for a feeling of being deprived. A feeling of consolation through food results. Obesity becomes a vicious cycle: Eating may provide momentary comfort, but obesity leads to a negative self-image and to being teased or seen as unattractive and unappealing by others, to feelings of being lonely or miserable, and thus to eating more. Eating as a source of comfort becomes a substitute for gratification from real life. Food often becomes a symbol of love, and commercial television messages often reinforce this idea.

Some children want to show that they are almost adults. Eating cake, popcorn, and sodas becomes a sign of being more grown up and therefore the child feels psychologically more adequate. Feeling more adequate is also achieved by behaving as part of a peer group. Eating junk foods and snacking frequently becomes a symbol of being accepted by others. Another adult or powerful feeling is the use of overeating as a weapon. Parents, and others, can be beaten in a power struggle since the child wins by eating too much and being obese. Children retaliate to parental anger and threats concerning weight by eating more. Layers of fat and bigness can be a sign to others that the individual is big, important, and a presence to be recognized. These reasons are all clear reflections of the lack of obtaining recognition and a good self-concept through means other than food consumption.

Obesity as a defense. Obesity may be a means of protecting oneself from any perceived danger. Interacting with others may be frightening or anxiety provoking, and obesity becomes a means of warding off interaction. Being fat becomes an excuse for not relating well since "nobody likes me and they tease me for being fat." Obesity becomes a focus which removes the spotlight from real personality problems. Similarly, many teen-agers (particularly girls) can avoid the anxiety over sexual feelings and behavior by being obese and unattractive sexually to others.

Feelings of boredom or loneliness can be dealt with by eating. Therefore, negative feelings are warded off by the process of overeating. The cause of the boredom is not dealt with, and the individual does not develop the insight or behavior to change the negative cycle. Obese children are often not sought by peers, and they usually do not participate in active games. They become more bored and lonely and eat more. Some children feel that they deserve to be fat, almost as a form of self-punishment. Naughty or violent thoughts may be handled and warded off by punishing oneself through being obese and taunted.

Learned overeating. Put simply, many children overeat to please their parents. Some parents believe that fat children are more healthy and/or happy. Parental behavior provides many verbal or nonverbal cues to children regarding the desirability of consuming large quantities of food. Therefore, the children learn to eat too much and are positively reinforced for doing so. "Have some more" is constantly heard, and smiles and compliments result from agreement. Distrust of a child's ability to self-regulate comes into play. When children say that they are not hungry, adults frequently reply that they should eat more and "it's good for you." Overestimating how much food children need is typical. Also, anxious parents sometimes overfeed children as a means of allaying their own worries or concerns.

Learning by imitating obese parents is frequent. Parents serve as a strong model. Obese parents have obese children, who have adopted the lifestyle which leads to obesity. Consumption of too much or the wrong type of food is typical. Snacks of fattening foods are part of obese family life. Also, obese children have learned to eat in response to visible food cues. The more they see food or references to food, the more they eat.

Insufficient exercise. We list this as a separate category since some obese children can eat the same amount of food as their peers but do very little physical activity. More typical is the child who overeats and underexercises. Family patterns are once again strongly influential. Walking, jogging, swimming, playing sports, etc., are *not* engaged in by these families. Eating together is the frequent and enjoyable family activity.

Insufficient exercise may develop as a habit learned in early childhood. Some children appear to have always been lazy, sluggish, or lethargic. This can be due to a combination of a constitutional predisposition and environmental (family, friends, school) influences. Some children lack confidence and see themselves as unable to exert much energy. They cannot imagine themselves as being able to run or play for long periods of time. Many girls at puberty, when fat accumulation naturally occurs, become less physically active. Vigorous exercise is seen as "unfeminine" and is avoided.

How to Prevent

Do not use food for psychological satisfaction. Food is one of the strongest reinforcers since it is physiologically satisfying. It is too easy for eating to become linked with relieving boredom or reducing anxiety. From the earliest age, food should not be used as a tranquilizer. Infants and toddlers can develop very strong habits of eating when stressed. Parents must carefully avoid encouraging this frequent pattern. Sweets and desserts as a reward promotes the conditioned response of eating as the most rewarding and gratifying experience. Logically, sweets are then sought as a source of good feelings. "Eat, you'll feel better" should never be heard.

Many teen-agers have been conditioned to experience good psychological feelings by overeating with relatives or friends. In some ethnic groups, enormous food consumption is an important and happy tradition. Obesity can be prevented by purposely altering the way food is consumed. Eating can be relatively quite enjoyable but *not* the main source of gratification.

Model and teach balanced eating and sufficient exercise. Obese children develop an increase in the number of fat cells, which leads to the need for a lifelong diet.[4] Clearly, appropriate weight should be achieved before age 6. There is some evidence that the pattern is set by age 2 and that infants should not be permitted to become obese. Therefore, the best prevention for obesity is to avoid the development of excess fat *from birth*. The vast majority of obese adults who were obese children cannot maintain weight loss.

Obese parents have obese children. These parents not only serve as fat models, but their lifestyles are learned by their children. Parents should serve as non-fat, active models! Meals should be enjoyable, slow-paced, well-balanced, and not too large. You must have the conviction that vegetables, fruits, lean meats, whole wheat, and oats are better than junk food. The sugar habit is to be avoided at all costs. The price of a ''sweet tooth'' is to have rotten teeth and excess fat. Dietary habits set in childhood often *persist throughout life*. The poor diet of sweets, refined starches, and animal fats not only leads to excess fat but interferes with consumption of nutritious foods. The sugar habit should be stopped before it begins. For example, fresh fruits and juices should be purchased, not sweet punch or fruits canned in heavy syrup. Foods with sugar added and sugar cereals should be totally avoided. Cookies with nuts, raisins, or oatmeal are better than those made with butter and sugar.

Snacks should not be candy, pretzels, or potato chips. Healthy snacks are fruits, nuts, raw vegetables, cheese, and granola. Lunch meat, lean sausages, and liver pates should be used at times. If a child is very hungry before a meal, part of the meal (like a salad) could be given rather than an extra snack. In fact, by school age it is quite feasible to decrease the frequency of snacks or eliminate them entirely. Many habits, such as late night snacks, may be traditions, but they should be ended for the sake of better health. Other customs, such as family conversations, can be substituted.

Promote general satisfaction and feelings of adequacy. Overeating as a source of psychological satisfaction is so frequent that great care should be taken to prevent this occurrence. Satisfaction should be available through accomplishments, friendships, and intimate family relationships. By aiding the growth of these satisfactions, obesity (and many other problems) can be prevented. Specifically, mealtimes should be sources of psychologically pleasurable interactions, not filled with tension and criticism. Eating does not become the best sensation in the context of negative feelings between people.

From birth, feeding should be a pleasant experience. Bottle feeding should be accomplished with affectionate, physical contact, and pleasant, relaxed feelings. As children develop, their own perceptions and feelings of adequacy should be encouraged. It is destructive to tell children, who say they're not hungry, to eat. This is very similar to parents telling a child who feels cold that it is very warm in the house. Children learn to mistrust their perceptions and have a feeling that their judgment is terrible. They have learned to respond to external cues (such as time of day or parental suggestions) rather than their own internal hunger cues. You must not inadvertently teach children to eat more than they need or want. Children must learn to recognize their own physiological hunger signs rather than to eat because of parental approval or disapproval. A major accomplishment is reached when a person says, "I eat only when I'm hungry and then I eat just enough to feel satisfied." Eating is then *not* associated with pleasing others or with a source of adequacy.

What to Do

Provide nutritional food. Since fattening foods (fats and carbohydrates) are frequently irresistible temptations, they must be *removed*. No junk food at home might be viewed as a penalty by nonoverweight family members. Therefore, a family discussion should take place regarding nutrition, health, and weight. It is possible that all will agree to the absence of candy and rich cakes. Some families have used locked cabinets successfully. Only nonoverweight individuals are given a key. However, since enduring weight loss is the goal, having only nutritional food is by far the best plan. Weight can be taken off slowly and surely. Less carbohydrates and less snacks will work. If necessary, nutritious snacks should be used to reduce hunger in between meals. Bread and sweets should be replaced by fruit, raisins, or nuts. Health food stores now have a variety of healthy, good tasting snacks. More seafood and less meat is advisable. Fruit juices, diet soda, fat-free milk, and especially water should be the drinks available. Adults can set the example. Even in alcohol consumption, adults can switch to wine rather than mixed drinks.

Teen-agers typically skip meals and consume many nonnutritious snacks. They actually require more protein, calcium, iron, and calories than they do as children or adults. Crash dieting is not healthy and should be avoided. Many adolescents have iron deficiency anemia, especially females. Adequate quantities of good food is the answer.

Change pattern of physical activity. Since obesity results from more calories consumed than expended, the solution is simple. Eat less and exercise more. Temporary large amounts of exercise is not the answer. Altering the pattern of physical activity leads to weight loss, which can be maintained if the new activities are continued. As weight is lost, skills and endurance improve. Children should be encouraged to become aware of their improving abilities. They can measure their walking or throwing farther. Exercising every day before breakfast can become a personal or family pattern.

Group activities should be strongly encouraged. This promotes both increased exercise and relating to peers. Local team sports can be very useful in this regard. After consulting with parents, the team coach can make weight loss a condition for remaining on the team. If the team has importance (peer prestige and spectators), weight loss may well become self-motivated rather than as a response to pressure from others.

A useful guideline is to increase already performed activities rather than instituting a major change. Walking further and playing longer are good examples. Climbing steps rather than using an elevator or escalator and standing rather than sitting are both good sources of naturally increasing exercise. The best activity to expend calories is rhythmically using large muscles for long periods. Jogging and walking are excellent. It is the *total time* of the activity that is important, not the intensity. Therefore, walking is often the most acceptable, and effective, exercise for many children.

Reward weight loss and self-control. With older children and adolescents, serious family discussions may be sufficient, or at least enhancing, sources of motivation. Maintaining normal weight should be discussed as a conscious decision concerning values and priorities. It can be stated that normal weight leads to feeling and looking better and living longer. By setting the tone that bodily condition should be a priority, eating more may well become less of a priority than it has been.

Positive reinforcement, contracts, and charts discussed earlier are good motivators, if necessary. Rewards should be tailored to the child's age and powerful enough to motivate. Many teen-agers would be motivated by extra allowance and use of the telephone or car for maintaining weight loss. For weight gain, disliked chores or activities may be good negative motivators. While using positive or negative reinforcers, criticism or angry feelings should be avoided. The success of the intervention lies in correctly using a method, and criticism is counterproductive.

Self-control approaches have consistently been more effective than other methods.[5] Weight and foods eaten should be recorded by the individual. This type of *self-monitoring* is often the key leading to the gradual assumption of real self-responsibility. Research has consistently shown that desired behavior often increases by simply recording that behavior. For example, food consumed may be immediately entered into a food diary. Many people begin to lose weight immediately since there is visible feedback concerning the time, quantity, and type of food consumed. Feedback of weight loss may also be used. Some individuals have successfully used reduced food consumption if they have not reached a set goal. For example, a teen-ager might want to lose 2 pounds per week. If the goal is not reached, 1 or 2 days of being careful after the weigh-in day can result in the desired loss during that week.

Similarly, *self-reward* rather than reward from others can be used. Older children and adolescents can quickly learn the valuable principle of setting a task, doing it, and then administering a self-reward. After eating a nutritious snack or engaging in exercise, a pleasurable activity can be engaged in. Television watching, reading, resting, listening to music, talking to someone, etc., may be used as self-rewards. Specific weight loss may be rewarded by going to a movie, making a special trip, buying a valued object, etc.

Planning the best environment for weight loss is invaluable and can become part of the child's developing self-control. Eating can be valuably *restricted* only to one room (usually the kitchen). The cues for eating become associated only with one place at home (stimulus control). It is much easier to control eating this way, as compared to eating, or especially snacking, in various rooms. The availability only of nutritious, nonfattening snacks fits the concept of planning a conducive environment. Similarly, food cues should *not* be obvious. Foods should be kept in closets and *out of sight*. The eating process itself should be altered to chewing more, slower pace, not gulping, and savoring more. This process leads to eating less and enjoying it more!

While rewarding weight loss, the self-control process of conflict resolution should also be rewarded. Children and teen-agers should be taught and rewarded for solving conflicts and for not having to use fatness as a weapon or defense. Attention should be gained for positive behavior, especially for improved coping skills, not by being obese.

Independence and self-control should be promoted and encouraged. By rewarding psychological growth, the use of weight as a symbol of independence is unnecessary. A teenage boy stated that his father could ground him and take away his allowance, but he couldn't take away his fat.

Case Report. Many children and teen-agers have responded to the approach used with a 13-year-old boy. He was 35 pounds overweight, engaged in very few sports or active games, and was doing fairly well in school. Straightforward counseling was used to modify the parents' behavior. The mother was quite obese and the father was of average weight. Both parents agreed to provide only nutritious snacks and food and to engage in family exercise. The whole family (including a slightly overweight younger brother) jogged for 1 half-hour before every dinner. On weekends, they developed 1- to 2-hour different walking tours of their area. Additionally, they encouraged (and arranged) more opportunities for him to be involved with peers. A Saturday afternoon swim and a 2-day-per-week after-school recreation program were set up.

Food was only permitted in the kitchen, and he stopped gulping his food and learned to appreciate it. He received much praise for his exercising and his growing self-control over eating. He recorded all consumed food and proudly showed his parents how he had cut out junk food, especially in school. Within 4 months, his weight was average and he continued the exercise which he enjoyed. While many cases are not this successful, the main ingredient here was the family spirit. When the parents are uninvolved or unwilling to change their habits, children's habits are more difficult to influence.

Books for Parents

American Medical Association, Monroe, WI: Pamphlets: *Your Age and Your Diet: Infancy through Adulthood* (1971); *The Healthy Way to Weigh Less* (1973).

Stuart, R.B. and Davis, B.: *Slim Chance In a Fat World: Behavioral Control of Obesity.* Research Press, Champaign, IL (1972).

Kaufman, Harry: *The Psychology of Slimming Down and Feeling Great.* Plantagenet Press, Dobbs Ferry, NY (1976).

Books for Children

Schwarzrock, Shirley and Wrenn, C. Gilbert.: *Food as a Crutch*. American Guidance Service, Circle Pines, MN (1970). Age 11 and over.

Causes of overeating are vividly portrayed. Consolation, self-rewards, and many snacks are used as crutches. A boy decides to diet and develop satisfying activities. Practical suggestions are offered for overweight teen-agers.

Danziger, Paula: *The Cat Ate My Gymsuit*. Delacorte, New York (1974). Ages 11 and over.

An overweight 13-year-old girl feels inferior and has many arguments with her father. A teacher encourages her to express her feelings. At home, the girl encourages her mother to be more independent. Various events at school are described, and the story ends optimistically with the girl seeing a psychologist and dieting.

Du Bois, William Pine: *Porko von Popbutton*. Harper and Row, New York (1969). Ages 9 to 12.

The problems of a very obese boy are vividly depicted. He becomes very involved with his boarding school's ice hockey team and loses 124 pounds. His poor eating habits and self-control problems are described.

Angel, Doris: *Next Door to Xanodu*. Harper and Row, New York (1969). Ages 9 to 11.

A lonely, overweight 10-year-old girl is frequently teased. With a girlfriend's help, she starts to diet. She learns how to develop friendships and lose weight.

Pinkwater, Manus: *Fat Elliot and the Gorilla*. Four Winds Press, New York (1974). Ages 8 to 10.

Elliot can't run or tie his shoes because he's so fat. An imaginary gorilla helps him exercise frequently and learn to feel good about himself.

Solot, Mary Lynn: *100 Hamburgers: The Getting Thin Book*. Lothrop, Lee and Shepard. New York (1972). Ages 7 to 10.

An obese 9-year-old boy loves fattening food and wishes he could eat 100 hamburgers. He talks to his physician about getting thin and receives advice about what kinds of food to eat. This book is one of the few that specifically describes realistic means of dieting for children.

Holland, Isabelle: *Heads You Win, Tails I Lose*. Lippincott, Philadelphia (1973). Ages 12 and over.

A 15-year-old girl is nagged by her parents to lose weight. Many serious family problems are depicted, including the father leaving home and the mother drinking heavily. The girl always became involved in parental arguments. After inappropriate use of pills, she gets straightened out with a little help from her friends.

References

1. Coates, Thomas J. and Thoresen, Carl E.: "Treating obesity in children and adolescents: A review." *American Journal of Public Health* 68: (1978), pp. 143–151.
2. Garn, Stanley M. and Clark, Diane C.: "Trends in fatness and the origins of obesity." *Pediatrics* 57: (1976), pp. 443–456.
3. Schaefer, Charles E., Millman, Howard L., and Levine, Gary F.: *Therapies for Psychosomatic Disorders in Children*. Jossey-Bass, San Francisco (1979).
4. Winick, Myron (ed.): *Childhood Obesity*. Wiley, New York (1975).
5. Abramson, Edward E.: "Behavioral approaches to weight control: An updated review." *Behavior Research and Therapy* 15: (1977), pp. 355 –363.

Eating too Little

Reasons Why

Power struggle and conflicts about food. Some fussiness is natural and does not mean that a child will be finicky or undereat for life. It is important to make sure that sickness, boring food, or a noisy confused atmosphere are not causing a poor appetite. However, a very frequent pattern is the power struggle resulting from parental overreaction to a child's eating style. Parents begin to plead, urge, threaten, punish, or reward eating. Unfortunately, children may perceive that eating is important to their parents and unimportant for them. Not eating certain foods becomes a means of controlling adults. Although hunger is not a naturally pleasant state, some children's undereating becomes a stronger gratification than feeling full. The giving up of food becomes a type of addiction to controlling, or getting even, with adults.

Also frequent is the use of inadequate eating as a sign of independence. "I can do what I want to" can take the form of only eating minimum amounts of food. This form of expression of individuality is especially likely when parents express great concern over food. Problem eating is compounded in situations where undereating is a means of expressing both independence and anger. Arguing about eating can become a chronic and more severe problem due to the resulting conflict and tension. A vicious cycle is set up where a tense family atmosphere is not conducive to proper eating. Children want to "get the meal over with."

Mothers may impose their own concepts of needs on the child and prevent the child from developing a realistic awareness of hunger.[1] These children do not learn to be separate individuals with a clear awareness of bodily needs. Often, they feel as if they never do things correctly. They may be perceptive about others, yet unaware of their own bodily perception. A faulty hunger and satiation awareness develops.

Never learned proper eating. Parents who model undereating are clear causes of similar behavior in their children. Children very easily imitate finicky adults or siblings. Less clear is the lack of proper teaching or reinforcement of proper eating. Children learn from verbal statements and nonverbal cues about the recognition of hunger and adequate satisfaction. They learn to feel and then say that they have eaten enough food. Parents may underestimate their influence in both teaching and *positively reinforcing* their children for eating sufficient, nutritious foods.

Some children never develop a flexible, adventurous approach to eating. Not unusual is an adolescent who only eats hamburgers, meatballs, and french fries. Early food preferences become rigid codes. Particularly vulnerable are those children who appear constitutionally relatively rigid, that is, they find it difficult to adjust to any change or to new things.

How to Prevent

Make eating a pleasant and relaxed activity. From birth eating can and should be a positive, relatively conflict-free experience. For the infant, the physical setting should be attractive, easily cleaned, quiet, and conducive to messy eating. A short, straight, broad-handled spoon makes eating easier. Infants can hold it and even put the wide part of the spoon in their mouths sideways. Later, a blunt fork can also be used. Food should be placed at stomach level so infants do not have to reach up. A low straight-backed chair provides the comfort of being able to keep feet on the floor, not in the air. Solid foods should be introduced at 6 months. Food that sticks together is easier to eat than soup. Most infants respond better to bland foods at first. Many foods with different tastes, textures, smells, and colors should be offered in very small portions. Most effective is serving these along with foods infants already like. Very small amounts of rejected food (such as vegetables) can be mixed with preferred foods. An excellent method is to use a rejected food in a different form. For example, if milk is rejected, it can be served as milk pudding, cheese, cream soup, etc.

A relaxed, nonpressured *adult attitude* is crucial. Eating should be fun, not a battle. Children should not be coaxed or forced to eat! Do not make an issue over rejected foods (other foods should be substituted). If parents react strongly, the child becomes the center of attention because of food. Food should be offered in a casual manner without urging. Nonstrained, relaxed mealtimes lead to good eating habits and prevent problems from developing. Belittling, teasing, or criticizing food habits should be strictly avoided.

Infants should be permitted to take their time. Adults must set aside enough time that hurrying is not necessary. Dawdling and playing with food are normal during infancy and toddler age. Feeding can be arranged in an orderly, yet flexible manner. Eating can stop if the child is not in the mood or ended by the adult after a reasonable amount of time (say 1 half-hour) has passed. Clean plates every time should not be mandatory. Prizes for eating should not be used, since prizes become more valued and food in itself loses value. The goals are for children to like to eat and be able to do so by themselves and with some choices.

Involve children in food selection, preparation, and learning about nutrition. Education about appropriate food should begin early and continue throughout adolescence. Children should be very informed by the time they buy their own food. They should learn to cook and be given choices. Practically, this means that children can choose peas or carrots and then be involved in preparing the food the way they prefer it cooked. Finicky children can create different shapes (clown face, airplane, etc.) with food and therefore be less bored. New foods should be combined with old favorites. Vegetables can be served raw with a dip or fried and crunchy. Disliked foods may be blended with preferred foods. Vegetables can be prepared in more acceptable ways such as in chicken pot pie, carrot cake, or soup. A dinner suggestion box is a means of involving all family members in being creative about menus. Family involvement in preparing specialties is a clear indicator of positive attitudes towards food. "Family service" is a useful device where everybody serves themselves from a large bowl. If children tend to take nothing, they can be asked to take only a very small amount. Seconds can be given only if all food is tasted. This increases individual responsibility.

For children who don't want breakfast, it can be made too good to miss. Some children can't resist a peanut butter sandwich and a milk shake. Teen-agers can blend fruit, eggs, ice cream, etc., for a delicious and nutritious treat. All children should be involved in learning about nutrition and experimenting with various combinations. Books, articles, pictures, movies, etc., about good food should be used. Family participation is very helpful. Discussions should take place concerning how to obtain more food value for your money. Milk and an apple is healthier and of more food value than soda and pretzels or potato chips.

What to Do (after a medical evaluation has ruled out any organic cause of undereating).

What to avoid. Do not force, bribe, coax, or remind children to eat. At times children are forced to eat even though they may be sick, tired, constipated, or stuffed with snacks. Avoid long meals where children whine or only pick at their food. If a meal is not eaten in 30 minutes, remove it with a friendly or neutral attitude. You might say, "I guess that you're not hungry today." Avoid paying attention to undereating since attention can serve to reinforce and increase eating problems. Sympathy, sad looks, overheard emotional conversations between parents, etc., are all forms of undesirable attention. Do not allow meals to be interfered with by noise, confusion, or other activities. Toddlers should not be distracted with conversation or games. Let them pay attention to eating.

Large portions are to be avoided. Several small portions are less scary to young children. Sandwiches may be cut in parts, and milk can be served in half-glass amounts (some children then ask for more). Clean plates and perfect table manners are not necessary. Do not allow between-meal snacks. Junk food is a typical hunger reducer. Food may have to be locked up to prevent access by non-meal eaters. If children appear to be eating very little at meals, do not panic. Children may not eat much during meals for a few days, but they won't starve. It usually takes 3 to 5 days for a new eating pattern to take effect. Some tolerance of anxiety is necessary during this period, or you'll give up too soon and the old pattern will reoccur. Do not judge adequate nutrition by the amount of food eaten, since there are wide differences in the amount of food necessary for individuals. Health, vitality, and growth are better indicators of sufficient nutrition. Food deprivation should never be used as a punishment! One exception is the often-used plan of no dessert unless each food served is at least sampled.

Avoid conflicts, arguments, and frustrations at mealtimes. Do not moralize or lecture children about the importance of eating. Don't say, "I hope you'll like this," but have an unconcerned, calm expectation that children will eat what is given. In general, don't become emotionally aroused about food.

Make eating a rewarding experience. Eating is controlled by hunger and appetite. Hunger results from an empty stomach, while appetite is a desire resulting from memories of previously satisfying eating experiences. Children may be hungry but have no appetite because eating has been an unpleasant experience. Wanting dessert after a big meal is an example of appetite with no hunger. Appetite is enhanced by pleasant, calm, unhurried mealtimes where good flavorful food is attractively served. Children are encouraged to eat, but their appetite should decide how much. Hunger is stimulated by regular mealtimes (with sufficient time between meals) and by exercise and fresh air. Only items such as fruit juice, fruit, crackers, or milk should be given between meals. Fatigued young children should rest *before* a meal.

Meals should be a time for family togetherness where experiences are shared in the context of pleasant and supportive feelings. Meals must be enjoyable for all! Picnics and barbeques are means of enhancing the positive experience of eating together. Children should be involved in food preparation. For example, they can prepare eggs the way they like them. New foods should be introduced at the beginning of a meal, when hunger makes for a greater likelihood of acceptance. Flavor is less important when one is hungry. Different foods should be introduced in small amounts and only one new food per meal. This process takes into account that children often do not like change and that they usually reject new tastes.

Preferred foods may be used to reinforce the eating of nonpreferred foods. For example, spaghetti may be served only after one stalk of asparagus is eaten. In the spirit of making eating as pleasant as possible, asparagus (and all foods) should be prepared in a tasty manner. Asparagus could be soggy and tasteless or served fresh in a tasty sauce. Similarly, a good homemade dressing can make the difference between liking or not liking salad.

As long as children are sampling foods, they could be allowed to serve their own portion and eat as much as they want. In general, refusal to eat nonpreferred food may be ignored. Eating new or disliked foods can result in the rewards of praise or special events. Parents might purchase a special game only to be played with a child after an appropriate meal is consumed. For underweight children, a reward system can be effectively employed for weight gain. For example, weight increase can lead to extra allowance. If necessary, weight loss could lead to a reduction in allowance. As in all reward systems, the details should be discussed, clearly spelled out, and agreed to by all parties whenever possible.

Case Report. A 7-year-old girl was 10 pounds underweight and a finicky eater who would not try any different foods. Intervention consisted of three parent counseling sessions. The parents agreed to stop coaxing, threatening, or making an issue over food. A reward system was tailored to the girl's interests. Best-liked foods were given after she tasted one new food introduced at the beginning of a meal. Consuming more than a taste of nutritious food (vegetables, cheese, fruits, etc.) resulted in playing for a half-hour with her parents. A special game (a hockey game on legs set up in the basement) was purchased for this purpose. In addition, a weight gain of more than one-half pound resulted in a special weekend trip. Weigh-ins were Friday nights. The larger the gain, the more special the event.

Progress was gradual and within 3 months her weight was average and she looked healthier. Everyone was pleased and a party was held to celebrate her newly developed adventurous attitude towards eating. Rewards were discontinued as no longer being necessary.

Books for Parents

Sloane, Howard N.: *Dinner's Ready: A Short, Step-by-Step Guide for Teaching Your Children to Finish Meals and Control Before-Meal Snacking.* Telesis, Fountain Valley, CA (1976).

Marbach, Ellen S., Plass, Martha, and O'Connell, Lily: *Nutrition in a Changing World.* Brigham Young University Press, Provo, UT (1979).

Nutrition education for preschool or primary grade level children.

Books for Children

Lord, Beman: *Quarterback's Aim.* Henry Z. Walck, New York (1960). Ages 8 to 10.

A young small-sized boy wants to compete with larger boys. Rather than trying to achieve unrealistic goals, the coach helps him develop special skills.

Van Leeuwen, Jean: *I Was a 98-Pound Duckling.* Dial Press, New York (1972). Ages 11 and over.

Various problems of a very thin 13-year-old girl are described. She learns to disregard the inappropriate suggestions of fashion magazines. The long road to self-acceptance is interestingly presented.

References

1. Bruch, Hilde: *Eating Disorders: Obesity, Anorexia Nervosa, and the Person Within.* Basic Books, New York (1973).

STUTTERING

Children try to say a word, hesitate, and try to say the word again. They may repeat the first letter or the whole word. There may be a silence for several seconds.

Stuttering is speaking with involuntary disruptions or blocking of speech, with a spasmodic repetition or prolongation of vocal sounds. Stuttering and stammering are used interchangeably. It is a disorder of speech rhythm, where the flow of speech is not smooth. Continuity of speech may be interrupted by spasms in muscles controlling speech. Some stutterers are fluent with friends or when alone, but stutter severely with others, especially with authority figures. All people have some periods of nonfluent speech, more so in children. Some children are seen as stutterers by everyone, but many only stutter under certain circumstances. Most stutterers do not stutter when singing or speaking in time with a metronome (an instrument marking time with a regularly repeated tick). In general stutterers are average or above in intelligence, whereas children with other forms of speech defects are often below average intellectually.

Some stuttering is typical and temporary in young children, and is called "developmental" stuttering. The onset is usually between 2 and 4 years and lasts only a few months. "Benign" stuttering begins from 6 to 8 years of age and may last for 2 or 3 years. "Persistent" stuttering starts between 3 to 8 years and lasts unless some effective intervention is employed. Stuttering occurs more frequently on sounds such as b, d, and g as compared to p, t, and k. "Secondary" stuttering, indicating a serious struggle with speech, is an indicator for immediate professional attention. Signs are facial grimacing, arm or leg movements, eye blinking, or irregular breathing. Stuttering appearing after age 5 is considered more serious than that appearing at a younger age.

The onset of stuttering occurs most frequently between the ages of 2 to 5 years. There are several million preschool stutterers, about 4 percent of that population. By school age, approximately 1 to 3 percent of children stutter. About 1 percent (2 million) of the adult population stutter. An important statistic is that 75 percent of 10 year olds who stutter remain stutterers throughout life.

Although about 80 percent of childhood stutterers do not stutter as adults, many of them develop personality problems such as shyness, withdrawal, and lack of confidence because of their experience. Fifty percent of severe childhood stutterers continue to be severe stutterers as adults. At all ages, there are from four to eight times as many male as opposed to female stutterers.

Reasons Why

Physiological. There is a widespread belief that a genetic predisposition to the development of stuttering exists. The likelihood of becoming a stutterer is in large part influenced by heredity. Males are at least five times as likely to stutter.

A direct physical cause is believed to be an auditory perceptual defect.[1] Individuals receive false or misleading feedback from their own speech, specifically a delayed feedback. This is called the "auditory interference theory."

Another theory is that stuttering is a neurologically-based language disturbance caused by a lack of appropriately developed cerebral dominance. One side of the brain has not achieved the level of influence necessary for smooth speech.

Two other possible physical causes could be called psychosomatic, because of the influence of psychological factors on the physical mechanics of speech production. A rather widespread theory is the presence of a "timing disorder."[2] This is any interference with the timing of the action of any of the speech muscles, including lips and jaw. There is a disruption in the precise linking of sounds and syllables. Word distortions result from any weakness in the great precision in timing required for smooth speech. A recent, but not widely accepted, belief is that there is an inappropriate reflex[3] during which the vocal cords open before speech, instead of remaining loosely together. Some children pause and the cords relax, while others force the cords shut and lock them, making speech difficult. The theory is that struggling against physically locked cords causes stuttering.

Parental Expectations. Unrealistic parental expectations lead to pressure on children, who become anxious. Many parents are not aware of child development, when and how speech develops, and the wide normal range of fluent speech at different ages. Tension and stuttering are caused by parents who try to get very young children to speak before they are sufficiently mature. Some 2 and 3 year olds have been pressured by parents to develop a good vocabulary, speak in complete sentences, and relate a logical story. Similarly, perfectionistic parents can cause the same types of tension. The children involved feel compelled to live up to a standard that is either impossible or extremely difficult. Different children are vulnerable to parental perfectionism at different ages. Therefore, it is possible that some children begin stuttering at different sensitive periods in their lives. The start of school or puberty is a vulnerable period when parents expect generally good behavior and improved speech.

Overconcern and overreaction to speech may cause stuttering. Some stuttering from ages 2 to 5 is normal. If parents overreact, problems result. When children stutter, some parents say ''Start over again and speak more slowly,'' ''Be more careful when you talk,'' or ''Slower, you're stuttering.'' Children often become anxious and stutter more. The point is that speech is smoother when one is not self-conscious about speaking. Additionally, by labeling children as stutterers, children and others accept the label and stuttering becomes more frequent. A child's forceful attempts to reduce the stutter in public often leads to more hesitation and ticlike movements. At the other end of the scale of too much pressure are too few expectations. Overprotective parents expect too little and try to protect their children from any demands or stress. In the first few years of life, parents may do everything for their children, and speech development is not necessary or encouraged. These children may not learn to express themselves well, and their feelings of inadequacy may show up in stuttering speech.

Reaction to Stress. A variety of stressful situations may lead to childhood stuttering. Intense or continuous family arguments are especially stressful to young children. A continued high tension level is conducive to stuttering. Children with normal speech will stutter when highly anxious or distressed. When a proneness to stutter exists, stressful situations will increase and exaggerate stuttering. Tension causes susceptible individuals to lose control of the delicate balance of speech muscles. With continued tension, a pattern often develops known as anticipatory stress. Children fear what will happen when they speak, become tense, stutter, and their fear is confirmed and becomes stronger. Anticipatory stress may have developed as a desire to speak more quickly. Fear of sounding slow or stupid and criticism from others can set up the anticipation of not speaking well and can result in tense, stammering speech.

Other sources of stress are fatigue, lack of readiness, and forced change. Feeling tired increases stuttering spasms. Any area of weakness is more easily triggered when fatigued. Fatigue may be caused by too much physical activity, insufficient nutrition, not enough rest, and too much emotional stress. When children are not emotionally ready for some situation, stuttering may be their way of indicating fear or reluctance. It is fairly frequent for a child who has been sick for a while to start stuttering when it is time to resume school attendance. Many children find public performances stressful and indicate lack of readiness by increased stuttering. A typical example is when left-handed children are made to use their right hand. In this situation, it is believed that in addition to stress, the part of the brain controlling the preferred hand is also associated with speech. Therefore, stuttering results from psychological stress and neurological interference. In other instances, the stress of forced change alone may cause or exaggerate stammering. An example is that naturally slow moving or slow speaking children may be inappropriately forced to be quicker.

Expression of Conflict. For many years, stuttering was believed to result from a conflict in the expression of aggressive or sexual impulses. Individuals presumably had strong feelings which could not be expressed because of social taboos or negative parental reactions. There is relatively little research support for this belief, but there are a considerable number of professionals who see this as a cause and state that relief of the conflict results in elimination of stuttering. Unexpressed feelings of anger are thought to be a primary cause of stuttering. Another type of conflict is that between expressing yourself and holding back. The result is pausing and hesitating because of the psychological ambivalence regarding expression. This would be exaggerated by children's unsureness in their ability to adequately express themselves. Finally, psychological conflict may result from traumatic experiences. Children who witness death, violence, or serious illness may experience great conflict about their safety and ability to cope. They may continue to feel torn apart emotionally by conflicting feelings. They may want to be close to others but fear being badly hurt. They may want to engage in heavy exercise but worry that they will become hurt or sick. Their continued experiencing of conflicting feelings may result in tense, stuttering speech.

How To Prevent

Teach and Strengthen Speech of Receptive Children. Children should not be pressured to learn or practice speech against their will. Receptive children should be encouraged and stimulated. With resistant children, games and rewards may lead to motivation and willingness to participate. Infants can strengthen speech muscles by blowing bubbles, then blowing up balloons, and later by whispering and singing. From age 2, you teach speech sounds and encourage vocabulary development in a fun filled manner. There are a large number of picture vocabulary books that are educational and very appealing to young children. You read these words to children while asking them to point to the correct picture. Then while pointing to pictures you ask for the correct word. When children lose interest, you immediately stop. Don't underestimate the powerful influence of the early association between speech and positive, pleasant experiences. In contrast, anxiety ridden attempts to promote speech may well lead to tension and stuttering. As children develop, speech should be a natural and fun experience with an accompanying feeling of pride and accomplishment.

Provide an Accepting, Harmonious, and Calm Atmosphere. A relatively peaceful and emotionally supportive family atmosphere is an excellent means of preventing the development of stuttering. However, it is essential to provide this atmosphere for children who begin to stutter more than occasionally. Keep in mind that tense or overly sensitive children do much better in a calm atmosphere where regular routines are the rule. Some families have a tendency to respond even to minimal stress with much concern and commotion. Many family members may not mind, or might enjoy, the excitement, but more fragile children do mind the chaos. Therefore, it may help tremendously to minimize chaos and provide some feeling of safety for that child. A calm word and specific suggestions help. For example, when it rains during a picnic, many people run for cover and generate a feeling of confusion. You make sure that the sensitive child does not get lost or overwhelmed in the confusion. At home, it is important to make sure that the general atmosphere is harmonious. When arguments and disagreements occur, let children know that these are natural, manageable, and do not mean that serious or terrible things will result.

Providing a relatively calm and accepting atmosphere begins very early. Feeding and toilet training must be at least neutral and hopefully a reasonably enjoyable experience for all. The key is to be relaxed, have perspective, and maintain your sense of humor. Much difficulty results from tense, angry, early training. Vulnerable children may well become tense stutterers. While providing a relatively harmonious climate, make sure that children have enough rest. Enthusiastic children often forget to take care of themselves and want to overdo everything. Fatigue, which may cause or exaggerate stuttering, should be carefully minimized. Early bedtimes and an afternoon nap are necessary for many preschoolers. For easily fatigued children, morning kindergarten is essential. There, children may cope more adequately with situations in the morning while they are more energetic.

If children begin to stutter somewhat, that is the time for an all-out effort to be accepting, warm, and not upset. Stuttering should be seen as a temporary situation to be handled in a very low-key manner. It is unnecessary and harmful to become anxious, worried, or self-pitying because your child is stuttering. The best approach is to ignore the stuttering and concentrate on making the child's world an even safer and more fun filled place.

Promote Adequacy and Reduce Tension. Similar to providing an accepting atmosphere, promoting adequacy prevents stuttering and is essential if mild stuttering begins. In a fun way, you teach children to be socially sensitive and to get along with others. You watch children and when you observe behavior that annoys others, you help children act more appropriately. The 5 year old who is too bossy and won't give anyone else a turn must learn to do so immediately. You play games with the child and focus on his more socially appropriate behavior, which you praise. In general, you try to teach children, through play, how to feel confident in relating to others. Preschoolers need practice with peers and with adults in playing by simple rules and beginning to care about others' feelings.

Even mild stuttering leads children to feel different and inadequate. It is crucial to help them feel relaxed and more socially skillful. Sensitive baby sitters or teen-age relatives may help provide a relaxed atmosphere where the child can relate socially without tension. You try to discover the cause of tension and then reduce it as much as possible. If you discover that children feel awkward and don't know how to react with others, you immediately help them learn. You use role playing, where you act like a child, in order for your child to *practice interacting* in a pretend, nonpressured situation. The repetition both reduces anxiety and improves social skills. Children learn by watching you express concern for others, let others do their favorite activity, take turns, etc. When traumatic experiences occur, encourage children to express their feelings and concerns. You provide empathy and reassurance. Do not correct any stuttering, and reduce tension by carrying on enjoyable activities. The child, who stutteringly tells of being beaten up, should be comforted. Afterwards, you discuss what happened and ask the child about other ways of handling situations. Do not increase tension by criticizing your child for not fighting back or for being scared. Your task is to promote feelings of adequacy by helping children to figure out the best way of handling difficult situations.

Slow speakers should not be rushed. Patience, acceptance, and reducing pressure helps. Do not correct speech by having children say a word or sentence over again. This increases self-consciousness. Do not insist or subtly pressure children to speak or perform for friends and relatives. If children do not want to show how well they speak, do not express subtle or blatant disappointment. In fact, it is unnecessary to feel disappointment if children won't perform. Keep in mind that your focus is on helping your child feel adequate and not on insisting on behavior that pleases you. A great deal of tension will be prevented by following this simple rule.

What To Do

Adapt Professional Methods for Home Use. The following methods may be effectively used by parents with cooperative children who want to stop stuttering. As with other problem behaviors, parents may have to increase motivation with some reward for cooperation. You try one method for several weeks in order to assess the effectiveness. Which method you use should be decided by your evaluation of its description here, by reading original sources, and by your judgment as to which might be suitable for your child.

Professionals use computers to analyze voice gentleness in Precision Fluency Shaping.[2] You can encourage children to slow down their speech and *start* each syllable *gently*. The idea is not to forcefully close the throat valves (vocal folds), which interferes with smooth speech. You encourage children to breathe with their abdominal breathing muscles, not with their chests. This procedure is to be practiced repetitively. You serve in providing helpful feedback about the gentleness of the start of each word. Another method[3] requires inhaling and exhaling before each sentence. The breathing serves to keep the vocal cords unlocked. The first syllable is begun slowly in order to avoid "speed stress." When children stutter severely when speaking too quickly, slow speech should be demonstrated and practiced.

There are many methods based upon *paced speech*,[4] which is the oldest means of improving stuttering. Children are shown how to speak in a rhythmically paced manner. You can purchase a metronome in any music store since it is commonly used by musicians to pace themselves. Professionals[5,6] use hidden metronomes behind the ear for training and for use in public. Children speak in time with a slow beat, then at normal speed, and then without its use. Very effective is rhythmic training and having children gradually speak in more and more fearful situations. Paced speech is especially effective with severe stutterers. Children benefit from this method more than adults and relapse is rare. It is useful for all types of stuttering except those caused by laryngeal disturbances. For most children, the use of a metronome is temporary, but a small percentage appear to require a hidden metronome in order to speak smoothly in public.

Desensitize Anxiety. The methods described above should be combined with a systematic plan to help children become less anxious in various situations. However, some children may respond very well with just this approach. The basic idea is to gradually expose children to increasingly more anxious situations as they show the ability to handle themselves well. With very anxious children, they can be shown how to *imagine* speaking in various situations. When they can imagine speaking without feeling anxious, then they can begin speaking in real situations. Speaking in front of relatives and friends is usually easiest. You start with one person, then two, etc., until the child can speak without anxiety in front of a small friendly group. After this is accomplished, you arrange for children to speak in front of acquaintances and finally strangers. The idea is to assess with children their fears from least to most. The use of a telephone usually causes a great deal of anxiety. Again, telephone use should be very slowly built up from saying "hello," to very quick conversations, and finally to normal telephone calls.

Some children respond very well to learning how to relax their muscles completely. You demonstrate muscle tension and letting go and children learn how to quickly and efficiently relax. They physically relax before speaking, and counteract tension by relaxing when they begin to tighten up. The key is to frequently practice so that relaxing becomes easy and natural.

Reduce Pressure. Reducing pressures may be used alone or in conjunction with other methods. The idea is that children who are trying to reduce stuttering are aided by feeling generally less tense. There is no substitute for analyzing an individual's activities and using a good strategy to eliminate unnecessary tension. Often, the elmination of activities that children do not like and which cause tension is required. Typical activities that might be dropped include music lessons, religious classes, tutoring, or visiting relatives. Children feel better when activities unpleasant to them are reduced. When stuttering is eliminated, activities considered very important may be resumed. Certainly, any pressure involving speech should be reduced. Comments of any kind about stuttering should be avoided. In general, greater acceptance and approval should be provided. This includes spending more positive time together and engaging in pleasant activities.

In some situations, parental expectations must be lowered. Some parents have open or subtle expectations that their child's speech must improve "or else." This exerts high-key anxiety, provoking pressure to change. Low-key help and encouragement are necessary. Often, there are other areas where parents have unrealistic expectations. Some parents are perfectionistic or think that their child should be doing much better. They overestimate their child's maturity and are not tolerant enough of inconsistencies and typically childish behavior. Silliness, giggling, babyish acts, etc., should be accepted at times without criticism.

Reward Fluent Speech. As a first step it is essential to not inadvertently reward stuttering. Without meaning to, some parents pay attention to children when they stammer. Any form of attention may serve to strengthen speech problems. Attention may take the form of criticism, sympathy, more time, or extra privileges. When using a reward system, stuttering should be literally ignored. At first, short time intervals of no stuttering should lead to praise or earning points. When arranged properly, all children should earn rewards immediately. The intervals should be short enough so that no stuttering is assured during that period. Intervals should be increased as the frequency of stuttering decreases. Therefore, the child is rewarded for the positive behavior of smooth speech. Some children respond very well to this approach alone. It is a way of increasing their motivation to improve speech. For those who can do it, it is a simple, efficient method.

Professional Evaluation. When children respond relatively quickly, no further efforts are necessary. With children whose stuttering remains the same or worsens, professional help should be sought. Very anxious or multi-problem children might be evaluated by a psychologist. This is especially appropriate if school problems are also present. A qualified speech and language therapist may be obtained through a referral from your school, family physician, or through the American Speech and Hearing Association, Washington, D.C. The speech therapist evaluates the problem, makes recommendations or a referral if indicated, or treats the child if necessary. Physical causes such as delayed auditory feedback must be pinpointed. In some instances, appropriate drugs might be prescribed by a physician. For children with significant psychological problems, psychotherapy is advisable.

Case Report

A 6-year-old boy began stuttering and fairly frequently repeated the first sound in a word. A consultation was sought after 2 weeks of continued stuttering. The parents had tried to help the child stop by having him repeat the word properly. Rather than helping, the boy became more anxious and stammered more. The parents were advised to not have him repeat words and to show him how to relax and start each word gently. Additionally, they were to praise periods of smooth speech and to provide an easygoing, enjoyable atmosphere. Without realizing it, the parents had become upset and were communicating their agitation in a variety of ways. This approach led to the disappearance of stuttering. It should be pointed out that the parents were extremely conscientious and the problem was of very short duration. However, it does highlight the importance of taking some action when stuttering appears to be worsening.

Books for Parents About Stuttering

Bryant, John E.: *Helping Your Child Speak Correctly*. Public Affairs Committee, New York (1970).

Cooper, Eugene B.: *Personalized Fluency Control Therapy: Behavior and Attitude Therapy for Stutterers*. Learning Concepts, Austin, TX (1977).

Schwartz, Martin F.: *Stuttering Solved*. Lippincott, Philadelphia (1976).

Stuttering: Its Prevention. Speech Foundation of America, Memphis, TN (1975).

Van Riper, Charles: *The Treatment of Stuttering*. Prentice-Hall, Englewood Cliffs, NJ (1973).

Books for Children About Stuttering

Fassler, Joan: *Don't Worry Dear.* Behavioral Publications, New York (1971). Ages 4 to 6.

Parents allow a little girl to outgrow stuttering naturally. They provide emotional support and acceptance of her speech difficulties. One aspect of support is provided by her mother who goes along with the girl's pretending that toy animals are real.

Lee, Mildred S.: *The Skating Rink.* Seabury, New York (1969). Ages 10 to 13.

A 3 year old witnessed his mother's drowning and stuttered ever since. People in his small town made fun of him, and he rarely spoke to anyone. At 16, an understanding roller skating rink operator encourages him to skate. He begins to develop self-confidence and decides to continue school rather than dropping out.

Madison, Winifred: *Growing Up In A Hurry.* Little, Brown, Boston (1973). Teen-agers.

A 16-year-old girl feels unloved and not accepted by anyone. She falls in love with a boy and does not stutter with him. Her stuttering is most severe in her parents' presence. She becomes pregnant, but her mother becomes concerned and helps her prepare for an abortion.

Watson, Sally: *Other Sandals.* Holt, Rinehart and Winston, New York (1966). Teen-agers.

A 12-year-old girl lives in a commune in Israel. She is an impulsive talkative child who stutters. The focus is overcoming prejudice, changing attitudes, and improving self-esteem.

References

1. Webster, Ronald L. and Lubker, Bobbie B.: "Interrelationships among fluency producing variables in stuttered speech." *Journal of Speech and Hearing Research* 12: (1969), pp. 677–686.

2. Van Riper, Charles: *The Nature of Stuttering.* Prentice-Hall, Englewood Cliffs, NJ (1971).

3. Schwartz, Martin F.: *Stuttering Solved.* Lippincott, Philadelphia (1976).

4. Hutchinson, John M.: "A review of rhythmic pacing as a

treatment for stuttering." *Rehabilitation Literature* 37: (1976), pp. 297–303.

5. Brady, John P.: "Metronome-Conditioned speech retraining for stuttering." *Behavior Therapy* 2: (1971), pp. 129–150.

6. Brady, John P.: "Metronome-Conditioned relaxation: A new behavioral procedure." *British Journal of Psychiatry* 122: (1973), pp. 729 –730.

TICS

Tics are any abrupt, repetitive nonpurposeful bodily movements. Muscles move in an involuntary, impulsive, and persistent manner. After eye blinking, face, neck, and shoulder movements are most frequent. The head and neck may suddenly be contorted or move in one direction. Verbal tics are repeated noises (sometimes, repetitive phrases such as "you know" are referred to as tics). Mild tics often come and go, particularly in relatively tense children. Nervous tics are different from organically caused problems, such as spasms and tremors. Nervous tics occur repeatedly, sometimes hundreds of times per day. Organically caused chorea movements are irregular, fragmented, and less stereotyped. Nervous tics are not painful and muscles do not deteriorate (atrophy). Children with tics are often restless, self-conscious, sensitive, excitable, stubborn, and overly dependent on others.

About 1 percent of the general population have tics.[1] Tics include eye blinking, squinting, frowning, grimacing, tongue pushing or clicking, coughing, and jerking of the head, mouth, cheeks, or shoulder. The usual age when tics begin is between 4 and 12 years. The average duration of tics is about 4 years, before professional help is sought. Most reports show that there are more boys than girls (as much as 3 to 1) with tics. The most frequent period is between the ages of 6 and 12, where about 10 percent of children have tics. The peak incidence is between 7 and 9 years. In the long term, the outlook is favorable in that only 6 percent of children continue to have tics as adults. The outlook is much worse for children who have multiple tics.

Tics usually become more intense and frequent under stress. During sleep, tics do not appear. Approximately 50 percent of children with tics have diffusely abnormal electroencephalograms. This means that their brain waves are not functioning normally, but that there are no focused findings which would indicate tumors, lesions, or epilepsy.

Gilles de la Tourette's syndrome is the name used to describe the combined presence of a muscular tic and a verbal noise. The problem usually starts with tic movements of the head and then spreads to other parts of the body. A repetitive noise is made such as throat clearing, whining, wheezing, or grunting. Most typical is a barking noise. The vocal tics may be the imitation of words spoken by others (echolalia). Some professionals have only used the term *Tourette's* if compulsive cursing occurs. While this happens fairly frequently with adolescents, children may have tics and noises without cursing and they also would be considered to have Tourette's syndrome. Most people who have not heard of this condition are shocked by hearing many obscene words from teen-agers who insist that they can't help it.

Reasons Why

Tension. Anxiety in children can stem from a large variety of sources. Peer and school pressures are the most frequent source of tension. Children often feel that they cannot cope with the demands placed upon them. This feeling of inadequacy combined with feelings of embarrassment and self-consciousness may lead to the development of tics. A helpful way of viewing this pattern is that a twitch is a natural physical reaction to tension. Continued tension produces the twitching which becomes habitual. Therefore, the tic habit is seen even under nonstressful conditions. Increased stress usually leads to more frequent tics. Many children react to teacher criticism as a very strong negative emotional experience. The tic often develops within the tense classroom atmosphere. Similarly, some peer groups engage in much teasing and competitive behavior. Some children do not cope well in this situation, need the peers for companionship, and feel continued tension.

Parental Behavior. Parents may serve as models to be imitated. The most obvious is the appearance of tics in children (especially those under 6 years) whose parents have the same, or another type of, tic. Unrealistic parental over-expectations may lead to a pressured feeling and to tics as an outlet. Without meaning to, parents may reinforce tics. When natural twitching occurs, some parents overreact with sympathy, attention, upset, or anger. Any of these responses serves to focus attention on the behavior and often increases that behavior of twitching. Finally, tics are most prevalent when parents are highly anxious, rigid, and strict. These characteristics serve as a model for children, and lead to highly pressured child-rearing methods. Punishment and criticism are heard frequently. The result is an atmosphere conducive to the development of tension and tics.

Reaction to Trauma. Frequently, children develop tics after an emotionally traumatic event, especially the sudden loss of a significant person. The departure or death of a close relative is particularly upsetting to children, especially to those who are quite sensitive or going through a difficult period in their lives. Some children become very upset at living with, or observing, a person who is terminally ill. Any frightening experience or fear of injury might lead to a defensive withdrawal by some groups of muscles. The tic often involves a few muscles from that original withdrawing response, since parents and others disapprove of the large repetitive movements. A usual process is that children have a normal reaction of twitching during and after an upsetting event. The twitch may serve as a release of muscular tension or may become an accustomed activity which focuses attention away from unpleasantness to some extent. The key is that the movement becomes a habit, which is repeatedly performed. This leads to the strengthening of specific muscles and the weakening of opposing muscles. Therefore, the tic becomes more and more entrenched and difficult to stop.

An example of a tic is rapid eye blinking. Children become very frightened while witnessing some event. They blink as a reflexive reaction to fear, as if they were trying to shut out the scary sight. Even minor fear may then trigger the excessive blinking. Eye blinking may then become a general habit. Even when most relaxed, the blinking may be present.

Unresolved Conflicts. A belief is that unexpressed strong feelings cause tics. Unacceptable aggressive or sexual impulses are the most usual sources of conflict. The individual is torn between wanting to express a desire and not wanting to because of societal and/or personal values. A typical example is the fear of directly or indirectly expressing anger. A verbal tic may develop such as a grunting sound or throat clearing. This is a symbolic way of trying to express anger. It may be a way of making sounds rather than expressing anger and using curse words. Also, it could be an indirect way of expressing anger by having people disturbed by the noises. A shoulder- or arm-jerking movement would be a symbolic way of expressing some type of striking movement. Rather than punching, the movement becomes a habitual beginning and holding back of striking out at others. Head jerking may be a symbolic way of saying "no" to a variety of stressful demands.

Sexual thoughts are often a source of much tension. There are many social taboos against the actual expression of, or even having thoughts about, sex. Young teen-agers often feel quite guilty about sexual fantasies. Fear and concern about sex is also quite frequent. The result is a building psychological pressure that may be expressed through tics. Head jerking may be a symbolic way of shaking out the bad thoughts.

Physical Causes. Nervous tics must be differentiated from organically caused spasms, tremors, chorea, and athetosis. A medical evaluation will pinpoint those diseases (such as St. Vitus Dance or rheumatic fever) which can cause repetitive movements. However, there is still a difference of opinion about the cause of Tourette's syndrome which includes a physical movement and a vocal tic, such as a barking noise or compulsive cursing. Some theorists believe that both types of tics are habitual, learned behaviors. However, others[2] have presented evidence that Tourette's syndrome is organically caused. It is believed that there is some impairment of the central nervous system that produces the tic.

How To Prevent

Encourage Expression of Feelings and Confidence. To prevent a build-up of tension, feelings should be openly expressed. Children must have adults or peers whom they can confide in. It is particularly effective when children feel that they can go to their parents with any type of problem. This is the opposite of situations where children only tell their parents about good things and are reluctant or fearful about discussing potentially embarrassing or confusing thoughts and feelings. The key is that *all* feelings and fantasies are acceptable to have and discuss. Some parents have a very hard time listening to "weird" or "dirty" thoughts. By being open to such feelings, much larger real-life problems may be prevented. One example is masturbation. Many children are concerned or worried about masturbation and feel guilty and tense about their behavior or thoughts. A matter-of-fact approach and willingness to talk about the topic is very beneficial. This is true no matter what position a parent takes. There is a clear trend towards open acceptance of masturbation as natural. However, even if parents do not approve, it is their nonshocked and nondisgusted approach that is vital.

Psychological conflicts over aggressive feelings is a significant cause of tension and tics. Helping children express anger appropriately is therefore crucial. Children should feel self-confident in their ability to cope with situations and assert themselves appropriately. You may have to teach (and role play) how to express anger clearly and without unduly antagonizing others. Any sign of passivity and helplessness should be a clue to seeking means to change that pattern. Successfully assertive children do not have to symbolically express anger through a physical or verbal tic.

Reduce Stress. When you see signs of tension in children, active steps should be taken to reduce stress. You might look objectively at your child-rearing patterns and possibly decide to be less strict, rigid, or punitive. You try to prevent the specific cause of conflict and tension. Sibling rivalry or frequent family quarrels may have to be lessened. Also, most children who develop tics are overly sensitive and easily fatigued and excited. Therefore, stress should be at a minimum and you should make sure that children get sufficient rest and take "calm" breaks during the day. A final stress reducer is the provision of clear and frequent reassurance. You tell children, and show by example, that the general situation is under control. Feelings of chaos or helplessness greatly frighten sensitive children. You reassure them that you love them and will always care for them, thereby preventing tension related to the threat of loss of love.

Do Not Overreact To Tics. At the first sign of tics, act in a very low-key manner. Do not nag or compare the child unfavorably to others. Overreactions of any type tend to increase tension and strengthen tics. Parental upset, anger, and concern frighten children. Most tics are temporary and will disappear without intervention. When a traumatic event occurs, be especially warm and supportive. If a tic appears, ignore it and concentrate on providing a feeling of security and confidence. If the tic continues for several days, it is then time to begin to use approaches described in this section in a low-key, positive, and nonpunitive way.

What To Do

Reward and Ignore. A simple yet effective method is to ignore tics and reward children for going for a length of time without tics. This method is especially useful when tics have just begun. It avoids the possible communication of overconcern, which may inadvertently reinforce and strengthen tics. Also, most tics are not long lasting so the unnecessary effort of a more complicated method is avoided. It is often helpful to explain tics matter of factly to children. Much anger and shame can be avoided by parents telling children that tics are not purposeful. At this stage, children are not told to do anything about tics but just to relax in general. Many children develop exaggerated tics by focusing on their movements and trying to suppress them.

When tics occur, you should pay no attention and make no response whatsoever. It is important that parents, teachers, and as many others as possible follow the same approach. An agreement is made to praise or reward children when they do not show a tic for some length of time (say 10 minutes at first). As the tic diminishes, the time interval is increased. The child is complimented in some manner at the end of the time period. "You really look nice and relaxed today," "It's nice to see you looking good and happy," etc. Even smiles and affectionate touching serve as a nonverbal reward for no twitching. After a week, if no improvement has been made, you might try the following procedures. Whenever intense tics occur, you might leave the room without saying anything. In some cases this method is effective, especially when attention seeking plays some role in the problem. The key for success is not to feel or express anger, but to act in a calm, purposeful way. Another method is to have children leave when tics occur. This is particularly appropriate when the tic bothers others. Loud noises and obvious jerking movements may be very distracting to others. The children are asked to take a "time out"[3] from the activity. It can be matter of factly explained that the time out gives them a chance to relax, prevents others from being disturbed, and will help them learn to control their tics. The most effective time out is for a few minutes to be spent sitting in a chair in a relatively bare room. Games and books should not be available. The idea is to make tic control more worthwhile and tic behavior undesirable.

Teach Anxiety Control. This method is also quite effective when tics first begin. You teach children how to handle anxiety and how to relax and feel calm in general. This is particularly effective with children who are obviously tense and fidgety. The general method is to show them how to completely relax their muscles. Some children find this very difficult at first. They slowly tense their muscles and then slowly let go more and more until they are limp. They remain limp for longer and longer periods. Stopwatches are very useful to help them build up the ability to remain still from 10 seconds (increasing 10 seconds each time) to several minutes. You might also include the imagining of pleasant scenes to enhance a calm feeling. If you know which are the tension-causing situations, you should add desensitization. While the child is relaxed, you describe the types of situations that cause anxiety. Each time you describe a more and more tension-producing scene, until the child can listen and not feel anxious. This helps desensitize the child to the cause of tension. This could be speaking in class, meeting new people, hearing arguments, playing with peers, etc. Finally, relaxed deep and even breathing is very useful for controlling anxiety and feeling more relaxed.

Self-Monitoring. When tics persist, you involve children in learning how to *control themselves.* A simple, yet often effective, method is self-monitoring. This has been successful for simple tics and for the multiple tics seen in Tourette's syndrome. For several days children are trained to become aware of and record the number of times that tics occur. At first, parents and teachers observe and record tic occurrence. Sampling periods should be from 10 to 20 minutes.

You watch children unobtrusively (without their awareness) for 10 minutes, recording on a pad each time the tic occurs. This gives adults an accurate picture of the frequency of tics. Children are then taught to be aware of their tics and count them. You may have to point out each occurrence matter of factly until children are able to recognize each tic. A very helpful device is a wrist counter which can be clicked for each tic. A running count is therefore available. Much to adults' surprise, just counting often leads to a greatly diminished number of tics or to complete disappearance. This is especially true if the habit is a few weeks or months old. For resistant habits, the following two methods should be used.

Practice Tics. It may be surprising, but intense practice often leads to the disappearance of tics. This has been called massed or negative practice. Prolonged practice[5] is followed by rest. Young children can play a game of making the tic as much as possible until they're tired. At least three times per week for a half-hour, the child voluntarily and rapidly does the tic over and over. It is explained that the practice is performed in order to break the habit. Most children want to eliminate the habit and this motivation helps a great deal. They should understand that practice helps get an involuntary movement under their control. An involuntary act is made voluntary! While practicing, they should think about the goal of control. They are making an effort to do what they previously had been trying not to do. They are helped to practice the *exact* movement of the tic, and they learn to perform it on cue. Voluntary control is then clear when the child can do it immediately when asked.

Habit Reversal. This method requires the most effort and is the most effective according to recent research.[1,6] This is a form of "overcorrection," which has been discussed as a method for other problems in this book. Children are taught to practice a response which directly *competes* with the habit. Competing responses should make the individual more aware of the habit, be incompatible with the habit (the habit can't occur while the response is being made), be able to be maintained for several minutes without others being aware, and should not interfere with normal activities. Children are told that they will practice a specific behavior that will counteract or compete with their habit. Nagging and scolding should not be used at all.

For head jerking, the chin should be held in and down as inconspicuously as possible. This is an "isometric" contraction where the muscles are tensed but kept still. Similarly, for shoulder jerking, shoulders are forcefully held down. For eye blinking and twitching, the opposing muscles of the eye and cheek are contracted. Another method is to voluntarily blink, keeping the eyes wide open between blinks. In the case of various throat noises, smooth breathing is the competing response. The mouth is slightly opened, and smooth breathing is practiced so that there is no stopping of the inflow and outflow of air. This is similar to rhythmic breathing while swimming, where a pause or catch of breath is inappropriate. Smooth breathing avoids fatigue and is incompatible with the pause necessary for grunting, throat clearing, or barking.

Awareness training is part of the procedure. You describe the tic to children, have them observe themselves in a mirror, and then reenact the movement. You watch and let the children know when a tic occurs. They should become aware of the *earliest sign* of the beginning of a tic. Also, they can become aware of what types of situations trigger tics. Often, it becomes apparent that they have more tics when with certain people or in situations where certain behavior is expected of them (school tests, socializing, performing, etc.). It is very helpful to have children ask others to help them control the habit by letting them know when the tic occurs. This could be embarrassing at first, but it usually then helps them feel less worried about others noticing and more aware of their tic.

Some children may need to have their motivation increased to stop their tic. You do this by reviewing the negative aspects of having a tic: It is inconvenient, embarrassing, and causes psychological pain. Relatives and friends should be enlisted to enhance motivation by complimenting efforts to stop and praising improved appearance during periods where tics are absent. They can also remind children to practice habit reversal.

Children act out the tic in slow motion while describing movements aloud. At least twice per day, they practice the competing response. They become aware of what happens just before the tic, such as touching their face, turning their head, looking up, etc. At the first sign of a tic, they immediately do the competing response for at least 2 or 3 minutes. Even when tempted to perform a tic, the competing responses should be practiced. There may be a need to make sure (promote generalization) that no tics occur in other settings. Self-monitoring and recording should be used at school and in the community. Some children find it very useful to imagine themselves in other situations and picture themselves engaging in various activities without having tics. The same approach of competing responses is very useful for other habits, such as nailbiting (grasp objects), eyelash picking (grasp objects), and thumbsucking (clench fists).

Drugs. Some consider drugs of little value and are concerned that drug use reinforces a helpless feeling. However, a variety of drugs are prescribed for simple tics with reported success. Drugs employed include butyrophenones, phenothiazines, methylphenidate, and dextroamphetamine. Haloperidol has been reportedly successful with simple tics and with the multiple tics in Tourette's syndrome. Most reports describe 80 percent improvement occurring by administering haloperidol to children and adolescents with Tourette's syndrome.

Case Studies

Two cases will be described. A 9-year-old girl had a head jerk to the left side for 2 months. It had continued to increase to a point where she exhibited this tic several times during an hour. The parents were told to reduce pressure by being more warm and supportive and by discontinuing piano lessons which she hated. Additionally, they taught her to be aware of the tic and to record each occurrence. Within 2 weeks, the tic diminished and disappeared. A 15-year-old boy had shoulder jerking and rapid, frequent eye blinks for several years. Psychotherapy for 1 year had no effect. Habit reversal was then successfully employed by the parents. He was very motivated to stop as he was extremely embarrassed about the habits. The parents taught him to be aware of and to count the occurrences. Eyes were held open for long periods and shoulders were contracted downward. At the first sign of either tic, 2 minutes of the competing response took place. After 3 weeks, shoulder jerking was eliminated and eye blinking greatly diminished. However, he stopped doing the competing response for eye blinking since the amount he did was not noticeable and didn't bother him.

Books For Parents About Tics

Azrin, N.H. and Nunn, R.G.: *Habit Control in a Day*. Simon & Schuster, New York (1977).

References

1. Azrin, N.H. and Nunn, R.G.: "Habit reversal: A method of eliminating nervous habits and tics." *Behavior Research and Therapy* 11: (1973), pp. 619–628.
2. Shapiro, A.K., Shapiro, E., Wayne, H.L., Clarkin, J., and Bruun, R.D.: "Tourette's Syndrome: Summary of data on 34 patients." *Psychosomatic Medicine* 35: (1973), pp. 419–435.
3. Lahey, B.B., McNees, M.P., and McNees, M.C.: "Control of an obscene verbal tic through time out in an elementary school classroom." *Journal of Applied Behavior Analysis* 6: (1973), pp. 101–104.
4. Thomas, E.J., Abrams, K.S., and Johnson, J.B.: "Self-monitoring and reciprocal inhibition in the modification of multiple tics of Gilles de la Tourette's Syndrome." *Journal of Behavior Therapy and Experimental Psychiatry* 2: (1971), pp. 159–171.
5. Tophoff, M.: "Massed practice, relaxation and assertion training in the treatment of Gilles de la Tourette's Syndrome." *Journal of Behavior Therapy and Experimental Psychiatry* 4: (1973), pp. 71–73.
6. Azrin, N.H. and Nunn, R.G.: *Habit Control In A Day*. Simon & Schuster, New York (1977).

4 ———

Peer Problems

INTRODUCTION

The focus of this chapter is on difficulties children have relating to one another. Characteristically this difficulty takes the form of either fight or flight. Included in this chapter are the following problems: fighting or aggression to one another, cruelty to younger children or animals, sibling rivalry, bad companions, and social isolation.

A major section of this chapter deals with the aggressive reactions of children to one another. Up to one-third of all children referred for mental health services exhibit aggressive or out-of-control behavior problems. Clearly, a pattern of persistent, excessive aggressiveness is a serious problem that should be controlled early. Not only does it lead to counteraggression, unpopularity, and even ostracism by a child's peers, but it has been found to be associated with later aggressiveness in adulthood. Long-term follow-up studies reveal that a large majority of highly aggressive children make inadequate adjustments as adults.[1] With proper parental management, it is likely that many of these children could have been helped at home.

Three types of aggression can be distinguished in children:

1. *Provoked aggression* wherein the child responds in self-defense to aggressive acts of peers.
2. *Unprovoked aggression*. This child is constantly in fights because she seeks to dominate or bother peers by hitting, teasing, or bossing.
3. *Outburst aggressiveness* or temper tantrums. This is the child who breaks up the house when he gets so mad and can't seem to control his anger.

The focus of this chapter will be on unprovoked aggression; temper tantrums will be discussed in the next chapter.

Research shows that aggressive children tend to reveal the following traits: assaultiveness, throwing temper tantrums when frustrated, quarrelsomeness, fighting to settle conflicts, and ignoring the rights and wishes of others.[2] Direct observation[3,4] of aggressive children reveals that they threaten or actually physically assault others, manifest a negative tone of voice, tease, embarrass others, and demand immediate compliance with their wishes. The Group for the Advancement of Psychiatry[5] characterized children with aggressive behavior as being antagonistic, verbally and physically assaultive, teasing, provoking, and quarrelsome.

There is no single cure or general prescription to reduce aggressiveness in children. Each child presents a different problem, and the remedy must be tailor-made to the needs of the child. Thus, this chapter presents a variety of techniques for changing aggressiveness, sibling rivalry, and cruelty in children.

References

1. Robins, L.N.: *Deviant Children Grown Up.* Williams & Wilkins, Baltimore (1966).
2. Quay, H.: "Patterns of aggression, withdrawal, and immaturity." In *Psychological Disorders in Childhood.* Quay, H., Werry, J., eds. Wiley, New York (1972).
3. Patterson, G.R. *et al.: A Social Learning Approach to Family Intervention.* Vol. 1. Castalia, Oregon (1975).
4. Werner, E. *et al.:* "Reproductive and environmental casualties: A report on the 10 year follow-up of the children of the Kauai pregnancy study." *Pediatrics* 42: (1968). p. 112.
5. Group for the Advancement of Psychiatry: *Psychopathological Disorders in Childhood: Theoretical Considerations and a Proposed Classification.* New York (1976).

AGGRESSION

Aggressiveness or hostility is a normal reaction in young children. Close to the surface, it readily emerges when the child needs to protect her safety, happiness, or individuality. Aggressiveness can be defined as behavior that results in personal injury to another.[19] The injury can be psychological (in the form of devaluation or degradation) as well as physical. This section will discuss unprovoked aggression, that is, the child who attempts to dominate his peers by physical assault (hitting, biting, kicking, throwing objects, pushing, and spitting) and/or verbal attacks (name calling, teasing, profanity, bossiness, derogatory remarks, quarrelsomeness, and threats of harm).

The child who is persistently and excessively aggressive tends to be impulsive, irritable, immature, inarticulate about feelings, and action-oriented.[18] Rather self-centered, the aggressive child has difficulty taking criticism or frustration. The low-IQ child has been found to be more prone to aggressiveness; perhaps more subtle and sophisticated ways of resolving conflict are harder to learn.

Between the ages of 3 to 7, most children make gains in the direction of greater control of aggression. Whereas the 2 year old may try to settle a dispute by hitting another with an object, the 4-year-old is more prone to argue with the other, at least some of the time. By the ages of 8–9, the child is fairly well controlled, although brief, intense quarrels will still occur. If the older child still engages in frequent and excessively aggressive acts, then the parents need to take this seriously and employ swift, effective action to curb this aggressiveness.[1]

The prevalence of overaggressiveness (verbal or physical) in boys and girls has been found to be almost equal. One study found that about 1 percent of 10-year-old children were persistently overaggressive.[3]

Reasons Why

There are many theories as to the causes of childhood aggression. Some believe that there is a universal fighting instinct in man,[8] while others maintain that young children learn many aggressive habits by observing the example set by others, such as parents, siblings, and peers. Also, it is apparent that aggressiveness is likely to be learned when children are rewarded for aggressive acts, that is, get their own way or get the adult attention they are craving. Other theorists assert that the frustrations of daily living trigger an aggressive drive in man; in other words, you react aggressively when an obstacle prevents you from satisfying a need or fulfilling a goal. Support for the frustation-aggression theory is seen in the fact that most quarrels of preschoolers start over a struggle for possessions (someone tries to take the toy of another). The number of quarrels of this type decreases with age but still holds the lead over other types at all ages.[9] Society's attitude toward aggression is another important variable. The steady rise of violent crime in this country (including wife and child abuse) most clearly demonstrates our inability to control aggression in ourselves, much less in our children.[11] The past decade has witnessed the glamorizing of violence by novels and the mass media, while punk-rock groups like Kiss glorify destruction and brutality. A sub-culture of violence seems part of the American scene. This sub-culture espouses such violence-related social norms as "an eye for an eye" and the "end justifies the means." Our society is also organized around competitive laws, and competition tends to foster aggression.

A child's capacity for fantasy also seems to be a factor related to aggression since there is evidence that children who produce more fantasies, even aggressive fantasies, are less likely to engage in aggressive acts.[10] Another variable is excessive drug use; alcohol, for example, is known to precipitate or worsen episodes of random violence in teenagers. Alcohol intoxication lowers ego controls and induces impulsivity. Finally, it has been noted that boys from homes where the father is absent or missing for an extended period tend to rebel against the feminizing influence of overinvolved mothers, by becoming excessively aggressive.[12] Many of these boys act as if they believe that hostile acts toward others are the earmark of masculinity.

It is probable that most of the above theories are partly true: They all seem to have a role to play in fostering childhood aggression. Because there are so many different theories of aggression, it is not surprising that numerous solutions have been proposed for solving the problem.

How to Prevent

Avoid Faulty Childrearing Attitudes and Practices. Research indicates that a combination of lax discipline and hostile attitudes by parents can produce very aggressive and poorly controlled children.[7] The lax or overly permissive parent is one who gives in to the child, acceding to his demands, indulging him, allowing him a great deal of freedom, being submissive toward him, or neglecting him. A parent with hostile attitudes is frequently unaccepting and disapproving of the child; this parent not only fails to give affection, understanding, or explanation to the child; but tends to use excessive physical punishment. When a hostile parent does exert authority, it is often done erratically and unpredictably. When this combination of low parental warmth and harsh physical punishment continues over a long period of time, it tends to produce aggressiveness, rebelliousness, and irresponsibility in the child.[4,5,6]

Limit Exposure to TV Violence. The power of television as a tool for learning aggression has been well established. A recent study,[5] for example, indicates that television habits established by age 8 or 9 influenced boys' aggressive behavior at that time and at least through late adolescence. The more violent are the programs preferred by boys in third grade, the more aggressive is the behavior both at that time and 10 years later.

Promote Happiness. Studies suggest that people who are experiencing positive affect (happiness) tend to be kind to themselves and to others in a variety of ways.

Minimize Marital Strife. Since the normal child learns a great deal of his social behavior by observing and imitating his parents, it behooves parents to ensure that children do not observe a high level of arguing, conflict, and aggressiveness between themselves.

Provide Physical Outlets and Other Alternatives. It is important for children to have opportunities for physical exercise and movement. Give plenty of opportunity for strenuous outdoor play and exercise so as to drain off tension and energy.

Change the Environment. Try to rearrange the home environment so that aggressive behavior is less likely to happen. The more physical space children have to play in, the less likely they are to be at each other. For this reason, outdoor play where there is plenty of room to roam is highly recommended. Music can also have a soothing effect on aggressive impulses. Arranging for the child to play with older children can help reduce fighting.

Provide More Adult Supervision. Very young or immature children seem to need much more adult involvement in their activities so as to prevent or ameliorate aggressive reactions. Showing interest in or becoming involved in what children are doing can head off trouble.

Also, the adult should be alert to the need to move physically closer to the child as a means of curbing aggressiveness. Young children are often calmed by having an adult nearby to act as an external ego.

It may also be necessary to cut down the length of time during which the child is allowed to play with others, and to cut down on the number of children with whom the child is allowed to play unsupervised.

What to Do

There are a variety of effective techniques for controlling aggressiveness in children.

Reward Desired Behaviors. Too often we adults take good behavior by children for granted and fail to reinforce it. The first step, then, in dealing with aggressive behavior, is to "catch the child being good" and to give plenty of positive reinforcement for nonaggressive acts such as playing cooperatively with a friend. *Each and every time* the child plays with a peer without fighting or yelling for a short interval of time (as little as 1 minute for some children), he should be praised by a parent.

With many children it will be necessary to combine the praise with a concrete reward. One way to do this is to make a game of it and have the child determine the reward by turning over a playing card in a previously shuffled deck. An ace could earn a penny candy, a number card could earn the same number of raisins as the number on the card, and a face card might merit a piece of bubble gum.

Another way to reward young children (ages 3 to 6) for nonaggressive behavior, *e.g.,* no teasing, is to set up a star chart on the refrigerator door (See Figure 1). Tell the child that each time a tease happens you will make a mark in one box on the star chart for that day. "If you go a whole hour

Star Chart

Name _____ Date _____

M	T	W	TH	F	S	SU

A star means going an hour without teasing.

Teasing Behaviors	M	T	W	TH	F	S	SU
9:00							
10:00							
11:00							
12:00							
1:00							
2:00							
3:00							
4:00							
5:00							
6:00							

Figure 1. Star chart.

without teasing, then you get a gold star in the box.'' Whenever the child teases say, "That's a tease!" and without scolding or nagging, place a check in the square for that day and that hour. When the child has gone an hour without teasing, say, "You've gone a whole hour without teasing! Should I put the gold star up or do you want to do it?''

Planned Ignoring. Rewarding prosocial behavior should be combined with the ignoring of aggressive acts. Unless the child's aggressiveness poses a serious threat to the physical safety of another, give absolutely no attention to it. Do not nag, scold, or punish the child for teasing or fighting. By ignoring the fighting you will be making sure that you are not inadvertently reinforcing this behavior by paying attention to it. In this regard there is research evidence that adults can dramatically reduce physical and verbal aggressive responses in children by systematically ignoring these aggressive behaviors while attending to and praising cooperative interactions among children.[13]

Additionally, in cases of unprovoked aggression, while ignoring the aggression you should give a great deal of attention and nurturance to the victim. Show great concern, empathy, and compassion for the injured party.

Teach Social Skills. Children often "fight it out" because they lack social skills such as "talking it out." Among the social skills that may need strengthening in some children is assertiveness.

Assertiveness. Research has shown that assertive responses provoke less anger and gain greater compliance than aggressive responses.[14] When being assertive you state your feelings and stick up for your rights in a reasonable way without being hostile to another person and without using coercive force to settle the conflict. When someone takes something of yours, you might say in an assertive way, "That's mine and I need it back. It makes me mad when you take it without asking me." Notice that the focus in assertiveness is on yourself (your feelings, rights, and needs), while the focus in aggressiveness is on the other person (attacking the other person verbally or physically).

One way of teaching assertiveness is to tell the child that it is important to let other children know when their behavior is bothering him, but that it is possible to tell them without hurting their feelings or provoking a fight. Ask the child to give an objective description of the offending behavior together with his personal reaction to the behavior; *e.g.*, "I was watching TV when you changed the channel. I don't like it when you do that." "You've been teasing me a lot, and that makes me feel bad." After the child has learned how to describe the behavior and express his feelings regarding it, you can then teach him the final component of assertiveness, namely, making a request for new behavior. Tell the child that sometimes other people will be willing to change their behavior if they receive a good suggestion about what to do instead—just telling them to stop what they are doing is not as likely to be effective. The request for new behavior involves one of four strategies: "Let's discuss it"; "Please move somewhere else or do something else"; "Let's share"; or "Wait now and you'll get it later." Once the child understands the assertiveness response, have her practice responding in this way to hypothetical situations that you describe.

Good problem solving or negotiation skills are an important part of effective assertiveness. Try to draw out of the child alternate ways of handling conflict situations other than fighting. If the child has trouble thinking of alternative solutions, you will have to suggest some, such as compromise, have an adult intervene, or walking away from a small child. Also, encourage the child to consider events which usually lead to fights (grabbing toys) and to think up ways to prevent such conflicts in the future (exchanging toys).

Develop Social Judgment. Good social judgment involves thinking before you act and anticipating the consequences of your actions for yourself and others. To develop this skill, try describing a past fight of the child's and pointing out the adverse consequences such as: loss of friendship and popularity; parent or school displeasure; bad mood in the child; bad feelings or physical pain in others, etc. Teach your child that he has the responsibility first to consider reasons, alternatives, consequences, and feelings of others when he is tempted to be aggressive, and to make an appropriate decision.

Another aspect of good social judgment is respect for the rights of others to have their own possessions. Since the fights of children are often over property rights (one child taking the toy of another), youngsters need to learn to distinguish between "mine and thine." From an early age, then, teach your children to respect the rights of others to own property. This means no "borrowing" things without prior permission.

Self-Talk. If your child is quite impulsive and has difficulty controlling her impulses, you might teach her a variety of aggression-inhibiting sentences that the child can say quietly to herself when tempted to attack others, such as "Count to ten," "Talk, don't hit," and "Stop and think before you act." Have the child repeat these sentences over and over until they become automatic guides to action.

If your child is generally delayed in verbal development, you should try to develop verbal communication skills by talking more with the child. Encourage the child to talk by showing a sincere interest in what he has to say. Children lacking verbal skills tend to fall back on their physical power as a way of dealing with peers.

Reduce Exposure to Aggressive Models. Most studies indicate that when children view aggressive acts by others, they tend to act more aggressively themselves. If the parents, for example, typically relate to one another in a hostile manner (arguing, criticism, belittling), then it is likely that the children will relate to others in a similar manner.

Since watching violent TV shows can also lead to imitation of aggressive acts by children, parents should consider strictly limiting the amount of time a child can view such shows. Parents can also mitigate the effect of a violent show on a child by watching it with him and helping the child distinguish between reality and fantasy violence, connecting the adverse consequences of a given aggressive act with the act itself, understanding the often complex motives for aggression, and disclosing nonviolent alternatives for handling the situation.[20] By discussing the show with the child, you can point out the self-defeating motives and consequences of violence, provide standards and moral perspectives by which the child can evaluate the TV actions, and make it clear to the child that she is watching purely fictional entertainment that is not an accurate model of the real world.

Provide Alternate Ways to Release Anger. An outlet for aggressive impulses can be provided in play activities. Play provides a gratification of wishes and impulses that may not be fulfilled in reality. For aggressive impulses, play allows symbolic gratification and release. The child cannot hit his brother, but he can hit a brother doll. Play, therefore, has cathartic value. Among the play objects that you might provide the child with for releasing angry feelings are an inflatable "Bobo" doll, punching bag, pounding clay, pegs to hit, and games of war or cowboys and Indians. Once released, these feelings may be quickly brought under control. Contact sports, such as football, also allow a socially acceptable outlet for aggressive, competitive impulses. A child may also draw or paint a picture depicting his aggressive thoughts and thus release them in an acceptable way.

Ensure Firm Discipline. Excessive aggressiveness can be a response to parental permissiveness.[7] Being firm means, first of all, making it crystal clear to the child that certain aggressive acts are not acceptable and not to be tolerated, namely, unprovoked hitting and teasing. Make it abundantly clear that you strongly disapprove of these acts and explain your reasons. Do not overlook such behaviors or condone them by saying, "He's all boy. He stands up for himself." Remember that a tolerant attitude toward such behavior may only serve to foster it. When the child acts aggressively, clearly label the act and be forceful in prohibiting the hurtful behavior. *"Look* what you did!" or "You must *never* poke anyone's eyes!"

Punishment. In addition to setting rules, firm discipline means consistently enforcing the rules. With preschool and grade-school children, a very effective form of punishment for aggression is the use of a "time out" penalty. Time out means that for a specified period of time the child must be isolated (perhaps in his room, the bathroom, or a specified area of the room) from ongoing social activity in which he can be reinforced.

Each time your 3 to 6 year old fights or teases, say, "You will have 2 minutes of time out. That means you go to the bathroom like this." (Walk with the child, open the door to the bathroom, and have the child go in.) "I will set the kitchen timer for 2 minutes. When you hear it ring you can come out."

Some guidelines for time out are:

1. For preschoolers, time out means 2 minutes alone in

the bathroom with the door closed. Time out for school-age children may be 5 to 10 minutes.

2. Each time the child teases or fights, send him immediately to time out. Say, "John, you forgot and teased. Go to time out." Don't argue or nag. If the child does not comply, physically escort the child while reminding him that he must spend an extra minute for not going alone.

3. The child is not to be spoken to while in time out.

4. If the child is noisy when the timer rings, reset the timer for another minute and have the child stay in time out—you may have to do this a number of times.

5. The child should clean up any mess made while in time out.

6. When the child returns from time out and is behaving appropriately, immediately reinforce this behavior with praise and attention.

7. If the child enjoys being alone and isolated, use some other form of punishment.

If time out is not feasible, you might take away privileges or require the child to make *restitution* to the injured party by apologizing or being extra nice (giving candy). If a blow was struck, the young aggressor (age 2–6) might be required to pat the injured area for a short period of time with the hand that administered the blow. If the child refuses, you could physically guide his hand through the required act.[15]

Physical punishment should be avoided. While it does tend to suppress the aggressive behavior immediately, it often generates hostility in the child and leads to further outbursts at some other time or place. Moreover, the parent who inflicts physical punishment provides an example of the use of aggression at the very time when he is trying to teach his child to be nonaggressive.

Arrange More Male Companionship. As previously mentioned, some boys may become excessively aggressive as a defense against too much exposure to females in the home. In homes where a father is present, he should endeavor to spend more time with the aggressive boy. Where there is no father available, efforts should be made to enlist uncles or male volunteers to act as "big brothers" to the boy.

A case in point is Tommy, age 10, who is considered to be a difficult child by all who know him.[12] He would rather fight than play with his friends, and he typically evokes anger rather than approval from adults. Chronically angry and troubled, Tommy lies, steals, and disrupts the classroom. Although he now has the presence of both parents in the home, he spent over half of his life without a father. His father, a navy pilot, was shot down in Vietnam and held as a prisoner of war for 5 years. Researchers at the U.S. Navy's Center for Prisoner of War studies have found that children whose fathers were held captive tend to display an excessive number of behavior problems, including rebelliousness, temper tantrums, nightmares, and proneness to crying.

Foster Altruism. Altruism refers to action designed to help someone in distress. The more a child shows concern for others, the less likely he is to harm them. Recent studies[14] have indicated that from at least the age of 1, children naturally show empathy and compassion for the feelings of others. They will, for example, try to comfort people who are crying or in pain. Parents can foster empathy and concern for others by asking the child how the victim must feel after being attacked, and by praising the child every time she shows concern for the suffering of others.

Undermine Defenses. Don't let your child justify aggressive acts and avoid taking responsibility by using such excuses as:

   "Everybody does it" (everyone does not do it, and even if they did it would not make it right).
   "He started it" (how else could you have handled it without fighting).
   "I didn't do it" (the facts indicate you did do it, and it will go easier for you if you own up to it).
   "He's a creep" (point out the inherent dignity, worth, and desirable characteristics of the other person).

Search for Underlying Reasons. Try to uncover some unmet need that may stimulate the aggressiveness.[21] Is the child living with constant criticism and not enough praise and appreciation? Does the child have a learning disability or physical handicap that makes it difficult to keep up with other children?

Some youngsters may respond in aggressive ways because of unmet needs for love and approval. A strengthening or redevelopment of loving feelings between parents and child may be necessary if the frequency of juvenile aggressive acts is to be lessened. Warm feelings of affection from parents are a powerful antidote to acting aggressively, especially when the child knows his parents strongly disapprove of aggressive behavior.

Case Reports

Case #1. Rorey was a 4-year-old boy who frequently fought with his peers.[17] He screamed frequently at them, continually told the other children what to do and how to play, and enforced his demands with punches, kicks, and slaps. With professional counseling, the parents implemented the following program to reduce the aggression.

1. Immediately after Rorey acted aggressively (physical aggression, yelling, or bossing), he was taken to the time-out room. One of the family bedrooms was modified for this use by having toys and other items of interest removed.
2. While escorting him to the time-out room, the parents said, "You cannot stay here if you fight." No other comment was made.
3. Rorey was quickly placed inside the time-out room, and the door was hooked so he could not leave.
4. The boy remained in time out for 2 minutes. If he cried or had a tantrum, the 2 minutes was timed from the end of the last tantrum or cry.
5. After time out he was brought back to his regular activities without further comment on the episode, in a matter-of-fact manner.
6. If the parents wished to give Rorey an explanation of the reason for time out, they had a brief discussion with him later in the day, when the aggressive behavior had not occurred.
7. The parents ignored minor aggressive behaviors which did not merit going to the time-out room, which means that they did not comment upon such behavior, nor attend to it by suddenly looking around when it occurred. The parents also ignored aggressive acts they learned about in retrospect.
8. Desirable cooperative play was reinforced frequently (at least once every 5 minutes) by the parents without interrupting it. Direct praise or such

comments as "My, you're all having a good time" were given by way of reinforcement.

9. Special treats, such as cold drinks, cookies, or new toys or activities, were brought out after periods of desirable play.

10. This program of rewards and penalties was followed 24 hours a day. After 3 days of this procedure, Rorey's aggressive behavior practically disappeared. Both Rorey's parents and several neighbors commented that he behaved like "a different child." On rare occasions when aggressive behavior did occur, it was usually in self-defense.

Case #2. Christopher, age 6, was the neighborhood "bully."[2] He laid down the law as to what games should be played and how, and he punished infractions with tripping or punching, so that the younger children were frightened and fearful when he was there. One day, Mrs. Brown, the mother of a 5 year old, invited Christopher to go to the beach with her family. Christopher's mother agreed but warned that he would probably ruin the day for everyone.

At the beach Christopher discovered a hidden talent in that he excelled at a nearby rifle range. This success buoyed his spirits, and he was extremely amiable for the rest of the day. After that Christopher frequently visited the Browns. At first the Brown children disliked him, but they soon agreed that he was "O.K. when he was nice." Christopher's mother and Mrs. Brown also became friends. As Mrs. Brown pointed out Christopher's good points and as his behavior improved, his mother came to like him more. Because his mother liked him, he felt better about himself and didn't have to show how important he was by bossing everybody and beating them up. Christopher, then, proved to be more of a neglected child than a problem child. Genuine warmth and interest—first by the Browns and then by his own mother—made a world of difference in his outlook and behavior.

Books for Parents about Aggression

Patterson, G.R.: *Living With Children: New Methods For Parents and Teachers.* Research Press, Champaign, IL (1971).

Describes the use of a system of rewards and penalties for dealing with childhood aggression.

Books for Children about Aggression

Sugarman, Daniel: *Seven Stories for Growth*. Pitman Publishing Co. (1965). Ages 6–12.

The first story deals with Johnny, who is hostile and destructive to others until he is able to discuss the cause of his anger with someone.

Greene, Constance: *The Ears of Louis*. Viking Press (1974). Ages 8–11.

A fifth-grade boy with big ears is the butt of name calling by his peers.

Stolz, M.: *The Bully of Barkham Street*. Harper & Row Publishers (1963). Ages 8–11.

A lonely, overweight sixth grader picks fights with younger children.

References

1. Robins, L.N.: *Deviant Children Grown Up*. Williams & Wilkins, Baltimore (1966).
2. Patterson, G.R. *et al.: A Social Learning Approach to Family Intervention*. Vol. 1. Castalia, Oregon (1975).
3. Werner, E. *et al.:* "Reproductive and environmental casualties: A report on the 10 year follow-up of the children of the Kauai pregnancy study." *Pediatrics* 42: (1968), p. 112.
4. Fairchild, L. and Erwin, W.M.: "Physical punishment by parent figures as a model of aggressive behavior in children." *Journal of Genetic Psychology* 130: (1977), pp. 279-284.
5. Lefkowitz, M.M. *et al.: Growing Up to be Violent: A Longitudinal Study of the Development of Aggression*. Pergamon, New York (1977).
6. Sears, R.R., *et al.:* "Some childrearing antecedents of aggression and dependency in young children." *Genetic Psychology Monograph* 47: (1953), pp. 135-234.
7. Becker, W.C.: "Consequences of different kinds of parental discipline." In *Review of Child Development Research*. Vol.

1, Hoffman, M.C., Hoffman, L.W., eds. Russell Sage Foundation, New York (1964), pp. 169–208.

8. Lorenz, K.Z.: *On Aggression.* Harcourt, Brace & World, New York (1966).

9. Dawl, H.: "An analysis of two hundred quarrels of preschool children." *Child Development* 5: (1934), pp. 139–157.

10. Goldberg, L.: "Effects of imitation, fantasy and frustration on aggression in children." Paper presented at the Eastern Psychological Association Convention, April 1975.

11. Pincus, J.H. and Tucker, G.J. "Violence in children and adults." *Journal of Child Psychiatry* 17: (1978), pp. 277–287.

12. Segal, J.: *A Child's Journey.* McGraw-Hill, New York (1978).

13. Brown, P. and Elliot, R.: "Control of aggression in a nursery school class." *Journal of Experimental Child Psychology* 2:(1965), pp. 103–107.

14. Hollandsworth, J. and Cooley, J.: "Provoking anger and gaining compliance with assertive versus aggressive responses." *Behavior Therapy* 9: (1978), pp. 640–646.

15. Pines, M.: "Good Samaritans at age two." *Psychology Today:* (June 1979), pp. 66–74.

16. Ollendick, T.H. and Matson, J.L.: "An initial investigation into the parameters of overcorrection." *Proceedings of the Midwest Association of Behavioral Analysis,* Chicago (1975).

17. Zeilberger, J.: "Modification of a child's problem behaviors in the home with the mother as therapist." *Journal of Applied Behavior Analysis* 1: (1968), pp. 47–53.

18. Quay, H.: "Patterns of aggression, withdrawal, and immaturity." In *Psychopathological Disorders of Childhood.* Quay, H., Werry, J., eds. Wiley, New York (1972).

19. Group for the Advancement of Psychiatry. *Psychopathological Disorders in Childhood: Theoretical Considerations and a Proposed Classification.* New York (1976).

20. Horton, R. and Santogrossi, D.: Mitigating the impact of televised violence through concurrent adult commentary. Paper presented at the American Psychological Association Convention, August 1978.

21. Wolf, A.: *The Parents' Manual.* Simon & Schuster, New York (1941).

SIBLING RIVALRY

Sibling rivalry refers to the hostility and jealousy that brothers and sisters develop toward one another. With two or more children in a family, there will always be some degree of bickering or arguing. Quarreling among siblings is one of the most common family annoyances. Parents often feel disappointed about this since they believe it reflects the lack of a happy, harmonious relationship in the home. However, bickering represents a normal developmental stage. Two year olds hit, push, and grab, while older children tease and are verbally abusive to each other at times.

Although squabbling, teasing, and competition among siblings must be considered normal, some children develop antagonisms or indifference to each other which often lasts a lifetime. Others form deep attachments from the early years. Typically, siblings show a liking and loyalty to each other which outlasts minor irritations. Thus, rivalry can be considered normal if the siblings share mutual satisfactions as well as frustrations, if they don't become overwhelmed by violent impulses and engage in life-threatening attacks on one another, if they don't harbor grudges, and if they don't react to every putdown as if it were a catastrophe.

Studies[1] show that children tend to become more competitive and rivalrous with increased age. So expect your 8 year olds to be more rivalrous than your 4 year olds, and 12 year olds to be even more competitive than 8 year olds. Rivalry is usually most prevalent in older siblings when they are fairly close in age (1 or 2 years) and when all are within the middle childhood years (8–12). Rivalry also tends to be greatest with two children of the same sex. Often the older child feels "replaced" by the younger. If the oldest is serious, hard working, and high achieving, the younger child is likely to seek a separate identity by becoming happy-go-lucky, sociable, and unconventional.

Minor squabbling among siblings can have a positive aspect. It can teach them how to defend themselves, stand up for their own rights, express their feelings, and resolve conflicts. Harmless teasing can also be a way of having fun together.

However, when sibling rivalry becomes excessive, it is time for the parents to intervene quickly. Excessive rivalry refers to fighting that is too frequent and/or too intense (bitter). Parents should not tolerate frequent destructive teasing wherein the goal is to make fun of the other and tear down the other's self-esteem. If one child has low self-regard anyway, this type of teasing can become very harmful. Once a teasing and squabbling pattern is well entrenched, almost any behavior, including just looking at one another, can trigger off a fight. These children are also eager to tattle so as to get the other into trouble. Of course, physical attacks or fights between siblings should not be allowed by parents under any circumstances. Although there is growing recognition in this country of the need to control child- and spouse-abuse, sibling-abuse (violence against one sibling by another) is just as serious a problem. In brief, parents need to take sibling rivalry seriously and protect their children from all forms of abuse by one another, including both psychological abuse (endless bickering, belittling, and battling) and physical abuse (violent acts).

Reasons Why

Among the more obvious reasons siblings feel jealousy and hostility toward one another are as follows.

1. Children depend so much on their parents for love, attention, and fulfillment of their needs that they do not like to share their parents with anyone.
2. There are normal conflicts and disagreements which result from close living with other people for extended periods.
3. Parental favoritism toward one child can spark resentment in the other children. In this regard, the Bible records the murder of Abel by his brother Cain due to jealousy over parental favoritism.
4. Sometimes hostile feelings toward parents are taken out on younger siblings.
5. Older siblings may be acting out a parent's unconscious dislike or rejection of a younger child.
6. When one sibling is clearly inferior in talent to another sibling who is close in age and of the same sex, the less well-endowed child tends to show more hostility toward the other.[2] For example, if one sibling has to live in the shadow of the achievement of a talented sibling, then he tends to feel robbed of his individuality. In this situation he feels that all of his actions and accomplishments are being compared with those of the other sibling.

How to Prevent

The following strategies can help head off some sibling rivalry.

Love Uniquely. Make each child feel loved and valued for himself. Make an extra effort to do this if one sibling is not as talented or attractive as the others. Show unconditional love for the less successful child, frequently express affection, point out her unique qualities, and help her find new roles in which she can gain family recognition and self-esteem. Try to love each child in a unique and special way.

Treat All Children Fairly. Avoid comparing one child with another, such as by saying, ''Why don't you work hard in school like your sister?'' We resent it when another is held up as an ideal.

Avoid having obvious favorites among your children. Appreciate the uniqueness and differing abilities of each child. Become more aware of subtle signs of favoritism such as:

1. Calling one child by endearing terms more often.
2. Getting along better with one child.
3. Babying one sibling.
4. Constantly belittling one child's interests, abilities, or performance.
5. Spending more time with one child.
6. Laughing more or talking more with one child.
7. Spending more money on one child (better clothes, more private lessons, more expensive college).

Do not rely on your judgment in this regard but regularly ask your children if they feel that you have a favorite.

Prepare Child for New Baby. Be sure to inform your children of the expected birth of a sibling well in advance. Let the siblings help with the new baby, and give them the feeling that this is their baby too. Gifts should be bought for all the children, not just the new baby. Tell the children that a new baby means lots of work for you; if they ever feel you are not playing with or loving them enough, they should be sure to tell you so that you can give them extra love and attention. Expect your children to show some resentment toward the new baby and/or step back into babyish ways. Do not criticize or punish them for this. Listen, be supportive, and reassure them of your love.

Individualize. Recognize that each child is different. You may give one more time because she requests it, another more compliments—but only earned ones—because he needs them, and a third a book or a tennis racquet because she will make good use of it. Don't buy all your children the same gift when you return from a trip. Individualize toys to meet the interests of each child. Don't insist upon the same bedtime for everyone. The older children will usually want to stay up later because they need less sleep.

Time Alone. Reserve some time each day to be with each child alone. Let the child be the center of your attention. Be his special friend for a short time. Don't talk about your other children. Rather, let that child be your only child for that time. This is the time for listening, caring, and mutual enjoyment. Remember that middle children, in particular, tend to suffer from parental neglect. The more you give of yourself to your children, the less they will have to compete for your attention.

Space Children. Sibling rivalry tends to be minimized when children are spaced 3½ to 5 years apart. By age 3 a child has started to learn to share parental attention, and much of the rivalry can be avoided.

Provide Privacy. Give each child as much privacy as possible. Try to arrange for separate bedrooms and closets. The more physical space there is in a house, the more likely conflict among children will be reduced. Encourage all family members to respect the privacy of the others.

Separate Ways. Encourage your children to have separate experiences. Living in close proximity to others for extended periods can lead to friction, as testified by submariners when forced to live together in a confined space for a long voyage. Do not ask older siblings to always let one of the younger ones "tag along" with them. Arrange for the children to spend several hours a day apart. Encourage different pursuits, different schedules, and different companions. A certain amount of physical separation fosters separate identities and helps reduce friction.

Teach Property Rights. Teach respect for private property early and train your children to ask rather than use the possessions of another child without permission. Try to minimize children having to share property such as toys and radios. Do not *force* the children to share their personal property.

Family Activities. Arrange for frequent family group activities of a fun nature, such as picnics, parties, and games. Having fun as a family builds up positive feelings which help counteract the negative ones.

Establish a System. Clearly define household chores and responsibilities (who does what and when). Arrange chores so children are not in each other's way. Rotate work assignments, and see to it that one child does not get all the good chores, while the others get the "dirty work." Label and clearly identify which toys and possessions belong to each child. Set a time limit (10 minutes) on how long children may talk on the phone.

Family Council. Set up a family council. This means that at certain times the whole family meets for discussion, sharing, griping, and planning. Children can ventilate feelings at these times and be assured of a fair hearing.

Parental Example. Your relationship with your spouse sets the example for all family interactions. Do you typically model for your children warmth, consideration, and constructive problem solving?

No Tattling. Instruct your children that we all do things wrong and that it is best to overlook much of this. Constantly telling parents about little things is called "tattling," and this tends to make life unpleasant in a family. Of course you need to know about serious misbehavior (*e.g.*, hitting).

Avoid Overprotection. Don't be overprotective of the youngest child in the family. She has to learn to respect the rights of others and to share your attention.

No Surrogate Parents. Do not force your older children to babysit or assume an adult role in caring for the younger children. If the older ones often correct and criticize the younger ones, be understanding but explain that it is your job to train and correct the children.

Concern for Others. Teach your children the basic values of cooperation, sharing, and family cohesiveness. Show them that you value these virtues as much as competitiveness and individuality. Encourage your children to strive for the good of the family and not just for personal advancement or enjoyment. Compare your family to an athletic team, and point out that best results are achieved when members assist one another in striving for common goals. Insist that your children be empathic to each other and consider how their behavior makes the other person feel. Reward unselfish acts by commendation and occasionally by some concrete reward. Teach good sportsmanship in games and athletic contests. Remember the observation of Charles L. Lucas: "Civilization is just a slow process of learning to be kind."

What to Do

The following procedures have been found useful in reducing arguing and fighting among siblings of all ages. Typically parents use a combination of these techniques.

Ignore. If the children seem evenly matched, it seems wise to let them settle minor squabbles on their own. In this way they learn to fight their own battles without undue dependence on adults. By completely overlooking minor hassles, you will find that when you do intervene, it will tend to be more effective.

Referee. You can help the children settle a number of their differences by acting as an impartial negotiator.

In most instances it will not be clear who is at fault. Rather than attempting to fix blame, your role in these instances will be to help the children resolve the conflict themselves. Initially, you will have to sit with the children and teach them effective problem-solving skills, such as the following.

Express angry feelings. Teach the children how to express feelings of anger or annoyance directly to each other. Letting angry feelings out is better than forcing them underground. Don't make children deny that they really hate their brother or sister at that moment. Letting your children know you understand helps them feel less guilty about their strong feelings. Tell the children that these feelings are normal. Instruct them that each should be assertive (state what their rights, needs, and feelings are) but not aggressive (no name calling, yelling, threatening, hitting) with the other.

Mutual problem solving. Encourage them to work out a solution. Frequently their ideas are much more fair, and their understanding of each other's motives more correct than yours. Each child should try to think of several possible solutions. Advise them that an effective solution often involves compromise in order to meet the needs of all concerned. Appeal to their strong sense of justice and fairness. If the children are too upset to negotiate, let them sit and cool off for a while.

Takes two to fight. Teach your children that they have a choice to accept or decline the invitation of the other to fight. The next time a sibling teases them, all they have to say is, "I'm sorry you feel that way," and pay no further attention.

By teaching the above skills, you give the children an alternative to aggression for solving conflicts. Once you have taught these skills, your role as referee will be one of encouragement. Show confidence in the ability of the children to solve their difficulty by saying, "I know you'll find a way to satisfy both your needs. Let me know what you decide," or "I'm sure you two will work it out."

Judge. When you have reason to believe one child is clearly to blame or the children are not able to solve the problem themselves, you may have to act as judge and jury. Bring the children together for a face-to-face hearing, or talk to each child separately. Be sure you hear both sides of the issue. Restate the conflict in your own words, and ask both children if you restated it fairly. Make sure all the opinions are clearly known, the arguments reviewed, and the decision, when reached, clearly understood by both children. Avoid taking sides predictably or constantly.

The noted child psychologist Haim Ginott[3] recommends that when you are gathering the facts, you ask the children to tell you what happened in writing. In 100 words or more, they should describe how it started, how it developed, what was said, and at the end include their personal recommendation for the future. Spelling doesn't count. Ginott reports that children do not always comply with this suggestion, but they always quiet down after it is made. Many parents find that children choose to settle their conflict, rather than write about it.

Once you have the facts, be fair, firm, and calm in giving your decision. For example, you might say, "Joan, the bike belongs to Helen, your older sister. You must ask her before you ride it. It is hers. Helen, be good to Joan. Sometimes you like to play with her toys." Children set great store by justice, and they also like order and control.

Sometimes it will be necessary to penalize a child who is bullying or disruptive to others by sending her to a time-out area for 5–10 minutes.

Group Rewards and Penalties. This is a very popular procedure with parents who have tried it. It eliminates the need to fix blame which is difficult to do in most cases. Often the teaser secretly welcomes and subtly provokes the teasing so as to get the other child in trouble.

Rewards. When two siblings are constantly fighting, say to them, "Look, if you two play together this afternoon without either of you hitting, fighting, or calling names, I'm going to give you both a surprise. I can't tell you what the surprise is now, but it will be something you both like. If I hear absolutely no fighting of any kind for the next 2 hours, then you both get the surprise. But if either of you starts arguing, then nobody gets the surprise, no matter who starts it. Do you understand?" As rewards, you might give each one a favorite snack, small toy, or trip to the park.

An alternative procedure involves setting the kitchen timer for variable intervals of time. When the bell rings on the timer, check to see if the children are getting along well. If they are, praise them or give a small reward.

The trick in rewarding cooperative play is to remind yourself to do it, since most parents are in the habit of attending primarily to negative interactions.

Penalties. Next time the children fight, say, "Now listen, since you can't get along peacefully together, you'll have to be apart. Each of you go to a separate room and stay there for 5 minutes. The kitchen timer will ring to signal you to come back. If you start fighting again when you return, you'll have to go to the time-out rooms again for a longer period. I don't care who started this; I'm finishing it. We can't have this yelling and fighting all the time."

Similarly, if the children are arguing over a toy or possession, take the object and tell them that they can have it back when they decide who is to get the object. If they squabble over the TV, say, "Q.K., from now on, nobody watches TV until you decide who's going to watch what shows. All of you together decide in your bedrooms. Nobody is to turn on the TV, at any time of day, until you can tell me what you've agreed on." Remember that the application of group penalties gives everyone a reason to make peace.

Release Anger. A certain amount of aggression in every child must be allowed to come out. Haim Ginott[3] suggests that a jealous older child who hits the baby be given a baby doll and allowed to hit or spank it to release anger. In another instance he advises parents to say to a child, "If you want to, you can throw stones at the tree and pretend it's your sister. If you want to, you can even draw her face on paper, stick it on the tree, and then throw stones, but she is not to be hurt." Some parents encourage an angry child to hit a pillowcase stuffed with soft clothes which is hung from the basement ceiling.

Set Limits. Make clear to your children, in no uncertain terms, that you will not allow them to harm each other physically (hitting) or with words (name calling, ridicule). Under no circumstances, then, will you tolerate physical violence between your children or any destructive teasing. As a general guideline do not allow your children to treat each other in ways that you would not tolerate if they were someone else's children. Do not permit violence in the family by condoning the belief that if someone is doing wrong, and "won't listen to reason," it is acceptable to hit that person.

Distraction. Your children may need more adult supervision of their play. Quietly join the group. Your presence alone may reduce tension. You might suggest a new game or see further possibilities in the old one. Saying, "How about this puzzle, does anyone want to solve it?'' might arouse interest in a constructive activity and diminish hostility.

Understand the Causes. Make a serious effort to understand the causes underlying destructive teasing. Eliminate all realistic reasons for one child to feel jealousy or resentment toward the others.

Separate. If two children are hopelessly abrasive to each other, consider adjusting their schedule (meal times, homework, leisure) in a manner that will keep them out of each other's way.

Case Report

Two brothers, ages 7 and 4, were engaged in an extreme form of sibling rivalry. Almost every look and gesture were grounds for verbal or physical battle. They continuously competed for attention from adults and children. The parents were most cooperative with a therapist's recommendation and tried two new techniques. For the younger boy, helping the child express his feelings in words had the effect of lessening the intensity of his feelings. Both parents focused upon his strong feelings and verbalized what they thought he felt. Particularly effective was their expressing his feelings of being picked on and of everyone being unfair to him. It was necessary to prevent the parents from moralizing, which was their usual behavior. Reflection of feelings was explained as a necessary and sufficient means of demonstrating their empathy for their son's feelings. The older boy required specific instructions to cool off and not to always respond in an excited, defensive manner. Additionally, cooperative play and friendly conversation were reinforced by the parents. They were told to praise this behavior in a natural and positive manner and to give an occasional concrete reward. The previous parental pattern was broken, wherein they had been moralizing the need for good behavior, focusing on rivalrous behavior by negative attention, and not mentioning or praising appropriate cooperative behavior. The boys had many periods of cooperative, friendly behavior, and their rivalry diminished to a more acceptable level.

Books for Parents About Sibling Rivalry

Neisser, E.G.: *Brothers and Sisters*. Harper & Row, New York (1951). An excellent book on sibling rivalry.

Ostrovsky, E.: *Sibling Rivalry. A Guide for Parents Who Want to Understand and Control Conflict Between Their Children*. Cornerstone Library, New York (1970).

Sloane, H.R.: *Stop that Fighting. A Short, Step-By-Step Guide for Turning Sibling Rivalry Into Peaceful Coexistence*. Telesis, Ltd., Fountain Valley, CA 92708 (1976). A short booklet about using group rewards and penalties.

Books for Children About Sibling Rivalry

Blume, J.: *Tales of a Fourth Grade Nothing*. E.P. Dutton & Co. (1972). Ages 8–11.

A fourth grade boy is convinced he must be nothing because his 2-year-old brother gets much more parental attention.

Colman, H.: *Diary of a Frantic Kid Sister*. Crown Publishers (1973). Ages 10–13.

Eleven-year-old Sarah has intense feelings of anger and jealousy toward her 16-year-old sister.

Hazen, B.S.: *If it Weren't for Benjamin (I'd always get to lick the icing spoon)*. Human Sciences Press (1979). Ages 4–8.

A sensitive, understanding look at the rivalry and love between two brothers.

Viorst, J.: *I'll Fix Anthony*. Harper & Row (1969), Ages 3–6.

An older sibling's unkind behavior toward his younger brother.

Zalben, J.: *Cecelia's Older Brother*. Macmillan (1973). Ages 4–6.

Cecelia's older brother is continually fighting with her.

References

1. Kagan, S. and Madsen, M.C.: "Rivalry in Anglo-American and Mexican children of two ages." *Journal of Personality and Social Psychology* 24: (1972), pp. 214–220.

2. Pfauts, J.H.: "The sibling relationship: A forgotten dimension." *Social Work* 21: (1976), pp. 200–204.
3. Ginott, H.: *Between Parent and Child.* Avon, New York (1969).

BAD COMPANIONS

Normal children tend to have a variety of friends, some good and some bad. The evidence suggests that children's imitation of peers is, in the main, constructive. Children are less likely than many parents fear to form an enduring relationship with peers who do not share parental values and standards.[1] The child's moral character is basically set by age 12. By this time, the influence of bad companions is generally not able to change the character formed at home. The child may experiment and test out differing ways, but he is not likely to drastically change his character and morals.

Although children are rarely made bad by undesirable companions, their own trouble-making inclinations may be triggered by other children. When a child frequently gets into difficulty with a certain friend, parents are well advised to take immediate action rather than hoping that this is a phase the child will outgrow.

Reasons Why

Often children realize that a particular friend or group is a bad influence on them, but they continue to associate with them for such reasons as:
1. Special attention and the chance to "belong" (little companionship or support at home).
2. Fun and excitement.
3. Similarity of special interests.
4. Status and prestige.
5. Temporary need to rebel and assert one's independence from parents.
6. Lack of self-confidence so child associates with friends who are younger, "duller" or "not as good" as herself.

In other instances, bad companions are the result, not the cause, of juvenile delinquency. The undesirable friends, instead of having led the child astray, may have been selected by him after his antisocial problems began, precisely because of a similarity of deviant interests.

How to Prevent

Get to Know Friends. Make your child feel that his friends are welcome at your house. Exert every effort to meet and get to know his friends and their parents. The more your child and friends are able to enjoy themselves at home, the less likely they will be to seek excitement elsewhere. Also, by spending time with the friends, you will be able to get to know them and their value systems. Your children will also measure their friends by the standards at home. In your home do not tolerate antisocial practices or people who practice them.

Ensure Variety of Friends. Help your child form a variety of friends by such strategies as sending your child away to summer camp, and back and forth visits with children of friends and relatives.

Use Reasonable Discipline. In one study[2] adolescents were more likely to model themselves after their parents and to associate with peers their parents approved of if their parents used reason to explain decisions and demands. Such a reasonable parent stands in contrast to the authoritarian parent who uses arbitrary, domineering, and exploitative methods.

What to Do

Tactful Criticism. Before your child reaches high school, you may be able to request that she not see a bad companion. With teen-age children, however, direct criticism of a friend challenges the child to stand up for his choice. Forbidding a friendship at this age only tends to add spice and intrigue to it.

Indirect criticism seems best with teen-agers. Try to plant a seed of doubt about the suitability of associating with the friend. For example, you might observe, "It seems that whenever you're around Jim you get into trouble." Or you might "wonder" if the companion is a wise choice for specific reasons such as bossiness or bullying behavior. You could "speculate" whether continued association will get the child into more serious trouble. You could also say, "In my opinion your friend tends to act in a self-centered way and rarely thinks about your needs."

If your child continues to get into trouble with an undesirable friend, you might try the mutual problem solving technique by saying, "Jane, whenever you're with Joann you get into trouble. This cannot continue. How do you think we can solve this problem?" Often children come up with good ideas, such as, "Well, I'll see her only at lunch, but not after school."

Encourage Individuality. Help your child see that it is both to his and his friend's advantage to broaden their interests and associations. Limiting their activities to those which they participate in together will eventually become tiresome and boring so that they will tend to lose interest in each other. If one child, slightly built, goes out for track, and his friend, huskily built, plays football, they will find more to talk about because of their different activities.

So encourage your children to develop their unique skills and broaden their friendships by joining organizations where prosocial children abound, such as Girl Scouts, boys' clubs, band, little league, Sunday school, or the "Y" program.

Examine Needs. Determine which of your children's needs are being met by bad company (excitement, adventure, caring, belonging, prestige) and arrange substitutes to meet these needs. For example, if your child seems to be seeking excitement, you might arrange a wilderness camping trip.

Believe in the Child. It is important that parents do not lose faith in a child or in the child's ability to cope with a difficult situation. Believe in the basic goodness of your child. Remember that childhood friendships are typically transitory and that children often go through a limited period of rebellion or mischief-making. Have trust in the child since his character is well established by age 10–12.

Strengthen Your Relationship. To counter the influence of bad companions make a special effort to develop closeness with the child by spending more time alone on mutually enjoyable activities and by talking more with the child in which you try to listen more respectfully and disclose more of yourself. By building companionship with your child, she will be more apt to identify with you and try to please you.

Promote Other Associations. Take steps to reduce your child's association with bad companions. Identify some potential friends with acceptable values and then arrange situations wherein the child comes into contact with these peers. Studies show that mere exposure to others is a strong incentive toward the formation of friendships.

Arrange Counseling. Try to get an adult the child is close to and likes to talk with the child and offer guidance about undesirable companions. It could be that a parent is the last one a child will confide in at the time. On the other hand, a teacher, guidance counselor, relative, or member of the clergy might be able to open lines of communication and act as a mediator.

Provide Structure and Limits. Establish a firm household schedule in which there is a set evening meal time. This will tend to limit escapades far from home.

Schedule family outings on weekends to limit undesirable associations. Arrange for a part-time job for the child. By filling up your child's leisure time, there will be little opportunity to associate with undesirable friends.

Although children have the right to associate with whom they choose, they must not be allowed to *act* in antisocial ways. If your child acts up in a way that violates the rights of others, then you must intervene since you are responsible for your child's behavior. You are well within your rights in prohibiting a disrespectful child from entering your home. If your child commits an act of vandalism, you should make sure he faces the consequences—working to undo the harm or paying for the damages.

Researcher Lee Robins of the Washington University School of Medicine reports that parents who are lenient with their children when they steal, commit acts of vandalism, or break the law in other ways are likely to end up with delinquents on their hands.

Distancing. When all else fails you may have to take more drastic measures such as moving to another neighborhood, sending your child to live with relatives for a temporary period of time, changing the child's school, or sending your child to a sleep-away summer camp or to a boarding school.

References

1. Segal, J. and Yahroes, H.: "Protecting children's mental health." *Children Today* 7: (1978), pp. 23–25.
2. *Parents as Leaders: The Role of Control and Discipline.* NIMH Division of Scientific and Public Information, 5600 Fishers Lane, Rockville, MD (1978).

CRUELTY

Cruelty to animals or younger children is commonly recognized as a passing phase in childhood that under parental pressure is channeled into more acceptable behavior as the child progresses beyond the early phases of his emotional development. Cruelty is defined as the premeditated deriving of pleasure by hurting others (usually younger children) or animals. It has to be differentiated from impulsive behavior, which is not premeditated.

Some children show unrestrained and persistent cruelty far beyond the usual age. They may, for example, take sadistic pleasure in torturing cats, dogs, or birds, organize groups for the purpose of whipping other boys, or be so cruel to younger siblings that they endanger their safety.

Children who bully others have been found to have distinct characteristics.[1] They tend to be males, hyperactive, disruptive, extroverted, and have lower IQ scores than their peers. They tend to have parents who have marital problems or conflicts at home, have been bullies themselves, and exhibit inconsistent or overpermissive approaches to childrearing. Children who are cruel to animals[2] also tend to be boys, are usually young (average age, $9^{1}/_{2}$), of normal intelligence, and show many other aggressive symptoms, such as bullying, fighting, temper tantrums, lying, or stealing. These children often had a chaotic home with aggressive parental models. Some children who are cruel to others show signs of underlying brain damage, such as an abnormal electroencephalogram.

What to Do

Reduce Aggressive Models. The behavior you yourself model is of crucial importance. If a child sees parents hitting each other or throwing dishes, he may quickly adopt these actions himself. If you use harsh physical punishment with the child, he may imitate the cruelty done to himself. So try to express your feelings in words and encourage your child to do so.

Set Limits. Cruelty in any form must not be tolerated. Whenever you observe this behavior, say immediately and emphatically, "No hurting. I can't let you do that." If needed, restrain the child physically, holding his arms against his body. Do not spank the violent child since meeting violence with violence sets a bad example. With younger children a few minutes of time out would be a logical penalty, while loss of privileges (playing with friends) is appropriate for older children. Do not plead with the child to stop and then do nothing. Also, avoid giving the impression that you respect such behavior or think that it is cute ("Oh, she's such a holy terror!").

Encourage Alternative Expressions of Feelings. If children cannot express angry feelings in some way, they seem to get bottled up and may erupt in violent form. Among the acceptable ways a child can express anger are:
1. Painting a drawing or mean picture. This might be a picture of a "horrible" father or sister. This is better than biting or kicking others.
2. Darts may be thrown at a board, or other objects can be thrown or hit, such as a punching bag.

Father Models Warmth. Fathers of sons who show cruel behavior should make extra efforts to be soft and loving and to express tenderness and warmth so the child sees this modeling and does not have to act supertough in order to be considered masculine. Also, the more time fathers spend with their sons in mutually enjoyable activities, the more likely the son will identify with the father and adopt his moral standards.

Foster Empathy. Whenever the child tries to injure others, explain that it "hurts" the other and try to stimulate empathic feelings by asking, "How would you feel if someone tied a can to your tail or hit you on the head with a stick?"

References

1. Lowenstein, L.F.: "Who is the bully?" *Home and School* 11: (1977), pp. 3-4.
2. Tapia, F.: "Children who are cruel to animals." *Child Psychiatry and Human Development* 2: (1971), pp. 70-77.

SOCIAL ISOLATE

Being socially isolated is an extreme form of disturbed peer relations. Little positive interaction can result when virtually no time is spent interacting with others. See the section regarding "Shy" children for additional information. Shy children typically want to socialize and make attempts to do so. Social isolation is a more severe reaction, where children actively seek to avoid others.

Socializing means to have companionship and interaction with a group and feeling a sense of belonging. *Isolation* is to be set apart from others—being seclusive and alone most of the time. Very frequently, detachment begins for reasons not under a person's control, and then the person more and more deliberately withdraws. The shy child feels uncomfortable but continues to seek social contact, while isolated individuals actively prevent any social interaction. Social isolation is highly correlated with other problems such as school difficulties, general personality maladjustment and, later, emotional problems as adults. Strikingly, isolated children often develop delinquent behavior, and isolated adults have a high incidence of bad conduct discharge from the Armed Services.

At times, bright creative children choose to be alone and not join any groups. These children may be able to be productive and feel happy. However, they are still prone to feeling different and receiving negative feedback from others. In our society, outgoingness is highly valued. Most isolated people feel fearful, uncertain, misunderstood, rejected, abandoned, and alone in a crowd. Approximately 10 percent of children in elementary school are not selected as someone to spend time with by any peer. These children may be actively rejected by others or merely ignored. The extreme form of isolation occurs when children totally or frequently withdraw into their own fantasy world. This type of problem requires immediate professional intervention.

Of great concern is that isolated children do not have many occasions for social learning. They more and more lack the experience and practice of relating to others. Some children are isolated from everyone, while others can relate relatively well either to peers, younger or older children, or to adults. Isolated children do not have the opportunity to develop friendships because friendships require mutual self-disclosure over fairly long time intervals. Closeness is deepened by continued sharing which is not possible when an individual is alone most of the time. Additionally, peer values are shared and are instrumental in individuals feeling that they "belong" to a group. Isolated people do not learn others' values and are not able to share their own views with others. Before puberty there are frequent shifts in group membership. Afterwards, there are more cliques who stick together and identify with each other. Therefore, by 12 years of age it is essential to be able to fit into some peer group. Otherwise, children may well remain isolated for the rest of their school careers and possibly for good. Children accept or reject others based upon personality traits and level of skill. Healthy, friendly, sociable, and easygoing children are valued. Withdrawn or hostile children are avoided. This section focuses on enhancing social desirability and the motivation to be sociable.

Reasons Why

Fear of Others. Fear of others is a powerful reason to remain alone. Fear takes many forms but basically results in a wish to escape negative feelings by avoiding others. Interaction has become equated with psychological pain. This pattern may be set very early by children experiencing strong negative reactions in the presence of parenting figures. Tense, angry, uncaring, ambivalent, or insensitive adults can cause infants and toddlers to want to withdraw from people. People become associated with pain, and solitude becomes associated with safety and pleasure. Similarly, early sibling or peer experiences can set the tone for later social interaction. Children who are teased, bullied, and embarrassed often become self-conscious, overly sensitive, and expecting of negative responses from others.

Lack Social Skills. Some children do not know how to relate to others. It is important to analyze social skills by age. By doing so, parents can pinpoint which skills are lacking. Preschoolers may not have learned the basic rules of relating to others such as taking turns, sharing, complimenting others, and contributing ideas for games. Older children may not know the methods involved in making and keeping friends. They may not have learned or practiced giving and receiving. They may not have learned how to talk to anyone about anything. Lack of exposure to others can result in the development of no interests in common with peers. Social relatedness is necessary for learning and sharing mutual concerns.

Parental Rejection of Peers. Negative consequences occur when parents have overly high expectations for their children's friends. What gets communicated openly or subtly is that the chosen friends are not good enough. This may directly discourage peers from associating with a child because they feel unwanted and rejected by the parents. The real blow comes when children learn to doubt their own judgment or feel that they can never please their parents in their choice of friends. Isolation becomes the unfortunate result. The pattern is set for obtaining satisfaction from solitary pursuits and others become irrelevant.

How to Prevent

Early Exposure to Others. It is important to provide early, *positive* experience with others. Problems can arise when very young children play unsupervised. Several negative experiences (being teased, bullied, or embarrassed) may greatly influence the young child to try to avoid others. Parental presence alone may well aid the sensitive child to feel safer when playing with others. Additionally, you should take the opportunity to analyze your children's style of interacting. Causes of problems with others may be identified and quickly remedied when spotted early. Children who always grab others' belongings must be identified so that the pattern of rejection by others and social isolation does not begin. Parental participation with groups of young children should foster sharing, taking turns, cooperation, and being able to tolerate not having one's own way.

While very young, children can learn to accept feelings of embarrassment and anger. Parents should acknowledge these concerns and accept them as natural. "We all get angry or afraid, but we quickly get over it and like each other again." Gradually, children should learn to mingle with others and feel comfortable in larger and larger groups. Some children experience their first large groups in kindergarten and cannot handle the excitement and interaction. Early and gradual exposure within a pleasant supervised context prepares children for being positive group participants.

Model, Teach, and Discuss Positive Group Belongingness. Social skills should be modeled and taught throughout childhood. Children learn by observing you getting along with friends and hearing you discuss the positive characteristics of others. Pointing out others' weaknesses and complaining about their behavior is to be avoided. Children then learn by observing models (you, siblings, and peers) and by being taught appropriate skills. You teach them how to get along with others and how to avoid fighting and complaining frequently. By talking and demonstrating, you show children negative social behavior. *Unpopular* children tease, insult, tattle, grab, bully, and do not contribute to the group. They are often unhappy, stingy, bossy, gloat when they win and cry when they lose, and their feelings are very easily hurt. What should be taught at every opportunity is what makes children valued group members. *Popular* children are generous, sharing, considerate, cooperate, and often do more than their own share which contributes to others. They have a good sense of humor, are cheerful, and frequently laugh. They ask permission to use others' belongings, and they are good sports about winning or losing. There is a willingness to follow majority rule and play according to the group standards. In essence, you aid your child in feeling more poised, self-confident, and creative. By expressing oneself in a positive manner, others are more accepting and seek one out as a friend.

At home you convince children that you really care about them by your behavior rather than by well-meaning words. Your family is a powerful, real-life model of group acceptance. Children who do not feel a sense of belonging and acceptance at home find it very difficult to participate in unfamiliar groups. Family relationships should be constantly improved, in terms of warmth, support, and openness to expression of feelings. With older children, discussion about peers should be actively encouraged. You provide a sympathetic ear and helpful suggestions at times. Complaints can be acknowledged, but a positive and optimistic view of group membership should be projected. You can be sympathetic when a child talks about a group of children who do not let others participate with them. Discussion can take place about cliques who stick together and resist accepting new members. This tendency makes it especially difficult for children who have to make several geographic moves. Also, you can acknowledge that some children just don't get along even if a child desperately wants to be accepted. Many people like a small number of individuals and are indifferent to the rest.

You can teach children that hierarchies naturally develop in groups. In some groups smartness counts; in others it is athletic skills. Children should learn to relax and to fit in. They can understand that it is quite normal to be a leader in a situation where they are quite skilled and a follower in another situation. In order to enhance children's awareness of social skills in groups, you might suggest that their school purchase or develop their own films regarding positive group participation. For example, research[1] has shown that viewing films can lead to increased positive peer interaction. The films show children having positive experiences when approaching others to play or talk.

Promote Self-Confidence and Risk Taking. Children should feel adequate and relatively secure. Developing early mastery and competency is the key. Children can be taught and coached in skills that others value. Physical coordination can be greatly enhanced by frequent practice with parents. Athletic skill, especially in boys, is greatly valued by peers. Outstanding athletes are rarely social isolates. Similarly, interest in one or two hobbies should be actively encouraged. You can observe and ask questions in order to assess what type of hobbies or skills are valued by the local similarly aged children. By buying really good presents, you can naturally promote interest in your child. For example, if many young teenagers listen to music and play instruments, you might buy an electric guitar for your somewhat withdrawn child.

When children feel relatively self-confident, they are able to take risks in spite of possible rejection. Tolerance of rejection is gradually built. You might tell your children of your own experiences of being rejected as a child or more recent examples of rejection. The attitude of acceptance is communicated. A person can be rejected, still feel worthwhile, and not feel crushed and humiliated. Approaching people implies taking the risk of being rejected. Children can learn that it is a risk well worth taking. The results can be very rewarding, and the risks are not earth shattering.

What To Do

Reward Any Social Interaction. Social isolation should not be criticized. Talking to or questioning others should be praised or tangibly rewarded. If children never interact with others, you can make a specific suggestion and reward the behavior immediately. Even if no communication occurs, it is important for the child to study or eat with peers. A child's favorite toy could be used as a reward only if she spends some time with others. Points could be earned to purchase privileges or small toys. Playing interactive games, following group rules, or being considerate of others could earn points. Good snacks should never be served during or immediately after a child is not participating with others. Parents underestimate the power of natural reinforcers such as food. Milk and cookies should be served while children are having fun and when your child has been interacting. Similarly, when children are relating well, they then may be taken for a treat such as bowling, a movie, or a sporting event. Some parents are concerned that praise or tangible rewards for increased peer interaction will become habitually needed. The evidence is clearly contrary, especially when reinforcement is gradually diminished. Once the good habit of social interaction becomes established, it is very frequently long lasting.

Actively Encourage Group Participation. Isolated children must be encouraged to interact with others under a variety of conditions. Pairing an isolated child with a popular peer is very worthwhile. Popularity rubs off! The isolated child becomes more acceptable to others. If a friend or relative has a popular child, they can be enlisted to help. Otherwise, you might ask your child who in class is popular and invite that child to go on a special trip. The popular child's parents might cooperate by rewarding their child for helping your child by playing with him. Parents must be creative enough to develop situations that make their child's company valuable. Trips to the theater, sports events, and amusement parks are excellent. Children enjoy trips and associate having a good time with being with others. This works both ways. Your child learns to like being with others, and they learn to like him. The goal is for others to reciprocate by inviting your child, thereby ending the socially isolated habit.

You can obtain a roster of names and telephone numbers of classmates. You should show an interest in who they are and request information about them from your child. When your child discusses others, be enthusiastic and make the conversation last as long as possible. Invite the classmates or neighboring children at every opportunity. Foster game playing by purchasing popular board games and making as many parties as feasible. Enroll your child in clubs or any type of specific interest group. People approach each other more easily in situations where they are engaging in activities together. If no clubs exist in the community, be active in creating some and being personally involved. Children should be encouraged to participate in school plays, chorus, or any special events. Do not be reluctant to approach teachers and request that they ask your child to join in. Isolated children become more accepted by peers when they participate in school events.

At home, equipment should be purchased which will attract others. Outdoor play equipment such as a jungle gym, fancy slide, elaborate sandbox, tether ball, basketball hoop, etc., are excellent investments for your child's social life. If financially feasible, a backyard swimming pool can be a powerful natural means of ending a child's social isolation.

Teach Specific Social Skills. You cannot assume that isolated children know basic social skills.[2] Even if they do, you cannot assume that they feel comfortable enough to use the skills in real social situations. Therefore, it is essential to teach them appropriate behaviors and give them plenty of *practice* in skill use. Children can watch parents pretend to act like children interacting. After saying "hello" in a friendly manner, things of common interest should be discussed. Current, local happenings and the people involved are good topics. You use open-ended questions and demonstrate expanded answers and interesting associations rather than one- or two-word replies. Questions about the other person's motives and reactions can be used productively: "What is it that you want to achieve? What is your opinion about what she did? Would you have handled that in a different way?" Conversations should be personalized where people discuss themselves and their reactions. A key is to give *more* than required. A good idea is to pretend to be disinterested by looking away, yawning, or making comments about having to do something else. The other person then demonstrates sensitivity by being brief, asking if the other would like to continue talking another time, and gracefully ending the conversation.

For teaching social skills to isolated children, the following guidelines[3] might help: (1) Teach communication skills, especially how to listen. Talking silently to yourself and asking questions about how to proceed should be demonstrated. (2) Show how to make friends. This includes a greeting, asking for and giving information, offering to include the other person in activities, and effective leave taking. (3) Show how to give and receive positive interaction. You show interest, attention, helpfulness, cooperation, paraphrase interesting aspects of what you hear, summarize what others say, comply with requests, give approval and support, and be affectionate. For children who feel different and inferior, a demonstration of the process behind deciding to interact can be interesting and relieving. Acted out is the feeling of wanting to interact, worry about possible negative consequences, debating different aspects of the problem, deciding what to do, approaching and greeting people, and asking for help or participation.

Once skills are taught, children must be *coached* in effective behavior in order to increase their acceptance by peers. Proper coaching and behavioral rehearsal leads to short- and long-term positive effects. Encourage the viewing of any type of good modeling. Children should watch others (on film or actual behavior) who interact positively. They should see children approaching each other, talking freely, and playing happily. It is very useful for them to be asked to observe well-functioning children playing games like Dominoes, Pick-up-Sticks, or Blockhead. They can see how children focus on the game, take turns, ask questions, and make comments.

With proper focus you can be very effective by guiding your child's play with one friend. Your child practices the above skills by playing with the peer. Immediately after, the experience is reviewed and you coach your child in alternative, better ways of handling the specific situation that occurred. Be sure to take notes of the significant events. Skills should be taught for the specific situation that arose. In order to maximize learning and assure generalization to other situations, ask the child for other examples in his life. Different situations (school, community, relatives' homes) should be discussed. Ask for examples of good interactions (sharing, expressing opinions, etc.) and of not-so-good behavior (withdrawing, silence, and insensitivity).

You explain to children why certain actions are important. Children can then give examples of when and how they could apply these actions. If children get stuck, you give ideas and examples. A good question to pose is whether they can figure out how to make a game more fun for others. Also, a powerful lesson is learned by discussing what behaviors make situations unpleasant or not fun for others. You instruct children to *try* these skills with others and to relate the results to you.

Case Report

Informal consultation was given to friends with a socially isolated 12-year-old boy. He related fairly well in school but showed no social motivation or initiative at other times. They were encouraged to praise any sociable behavior and stop making critical remarks about his lack of interest in others. Since he rarely left his room, they had to assure his being in contact with others by insisting upon a minimum of group participation. He had to earn his allowance by joining a Saturday recreation program at a local recreation center. Additional money could be earned by spending time away from home. This proved to be most effective since he began to find boys to play with while walking around the neighborhood. By rewarding time away from home, the natural course of events led to interaction with others.

Books For Parents About Social Isolation

Ernest, Reta and Siegel, Paul: *Help for the Lonely Child.* Dutton, New York (1974).

Goldstein, A.P., Sprafkin, R.P., Gershaw, N.J., and Klein, P.: *Skillstreaming the Adolescent: A Structural Learning Approach to Teaching Prosocial Skills.* Research Press, Champaign, IL. (1979).

Books For Children About Social Isolation

Fitzhugh, Louise: *Harriet the Spy.* Harper & Row, New York (1964). Ages 10–12.

Children discover an 11-year-old girl's diary which contains many critical observations of them. They ostracize her and tease her mercilessly. Rather than face the situation, she pretends to be sick and avoids school. A letter from a former governess advises her to apologize and be nicer to others, which she does successfully.

Godden, Rumer: *The Diddakoi.* Viking, New York (1972). Ages 10–12.

Children ostracize a 7-year-old gypsy girl because of her different lifestyle. Gradually, she accepts food and kindness from her new guardian.

Guy, Rosa: *The Friends.* Holt, Rinehart & Winston, New York (1973). Ages 12 and over.

A 14-year-old girl is avoided by others because of her accent, fancy clothes, and good schoolwork. Only one poor girl befriends her. The family's false pride makes the relationship difficult to maintain.

Keith, Harold Verne: *The Runt of Rogers School.* J.B. Lippincott, Philadelphia (1971). Ages 9–12.

A short, inept fifth grader is rejected and teased by schoolmates. He finally proves himself and is accepted by doing well on the school football team.

Limbacher, Walter J.: *I'm Not Alone.* Pflacim, Dayton, OH (1970). Ages 9–10.

Children are helped to understand and accept the positive values of group membership. Growth and self-acceptance are stressed.

Schick, Eleanor: *5A and 7B*. Macmillan, New York (1967). Ages 3–5.

Two very lonely girls live in the same apartment building. They finally meet, become friends, and play together.

Wrenn, C. Gilbert and Schwarzrock, Shirley: *Living with Loneliness*. American Guidance Service, Circle Pines, MN (1970). Teen-agers.

Examples of loneliness are described with methods for overcoming lonely feelings. Teen-agers are shown that others are also lonely and told to get to know other lonely people. Joining groups is recommended and discussed.

References

1. O'Connor, R.D.: "Relative efficacy of modeling, shaping and the combined procedures for modification of social withdrawal." *Journal of Abnormal Psychology* 79: (1972), pp. 327–334.
2. Oden, Sherri and Asher, Steven R.: "Coaching children in social skills for friendship making." *Child Development* 48: (1977), pp. 495–506.
3. Gottman, John, Gonso, Jonni, and Schuler, Philip: "Teaching social skills to isolated children." *Journal of Abnormal Child Psychology* 4: (1976), pp. 179–197.

5 ———

Antisocial Behaviors

INTRODUCTION

In this chapter we will discuss a variety of antisocial behaviors which bring the child in conflict with society. Such behaviors include disobedience, dishonesty (lying, stealing, cheating), profanity, destructiveness, firesetting, prejudice, and running away from home and school. Although disapproving of these behaviors, our society does tend to foster their development by favoring competition over cooperation, individualism over conformity, and narcissism over altruism. In regard to prejudice, homogeneity of ethnic contact also seems to be the norm in our society rather than cultured diversity.

Another factor associated with antisocial behaviors by youth is prolonged adolescent dependency. Adolescents in our society have the talent and energy to assume adult responsibilities, but there is little for them to contribute in the way of constructive work and little opportunity for them to assert their independence from their parents. The student role taken by most of them tends to afford few chances for them to become fully independent, competent, and responsible. This prolonged dependency on others may, in part, account for the fact that criminal and violent behaviors are disproportionately high among the young. Perhaps more opportunities for youth to engage in meaningful work-study programs and altruistic behaviors (tutoring young children, caring for the elderly) will help resolve this problem.

Methods for decreasing antisocial acts are described, including the use of punishment. Even more important, however, is the emphasis in this chapter on positive approaches which are aimed at increasing prosocial behaviors by the use of praise and rewards. By strengthening prosocial behaviors such as compliance and honesty, the negative behaviors are less likely to occur. Usually the child knows the appropriate ways of behaving, but needs to be motivated to perform them. Behavioral techniques, such as the contingent use of rewards and penalties, ignoring, and modeling prosocial behaviors, have proven particularly effective in reducing antisocial actions. Relationship factors such as understanding and affection are also stressed in this section. Many antisocial acts result from the child feeling alienated from her parents. The child's needs for companionship, guidance, and love may not be met. As a result, the child turns to the peer group to satisfy these needs. Often the peer group has rebellious, antisocial tendencies.

In light of the above, it is not surprising that research has shown that broken homes or loss of a parent for an extended period can often lead to antisocial behaviors in children. A crucial relationship has been interrupted, and the child does not know how to cope with it except by striking out against society. Unable to tolerate the sad, unhappy feelings that result from the loss, the child tries to shut out these feelings by engaging in antisocial behaviors such as stealing and vandalism.

Discipline may be another unmet need of the child. Parents who overlook, condone, or derive vicarious satisfaction from the antisocial actions of their children are preparing the child for a delinquent life style. Children's behavior must be closely supervised, and unacceptable behavior immediately confronted and dealt with.

Over time every child will engage in isolated, infrequent antisocial acts, such as disobedience and lying. Most of these youths will not grow up to be delinquents or criminals. It is important that parents do not label or stereotype a child as "delinquent" or "bad" because of certain antisocial behaviors, such as petty stealing. Such labels and expectancies foster a negative self-image. Once the child sees himself as "bad," he will continue to act that way and seek out others who are perceived in the same light. This process is an example of the "self-fulfilling prophecy," wherein predictions about a child set into motion factors that actually bring the beliefs and expectations into reality. So avoid making matters worse by overreacting to an antisocial incident. We simply must control our emotions and not take these behaviors as a personal affront or sign we are ineffective parents.

Whatever approach you use to combat antisocial tendencies in your child, you should be aware that working on too many problem areas at one time is prone to lead to failure. The best approach is to select one specific misbehavior to work on at a time. Try to select a behavior that occurs fairly frequently and is most disturbing to you or others. Also, when working on your child's problems, you must be flexible and open with yourself, that is, willing to examine and when necessary change your attitudes, values, and behaviors. Finally, rather than standing back and hoping the child will outgrow the misbehavior or that other adults will handle the problem, you must be actively involved and willing to invest your time and energy to help the child.

DISOBEDIENCE

The question parents ask the most in regard to childrearing is: "How can I teach my child to do what he is told?" It is estimated that about one-third of the problem behaviors exhibited by children are related to noncompliance.[15] Other investigators feel that the problem is more widespread and that most children referred for professional guidance have noncompliance as the major problem.[17] Compliance or obedience is defined as doing what a parent requests when it should be done. Most of the time children comply with parental directions, even during the first and second years of life.[1,2] Nevertheless, one of the hardest lessons for children to learn is that they must do something when it has to be done, whether they like it or not. Indeed, this is a lesson many adults continue to have difficulty with.

Of course all children are disobedient at times and refuse to respond positively to reasonable rules set by parents. Noncompliant behavior first reaches a peak incidence during the legendary "terrible twos" and normally diminishes thereafter. Negativism becomes prominent again during the adolescent years.

Reasonable amounts of noncompliance should be seen as a healthy expression of a developing ego seeking independence and self-direction. Don't take a child's refusal personally, as a sign that you an incompetent parent or that the child is deliberately trying to anger or humiliate you. Some youngsters, however, are consistently disobedient and automatically resist every request or command. Abnormal noncompliance occurs more frequently, more intensely, or over a longer period of time than the normal type.

There are three main forms of disobedience:

1. The passive resistant type where the child delays in complying, pouts, becomes sullen (quiet, withdrawn), or whines about having to comply, or conforms to the letter but not the spirit of the law.
2. The openly defiant "I won't do it" child who may be prone to be verbally abusive or to throw a temper tantrum to back up his position.
3. The spiteful type of noncompliance results in the child doing the exact opposite of what she is told. For example, the child who is asked to be quiet screams louder.

If disobedience becomes a way of life for a child, he may develop the habit of negativism wherein he opposes opinions and principles offered by others. He disagrees with other persons on all points, without rational grounds for his disagreement.

Reasons Why

Among the more common reasons for persistent noncompliance in children are:

1. Lax discipline by permissive parents who try to refrain from saying, "No," to a child.
2. Unduly harsh or restrictive discipline by parents who tend to be authoritarian, excessively critical and perfectionistic, nagging, or domineering. Such parents tend to demand "instant" obedience from children.
3. Inconsistent discipline by parents who cannot agree on standards of behavior and enforcement of rules. When parents disagree, the children themselves will try to decide what is all right and not all right.[4]
4. Parents in stress or conflict. One or both parents may be neglecting the parenting role because of job demands, disinterest, personal problems, divorce, or marital conflict.
5. A particularly creative or strong-willed child will tend to be a noncomformist and dance to his or her own drummer.
6. By drawing off all the anger and disappointment of the family members, the noncooperative child may

be enabling the rest of the family to live in relative peace.

7. Parental attitudes toward authority will influence a child's proneness to obey. If parents show little regard toward the law or law enforcement agents, then their children are likely to be less respectful toward adults.

8. The more intelligent the child, the more likely she will be to obey legitimate requests. Intelligent children can anticipate the consequences of their actions, and can postpone immediate gratifications for long-term goals.

9. Children are less likely to obey when they are tired, ill, hungry, or emotionally upset.

How to Prevent

The key to instilling a cooperative attitude in children is to avoid the extremes of authoritarian or permissive child-rearing. Rather, adopt a middle ground wherein you are not afraid to set a few necessary rules, but you do so in a way that is combined with love and reason. This has been called authoritative parental control.[7] The demands you make on a child should be balanced by warmth, reason, praise, and responsiveness to the child's needs. When children experience both love and limits, their inclination to rebel is minimized. Remember, your goal is firmness but not domination.

Build a Close Relationship. The more you and your child like each other, the better the child will accept your directions. When you are friends with someone, you want to try and please them. So take some time each day to give undivided attention as your child works or plays. Bedtime is also an excellent time for companionship. Try to make this a pleasant, relaxed time in which you share some of the interesting experiences of the day.

Be Responsive. The more you comply with your child's requests, the more you can expect your child to comply with your wishes and instructions.[2] This is the Law of Reciprocity, that is, "If you scratch my back, I'll scratch yours."

Studies show that a disposition toward obedience emerges

in infants when their parents are tuned in to the baby's signals (respond immediately to baby's cries) and are able to see things from his point of view.[5] The insensitive parent, that is, one who is more concerned with his own wishes, moods, and activities, is less likely to have a child who willingly responds to parental directions. So the more cooperative you are with a young child and the more sensitive you are to her needs and distress signals, the more you will be developing an obedient child.

Don't Be a Dictator. Don't give a command if a request would do as well. Rather than assuming a dictatorial role by bossing a child around a great deal, try giving more requests and suggestions rather than direct orders. You are likely to get more compliance this way.[3] Of course, if the child has no choice but to comply, give a clear, direct order lest you confuse the child.

Whenever possible, give your children a voice in setting up rules; they will be more apt to obey them this way.

Don't expect instant obedience from children all the time. If you give them a little advance warning ("5 minutes until bedtime"), they will comply more readily. So allow leeway and give playing children a few minutes to finish their game before coming in.

Also, allow your children to grumble a little when they are obeying an unpleasant rule. This will provide a release of upset feelings and body tension. We can be accepting and understanding of some "back talk" then, as long as it does not turn hostile or insulting.

Permit "feeling" statements: "I hate doing the dishes," "I'm sick of cleaning this crummy room." These are not "I won't" statements. They are statements about how the child feels. Children have a right not to like something. Respect their feelings and help children express them appropriately. We can expect children to do what we ask, but not necessarily to be happy about it. Typically, a child will complete a task assigned, once he has expressed displeasure.

Set the Example. If you have a positive attitude toward authority and laws, your children are likely to show respect for authority. If you disregard stop signs, litter streets, or speak disparagingly of the police, your children will tend to imitate this example.

Setting Rules. Any demand placed on a child is a rule. The child has no choice but to obey. Some guidelines for establishing rules follow.

Individualize. You are in the best position to decide what rules are needed by your child. You know the child better than anyone else and are the best judge of what rules will suit the child's particular personality, level of maturity, and special circumstances. You should take into consideration but not blindly follow the rules under which the child's age-mates are governed. The rules set for other children may be leading them toward behavior problems.

Be specific. In stating a rule, be sure the child knows exactly *what to do* and *when it should be done* (the time limit). Don't say, "Clean your room"; say, "Hang up the clothes in your room, make the bed, and put the toys away." The child should know immediately when he breaks a rule. For example, you might say, "You are to take out the trash every evening before dinner. This means emptying the garbage can in the kitchen and the baskets in all the bathrooms."

State the reason. Most studies have found that when you explain the reason for a rule, children more readily comply with it.[6] Do not require blind obedience because this inhibits the development of moral reasoning in a child. The more legitimate your demand, that is, the more it involves the needs or rights of others, the more obedience you will get, especially from adolescents.

Also, children obey rules more readily when both you and they benefit from the rule. If only you or other adults benefit from the rule, you can expect more resistance to the rule.

Expect obedience. When you ask your child to do something, behave as if you expect her to obey. Never let her sense that you expect her to do otherwise. If adults seem confident of compliance, they are more likely to get it from children. Remember that the research shows that more often than not children do obey their parents, even during the "terrible twos." Just beneath the surface of the obstinate child is a good child who wants to please you.

Make few demands. Make as few demands as needed but be sure these are carried out. It is better to give five rules that can be remembered and enforced 100 percent of the time than to make ten rules which you enforce 50 percent of the time. Most parents set too many rules and don't enforce them consistently. Studies have shown that the more rules you make, the more opposition you receive from your children.

State impersonally. The less personal you are in stating a rule, the less resistance you will get. Thus, it is better to say: "The rule is no throwing balls in the house" rather than: "I do not want you throwing balls in the house."

Be sure to make a *direct statement,* "Time to go to bed now," rather than coaxing the child by saying, "I'd like it if you went to bed now, please go."

State in positive way. Express the rule in a positive way if possible. Tell the child what to do (prescriptive approach) rather than what not to do (proscriptive).

For example, say, "Talk in a quiet way," rather than "Stop shouting." Say, "Please use your knife and fork," rather than "Stop eating with your fingers."

Watch your manner. In stating a rule, watch your tone of voice, manner, and the words you use. All of these can arouse a child toward opposition. A pleading or coaxing manner, a hurt-feeling manner ("How could you do this to me?"), an angry, hostile manner (glaring), and a critical remark ("Don't be so lazy; go clean up this mess") can make the child feel bad and trigger oppositional behavior. Be calm, matter-of-fact, and relaxed when giving orders so as to signal that you are positive toward the child and confident he will follow your direction.

Give a choice. In issuing a demand, try to give the child some freedom of choice. Thus, you might say, "Either play quietly or go outside to play," "Would you like to go to bed right after the TV program or right now so there will be time for me to read you a story," "O.K. you can sit in this chair until you are ready to do the dishes," and "Do you want to take your shower in the upstairs or downstairs bathroom?" Giving choices is more likely to increase independence and decision-making ability in a child.

Be flexible. The boundaries you place on a child should be gradually relaxed as she matures, to give her more and more freedom and self-responsibility.

Enforcing Rules
Be consistent. Whatever rules you set, they should be enforced consistently. Don't be lax one day and strict the next. When children are subjected to constant changes in rules, they test the rules at every opportunity. Only let a child break or bend a rule on the *rarest* circumstances that border on emergency situations. The first time or two that the child breaks the rule, ask her to tell you what rule has been broken. Do not accept lame excuses or permit the child to bend the rule. Let the child know that the rule is firm. If the child continues to break the rule, you will have to penalize the child to ensure compliance. Quietly carry out the penalty and ignore any emotional outbursts from the child. Never allow a child to break a rule by throwing a tantrum.

Use reasonable penalties. Try to make the penalty fit the crime. A loss of privileges is a reasonable punishment for many forms of noncompliance: no regular supper if late coming after being called; no use of toys for a week if left lying around; running into the street means he must play indoors; hitting little sister means staying in his room alone.

Avoid excessively harsh punishments, including the use of spanking, straping, slapping, or screaming at the child. These methods of punishment are apt to trigger resentment in a child and lower the likelihood of your child identifying with you and your moral standards. Severe punishment brings with it severely upset emotions (fear and anger), and these get in the way of learning and thinking.

What To Do

First, some don'ts. Don't launch a crash program of "cracking down" on a child by becoming very restrictive (many rules) and punitive (harsh punishment). Avoid nagging and then wacking, yelling, threatening, or namecalling. These techniques are likely to backfire and breed resentment and further rebelliousness in a child.[2,3] Rather, carefully plan a program which focuses on the enforcement of one or two rules and the gradual development of a compliant, cooperative attitude in a child.

The following are some techniques that often have been found effective in reducing oppositional tendencies in children.

Positive Reinforcement. Instead of taking obedience for granted, parents should make a special effort to praise the child for each time he does comply with their demand. Typically parents seldom praise compliant behavior while frequently reprimanding noncompliance.[12] When one mother tried praising her 7-year-old daughter's compliant behavior while simultaneously ignoring the child's arguing, yelling, and noncompliance, she found that the undesirable behavior was markedly reduced within 10 days.[8]

In addition to praise and appreciation, concrete rewards for compliant behavior have worked well with children aged 12 and younger. Every time the child complies with a parental request, she is given a poker chip, point, or star which can be exchanged on a regular basis for privileges (watching TV) or food (cookies, candy). Select rewards that you feel will particularly appeal to your child. Let the child have some voice in deciding on the rewards you use. By making the rewards in the home contingent upon obedient behavior, you can motivate a child to behave in a cooperative way.

With children aged 7 to 12, try a compliance point system. The children receive one point on a posted chart each time they comply with a rule. When 25 points are earned, praise the child for complying and give a previously selected activity reinforcer, such as a movie or trips to the park (see Figure 1). When the percentage of compliance remains over 75 percent for 2 consecutive weeks, gradually increase the number of points required for obtaining a special treat.

For children aged 2 to 5, give a star or happy face on the chart for each compliance. When they collect five faces, give a concrete reward like candy or a small toy, together with praise and an explanation of why the reward was given.

In one family the three children were not complying with the parents' requests to help with household chores. The parents then instituted the following system. The children earned a specified number of points for each chore they completed. They received 5¢ for every ten points they earned and could either spend the money immediately or

PROGRESS CHART

Child's Name _____

TASK	Monday	Tuesday	Wednesday	Thursday	Friday	Saturday	Sunday
Make bed by 9 A.M.	X	X	X	X			
Take out trash		X	X	X			
Feed cat at 6 P.M.			X	X			
Be in bed by 8:30 P.M.	X		X	X			
Finish breakfast within 30 minutes	X	X		X			
Daily Total	3	3	4	5			

Twenty-five points earns a movie with Dad.

Figure 1.

designate some item or privilege they wished to save for. One point was subtracted for each chore they did not finish. No other punishment (e.g., spanking) was used. The parents kept a weekly chart for each child of the number of points earned for each chore. On the chart one column listed the chores, and there were columns for each day of the week in which the points were marked. This procedure resulted in an immediate increase in completing the chores.[10]

Penalties. A very effective way to stop disobedience is to teach the child that this behavior results in unpleasant consequences. For example, every time he comes late for supper, he may have to eat milk and crackers. The key is to be consistent in applying penalties (100 percent of the time) and to set reasonable consequences.

Some penalties that parents have found effective follow:

If a child is not doing his chore of taking out the garbage, set the rule that the garbage is to be taken out by 8 P.M. each evening. If the child fails to do it, the mother will do it and receive 50¢ from the child's weekly allowance of $3.00. An alternative penalty is not to allow the child to go to bed until the chore is done.

If a 16-year-old girl is late returning home from dates, set the rule that curfew is 10 P.M. on weekday nights and midnight on weekends. Each 15-minute period over curfew means the loss of a night's privilege of going out. So if the teen-ager is 45 minutes late Friday night, she can't go out Saturday, Sunday, or Monday. If the child argues, tell her you will listen to a good case for extending the time of curfew but that it had better be good.

Give A Reprimand. Express your disapproval for noncompliant behavior by a statement that points out the adverse effect for you of noncompliance and your feelings about it. You might say, for example, "Joan, when you don't complete your chore of making your bed in the morning it means more work for me, and this makes me very unhappy!"

An ineffective reprimand is one which is designed to hurt or put down the child, such as sarcasm, name calling, ridicule, or threats of physical harm or loss of love.

The reprimand might also include a warning about the unpleasant consequence that will ensue for the child if she continues the noncompliance: "If you don't pick up your coat now, you'll have to go to your room."

Combined Carrot and Stick Approach. This approach combines rewarding (praising) a child for complying or doing what you tell her to do, and penalizing a child for failing to obey. First decide on one task that must be done on several different occasions during the week. Tell the child to do it in a clear, matter-of-fact way. Praise the child if she does it. If the child refuses, ask her to tell you what she is to do, so you are certain she understands. Praise her for telling you and then tell her to do it. If she complies, praise her. If she refuses, tell her nothing else happens until she does it. Express your displeasure with the refusal and restate the reason why the behavior is needed. If she persists in noncompliance, take her to her room to settle down. Wait until the child is quiet and then go back to step one. The child will soon learn that it is to her advantage to obey.

Another combined reward and penalty approach for noncompliant children aged 2 to 9[16] involves rewarding the child with praise and special treats every time he obeys a command within 5 seconds. If the child does not comply, a warning is given to the child that continued noncompliance will result in a time-out penalty. If compliance does not occur within 5 seconds following the warning, the child is placed in a time-out chair in a corner of the room. The parent tells the child, ''You did not do what I told you right away, so you are going to have to stay in the corner of the room,'' takes the child by the hand, and leads her to the corner. If the child leaves the chair, a warning is given that a spanking would occur if he left the chair again. The child is then returned to the chair. This procedure is repeated until the child stays quietly on the chair for 4 minutes. The child is then returned to the uncompleted task and given the initial command. Compliance by the child results in praise by the parent; continued noncompliance leads to a repeat of the time-out procedure. Research indicates that this time-out method is very effective in reducing disobedient behavior in children aged 2 to 6.[18] The time-out duration should only be 4–5 minutes because this has been found to be just as or more effective than longer or shorter intervals.[18]

Strengthen Your Relationship. Try to show more love and affection for the child. Spend some time with him so as to form a close relationship. In this way the child will be more likely to accept your discipline. Seek more time to cuddle, confide in, and be supportive of one another. Engage in pleasant activities that will allow you to be together for the sole purpose of mutual enjoyment. Play baseball, make scrapbooks, take little trips, horseplay during swimming, and so on. When there is an abundance of affection between parent and child, then control is more readily accepted.

The bottom line is that how children feel about us determines how they react to our discipline. If they feel only marginally accepted or frequently criticized, they are prone to respond in a negative way to punishment. Our need to be the child's friend should be stronger than our need to be a policeman.

Ignoring. Research indicates that parents pay attention to a child's oppositional behavior almost 100 percent of the time.[9] Paying attention means looking at the child, touching, or talking to the child. Since parental attention, even negative attention in the form of scolding, can reinforce a child's misbehavior, it is advisable to pay no attention to as much of the noncompliant behavior as possible, especially for minor incidents. Ignore minor defiance and do not get into an argument with the child. When giving less attention to noncompliance, give 100 percent attention to compliant behavior. Such a planned shift in parental attention has been found effective in significantly reducing oppositional behavior in preschool children.[9]

While ignoring the child's resistance, try distracting the child and interesting him in something else. For example, if a child comes home from school tired and irritable, and refuses to take his coat off, an inexperienced parent might argue, threaten, or use brute force to make him comply. A skillful parent, on the other hand, is more apt to back off the confrontation and start a friendly conversation or game and possibly jolly him out of his antagonism. The mother might say, ''Let's see how the goldfish are doing.'' After becoming interested in the fish, the child is likely to lose interest in annoying grownups.

Of course, if distraction or the temporary ignoring of oppositional behavior does not work and the child persists in defying you, you will have to take a stand and insist that the child either comply with the rule or be penalized.

Contract. An approach that works well with teen-agers[17] is to have the child sign a written agreement that indicates her commitment to reducing oppositional behavior. The parents also agree to comply with certain wishes of the child so that a reciprocal exchange is effected. A contract is an agreement in writing which says what a child will do and what a parent will do in return. A sample contract follows:

> I hereby agree to reduce my noncompliance to my parents' requests and commands. If during the first week of this agreement, I comply with my parents' directions 90 percent of the time, my parents have agreed

to give me a special treat, namely a new baseball glove.
I will keep a posted record of my progress.

_____
Signature (child)

_____
Signature (parents)

Date _____

These contracts serve to define and underscore what is
expected of both parent and child, and to strengthen the
commitment of the child to change. It is important that the
contract be written so that small gains are agreed to rather
than expecting the child to be immediately obedient 100
percent of the time.[19] Sometimes it will be necessary to
write the contract to cover one day at a time.

Give Clear Directives. Be sure the commands or rules you
give are direct, concise, and very specific. They should tell
the child exactly what to do and when to do it. Instead of a
vague "Do something about this mess," say, "Pick up all
your toys and books from the floor of the playroom and put
them on the shelf." Give a clear time limit on when you
want this done: "I want the mess cleaned up right now" or
"The mess has to be cleaned up before dinner."
  Avoid giving any of the following ineffective commands:[16]
  1. Commands which are so vague that proper action for
     compliance cannot be determined.
  2. Commands interrupted by further talk by a parent be-
     fore enough time has elapsed for the child to comply.
  3. Commands that the parent carries out before the child
     has an opportunity to comply.

Allow Some Rebellion. If you have teen-agers, you should
allow some oppositional behavior that stops short of im-
morality or illegality. Let them wear the clothes they prefer
and the hair style they like. The same policy applies to
younger children. Let them win a few battles or disagreements as long as their behavior does not cause harm to the
child or to others. We should not completely crush a child's
striving to be independent and think for herself. The wise
parent will yield occasionally to the child's desires in areas
where the stakes are not particularly high.

Stop the World. One technique designed to achieve compliant behavior from a child involves depriving the child of all family interactions and services until the child obeys the rule. If the child refuses to make his bed, for example, the whole family acts as if the child is not there. The child is not spoken to, played with, or served a meal until the original request is complied with. Other children are told, ''Bob can play with you when he makes his bed.'' The first few times you use this ''stop-the-world'' technique, you can expect the extremely oppositional child to wait a long time before compliance. A wait of several hours or even a full day is not unusual with children aged 9 to 12 years. If parents succeed in holding out on the first few occasions, however, delays before giving in become more infrequent and of shorter duration.

''Bronco Busting.'' The ''bronco busting'' technique has been used effectively to clearly let children know that they are not the boss in the house.[13] It has been particularly successful in single parent families when one child has assumed the role of a parent and the child believes she is as powerful as a parent.

The ''bronco busting'' technique involves having the child sit on the parent's lap with one of the parent's legs over the child's body to entrap it. The parent's arm should encircle the child's torso and grasp the child's hands. With older children, the child should lie face down on the floor and the parent should straddle the back of the child with the hands pressing firmly down on the shoulders or clasping the hands. In either case, the area surrounding this activity should be unencumbered, and no sharp or hard surfaces should be exposed. Glasses, pens, shoes, and other harmful personal objects should be removed before the process begins. With larger and stronger children, it is desirable for a parent to have a relative or friend help in maintaining control, usually by holding the legs down so that the parent appears to have the most control.

When the parent and child have assumed this position, the parent should ask the child, ''Who is the boss?'' repeatedly until the child answers that the parent is the boss. The child should state this in a complete sentence while maintaining eye contact with the parent.

Often the child's first reaction to this technique is that it is a game. But as the process develops, the child becomes angry and should be encouraged to express this anger through struggling, screaming, and pounding his fists on the floor. The parent must keep her own anger under control and maintain a position of loving firmness and control.

In the early phase of this procedure, while asking who is the boss, the parent may need to confront the child by saying, "If you are the boss, why can't you get up?" "How can I do this to you if you are the boss?"

When the child passes through anger to eventual exhaustion and giving up, the parent should shift from a confronting approach ("Who is the boss?") to a supporting position ("I expect you to fight and you're putting up a good one. It hurts me that I didn't settle this a long time ago. It is enough for you just to be responsible for yourself. I am the parent and I will start taking care and charge of both of us from now on. I want you to enjoy being a child and I will take responsibility for being in charge").

This process may take 2 or 3 hours, and you must be sure you have adequate time to devote to it before initiating it. If the father does the procedure, he should tell the child at the end that in his absence the mother is the boss and that he backs her up in whatever she may choose to do. The child will probably continue to test limits after this procedure, and the parent(s) should concentrate on enforcing one specific rule the following week.

A similar holding technique is described by professionals at a child guidance center.[14] The child is placed in a sitting position across the parent's lap, with the child facing the parent's right or left. When the child faces the parent's right, the parent's left arm encircles the child's back and restricts the child's left arm. The child's right arm is tucked under the parent's left and behind the parent's back. The parent's right arm controls the child's legs. Before beginning this technique, the parent should wear sturdy, comfortable clothing that permits free movement. The parent says to the child, "Johnny, I'm going to hold you like this until you tell me I'm the boss. Who is boss, Johnny?" This approach is used with children who feel omnipotent and in control of their parents. Before attempting this method, the parent must be determined to win the struggle, no matter how long the child rages, and shift the power back in favor of the parent. If the child acknowledges the parent as boss but fails to carry out a specific parental direction thereafter, the procedure is resumed. The holding technique has been used with children aged 2 to 9 years, although it seems most appropriate for children aged 3 to 6. The method has been reported effective in establishing parental authority in 75 percent of the cases, and in no case has it been found to be detrimental to the authority relationship. In view of its stressful and strenuous nature, the holding technique should only be attempted by parents who are physically and psychologically strong. The goal of the technique is not to break the child's spirit but to break the child's thoughts of omnipotence.

Alternative Caretakers. A nursery school experience may be helpful for teaching an oppositional child to conform to authority. Similarly, camp or boarding school experiences may be best for an older, rebellious child.

Case Reports

Case #1. The following procedure proved successful with a very oppositional 5-year-old boy.[11] The parents discontinued their attempts to reason with or seek an explanation of why the boy was disobeying. Instead they asked the child no more than twice to do a task. If he complied with either of their requests, he received a star on a posted chart and was warmly praised. A certain number of stars earned him the privilege of playing in a special playroom. In the event the child failed to comply with the second request, he was placed in his room for 15 minutes as timed by a kitchen timer. He was told before going to his room: "You cannot stay here if you do not do what you are told." No other comment was made by the parent. Leaving the room before the end of the 15 minutes resulted in his having to spend an additional 5 minutes in his room.

Case #2. A 4-year-old boy, the third of four children in a middle-class family, was unmanageable at home.[20] Prominent among his defiant, disruptive behaviors were the following: (1) biting his shirt or arm, (2) sticking out his tongue, (3) kicking or hitting himself, others, or objects, (4) calling someone or something a derogatory name, (5) removing or threatening to remove his clothing, (6) saying "No!" loudly and vigorously, (7) threatening to damage objects or persons, (8) throwing objects, and (9) pushing his sister. With professional counseling, the mother switched from the use of persuasion, arguing, or distraction to control these behaviors, to the procedure of first telling her son in a firm voice to stop these acts whenever one appeared, and if this proved ineffective, to immediately place the boy in his room and lock the door. He was required to remain in his room for 5 minutes and to be quiet for a short period before he was allowed to come out. All objects likely to be used as playthings had been previously removed from the room. On the few occasions when the boy broke a window in his room while being punished, his mother entered the room, swept up the glass, reprimanded him for breaking the window, attended to his wounds if any, and left. The mother also gave the boy attention, praise, and affectionate physical contact when he was behaving appropriately. This combined reward-penalty procedure was effective in quickly reducing the frequency of the objectionable behaviors.

Case #3. Jerry, 7 years old, had to be called by his mother three or four times to wash his hands and come to supper.[21] After arriving late for the meal, he would eat quickly and carelessly to get back to his play. He was a daydreamer and seemed preoccupied with his play when his mother called him. The mother decided to enforce a new rule. Jerry would be called just once for supper. He was to wash his hands immediately and be seated at the table before his mother sat down. Moreover, he was to eat slowly and remain at the table until the whole family was finished. He was informed that failure to comply would mean his supper would consist of a bowl of soup.

The following evening he failed to heed his mother's call and arrived late for supper. When asked the rule, he was able to repeat it. Jerry then washed his hands and waited for his mother to finish eating so she could heat his canned soup. The next evening Jerry did a little better. He continued to watch TV for a few minutes, washed his hands, and returned to the TV for 2 or 3 minutes before going to the table. By this time the family was seated and was passing the food. His mother asked him, "What's the rule?" Jerry stated the rule and added, "Soup again?" His mother nodded.

On the third evening his mother prepared spaghetti for supper (Jerry's favorite dish). He responded immediately, ate slowly, and talked with his brothers and sisters. On a subsequent occasion Jerry tried to test the rule again. He came to the table without washing. His mother observed the rule violation. Jerry protested, saying he had washed after coming home from school. His mother said, "I'll fix you soup after everyone else has finished."

Case #4. The effect on obedience of strengthening your relationship with the child is seen in the following incident reported by a professor of psychology:[22]

"Many years ago, when my boy was in second or third grade, I was on a very hectic schedule lecturing on 'How to be good parents and teachers.' I began to notice that I was not getting the same results with my boy that I used to. I finally decided to take a day off and spend it alone with the boy on the beach. We did. We played with balls and kelp and did all the things one does on the beach. At the end of the day I was completely exhausted and even my boy was kind of tired—but extremely happy. On the way home, he said quite suddenly, "Didn't we have a good time?" After I agreed, he said, "You know, I am going to do everything you ask me to do from now on."

Case #5. Pat, age 3½, was brought for testing because she was not learning her ABC's in nursery school.[14] When Pat refused to be tested or to solve puzzles her parents said she could do easily, her father spanked her. She still refused to cooperate with the counselor. When her parents said that nothing seemed to work when Pat made up her mind to disobey, the counselor suggested the holding technique. At first, Pat was relatively passive while her father held her. Once she realized its purpose, she became tearful, annoyed, and resistant. She seemed to expect her father to give in. After 10 minutes when she realized her omnipotence was being challenged, she became angry, screamed, and struggled to free herself.

Although worried at first that Pat was being hurt, her mother was reassured by the counselor that the crying did not mean that the child was in pain, but was a manipulative technique to win the confrontation. After 25 minutes, Pat gave in and said to her father "You're the boss," and followed her father's instructions. However, she balked at attempting a second puzzle her father set up for her, and the father had to use the holding technique again. Only after 20 minutes when she became convinced that her father would not give in, did she complete the puzzle.

The counselor advised the parents to reduce their demands that Pat learn in school, stop their usual punishment, and use the holding technique to establish parental authority. The next week both parents used the holding technique when Pat disobeyed. It was becoming obvious to the parents that Pat was capable of doing many things that she had previously resisted. Pat was now asking that her parents spank her rather than use the holding technique. When the counselor contacted the parents 2½ months later, they reported that they still used the holding technique on occasion. They felt that Pat was much more answerable to their authority and was performing age-appropriate tasks at home and in school.

Case #6. A divorced mother brought her 11-year-old daughter for counseling because the girl defied her and was out of control. The mother had been inconsistent in setting limits with the girl and frequently gave in to the daughter's demands, such as buying whatever she wanted at the grocery store and cooking whatever she wanted for breakfast.[13] When asked by the counselor, "Who is the boss?" the daughter quickly answered that her father was. When the question was asked again with regard to her relationship with her mother, the girl said she was the boss of her mother. In a move designed to reestablish the mother's authority, the girl was asked to sit on her mother's lap. She refused the request. Then, the counselor asked her to lie face down on the floor. She agreed, and the mother was instructed to straddle the daughter's back in accordance with the "bronco busting" procedure described earlier. The mother was instructed to repeatedly ask, "Who is the boss?" At first the daughter regarded the event as a game. Later, she started to fight back and at times cried to be released. The counselor had to support the mother's hold by securing the daughter's legs. The session lasted 1½ hours before the daughter unequivocally responded that her mother was the boss. In this family the bronco busting technique marked a breakthrough and a new beginning. The mother began to assert her rightful power and authority so that her daughter could be free to be the child she needed to be.

Case #7. Keith, age 9, refused to obey his mother's commands, argued, and often exhibited temper tantrums.[23] Moreover, Keith's 6-year-old brother, Glen, recently had become disobedient at times. With professional counseling, the mother decided to enforce, one at a time, the following four tasks:

Glen's Room Cleanup: Pick up clothes and put away toys within 10 minutes.

Glen's Bath: Glen had 15 minutes to go upstairs, take off his clothes and put them away, take a bath, put on his pajamas, and return downstairs.

Keith's Room Cleanup: Change clothes, pick up clothes, put toys away, and put books on chest within the 10 minutes allowed.

Keith's Kitchen Cleanup: Remove dishes from the table and put them in the dishwater within the 20 minutes allowed.

The following procedure was used to enforce these rules. After issuing a command, the mother silently counted to 10. If the child complied within this time, she praised the child and reminded the child of the time allowed to complete the task. She then set a kitchen timer for the interval allowed and left it in the child's view. If the task was completed, the child was praised. If the task was not completed, the mother took the child to a corner where he was required to stand for 2 minutes plus fulfillment of a 5-second quiet period. While putting the child in the corner, the mother said, "You did not finish in time so you have to stand in the corner." After removing the child from the corner, the mother took him back to the task area and said, "You have 2 minutes to finish this task." The timer was set for 2 minutes.

If the child did not begin the task within 10 seconds of the original command, the mother counted out loud, "5, 4, 3, 2, 1." If the child did not initiate compliance before the mother finished this countdown, he was placed in the corner. His mother would say, "You did not do what I said, so you have to stand in the corner." After 2 minutes and fulfillment of the 5 second quiet time, the mother removed the child from the corner and restated the command. If he did not begin the task, the countdown procedure was repeated. If he complied before the countdown ended, he was praised.

This procedure proved effective in achieving compliance with the assigned tasks within the time allowed. It is noteworthy that the mother started this method with the younger and less difficult child.

Case #8. Jerry first began wearing an orthodontic device when he was 8 years old.[24] The dental mechanism consisted of a removable head band held in place by a plastic band around his neck. Although the recommended wearing time was 12 hours a day, Jerry used the device only a few hours daily. After 8 years, four dentists, and over $3000 in dental fees, Jerry's orthodontic condition was essentially the same.

The followed procedure was implemented by the mother. Five times a day at fairly regular times, she observed the boy to determine if he was wearing the device. If he was she praised him (and refrained from reprimanding him when the bands were not in place). After 9 days this resulted in the device being in place 36 percent of the time. Not satisfied with this progress over his previous rate of 25 percent, the mother decided to immediately give the boy a quarter if he was wearing the device during each of the five checks. Within a few days this monetary pay-off brought the rate of wearing the device to 97 percent. After about a month of this procedure, the mother informed the son that she would be making the observation (and pay-offs) less frequently and at more variable times. She was soon making the checks only every 2 weeks, but the bands were consistently in place. Eight months after this procedure was initiated, the dentist reported great progress in Jerry's mouth structure and that it was no longer necessary to wear the apparatus.

Case #9. Antoinette, age 10, was expected to perform eight routine household tasks each day, such as putting her clothes and personal articles away, sweeping the floor, and making her bed. Despite verbal reminders and assorted punishments, the mother was having little success in getting Antoinette to complete these tasks.

With professional guidance, she implemented the following procedure. Each task was precisely spelled out (make bed—covers straight, neat and smooth, sheets not visible, pillows covered, blankets folded, no other items on bed) and assigned points (5, 10, or 20) depending on the difficulty or amount of work involved. Each evening at 6 P.M. the mother checked the tasks and if completed recorded the points for each task on a chart posted on Antoinette's bedroom door. Before the point system, the girl's work would only have merited about a point a day; immediately after the point system was in effect, the girl was averaging over 16 points a day. When the mother then started a new procedure of giving the girl a penny for every point earned, the mean number of points earned a day increased to over 36. During the final day of this pennies procedure, Antoinette asked her mother for permission to join the Campfire girls. Her mother told her yes and that she could save the points she earned and exchange them for the blouse and skirt of the uniform that Campfire girls required. Each item of the uniform could be obtained for 100 points. By the 19th day of this procedure, Antoinette had earned over 800 points and was able to buy the uniform. The mean number of points earned was 42 a day. Subsequently, she was earning points to buy Christmas presents at the exchange rate of one penny per point.

Case #10. A 5-year-old boy rarely complied with parental requests and was often openly defiant. Upon review of the situation, it emerged that the parents were quite inconsistent in their response to disobedience. Each parent was not only inconsistent as an individual, but they often could not agree on any unified action. They agreed to consistently enforce a few basic rules (after a focused discussion concerning the existence of too many unenforceable rules). As individuals, they were able to insist upon compliance and verbally praise their son for prompt obedience. This approach, tried for several weeks, was not successful.

In discussing the lack of any improvement, it became clear that the parents still argued about the rules and about their differing expectations. The father expected immediate compliance, while the mother felt that this was unrealistic. Some improvement in their approach resulted whereby each somewhat modified their positions. However, the significant effective strategy resulted from a suggestion that they both refuse to talk to their son for a 10-minute period after open defiance. This specific method served to unify the parents and apparently convinced the boy that his parents were together and meant what they said. They had explained, in a positive manner, that they could not speak to a boy who was so uncooperative.

Books for Parents About Childhood Disobedience

Dardig, J.C. and Heward, W.C.: *Sign Here: A Contracting Book for Children and Their Parents.* Behaviordelia, Kalamazoo, MI 49005 (1976).

Patterson, G.R. and Gullion, M.E.: *Living With Children: New Methods for Parents and Teachers.* Research Press, Champaign, IL 61820 (1971).

A how-to manual for using rewards and penalties to reduce noncompliance.

Books for Children About Disobedience

Charnley, N. and Charnley, B.J.: *Martha Ann and the Mother Store.* Harcourt Brace Jovanovich, New York (1973). Ages 5–9.

This imaginative story describes a young girl who rebels against her mother's discipline. As the girl explores alternatives, she finds that she is not really happy without guidelines and reasonable limitations.

Potter, B.: *The Tale of Peter Rabbit.* Frederick Warne & Co., (1902). Ages 3–7.

This timeless story describes Peter's foolhardiness in disobeying his mother's instructions and the danger that results.

References

1. Minton, C. *et al.:* "Material control and obedience in the two-year-old." *Child Development* 42: (1971), pp. 1873–1894.
2. Lytton, H.: "The socialization of two-year-old boys: Ecological Findings." *Journal of Child Psychology and Psychiatry* 17: (1976), pp. 187–304.
3. Lytton, H. and Zwiner, W.: "Compliance and its controlling stimuli observed in a natural setting." *Developmental Psychology* 11: (1975), pp. 769–779.
4. Brehm, S.S.: "The effect of adult influence on children's preferences: Compliance versus opposition." *Journal of Abnormal Psychology* 5: (1977), pp. 31–41.
5. Stayton, D.J. *et al.:* "Infant obedience and maternal behavior: The origins of socialization reconsidered." *Child Development* 42: (1971), pp. 1057–1069.

6. Lytton, H.: "Correlates of compliances and the rudiments of conscience in two-year-old boys." *Canadian Journal of Behavioral Science* 9: (1977), pp. 242–251.

7. Baumrind D.: "Current patterns of parental authority." *Developmental Psychology, Monograph* 4 (1): (1971).

8. McDonald, J.E.: "Parent training in positive reinforcement and extinction to effect a decrease in noncompliant child behavior." *Journal of the Association for the Study of Perception* 12: (1977), pp. 16–21.

9. Peisinger, J.J.: "Parent-child clinic and home interaction during toddler management training." *Behavior Therapy* 8: (1977), pp. 771–786.

10. Stein, T.J. and Gambrill, T.: "Behavioral techniques in foster care." *Social Work* 21: (1976), pp.34–39.

11. Ayllon, T. *et al.:* "Behavioral treatment of childhood neuroses." *Psychiatry* 40: (1977), pp. 315–322.

12. Daly, P.B. *et al.:* "A comprehensive early intervention program for families with problem children." Mimeographed Report (1978).

13. Johnson, J.W. *et al.:* "Bronco busting or 'Who is the boss in the family'." Mimeographed Report (1978).

14. Friedman, R. *et al.:* "Parent power: A holding technique in the treatment of omnipotent children." *International Journal of Family Counseling* 6: (1978), pp. 66–73.

15. Johnson, S.M. *et al.:* "How deviant is the normal child? A behavioral analysis of the preschool child and his family." In *Advances in Behavior Therapy.* Vol. 4. Rubin, R.D., Brody, J.P., and Henderson, J.D., eds. Academic Press, New York (1973).

16. Peed, S. *et al.:* "Evaluation of the effectiveness of a standardized parent training program in altering the interaction of mothers and their noncompliant children." *Behavior Modification* 1: (1977), pp. 323–350.

17. McAuley, R. and McAuley P.: *Child Behavior Problems: An Empirical Approach to Management.* Macmillan, London (1977).

18. Hobbs, S.A. *et al.:* "Effects of various durations of timeout on the non-compliant behavior of children." *Behavior Therapy* 9: (1978), pp. 652–656.

19. Dinoff, M. and Richard, H.C.: "Controlling rebellious behavior through successive contracts." *Child Care Quarterly* 1: (1972), pp. 205–211.

20. Hawkins, R.P. *et al.:* "Behavior therapy in the home: Amelioration of problem parent-child relations with the parent in

a therapeutic role." *Journal of Experimental Child Psychology* 4: (1966), pp. 99–107.

21. Moore, D.J.: *Preventing Misbehavior in Children*. Charles C. Thomas, Springfield, IL (1972).

22. Sheviakov, G.V.: "Some reflections on the problem of discipline." In *From Learning for Love to Love of Learning*. Epstein, R., Motto, R.L., eds. Bruner, Mazel, New York (1969).

23. Resick, P.A. *et al.:* "The effect of parental treatment with one child on an untreated sibling." *Behavior Therapy* 7: (1976), pp. 544–548.

24. Hall, R.V. *et al.:* "Modification of behavior problems in the home with a parent as observer and experimenter." *Journal of Applied Behavior Analysis* 5: (1972), pp. 53–64.

TEMPER TANTRUMS

A temper tantrum is a violent outbreak of anger. The fits of anger are easily provoked, and the reactions are almost volcanic in intensity. The rage is manifested by a complete loss of control as evidenced by screaming, cursing, breaking things, and rolling on the floor. Younger children may vomit, pass urine, or hold their breath. On rare occasions the child will physically attack an adult by kicking or hitting.

Temper tantrums are not unusual in young children, and they are very rarely a sign of a serious emotional disturbance in the preschool child. Tantrums are most common at ages 2 to 4 years when children first exhibit negativism and independence. As children grow older (ages 5 to 12) and are able to express their thoughts verbally, temper tantrums tend to subside, and occur only sporadically in the early teens. A substantial number of people never really outgrow this behavior and continue to have fits of temper (yelling, hitting, throwing objects) through their adult years.

According to the psychologist Albert Trieschman, a tantrum is not a single disruptive event, but a series of events. Typically a tantrum evolves through different stages. The first stage is familiar to every parent and is termed the "rumbling and grumbling" stage. The child will grumble, look grouchy, and sulk around the house. No matter what activity you suggest, nothing really satisfies. The child is tense, restless, and moody. With the slightest provocation or criticism from a parent, the explosive outburst of the tantrum may emerge. The child may shout, curse, or break something. If the child resists parental effort at control at this outburst stage, he may increase his opposition to parental words and actions. If you suggest quiet, the child shouts. This is the "no! no!" stage. It is best to say to the child at this stage, "You can be in charge of yourself when you can stop all this yelling and thrashing about." The tantrum gradually runs down after this stage, and depression replaces aggression. In the next, "Leave me alone" stage, the child becomes sad and placid. He does not want to interact with his parents, although he may accept a glass of water. In the final "hangover" or posttantrum stage, the child, a little tired and red-faced, is ready to resume normal activities. The child may act as if nothing has happened.

Also noteworthy is that there is a definite pattern to the reduction of temper tantrums.[1] The first observable change will be fewer tantrums and a longer time between tantrums. This may be somewhat disappointing since parents often wish that the intensity of the tantrums would decrease first. Unfortunately, this is not the reality. By keeping a record of when and under what circumstances tantrums occur, you will be able to spot the first signs of progress. The first important change occurs as a result of the child omitting a tantrum altogether if he feels his parents would regard it to be a fuss over a minor issue. So the child starts to make judgments rather than flying into a blind rage. His pouting time after a tantrum also tends to be shorter. Another sign of progress is a quiet reaction in the child after a tantrum and expressions of regret and/or affection for the parents. The next change in the temper tantrum reduction pattern is a decrease in the tantrum time. The time may decrease from 15 minutes to 1 or 2 minutes. The final stage in the resolution of tantrums is when parent and child can talk things out together while keeping a lid on their anger.

Temper tantrums reflect a serious behavior problem when they become the sole or favorite means of problem solving by a child over a long period of time.

Almost invariably, one finds that temper tantrums that are habitual have worked out to the child's advantage. Parents often surrender and agree to the wishes of an angry child in order to avoid further unpleasant scenes. In this way the child quickly learns that he can control his environment. The temper display is out of all proportion to the demands of the situation, and the child readily stages a violent tantrum to get his way.

Coping with children's anger can be puzzling, draining, and distressing for parents. In fact, one of the major problems in handling tantrums in children is our difficulty in controlling the anger that the child's temper stirs up in us.

Reasons Why

Anger is a normal, instinctual reaction when we are frustrated or attacked or when our expectations are not met. According to Ashley Montague, a bad temper is generally a result, not of a wrong done you, but of a frustration. You did not get what you expected to get. In an attempt to solve the problem, you communicate intensity of feelings rather than logic of ideas. Unfortunately a fit of temper is not the most effective way to solve problems.

Another contributing factor to anger outbursts in children is exposure to adults in the house who readily display temper themselves.

A third factor is the inability of children to perceive when they are becoming irritated or frustrated so they can't communicate these feelings to others except when they erupt in a full-blown tantrum. The expression of irritation or anger seems to be an "all or none" thing. Often hours will pass between the incident to which the child said she was objecting and the explosive episode that let people know of her objection. This results in the tantrums being described as "unprovoked." These children have been told many times to control their feelings and not express their anger.

How to Prevent

Parental Example. Do you tend to react to frustrations by "flying off the handle?" Remember that your children are very likely to imitate your example in handling frustrations. You can't expect your children to control themselves when you have a "hair trigger" temper and explode when things go badly.

Physiological Needs. When children are hungry or fatigued, they are more likely to have temper outbursts. So make sure your child is getting enough sleep and having her meals on time. A snack after school should also be provided. Be sure your children have plenty of opportunity to play freely outdoors.

Minimum Demands. Do not be excessively restrictive in managing your child by setting too many unnecessary or arbitrary prohibitions which tend to induce temper outbursts. Anger and resistance are natural reactions to "stop" signs. So limit controls over your children to most necessary ones.

Early Warning. Encourage your children to express minor irritations in a socially acceptable way. When a child starts rumbling and grumbling and seems to be headed for an eruption of temper, suggest to the child that something seems to be bothering her and you would like to be helpful. If the child has difficulty expressing herself, you might try to put into words what you suspect the child is thinking and feeling. If you have no idea what is bothering your child, ask some questions such as, "Did anything happen in school today?" "Are you angry about having to clean up your room?" Even if the child denies that you are correct about what is bothering her, but calms down markedly, it's a good bet that your diagnosis was on target even though the child is too upset to admit it. Parental understanding and concern can go a long way toward reducing unpleasant feelings even if the parent cannot satisfy the child's immediate desire.

Relaxation Training. Teach your child how to relax by tensing and relaxing different muscle groups. Emphasize mental as well as physical relaxation by having the child picture a particularly relaxing scene. Deep breathing exercises should supplement the muscle relaxation training. By becoming more aware of mental and physical tension, the child can counter rising agitation using relaxation methods.

What to Do

The simple truth is that there is no best way to deal with tantrum behavior. All of the following tactics have been proved effective in a certain percentage of the cases. Parents often find it helpful to combine management procedures.

Thus, ignoring might be combined with reinforcing intervals of nontantrum behavior.

The least effective ways of dealing with temper outbursts in a child are to yell and lose control of your own temper, meekly give in and let the child have his own way (this leads to the child throwing tantrums all the time), arguing with the child when you are both extremely upset, or using physical punishment or harsh threats.

Ignore. Deliberately ignore tantrum behavior that can be tolerated. At times it is best to simply walk away and refuse to be a spectator or participant in the child's temper outburst. You might go to your bedroom and play the radio really loud. One expert on child care, Rudolf Dreikurs, recommends that you withdraw to the bathroom since the child will be more likely to respect your privacy there. Take a book with you and do not come out until the tantrum has ceased. If the main goal underlying the tantrum is to get your attention or get you to give in, this bathroom technique should gradually reduce the temper displays.

Of course if the child is likely to destroy property or physically harm someone during a tantrum, you will have to remove the child to a secure time-out room before you ignore the tantrum.

Some children hold their breath during a tantrum until they turn blue. Do not become unduly concerned about this and capitulate to the child's demands. There is a physiologic "cut off" at which carbon dioxide accumulation stimulates the respiratory center, and the child will breathe even if he tries not to. If the child loses consciousness, you should apply a cold sponge to the child's face which tends to restore breathing. In normal children these breathholding attacks disappear spontaneously by the fourth year when the child has less need to control the environment.

Appropriate Anger Expression
Verbal expression. There is a place for anger and its expression. Both parents and children should be able to accept their angry feelings and put them into words. This should be done, however, in an assertive way (sticking up for one's rights) rather than in a hostile manner (attempting to hurt or deprecate the other). A mother, for example, might tell her 5-year-old son, "I get very upset when I see your toys scattered all around your room. It looks messy

and it means more work for me." By so doing, she serves as a model for her son, so that he can learn to appropriately state his feelings. If he can tell his parents that he feels bad because they are going out so much, maybe the series of temper tantrums won't begin in the first place.

The ultimate resolution of tantrum behavior is when child and parent can *talk out* differences of opinion. The discussion may be heated and emotional, but throughout it all both must remain in control, refrain from putting the other down, and try to negotiate a solution acceptable to both.

Physical release. When a child is too upset to talk, encourage the release of her anger by such physical activities as running around the block, going in a closet and screaming, throwing things at a target, drawing a mean face, pounding clay, or dancing to records.

Striking a punching bag is another acceptable release. Suitable punching bags for this purpose can be constructed from old pillow slips and some discarded clothing. Fill the pillow slips until they are packed solidly. Then hang them from a doorway or basement ceiling and allow your child to hit away until the anger dissipates.

Remember that one's goal should not be to repress or destroy all angry feelings in children, but rather to accept the feelings and to help channel and direct them into constructive ends. Unexpressed anger tends to build up and emerge in an explosive way later on. If the tension remains bottled up in the body, it can lead to a variety of psychosomatic disorders, such as migraine headaches and recurrent abdominal pain.

Rewards. Give the child a positive incentive for nontantrum behavior. Post a star for each half-day of nontantrums. When the child earns four stars in a row, a special treat is provided. Gradually, more and more stars are needed before the special treat is given.

Also, be sure to praise the child for being good and for handling frustration without becoming upset. For example, you might make such comments as, "I appreciate your hanging up your clothes even though you were in a hurry to get out to play," "I'm glad you shared your toy with your sister," "You were really patient while waiting your turn in line."

Mild Penalty. To help teach your child that temper tantrums will not work to his advantage but, rather, will result in isolation, impose a penalty of 5–10 minutes in a time-out room whenever a tantrum occurs. Be firm and matter-of-fact in enforcing this rule (show no sympathy or anger). If the child is still disruptive at the end of the time-out period, he receives additional time in isolation.

More Supervision. Very young children seem to need more adult involvement in their interests. A child who is becoming upset is sometimes easily stopped when an adult moves physically closer to the child, expresses interest in the child's activity, or offers a hug. When a child first gives signs of becoming frustrated or upset, an adult might also suggest ways of solving the problem. Focus on the issues and the child's objectives in a rational, realistic way. Suggest several different solutions and leave the final choice to the child.

If your child is only mildly upset, setting a limit may be effective. By saying, "no," you may be able to check the anger expression before it escalates into a full blown tantrum. You might say something like:

"That's enough. You are upsetting us all and making yourself more and more unhappy. We cannot have a pleasant evening if you are going to be unhappy."

"No hitting your sister. If you are angry with her, tell her what is bothering you."

Role Playing. Help your children control their temper by exposing them to hypothetical situations which would normally cause them to get angry. Once they learn to expect and handle such situations, they can roll with the punch instead of becoming angered. So defuse provoking situations by diminishing their power to arouse anger in the child. This is achieved by desensitization procedures.[2]

First discuss situations that typically trigger a child's temper problems, such as a scolding from a teacher. Then ask the child to role play his typical responses to authority figures. To provide your child with a mirror of his behavior, you should act out how he behaves during a typical temper tantrum. Discuss the adverse consequences for the child that result from such a temper display.

Then identify more socially adaptive responses to the situation. In the case of the teacher criticism, you might specify three behaviors: eye contact, moderate tone of voice, and a socially cooperative response (for example, if asked where his assigned homework was, a cooperative type of response would be, "My mistake—I'll get it from my locker where I left it"). Periodically play the role of a teacher confronting the child and have him practice giving an appropriate response. Praise the child whenever he plays his role in a cooperative manner.

Self-Talk. Train your children how to talk themselves out of their anger. Teach them how to counterbalance frustration and insult by saying quetly to themselves calming thoughts, thoughts of self-control, or thoughts which put the situation into perspective. If a playmate has hurt your child's feelings, for example, he can soften his anger by saying to himself: "When kids are mean to me, I feel sorry for them. They must be feeling pretty bad themselves to act so mean," or "Well, names can't really hurt me so I'll just ignore them," or "That is not really upsetting. It is not worth getting bothered about." If a child spills her paints, she can reduce her feeling of inadequacy, by saying, "When I do something wrong I try to think of all the things I do right."

Promote Insight. After your child has fully recovered from a tantrum, discuss the event with her to promote greater understanding. The discussion should include a description of how you and the child each felt during the episode, the causes and early warning signals of the difficulty, and alternative ways to solve such problems in the future. Be sure to listen respectfully to the thoughts and feelings of the child.

Holding. Occasionally a child may lose control so completely that he has to be physically restrained or removed from the scene for safety's sake, that is, to prevent him from hurting himself or others, or from destroying things. This approach should not be viewed as punishment but as a means of saying, "You can't do that." Some children need reassurance that they will be controlled when they lose self-control.

So when a child is in danger of hurting himself or others or of breaking property, you have no choice but to physically restrain him. As quickly as possible, move the child to a comfortable and private place. This will avoid upsetting other children in the household. Out-of-control children often do things that would be quite embarrassing for them once they regain control. Try to hold the child from the back since there is less risk of physical injury this way. It is easier to avoid kicking and biting when the child is not facing you. If possible sit down and hold the child on your lap. Do not hold the child any tighter than is necessary. As the child regains self-control, your grip should relax accordingly.

Talk to the child in a low, soothing voice. The calmer you remain, the quicker the child will regain his own composure. Avoid discussing what is upsetting the child and keep reassuring him that as soon as he calms down you will release him. Do not threaten to punish the child. Console the child by saying, "I know it feels bad to be so angry; I'm sorry you feel so bad."

When the child has recovered and is in control, offer a glass of water for his dry throat and a cool cloth for his face. Be soothing and reassuring and do not attempt to confront the child at this stage. Let the child sleep or be alone if he wishes.

Later, when the child has resumed normal activity, you can discuss the episode, including how angry his behavior made you. Reassure the child of your basic liking for him and confidence in his ability to overcome this problem in the future.

Paradoxical Task. Paradoxical tasks are those which appear absurd because they exhibit an apparently contradictory nature, such as requiring children to continue temper tantrums, rather than requiring that they stop the tantrums, which is what everyone has been demanding. By instructing a child to carry out and even exaggerate tantrums, he may actually decrease this behavior because he resists being told what to do.

In one family,[3] the 4-year-old son was exhibiting almost daily temper tantrums. The parents had tended to be overprotective and used a "reasoning" approach with the child. With professional advice they instructed the boy that he could have his tantrums but only in a chosen tantrum place at home. If he started to tantrum at any other place, he was to go, or be taken, to the tantrum place. If he was away from home when he started to tantrum, he was told that he would have to wait until he got home to go to the tantrum place. The following week the boy was told that he could tantrum, but only at a certain time of day (and in the tantrum place). The parents picked a 2-hour period that had been the most frequent time of tantrums. By the third week of this strategy, the boy's tantrums had decreased so markedly that he was explicitly told to tantrum during the following week. The boy failed to follow this direction and now revealed complete control of his temper.

Case Reports

Case #1. Billy was experiencing a great deal of difficulty controlling his temper in elementary school.[4] Typically he would have about 100 outbursts over the course of the school day. After he was expelled from school for cursing a teacher, his homeroom teacher decided to implement new rules. Billy was told that his outbursts would be recorded and every time he went over 25 a day, there would be a penalty. He would have to sit in a time-out area—a small desk in a corner away from the rest of the class. Although Billy did not like this, he asked and was granted permission to try to stay under five outbursts instead of 25. Every day he exceeded this limit, he went to the corner. In addition, each time he stayed under five for the day, he received a reward (small treat or privilege, such as going out to recess early). This procedure was successful in markedly reducing the incidence of tantrums within a few days.

Case #2. One mother of a preschool child would sit quietly with her knitting in the room where her child was thrashing about, kicking furniture, and occasionally throwing things. Once in a while she moved an object to a safer place and occasionally got up to hold the child from kicking in the door panels. She was firm and she made it quite clear that she disapproved of such behavior, but she was not agitated—at least not outwardly.

She would say quietly during the momentary lull, "Of course you are angry at me. You are angry because I can't let you do what you want. Mothers sometimes have to stop their children from doing what they want."

She listened to a barrage of unjust accusations until the storm gradually lessened, and she was able to engage him in friendly conversation about other matters. She did not demand an apology, impose a penalty, moralize, or refer to the cause of the original tantrum. The child learned that his mother had control of the situation and of her emotions.

She also demonstrated that she disapproved of the behavior, not of the child.

Case #3. Greg was a boy who found it hard to directly express his angry feelings.[5] There were several reasons for his inability to tell others when he was mad: First, his language development was delayed, and he had difficulty finding the right words to express his anger. He also felt unable to stand up to other boys his age, so when he was angry at another boy he would strike out at the nearest adult who he knew would not retaliate. The following concrete approach was used to control his temper attacks. A reward system was established to give Greg a piece of candy for each 30-minute time period in which he did not hit, push, or kick at an adult. In school Greg was given an additional reward of spending special time with the teacher for each day that he did not hit at all. He was also praised and encouraged for legitimate expressions of anger. In addition to verbalizing that he was angry at someone, Greg was instructed to explain why.

An alternative release for Greg's anger was provided. If he felt the need to strike out, he was permitted to go to the exercise room and punch the heavy bag. He was praised and encouraged for making this choice in the same way as if he had made a verbal expression of anger. On the other hand, if Greg tried to hit an adult, he was removed to his room until he was able to express himself more appropriately. These methods very quickly reduced the amount of hitting he did.

Case #4. Peter, a 4-year-old boy, exhibited frequent temper tantrums and disobedience. He often kicked objects or people, removed or tore his clothing, called people rude names, annoyed his younger sister, made a variety of threats, hit himself, and became angry at the slightest frustration. He demanded attention almost constantly and seldom cooperated with his mother. He was described as an overactive boy of borderline intelligence who was possibly brain-damaged.

In the past his mother would try to control him by explaining why he should not misbehave, and attempting to interest him in another activity by giving toys or food. The mother had difficulty enforcing penalties of any kind. With professional guidance the mother instituted the following child management procedures. She was to give commands in a clear, firm manner and not "give in" after directing Peter to do something. When Peter did not comply with a command to stop misbehaving, he was immediately placed in his room and the door was locked. When placed in his room, he was required to remain there for at least 5 minutes. Moreover, he had to keep quiet for a short period before he was allowed to come out. All playthings had been removed from his room, and he had little opportunity to amuse himself there. His mother also made a special effort to give Peter attention, praise, and affectionate physical contact whenever he played in a desirable way. This new procedure reduced his temper tantrums and disobedience to low levels.

Books for Parents about Temper Tantrums

Wiggins, J.G.: *Dealing with Temper Tantrums.* Personal Growth Press, Berea, OH 44017 (1969).

8 Ways to Vent your Anger: A Book of Anger Exercises. Crescent Publishers, Dept. PT, 4201 E. 3rd, Bloomington, IN 47401 (Cost, $3.95).

Books for Children about Temper Tantrums

Preston, E.: *The Temper Tantrum Book.* Viking Press, New York (1969).

References

1. Wiggins, J.G.: *Dealing with Temper Tantrums.* Personal Growth Press, Berea, OH (1969).
2. Kaufman, L.M. and Wagner, B.R.: "Barb: A systematic treatment technology for temper control disorders." *Behavior Therapy* 3: (1972), pp, 84–90.
3. Hare-Mustin, R.: "Treatment of temper tantrums by a paradoxical intervention." *Family Process* 14: (1975), pp. 481–485.
4. Chase, E.: "Improving the behavior of a second grader." *Educational Technology Monograph* 1: (1968), pp. 7–8.

5. Krueger, M.A.: *Intervention Techniques for Child Care Workers*. Franklin Publishers, Milwaukee, WI (1978).

DISHONESTY

It takes time for children to develop a sense of honesty. It is not something they are born with. In this section we will discuss the so called "white-collar" offenses of lying, stealing, and cheating. These nonviolent offenses involve elements of deceit, concealment, misrepresentation, and breach of trust. They are committed by people of all ages, and by members of all social orders.

Contributing to the dishonesty we find in children is the moral crisis that is so prevalent in America today.[1,5] Many adults cheat on income taxes and steal from employers. The result is a "rip-off" mentality and a self-centered, "What's in it for me" orientation. The Watergate episode indicated that deliberate deceit exists even at the highest level of government.

"The culture of narcissism" is the way Christopher Lasch described our society in a recent book. Self-preoccupation is so strong in America, according to Lasch, that it seems to allow little room for moral values of any kind.

For parents, it is easy to forget that little acts of dishonesty at home are related to the big acts of dishonesty like nursing home scandals and big corporation payoffs. The difference is largely one of degree. Personal dishonesty by anyone in the family encourages other family members to lower standards. Children tend to identify with the basic moral character of their parents. Honesty, then, is a significant moral behavior, and without it families and societies become unlivable.

Stealing

Stealing can be defined as the possession of an object not clearly (in the adult's judgment) belonging to the child. For an incident to be called stealing, the child must have known that it was wrong to take the object without permission of the owner. Minor stealing incidents in early childhood are quite common. Stealing by children tends to reach a peak incidence around the ages of 5–8 and then taper off. The development of a conscience proceeds slowly in children as they gradually move away from a self-centered orientation and a desire for immediate gratification of their impulses. Of all the behavior problems of childhood, stealing worries some parents the most. These parents see it as behavior typical of criminals, and this strikes fear in their hearts. They also feel that neighbors will judge them on the behavior of their child. Fortunately, there are definite steps parents can take on their own to deal effectively with childhood stealing. If regular stealing persists after age 10, then it is most likely a sign of serious emotional disturbance in a child which requires immediate professional assistance. Each year about 25,000 children go to juvenile court for stealing.

Reasons Why. Children steal for a variety of reasons. Very young or immature children may simply not understand that others have a right to private property that must be respected. These children have trouble distinguishing between borrowing and stealing.

1. There may be something seriously lacking in the child's life, so that stealing may be a symbolic replacement for the absence of parental love, attention, respect, or affection. It is not unusual for stealing to start after one parent has left home or died.

Also noteworthy is the finding[2] that juvenile delinquents who repeatedly engage in a variety of antisocial acts tend to come from homes characterized by parental alcoholism, criminality, and associated poor childrearing or often total neglect of the children.

2. Another reason for a child's stealing is the fact that some parents obtain a vicarious unconscious pleasure from their child's misdoing, as it gratifies some of their own hidden rebellious feelings. The child senses this and is stimulated to continue.

3. The child may have selected a poor example to admire. Perhaps he has seen a parent, friend, or brother or sister stealing and has identified with this person. Stealing to gain approval from a gang is not uncommon.

4. Some children steal to bolster their self-esteem. They exhibit the stolen goods to prove to others their toughness, manhood, or competence. Other children enjoy the excitement and sense of adventure involved in stealing.

5. Children from low socioeconomic backgrounds may steal because they simply have no money to buy the things they want. Having so little themselves, it is hard for them to respect the property of others.

6. Stealing may be a child's way of unconsciously getting even with a parent. If a parent forbids a child to wear make-up, the child may steal from a store with the unconscious wish to get caught and thereby embarrass the parent.

7. Stealing may be a sign of internal stress in a child, such as depression, jealousy over a new baby in the home, or anger. The child is trying to reestablish a comfortable feeling inside by the stealing. Another reason may be that the child has a very low frustration tolerance and has great difficulty resisting temptation.

How To Prevent

Teach values. Parents who place a high value on personal honesty and respect for the property of others, who are more concerned about the common good rather than personal gain, and who are clear about these values and live up to them in their daily lives are less apt to have children with a stealing problem. Parents who have consistently respected the child's right to personal property are also less likely to experience a problem in this area, that is, parents who would never borrow a child's personal property or savings without the child's permission.

Develop a close relationship. If closeness to the child is lacking in the home, endeavor to develop a warm parent-child relationship. In this way the child will be more likely to strive to please you and identify with your values.

Ensure regular income. Be sure your child has a regular source of income to buy the things he needs. This income could come from an allowance, or a part-time, after-school job.

Also, let your children know that they can come to you when they have a real need for money and that you will try to help.

Close supervision. Parents who keep in touch with the daily activities of their children will not allow a habit like stealing to gain much headway before they become aware of it. The earlier the stealing habit is detected, the better. Also, be sure to provide your child with plenty of constructive, exciting activities to engage in during leisure hours.

Set the example. Be sure to show integrity of character in your daily activities. Return found property and do not shortchange others, cheat at the turnstile, or "lift" things from your employer.

Property rights. Clearly establish property rights in and out of the home, with the rights of all respected. Tell your children how to borrow and return property belonging to others.

Remove temptation. Do not leave loose change, wallets, piggy banks, and unlocked coin collections about.

What To Do

Take immediate action. Rather than overlooking or minimizing the antisocial tendencies of their children, parents should take the time to understand, confront, and correct this behavior which should be as unacceptable at home as it is outside.

  Correct: The most reasonable penalty for taking something belonging to another is to make restitution by either returning the object with an apology, or making a monetary payment to replace the object. Thus, when a child takes candy or other objects from a store, the parent should escort the child to the store and require the child to personally return the object. Do not require young children to apologize to the storeowner since they often become so embarrassed that they cannot talk. When a stolen object has been damaged or lost, the child should be required to schedule reimbursement from an allowance or other personal source of funds. In this regard, care should be taken not to pauperize the child because this will only encourage more thefts. Repayment should inconvenience the child and necessitate going without certain material things the child could have had from the allowance. If for some reason restitution is not possible, the child should be deprived of something, such as loss of TV privileges, to reinforce the ethical issue. It is important to *immediately* and *consistently* set penalties for stealing incidents. Apologies, explanations, and promises to reform by the child should not be allowed to undermine the *certainty* of the consequences. The child must assume personal responsibility for correcting the misdeed.

Confront: Along with requiring restitution, parents should verbally confront the child (when both have calmed down) about the seriousness of the behavior. This means explaining why the act is inappropriate and making it clear that the behavior will not be tolerated. Rather than using euphemisms such as ''borrowing'' or ''sticky fingers,'' the parents should clearly label the act as ''stealing'' so that the child understands the true nature of the misdeed and cannot minimize it.

Confront the child about the stealing in a simple, honest way rather than giving a sermon. Point out the unfairness of the act, explain the right of people to private property, and examine the feelings others have toward people who steal. It is also helpful to show the child that you understand the motive for the act (''It looked too tempting and you always wanted it'') and to end the confrontation on a positive note by expressing affection, appreciation, or positive expectations for the child.

Encourage empathic responses from your child by saying: ''How would you feel if someone took something you really valued?'' ''How do you think the owner of his wallet will feel if you call him up right now and say you found it?''

In a situation where you suspect a child of stealing but are not certain, you might say: ''John, I'm not sure you took money from my purse, but if you did because you felt you really needed it, and if you can give it back, I'd be very proud of you. But even more important than my being proud of you is for you to be proud of yourself. You have to live with yourself and be happy with yourself and that would be hard to do if you're not honest and fair with other people.'' Often a child will return the object in a few days after such a talk.

Understand: Asking children ''why'' they stole something is usually fruitless because they lack the sophistication to give a valid answer. It is better to consider the facts yourself and try to determine what the child got out of it. By understanding the child's basic motives, you will be in a better position to get at the root causes and thus prevent further reoccurrences of the problem. As previously mentioned, some of the reasons school-age children steal are as follows.

Economic deprivation: Some children have insufficient money to meet their needs for occasional candy, movies, and so forth. They want what their friends have and have no other way to get money. *Solution:* Provide more material things or source of income.

Emotional deprivation: Feeling deprived of love, affection, and caring from their parents, these children steal to fill the empty feeling inside. *Solution:* Greater efforts by the parents to love, like, and spend time with their children.

Immaturity: Some school-age children (aged 7 and up) steal because they haven't developed a mature conscience or level of moral judgment. They tend to be self-centered and seek immediate gratification of their impulses. Unable to plan ahead and save money, these children steal to get what they want *now.* They have little sense of private property or knowledge of the distinction between borrowing and stealing. They feel little or no guilt over taking things. *Solution:* Repeated setting of consequences and teaching of moral principles *(e.g.,* concern for others).

Excitement-machismo-prestige: Some children steal for the "thrill" of it (risking danger, putting something over on someone else), to win the approval or admiration of the peer group, or to prove how "tough" or "slick" they can be. *Solution:* Provide or offer guidance as to alternative sources of excitement, friendships, and prestige.

Parental reinforcement and modeling: Some parents derive unconscious, vicarious pleasure from a child's stealing since it satisfies their own hidden rebelliousness or antisocial tendencies. For example, they might really believe that it's acceptable to loot during a blackout because the shopkeepers have long been "ripping off" the community. Other parents may often steal themselves (or cheat on their income taxes) and do little to disguise this behavior from the children. *Solution:* Behavior and attitude change in parents.

Examine the possible reasons for childhood stealing and decide which best apply to your child; then take steps to solve the underlying cause(s).

React with self-control. In coping with a child who steals, it is important for parents to control their emotional upset and not be overly shocked, angry, or despairing. Do not take stealing as a personal failure or affront to you. Since children tend to be egocentric and pleasure seeking, one has to expect some stealing episodes. You can express your disapproval in a firm way without unnecessary yelling or excitement. Avoid exaggerating the incident and making the child feel like a criminal. In other words, don't become a "prosecuting attorney" who verbally browbeats a child by labeling him or her a "little thief" and/or making dire predictions ("You're going to wind up in Sing Sing"). When you give a child a bad label or suggest a bad outcome, a child may become convinced that you are right. Too intense a reaction from you may convince a child that making amends can never undo the crime, may stir up uncontrollable guilt or shame, and may seriously impair your relationship with the child. Don't demand a confession which will only force a child to lie. Remember that when a child is in trouble, she needs your affection and confidence more than ever. Rather than saying, "Did you take my money?" when you are sure your daughter took the money, say something like: "I know you took the $5 from my purse, probably because there was something you really wanted, and you didn't know how else to get it. In the future when you want to buy something, please tell me about it and we'll discuss it."

Rather than becoming a prosecuting attorney, some parents handle their feelings of shock and humiliation by completely denying the incident and thus becoming the child's defending lawyer: "My child would never have done anything like that. I don't want to talk about it any further." The best attitude to take is an open mind which seeks all the facts, both sides of the story, and tries to understand the causes or underlying motives behind a stealing incident.

Monitoring. Research shows that people cheat, steal, and lie less if the risk of detection is high. Children who habitually steal need close surveillance by their parents so that whenever they steal there is a high probability the incident will be detected. Studies have shown that these children often come from homes where both parents work and thus do not keep in touch with the daily activities of their children.[3] Consequently the habit has gained considerable headway before it is uncovered. Children who frequently steal (an average of one or more thefts every 2 weeks) should not be allowed to keep any objects that do not clearly belong to them and should be told that they can expect regular "pocket-emptying" and "room-searching" inspections until the problem is corrected. In other words their right to privacy will be temporarily suspended until they learn to respect the rights of others. These children need the certain knowledge that they can't get away with stealing, despite clever lies or cover-ups. They should be confronted with each stealing episode, and no explanations or excuses should be accepted.

Arrange regular income. Research has indicated that children who engage in petty thievery tend to have been brought up in homes where their financial needs were ignored or else where their parents gave them large sums of money. School-age children should be assured of a regular, modest source of income such as an allowance and/or a part-time job.

Case Reports

Case #1. A mother became very angry at her 9-year-old daughter who was detected stealing money from a teacher's desk.[4] The woman, who was in therapy, told her therapist that she knew her daughter Margaret had occasionally taken nickels from her purse since Margaret was 6 or 7, but she had said nothing, believing that Margaret would "outgrow it." "Besides," the mother said, "it was never serious, so the less said, the better." This mother told the therapist that she had frequently stolen during childhood, and her mother had always protected her. The therapist helped the mother see that she had been dismissing significant stealing episodes as unimportant. The mother was subsequently able to take a definite stand against stealing and to consistently require the child to take responsibility for these acts by making restitution.

Case #2. A 14-year-old boy had stolen some goods belonging to neighbors as well as his family's car, and had run away from home. After the boy was caught, the parents' primary complaint was that the boy showed no remorse. No punishment was given for any of these misdeeds. In fact the mother reported that she very seldom punished the boy except when he expressed anger at her. Typically, she would try to reason with him when he misbehaved. The parents were counseled that they should set and enforce limits on the boy's behavior. He should be required, for example, to earn money to pay back the goods which were stolen and lost.

Case #3. An 11-year-old girl stole objects and money at home, school, and occasionally from stores. The parents had fallen into a pattern of sporadic but extreme punishment and frequent references to their daughter being a criminal. After much discussion, they agreed that immediate consistent action was more appropriate. They set penalties (removal of money in the amount of the stolen object from her bank account) and insisted upon restitution to the victim. The stealing had been a source of extreme embarrassment, and neither the parents nor the child had been able to face the prospect of returning objects or money to the victim. This was an important step since it made it clear to the girl the seriousness of the behavior and the necessity of restitution. For her, facing a person and apologizing was a very powerful motivator to cease stealing. The parents informed the child that in the future she would not be allowed to keep any objects she "found" or that the parents felt did not clearly belong to her. In this case, these simple steps were immediately effective.

Books for Children About Stealing

Cole, J.: *The Secret Box*. William Morrow (1971). Ages 6–8.

A primary-school girl begins stealing objects from the classroom. She quickly stops when she discovers how unhappy this makes others feel.

Slate, A.: *Tony and Me*. J.B. Lippincott, Philadelphia (1974). Ages 8–12.

Two fifth-grade boys are caught shoplifting a baseball from a sports store.

Wilson, A.: *A Country Wedding.* Addison Wesley (1969). Ages 5–9.

Stealing food and wine by a fox and a wolf does not pay off.

References

1. *Behavior Today:* (May 21, 1979), p. 15.
2. Zabcznska, E.: "A longitudinal study of development of juvenile delinquency." *Polish Psychological Bulletin* 8: (1977), pp. 239–245.
3. Patterson, G.R. and Reid, J.B.: "Intervention for families of aggressive boys: A replication study." *Behavior Research and Therapy* 11: (1973), pp. 383–394.
4. Szurek, S.A. and Berlin, I.N.: *The Antisocial Child.* Science and Behavior Books, Palo Alto, CA (1969).
5. Bok, S.: *Lying: Moral Choice in Public and Private Life.* Pantheon, New York (1978).

Lying

Lying can be defined as making an untrue statement, with knowledge of the falsehood and with the intent to deceive another so as to gain an advantage or evade unpleasantness. Although all children lie on occasion, parents tend to regard honesty as an essential character trait above all others and get very upset when a child is dishonest. During the pre-school years, children have difficulty distinguishing fantasy from reality. As a result they are prone to self-deceptions, exaggerations, and wishful thinking. The school-age child, on the other hand, is more likely to tell the "antisocial" type of lie, wherein a falsehood is deliberately told to avoid punishment, gain an advantage over others, or demean others. Children differ in their level of moral development and understanding of honesty. Piaget distinguishes three stages in children's beliefs about lying. In the first stage the child believes that a lie is wrong because it is an object of punishment by adults. If the punishment were to be removed, the lie would be acceptable. In stage two, a lie becomes something that is wrong in itself and would remain so even if punishment were removed. In stage three, "A lie is wrong because it is in conflict with mutual respect and affection." In order to understand the level your child is at, try asking the following questions: "Why is it naughty (wrong) to tell lies?" "Would it be all right to tell a lie if you don't get caught and if no one punishes you for it?" By age 6 most children are at stage two, while at age 12 about one-third of the children in our society are at stage three.

Lying by children takes many forms, including:

1. *Simple reversals of truth:* The child says he has done his homework when he has not.
2. *Exaggerations:* A child magnifies her father's strength when talking with peers.
3. *Fabrications:* A child tells friends of a vacation trip that never happened.
4. *Confabulations:* A child tells a story that is partly true and partly false.
5. *Wrong accusations:* The child blames a sibling for spilling the milk when he did it.

Reasons Why

Among the common reasons children lie are the following:

1. Self-defense: To escape the unpleasant consequences of behavior, such as parental disapproval or punishment.
2. Denial: A way of handling painful memories, feelings, or fantasies.
3. Modeling: Copying the example of adults.
4. Ego-boasting: Boasting or bragging to receive attention and admiration.
5. Reality-testing: Attempting to find out the difference between reality and fantasy.
6. Loyalty: Protection of other children.
7. Hostility: Act of general hostility toward others.
8. Gain: To get something for oneself.
9. Self-image: The child has been told repeatedly that she is a liar and has come to believe it.
10. Distrust: Parents tend not to trust and believe a child when he tells the truth, so the child prefers to lie.

How To Prevent

1. Do not demand that children testify against themselves by demanding a confession. We are all tempted to lie when asked to incriminate ourselves. Rather than forcing a child to confess, we should gather all the facts from other sources and base our decision on the evidence. When in doubt as to a child's guilt or innocence, it is better to avoid the issue and forego discipline rather than force a child to lie or confess.

If you know a child did poorly on a test at school, don't ask, "Did you pass your exam?" Rather, state, "Your teacher called me to inform us that you failed the test. We are worried. We wonder how to be of help."

2. Establish the same standards of honesty. If we as adults feel free to bend the rules a little in regard to honesty, such as by telling "white lies," children should not be required to always tell the whole truth.

3. Discuss moral issues. Have family discussions of why it is not good to lie, steal, or cheat. Make these discussions interesting and informative.

4. Avoid too severe or too frequent punishment which tends to promote lying as a means of self-protection. Children will also lie to preserve their self-esteem when parents are continually criticizing them for ineptness and failure. The best strategy is to make frequent use of praise and appreciation so children will feel secure enough to admit mistakes and misdeeds.

5. Make a practice of being truthful yourself. Do not try to dodge unpleasant situations by telling the child the doctor's needle won't hurt, or to disguise personal weaknesses by engaging in obvious falsehoods, excuses, or broken promises. Honesty to the facts is a learned behavior that children acquire best by imitating parental example.

Try to become more aware of any tendencies you might have to:

1. Exaggerate a story.
2. Fib to escape an unwanted appointment.
3. Deny a mistake made.
4. Give instructions to inform a caller that you are not home.
5. Tell your child that you are going to be home when you are not.

What To Do

Penalize. Help your children learn by experience that lying to you tends to be unsuccessful and only works to their disadvantage. Show them that being honest is a mitigating circumstance (will tend to reduce their punishment for a misdeed) and that lying to cover up an antisocial act will only result in additional punishment for lying. In the case of the cover-up lie, the child should be punished *both* for the act of lying and for the misdeed that prompted the lie. Two punishments may be appropriate; this may involve the loss of two different sets of privileges, or a double punishment.

You should also explain the value of truthfulness by repeating over and over that if they tell you the truth about a troublesome situation, you will do all in your power to help them, for in knowing the real facts you can deal with any misstatements by others. If, however, they lie to you, you can't be of much help because you can't depend on them for the truth. Remind and reassure your children that you are on their side and that they do not have to be afraid of the truth.

Teach moral values. Do not overlook or downplay the significance of childhood lying. Rather, teach your children that dishonesty in any form is immoral and destructive to oneself and others. Explain that mutual respect and trust are built upon honest communication and that their "word" is of great importance. Remind the child of the story of a boy who "cried wolf" too often so that no one believed him when he was telling the truth. Show the child that truthfulness is expected from everyone in the family since it is part of the family's moral code.

You might reinforce the moral message by reading the following poem to your children:

> *The History of a Lie*
> *First somebody told it,*
> *Then the room wouldn't hold it,*
> *So the busy tongues rolled it*
> *Till they got it outside:*
> *Then the crowd came across it,*
> *And never once lost it,*
> *But tossed it and tossed it,*

> *Till it grew long and wide.*
> *This lie brought forth others,*
> *Evil sisters and brothers,*
> *A terrible crew,*
> *As headlong they hurried,*
> *The people they flurried*
> *And troubled and worried,*
> *As lies always do*
> *So, evil-boded,*
> *This monstrous lie goaded,*
> *Till at last it exploded,*
> *In sin and shame.*
> *But from mud and from mire*
> *The pieces flew higher,*
> *Till they hit the sad liar,*
> *And killed his good name.*
> —Reader of Ann In The Monett Times

Reality feedback. When a preschool child tells a tall tale, let him know you regard it as a very good story and nothing more by such remarks as, "Well, now, that's a very interesting story. But how did you tear your shirt?" You might help a child distinguish truth and fantasy by asking, "Is it true or a fairy tale?" When you know a story is not true, you might say, "Now tell me the true story. That was make-believe. Tell me the true story now." Also, when reading stories to a child, point out which stories are pretend and which are about things that really happened.

Promote self-awareness. When children lie by denying they did something, help them recognize their role in a troublesome situation by getting them talking about every phase of the situation. Say, "I want to know everything that happened from start to finish." Help them focus on their own involvement by asking pointed questions about what has been told, to show you suspect that certain parts are not accurate or believable. As a child probes and examines the situation, he may see for himself where he is wrong or where he stretched the truth. Be sure to agree with the child whenever he is right and obviously telling the truth.

Search for underlying causes. Try to find out what prompted the child to lie so that you can prevent future reoccurrences of the lying. As discussed earlier, the most common reasons children lie are:

1. *Get praise, attention, or prestige.* Solution: Give child more praise and appreciation for what he or she is and does so the child does not have to lie to feel good.
2. *Avoid punishment, guilt, or embarrassment.* Solution: Be less severe if child has been receiving harsh and unjust punishment in the past. Set a reasonable penalty for lying, and make honesty more rewarding.
3. *Lies of imitation* (imitate parents who tell "white lies"). Solution: Set better example at home.
4. *Fear of disapproval for failing a difficult task.* Solution: Don't expect so much so soon from the child.
5. *Get something for self.* Solution: Help child explore other ways to get the desired object.
6. *To belittle or exploit others.* Solution: Discuss fairness and good sportsmanship.
7. *Be loyal and protect other children.* Solution: Gather the facts from other sources.
8. *As act of general hostility.* Solution: Professional counseling for child and family.

Case Reports

Case #1. A 9-year-old boy frequently lied to parents, teachers, and peers. The lying involved either an attempt to avoid punishment or a means of making himself appear heroic or important. As a first step, the parents agreed to set reasonable, agreed-upon penalties for lying. After a discussion between the boy and the parents, it was decided that television was not to be viewed during any day in which a lie was told. This method was used since television viewing was an important activity to the child. This loss was seen as significant (and fair) by him. Additionally, if two "lying days" occurred during a week, he would lose $.25 of his $1.00 weekly allowance.

His need to feel important was handled by the parents' increasing their praise and appreciation of him. This was accomplished by a general increase in positive statements to the boy. Also, comments were made by the parents about their delight in their seeing an increase in honesty. Specifically, they agreed to comment about the boy's honest reporting of events and admission of his difficulties. The parents admitted that their previous reaction was never to praise good behavior, but to scold and criticize bad behavior (especially lying).

During the first month, there were 2 weeks where $.25 was lost (lying during 2 days 1 week and 3 days of another week). During week 3, only 1 day of television loss occurred and week 4 was perfect. The parents were told to engage in a special treat that weekend. On Sunday, the father went bowling only with his son and then treated him to an ice cream sundae (the boy's choice was the special—a banana barge). Much to everyone's satisfaction, lying markedly decreased after 1 month. The system was then discontinued since all felt it was no longer necessary.

Case #2. Ann, age 9, was caught in a lie. She stated that she had lied to save herself embarrassment. Her mother replied, "In our family we trust each other. When truth is bent, it creates distrust." Ann apologized and said she would not do it again. Her mother replied, "I accept your word." By stating her disapproval and family values, this mother was able to keep lying incidents to a minimum in the family.

Case #3. Joey, age 13, was in a residential treatment center because he enjoyed doing whatever he wanted at the moment rather than following family rules.[1] To achieve his ends he had learned to lie and steal. He would lie at a rate of two to seven times a day. To decrease his dishonest behavior, both he and his counselor recorded each incidence of lying and stealing behavior. For periods of time when no dishonest behavior occurred, Joey received poker chips which could be turned in for various privileges and rewards, such as games, treats, and freedom to play in specified areas around the house. This procedure quickly brought the lying and stealing under control.

Readings for Parents About Childhood Lying

Leshan, Eda: "When a Child Lies . . ." *Woman's Day:* (November, 1976), p. 107.
Lying and Stealing: What makes my child dishonest? Human Relations Aids, 119 Park Ave. South, New York, NY 10016.

Books For Children About Lying

Brink, C.R.: *The Bad Times of Irma Baumlein.* Macmillan (1972). Ages 10–13.

A lonely girl in elementary school gets into more and more trouble after lying about owning the largest doll in the world.

Fife, D.: *Who's in Charge of Lincoln?* Coward, McCann & Geoghegan (1965). Ages 8–10.

Because an 8-year-old boy is in the habit of telling tall tales, people do not listen to him when he tells the truth.

Gardner, R.A.: "The $100 lie." In *Dr. Gardner's Stories About The Real World.* Prentice Hall (1972). Ages 6–12.

A story describing the adverse effects of lying by a child.

Little, J.: *One to Grow On.* Little, Brown & Co. (1969). Ages 10–12.

Jamie, a junior-high-school student, tells lies to make herself appear important until her godmother helps her with the problem.

Ness, E.M.: *Sam, Bangs, and Moonshine.* Holt, Rinehart & Winston (1966). Ages 4–8.

Sam, a young girl, falsifies so many things that people feel they cannot believe anything she says. A near tragedy forces her to pay more attention to reality.

References

1. Todd, D.R. *et al.:* "A unique approach to comprehensive mental health services for children." Paper presented at the annual meeting of the Association for the Advancement of Behavior Therapy, San Francisco, 1975.

Cheating

Like lying and stealing, cheating is a very common behavior in youth. Studies have confirmed that nearly everyone cheats sometime, depending on the situation. It is not surprising, then, that a poll conducted by Princeton University's campus newspaper in 1979 revealed that over 30 percent of the college's students had cheated on in-class examinations.

During the years 8 to 12, games with rules are the preferred play activity of children. Quite competitive during these games, the children believe in strict adherence to the rules. Some children, however, find it difficult to accept defeat and will generally cheat at games. Often these children will be having difficulty with academic learning. When confronted about the cheating, the child will typically become quite angry, accuse the other of cheating, and act as if he has been sorely mistreated. School-age children will not continue to play with a child who constantly is unable to abide by rules and "play fair" without losing her temper.

A chronic tendency to cheat seems related to the personality charcteristic called "Machiavellianism."[1] Persons high on this trait are characterized as being manipulators, leaders, and individualists. They are reluctant to cheat at the behest of others, but do so whenever they themselves deem it desirable. When caught cheating, these persons are likely to vigorously deny any wrongdoing.

Reasons Why. Among the common reasons for cheating at home or in school are:

1. External pressure to be tops in the class. The child has a "win at any cost" mentality because of parental pressure to overachieve. It seems that cheaters have a stronger need for adult approval than noncheaters.[3]
2. Before the age of 7, children tend to be egocentric. They see themselves as the center of the universe, and demand to be first, to be best, and to win at all games.
3. Children who feel poorly prepared or generally inadequate and thus expect to fail at a task are more likely to cheat.

How To Prevent

Provide close supervision. Studies have shown that whenever people feel they are likely to get away with it, they are more likely to cheat.[2] By providing close adult supervision when children play games or take tests in school, you will minimize cheating behavior. A consistent finding in the literature is that fear of detection is the most effective deterrent of cheating.[4]

Teach moral principles. Although most school-age children will not cheat because they want to please adults or because it is against the rules, teen-agers should begin to understand the general moral principle involved, honesty, and to freely choose this behavior because it is the logical and right way to act for the good of society. In other words, try to influence your children to be honest because of universal ethical principles which they have thought through and chosen for themselves.

Give a handicap. When your child is at a disadvantage in a game because of a lack of skill or experience, try giving the child a handicap to equalize the situation. For example, you might play with fewer checkers than the child. In this way the child will be less likely to cheat to avoid defeat in games of skill.

What To Do

Express disapproval. When a child cheats, you might verbally confront him by saying, ''I'm really upset because you are not following the rules. It makes me feel you are only interested in winning and not in having a good time together. It's no fun to play with you when you cheat.'' If a child cheats again after such a confrontation, you should immediately stop playing the game, saying, ''I don't want to play since you are cheating.'' Thereafter, continue to stop playing a game whenever the child begins to cheat. Advise other members of the family to do the same. If you follow this procedure consistently, the cheating behavior should gradually decrease.

Moralize. Teach your child that dishonest behavior leads to a lack of trust by others. If you are not able to play by the rules of a game, you give yourself an unfair advantage so that no one will want to play with you. When you are dishonest then, you are really cheating yourself as well as others. Personal integrity is a tremendously important trait if you are to be accepted by others. You will be greatly disadvantaged in life if you do not have it.

Ignoring. Young children find it intolerable to lose at any game. Since this behavior is so common in children, parents can overlook a lot of it and not make a big fuss. In time the child will be less self-centered and will develop greater frustration tolerance.

Teach self-talk. If a child feels the need to win at games all the time, you might train the child to say quietly to herself when tempted to cheat, "It would be nice to win, but if I don't, it will still be okay." Have the child repeat sentences like this over and over to be sure she has internalized the message.

Give unconditional support. By your words and deeds show your child that your approval and love are not dependent on the child achieving at a high level in school or at games or sports.

Build self-esteem. To help the child accept his real capabilities and limitations give realistic praise for the child's skills in playing games. Feeling generally inadequate, the child may need to have his good moves recognized and encouraged. Many children are unable to recognize, much less accept and approve, gradual improvement in their performance. They have an "all or nothing" attitude; either they win or they are total failures.

You can also help the child by conveying your own stable sense of worth, even in the face of repeated defeats. If the child makes derogatory comments about you when you lose, ask the child if she feels stupid or worthless whenever she loses at a game.

Of course, when the child plays fairly, permit her to win more games, even if you have to play poorly or give a handicap. This will help bolster the child's self-esteem and reinforce fair play.

You might also explain to the child that your expertise at a game is the result of learning and experience, not some magical quality. Point out that one gradually improves at a task by patient effort. There is no instant or magical success.

The final technique is to suggest that cheating is a "no-win" strategy. Victories achieved this way can never be a legitimate source of pride. Even if others do not detect the cheating, the child has an inner awareness that the victory was not real and will always doubt his own abilities. Thus you are only cheating yourself when you cheat.

Case Report. Charles, the oldest of three brothers, was referred for therapy at age 9 because of poor school performance and general immaturity.[5] Charles's mother had returned to work when he was 6 weeks old, and the lady who cared for him during the day was able to offer him very little individual attention. The early separation from his mother was accompanied by a strong push for precocious independence which did not permit the gradual development of a sense of mastery. To avoid anxiety he would pretend he could master any situation, and he avoided those which might reveal his felt inadequacy.

When playing games in therapy, he would cheat to avoid losing. In card games he switched the cards he did not want. In darts he hand-carried the missiles to the bull's eye whenever he needed points. Needless to say, he won all the games. After winning he would taunt the therapist and chant "Ya, ya, ya, ya, ya."

After this went on for several weeks, the therapist commented that winning seemed very important to him. In a tone of mock solemnity Charles said, "If I lose, my father will kill me." Later he stated that his father had told him, "It's not how you play the game that counts, it's whether you win or lose." Subsequently the therapist suggested that Charles cheated at games because he felt he did not have the skills to win fairly. The therapist said firmly that he believed Charles had such abilities but was afraid to use them. Charles listened quietly, then asked, "You really believe that?" In later therapy sessions the cheating appeared periodically, usually accompanied by "clowning" but became increasingly rare. Charles became more interested in learning to play more skillfully. He was very pleased that he was able to beat his father at times by playing fairly. Defeat remained hard for him to bear, but it was now tolerable because of the support he had received from the therapist. The therapist's goal had been to bolster realistic self-esteem in the boy, clarify the futility of cheating, and encourage a reliance on the gradual development of playing skills. A similar strategy might be followed by parents.

References

1. Christie, R. and Geis, F.L. (eds.): *Studies in Machiavellianism.* Academic Press, New York (1970).
2. Leming, J.S.: "Cheating behavior, situational influence, and moral development." *Journal of Educational Research* 71: (1978), pp. 214–217.
3. Millham, J.: "Two components of need for approval score and their relationship to cheating following success and failure." *Journal of Research in Personality* 8: (1974), pp. 378–392.
4. Dickstein, L.S. *et al.:* "Cheating and fear of negative evaluation." *Bulletin of the Psychonomic Society* 10: (1977), pp. 319–320.
5. Meeks, J.E.: "Children who cheat at games." *Journal of Child Psychiatry* 9: (1970), pp. 157–170.

BAD LANGUAGE

Bad language in children falls into three major categories: *profanity,* or speech involving disrespect for something that is considered sacred or holy, such as the name of God; *cursing,* or speech reflecting the wish to harm someone, *e.g.,* "Damn you"; and *obscenity,* which is referring to sexual or elimination topics in a jocular or sneering way, *e.g.,* "Screw you." Almost all children use bad language sooner or later. This kind of language is on the increase in recent years since our society has relaxed its prohibitions against it.[2]

Reasons Why

Attention. Some children use "bad words" to get attention. It's one way to be sure you'll be noticed.

Shock. It's great fun for a child to shock adults and make them feel uncomfortable. When you shock someone, you tend to feel superior to that person.

Release. People tend to curse in an impulsive way when they feel frustrated or angry; it's a release of physical tension.

Defiance. For some, bad language represents an act of defiance. They may come from home environments where swearing is strictly taboo. So the rebel in them wants to assert his independence.

Maturity. Others use bad words because for them it's a symbol of adulthood. They have heard adults use these words, so they feel it's their turn now.

Peer Acceptance. When "horsing around" with their friends, some youths use bad language to gain approval. They may feel that cursing promotes the macho or tough guy image.

Infantile Pleasure. Young children become fascinated with bathroom functions and delight in discussing elimination functions. Later, sexual awareness emerges and children revel in speaking of the organs and acts of sex. By talking about these topics, children seem to derive some kind of infantile sexual pleasure.

How To Prevent

Set the Example. Children often learn undesirable language by observing their parents. If you are able to inhibit your tendency to use profane or vulgar language, your children are likely to imitate this control.

Impulse Expression. If your child feels free to express hurts and anger to you directly, she will be less apt to use curse words to communicate negative feelings.

Discussion. One family made it the practice to regularly discuss bad words with their children. The parents freely talked with the children about every one of the commonly used dirty words. The words were written down, defined, and then discussed. This approach proved effective in preventing the use of foul language by the children.

What To Do

Ignore. If children find bad language is not startling or up-setting to you, they may not have a reason to continue using the words. Therefore, sometimes simply ignoring this language is enough to eliminate it. Even if the child continues to use certain words occasionally, they may serve the adaptive function of releasing excessive energy and conveying strong emotion.[4]

According to Montagu,[4] the function of swearing is to provide an outlet for aggressive feeling and thus to restore the "psychophysical equilibrium of the individual."

"Play Dumb." Rather than appearing shocked or disturbed, parents can take the wind out of the child's sails by playing dumb. Dreikurs[3] recommended that you reply by saying, "What is that word you used? I don't understand. What does it mean?" The child is likely to abandon a tactic which puts him in this position.

Be Empathic. When the child curses as a response to underlying frustration, try to recognize the child's distress and needs by responding empathically, "Looks like these are a little hard for you, Karine," and offering support: "Let me help you."

Express Disapproval. You might tell your child that "I can fully understand that you are angry but I wish you wouldn't use bad language," or "You may not use that word in this house," or "While other people may speak that way in their homes, we do not talk that way in ours," or "I don't talk to you that way and I don't expect you to either."

When disapproving, explain that certain words show poor manners, like belching or not saying, "Excuse me," at the proper time. Point out that people do not like to hear these words used that way and you would appreciate the child not using them and thus respecting the feelings of others.

Penalize. If the child continues to use bad language after you have forbidden it, you may have to enforce a penalty such as going to a time-out area for 5–10 minutes. This brief isolation seems a more logical consequence than washing the child's mouth out with soap and water.

Reward. Record the number of times a child uses bad language each day. Then tell the child that he will receive a star on a posted chart for each hour (or other set interval) that he does not use this language at home. A certain number of stars earns the child a treat or privilege. Be sure to praise the child each time you post a star and give a reward.

Teach Discrimination. Explain to your child that certain words, like asshole, are disrespectful to people and should not be used. Teach your child more acceptable ways to express anger toward others. Children also need to learn that while certain words may be permissible at home, they are not to be used in polite society or when company is present. For example, when in school the child should say, ''Can I got to the bathroom?'' rather than, ''Can I go Pee Pee?''

Encourage Creative Use. The overuse of certain four letter words is not only boring but degrades our language and manners. You might encourage a child, then, to be more imaginative in his choice of expletives. One student in a high school creative writing class felt that war rather than sex or elimination was obscene, so he invented the obscenity ''Bombschmutt.''[1]

Case Report

One mother used a tolerant attitude toward dirty words. When her 8-year-old daughter returned home from summer camp with a colorful vocabulary, the mother calmly repeated all the words back in a sentence and then said, ''Sounds as if you had a fun week learning lots of new words.''

The mother later told her daughter the origin of one very popular four letter word. It comes from a German word *ficken,* meaning to plant seeds in the soil. Over the years it became the slang word *fuck,* meaning to plant seeds in a human.

The mother explained to her child that there were times and places when it was appropriate—and not appropriate— to use four-letter words. The child was permitted to use the words as often as she wanted at home but not outside. Having been granted this permission, the child hardly ever used it.

Pornographic material was handled in the same manner. The parents brought porno magazines home and gave the child permission to look through them as much as she liked.

References

1. Cohen, S.S.: "Four-letter words." *Westchester Magazine:* (June, 1978), p. 65.
2. Bloom, R.B.: "Therapeutic management of children's profanity." *Behavioral Disorders* 2: (1977), pp. 205–211.
3. Dreikurs, R.: *Children: The Challenge.* Hawthorne, New York (1969).
4. Montagu, A.: *The Anatomy of Swearing.* Macmillan, New York (1967), p. 72.

FIRESETTING

Watching fires and learning to light fires and extinguish them are exciting and pleasurable for most children. Fire also fascinates adults, as evidenced by the fact that a major fire draws a large crowd. When a child repetitively engages in this activity without parental supervision, however, there is cause for alarm. This is the child who lights "fun fires" in fields or in wastepaper baskets, or who accepts money to burn down buildings. Fortunately, the firesetting habit is a very infrequent behavior among children.

The child who deliberately sets fires poses a serious threat to the well-being not only of his family but the entire community as well. Because of the obvious danger, the correction of this behavior must be a high priority for the family. It is crucial that parents see this behavior as a serious problem and that they do not overlook or excuse it.

Reasons Why

Typically, the vast majority of firesetters are boys.[1] Firesetting is a complex act with many causes. The following are some of the more common reasons for the act:

Poor Impulse Control: Often the firesetter has poor control of his impulses, particularly his aggressive tendencies. He often shows other aggressive behavior, such as stealing and fighting.

Unmet Needs: In some cases the firesetting is the act of an unhappy boy whose needs for parental supervision and companionship—particularly by the father—have not been met.[2]

Revenge: Younger children sometimes set fires as an act of revenge against some significant person in their life.

What To Do

Promote Understanding. Be sure the child understands the seriousness and potential harm that can result from firesetting. Be very explicit about the destructiveness and personal harm that fires can cause. Discuss the illegality of the act.

Set Limits. In no uncertain terms tell the child that he may not play with matches or light fires without permission. Explain what the penalty will be for violation of these rules. Provide extra supervision so that you will know immediately if these rules are broken. You might combine penalties with rewards for not striking matches or intervals of no firesetting.

Find Acceptable Outlets. Seek an appropriate alternative to match or fire play. One mother of a 4 year old who liked to play with matches found she could keep this behavior under control without forbidding the use of matches by appointing the boy waste-paper burner in the family. Every morning the boy's task was to go through the house collecting the waste paper from the baskets and then burn it in the incinerator. The boy had agreed not to take any matches except to burn the paper.

Other parents have scheduled regular times for their child to light matches. The only stipulation is that they must strike hundreds of matches at each time. In this way the parents hope the child's fascination with fire will soon disappear and be replaced with boredom and fatigue.

Case Reports

Case #1. A 7-year-old boy was referred for therapy because of firesetting behavior.[3] Employing a "satiation" technique, the therapist brought in 20 boxes full of small wooden matches and asked the boy if he would like to learn how to properly light them. The boy agreed and was told how to close the cover before striking, how to hold it over an ashtray, and how to hold it until he felt its heat on his fingertips and then to blow it out. In the first 40-minute session, the boy soon became restless and was allowed to do something else at the end of the session. The boy showed no interest in striking the matches at the next session and was allowed to play after striking ten matches. At home, the parents reported that the boy no longer seemed fascinated with fire play. The boy was seen in traditional play therapy for several more months, during which time the firesetting behavior did not return.

Case #2. Robert, age 7, had the habit of setting fires at home.[4] He would set fires whenever he found matches and his parents were out of the house or in bed. Punishments such as being slapped, locked in his room, and touched with a smoldering object were only effective for a short time.

With professional advice, the father carried out the following plan. He told Robert that if he set any more fires he would permanently lose his highly prized baseball glove. Robert was also told to immediately bring to the father any matches or matchbook covers he found around the house. When Robert brought an empty matchbook cover the father had conspicuously placed on a table, he was immediately given five cents and urged to go to the store to spend it, which he did. The next few nights the father continued to leave packets containing matches around the house, which Robert promptly brought to him. Robert was receiving one to ten cents a day for his efforts. Matches or covers found outside during the day were saved by the boy and given to the father at night.

To further strengthen the program, the father informed the boy about a week after the program started that he could strike a full packet of matches if he liked under the father's supervision. Twenty pennies were placed next to the pack, and Robert was told that for every match left unstruck he would receive one penny. But one penny would be removed for every match he used. During the first session, Robert struck ten matches and received ten cents. The next evening he earned 17 pennies and on the third evening, 20 pennies. In further sessions, he consistently decided not to strike any matches. By the end of 4 weeks, the firesetting had disappeared, and it had not returned at an 8 month follow-up.

Case #3. The following case involves an emotionally disturbed boy; extensive therapy was needed for the boy and his family. The boy was 7 years old, and he repeatedly set fires as an angry reaction to parental neglect and hostility. His father worked long hours and was seldom at home. When the father was present, he was irritable and impatient with the boy. The boy's mother was absorbed in difficulties with her husband and relatives. She favored the boy's 3-year-old sister and was typically critical of the child. He was an odd, isolated boy who played a good deal by himself, and he did poorly in school despite adequate intelligence. At the age of 6 he began to set small fires in his home despite parental punishment, cajolery, and threats. As his firesetting increased, he ceased to attack his sister; the firesetting seemed to provide a release for his hostility toward her and his parents. The boy's firesetting only stopped after the family spent 2 years in weekly therapy sessions. Much of the therapy was devoted to helping the parents improve their attitudes toward the child and in resolving their marital problems.

References

1. Vandersoll, T.A. and Wiener, J.M.: "Children who set fires." *Archives of General Psychiatry* 22: (1970), pp. 63–71.
2. Macht, L.B. and Mack, J.E.: "The firesetter syndrome." *Psychiatry* 31: (1968), p. 277–288.
3. Welsh, R.S.: "Stimulus satiation as a technique for the elimination of juvenile firesetting behavior." Paper presented at the Eastern Psychological Association Convention, Washington, D.C., April, 1968.
4. Holland, C.J.: "Elimination by the parents of firesetting behavior in a seven-year-old boy." *Behavior Research and Therapy* 7: (1969), pp. 135–137.

DESTRUCTIVENESS

Destructiveness refers to the act of damaging or destroying property. Because it is wasteful and often costly, destructiveness by children tends to really upset parents. Children who destroy things can be divided into two groups:[1]

1. Those who do it innocently or unintentionally. (Clumsy type of child; doesn't realize his own strength; or is very curious and likes to disassemble objects.)
2. Those who do it deliberately with malice. (Hostility or boredom may trigger this behavior.)

Reasons Why

Among the main causes of deliberate destructive acts are:

1. *Pranks:* On Hallowe'en and other occasions, it is not unusual for a neighborhood gang to break windows, remove gates, or perform other destructive pranks. Rather than destructiveness per se, the main motives are excitement, nothing better to do, the desire to impress peers, and the wish to be independent of adults. Children aged 10 to 15 are particularly prone to this behavior. In a group they will do things they wouldn't dream of doing on their own. Parents and the community have to be a little tolerant of such mischief and not label a child a juvenile delinquent because of one incident.

2. *Frustration:* Anger and aggression are natural responses to frustration. Young children are especially prone to react with destructive rage when having a temper tantrum.

3. *Maliciousness:* Some children destroy in a deliberate way, out of hostility. They may set fire to curtains, flood the bathroom, or smash a valuable object to get even with a parent. This is the most difficult kind of destructiveness to handle, and the behavior often signifies a deep underlying emotional disturbance. For example, the authors know of one 15-year-old girl, who, in a burst of resentment against her family, took a baseball bat and smashed every mirror, lamp, and window in her home shortly before she took refuge in a local residence for homeless girls. Also, teen-

age boys may deliberately smash the family automobile or engage in public vandalism as acts of rebellion against their parents. A general discontent and pent-up sullenness can lead to a chronic destructiveness at home and/or in the community.

It is estimated that only a small proportion of youth who are destructive have such serious psychological problems. The usual estimate is that 5 to 20 percent of destructive children have deep-seated internal difficulties.

What To Do

Confront. You must take immediate action to stop destructive behavior whenever it occurs.

1. Interrupt the child's behavior.
2. Give a verbal command: "You cannot break your brother's toys."
3. Explain the reason (value of property; rights of others).
4. Remove the child to a time-out area for 2 to 5 minutes to calm down. Praise him for quieting down.
5. Help the child "undo" the damage. Examples: "You will have to pay for the window you broke." "You must wash the pencil marks off this wall." "This mess has to be cleaned up." "You have to fix this truck." Praise the child for following through on the consequences.
6. Assist the child in figuring out a better way of handling his feelings next time. Examples: Pound a pillow when upset; ask brother to share his toys.

Understanding. When a child is willfully destructive, try to find out *why*. The problem may start with jealousy of a brother or sister, difficulty in school, lack of playmates, or worry about family fights. Be a good listener and try to get the child to talk about his feelings. Be observant and note what usually happens just before the destructive acts. Talk to the child's teachers, counselors, or friends to see if they can shed light on the cause or suggest remedies. Understanding the child's motives can be more important than punishment for the act.

Appropriate Release of Anger. Some children act out their anger because they have not been taught appropriate ways to release their feelings. You might suggest that the child pound a pillow or plastic blow-up toy, hammer or chop wood, tear up magazine pictures, or express feelings through painting, drawing, or working with clay.

Constructive Alternatives. A destructive gang can often become a constructive group with a little help. In one case, a gang of boys had been destroying property and had seriously annoyed the neighborhood by their nightly escapades. The mother of one of the boys was wise enough to offer a small building in the back yard to be used by the gang as a clubhouse. The boys took great pride in fixing it up and equipped it to suit themselves. It gave them a constructive interest in property and as a result these destructive tendencies disappeared.

Community resources might also be tapped. The department of parks and recreation, scout masters, school principals, and local parent-teacher associations can help. Trips to a firehouse, bakery, or soft-drink plant can be educational and fun. Team sports or increased outdoor play can aid in draining energies that tend to erupt in a negative way. Day camps, scouting, and teen centers are positive alternatives that help channel youthful energies.

Reward. Carefully observe and record the number of times each day the child destroys or attempts to destroy property. Post the daily totals on a chart. Reward the child with a treat or special privilege for making a significant reduction in the average number of daily incidents.

References

1. Coffman, H.C.: "Techniques of guidance." *Child Study* 3: (1933), pp. 100–110.

RUNNING AWAY

Running away, quite simply, means leaving the home of one's parents or adult guardians, before the appointed and approved time. Brief infrequent episodes of running away by children aged 6–12 are fairly common. The precipitating causes such as arguments or the search for adventure are easily discovered.

The child typically forewarns his parents with threats of running away. He stays only a few hours and ends the incident with a tearful reunion at mealtime or bedtime. Common sense and talking out the problem with the child will usually resolve the underlying cause.

A far more serious problem is the repeated and/or prolonged running away by about 200,000 youth each year because of deep-seated personal or family difficulties. Such running is more common in older children and adolescents. With increased age comes greater skill in traversing long distances and providing for oneself. Most incidents of running away are poorly planned and in time end in voluntary or forced returns home.

A report by the University of Michigan Institute for Social Research estimated that 6 percent of the adolescents in America ran away from home between 1969 and 1972. The most typical runaway is a 15- to 17-year-old child who leaves for only a few days or weeks. At least half of these children are females. About 70 percent of runaway youths simply run to the house of a friend or relative. Only 13 percent of them go "on the road" and leave the city or community. When the runaway returns home, she is likely to leave once again if she feels the family situation has not significantly changed.

Only drug abuse rivals the runaway reaction in importance as a problem for teen-agers.

Reasons Why

Family Conflict. Many runaways experience conflict with their parents before they run. They feel rejected by their parents and turn to their peers for help with problems. Almost half the children who run away have experienced strong disagreements with their parents for 2 years or longer.[1,2]

A large proportion of runaways come from broken and nonnatural parent homes. Difficulty relating to stepparents and foster parents is common. A high incidence of parental discord is found in the homes of runaways. A number of runaways come from families where the parents have alcohol problems and/or physically abuse the children.

It is little wonder, then, that trouble at home is the primary motivating force which prompts a child to take off. Parental confrontation over the child's life style often sparks runaway episodes: Mode of dress too casual, violation of curfew hours, choice of friends, and differing values—all are reasons for a child leaving home. In some instances, the child interprets parental preoccupation with making money or inattentiveness to the child's problems as rejection.

Sometimes running away is a desperate act by the child to communicate something to his parents which he has tried to tell them, but which they have not heard. Typically communication with the parents has stopped, and the child feels that she is misunderstood and her actions generally disapproved of.

Sudden Crisis. Some children run away when they find themselves facing a sudden crisis that they believe is overwhelming and cannot possibly be solved. Examples of such crises are: missed menstrual periods that prompt fears of pregnancy; damaging the family car which had been borrowed without permission; bad report cards that seem to end all hope of entering college; and breakup of a long relationship with a boy.

School Difficulties. Teen-age runaways tend to have poor school grades and a relatively high number of absences, latenesses, and retentions prior to running.[4]

Personal Characteristics. Several studies have indicated that runaways tend to be impulsive individuals who often make quick, poorly planned decisions. They tend to see themselves as inadequate and friendless. They have difficulty forming deep, lasting relationships with anybody.

Intimidation. Inept or indulgent parents can easily be intimidated by the child's running away and give in to a child's demands. It is a very frightening thing for parents to feel that if they say or do the wrong thing the child will run away. The child can use running away as a weapon.

Adventure. The lure of the open road is a normal human emotion. Everyone, at times, wants to escape his routine and responsibilities, to try something new, and to prove that it's possible to live by one's own devices.

Independence. Some adolescents feel the need to experience freedom and independence from their parents. They believe their parents are imposing values and career goals on them and they want to find their own way.

"Throwaways." About 3 percent of all runaways do not leave home because they want to, but rather because they are forced to. They are literally "kicked out" by their parents. Others, the "walkaways," leave by mutual consent of child and parent.

How To Prevent

The best medicine is preventive medicine, and in that light the best way to deal with a runaway situation is to see that it doesn't happen in the first place.

Communicate. Keep lines of communication open with your child. Find out how your child is feeling about his life, the world around him, and the family. It is never too late to reestablish communications with a child and to resolve—or at least make bearable—some of the problems that make life so difficult for the child.

Have you become so absorbed in your own problems that you have been unable to see the world as your child does?

Remember that running away is usually a desperate act by a young person to communicate something to her parents which she has tried and tried to tell them, but which they have not heard.

Observe. Watch for the early warning signs that your child is in trouble or under stress: lying, stealing, cheating, irritability, sleeplessness, using alcohol or other drugs, run-ins with teachers, friends, and siblings. There will usually be more than one sign of anxiety. If you ignore your child's cries for help, you may be forcing the child to seek assistance outside the home.

Relate. Children who feel their parents never have time, praise, or affection for them are likely to feel emotionally rejected. They may turn to the streets to feed their starving egos.

Support. When a child is upset and threatens to run away, don't encourage it by saying, "Good I'll help you pack," or "Go already and live someplace else if you think we're so awful." Such responses can make a child feel frightened and more rejected. Rather, express concern, warmth, and a desire for them to stay: "If you run away I will really worry about you because I will be thinking of all the terrible things that could happen to you." Then encourage further discussion by saying, "What's bothering you—maybe I can help." Either is better than saying, "You shouldn't run away, its dangerous," which leaves the child only the option of backing down or fighting back.

Give Independence. Remember that there is a developmental thrust toward autonomy in adolescence. Be flexible and gradually give your teen-ager more and more freedom over her life, values, and choice of friends. Avoid the extremes of total permissiveness and total rigidity in relating to your adolescent. Parents often say they want their child to be on his own, but when the child begins to show signs of independence, they try to stop it from happening.

What To Do

Better Communication and Problem Solving. Avoid the temptation to take immediate ill-planned action that is designed to punish the child and/or yourself. Rather than "throwing the child out" or completely giving in to the child's wishes, follow a step-by-step procedure involving establishing better communication and problem solving. Start by telling the child that you missed her, you're glad she's back, and you were very worried about her. Explain that such behavior poses a serious threat to her safety and to your peace of mind. Explain that you are going to have a long discussion with her to talk about the reasons for such behavior and ways to prevent it from happening again.

Communicate. One solution is greater communication and understanding between parents and child and a willingness by both sides to really listen to each other, to accept some responsibility for the problem, and to negotiate a resolution of major conflict areas. View the problem and the family confrontation as an opportunity for growth.

To effectively resolve the situation, parents must be willing to recognize that they are part of the problem. All too often "scapegoating" or putting the family's problems onto one child is common. A long, hard process of negotiation is often needed to resolve underlying difficulties.

It is absolutely necessary for parents and child to sit down and talk honestly, openly, and with utter candor. If a heart-to-heart talk proves impossible, you will have to seek help from a professional counselor, clergyman, or favorite teacher.

Problem Solve. After the issues are fully aired, the problem solving part of the process must begin. This usually means more stringent demands will be made of the child in some areas, and greater freedom will be given in others. For example, you may stop giving the child money or increase his chores on one hand, while backing off about his values or how he spends his own time, on the other. In this way, the adolescent feels he has at least some control over the troubled family situation. The parents also show their commitment to make some effort for positive change.

It is often helpful to write out the agreement in the form of a contract. A sample contract[6] is presented in Table 1.

Give A Choice. After the necessary corrections have been made in the home, the final part of the process is to give the child an honest choice of whether to live at home or to leave if he finds it intolerable. It should be understood that if the child leaves, the parents will not contribute money, clothing, or any other material support. In the vast majority of cases, children given this freedom of choice elect to stay at home. In cases where the child decides to leave, the benefits of this increased freedom and responsibility may be the best thing for him.

Relationship Building. Parents often need to develop a closer, more caring relationship with the child. The most pressing need for many runaways is to experience greater love by their parents.[3] Often a trip or vacation with the child can help mend relationship fences.

When parents examine with the child the real issues that divide them, they often discover the real conflict is not about curfews or messy rooms: It's about the parent-child relationship. The teen-ager feels rejected or overcontrolled; the

CONTRACT

Clients: Frank, age 13, and his parents are in conflict about curfew times and household rules and duties. The parents are rigid and complaining while Frank deliberately irritates them. This initial contract focuses only on concerns about curfew and parental nagging.

Goals: Frank is to maintain a curfew of 9 P.M. on weeknights and 11 P.M. on weekends. His parents are not to nag and will provide an allowance of 40 cents daily for several mutually agreed upon household duties.

Terms:
1. IF Frank returns home weeknights by 9 P.M.,
   THEN: His parents will not complain about his friends and will agree to 11 P.M. weekend curfew.

Bonus: If Frank is home on time and his parents question or criticize him about his friends, his allowance is doubled for that day.

Penalty: For every ½ hour Frank is late during a weeknight, he forfeits 20 cents of his allowance. If his entire allowance is used up during a single week, he then will forfeit ½ hour of weekend time for every ½ hour late.

2. IF Frank has maintained his weeknight curfew and has followed and completed the previously agreed-upon posted duties and has specifically stated where he will be,
   THEN: He may stay out until 11 P.M. Friday and Saturday nights with no questions or nagging from his parents.

Bonus: If Frank is home on time and is nagged, the nagging parent has to miss 1 hour of a favorite television show the next night.

Penalty: For every ½ hour he is late, he loses an hour off next weekend's curfew. If he is not at the place he indicated, he is grounded for the next weekend.

CONTRACT TO BE MONITORED BY:

_____ (Frank's older sister)

CONTRACT DURATION

_____ Nov. 1st to Nov. 30th, 1979.

SIGNED BY:

_____ (Frank)

_____ (Mother)

_____ (Father)

Table 1 Sample Contract

parent unloved or unappreciated. Each side feels that "If you loved me, you wouldn't . . ." Frequently there is a real need for everyone to express their feelings of caring about one another.

Alternative Care. When all else fails, a child may need to live for a period of time with a relative. The last resort for a minor who is out of control at home is to place him in a residential treatment center. Although parents are legally bound to provide care for a minor, such care does not have to be at home when the child is not amenable to parental supervision.

Case Report

Kim was an attractive high school junior who had always been popular and successful.[5] The mother had pushed Kim to achieve in school and sports, and to be popular with boys and in school politics. When Kim's parents decided that her boyfriend was not good for her, they required her to give a full account of whom she was with and where she was when away from home. Kim reacted to this by lying, staying out late, and coming home intoxicated. The second time Kim returned home drunk, her mother kept her up all night interrogating her. Kim left home the next day and stayed with a college student. She contacted her parents after 3 days and expressed the wish to live with her widowed grandmother.

The parents sought professional counseling and were advised to make some changes at home and then let Kim decide whether to stay or not. In some areas the parents were counseled to let up on Kim: not require her to continually report her whereabouts or what she was doing, and to allow her to drive the family car. In other areas the parents were advised to toughen up: a 10:00 P.M. curfew weekdays, a 1:00 A.M. curfew on weekends. For each 15 minutes she returned late, she lost the privilege of one night out. Kim was also not to receive an allowance until the parents felt confident she was not spending it on drugs.

A few weeks after moving back home, Kim admitted she had experimented with drugs but assured her parents she had quit. Her parents decided to trust her and restore her allowance. Kim's parents were able to follow through on giving her increased freedom in a number of areas such as her friends, dates, her studies, whether or not she ran for office, her tennis, and her cheerleading. Her relationship with her parents improved drastically, and she elected to attend college while living at home.

Books For Parents About Runaways

Ambrosino, Lillian: *Runaways*. Beacon Press, Boston (1971).

A short, practical book addressed to runaways and their parents. The author points out that running away may indicate a healthy response as well as a cry for help.

Raphael, Maryanne and Wolf, Jenifer: *Runaways*. Drake Publishers, New York (1974).

Provides a sympathetic and perceptive look at youthful runaways in the 1970's. Features ten detailed case studies.

Books For Children About Runaways

Finlayson, Ann: *Runaway Teen*. Doubleday, New York. Ages 9–13.

The story of a 16-year-old girl who runs away to Chicago because she resents her new stepfather and thinks her 16th birthday has been forgotten.

Kwolek, Constance: *Loner*. Doubleday, New York. Ages 9–13.

The story of a girl who runs away from home and school to New York City and realizes she really wants an education and must do something about it.

Sources of Assistance for Runaway Youth

The runaway child's most immediate need is for lodging and guidance. The phone numbers below offer help. The phones are answered 24 hours a day by understanding counselors and the numbers are toll-free—the child will even get his dime back.

1. *National Runaway Switchboard:* People to help you think things out. They can connect you with the nearest runaway center or suggest other places you can

go if you need help. You don't have to give your name
or location. The counselor will not get police or parents onto you.

In Illinois: 800-972-6004

Anywhere else in country: 800-621-4000

2. *Peace of Mind:* They'll refer you to a runaway center
and will even take a message to your parents without
giving them your location. You can call them back
for a message from your parents.

In Texas: 800-392-2352

Anywhere else: 800-231-6946

References

1. Jenkins, R.L.: "The runaway reaction." *American Journal of Psychiatry* 128: (1971), pp. 168–173.

2. Beyer, M. *et al.:* "Runaway youths: Families in conflict." Paper presented at the Eastern Psychological Association Convention, Washington, D.C., May, 1973.

3. Riemer, M.D.: "Runaway children." *American Journal of Orthopsychiatry* 10: (1940), pp. 522–526.

4. Elliott, E.: "New look at runaways." *Youth Reporter:* (May, 1975), pp. 5–7.

5. Wright, L.: *Parent Power.* Psychological Dimensions, New York (1978).

6. Martin, R.D.: "Behavioral contracting with adolescents and their families." *Canadian Counsellor* 12: (1977), pp. 62–65.

TRUANCY

The truant is a child, aged 6 to 17 years, who absents himself from school without a legitimate reason and without the
permission of his parents or the school officials. The truant
usually does not go home until his usual time so his absence
from school is not noticed by his parents. If truanting is
repeated so that the child is consistently missing several
days of school a month, then it should be considered a serious problem. High absenteeism from school is associated
with decreased grade point average and delinquency tendencies.

Many more boys than girls become truants. Excessive absence begins at a very young age and continues through

secondary school. One study of males who were excessive truants in primary school found that 82 percent were frequently absent during their first 2 years at school.[1] So the time to take action about the problem is when the child is very young. Truancy is a problem which increases steadily in incidence the older the children get and is most frequent at age 13. The longer the child remains out of school, the more nonattendance becomes a habit.

Attendance rates in the nation's schools are plummeting. While it once was the case that a 5 percent absentee rate was "normal," today rates of 15 percent are not uncommon, and in some urban districts they exceed 30 percent. In fact, truancy has become so widespread that the nation's principals now rank it as their biggest problem, outstripping discipline by 2 to 1. In the New York City public schools, more than 200,000 of the city's 1.1 million pupils are not in school daily. Officials estimate that 60,000 are absent for illness and another 50,000 slip away each day after homeroom attendance is taken. Many of the rest have just stopped going to classes and never bothered to say goodbye.

Reasons Why

Among the many factors that have been reported to contribute to truancy are the following:

1. Parental indifference toward school appears to be the most common cause of truancy. Many times the mother works and wants the child at home to help with the housework. The child is frequently from a broken home.

2. Difficulty with school work ranks high as a cause for school absence. Anxious over school work which she finds hard, the child stays away. This results in a vicious cycle—the child falls further behind and stays away more and more. The child is often rejected by her classmates because she is overage for the class.

3. Some students are intellectually too advanced for their class and stay away because they find the work dull and uninteresting. Such children are often regarded at school as behavior problems. Advancing the child one or more grades in school often solves this truanting problem.

4. Still other students are absent because they fear vio-

lence in school, are on drugs, or are seeking adventure. The persistent truant, however, is more likely to be running away from something than to be seeking excitement.[2]

What To Do

Express Disapproval. You must believe and convey to your child your conviction that school benefits are important. Give your child the firm and consistent message that he must attend school. Establish a close liaison with the school so that you know immediately if the child cuts a class or does not attend school. You must take personal responsibility for ensuring that the child attends school. Blaming the problem on the school, teacher, or child is no solution.

Be Understanding. Listen to the child's reasons for not attending school and encourage him to express his feelings about it. By actively listening to the child, you will be most likely to discover any underlying conflicts which may be causing the excessive absenteeism. You may find that the child is afraid of a class bully or is afraid of failing an examination. Give whatever remedial or guidance supports the child needs to handle his particular difficulty. Sometimes a vocational school may best meet the needs of a child who is not academically minded. Traditionally, vocational schools have had the best attendance records.

Provide Incentives. You can motivate a child to attend school by clearly spelling out the rewards for doing so and the penalties for nonattendance.

Often it is helpful if you write a contract wherein the child earns money, special privileges, or special rewards for attending school on a regular basis (verified by daily notes from the school), and loses money and privileges for failure to attend school consistently. This formal agreement should be signed by both parents and the child. Be sure to be very specific. For example, you should specify the number of days of school or classes a day the child must attend in order to receive privileges such as an allowance.

The incentive approach can be used by school systems as well as by parents. One school system (Dade County, Florida) came up with a novel incentive system to cut down truancy. They lured truants back to the classroom with prizes for good attendance, such as Frisbees, T-shirts, yo-yo's, and hamburgers. Teachers were also awarded. Those having the best attendance records received free gasoline, record albums, and dinners.

Case Report

Claire, a bright 16-year-old girl was referred to a probation agency because of repeated truancy.[3] Previous efforts by the mother to stop the truancy by punishment had failed. The mother had stopped the girl's spending money, use of the telephone, and dating privileges. It was not made clear to the girl, however, how these important privileges could be regained. With professional guidance, the following plan was implemented. The school attendance office gave Claire a note if she was present at all her classes during the day. The mother exchanged this note for certain privileges that were spelled out in advance. If Claire received a note, she earned telephone privileges that day (both receiving and calling out). If four out of five notes were obtained during the week, one weekend date was earned; two weekend dates were earned if five out of five notes were sent home. The use of the phone on the weekend was not included in the plan. Claire accepted the plan and attended school regularly from the first day it was initiated. The plan was modified after a month so that Claire would have to receive only two notes a week. If classes were attended on Monday, Tuesday, and Wednesday, one note was required to verify this; and this note earned the privilege of one weekend night out. A second note, on Friday, certified to the full attendance on Thursday and Friday, which earned a second night out on the weekend. Telephone privileges were removed from the plan. Claire improved so much over a period of 7 weeks that the notes were stopped altogether. Claire was illegally absent only twice while the program was in effect, and she was never absent during the next semester of school. Her work, attitude, and interest in school also improved.

Books For Children About Truancy

Alcock, Gudrun: *Run, Westy, Run.* Lothrop, Lee & Shepard Co. (1966). Ages 10–12.

Eleven-year-old Westy has run away from home many times. Westy is lonely because his family never shares time together and he is not allowed to bring friends home to visit. When the story begins, the truant officer is looking for Westy because the boy has missed too much school. Gradually the boy learns that he cannot avoid problems by running away. With outside help, he and his parents recognize their mistakes and begin to change.

Fife, D.: *Ride The Crooked Wind.* Coward, McCann & Geoghegan (1972). Ages 10–12.

Twelve-year-old Poito's parents are dead, and he lives with his grandmother on an Indian reservation. Poito often plays hooky from school because he does not like the white man's education. After considering the downtrodden condition of others in the village, Poito decides that the white man's education at the Indian school could be beneficial and that it will not change his cultural heritage; so he returns to school.

References

1. Robins, L.N.: "Antecedents of character disorder." In *Life History Research in Psychopathology.* Roff, M., Ricks, D.E., eds. University of Minnesota Press (1970).
2. Hersov, L.A.: "Persistent non-attendance at school/refusal to go to school." *Journal of Child Psychology and Psychiatry* 1: (1960), pp. 130–136.
3. Thorne, G.L. *et al.:* "Behavior modification techniques: New tools for probation officers." *Federal Probation* 31: (1967), pp. 21–27.

PREJUDICE

Prejudice refers to the negative perception of people belonging to other ethnic groups.[1] Ethnic groups are populations distinguished by the possession of specific inherited physical characteristics ("race") or by differences in language, religion, culture, national origin, or any combination of these. The negative evaluation of others is a prejudgment reached before the relevant information has been collected or examined and is therefore based on inadequate or even imaginary evidence. The hostility which prejudice breeds and the discrimination to which it may lead on the part of the dominant population toward minority ethnic groups has caused enormous human suffering.

Children are not born with prejudice but rather learn it early in life from their social environment, usually their parents. Children start showing signs of prejudice toward other ethnic groups around age 5, but it is during the early school years that active prejudices become solidified. In these early years there is a close relation between ethnic attitudes of parents and children; somewhat later a similarity is noted between teacher's and their pupils' attitudes.

What type of child is most likely to be prejudiced? Studies[6] show it is the child with a low self-esteem who rigidly conforms to approved social values and moralistic condemnation of others. The child tends to reject all who are weak or different and shows a rigid conception of appropriate sex roles. Thus, the child tends to be intolerant of passive or feminine behavior in boys and masculine or tomboyish behavior in girls. The child's parents tend to be rigid, authoritarian, highly conforming, and overly moralistic.

Reasons Why

Among the most common reasons societies foster prejudice are:

1. There is a tendency for preliterate societies to fear strangers, which can foster hostility toward others.
2. Historical factors, such as slavery and colonization, have led white people to believe their culture was superior to others.
3. Religious influences have played a role in instilling anti-Semitism.
4. Nationalistic loyalties have cultivated ethnocentric prejudice and hostilities toward other nations.
5. Prejudice and discrimination enables the dominant group to make others subservient and to keep them "in their place." This enables all members of the dominant group to feel superior to the minority.

What To Do

Provide Information. Among the facts that you can give your children to counter prejudice are:
1. There is no acceptable proof of the inherent inferiority of any ethnic group.
2. Outstanding individuals are found within all groups.
3. Basically people are more similar than different.
4. Discuss the interesting customs of different groups of people (foods, dances, arts and crafts, music, architecture).

Implant Values. The brotherhood of man should be established as a high value for you and your family, as opposed to a competitive "we are better than others" mentality.

Also, the teaching of general moral principles should help, since research has indicated that the higher the level of moral development your child has achieved, the less likely the child is to be prejudiced.[3]

You can help implant democratic values in children by disapproving of expressions of prejudice by your children. Also, encourage your children to describe people in personal (individual) terms rather than in a stereotype (group) manner.

Arrange Contact and Cooperation. Contact between children of different ethnic groups can have a positive effect when the contact is between children of equal status and ability levels.[2] This contact is best when the children strive for a common goal to be achieved by joint effort.[4,5] Thus, you might try to arrange for mixed groups of children to work together on projects in school or on after-school arts and crafts projects or athletic activities.[7] In this way mutual trust and respect will be fostered, and the child will grow up feeling comfortable with members of other groups.

Children living in ghetto areas or in suburbs containing a homogeneous group of people particularly need this kind of mixed group contact. Interracial nursery schools and camps have been found to be quite effective in preventing prejudice from developing.

Encourage empathy. Whenever possible train your child to put himself in the shoes of a person who is discriminated against. Better understanding and acceptance tends to result when we attempt to see a problem from another person's viewpoint. You might for example, arrange for your child to read books describing the experience of people from minority groups, such as biographies of Martin Luther King.

Parental Modeling. Whether we like it or not, young children pick up our unconscious and conscious prejudices without being taught, and they often retain these beliefs longer than ideas learned in school. Parents can subtly instill prejudicial attitudes in children by the tone of voice they use in talking about certain people, or by simply inquiring about racial, ethnic, or religious differences among people when this distinction had not occurred to the child.

As parents then, we should try to become more aware of our prejudices and strive to overcome them. At the very least we should openly acknowledge our prejudices to our children and our desire to change them. We must realize that it is just about impossible to conceal our prejudices from our children, and that our attitudes, and the attitudes of other authority figures the child comes in contact with, will have the strongest influence on the child.

Books For Children About Ethnic/Racial Prejudice

Alexander, A.: *Trouble on Treat Street.* Atheneum Publishers (1974). Ages 10–12.

The author clearly shows how boys from two different ethnic groups (Chicano and black) can work together on a common problem (gang intimidation) and, in the process, form a loyal friendship.

Blume, J.S.: *Iggie's House.* Bradbury Press (1970). Ages 10 and up.

This realistic story illustrates the emotions a young white girl experiences when she encounters racial prejudice for the first time (black family moves into her neighborhood).

Carlson, N.S.: *The Empty Schoolhouse.* Harper & Row (1965). Ages 8–12.

This story describes some of the difficulties faced by children during the early phases of school integration.

Clayton, E.T.: *Martin Luther King: The Peaceful Warrior.* Prentice-Hall (1964). Ages 8–10.

This is a very readable biography written by one of Dr. King's closest associates. It touches on the major events in Dr. King's long struggle for his people's freedom.

De Angeli, M.K.: *Bright April.* Doubleday & Co. (1946). Ages 8–10.

April Bright is the youngest member of a united, hard-working Afro-American family. This book portrays her beginning awareness of the reality of racial prejudice.

References

1. Allport, G.W.: *The Nature of Prejudice.* Addison-Wesley, Reading, MA (1954).
2. Bullock, C.S.: "Contact theory and racial tolerance among high school students." *School Review* 86: (1978), pp. 187–216.
3. Davidson, F.H.: "Ability to respect persons compared to ethnic prejudice in childhood." *Journal of Personality and Social Psychology* 34: (1976), pp. 1256–1267.
4. Goldstein, C.G. *et al.:* "Racial attitudes in young children as a function of interracial contact in the public schools." *American Journal of Orthopsychiatry* 49: (1979), pp. 89–99.
5. Amir, Y. and Garti, C.: "Situational and personal influence on attitude change following ethnic contact." *International Journal of Intercultural Relations* 1: (1977), pp. 58–75.
6. Frenkel-Brunswik, E.: "A study of prejudice in children." *Human Relations* 1: (1948), pp. 295–306.
7. DeVries, D.L. and Edwards, K.J.: "Student teams and learning games: Their effects on cross-race and cross-sex interaction." *Journal of Educational Psychology* 66: (1974), pp. 741–749.

6

Other Problems

In order to cover all of the common problems of children, this chapter contains behaviors which do not fit into the five general categories. Drug abuse, sexual misbehaviors, being unmotivated in school, and poor study habits are discussed. Drug abuse and sexual problems among teen-agers are concerns that are serious and frequent. Our's is a drug oriented culture where a variety of consciousness altering substances are consumed. The frequency of the problem depends upon the type of drug. We cover tobacco, alcohol, marijuana, inhalents (glue, gasoline, etc.), stimulants, sedatives, narcotics, and hallucinogens. Sexual misbehaviors range from mild temporary problems to more serious difficulties. Masturbation, sex play, deviant sex roles, and premarital pregnancy are reviewed.

A recent survey[1] of 2200 children aged 7 to 11 years highlights the frequency of school related problems. Many American children describe schoolwork as a source of anxiety, shame, frustration, and unhappiness. Approximately 50 percent of the children felt angry when they had trouble learning new things and agreed that "I sometimes feel I just can't learn." Roughly two-thirds worried about tests and felt ashamed when they made mistakes. Helping children to be more motivated and study more effectively are possible ways that parents may counteract their children's negative attitudes about school. Suggestions are also made for parents to influence the schools to be more positive and stimulating places for children.

References

1. *National Survey of Children*. Foundation for Child Development, New York (1976).

DRUG ABUSE

From aspirin to sleeping pills, from tranquilizers to the "pill," Americans of all ages are ingesting drugs in greater variety and in greater numbers than ever before. In this section we will be discussing "psychoactive" drugs, that is, substances which bring about a chemical action in the brain that affects feelings, thinking, and behavior. There are different types of psychoactive drugs, including stimulants, sedatives, and narcotics.

Drug abuse is the use of any chemical substance, legal or illegal, which causes physical, mental, or social harm to a person or to people close to him or her. Of course, drug abuse is not new—it has been with us throughout recorded history. People in every era, in every generation, and in every country have turned to drugs to reduce the pain of existence or to produce a special experience which was otherwise not available. What is new in our time is the greater availability of drugs and their ever-increasing use by progressively younger age groups.

Drug Addiction

What is drug addiction? When is a child addicted? As defined by the World Health Organization, it is a state of periodic and chronic intoxication detrimental to the individual and to society, produced by the repeated consumption of a drug. Its characteristics include:

1. An overpowering desire and compulsion to continue taking the drug—and to obtain it by any means.
2. A tendency to increase the dose.
3. A psychological, and sometimes physical, dependence on the effects of the drug.

Too often one is unaware of his progress from habit, to dependence, to addiction—until it is too late. By then, he is "hooked."

Drug dependence is a state of psychological or physical

dependence, or both, which results from chronic, periodic, or continuous use. Habituation is another name for psychological dependence; it means the psychological desire to repeat the use of a drug intermittently or continuously because of emotional reasons. A teen-ager who can't give up smoking marijuana has a psychological dependence. He depends on the drug to feel better. When he can't get the drug, he feels rotten and all he can think about is getting more of the drug.

Addiction is the term for physical dependence upon a drug. Its scientific definition includes the development of tolerance and withdrawal. As a person develops tolerance, he requires larger and larger amounts of the drug to produce the same effect. Also, when the addicting drug is stopped abruptly, the withdrawal effect is present, characterized by such symptoms as vomiting and convulsions. Although a narcotics addiction is well known, it is also a fact that barbiturates, certain tranquilizers, and stimulants in large doses can be addictive.

Recent statistics point up a shocking truth: Drug abuse and narcotic addiction are young persons' diseases. Ninety percent of known addicts started as teen-agers, using such nonaddictive drugs as glue and marijuana. Young people are vulnerable to drug abuse because its contagion so easily spreads from one to another. Usually addiction is spread—not by professionals—but by a "friend." The highest incidence is among the 16–28 year age group.

The focus of this section will be on the "gateway" drugs, so called because they are usually the first ones young people encounter in our society. These drugs are tobacco, alcohol, marijuana, and inhalants.

Tobacco

Children take up the smoking habit when quite young, and the age has significantly lowered in recent years. A survey conducted in Portland, Oregon, for example, found a steady increase in smoking experimentation through grade school. After the ninth grade the rate slows, indicating that most children today begin trying cigarettes in junior high school, that is, seventh, eighth, and ninth grades.[1] By the time young people are 18, 42 percent of the boys and about 28 percent of the girls are regular smokers. The smoking incidence among young men has been stable in recent years, while the proportion of female adolescents smoking has been rising. Once a teen-ager starts to smoke regularly, it is very hard to stop. One develops a psychological dependence on tobacco which is very strong. There is some recent evidence to suggest that a physical dependency also occurs with heavy smoking—due to the nicotine content.

The World Health Organization reports that four characteristics seem to be more common among young smokers than among nonsmokers of the same age: (1) They are likely to have parents who smoke; (2) they are likely to be children who are doing less well in school; (3) they are likely to have friends who smoke—although it is not clear whether a smoking group influences a young person to smoke, or whether smokers merely seek out other smokers; (4) finally, some children are likely to use smoking as a symbol of independence and rebellion against their parents.

Reasons Why. A child's first cigarette is rarely enjoyable. The main reason that students themselves give for their starting to smoke is peer pressure, especially from a "favorite peer."[1] The young person who accepts an invitation to smoke gains greater acceptance from smoking peers and gains the appearance of being "tough," "cool," mature, and adventurous.

In addition, young persons are more likely to become smokers if their parents or older siblings smoke. Smoking is also a social class phenomenon since young people who do not plan to attend college are more than twice as likely to smoke as are their more economically and educationally advantaged, college-bound peers.[1] Educationally deprived youngsters seem to experience more stress and greater pressure to adopt behaviors which reflect independence and maturity. Moreover, scholastic achievement and/or participation in sports are negatively associated with smoking.[2]

In the early school years, children almost invariably express strong negative and moralistic attitudes toward smoking, and they often nag adults to stop the habit. Once they reach adolescence, however, they tend to be much less likely to absolutely condemn the habit. This shift seems to be due to a transition from the absolute moralization of the child to the more relativistic and tolerant thinking of the adolescent.[3] This leads to a questioning of adult values and sometimes to experimentation with new, previously condemned behaviors.

Effects of Smoking

Immediate. Tobacco smoke is a very complicated mixture of gases and chemicals. When smoke is inhaled into the lungs, bits of poison particles remain and make it hard for the body to do its work. The smoker's mouth, tongue, throat, and lungs become irritated. Appetite for food can decline and breathing can become difficult.

Tobacco smoke contains tiny amounts of:

Tars—These particles coat the lungs and slow down its normal action. An average smoker inhales more than a quarter of a pint of tars from cigarettes in a year. Tar is an important factor in the development of cancer of the lungs and throat.

Nicotine—A stimulant drug that makes the heart beat faster, raises blood pressure, and quickens the breathing. This is a great handicap in all strenuous activities. Nicotine, in pure form, is a poison that can kill instantly. Recent evidence indicates that inhalation of nicotine may be so pleasurable and physically addictive as to be very difficult to give up.

Long-term hazards. The incidence of certain deadly diseases in this country seems to be growing despite all efforts at control. Among these are lung cancer, heart attacks, strokes, and such respiratory diseases as chronic bronchitis and emphysema. Since these diseases are associated with cigarette smoking, cigarettes have come to be regarded as the primary public health problem in the United States. The grave threat to health caused by cigarette smoking has been well known since the first report in 1964 by a distinguished committee of scientists appointed by the U.S. Surgeon-General. A second, updated Surgeon-General's Report was issued in 1979 which reviewed thousands of more recent studies and vastly strengthened the indictment against cigarettes contained in the original report. The following is a summary of the basic facts contained in the second report:

—The overall death rate for current cigarette smokers is 70 percent higher than for nonsmokers. It increases with the amount smoked, but 10 to 15 years after they quit, the ex-smokers' death rate is about the same as nonsmokers'.

—Cigar and pipe smokers have "slightly higher" mortality rates than nonsmokers, but "substantially lower" than cigarette smokers.

—For low tar and nicotine cigarette smokers (less than 17.6 mg. tar and 1.2 mg. nicotine), the death rate is 50 percent above nonsmokers.

—"Coronary heart disease is the chief contributor to the excess mortality among cigarette smokers," followed by lung cancer and chronic obstructive lung disease.

—Cigarette smoking is a major factor in the risk of heart attacks and sudden death in both men and women. Smoking increases the risk of heart attack tenfold in women using birth control pills.

—Cigarette smoking is causally related to lung cancer in women and men. Lung cancer may surpass breast cancer in a decade as the leading cause of cancer deaths among women.

—Smoking is a causal factor in cancers of the larynx, mouth, and esophagus. Epidemiological studies have shown a "significant association" between cigarettes and bladder cancer. Cigarettes are associated with kidney cancer in men but not in women.

—Cigarettes are "significantly associated" with peptic ulcer disease and increase a person's risk of dying from it.

—"Workplace chemicals may be transformed into more harmful agents by smoking."

—Babies born to mothers who smoked during pregnancy weigh an average of 200 grams less than those born to nonsmokers.

—Maternal smoking "increases the risk of spontaneous abortion, of fetal death, and of neonatal death in otherwise normal infants."

—"Evidence is growing" that children of smoking mothers may have deficiencies in physical growth and mental and emotional development.

—Children whose parents smoke "are more likely to have bronchitis and pneumonia during the first year of life."

An average man aged 25 who has never smoked regularly can expect to live 6½ years longer than a man who smokes a pack a day or more. It is estimated that the average heavy smoker shortens his life by 6 minutes for every cigarette he smokes—a minute of life for every minute of smoking.

Perhaps more important to the young smoker is the fact that the ill effects of smoking are felt early in the game. Shortness of breath, nagging smoker's cough, and an elevated heart rate may all occur in relatively young smokers. As smoking continues, these symptoms may develop into serious illness. Smokers suffer more illness, especially chronic conditions, than people who do not smoke and as a result lose more time from their job or school. More specifically, there are 11 million more cases of chronic illness yearly in this country than there would be if everyone had the same rate of sickness as those who never smoked. Smokers spend over one-third again as much time away from their job because of illness as those who never smoked.

How to Prevent. The difficulties of helping adult smokers give up the habit are well documented. To date, parents have not been very successful in influencing young people not to begin the smoking habit. The main approaches to smoking prevention seem to be parental modeling and drug education at home and in school.

Parental modeling. The best thing parents can do to deter their children from smoking is not to smoke themselves. Children are far more likely to be influenced by your example than by your injunctions. The Surgeon-General's report indicates that if both parents smoke there is a very good chance the child will smoke also. More specifically, if both parents and an older sibling smoke, it is four times more likely that a child will smoke than if all three do not smoke. If one parent smokes, there is a somewhat greater probability the child will smoke.

Drug education at home. A candid discussion about smoking in which you objectively present the facts can have an effect on some children. There is a difference between a parent who says, "You do anything you want, I really don't care," and a parent who tells a child, "I will let you choose, but I care about you and will help you make an informed decision."

Since fear of long-term consequences such as lung cancer does not in itself seem sufficient to discourage a substantial number of children from beginning to smoke, it appears better to focus on the *immediate* consequences of smoking such as shortness of breath and greater likelihood of sickness. In this way children will be less likely to see the dangers as remote. Also, since young people tend to view smoking as exciting, strong, daring, and sexy, they need to know how much adults who smoke don't like it and consider it a monkey on their backs. They need to be reminded that two-thirds of the adults in this country do not smoke and that nonsmoking is an acceptable and respectable alternative.

Remember that most children begin experimenting with cigarettes in the seventh, eighth, and ninth grades, so be sure they have the facts about tobacco before they enter seventh grade, that is, in the sixth grade.

Antismoking educational programs in schools. A very promising approach to smoking prevention is the implementation of antismoking campaigns in the schools. Recognizing the power of the peer group in early adolescence, the really effective programs enlist peer leaders to promulgate the message. Evans,[4,5] for example, developed an intervention strategy with several innovative features. Since children tend to be more present-oriented than future-oriented, the education program stressed the immediate physiological effects of smoking on a child. Thus, the children were shown evidence demonstrating the relationship between smoking and sudden increases in the levels of toxic agents in the body such as nicotine and carbon monoxide. The program also taught entering seventh graders to recognize the strong pressures to smoke that come from peers, parents, and the media. The children were then presented with detailed techniques for coping with these pressures. This program proved effective in reducing the incidence of smoking among participating students. Peer teaching, employed in the Evans program, has come to be recognized as an efficient means of providing health education to large numbers of elementary school children.

Also noteworthy is the fact that preventive educational programs are relying heavily on the principle of "psychological inoculation." Basically, this involves teaching children skills by which they can role play giving verbal responses to various inducements to smoke. For example, when called, "chicken" for not accepting a cigarette, they learn to respond by saying, "I would be a chicken if I smoked just to impress you."

A program combining inoculation techniques with teaching by peer leaders in the sixth and seventh grades was developed by McAlister[3] at the Harvard School of Public Health. Encouraging short-term results were found with this new approach. Interviews with the 11- and 12-year old students who participated in the study disclosed that "hardly anybody smokes now" and "It's not cool" to smoke anymore.

What to Do. What can a parent do if a child is already a regular smoker?

Confrontation. Ensure that the child is fully aware of the serious threat of smoking to health and that she sees it as a personally relevant hazard. It is helpful if the child admits the possibility of stopping and the value to be derived from quitting. Some of the short-term benefits of quitting are: much better "wind" for athletics; food will taste better; feelings of independence and self-control; physical well being; no more ugly stains on teeth and fingers; and more money for other things. Long-term benefits include: greatly reduced risk of respiratory diseases, heart disorders, and lung cancer.

Many young people seem to believe that by the time they have smoked long enough for it to affect their health—perhaps 20 years—scientists will have found "miracle cures" for cancer, heart disease, and respiratory ailments. This is simply wishful thinking. Children need to be reminded that scientists have been trying for over 50 years now to find some way to prevent or cure cancer. The success so far has been very limited. Such lung diseases as emphysema are still on the rise, and there is no sign of any breakthrough in regard to treatment.

Another step is to enlist the aid of doctors, other health professionals, and coaches who, by confrontation, can have a powerful influence on a teen-ager's smoking. Experience has shown, for example, that as many as one-fourth of all smokers will quit if sufficiently warned by the family doctor.

Assistance to quit. Most young people have the desire to stop smoking but feel they lack the will power. For the teen-ager who wants to quit but is finding it hard to kick the habit, there are a variety of self-help materials and books available. For instance, the National Clearinghouse for Smoking and Health has prepared "The Smokers Aid to Non-smoking: A Scorecard." To start a new habit—not smoking—the reader is encouraged to think of the positive effects of not smoking, the "nice" things to look forward to. The Scorecard provides weekly "Tickets" on which the new non-smoker can check off each day that he or she doesn't smoke and note how much money he has saved. Tickets cover 8 weeks—56 days of a new habit. For copies, write to: Scorecard, Rockville, Maryland 20852.

Children who find it difficult to quit smoking on their own initiative may find it helpful to attend an antismoking clinic, such as Smoke Watchers International or Smokenders. These clinics offer both group support and a scientific approach to breaking the habit.

It is estimated that about one-third of smokers who try to stop are successful. Thus many millions are successful each year. Light smokers are more successful than heavy smokers. Those who attend clinics have a somewhat higher success rate. The overall clinic cure rate is now conservatively estimated to be 35 to 40 percent. This rate is up from 5 or 6 years ago when the proportion of attenders who stopped smoking was only 10 to 15 percent.

Reduce the risk. If quitting entirely does not seem feasible to the child, the next best thing is to help the child reduce the hazards of smoking. At the World Conference on Smoking and Health, held in London in 1971, five positive steps were identified by which a smoker may avoid at least some of the harmful effects of smoking. These steps are:

1. Choose a cigarette with less tar and nicotine.
2. Don't smoke your cigarettes all the way down. The last third of the cigarette yields 50 percent of the total tar and nicotine, and these poisons are particularly concentrated in the last few puffs. Also, avoid the longer cigarettes since they concentrate more of the peril.
3. Take fewer draws on each cigarette. Try reducing the number of times you puff on each cigarette.
4. Reduce your inhaling. Remember that it is the smoke that enters the lungs that does most of the damage.
5. Smoke fewer cigarettes a day. Try picking a specific time of the day, or several times a day, when you

promise yourself not to smoke; make a habit of asking yourself, "Do I really need this cigarette?"

References

1. Johnston, L.D., Bachman, J.G., and O'Malley, P.M.: *Drug Use Among American High School Students, 1975–1977.* National Institute on Drug Abuse, Rockville, MD (1977).
2. Horn, D.: "Modifying smoking habits in high school students." *Children* 7: (1960), pp. 63–65.
3. McAlister, A.L. *et al.* "Adolescent smoking: Onset and prevention." *Pediatrics:* (1979), in press.
4. Evans, R.I.: "Smoking in children: Developing a social-psychological strategy of deterrence." *Journal of Preventive Medicine* 5: (1976), pp. 122–127.
5. Evans, R.I. *et al.:* "Deterring the onset of smoking in children." *Journal of Applied Social Psychology* 8: (1978), pp. 126–135.
6. McRae, C.F. and Nelson, D.M.: "Youth to youth communication on smoking and health." *Journal of School Health:* (October, 1971), pp. 445–447.

Alcohol

Alcoholism is one of our country's most extensive and serious drug problems. While about one-third of adults are abstainers, one of every ten Americans who drink are alcoholics or problem drinkers. This means at least 9 million Americans are alcoholics. Alcohol abuse has become so widespread that about one out of every five Americans polled says it is causing serious trouble in his or her family. So troublesome is this problem that about 20 percent of the adult population now favors a return to prohibition.

The National Council on Alcoholism reports that problem drinking is increasing significantly among boys and girls as young as age 12. A recent survey[1] indicates that most teenagers begin drinking at ages 13 or 14, and about 70 percent of teen-agers have had a drink. Nearly half of teen-age drinkers say they have been drunk at least once, and nearly one-fifth report that they get intoxicated one or more times per month. Beer is the beverage of choice for teen-agers, the most common setting for drinking is the home, and peers are the most common drinking companions. This survey[1] also found a high correspondence between drinking practices of teen-agers and the drinking patterns of their parents and peers.

According to the National Institute on Alcohol Abuse and Alcoholism, there are about 1.3 million teen-agers and preteens who drink to excess. Half of those killed in alcohol-related car accidents are teen-agers. Moreover, the incidence of problem drinking among youth in this country has about doubled in the past decade. Alcohol costs less than other drugs, is very much easier to get, and its use is more acceptable to adults than other drugs.

Reasons Why. Why are more young people drinking?

One reason is peer pressure—the influence of friends. "All my friends drink," said one young person as a typical statement. Another said, "I didn't want to look 'square' so I started drinking."

As with adults, many young people drink because, as one said: "Drinking makes me feel happy and helps me have a good time." Some other reasons young people give are: They are bored with life, have problems at home or in school, or fear the future in a world of uncertainty and harshness.

The most common reason given by young people for drinking is the influence of parents and adult society in general. In a society where heavy drinking is condoned, and where millions of adults are dependent on alcohol, it is little wonder that more and more young people are dependent on it also. If children live in a society where heavy drinking or drunkenness is portrayed not only as common but at times even as humorous, then the stigma against alcoholism lessens.

Effects of Alcohol

Immediate. Alcohol is a natural substance formed by the reaction of fermenting sugar with yeast spores. Although there are many alcohols, the kind in alcoholic beverages is known scientifically as "ethyl alcohol," a colorless, inflammable liquid which has an intoxicating effect. Alcohol is a mind-altering drug that works like a sedative or depressant. Rather than being broken down by the stomach and small intestine, alcohol is quickly absorbed into the blood stream virtually unchanged in form. The liver begins to oxidize or break down about 20 percent of the alcohol in the blood; the rest is carried to the heart which pumps it through the circulatory system to other parts of the body, including the brain. In the brain, it starts to slow down parts that control thinking and motion, so the person feels less inhibited and freer. The individual is also less able to perform complex tasks that require some degree of skill and attention, such as driving a car. Drinkers are also less able to make good judgments so that embarrassing behaviors, fights, accidents, and crises are more likely to happen when a person has been drinking.

When intoxicated or drunk, the person is in a state of physical and mental incompetence. Vision becomes impaired, depth perception is distorted, the pupils react more slowly to light, speech becomes thick, coordination deteriorates, ability to solve problems is reduced, emotion and mood become unpredictable, ability to recall past events and knowledge diminishes, and the mind's ability to integrate information deteriorates so that judgment becomes poor. The immediate effects of alcohol depend upon three conditions: how much a person drinks, how much a person weighs, and whether there is food in the stomach. The more alcohol a person has drunk, the longer the time required to get over the effects of it.

Long-term hazards. Drinking alcohol in moderation appears to do the body no permanent harm. Indeed, according to Dr. Morris Chafetz,[2] Director of the National Institute of Alcohol Abuse and Alcoholism, moderate drinking not only cheers people up and promotes conviviality, but it has beneficial effects on the body. Moderate drinkers tend to live longer than teetotalers and are less likely to develop heart disease. Dr. Chafetz defines moderate drinking as three drinks or less per day.

When taken in large doses over long periods of time, however, alcohol can be physically destructive, reducing a person's life span by about 10 to 12 years. Damage to the heart, brain, liver, and other major organs can result from prolonged heavy drinking. Heart disease is frequently found among alcoholic persons, and alcohol in large quantities is now believed to be directly toxic to the heart. The lungs can also be affected by heavy drinking. Liver damage is common among alcoholic people; cirrhosis of the liver occurs about six times more often in alcoholic people than in the general population.

When alcohol is consumed in large quantities, the gastrointestinal system can become irritated, and there is increased susceptibility to gastritis, ulcers, and pancreatitis. Heavy drinkers are also more susceptible to pneumonia and other infectious diseases.

Over many years, heavy drinking can also result in serious mental disorders or permanent damage to the brain and nervous system. Mental functions such as memory, judgment, and learning ability can deteriorate, and an individual's grasp on reality may come apart as well.

Excessive drinking is involved in a major portion of car accidents and fatalities; other accidents at home and on the job; and in suicides, assaults, and homicides. Nearly two-thirds of all murders and almost one-third of all suicides are alcohol-related, as well as half the fire deaths and drownings.

Among the most innocent victims of alcoholism are babies. Dr. Jaime Fries, director of a birth defect center at the University of Florida, states:

> From the clinical data now gathered, it can be stated accurately that a woman who drinks alcohol chronically during pregnancy stands a 50 percent chance of having a child with some degree of mental retardation and a 30 percent chance of having a child with additional multiple physical defects.

This damage to babies is irreversible, and many victims require special care throughout life, either at home or in institutions. The National Institute on Alcohol Abuse and Alcoholism is now strongly urging all pregnant women not to drink more than *two* drinks a day.

Teen-ager drinking and driving. To combine inexperienced drinking with inexperienced driving is clearly asking for trouble. The last thing learned is first forgotten in an emergency. Driving in today's vehicles in today's traffic calls for split-second decisions. Such decisions are made repeatedly and successfully by adults who have miles and years of experience upon which to draw.

Also, new drinkers do not have enough experience to know their own personal responses to even one drink. They have neither built up an awareness of their tolerance nor learned that the effect of alcohol is more potent on an empty stomach, that it is compounded when mixed with prescription or other drugs, and that emotional factors such as anger and physical factors such as fatigue can alter one's tolerance. Traffic fatalities are among the leading causes of death among teen-agers. A Michigan study found that students who drove after they have been drinking are three to four times more likely to have an accident. This is one reason why automobile insurance rates are so high for young drivers. By the time the blood alcohol level reaches 20 percent—the level at which most drunk drivers are arrested—the risk of an accident is 100 times that of the nondrinking driver.

How to Prevent. Where drug abuse is concerned, it is certainly true that "an ounce of prevention is worth a pound of cure." It is much better for a child not to become dependent on alcohol than to do so and then have to face the consequences. Young people should learn from their parents the responsible, sensible use of alcohol. Parents have an enormous influence on their offspring by what they say and do. Among the ways parents might head off a drinking problem in their children are the following.

Parental example. More than 50 percent of alcohol and drug abusers have parents or "significant others" who were substance abusers themselves. Thus, it is important that parents do not expose children to the idea that the stresses of daily living require chemical relief. Rather, parents should model the rational use of alcohol which means abstinence or moderate use. Moderate use involves the following: Parents may have a drink or two each day to slow down and relax, to increase their pleasure socializing with others, to enjoy the flavor of the beverage and of good food. They drink slowly, sipping the beverage, never gulping it. They space out their drinks and limit themselves to the few drinks they know they can handle without losing control of their behavior. They try to make a habit of eating before and while drinking. They don't drink when they "need" one, saying, "No, thanks," if they are overtired, anxious, or depressed. They can enjoy themselves without an alcoholic beverage. When parents keep their own drinking well within the limits of moderation, their children will not grow up thinking that habitual and heavy drinking is normal for adults.

Parents who use alcohol moderately are helping children form a constructive attitude toward drinking, a general point of view that responsible drinking can contribute to feelings of social fellowship, of celebration, and of relaxation. In addition to modeling, it seems helpful for parents to gradually integrate the child into the family drinking pattern. Attitudes are formed slowly, over a long learning period. When parents supervise a child's early drinking experiences and teach sensible practices, such as how to sip and space drinks, the child is less likely to imitate the irresponsible practices of peers. The child is also less likely to regard drinking as something that is done secretly, quickly, and with mixed feelings of guilt and pleasure.

Results of scientific surveys over the past two decades have consistently shown that most young people who drink are imitating adult behavior. Abstinent parents are more likely to have abstinent children, and alcoholic parents are much more likely to have children with drinking problems.[3] Studies have shown that half as many children with parents who are responsible drinkers are having problems with alcohol as compared with children whose parents are heavy drinkers.

Discuss the facts. Most young people do not feel free to discuss drinking with their parents—but they definitely wish they could. One teen-ager said, "Do you know what adults teach us about drinking? Nothing. All they say is don't drink because you're not old enough." Children need and want to be taught how to make intelligent, responsible decisions about alcohol.

A recent survey[1] revealed that about half the teen-age population in this country feel that more information about alcohol would be personally useful. About 9 percent of the youth using alcohol feel that, on occasion, their own use of alcohol presents personal problems that they would like to discuss with another person. Most teen-agers said they would most likely discuss an alcohol problem with a parent (55 percent), with a friend (32 percent), and/or with a sibling (31 percent).

Unfortunately, most adults are poorly informed about alcohol. Those discussing alcohol frequently repeat and believe statements which have no basis in fact. For alcohol education to be effective, it must be scientifically correct, and above all, it must have immediate practical value for young people. They need to know immediate effects such as impairment of driving, typing, or athletic skills, and the effects on judgment or reasoning. As a rule of thumb, you should start talking to your child about alcohol by the sixth grade. The beginning of junior high school is considered to be the ''danger zone'' for a child's initiation to drinking. In talking to a child, don't preach, frighten, or simplify; and don't expect too much too soon from too little talk. Avoid ''scare'' tactics that exaggerate, but point out dangers of alcohol abuse in objective terms. Show that excessive alcohol use can be harmful.

The goal of alcohol education is not proabstinence or prodrinking, but prorationality and responsibility in regard to drinking—which for some will mean moderate drinking, while for others, abstinence.

With older adolescents, it is no longer effective to set down rules which must be obeyed. We have to realize that these adolescents are going to make their own decisions about drinking. One of our obligations is to give them enough factual information so that they can make an informed choice about whether to drink or not.

Thirty-two percent of our adult population are nondrinkers. Abstinence is certainly an acceptable and popular choice. Among the most frequent reasons people give for nondrinking are:

1. Adverse reaction to it.
2. A desire to be one's natural self and not to be influenced by drugs.
3. Health reasons, such as fattening effect of alcohol.
4. Just don't like the taste or effect.
5. Can't handle it.

Moderate drinking. A person who uses alcohol moderately is not likely to develop drinking problems. Moderate use[2] means that no more than 1½ ounces of pure alcohol are consumed per day. This is the equivalent of four 8-ounce glasses of beer, a half-bottle of wine, or three 1-ounce shots of 100 proof whiskey. This limit, of course, is a statistical average. Even one drop of alcohol for some people is too much.

The manner of drinking is also important, and the following guidelines should be taught to a child:

—*One should always sip alcohol slowly.* Alcohol is an unusual food in that a substantial amount of it is absorbed directly from the stomach into the blood stream. So gulping produces a sudden, marked rise in the alcohol level in the blood and hence in the brain. Adults tend to sip alcohol slowly in a relaxed manner which minimizes the intoxicating effects. Young teen-agers, however, frequently gulp, since they drink furtively, in a "hurry-up-so-we-don't-get-caught" manner. It is also not unusual for them to chug-a-lug their drinks to prove their prowess.

—Avoid drinking on an empty stomach. Food in the stomach, preferably protein foods, effectively delays alcohol's entry into the blood stream. Food covers the stomach wall, making capillaries less accessible. It also sponges up the alcohol and carries it gradually through the digestive process, slowing absorption and allowing the metabolism and brain to adapt.

—Choose the time and place. Carefully select the best time, place, and circumstances for drinking. Clearly, if you are about to perform complex mental or physical activities, such as driving, writing, or business, it is inappropriate to be under the influence of alcohol. On the other hand, if you are going to engage in relaxed socializing, alcohol can facilitate the process.

—Do not use alcohol to escape. If you use alcohol for its own sake, for its anesthetizing effect on the body and mind, you are more likely to become a problem drinker. It is best not to take alcohol when physically or emotionally upset, lonely, or in need of solace. In these states, one tends to overindulge and become intoxicated and dependent on alcohol. Studies have shown that the liquor-for-its-own-sake attitude leads to drinking problems. Shearn and Fitzgibbon,[13] for example, found that when youth attempt to cope with life difficulties and intrapsychic stress by drug use, problems are compounded. Rather than proving to be an effective way of coping, the use of drugs, because of their effects on the physiology of the body and because they place the heavy user in a deviant position with regard to social standards, adds further stress to an already overstressed person.

—What you expect is what you get. As with most drugs, expectation is strongly related to outcome. If you are part of a group that wants to act drunk, even with small doses of alcohol, you'll feel drunk.

—Teen-agers face special risks. Because most teen-agers are smaller and weigh less than adults, their bodies are

less able to dilute the alcohol consumed. One ounce of alcohol consumed by any slightly built person will produce more pronounced effects. Also, psychological intoxication is greater for teen-agers. Transition from childhood to adulthood is not easy for young people, and they experience a wide range and intensity of emotions during this period. Finally, adolescents are particularly susceptible to car accidents. They tend to overestimate their skills and the capability of the vehicle. Also, young people are more willing to take chances and crave excitement.

Supervise initial use. Evidence[4] indicates that parents who are moderate drinkers and who permit their children to drink small quantities of diluted alcohol at home—for example, wine mixed with water or soda during meal times—are likely to bring up children who have a healthy attitude toward the use of alcohol. Parents who go to either extreme—drinking to excess or, on the other hand, expressing abhorrence for alcohol as something sinful—run the risk of inculcating dangerous attitudes in their children. In addition, studies comparing social drinkers with persons who have drinking problems show that for the most part the latter were introduced to alcohol later in life, began with hard liquors, had their first drinking experience outside the home, and got drunk the very first time. Conversely, responsible drinkers usually first tasted alcoholic beverages with their family when they were young, drank occasionally at home, started with a sip of wine or beer, and did not get drunk.

So rather than being overly restrictive in regard to alcohol use, it seems best to supervise a child's introduction to alcohol by gradually letting the child explore the effects of it in the protective home environment rather than allowing the child to be abruptly introduced to drinking at a later age.[4,5]

Provide alternatives. The alternatives concept has developed in the past decade as a major prevention approach to drug abuse. The basic assumption is that drug abuse becomes a less attractive outlet for youth who are involved in constructive activities of their own choosing. The emphasis in the alternatives approach is on process rather than product[6] . . . of more importance than the specific activities is the process that takes place within the individual of exploring ways to satisfy inner needs.

In searching for alternatives, it is important to identify

the particular interests and motives of a child. An energetic, excitement-seeking youngster might be channeled into physical risk-taking activities such as sports and athletics. Yoga and meditation can not only help a tense child relax and manage stress, but they can also provide a better alternative to drugs as a way of getting "high." As Brecher and the editors of Consumer Reports[7] point out:

> One sees a great many drug takers give up drugs for meditation, but one does not see any meditators giving up meditation for drugs.

Weil[8] gives a detailed presentation of drug-free methods of altering consciousness.

Another alternatives category relates to a young person's self-esteem and self-concept. The greater a person's self-esteem, the less likely he or she is to yield to social pressures to drink or to feel the need to "prove" oneself by reckless drinking. Various approaches to increasing self-esteem have been developed.[9]

A common teen-age complaint is "not having anything to do." Providing a place where young people can get together to dance, listen to music, or simply to "rap" can perform a very useful service. A youth center gives the teen-agers something to do with their time in a supervised environment. It is also a good place for adults to establish rapport with youngsters who may be having problems associated with drugs. Moreover, a teen-age social center is also a prime outlet through which to dispense drug abuse information materials.

School education programs. Traditional educational programs designed to prevent drug abuse have the same unimpressive record of success as the early smoking prevention efforts. In fact, poorly or naively conducted drug and alcohol education may actually increase drug use.[10] However, more innovative approaches such as the application of the "psychological inoculation" approach described in the previous section seem to hold promise. Using this approach, young people could be forewarned of influences toward foolish patterns of drug or alcohol experimentation and systematically trained in assertiveness skills for resisting these influences. A pilot test of his notion was conducted by McAlister,[11] using seventh grade peer leaders to discuss situations in which a young person would be pressured to drink alcohol or smoke marijuana. A contest was held in each classroom and LP records of popular youth entertainers (whose music did not encourage drug use) were offered as prizes for whoever could come up with the best ways of resisting the pressures. The best responses were acted out in front of the class. After the contest all students were given buttons which read, "I'm naturally high." The students were told that was what college students sometimes say when they are pressured to drink or use drugs, and the students discussed the meaning of the phrase. The results suggest some beneficial impact of this program in reducing the use of these drugs by the students.

Other school systems have attempted to reduce drug abuse by helping children clarify their basic values. The morality involved in drunkenness, such as the right to destroy self and others, is discussed. The responsible use of drugs is highlighted. Preliminary research[12] suggests that enhancing moral decisions through the values clarification approach may reduce the incidence of drug abuse among youth.

Children need to examine the basic values of freedom and responsibility and how they are related. Maximum freedom *depends* on finding those minimal restraints on individual freedom which are necessary to ensure freedom for everybody, as the Harvard Law School graduation ceremony calls them: "the wise restraints that make men free." Responsibility involves thoughtfulness, caring, being other-people-centered rather than self-centered, and controlling impulsive actions which may have adverse effects for others or self. A responsible person is one who has learned to predict what the consequences of his or her actions may be.

In general, young people underestimate the danger to society that a drug-intoxicated person can be. They must learn to see that their own acts of drug abuse can have a damaging effect on the rights of others and that society has a right to protect its members by enacting and enforcing laws.

Signs of a Drinking Problem. Too often parents try to avoid a child's drinking problem or deny its existence. One should not wait until the child acts "alcoholic" as pictured on skid row. The common factor in all drinking problems is the negative effect they have on the health or well-being of the drinker, and on others.

Authorities in the alcohol field have suggested these criteria for identifying a problem drinker:

1. Anyone who must drink in order to function or to "cope" with life has a severe drinking problem.
2. Anyone who by his own personal definition, or that of his family and friends, frequently drinks to a state of intoxication.
3. Anyone who goes to school or work intoxicated.
4. Anyone who is intoxicated while driving a car.
5. Anyone who sustains a bodily injury which requires medical attention as a consequence of an intoxicated state.
6. Anyone who comes into conflict with the law as a consequence of an intoxicated state.
7. Anyone who, under the influence of alcohol, does something he avows he would never do without alcohol.

In some cases a beginning alcohol problem becomes more serious and severe. These signs may be present, indicating the presence of a real alcoholism illness:

1. The need to drink increasing amounts of alcohol to achieve the same effects that once took place after just a few drinks.
2. Eventual loss of control over drinking.
3. Specific and painful physical and psychological reactions to the sudden withdrawal of alcohol.
4. "Blackouts," or the inability to remember what happened while drinking.

It is hard to draw the exact lines between social drinking, problem drinking, and alcoholism. Generally speaking, however, social drinking becomes problem drinking when drinking repeatedly harms the child or those close to him. Alcoholism, or alcohol dependence, may come early in a drinking career, but it often develops over a period of years.

What to Do. What can parents do to help a child with a drinking problem?

Talk it out. First, you become factually informed about alcohol abuse. You should talk to the child about it and try to understand why this behavior is taking place. Underlying problems might include poor self-esteem, rebelliousness, or desire for peer approval. Keep lines of communication open. Don't be afraid to talk about the drinking problem honestly and openly. It is easy to be too polite, too protective, or to avoid the issue by considering it the child's private affair.

As previously mentioned, most children with drinking problems really want to talk it out.

Try to remain calm and factually honest in discussing the drinking problem and the consequences for all concerned. Let the child know you are learning as much as you can about alcohol problems. Since a child's drinking problem affects all family members, you might have a family meeting to discuss it. This council meeting should involve listening, empathy, confrontation, and a mutual search for solutions. The key is for the child to honestly accept the fact that he or she has a drinking problem.

In talking with a child, do not threaten, bribe, preach, or try to be a martyr. Avoid emotional appeals that may only increase the child's feeling of guilt and the compulsion to drink. Never argue with the child when he or she is drunk. Above all, do not accept guilt for irresponsible behavior that rightly belongs to the child.

Be supportive. Let the child know you care. Show warm, human concern and caring. Be willing to participate with the child in counseling sessions if needed. Try to arrange more time alone with the child. Increased family interest and involvement in the child's daily activities can help.

Constructive coercion. Lack of motivation to change is often a big problem when one has a drinking problem. Parents must become a motivating force for their children. One way is to insist that the child refrain from heavy drinking and let him know that his drinking will be closely supervised. Becoming intolerant of drunkenness is one of the best methods for reducing drinking problems in youth. Insist that the child drink no more than two or three drinks in any day, paced at one drink per hour for a male, and one per hour and a half for a female, because of the weight differences. The point you want to get across is that alcohol abuse cannot continue as long as the child is under your care. Once you have confronted the child with the facts about his drinking problem and your determination that it is not to continue, give him time to think it through. Then discuss the matter a second or third time—but don't let things run on indefinitely. You must confront the child so that denial is overcome and the child is convinced to take action. Be sure you do not have an ambivalent attitude toward intoxication. In no way show that you think it is "funny" or a sign of manhood or adulthood. Both parents must give an unqualified disapproval of drunkenness. On the whole, young people abide surprisingly well with whatever limits their parents clearly set. You must help the child discriminate that moderate drinking is one thing, but drunkenness is another.

After taking a firm stand against any drunkenness and irresponsible behavior, it is important for parents to follow through with close supervision and strict enforcement. Studies by Dr. John E. Donovan of the Institute of Behavioral Science at the University of Colorado have indicated that for many teen-agers with a drinking problem, the drinking is just one aspect of a broader difficulty involving stealing, fighting, destruction of property, and truancy. These teen-agers do not do well in school and are concerned with acting "independent." They are more influenced by peers than parents and have friends who drink and use marijuana. They seem in dire need of close adult supervision and guidance. They need parents who can set limits and who have the time, energy, and caring to become closely involved in their lives.

A nudge or push at the right time can help a child change. It also shows you care and will not stand idly by while the child destroys himself or others. Of course, this pressure is best given before a child's will power is weakened by physical addiction or psychological dependency on alcohol.

There is often a need to reach and impress upon the child the reality of his problem. In some instances, it may be necessary to pressure a child into counseling or therapy or if the child is unwilling to accept this, a short stay in jail or in a youth shelter sometimes allows the teen-ager to experience the reality of what he has done and its consequences. The child may then become willing to alter his life style.

Various sources of professional help are available, such as mental health counseling. The Alcoholics Anonymous program is open to all age groups, and the earlier treatment is started, the better the chances for recovery. Community groups such as crisis intervention referral services and hotlines can direct users to appropriate programs.

Discuss alternatives. There is no limit on the interesting, pleasurable activities that can be substituted for alcohol abuse as a response to boredom, frustration, loneliness or pain. Among the alternative activities that you might sug-

TABLE I

LEVEL OF EXPERIENCE	CORRESPONDING MOTIVES (Examples)	POSSIBLE ALTERNATIVES (Examples)
PHYSICAL	Desire for physical satisfaction, physical relaxation, relief from sickness, desire for more energy, maintenance of physical dependency.	Athletics, dance, exercise, hiking, diet, health training, carpentry or outdoor work.
SENSORY	Desire to stimulate sight, sound, touch, taste; need for sensual-sexual stimulation; desire to magnify sensorium	Sensory awareness training, sky diving, experiencing sensory beauty of nature
EMOTIONAL	Relief from psychological pain, attempt to solve personal perplexities, relief from bad mood, escape from anxiety, desire for emotional insight, liberation of feeling, emotional relaxation	Competent individual counseling, well-run group therapy, instruction in psychology of personal development
INTERPERSONAL	To gain peer acceptance, to break through interpersonal barriers, to "communicate," especially nonverbally, defiance of authority figures, to cement two person relationships, relaxation of interpersonal inhibition, solve interpersonal hangups	Expertly managed sensitivity and encounter groups, well-run group therapy, instruction in social customs, confidence training, social-interpersonal counseling, emphasis on assisting others in distress via education
SOCIAL (Including Socio-Cultural and Environmental)	To promote social change, to find identifiable subculture, to tune out intolerable environmental conditions, e.g., poverty, changing the awareness of the "masses".	Social service, community action in positive social change, helping the poor, aged, infirm, young, tutoring handicapped, ecology action
POLITICAL	To promote political change, to identify with antiestablishment subgroup, to change drug legislation, out of desperation with social-political order, to gain wealth or affluence or power	Political service, political action, nonpartisan projects such as ecological lobbying, field work with politicians and public officials
INTELLECTUAL	To escape mental boredom, out of intellectual curiosity, to solve cognitive problems, to gain new understanding in the world of ideas, to study better, to research one's own awareness, for science	Intellectual excitement through reading, through discussion, creative games and puzzles, self-hypnosis, training in concentration, synectics—training in intellectual breakthroughs, memory training
CREATIVE-AESTHETIC	To improve creativity in the arts, to enhance enjoyment of art already produced, e.g., music, to enjoy imaginative mental productions	Nongraded instruction in producing and/or appreciating art, music, drama, crafts, handiwork, cooking, sewing, gardening, writing, singing, etc.
PHILOSOPHICAL	To discover meaningful values, to grasp the nature of the universe, to find meaning in life, to help establish personal identity, to organize a belief structure	Discussions, seminars, courses in the meaning of life; study of ethics, morality, the nature of reality; relevant philosophical literature; guided exploration of value systems
SPIRITUAL-MYSTICAL	To transcend orthodox religion, to develop spiritual insights, to reach higher levels of consciousness, to have Divine Visions, to communicate with God, to augment yogic practices, to get a spiritual shortcut, to attain enlightenment, to attain spiritual powers	Exposure to nonchemical methods of spiritual development, study of world religions, introduction to applied mysticism, meditation, yogic techniques

gest to a child are: jogging, bicycling, acting, flying, animal shelter work, and sculpture. You must search with your child for activities that are personally meaningful to the child. The activity should take into account the motives that influenced the child to drink. A list of common motives for drug use and corresponding alternatives for these motives has been prepared by Cohen[6] and is presented in Table 1. Alternatives are no different from the thousands of things people do every day to add excitement and pleasure to their lives. The range of activities that can capture a child's imagination is nearly infinite. The alternatives selected must be realistic, attainable, and meaningful. They should help the child find self-understanding, improved self-image, and feelings of excitement.

Brief Case Study. Katie, now 15, was 9 the first time she and her sister got drunk on beer they found in the refrigerator at home. "In my school you weren't normal if you didn't drink," she said. "Vodka—that was my specialty. When I was drunk, after a couple of years, I began going through this whole personality change. I used to be really friendly and I got paranoid, didn't want to be bothered while I was drinking." When she was 14, she took a trip to Florida with a man who had a wife and four children, became frightened of what was happening to her, and went to Alcoholics Anonymous. She is back in public school in the Bronx, New York where she lives and has not had a drink in nearly 8 months.

Books for Parents About Alcohol and Youth

Addeo, E.G. and Addeo, J.R.: *Why Our Children Drink.* Prentice Hall, Englewood Cliffs, NJ (1975).

Bacon, M. and Jones M.B.: *Teenage Drinking.* Thomas Y. Crowell, New York (1968).

Coles R. *et al.: Drugs and Youth. The Medical, Psychiatric and Legal Facts.* Human Sciences Book Service, New York (1976).

Land, H.: *What You Can Do About Drugs and Your Child.* Hart Publishing, New York (1969).

Staff, Child Study Association of America: *You, Your Child and Drugs.* The Child Study Press, New York (1971).

Sources of Information on Alcohol and Youth

National Institute of Alcohol Abuse and Alcoholism
U.S. Department of Health, Education, and Welfare
5600 Fishers Lane
Rockville, MD 20852

National Council on Alcoholism
733 Third Avenue
New York, NY 10017

National Clearinghouse for Alcohol Information
Box 2345
Rockville, MD 20852

Alcohol and Drug Problems Association of North America
1101 Fifteenth Street N.W.
Washington, D.C. 20005

Al-Anon Family Group Headquarters
P.O. Box 182, Madison Square Garden
New York, NY 10010

Alcoholics Anonymous
P.O. Box 459
Grand Central Station
New York, NY 10017

References

1. Blane, H.T.: *Alcohol and Youth Report.* National Technical Information Service, Springfield, VA (1978).
2. Chafetz, M.: *How Drinking Can be Good For You.* Stein and Day, New York (1978).
3. Hoff, E.C.: *Decisions About Alcohol.* Seabury Press, New York (1964).
4. Bacon, M. and Jones, M.B.: *Teenage Drinking.* Thomas Y. Crowell Co., New York (1968).
5. *Alcohol and Health, New Knowledge.* Second Special Report to the U.S. Congress. U.S. Dept. of Health, Education, and Welfare (June, 1974).
6. Cohen, A.Y.: "The journey beyond trips: Alternatives to Drugs." In *It's So Good You Don't Even Try it Once: Heroin*

in Perspective. Smith, D.E.; Gay, G.R., eds. Prentice-Hall, Englewood Cliffs, NJ (1972).

7. Brecher, E.M. and Consumer's Reports editors: *Licit and Illicit Drugs*. Consumer's Union, Mount Vernon, NY (1972).

8. Weil, A.T.: "Altered states of consciousness." In *Dealing with Drug Abuse*. Wald, P.M.; Hutt, P.B., eds. Praeger, New York (1972).

9. Washington, K.R.: "Success counseling: A model workshop approach to self-concept building." *Adolescence* 12: (1977), pp. 405–410.

10. Louria, D.B.: "Youth involvement in drugs." *The Futurist:* (June, 1978).

11. McAlister, A.L. *et al.:* "Adolescent smoking: Onset and Prevention." *Pediatrics:* (1979).

12. Carney, R.E.: *Summary of Results From 1969–1972. Values-Oriented Drug Abuse Prevention Programs*. Educational Assistance Institute, Santa Monica, CA (1972).

13. Shearn, C.R. and Fitzgibbons, D.J.: "Pattern of drug use in a population of youthful psychiatric patients." *American Journal of Psychiatry* 128: (1972), pp. 1381–1387.

Marijuana

Marijuana—also called pot, grass, weed, maryjane, tea, and dope—is a drug found in the flowering tops and leaves of the hemp plant (cannabis sativa); it grows in mild climates in countries around the world. The leaves and flowers of the plant are dried and crushed or chopped into small pieces and smoked in short cigarettes or pipes. It can be sniffed or taken in food. The cigarettes are commonly called reefers, joints, and sticks. The smoke is harsh, and smells like burnt rope or dried grasses, with a sweetish odor. Its use is restricted and subjected throughout the world to legal sanctions. Next to tobacco and alcohol, marijuana is almost certainly the most widely abused drug, and nearly 100 million a year is spent illegally on it.

Incidence. Nationwide it is estimated that between 35–50 percent of high school and college students may have tried it at least once, and its use has begun to spread to junior high school and grade school students. Of those who have smoked marijuana, about 65 percent are experimenting, trying the drug from one to ten times, and then discontinuing its use. Some 25 percent are social users, smoking marijuana on occasion, when it is available, usually in a group context. Ten percent can be considered chronic users who devote significant portions of their time to obtaining and using the drug.

Smoking pot has become so widespread and prestigious among the young that the temptation to experiment is very strong and often irresistible. Parents should anticipate that well-balanced, reasonably mature youngsters may try marijuana. Marijuana can become a problem to the heavy user who organizes his or her life around it so that other interests and activities dwindle. The use of marijuana is roughly comparable to the use of alcohol, wherein only a relatively small proportion of occasional drinkers move steadily in the direction of chronic alcoholism.

Reasons Why. The well-known drug researcher, Dr. Donald B. Louria,[1] found that in a study of 20,000 junior and senior high school students, the search for pleasure was cited by the students themselves as the primary reason for drug experimentation. A continuation or intensification of the hedonistic ethic in our society will certainly encourage drug use. We need to reorder our priorities in such a way that other values gain in importance relative to the pursuit of personal pleasure. The spread of a leisure/pleasure orientation in American society, without the ability to use free time constructively, leads to the state of boredom that also is conducive to drug use. Also noteworthy is Louria's observation that many young people who were bored perceived their parents as bored individuals, unhappy with their own lives. So boredom seems infectious, especially among the young.

Young people may also turn to drugs because they feel alienated—that there is little to look forward to and that war, crimes, and inflation are insolvable. Futility and apathy set in: Since you cannot alter the world or the direction in which it will go, you must alter your state of consciousness and see the world through a "high." All that is important is your subjective state.

Among the reasons that have been put forward to explain the current popularity of marijuana are:

1. The belief that drugs can solve all problems.
2. The widespread access to various drugs.
3. The "peer pressure" which leads a young child to

conform to current styles in behavior, entertainment—and drugs.

4. The search for different perceptions and ideas which some persons believe they can obtain from mind-altering drugs.

5. The use of marijuana in a role similar to alcohol in a social context.

6. Rebellion against parents.

Obviously the factors contributing to marijuana use and misuse are complex and varied. Youngsters who use drugs heavily almost always have more than one reason for doing so. Not one but many forces are operating.

Effects of Marijuana.

Immediate. Marijuana is a common plant that grows in almost any temperate climate. People have known for 3000 years that the dried tops and leaves of the marijuana plant produce a state of relaxation when smoked or eaten.

Not too long ago, scientists identified THC—the complex chemical in marijuana that produces psychoactive effects. The amount of THC in a marijuana plant varies, depending on the type of plant, where it is grown, and the growing conditions. Marijuana from the South American countries and the Near and Far East is usually stronger in THC than marijuana grown in this country. Hashish or "hash" is a dark brown resin from the tops of the marijuana plant. It contains more THC than the dried plant itself. On the average the marijuana being sold today is at least twice as potent as marijuana grown and sold 5 years ago.

Marijuana acts as a mild intoxicant or as an hallucinogen depending upon the amount that is used and upon the predisposition of the user. Because it may cause hallucinations when taken in very large doses, it can be classified as a mild "hallucinogen." Some individuals are sensitive to minute quantities, whereas others can take relatively large doses without apparent effect. The user's personality, his emotional state, his expectations, the setting in which he takes the drug, and his previous experience with it blend to affect his reactions. This complexity makes it difficult to predict the drug's effects.

In ordinary low doses, marijuana usually produces a mild euphoria. At the start of a "high," many marijuana smokers are giggly, even hilarious; later they become more passive and may lapse into quiet reverie. Most marijuana users report alterations in sense perception. They say they see colors and shapes more vividly; they report hearing subtleties in music not usually apparent to them; time seems to stand still. These experiences are characteristic of the majority of low-dosage marijuana users. Some users, however, who are emotionally or biochemically fragile, have unpredictably severe reactions. Temporary panic and even hallucination can occur.

The more obvious physical reactions include rapid heartbeat, lowering of body temperature, and reddening of the eyes. The drug also changes blood sugar levels, stimulates the appetite, and dehydrates the body. Effects on the emotions and senses vary widely, depending on the amount and strength of the marijuana used. As previously mentioned, the social setting in which it is taken and what the user expects also influence his or her reaction to the drug. Usually, the effect is felt quickly, in about 15 minutes after inhaling the smoke of the cigarette, and can last from 2 to 4 hours. Reactions range from depression to a feeling of excitement. Some users, however, experience no change of mood at all.

Sense of time and distance frequently become distorted. A minute may seem like an hour. Something near may seem far away. Any task or decision requiring good reflexes and clear thinking is affected by the drug. *For this reason, driving is dangerous while under its influence.* Many teen-agers are not aware of the fact that police records contain many incidents of people involved in car accidents, suffering marijuana-impaired judgment, vision, and reaction to speed. Some marijuana victims said their foot on the gas pedal felt so light that it seemed necessary to press down hard to get going. Others said their car seemed to be going slowly because impaired peripheral vision made it seem that things moved past them slowly. Some who looked at their speedometer thought it was malfunctioning and thus pushed their car to 80 and 90 miles per hour.

Other users of marijuana have experienced feelings of power under its influence and attempted feats they would never think of under normal circumstances. A 5-ft., 6-in. tall youth—under its influence—attempted to take on the largest policeman on the Manhattan force, before a huge crowd in Times Square. And there is the case of two young girls attempting to hold up a bus full of people while it was crossing the George Washington bridge.

Long-term hazards.   The long-term physical effects are still not known. The drug cannot yet, therefore, be considered medically safe. The research needed to weigh the effects of chronic use is in its earliest stages. Recent synthesis of the drug's active ingredient, tetrahydrocannabinol, now permits such investigation.

We do know that there is nothing in the chemical make-up of marijuana that will cause one to crave "harder" drugs. It does seem that people who experiment with one drug are more likely to experiment with another. Surveys show that most marijuana is not physically addicting in that no with-drawal symptoms accompany termination of its use, but it can be psychologically habituating. Tolerance to mari-juana—the need for increased doses for the same effect—has been confirmed. An overdose of marijuana or hashish has never been known to cause permanent damage to bodily functions.

Real risks.   Many young people are inclined to minimize some of the potential physical, emotional, and legal hazards of marijuana. They may discount the dangers of driving un-der the influence of marijuana. To date, there is evidence that the drug impairs perception of distance and the ability to think clearly.

Young people may also be unaware of the extent to which habitual marijuana use can limit their psychological devel-opment. When marijuana is used as an easy way out of anxiety, restlessness, and self-questioning—troubles tradi-tionally associated with adolescence—normal adolescent development may be slowed down or postponed indefi-nitely. The task of growing up cannot be accomplished without a certain amount of struggle and pain. So the chronic user of marijuana may encounter a number of psy-chological problems if he is using the drug to escape life stress. His mental growth is impaired by not learning how to deal with frustrations and problems. He tends to with-draw from here-and-now reality, loses ambition and drive, and sustains a loss of motivation. He is present-oriented rather than future-oriented. He may drop out of active in-volvement in school or work. Chronic heavy use of mari-juana does seem to result in a "burnt out" syndrome. One becomes listless and does not think about the future. What has research shown on the relationship of marijuana and cancer? In a recent UCLA study, researchers found that smoking five joints of marijuana had the same effect on human lungs as smoking 112 cigarettes. This is due, in part, to the fact that marijuana has more cancer-causing compounds than an equal amount of tobacco, and also to the fact that marijuana smoke is held in the lungs as long as possible to get the greatest effect from the drug. So chronic inhaling of marijuana seems related to a higher incidence of cancer.

Legal Status of Marijuana Use. The facts are that use of liquor is legal and the use of marijuana is not. Federal penalties for simple possession of marijuana were reduced in 1970, when Congress passed legislation classifying the drug as a hallucinogen, not a narcotic. But arrest and conviction can still have far graver implications for a young person's future than is generally realized. The first offense for possession is a misdemeanor, and the penalty is at the judge's discretion. The second offense is a felony, as is any selling of the drug "for profit." Convictions for felonies result in loss of the rights of citizens, such as the right to vote. Federal penalties for possession of marijuana are up to 1 year in prison for first offense, and a fine of $5000 may be imposed.

In some states, users who possess any amount of marijuana can face criminal charges. Other states have changed their laws to lower the criminal charges for possession of small amounts of marijuana. This is sometimes called decriminalization. These states have made possession of small amounts of marijuana punishable only by a fine. In all 50 states, selling marijuana is still a criminal offense. So while some citizens argue for a repeal of all laws against marijuana, it is still illegal, and parents have the responsibility of informing and reminding children of this fact and the consequences thereof. Since marijuana is illegal, one often has to come in contact with the criminal element to obtain it.

How to Prevent

Discuss the facts. Very little can be accomplished by belaboring young people with prohibitions and warnings. They need information, calmly offered, about the real dangers—including the legal hazards—involved in marijuana use. Even quite young children tend to see through "scare" tactics. Exaggeration is usually found out sooner or later, and this results in some breakdown of trust and communication. What is needed is open, honest, and continuing communication between parents and children about marijuana use and misuse.

Fortunately, many children seem to have a healthy respect for the facts and for the findings of science. The current wane in the use of LSD, for example, may be traced at least in part to the reported possibility of genetic damage. Skillful presentation of factual information can often change a child's attitudes and beliefs. Study up on marijuana facts. Let the subject of marijuana use and abuse come up naturally, as per a newspaper article, rather than give a formal lecture. Try to emphasize the immediate dangers of marijuana use such as car accidents. Do not stress unproven dangers in an effort to deter the child.

Take a stand. After studying all the known facts, take a reasonable stand about marijuana use by young people. It is our duty to tell our youngsters where we stand and why. This can be a very positive influence on the decisions young people make. It seems best to take a stand on various drugs individually rather than collectively, and to base these positions on facts which we can convincingly document, and values we strongly believe in.

Remember that it is unreasonable to contend that adults need to have direct experience with all drugs in order to take a valid position about them. There are a whole range of social problems—poverty, racial inequality, genocide—about which we have to take a stand although we may not have experienced them. If our children suggest we are not qualified to talk about certain drugs because we've never tried them, we have an opportunity to explain the difference between knowledge through immediate experience and knowledge which does not require such experience.

Youngsters want—and have the right to expect—that we will be conscientious and consistent in upholding our convictions about what is worthwhile in life. In the eyes of our children, the credibility of our warnings about drugs is directly related to the sincerity of our concerns about fundamental human values.

Set an example. Three recent large-scale studies show that in cases where parents are users of legal tranquilizing or stimulant drugs, their offspring are substantially more apt to get into illegal drugs. Dr. Donald Louria,[1] of the College of Medicine and Dentistry of New Jersey, told a Senate subcommittee that one of these studies found that ''if the mother is a daily tranquilizer user, the child is three times as likely to use marijuana, heroin, LSD, or stimulants as those whose mothers are not daily tranquilizer users.''

Louria has also noted that studies conducted in the United States and Canada have concluded that ''if either parent smokes more than one pack of cigarettes a day, or uses stimulants or tranquilizers regularly . . . the children are two to seven times more likely to experiment with drugs themselves.'' So you yourself should be a model of responsible, moderate drug taking.

One of the points made to parents by pot-smoking youngsters concerns the responsible use of alcohol by adults: ''Well, you drink, don't you?'' In the first place, the use of alcoholic beverages by adults is not against the law; secondly, moderate social drinking assumes that adults are able to make mature decisions as to their behavior. Finally, there is the irrefutable fact that the young years of personality growth and development are dangerously inappropriate for any chemical means of confounding reality.

Maintain close family relationships. The link between family breakdown and drug use has long been recognized. Studies show that family discord increases the likelihood of drug abuse. As family ties weaken, peer group influence grows. This influence already rivals that of the family in determining whether a young person will become involved in drugs. So one key to drug prevention is a close relationship between husband and wife, open communication, and close involvement of parents in the lives of their children.

Positive addictions. Help your child find a number of positive activities which provide pleasure, excitement, and achievement. Running, horseback riding, music, and many other activities can give a ''high'' or be rewarding so the child will be less prone to turn to drugs. People of all ages need something to give their lives meaning and purpose. They need activities that interest and engage them. They need to feel exhilarated by life without drugs. They need to gain a sense of self-worth through personal accomplishment.

Signs of a Marijuana Problem. First, look for signs that the child may be under unusual stress, such as retreat into self, instability, or intense sibling rivalry. Such signs indicate the need for parents to be available, ready to listen, and supportive. You might ask, "Is something wrong?" or "Can I do anything for you?"

Some of the specific signs of marijuana misuse are:

1. In the early stages of marijuana usage, the child may appear animated with rapid, loud talking and bursts of laughter. In later stages, he or she may be sleepy.
2. The pupils may be dilated and the eyes get pink. The child may try to hide this with sunglasses.
3. The child may have distortions of perception and, rarely, hallucinations.

The marijuana user is difficult to recognize unless he is actually under the influence of the drug, and even then he may be able to work reasonably well. The drug may distort his depth and time perception, making driving or the operation of machinery hazardous.

Early intervention is important in cases of drug abuse. By knowing and being alert for signs of heavy drug use, you will be in a position to move in quickly with effective action. Be sure you have strong evidence before accusing your child of drug abuse.

What to Do. What can parents do to help a child who misuses marijuana?

Talk it out. Talk with—not at—the child. Listen to the child and show by your attitude that you want to talk frankly, even though you may not share his or her views. Find out as much as possible about the situation from the child's point of view, particularly the underlying motives for marijuana use. Don't appear overanxious or indifferent about the problem. A good rule of thumb is to keep yourself under control and to express your concerns openly and frankly. This makes for the kind of authentic human encounter that most young people respond to with the best in themselves.

As important as expressing your concerns, however, is the ability to listen to the child. We are accustomed to thinking of communication mainly in terms of what we say and how well we say it. Listening, on the other hand, is a communication skill that is relatively underdeveloped in many adults. They particularly find it hard to listen when the topic is emotionally charged, like drugs. Anxiety often drives parents to talk more and listen less at those times when youngsters are most in need of being heard. Parents also need to develop the capacity to listen to feeling as well as words. What seems like belligerence in a child is often uncertainty.

Crisis situations can be productive. They can provoke parents and children into communicating more honestly with each other than either had hitherto considered possible. Talking openly about disturbing, emotionally-laden issues often moves families to new levels of intimacy. A 16-year-old boy said:

After my parents got me released in their custody (from jail on a drug-possession charge), they went into their usual what-have-we-done-to-deserve-this act and I told them to cut the shit. I must have been pretty desperate. Things were sort of tense for a while. I let it all hang out and they did too. When we got home we were talking to each other like we haven't done in years. Would you believe my parents actually have a sense of humor and all of a sudden I realized I can make them laugh?

Good communication between parent and child is characterized by mutual respect and an acknowledgment of different levels of knowledge, experience, and competence. To ensure real communication, we adults must show in our actions and our beliefs that our children have the capacity to think and reason clearly. We must also demonstrate our own ability to think and reason clearly, which means concentrating on important issues and letting some things slide.

Be supportive. Above all else, don't give up on a drug abusing child. He or she particularly needs your help to change. Don't "disown" or disassociate yourself from the child because of your shame, guilt, or disgust over the drug abuse. Remember that hostility and/or panic won't help either of you. Don't overreact; many young people experiment with drugs at some time in their lives but most will not become drug dependent. Show faith in your child's capacity to bounce back, change directions, develop new attitudes, and find new interests. The potential for health and growth is there to be tapped in the young.

Consult others. Friends, clergy, or doctors who have provided previous support to the family may be called upon for assistance. Your child may feel freer to discuss the problem with a doctor experienced in drug use.

Consult with parents of other teen-agers involved. Peer pressure is a very powerful force in promoting drug use, but that pressure can be broken up by several parents acting together to affect the group.

Be firm. Let the child know that you will not tolerate drug abuse as long as he or she lives in your house. Insist that the child act in a responsible manner. Explain to the child that his irresponsible use of marijuana will result in a reduction of freedoms, such as grounding, loss of car privileges, or supervision of social life.

Seek positive alternatives. Be alert for positive alternatives and assist your child in discovering physical, recreational, emotional, mental, or spiritual activities that are just as meaningful and exciting as the drug experience.

Case Report. Richard, age 16, was arrested for possession of narcotics, and his parents were informed of this fact at 2 A.M.[2] This came as a great shock to the parents since their son had long assured them he had never even considered trying drugs. When they arrived at the police station, they were told their son and two companions were discovered smoking marijuana in a deserted parking lot. Because it was his first offense, Richie was released into his parents' custody. On arriving home, Richie told his parents that he had been smoking marijuana regularly for over a year and had experimented with other drugs. He had even been in on the sale of some. He belligerently informed his parents that all the kids he knew smoked and that his parents were "living in the ice age" by denying this fact. He told his parents there was nothing they could do about this very normal habit which he found quite enjoyable.

This confrontation jolted the parents, and they realized they had given the boy too much freedom and trust which he was not ready to handle. Deciding not to be cowed by the boy's challenge, they resolved that the boy was in their charge for at least 2 more years and that he would live by their rules of the house. After discussing strategy all night, the parents gave the boy an ultimatum the next morning:

No mre drugs—period. No further association with people who use them. He was also told that trust would have to be earned now, that the truth of everything he said would be checked. When he went out, the parents were to know where he was going, with whom, and why. He was to be home every evening unless attending a special function for a set time. His bedroom door was to be kept open except when he was dressing. The only parties he could attend were those held in his home or in the homes of people his parents knew and trusted. And, finally, he could not use the family car since his parents could not be sure he would be in control of his driving.

Richie reacted with anger to this ultimatum, threatened to run away, and he put his parents through several months of hell. He hardly spoke to them, and when he did it was always in an outburst of anger. His parents expressed understanding of his anger and expressed their love for him in spite of it. The boy's older sister came home from college for summer vacation and unexpectedly supported the parents' position. A family camping trip also helped to provide the boy with interesting activities and a chance to meet new friends. The boy did not return to drugs the next year and his grades improved. He finally said to his mother, "I love you. I don't agree with all the things you and Dad think, but I love you. I know you care about me, and you're trying to do what you think is right even if maybe it isn't."

Readings for Parents about Marijuana

Saltman, Jules: *What About Marijuana?* Public Affairs Pamphlet No. 426. Public Affairs Pamphlets, 381 Park Ave. South, New York, NY 10016.

Further information about marijuana and other drugs is available from the:

National Clearinghouse for Drug Abuse Information
Box 1701
Washington, D.C. 20013
Telephone: (301) 496-7171

The National Clearinghouse will give you a list of counseling or treatment centers in or near your community.

Additional information about treatment for drug problems is available from the:

Family Service Association of America
44 East 23rd St.
New York, NY 10010
Telephone: (212) 674-6100

References

1. Louria, D.B.: "Youth involvement in drugs." *The Futurist:* (June, 1978).
2. "Our 16-year-old son was on drugs." *Good Housekeeping:* (June, 1977).

Inhalants

The fads in inhalant use keep changing; they have included sniffing glue, gasoline, paint thinner, lighter fluid, cleaning fluid, nail polish remover, hair spray, and furniture polish—substances that are easy to come by in many homes. Inhalants are unpleasant to use and can be deadly. Fortunately, most young people who use an inhalant do not go on to use it regularly. Young people who use inhalants are likely to be in the younger age groups—some as young as ages 6 and 7. They are motivated by curiosity and pressure from peers to try something new, just for kicks. Boys are more likely to sniff inhalants than girls. Inhalant sniffing by children may seem harmless enough, but it is a very serious and dangerous practice that must not be overlooked.[3]

Effects of Inhalants

Immediate. The immediate effects are those of acute brain damage and are similar to those produced by alcoholic intoxication. A period of excitation lasting some minutes precedes a period of depression. Some or all of the following may be present: exhilaration and excitement; giddiness; somnolence; disorientation; dizziness; lethargy; irritation of the eyes; double vision; ringing in the ears; sneezing; nausea; diarrhea; pains in the chest, neck, head, and legs; cramps in the hands; paleness; muscular incoordination;

amnesia; slurred speech; blurred vision; dilated pupils; tremors; epileptiform seizures; and tingling and numbness in hands and feet.

The vast majority of children report that during their high they feel strong, invulnerable, and imbued with feelings of amazing capabilities. One of the common feelings is that of being able to fly. Some children feel insensitive to pain and will beat on concrete, self-administer cuts, and otherwise test their insensibility to pain. Visual hallucinations and illusions are common and frequently terrifying.

The body builds a tolerance to inhalants, just as it does to the so-called hard drugs. Increasing amounts are needed to produce the same effect. An inhalant "high" usually lasts for a relatively short period of time—only about an hour.

Hazards of heavy use. Reports have listed the following long-term effects; fatigue and reduced physical activity, mental depression, loss of appetite, weight loss, irritability, inattentiveness, irritation of skin and respiratory tract (especially nasal and oral mucous membranes), excessive oral secretions, halitosis, tremulousness and unsteadiness, deterioration of handwriting, forgetfulness, bone marrow inhibition, low blood pressure, various anemias and white blood cell abnormalities, congestion and hemorrhage of lungs, cerebellar degeneration, elevated spinal fluid pressure caused by cerebral edema, and liver and kidney damages. By freezing the larynx and the respiratory system, the gas in spray products can kill in seconds.

How to Prevent. Many children are unaware of the hazards of inhalant sniffing. It is important, then, for parents to provide early information about this danger, as well as sensible supervision. Information should be given in a calm, matter-of-fact manner, avoiding exaggeration or "scare" tactics. It is usually sufficient to tell your children before they start school that sniffing is one of many dangerous situations to which they will be exposed in the course of growing up. Just as they must learn to be careful crossing the street, so they must learn to avoid dangerous drugs as part of becoming responsible and more grown-up. Since your children will be curious about why sniffing is dangerous, explain the potential dangers described previously. Noteworthy is the fact that other people have taken steps to prevent inhalant use by children. The manufacturers of one kind of airplane glue have added a foul-smelling ingredient to their product to discourage sniffing. Local laws prohibit the sale of some inhalants, like glue, to minors.

Signs of Inhalant Use. How can I tell if my child is inhaling solvents or glue? The common signs of inhalant misuse follow:
1. Odor of substance inhaled on breath and clothes.
2. Excessive nasal secretion and watering of the eyes.
3. Poor muscular control (staggering) within 5 minutes of exposure.
4. Drowsiness or unconsciousness.
5. Presence of plastic or paper bags or rags containing dry plastic cement.
6. Slurred speech.
7. Bad breath.

What to Do. When the dangers of inhalant use are described and parents take a firm stand against inhalant use, most children will discontinue its use. If a child continues sniffing after the dangers have been pointed out, he or she needs more careful supervision and, usually, psychological treatment to uncover the cause of this compulsion to do what is forbidden and dangerous.

Case Reports of Inhalant Use. In one city, Dave, a high school student with a good record, found himself locked in a city jail. He told the judge that he went to visit a friend and he found a glue-sniffing party in the basement. Some were holding brown paper bags to their faces. He recognized two girls who were present, and they invited him to join in. He said he had to leave—but Marge, a girl he liked said, "He's chicken, let him go." So he thought he'd give it a try, and *then* leave. He told the judge, "I reached for the bag Marge was sniffing and tried it." He remembered nothing of what followed.

The police had received a call that an intruder was caught in a private home. The owner had come into the kitchen and found Dave in a confused state, drinking water at the sink. His parched throat was burning from the chemicals in the glue he had sniffed. When the home owner tried to turn the water off and hold him for the police, Dave became violent. He paid quite a price for experimenting: a year's probation, no driving for a year, reporting weekly to the probation officer, abiding by a nightly curfew, and—worst of all—a permanent police record. However, as bad as Dave's experience was, he was luckier than other glue sniffers.

One young boy suffocated when sniffing glue with a plastic bag over his head. Another, sniffing glue on a rooftop, was under the hallucination of being able to fly off the roof like a bird. He was killed when his body crashed in the courtyard below.

A 15 year old, "high" on glue, had gone berserk when his glue was confiscated, forced five members of his family out of their home, and shot himself in the leg.[1]

Michael,[2] age 15, had been sniffing glue or gasoline for 1 year and at least every second day. After sniffing glue, he said he felt light-headed, followed by a feeling of strength, bigness, and omnipotence. At times he would see dots before his eyes, strange birds flying about, or strange animals crawling in his room. He experienced difficulty in thinking and his thoughts seemed jumbled. He felt reckless and at times had felt he could fly. There was always some amnesia for part of the high and some difficulty in thinking clearly for at least 48 hours after.

Michael had a long history of parental rejection, school difficulty, and delinquent acts such as shoplifting. When excited he often tried to mutilate himself such as by slashing his wrists with a razor blade. He was placed in a residential center for disturbed youth.

References

1. Bass, M.: "Sudden sniffing death." *Journal of the American Medical Association* 212: (1970), pp. 2075–2079.
2. Barker, G. and Adams, W.: "Glue-sniffers." *Sociology and Social Research:* (August, 1963), pp. 298–310.
3. Chapel, J.L. and Taylor, D.W.: "Drugs for kicks." *Crime and Delinquency* 16: (1970), pp. 1–35.

Other Drugs

The drugs most commonly abused by young people—tobacco, alcohol, marijuana, and inhalants—have been discussed in the previous sections. In this section we will briefly review the other drugs that youths sometimes misuse, namely, stimulants, sedatives, narcotics, and hallucinogens. The procedures for prevention and intervention are similar to those described previously and will not be repeated in this section.

Stimulants. A stimulant is a drug that stimulates the central nervous system so as to increase alertness, activity, and speed up bodily processes. The stimulants or "pep pills" include amphetamines, cocaine, caffeine, and nicotine. Except for cocaine, these drugs are legal, easily available, and relatively inexpensive. Since cocaine is not available by prescription, it is only obtained through criminal sources. Cocaine is a white powder that is usually snorted (inhaled by sniffing). A cocaine high is much like a high from a large dose of amphetamines; the user becomes overalert, talkative, and feels surges of power and joy. The high does not last long, and the user may crave more of the drug to combat crashing.

Amphetamines, first produced in the 1920's, are best known for their ability to combat fatigue and sleepiness; they are also sometimes used to curb appetite. Under the supervision of a physician, they may be used legally for medical reasons.

The most commonly used amphetamines are Benzedrine ("bennies"), Dexedrine ("dexies"), Methedrine ("Meth," "speed," or "crystal"), and Dexamyl (which combines an amphetamine with a barbiturate). They are prescribed medically for relief of fatigue, for weight control, and as mood elevators for depressed or mentally ill people. Although it happens rather slowly, a large degree of tolerance can develop for amphetamines.

Effects
Immediate: The effect of Methedrine or Dexedrine on the body is to increase heart rate, raise blood pressure, cause palpitations, dilate pupils, and cause dry mouth, sweating, headache, diarrhea, and paleness. Action of the heart and metabolism is speeded up through stimulation of the release of norepinephrine, a substance stored in nerve endings, which then becomes concentrated in a higher brain center. Abuse of these drugs may produce exhaustion and temporary psychosis—conditions which may require hospitalization.

The injection of Methedrine into a vein, a practice called

"speeding," may result in critical serum hepatitis. When injected in unaccustomed high doses, the drug can cause death.

Long-term hazards: One of the most insidious dangers of the "up" drugs is that they mask the symptoms of fatigue, so that a user may push himself beyond his physical endurance, going without food or sleep for several days. When the effects of the drug subside, extreme exhaustion and depression commonly follow. Taking more pills to counteract these reactions sets up a cycle of drug use that is hard to break.

Long-term heavy users tend to lose weight and are usually irritable, unstable, and, like other chronic drug abusers, show social, intellectual, and emotional breakdown. Extremely heavy users may end up with a full-blown amphetamine psychosis—confused, frightened, and out of touch with reality.

Signs of stimulant misuse. The more obvious signs of heavy use of amphetamines are:
1. The child may be excessively active, irritable, argumentative, and nervous.
2. Excitation, euphoria, and talkativeness.
3. Pupils dilated.
4. Long periods without eating or sleeping.

Sedatives. Sedatives (barbiturates, tranquilizers, alcohol) belong to a large family of drugs which relax the body's muscles, relieve feelings of tension and worry, and bring on sleep. Barbiturates ("barbs" or "goofballs") include Seconal, Nembutal, and phenobarbital.

Taken in normal, medically supervised doses, barbiturates mildly depress the action of the nerves, skeletal muscles, and heart muscle. They slow down the heart rate and breathing and lower blood pressure. In higher doses, the effects resemble alcoholic drunkenness: confusion, slurred speech, staggering, and deep sleep. These drugs produce physical dependence. Body tolerance to them requires increasingly high doses.

Barbiturates are extremely addictive, and it is very hard to stop using them. Because barbiturates produce pleasant, relaxed feelings, they are often used by people who don't need them, such as teen-agers. They find sleeping pills in the family medicine cabinet.

Addicts may take 10 to 20 pills a day. Their sedative effect is so strong that an addict may fall asleep while smoking. Many carry telltale burns on their fingers from smoking cigarettes; they were unaware of it because the pain was blocked out.

Withdrawal from barbiturates is even more difficult and dangerous than from heroin. Abrupt cessation can cause convulsions, hallucinations, and death.

If the drug is withdrawn abruptly, the user suffers withdrawal sickness with cramps, nausea, delirium and convulsions, and in cases, sudden death. Withdrawal must take place in a hospital over a period of several weeks on gradually reduced doses.

Large doses are potentially lethal. Any dosage may cause accidents because perception of objects becomes distorted and reactions and responses are slowed. Barbiturates, especially when taken with alcohol, are a leading cause of automobile accidents. Users may react to the drug more strongly at one time than at another. They may become confused about how many pills they have taken and die of an accidental overdose. Barbiturates are a leading cause of accidental poison death in the United States and are frequently implicated in suicides.

Signs of barbiturate misuse. Signs that a child is a heavy user of barbiturates include the following:
1. Symptoms of alcohol intoxication, but without the odor of alcohol on breath.
2. Staggering or stumbling.
3. Falling asleep while working.
4. Appearing disoriented.
5. Slurred speech.
6. Pupils dilated.
7. Difficulty concentrating.
8. Quarrelsome disposition and quick temper.

Tranquilizers. These are sedatives used to quiet or calm a person's emotions without changing the person's ability to think clearly or stay alert. They do not have as strong a sedative effect as barbiturates, but they can relax a nervous person so that sleep is possible. It is possible to develop a physical and psychological dependence on them.

Narcotics. The term *narcotic* refers to opium and pain-killing drugs made from opium, such as heroin, morphine, paregoric, and codeine. These and other opiates are obtained from the juice of the poppy fruit. Several synthetic drugs, such as Demerol, are also classed as narcotics. Heroin, a white powder with a bitter taste, is the narcotic most abused by Americans. Studies have shown that heroin addiction is found chiefly among young men of minority groups who live in ghetto areas. The possession or sale of heroin is illegal, and federal and state laws establish severe penalties for narcotics violations.

Effects of heroin. Typically, the first emotional reaction to heroin is reduction of tension, easing of fears, and relief from worry. Feeling high may be followed by a period of inactivity bordering on stupor. Heroin is usually mixed with a liquid solution and injected into a vein. It appears to dull the edges of reality, and addicts report that it "makes my troubles roll off my mind," and "it makes me feel more sure of myself." The drug depresses certain areas of the brain and tends to reduce hunger, thirst, and the sex drive.

Like other opiates, heroin is addictive, and the body develops a tolerance for it. Once the habit starts, larger and larger doses are required to get the same effects. One of the signs of heroin addiction is withdrawal which occurs about 18 hours after the addict's last dosage. When the drug is stopped, the addict may sweat, shake, get chills, nausea, and suffer sharp abdominal and leg cramps.

Sniffing heroin is no safer than mainlining, although many young people like to think it is. When a 17-year-old Barnard College freshman died after sniffing heroin, the medical examiner observed: "The girl showed the common effect of a heroin overdose—froth at the nose and mouth, congestion of the internal organs, edema of the lungs. Her lungs were almost like you see in drowning cases."

Hallucinogens. Hallucinogens are drugs taken for their "psychedelic" or "mind-expanding" effects. They tend to make the users see things that are not there and often produce hallucinations and delusions. The most famous is LSD or lysergic acid diethylamide. It is one of the most powerful chemicals known; an amount almost too small to see with the naked eye is enough to cause disorientation for up to 12 hours. Advocates of LSD maintain it enhances perception in such experiences as religion, music, vision, and sex. However the positive properties are offset by the clearly destructive ones. A "bad trip" can lead to definite, long-lasting, and sometimes permanent mental derangement. Terrifying delusions have led to suicide. A peculiar property of the effect is that it may return months after it has supposedly ended, a frightening recurrence that may lead to disaster—if the flashback occurs behind the wheel of a car, for example. Because the LSD user may sometimes have paranoid feelings of invulnerability or even the ability to fly, there have been cases of accidental death resulting from these beliefs. Users have been known to walk in front of moving cars or to attempt to fly—*e.g.*, from a high window—with deadly consequences.

A number of studies have been conducted on the effects of LSD on chromosomes. While some scientists have found chromosomal defects in animals and in man, other investigators have not. Thus, whether LSD can cause birth defects remains an open question, and further studies are underway. Because of the risk factors, women of child-bearing age are particularly urged by medical authorities not to use LSD.

The Comprehensive Drug Abuse Prevention and Control Act of 1970 makes the possession and sale of LSD illegal. There are heavy fines and imprisonment associated with its use.

PCP (Angel Dust). Phencyclidine (PCP) is an animal tranquilizer often used in animal hospitals and, therefore, easily diverted to "street" drug use. Street use of PCP has been generally confined to oral ingestion or inhalation by smoking the drug as "Angel Dust," when it is sprinkled on parsley, marijuana, tobacco, or other smokable substances.

The immediate effects of PCP usually proceed in three stages:

1. Changes in body image, sometimes accompanied by feelings of unreality.
2. Perceptual distortions, infrequently manifested as visual or auditory hallucinations.
3. Feelings of apathy or estrangement.

The experience often includes feelings of drowsiness, inability to verbalize and feelings of "nothingness" or "emptiness." Reports of difficulty in thinking, poor concentration, and preoccupation with death are frequent. Many users have reacted to its use with an acute psychotic episode. It often leads to paranoia and has been linked with serious violence.

Youngsters desperately need to be given information about the risk factors in PCP use. The drug is unpleasant to use, and it tends to produce feelings of apathy and isolation. Its possession and sale are illegal under the Comprehensive Drug Abuse Prevention and Control Act of 1970. Illegal possession of PCP could result in a sentence of a term of imprisonment of 1 year and/or a fine of $5000.

Other Hallucinogens. Mescaline is the active ingredient in the peyote cactus. Psilocybin is the psychedelic drug in the so-called magic mushroom found in Mexico. Among the newer synthetic hallucinogens produced by the black market laboratories are "STP," which is very dangerous, and "MDA," which seems to act as a stimulant as well.

Books For Young Children About Drug Abuse

The following books are available from New Dimensions Publishing Co., New York:

Nelson, Natalie: *Things That Happen To Us.* Ages 6–10.

At school a teen-ager tries to sell drugs in the form of candy to a child.

Nelson, Natalie: *More Things That Happen To Us.* Ages 7–11.

Bob's older brother offers him some drugs, saying they will make him feel good. Bob refuses and tells his brother to stop ruining his life with drugs.

Rodriguez, Juan: *Why We Lost The Series.* Ages 8–12.

Tom, a pitcher, begins to act strangely and refuses to play in the final game of the series the team has been winning. The team loses and they find out Tom has been on drugs.

Hines, John: *In Memory of Jerry.* Ages 9–13.

Jerry decides to "turn on" with his friends who have gotten some drugs. He dies of an overdose.

Hines, John: *The Outsider.* Ages 9–13.

Roslyn, a teen-ager, at first refuses to take drugs, but when her friends reject her, she changes her mind. Dick, a young addict, pleads with her not to do it.

The following book is available from Doubleday & Company, New York:

Austrian, Geoffrey: *The Truth About Drugs*. Ages 9–13.

The story about drugs, their use, what is being done about them, and the reasons people take them.

SEXUAL MISBEHAVIORS

Sexual attitudes, morals, and beliefs have changed substantially in recent years. What was considered deviant sexual behavior in youth a few years ago may not be deemed abnormal today. In this section we will discuss the most common sexual behaviors of children and teen-agers (masturbation, sex play, deviant sex roles, and premarital pregnancy), with a view toward ascertaining what constitutes problem behaviors and what are the most helpful actions that parents can take.

Excessive Masturbation

The tendency to manipulate the genital organs for the sake of pleasure is present in all human beings. As infants, children discover that there is a pleasant, enjoyable feeling to be had from touching or rubbing the genitals. Quite common in children from the ages of 1 to 6, it also occurs often in teen-agers. For adolescent boys, masturbation is the main sexual activity. Kinsey reports that 94 percent of males masturbate during adolescence.[2]

Although most modern parents have heard, read, or personally experienced the fact that masturbation is harmless and that it does not stunt growth or cause insanity, sterility, or impotence, some still feel anxious when their children do it. Instead of ignoring the act, they severely scold or punish the child which tends to make the child feel guilty or anxious about it.[1]

Of course a child may engage in masturbation excessively or inappropriately, *e.g.*, in public places. A child may turn to excessive masturbation because he has too few sources of other pleasures in life, feels unwanted or unloved by his parents, feels lonely or disliked by others, or feels incompetent at school or in other areas of his life.

What To Do

Promote other interests. Your child may be too inactive, and his time by himself may be too long. Try to turn the child's attention away from continually seeking pleasure from his own body by encouraging him to find enjoyment in outside interests, such as work, study, projects, and recreation. To develop more social participation by the child, suggest his inviting more friends over to the house, joining clubs, or attending camp.

You may have to make yourself more available to the child and give more of your time and affection. Try to schedule more trips and activities together.

Distraction. To distract the child from masturbating, you might suggest playing a game together or running an errand for you. One 5-year-old girl would masturbate during nap time in kindergarten because she was bored. She frankly admitted to her mother that she "tickled herself" at this time. The mother purchased a number of inexpensive little games and puzzles that the child could do during this time. This procedure immediately stopped the masturbation.

Confront. In a matter-of-fact way, explain to the child that masturbation is not done in public. Tell the child that masturbation is permitted in the privacy of one's own room. Explain that most children want to do it sometime or other but that they can wait to do it in private. Reassure the child that such activity is normal and not perverted.

Understand. Try to review ways in which the child has been placed under too much strain and tension of late. The child may be masturbating because of nervousness or worry. The task here is to uncover the cause of the tenseness, instead of attacking the masturbation directly. Perhaps, the child is terrified a sick parent will die, or doesn't know how to get along with other children.

References

1. Dranoff, S.M.: "Masturbation and the male adolescent." *Adolescence* 9: (1974), pp. 169–176.
2. Kinsey, A.C. *et. al.: Sexual Behavior In The Human Male*. W.B. Saunders, Philadelphia (1948).

Sex Play

Like masturbation, sex play and sex exploration with other children are aspects of normal sexual development. Sexual curiosity may prompt boys and girls to see and touch each other's nude bodies. Games such as "playing doctor" and "playing father and mother" are quite common. The range of sexual behavior exhibited by preadolescent children includes sexual language and gestures, exhibitionism, homosexual acts, and attempts at heterosexual intercourse.

The Kinsey Reports and other surveys indicate that about 50 percent of preadolescent boys report homosexual prepubertal play and 34 percent report prepubertal heterosexual play. The incidence of sexual play in girls is somewhat lower but also shows an increase with age. Homosexual play, that is, sex play between children of the same sex, usually takes the form of children handling each other's genitals. There is no convincing evidence that this transient phase of homosexual activity has any bearing on long-term adult homosexuality.

The reasons children engage in sex play include sexual curiosity, the mystery and "forbidden fruit" aspect of sex, peer pressure, and overt sexual activity by parents in the home. The sex drive itself does not appear to be that strong in prepubertal children.

What To Do

Confront. Children often need parents to put limits on their sex play. Explain to the child that sex contacts are for grownups and that children must learn to wait. Be clear, firm, and matter of fact. Avoid making the child feel as if he has done something extremely wrong or sinful. Let the child know that you consider the desire to engage in such behavior to be normal but that it should be controlled. Clearly prohibit further activity by stating, "I don't want you to do that again.'' There is no need to give a long explanation or lengthy sermon.

Encourage alternative activities. Children who have plenty of interesting, satisfying activities at home and in the neighborhood are generally less apt to be fascinated by sex play or to turn to it as a substitute source of pleasure.

Supervise. Do not let children play alone in a closed room for hours at a time without occasionally coming in to see what they are doing.

Sex education. A child's sexual curiosity can be lowered by talking to the child about sex in the home and answering all her questions in a frank, matter-of-fact way. Studies have found that about 65 percent of preadolescents have poor sexual information, 13 percent have distorted information, and 5 percent have no information.[1] Children who have their sex questions answered truthfully and within the bounds of their understanding are less likely to engage in sex play. Sex will no longer be such a mystery to them.

Parental example. Do not let children watch you in the act of intercourse. Even a child of 9–10 cannot fully comprehend the moral aspects and limits of such behavior.

References

1. Thornburg, H.D.: "Educating the preadolescent about sex." *The Family Coordinator* 12: (1974), pp. 35–39.

Deviant Sex Roles

When extreme and rigid, atypical sex roles can be a problem for children.[1,2] We are referring here to extreme effeminate behavior in boys and masculine behavior in girls. Such behavior is often associated with high anxiety, low self-esteem, and low social acceptance for the child. Boys, in particular, are apt to find society quite intolerant of extreme effeminate behavior. As a result, many more boys than girls are referred for therapy because of atypical gender development (ratio of 15:1). One of the main responsibilities of parents is to assist their children in the establishment of a sexual identity. "Sex typing" is the process by which the child learns the behaviors and attitudes culturally appropriate to his sex. The child, in other words, learns "sexual-role standards," those psychological characteristics which are considered appropriate to one sex in contrast to the other. He acquires "gender identity." Gender identity, *i.e.*, feeling oneself to be a boy or girl, and sexual-role standards are acquired during early childhood. Preference of one sex role or the other emerges early in life, probably by the third year. Thus, it is difficult to bring about a major realignment of sex role and gender identity after 3 years of age.

The importance of not overlooking cross-gender behavior in children is attested to by the fact that adult transvestites (who enjoy dressing in clothes of the other sex but do not want surgical or hormonal sex change), transsexuals (who want surgical, hormonal, and legal sex reassignment), and some homosexuals recall their youth as characterized by an aversion to activities typical of same-sex peers and a strong attraction for cross-gender play interests.[2] So parents should not just consider this a passing phase that the child will grow out of. For a large majority of the cases, the emotional stress, discomfort, and pain continue into adulthood.[3]

While being tuned in to signs of a serious sex role identity problem, parents should not go to the extreme and become concerned just because their son enjoys more passive artistic activities to competitive sports. In recent years there has been a growing realization that we should not force children to conform to rigid and narrow sex role stereotypes, such as pressuring boys to inhibit tender feelings and conform to the "John Wayne" type of masculinity. It is now generally recognized that the healthy personality combines elements of both "masculine" and "feminine" characteristics. The psychologically *androgynous* person is one who freely engages in both "masculine" and "feminine" behaviors, is both instrumental (task oriented) and expressive (socio-emotional), and is both assertive and yielding, when the occasion calls for such behavior. Research shows that rigid adherence to narrow sex typing in either direction—masculine or feminine—restricts a person's adaptability and self-expression. By contrast, the research indicates that the androgynous person displays behavioral adaptability across situations, and engages in whatever behavior is appropriate, regardless of sex role stereotypes. For example, androgynous males display a high level of nurturance and playfulness (so-called "feminine" behavior), and females display a high level of independence from social pressure (so-called "masculine" behavior).

Studies of college students have found that about 50 percent show traditional sex roles, about 15 percent are cross-sex typed, and about 35 percent are androgynous. This is in keeping with other research[5] which found that 50 percent of adult women report having been "tomboys" in childhood. Tomboyish behavior, such as preferring active, outdoor games, playing with boys, and wearing jeans is thus quite common among females. If the girl is also interested in "feminine" activities and is comfortable with a feminine identity, she would be considered androgynous and well adjusted. Similarly, a boy who lacks aggressiveness, avoids rough and tumble play, and maybe daydreams a lot should not be considered a problem if he is happy being a boy. The critical issue, then, is whether the young child accurately classifies himself according to biological gender—and is happy about this classification.[6]

The following are signs to look for that a child has a sex role or identity problem:

1. The young child expresses a continuing preference for a cross-sex identity. A young boy might say, "I am a girl," or "I want to grow up to be a mommy and have children."
2. Persistent dressing in opposite-sex clothing strongly suggests a gender identity problem.
3. Cross-gender interests and role playing is another sign. This is a problem when a boy not only prefers games and toys which are labelled "feminine" but also shows a *persistent aversion* to boys' activities and male playmates. In fantasy games the child may insist upon playing the role of the opposite-sex parent.
4. The child's physical appearance may closely resemble that of the opposite sex. A girl, for example, may be frequently mistaken for a boy in early childhood. A boy may have delicate, attractive features which elicit affectionate responses from adults.
5. The behavior of gender-disturbed children frequently causes them to be rejected by their peers.
6. Mannerisms, gestures, and vocal tone of the opposite sex are exhibited, and the child finds it very difficult

to suppress these behaviors even under strong social criticism.

When parents attempt to help a child with a sex role or identity problem, the goal is not to turn the child into a sex role stereotype, but to enlarge the range of choices among various behaviors and offer the child the possibility of becoming an androgynous person who is comfortable with his or her sexual identity.

Studies have shown that feminine boys, unlike men with postpuberty gender identity disorders, are remarkably responsive to changes in the way their parents treat them. When treated between the ages of 4 and 12, the boys tend to become less feminine and more masculine. Cross-dressing, feminine mannerisms, and fantasy play diminish rapidly, and the boys become more aggressive toward their parents. Teasing and social rejection by male peers decreases and is replaced by acceptance. No matter how extreme the cross-gender behavior, the evidence indicates that this gender orientation has not yet crystallized in childhood and is amenable to change.

Reasons Why

1. Studies show that preschool boys raised in homes without fathers or where the father is absent for extended periods show feminine interests, attitudes, and behaviors.[4]

2. An overly close relationship between a child and the opposite-sex parent may be present. The child and parent tend to have extremely intimate physical and psychological contact, and the parent often reports that an "inseparable" relationship exists. Thus the child has little opportunity to identify with the same-sex parent and develop appropriate sex role behaviors.

3. Some parents, desiring an opposite-sex child, may attempt to make a girl act like the boy they never had, or vice versa.

Thus, parents should always be alert to reassure their little girl that they are pleased that she is female and the same goes for little boys as males. Friends and relatives who commiserate with parents about having "another girl" or "another boy" should be cut short. It is very important that parents accept whatever sex they get in their children.

4. A mother who hates and envies maleness may foster effeminate behavior in her boy. The mother may associate

masculinity with physical violence and aggressiveness, sexual license, and boorishness. She may prefer her son to be gentle.

5. Genetic or hormonal influences can play a role, but this is usually not the primary cause.

What To Do

Develop closer relationship with same-sex parent. In order to promote more appropriate identification, the same sex parent should spend a lot of time with the child and model alternative behavior patterns. For at least 1 to 2 hours a week, the child and same-sex parent should spend time alone together engaged in activities of common interest, such as bowling or miniature golf.

If for some reason the same-sex parent is not available, alternative role models of the same sex should be sought from among relatives, friends, scout leaders, teachers, or perhaps from a therapist. For effeminate boys a male college or graduate student might be hired to act as a companion or big brother and to play baseball and other games with the boy. Whenever possible a male teacher and baby sitter should be sought for the effeminate boy. The child should be encouraged to read books about heros of the same sex.

Initially the child is likely to reject the reaching out of the same-sex adult. A lack of common interests may also be a problem. The adult should persevere, however, and be determined to establish a relationship with the child. Sometimes, a group activity involving several adults and children helps maintain the motivation of the adults. An effort should be made by the same-sex adult to openly express emotions and feelings of warmth toward the child.

Parental reinforcement of appropriate sex-typed behavior. Whenever the child engages in behaviors appropriate to his or her own sex, the parents should verbally praise and encourage the act. Thus, an effeminate boy should be praised for activities using large muscles or for bravery, such as climbing high on monkey bars, plunging head first down a slide, running, or kicking a ball. Even inept attempts at handling a ball or climbing should be strongly praised, with considerable encouragement toward continuing.

Praise should contain the frequent use of either masculine or feminine nouns (whichever is most appropriate). For example, you would say to an effeminate boy, "That's a good *boy.*" "You're getting taller; you're going to be a big *man* when you grow up."

You might also establish a point system whereby the effeminate boy is given five points on a chart for engaging in masculine behavior, such as masculine play with a younger brother. A certain number of points could be exchanged by the child for candies and rewarding activities *(e.g.,* TV time). After a few weeks of this procedure, you could stipulate that in addition to earning points for masculine behavior, the boy will now be "fined," *i.e.,* will lose points for one particular kind of feminine behavior, such as feminine gesture. In this way the child's feminine behaviors could be gradually reduced. In the classroom, the boy's teacher should similarly reward masculine behaviors and penalize feminine behaviors.

Verbal disapproval. Cross-gender behaviors should be clearly disapproved of. Thus, you might say to an effeminate boy, "Hey, don't run like that." "You don't look much like a stewardess. You look more like a pilot. I think you'd make a better pilot." In other words, give the child specific feedback and prompts as to what are "girlish" interests ("that's a girl's toy") and mannerisms. If an effeminate boy starts to talk with you about a feminine topic, pay no attention to the child. Look away and do something else. If the child directly asks you a question about a feminine topic, express your disinterest by saying, "I'm not interested in that" or "I don't want to talk about that—that's girl talk."

Sublimation. Provide outlets for the sublimation or channeling of continuing feminine interests (if a boy). Playacting with costumes, for example, will cause less social hardship than wearing a sister's dresses. A girl with masculine interests might be encouraged to play baseball or participate in other competitive sports.

Case Reports

Case #1. Bobby, a 5-year-old boy with delicate good looks and a gentle manner, had a long history of cross-dressing and cross-gender play.[7] He frequently expressed his wish to be a girl. A physical exam and chromosome analysis revealed that he was a normal male child. With professional help, the mother was trained to praise and reinforce his play with masculine toys and to verbally prompt her son not to play with girls' toys. This strategy resulted in the rapid elimination of feminine sex-typed play behavior.

Case #2. Kraig, aged 4 years, 11 months, was referred for therapy because of cross-gender identification.[8] He had been cross-dressing since age 2, and he continually displayed feminine mannerisms, gestures, gait, and vocal quality. He resisted ''rough-and-tumble'' play with the boys in his neighborhood, and preferred to play with girls. He invariably insisted on playing the role of the ''mother'' in his play and assigned the part of ''father'' to a girl. He was overly dependent upon his mother and demanded her attention almost continuously.

With professional help, the mother took the boy to a playroom at a clinic several times a week and praised him whenever he played with masculine toys, such as dump trucks or toy soldiers. When he played with dolls or other feminine toys, the mother completely ignored him and read a book. At home the parents gave points exchangeable for treats whenever the boy engaged in masculine behaviors, *e.g.*, masculine play with his brother, and punished the boy for feminine behaviors (doll play, play with girls, feminine gestures) by either taking away points, isolating him for a brief time, or spanking the boy. This combined treatment resulted in the normalization of the boy's sex-typed behaviors.

Books For Children About Deviant Sex Roles

Female
Arthur, R.M.: *My Daughter, Nicola*. Athenuem Publishers (1965). Ages 10–13.

Nine-year-old Nicola's mother died soon after she was born. Feeling an intense need for the love and approval of her father, she tries to succeed at boys' activities. She finally feels secure when she learns that her father loves her as she is.

Male
Zololow, C.S.: *William's Doll*. Harper & Row Publishers (1972). Ages 4–7.

William wants a doll to care for and be a father to. This story reveals there is nothing wrong with this motive.

References

1. Rekers, G.A.: "Atypical gender development and psychosocial adjustment." *Journal of Applied Behavior Analysis* 10: (1977), pp. 559–571.
2. Green, R.: "Sissies and tomboys." In *Sexual Problems: Diagnosis And Treatment in Medical Practice.* Wahl, C., ed. Free Press, New York (1967).
3. Rekers, G.A. *et al.:* "Child gender disturbance: A clinical rationale for intervention." *Psychotherapy: Theory, Research And Practice* 14: (1977), pp. 2–11.
4. Hetherington, E.M. and Deur, J.C.: "The effects of father absence on child development." *Young Children* 18: (1971), pp. 233–248.
5. Hyde, J.S. *et. al.:* "Tomboyism." *Psychology of Women Quarterly* 2: (1977), pp. 73–75.
6. Pleck, J.H.: "The psychology of sex roles: Traditional and new views." In *Women And Men: Changing Roles and Perceptions.* Cater, Scott, Martyna, eds. Aspen Institute for Humanistic Studies, (1976).
7. Rekers, G.A. *et al.:* "Childhood gender identity change: Operant control over sex-typed play and mannerisms." *Journal of Behavior Therapy and Experimental Psychiatry* 7: (1976), pp. 51–57.
8. Rekers, G.A. and Lovass, O.I.: "Behavioral treatment of deviant sex-role behaviors in a male child." *Journal of Applied Behavior Analysis* 7: (1974), pp. 173–190.
9. Bates, J.E. *et. al.:* "Intervention with families of gender disturbed boys." *American Journal of Orthopsychiatry* 45: (1975), pp. 150–157.

Premarital Pregnancy

Nearly one in four 15 year olds and about one in two 19 year olds in this country are sexually active, *i.e.*, they engage in sexual intercourse. Over the past two decades, there has been a dramatic increase in premarital sexual activity among teen-agers.[6] Many are sexually active earlier and with a much greater frequency than before. As a result, there has been a corresponding increase in the number of premarital pregnancies. In 1976, for example, 780,000 pregnancies occurred premaritally to teen-age women aged 15–19 years old.[5] About one in every ten white girls between the ages of 15 and 19 has had a pregnancy. Over half of these pregnancies end in abortion. The increased incidence of teenage pregnancies is recognized as a serious social issue.

Numerous medical problems are associated with teen-age pregnancy, including higher risks of infant mortality, prematurity, and congenital neurological impairments, such as blindness, deafness, and mental retardation.[2] Psychological difficulties also abound. For adolescent parents, the pregnancy interrupts or terminates education; the result is often reduced earning power and dependency on the social welfare system. Teen-age parents encounter additional stresses of ill-considered marriages and increased likelihood of marital problems and divorce.[3] There is also a strong likelihood of more babies before the young woman turns 20.

Reasons Why. A recent survey of adolescents which investigated their sexual attitudes and behaviors revealed that 81 percent of the respondents felt that rebellion is a significant cause of adolescent sexual behavior, and 87 percent said that sex education during childhood and adolescence helps to avoid sexual and other problems.[4]

Among the other reasons for increased sexual activity and unwanted pregnancies among teen-agers are: a craving for love and tenderness, the wish to become an adult, and the pursuit of physical pleasure.

How To Prevent. There are two major approaches to preventing premarital pregnancies in teen-agers: (1) teaching abstinence, or (2) teaching the effective use of contraceptives.

Teaching abstinence. The only birth control method that is 100 percent effective is complete abstinence from intercourse. If after carefully considering all the factors, including moral, religious, psychological, and social factors, you feel this is the best course for your children, you should clearly express your position and the reasons which underlie it. Your main concern should be the quality of your children's lives and their relationships with others rather than what other people may think. Remember that surveys by the

Planned Parenthood Association show that one-half of all 19-year-old teen-agers today still elect not to engage in sexual intercourse. So have honest and open discussions with your child in which you state your values and beliefs about teen-age sex. Discuss questions as "How can I say, 'No' and still be liked?" "What will my friends think of me if I stay a virgin?"

Explain that a lasting and meaningful relationship with a member of the opposite sex can be maintained without full sexual commitment until marriage.

Point out that we form the deepest human relationships when sex and love are combined. The pursuit of pleasure alone can lead to sexual promiscuity. The sexually promiscuous male ("Don Juan" syndrome) often complains that he is unable to form a lasting or meaningful relationship with a female. Similarly, sexually promiscuous females state that they enjoy sexual encounters but only so long as they are brief and with relative strangers. In general, sexually promiscuous persons tend to see others primarily as objects to be used for their own satisfaction.

What kind of parents tend to have teen-agers who abstain from premarital intercourse? Studies show virgin female high school students were likely to have mothers who were affectionate, held traditional values, and applied firm discipline. Nonvirgin females typically came from homes where values were obscure, conflicting, and poorly communicated. Thus, clear and consistent values are important to apply to the young in regard to premarital sex. Don't be permissive and encourage your children to do their own "thing" and then expect them to avoid premarital pregnancies.

Discourage early dating. If premarital abstinence makes sense to you, you will probably want to prohibit early dating by your children. Some parents take a lot of pressure off their young children by stating, "No dating until you are 16." Certainly you will want to discourage heterosexual involvement by your preadolescent children. They are not ready for it physiologically or psychologically. Dating in grade school and playing kissing games at parties tend to both confuse and embarrass preadolescents. So even if you think it is cute, don't keep asking your young children if they have a boyfriend or girlfriend. This will only make them think they should be involved with the opposite sex before they are ready.

Remember that the more sexual experiences one has, the more liberal one's sexual attitudes tend to be. Also noteworthy is the finding that youngsters of both sexes who start dating and kissing at an early age are more likely to have early sexual intercourse.[7]

Identify other sexual outlets: Setting realistic curfews for your teen-agers and requiring information as to whom they are with and where they will be also serve to decrease the chances your teen-agers will encounter situations they cannot handle.

Dr. Eleanor Hamilton, author of *Sex With Love*, favors abstinence for teen-agers because she feels they do not have mature enough judgments to have intercourse nor the experiences to enjoy it fully. However, she believes that parents should teach children in late adolescence that there are alternative ways to derive sexual pleasure such as personal masturbation and petting to orgasm. Children mature sexually at the average age of 12, yet the average age of marriage is 22. So during this decade teen-agers must be taught responsible and acceptable ways to release sexual tension. Too often, Dr. Hamilton observes, parents seem to their teen-agers to be against all sources of sexual pleasure.

So you might want to seek the middle ground between a blanket prohibition against sex as in the Victorian days and a completely permissive approach to sex which offers the teen-ager no guidance at all. The latter seems too difficult for teen-agers to handle since they are still half adult and half child.

Teach effective use of contraceptives. Studies show that eight in ten of those teen-agers who have an unwanted pregnancy are not in fact using any contraceptive method when the pregnancy occurs.[5] It is clear that if a sexually active young woman uses a contraceptive regularly, she runs a relatively low risk of becoming pregnant (11 percent), and if she uses a medical method of contraception regularly, she runs an even lower risk (6 percent). It is also the case that a sexually active young woman who never uses a method is exceedingly likely (58 percent) to become pregnant.

If you feel that contraceptive use is the best way for your teen-ager to avoid pregnancy, you need to be sure your child has accurate information about human sexuality, reproduction, and birth control methods. Your child will need early and on-going instruction about pregnancy prevention methods. Ask your child to summarize the presented material to be sure the information is received. Try to dispel the common myths adolescents have about pregnancy ("It can't happen to me," "I can't get pregnant during my period"). It is important that teen-agers understand the very real risk of unprotected intercourse. Adolescents also need to know how to anticipate when intercourse is likely to happen and how to obtain contraceptives without embarrassment. Effective contraception also entails the ability to talk to your partner about it and the realization that the contraceptive method must be used *every time* intercourse occurs.

If you find it very difficult to talk to your child about sex and contraceptives, you might send your child to a teen clinic of the Planned Parenthood Association, wherein the teen-ager will receive accurate information about contraceptive methods and risks.

Parental love. A third approach to preventing premarital pregnancies in teen-agers is to make sure your teen-agers feel loved and wanted so that they will not seek a baby of their own in order to experience love. Some psychological studies of teen-age pregnancies have found that the felt lack of parental love is a factor in a number of cases. Feeling alienated from their parents, adolescents are more likely to seek sexual intimacy with their peers as a compensatory measure. So endeavor to keep the lines of communication open and do frequently express your love and affection for your teen-ager. Remember that most adolescents find it absolutely necessary to have someone in whom they can confide and tell their most pressing problems. Studies have shown that teen-agers who felt that their parents very rarely found time to do things with them during childhood were most favorable toward premarital sex.[8]

Church attendance. Kinsey and his associates found in the early 1950's that low church attendance was a good predictor of premarital sexual activity. In general this relationship was higher for females than for males. A further study in 1967 confirmed that for whites, low church attendance was associated with greater sexual permissiveness. This is probably the result of religious beliefs, which preclude sex before marriage.

What To Do. Apart from ensuring the teen-ager of continuing love and support, parents can help their unmarried child who is pregnant by discussing all the available alternative courses of action (abortion, adoption, marriage, raising child on her own), and the implications of each. In discussing the possibility of an abortion, for example, parents should point out that more than one abortion during adolescence produces a far greater risk of premature delivery or of miscarriage later on.

The decision should take place within the context of feelings, values, and attitudes, not only of the adolescent, but of her partner, her family, her peers, and within the context of the community and the alternatives offered by the community.[1]

Pregnancy is a crisis in the adolescent's life. As with all crises, it offers the opportunity for growth. Parental guidance should promote the developmental growth of the teen-agers involved, including an increased sense of autonomy, responsibility, and identity.

Books For Parents About Adolescent Sexuality

Welsh, M.M.: *Parent, Child And Sex.* George A. Pflaum Publisher (1970).

How To Talk To Your Teenagers About Something That's Not Easy To Talk About. Pamphlet by Planned Parenthood of America, New York, NY 10019 (1976).

Books For Teen-agers About Premarital Sex

Bohanna, P.: *Love, Sex And Being Human.* Doubleday, New York (1969).

Contraception: Comparing The Options. U.S. Dept. Of H.E.W. Public Health Service Pamphlet. Food and Drug Administration, Office of Public Affairs, 5600 Fishers Lane, Rockville, MD 20857. H.E.W. Publication No. (F.D.A.) 78-3069 (1978).

The Hassles Of Becoming A Teenage Parent. U.S. Dept. of H.E.W. Publications No. H.S.A. 75-16013, U.S. Government Printing Office, Washington, D.C. 20402.

Laing, F.: *The Bride Wore Braids*. Four Winds Press (1968). Ages 12 and up.

The characters and events in this story realistically portray a teen-age couple coping with marriage. It shows that poor jobs, parental disapproval, and unpleasant living conditions can put almost overwhelming stress on the emotional climate of a marriage.

Madison, W.: *Growing Up In A Hurry*. Little, Brown & Co. (1973). Ages 12 and up.

Feeling unloved by her parents, 16-year-old Karen finds a boyfriend who fills her need for love and approval. When her boyfriend abandons her because she is pregnant, Karen has to cope with the difficult task of having an abortion.

Shirbune, Z.: *Too Bad About The Haines Girl*. William Morrow & Co. (1967). Ages 12 and up.

Seventeen-year-old Melinda wishes her pregnancy were only a dream. She feels confused, worried, and ashamed that she has betrayed her parents' trust. She, her boyfriend, and her parents agonize over her choices now.

Teensex? It's Okay To Say No Way. Planned Parenthood Federation, 810 Seventh Avenue, New York, NY 10019.

Supports the decision of millions of teens who have chosen not to be sexually active. Effectively dispels the myth that "everybody's doing it."

References

1. Hertz, D.G.: "Psychological implications of adolescent pregnancy: Patterns of family interaction in adolescent mothers-to-be." *Psychosomatics* 18: (1977), pp. 13–16.
2. Hunt, W.: "Adolescent fertility: Risks and consequences." *Population Report Series Journal* 70: (1976), pp. 157–175.
3. Lorenzi, *et.al.*: "School-age parents: How permanent a relationship?" *Adolescence* 12: (1976), pp. 13–22.
4. *Behavior Today:* (January 8, 1979).
5. Zelnik, M. and Kantner, J.F.: "Sexual and contraceptive experience of young unmarried women in the United States, 1976 and 1971." *Family Planning Perspectives* 9: (1977), p. 55.

6. Miller, P.Y. *et al.:* "Adolescent sexual behavior: Context and change." *Social Problems* 22: (1974), pp. 58–76.
7. Rutter, M.: "Normal psychosexual development." *Journal of Child Psychology and Psychiatry* 11: (1971), pp. 259–283.
8. Streit, F.: *Parents and Problems: The Sexual Adolescent.* Essence Publications, Highland Park, NJ (1979).

UNMOTIVATED IN SCHOOL

A motive is something that causes a person to act. It is an inner state that causes and guides behavior. Any activity is initiated and continued because of some motivation. Children are motivated to *attain rewards* and *avoid punishments.* An incentive is a concrete or symbolic reward. Children are at first dependent upon parents for affection and other rewards. They seek attention and praise for their accomplishments. Then, self-evaluation (independence) is used to assess the successful completion of tasks. Children judge their performance according to some standard or expectation of others, and feel successful or not successful. Older children respond to reason. Education can be seen as important because it's fun to know things, it helps you deal with the world, it's necessary to obtain a good job, etc. A general motive is to *please* parents and teachers. Action follows a motivated belief. "I want to please my parents. I enjoy doing well in school. Therefore, I'll work hard." Another general motive for learning is to gain mastery and competence in dealing with environmental demands.

Following *wanting* to learn is the feeling of being able to learn. It is the expectancy that an outcome (learning) will follow an act (reading, listening, etc.). A self-fulfilling prophecy exists when children do not believe that effort results in success. If they feel that their effort is likely to attain good results, then they feel responsible (called internal locus of control). A child's tendency to be curious, explore, and manipulate can be enhanced.

Children are often eager to learn and achieve. This desire to do things well has been called "achievement motivation."[1] Individuals with high achievement needs believe that success is due to hard work and that failure results from a lack of work. Highly motivated people set goals that are high-enough—challenging but reachable. They experience satisfaction in meeting short-term goals. Additionally, wanting to succeed often leads to more persistence than wanting to avoid failure. Lack of motivation leads to "underachievement." Children are not motivated and therefore do not work up to their potential. Estimates of underachievement range from 15 to 40 percent of all children.[2] More boys than girls are underachievers. A significant period is when children are approximately 6 years old. They begin to engage in competition with others and can become discouraged and lose motivation at this point. Underachievement in school begins early and often gets worse if no effective intervention takes place. By high school, many underachieving teenagers are irresponsible and break appointments, cut classes, and turn in papers late or not at all. Their feelings of frustration or conflict do not lead to a positive arousal to solve problems, but to a lack of motivation to address problems.

Many children see no personal meaning in an academically oriented curriculum. Children from disadvantaged backgrounds are especially prone to be unmotivated in school. Many children are not motivated because their needs or special interests are not met in school. Teachers describe unmotivated children as not being interested in things or relationships, easily discouraged, having nothing that holds their interest for long, and generally unenthusiastic in situations that greatly interest their peers.

Reasons Why

Reaction to Parental Behavior

Expectations too high or perfectionistic. When parents expect too much, children often develop a fear of failure and low motivation. Research[3] has shown that children can develop a lack of motivation to learn reading skills as a result of high maternal pressure to achieve. This is especially true when parents use rigid, authoritarian, and overly controlling approaches. Typically, children may get even with parents as a form of revenge and punishment for parents perceived as being unfair. When parents expect perfection, a frequent reaction is for children to give up. Since they cannot consistently be good enough to please their parents, they stop trying or give minimal effort. These children feel like failures and that everything they do is wrong. Overt perfectionism is easy to spot, but subtle messages can be just as destructive. Parents may communicate disappointment that their child is not one of the best in the class. Children are very sensitive to the nonverbal cues that come from adults.

Expectations too low. Parents may seriously underestimate their children and communicate very low aspirations. Children literally learn that little is expected of them and they respond accordingly. There is no encouragement to prepare, work hard, or do well on examinations because the parents believe that the child is not capable. Often, infantile behavior is accepted and subtly encouraged. Children are expected to be subordinate and dependent! Independence and self-reliance are not fostered. Siblings and peers may also expect too little of a particular child (because of size, appearance, or behavior).

Disinterested. Parents may become so absorbed in their affairs and problems that they express no interest in their child's schoolwork. It is as if learning is of no concern. From an early age, parents may not foster good verbal fluency. There is minimum communication and no real give and take with their children. When infants are responded to (held, talked to, played with), they become more motivated and confident in their ability to influence their environment. Some parents may be interested in achievement, but not in the process that leads to achievement. This form of disinterest can be just as detrimental. Underachievers (as compared to achievers or overachievers) do not want to please their parents who are disinterested and not proud of good school performance.

Permissive. Parents who are permissive do not set limits nor expect compliance. Children are allowed to go it alone. Discipline is not a part of daily life. Some parents believe that permissiveness will result in an independent and motivated child. Instead, permissiveness often leads to insecure children with little motivation to achieve. They have not learned a disciplined approach to everyday or school tasks. They not only do not comply to the demands of others, but they have not learned to set goals and comply with the demands involved. Self-discipline does not develop properly. These parents have often been brought up in a laissez-faire atmosphere (in school or at home) themselves. There is a deliberate attempt to not direct or interfere with children's freedom. A frequent result is that children do not learn how to work hard or act effectively under stress.

Serious family or marital conflicts. Family problems can preoccupy children and leave little desire to succeed in school. How can school be important when they perceive continuous serious threats to their security? Frequent heated arguments or a high degree of tension may lead to a depressed child who cannot mobilize any interest in schoolwork. There also may be little motivation to please parents who are continuous sources of tension to the child. Parental alcoholism can have the same effect. Some children may be able to become absorbed in school as a means of forgetting family problems. However, most feel insecure and lose the desire to achieve. Some are particularly vulnerable to escapism types of behavior such as daydreaming, drugs, or delinquency. At times, school problems may be focused upon rather than parents facing family conflicts. Improved schoolwork might lead to a family crisis.

Rejection or frequent criticism. Rejected children can feel helpless, inadequate, or furious. Doing poorly in school and not caring are frequent means of getting even with rejecting parents. Intense and/or frequent criticism may cause a similar reaction. Criticized children often feel rejected even when parents honestly believe that they are quite accepting of their children.

Overprotective. Many parents overprotect their children for a variety of reasons. Most typical are fears for children's safety and wanting their offspring to have it better than they did. Some parents feel guilty because they didn't really want children or feel great rage because their children are ruining their lives or are great disappointments. Parents who feel guilty are frequently overprotective. These children do not learn to be self-motivated, to set tasks, nor to work under even minimal stress. They often remain immature and unmotivated in school.

Low Self-Esteem. Low self-esteem results in very little academic motivation. Low self-regard can be caused by a variety of factors, including the parental behavior listed above. It is important to understand that feeling worthless is a major factor in lack of motivation. These children often see themselves as helpless pawns who cannot really influence the environment or achieve success. They may appear to want to fail, almost as if failure confirms their poor self-image. Frequently, they can't express anger, feeling too worthless to be able to assert themselves in any way. Anger may be turned inward, and they blame themselves for all difficulties. They feel that they deserve to fail and lack any motivation to successfully complete tasks. The end result of a poor self-concept is to feel an "I can't" attitude. These children often think of themselves as nonlearners and underestimate their abilities. Disadvantaged children frequently think little of themselves and have very low academic or vocational aspirations. Their goals are immediate and self-centered, and symbolic rewards have little value.

Children with low self-esteem are most frequently nonassertive. They might be aggressive and belligerent, but when analyzed, their behavior is not assertive in the sense of their truly accomplishing what they would like. Underneath, they are often quite fearful, particularly about failing or being exposed as worthless. It's safer not to try. Any type of evaluation is avoided by isolating themselves. Instead of seeking success, they are motivated to avoid failure. They come across as relatively defensive and helpless. At times, children who are angry and feel worthless behave like compliant, "good" children who are passive and unmotivated. Parents often do not understand that these children handle aggressive feelings by being overly good, and pay the price of being stultified and unmotivated. An interesting sex difference is that boys often blame the teachers for their problems while girls often blame themselves. The result is a girl who accepts herself as a nonlearner and a boy who blames others while accepting no personal responsibility.

At times a conflict of values can lead to poor self-esteem. A child might be artistic, creative, idiosyncratic, or easygoing, whereas the parents are neat, conservative, perfectionistic, and mainly interested in academic grades. Instead of feeling good regarding uniqueness, the child may feel guilty and worthless. In a conflict of values, children often blame themselves for not measuring up to parental expectations. Children who do not feel satisfaction at home often seek peer approval. Unfortunately, they may associate with other angry, rebellious, and academically unmotivated students. Peer support reinforces the intellectually inferior feeling, and gratification may be sought through socially undesirable activities.

Poor School Environment. Parents must be aware that the learning atmosphere in a school system and in a particular class can lead to a large number of unmotivated children. The tone is set by the combination of administration and teaching staff. When staff morale is good, the "feel" of a school is one of excitement and optimism about learning and relating to others. Early grades are most important since achievement striving is relatively stable. Children develop an interest in learning, a tolerance for competition, and do not anticipate failure. Parents have been very effective in positively influencing educational systems through parent-teacher associations. Active, interested parents can apply positive pressure and help in making education more exciting and relevant to children. Administration is often responsive to a vocal group of parents who want to aid and who will not tolerate educational practices that turn children off. Parents can speak to classes about their own areas of expertise and interest or have children visit their places of employment. There is no substitute for the *demonstration* of parental interest and excitement about the educational process.

Teachers who "go through the motions" must be influenced or terminated from employment. This is a very sensitive area since tenure means that teachers remain employed unless gross incompetence or mistreatment can be documented. Parents are justifiably concerned that teachers should maximally motivate children and then help them learn to the fullest extent possible. It takes well-trained and *enthusiastic* teachers to accomplish these goals.

Developmental Problems. Children who develop at a slower rate than their peers, by definition, are less motivated. That is, their view of themselves as learners may be 2 or 3 years below expectations. They act and view themselves as less capable, even though intellectually they may be average or above average. These children are often described as physically, psychologically, and socially immature. They lag behind others and are often "late bloomers." In a sense, their lack of motivation may be seen as appropriate motivation for a much younger child.

Children with constitutionally-based learning disabilities

must be identified. These children very frequently have a general motivational deficit based upon an inefficiently functioning central nervous system. They lack persistence, frustrate easily, and lose interest quickly. They process information more slowly and inefficiently than their peers and become more and more discouraged. The consequences of their efforts often do not please themselves or others. Therefore, there is a deadly combination of inefficient learning and psychological discouragement. The result is an unmotivated learner.

How to Prevent

Be Accepting and Encouraging. The key is always to encourage the "I can" feeling. From the earliest age, children should be encouraged to try, do the best they can, and be able to tolerate frustration. This is the origin of the self-concept as a motivated learner. Parental "acceptance" is demonstrated by trust, mutual respect, and really listening to children. You should encourage and support children's attempts to understand. Teasing and sarcasm are to be avoided! Some parents make the mistake of linking self-worth with achievement. Actual achievement should certainly be encouraged, but tolerance for frustration comes with still feeling good about yourself even if you don't succeed. You can ask for help or temporarily lower your goals. The child who cannot do various tasks must still be, and feel, accepted by the parents.

Toddlers' exploratory behavior should be encouraged and stimulated within a supportive context. It is essential to encourage verbal (vs. nonverbal) communication. As toddlers learn to use language to express themselves, parents must be encouraging and patient. Criticism at this stage may very well squelch the motivation to communicate effectively. The same reasoning applies to language development throughout childhood. The basis for lifelong motivation to learn stems from adult acceptance of the child's attempts to cope with the environment.

Set Realistic Goals. It is extremely difficult to "accept" children if they continue to fail to reach goals. Adults (and the children themselves) begin to see the individual as a failure who rarely accomplishes tasks. The relatively immature (or learning-disabled) child does not accomplish in the same manner as more mature peers. The groundwork for lack of motivation is then set. In these cases, adult expectations may have to be dramatically changed. Great success has resulted when immature children have begun school later than usual. Much difficulty is typical when the immature just-6 year old tries to learn at the same rate as more mature children who are almost 7. Our society has often placed a value on speedy progress at all cost. Therefore, there is often much pressure felt by parents to have their child in the same grade as his agemates. This is related to the often discussed concept of "readiness," which is the art of not expecting too much or too little. The job of adults is to be sensitive to the readiness of children to benefit from new experiences. When the demands are within the child's abilities, limits can be set and adhered to. There can then be a realistic expectation for children to apply themselves and achieve. When children are not able to begin or progress at the same rate as others, more realistic goals can result in happier, more motivated children.

At approximately the age of 5 years, children can begin to understand short- and long-term goals. This is the origin of short- and long-term motivation. Children know the satisfaction of immediate accomplishment. They must learn to work toward longer-term goals. Young children see tomorrow as the far distant future and are unwilling to work for a reward that will happen tomorrow. This "delay of gratification" can be taught and encouraged. "Let's work on this model a little at a time so we'll be finished in a few days." The child can then see the progress and celebrate the final completion. In school, high achievers prefer to delay immediate gratification in order to achieve a later, larger reward. Poor achievers have not learned to do this. There should be a natural growth of aspiration level along with physical growth. The key is for adults to help children set realistic goals and assist them in overcoming obstacles toward those goals. Adults are then seen as sources of support and encouragement, rather than as criticizers.

Teach and Model Active Learning and Problem Solving. You can show children how curiosity can be satisfied. Your own curiosity can be verbalized, and you can share with children the discovery of why and how things work. This is the active approach to learning, where questions are posed and answers sought. Facts are assembled, organized, classified, and summarized. Discussion, at a simple level, should take place focused upon the meaning and application of knowledge. Some bright children have no idea of how their home is heated. This important, necessary-to-life function can be explained and shown in an exciting and informative manner. Parents often underestimate their teaching ability, and its beneficial effects. You can explain the parts of a heating system by answering the following questions: Where does heat come from? How does heat get to different parts of the house? Why is one room colder than others? If you don't know information, you can look it up in a book that explains how things work.[4] Children can read along or be read to, thereby participating in a practical learning process. Excitement about learning and discovery is catching!

From an early age, children can be taught to attend to the environment. They can be shown how to focus their attention, stick to a task, and complete what they start. The value of learning should be taught. Children then develop the desire to learn because they believe in and see the benefits. You can demonstrate for children by describing the learning process. You learned what you know by study, experience, and application of skills. You can then help children imagine how mastery will aid them in achieving their own goals. They can picture the image of their taking music lessons and practicing leading them to be able to play well and be admired by others for having that skill.

Reward Interest in Learning and Actual Academic Achievements. Adults praise and reward behavior whether subtly or openly. The value of education and fulfilling one's potential can be continuously positively reinforced. Recent research[5] clearly highlights that both success in academic tasks and positive personality characteristics are directly related to the concern for and reward of achievement provided by the home. A positive self-concept and feelings of effectiveness come from a series of competent achievements. This results from parents appropriately rewarding actual academic achievement in school. This clearly depends upon factual and clear feedback from teachers to parents.

Self-responsibility for achievement can be modeled by parents and positively rewarded. Underachievers often lack the feeling of personal responsibility. Excuses should not be accepted, but punishment is not necessary. Children can be assisted in becoming more responsible and should be shown how goals can be met. The progressive assumption of more responsibility should be met with effective rewards. The adults' task is to discover what types of rewards are effective for their children. Some children are very responsive to praise, while others require tangible rewards before learning becomes gratifying in itself. However, for many people earning rewards by achievement is an acceptable lifelong process. Adults earn money by working, and many families use material rewards (toys, stereophonic equipment, bicycles, etc.) to continuously reinforce academic accomplishments.

What to Do

Use Powerful Incentive System. For unmotivated students parental rewards for classroom performance are very powerful. Even parent and teacher attention, if used properly and purposefully, can become a strong motivator. Cards may be signed by teachers and brought home. Depending upon satisfactory work, a variety of rewards can be forthcoming. Effective rewards may be verbal praise, allowance, holding or attending parties, use of television, ham radio, or family car, extra playtime, or special trips. Not used nearly enough are rewards for reducing negative behaviors that interfere with learning. Rewards may be earned when teachers report less daydreaming, disruptions, talking, teasing, etc. Extra points or credits should be earned for extra work, completing assignments ahead of time, or showing enthusiasm and participation in class. Rewards can also be given for longer study time at home and for allowing fewer distractions to occur. The positive note (instead of the usual complaining one) from teacher to parent has been demonstrated to be very effective for academic achievement and better school behavior.[6]

Point systems should be flexible and permit the earning of meaningful rewards. These systems are most effective when school and home work together. However, they can be effective in either place alone. Good reward systems can be very effective with adolescents. When standards are set and made clear, adolescents can become motivated to earn rewards and privileges. The key ingredients are specificity and accountability. For example, the adolescent could bring a card home every day specifying appropriate materials brought, completed assigned work, and a daily grade. Satisfactory reports could lead to positive rewards preselected by the students. They are therefore held carefully accountable for their daily performance. Daily measures and feedback increases both learning and motivation.

Use of rewards have improved academic performance believed to be at the maximum.[7] Thirty fourth graders who were given one token for each correct answer improved their scores on the typically-employed standardized tests. The earned tokens were used to purchase selected toys and privileges.

Teach Effective Motivating Strategies. In contrast to the above adult administered rewards, children may be taught various self-control methods. After completing a considerable amount of homework, children can engage in self-rewards such as having a snack, watching television, or taking a walk. An excellent advantage is that self-reward increases both performance and self-concept. The child feels more adequate and independent. The student is given more responsibility. For example, the teacher and student can make a contract[8] for work to be done in a certain amount of time. The teacher thereby aids in setting objectives, knowing students' strengths and weaknesses, and discussing a realistic contract. The student is responsible to do the work, while the teacher offers good study methods and evaluates the results. This procedure was effective in motivating students both in elementary and secondary schools. Parents can effectively use the same approach at home.

The key here is to assist children in helping themselves attain goals. They can be told that by not allowing interruptions or distractions, they can concentrate better. If they become anxious about their ability to study and learn, parents can help by teaching children how to relax their muscles and calm down by thinking about pleasant images. If they have trouble concentrating, they can be taught "stimulus control." The desk should only be used for study and for nothing else. Letter writing, reading for pleasure, daydreaming, etc., should be done elsewhere. On-task concentration can also be aided by asking oneself questions and saying helpful comments to oneself such as, "Keep going, it'll come," "Don't give up," and "Get back to the point."

Kitchen timers can be used to record length of study times. If children become sleepy while studying, they can be shown how to take breaks, use a brighter bulb, and rest before studying. Parents can then be seen as people who can offer practical assistance.

A direct way of promoting "achievement motivation" is to change the way people think about themselves and the environment.[1] Performance can be changed by modifying the fantasies and images of the individual. Much research has gone into helping people become more motivated to solve problems and find new ways of doing tasks. This research concluded that four steps are necessary: (1) accomplishment feedback-rewards for each step; (2) discover and find out about models who are achievers; (3) change self-image to one of success and responsibility; (4) stop negative thinking and have encouraging, positive fantasies about your accomplishments.

Influence the School to be More Motivating. Parents should do everything possible to make education a more stimulating and rewarding experience. This can range from supporting school budgets, which provide for adequate teacher salaries, in-service training, and excellent curriculum materials, to becoming a member of the board of education. For most parents, joining the parent-teacher association is a practical and potentially meaningful step. Parent groups can strive to make the school environment more motivating. They can influence and modify the curriculum to be more relevant and exciting. They can encourage and raise funds for speakers, special programs, and educational trips. Just as children need motivating at times, so do educational systems. Parents who feel ineffective and pessimistic about influencing schools are negative models for their children. Parents who take an active interest and accomplish changes are living examples of positive motivation.

Reassess and Possibly Change Expectations. If you discover, upon analyzing the situation, that your goals for your children are unrealistic, the goals should be modified. As simple as this sounds, it could lead to a dramatic reduction in anger and disappointment and a corresponding increase in positive feelings. This is especially true if school problems are more than purely motivational. Children may be poorly motivated *and* have a variety of subtle learning difficulties. Hiring a tutor could be one way of enhancing any motivational system. A tutor can not only teach subject matter, but also aid the child in feeling more confident as a learner. Competent high school students are able to both tutor and serve as a positive model for unmotivated children.

For younger children, parental empathy and sensitivity is extremely important. Without meaning to, parents of young children often communicate a lack of respect for children's autonomy. Empathy and a certain kind of permissiveness can be learned and displayed by parents.[9] Children's feelings can be reflected and verbalized by parents. Intellectual performance and motivation is increased when children experience being understood, not being criticized, and having freedom of choice at home. Parents can change their expectations of children and see things more from their children's point of view.

Case Report

A 14-year-old boy who had done relatively well in elementary school became extremely unmotivated after 1 month of high school. The parents and boy could not account for the change except for a vague feeling he had that high school was more stressful. One consultation with the parents sufficed to change the situation. Strategies of self-control were reviewed with them. This was done, rather than psychotherapy with the boy, in order to maximize the boy's view of his parents as helpful. Stimulus control and self-reward were successfully used. He followed the parents' suggestion of studying only at his desk and engaging in no other behaviors there. After intervals of study, he rewarded himself with pleasurable activities. The parents also used additional allowance and special monthly events based upon increased performance in school. They met with the teacher who was happy to send daily and weekly reports home.

Books for Parents about Lack of Motivation

Atkinson, J.W. and Raynor, J.O.: *Motivation and Achievement.* Winston, Washington, D.C. (1974).

Chess, Stella: *How to Help Your Child Get the Most out of School*. Doubleday, New York (1975).

Felton, Gary S. and Biggs, Barbara E.: *Up From Under-Achievement*. Charles C. Thomas, Springfield, IL (1977).

Martin, Reed and Lauridsen, David: *Developing Student Discipline and Motivation*. Research Press, Champaign, IL (1974).

Smith, Charles P. (ed.): *Achievement-Related Motives in Children*. Russell Sage Foundation, New York (1969).

Volks, Virginia: *On Becoming an Educated Person*. Saunders, Philadelphia (1970).

Books for Children About Lack of Motivation

Eyerly, Jeannette Hyde: *Drop-Out*. Lippincott, Philadelphia (1963). Ages 13 and up.

A teen-age boy lacks interest in school and is mainly involved with cars. He and his girlfriend marry and drop out of school. Clearly presented is the difficulty in finding suitable jobs. They realize the negative aspects of lack of interest in, and not completing, school.

Scarry, Richard: *What Do People Do All Day?* Random House, New York (1968). Ages 3 to 8.

This is a stimulating and humorous book about the everyday activities of people. The illustrations are vivid and hold the interest of preschoolers. This book could serve both as a preventive and as a stimulator for lack of motivation. It could interest young children in everyday activities and lead to their wanting to learn more about a particular occupation or profession.

Wrenn, C. Gilbert and Schwaryrock, Shirley: *Grades, What's So Important About Them, Anyway?* American Guidance Service, Circle Pines, MN (1970). Ages 13 and over.

Topics include the meaning of grades and how to communicate with teachers. Described are the interviews a high school senior has regarding a job in a bank. There is also some discussion of how to improve study skills. The importance of grades and evaluation are clearly and effectively depicted.

References

1. McClelland, D.C.: *Motivational Trends in Society*. General Learning Press, New York (1971).
2. Asbury, Charles A.: "Selected factors influencing over- and under-achievement in young school-age children." *Review of Educational Research* 44: (1974), pp.409–428.
3. Goldman, Margaret and Barclay, Allan: "Influence of maternal attitudes on children with reading disabilities." *Perceptual and Motor Skills* 38: (1974), pp. 303–307.
4. *The Ways Things Work: An Illustrated Encyclopedia of Technology*. Simon & Schuster, New York (Vol. 1, 1967; Vol. 2, 1971).
5. Kifer, Edward: "Relationship between academic achievement and personality characteristics." *American Educational Research Journal* 12: (1975), pp. 191–210.
6. Hawkins, Robert P. and Sluyter, David J.: "Modification of achievement by a simple technique involving parents and teachers." *Journal of Learning Disabilities* 5: (1972), pp. 20–28.
7. Ayllon, Teodoro and Kelly, Kathy: "Effects of reinforcement on standardized test performance." *Journal of Applied Behavior Analysis* 5: (1972), pp. 477–484.
8. Christen, William: "Contracting for student learning." *Educational Technology* 16: (1976), pp. 24–28.
9. Guerney, Bernard, Stover, Lillian, and Andronico, Michael P.: "On educating disadvantaged parents to motivate children for learning: A filial approach." *Community Mental Health Journal* 3: (1967), pp. 66–72.

POOR STUDY HABITS

In general terms, studying is the application of mental faculties to acquire knowledge. Material is carefully considered, examined, or analyzed. Typically, details are reviewed attentively, and material is read with the intention of learning and remembering. When this process is usually accomplished ineffectively or inefficiently, we say that a child has poor study habits. Throughout life, studying is done primarily outside the classroom. The most frequent form of studying is homework, where a student is given an assignment to complete. In many families, homework is one of the greatest sources of conflict. Homework could be considered as the equivalent of adult work. Children use their learned skills and work habits to complete various tasks. The key concept is to do the work *independently.* Good study skills should be taught throughout elementary school. However, ". . . the greatest need for improved study habits is at the high-school level, where students are expected to take substantial responsibility for their own academic performance and homework, but where both motivation to learn the material and knowledge of how to study efficiently may be lacking."[1]

A recent informative survey[2] revealed that 60 percent of 17 year olds in the U.S. do less than 5 hours of homework per week. Reportedly, 7 percent have homework but do none of it, and 6 percent say they have no homework. Only 6 percent did more than 10 hours per week. These figures are striking in view of the widespread belief in the importance of homework, especially for high school students. Additionally, high school study habits prepare the student for the rigors of college. Poor study habits are the major cause of failure and inefficient learning in college. The other interesting aspect of the survey concerns a mathematics test that was completed by the respondents. The students who spent the most time doing homework and the least time watching television did best on the mathematics test.

Poor study habits often lead to underachievement (see previous section entitled "Lack of Motivation" for another cause of underachievement). The underachiever's performance is below that predicted by some test of intelligence or aptitude. Two years below grade level is a widely accepted rule. Underachievers have low expectations, are easily distracted, and do not complete work or hand in assignments. Reading skills are typically poor. To study effectively, the child must have the skills, be able to vary the rate depending upon the type of material, comprehend, and make inferences. A helpful guideline is for the reader to use what is studied and learned to solve real problems.

Reasons Why

Not Know How to Study. Many children do not know how to study. They may never have learned the skills involved. Their poor study habits are a result of using whatever approaches they have naturally developed or picked up from a variety of sources. It is possible that study skills were never taught to them in school. If taught, the children may not have understood or have been motivated enough to apply the skills. Students may not know how to use the library or a dictionary or read a map, graph, or table. A very frequent comment heard in schools is that there are many effective methods of study, but the major problem is getting students to use them.

Studying or homework assignments are the student's responsibility. Parental overinvolvement can prevent children's development of *independent* study skills. Similarly, parents who tutor children may inadvertently discourage good study habits. Homework should be a matter between teacher and child. Parental overconcern or nagging may imply that children are not capable of working on their own. Also, nagging may result in the perception that being nagged is a necessary condition for studying.

Learning Problems. Any form of mental retardation is an obvious cause of study problems. Less obvious, but relatively frequent, is some form of learning disability. Estimates of the number of neurologically-based learning disorders have ranged from 5 to 20 percent of school age children. Many forms of serious reading problems (dyslexia) may go unrecognized. Any weakness in the process of reading (perception-organization and integration—comprehension—recall) is a direct cause of study problems where reading is required. Audio tapes of books have been extraordinarily useful for problem readers. Difficulties with specific subjects (math, spelling, science) may result from a specific learning disability which must be pinpointed by appropriate psychological and educational testing. Language deficits greatly impair study efficiency. Thinking and reasoning require the manipulation and integration of symbols (words). Any measurable weakness in this area is significant and must be evaluated.

Much less understood are the behavioral control problems that accompany learning disorders.[3] Children who can't sit still, focus, avoid distractions, express ideas, accept mistakes, or are impulsive cannot study efficiently. These behaviors are often mistakenly believed to be due to emotional difficulties, when they may be a result of neurologically-based self-control problems. The reason for poor study habits may therefore be related to an improperly functioning central nervous system. It is the brain that determines and controls both learning as such and self-control behaviors necessary for acquiring information.

Psychological Problems. Many psychological problems can lead to difficulties in studying. Tension caused by family or peer interaction can lead to difficulty in concentrating. Anxiety, sadness, and worries are also detrimental. Daydreaming or fatigue similarly interfere with efficiency. Fear of failure, dependency, feelings of inadequacy, and pessimism can lead to not wanting to try to study or to ineffective studying. Perfectionism can lead to procrastination or never completing parts of assignments. Poor homework and studying may be used as a weapon by children who want to worry, or get even with, their parents. Lack of motivation to study can come from many sources, including lethargy from medication or drug consumption. A useful overview is that some children have a wish to remain dependent, and poor study habits confirm that image. Fear of success and a wish to fail have the same effect. Some children have learned to be lazy and do not put out real effort. In order to study for long periods of time, children must have incorporated the idea of delay of gratification. They have to work hard now in order to obtain the long-term rewards of good grades, knowledge, or adult approval.

Cultural values have strong psychological impact on children. For example, if families do not value education and the study process, most children will incorporate those values. Some poor children have been "tracked" in classes where expectations are low and their potential underestimated. This is a self-fulfilling prophecy where the children do not study and perform as well as expected. Additionally, in working class families there is often less abstract reasoning, impoverished vocabulary, and a focus on objects and action. In middle class families, language is more complex and concerned with social relationships. The result is that school language and independent study expectations are not familiar to a large group of children. These children have been exposed to more absolutistic reasoning ("do it because I say so") instead of a problem solving approach. Therefore, the foundation for the study process is extremely weak for those children who grow up in families with certain cultural and psychological value systems.

How to Prevent

Provide the Most Favorable Study Conditions. Work is an adult responsibility, and homework and study are children's responsibilities. Adults should provide the best possible conditions for the children to study on their own. The setting should be as quiet and uncluttered as possible. A desk in a bedroom is ideal. A bright light should come from the direction opposite the writing side. Glare and shadows should be avoided. Interruptions and distractions should be minimized. Study times and schedules should be arranged (possibly during a family discussion). During study time, callers could be told that telephone calls are not permitted during study time. Some parents find it very helpful to have children spend time in the study area even if they have no homework. They can spend some time on school-related work or can read. This avoids reinforcing those children who do not bring work home. It also emphasizes the notion of working regularly so that tasks do not pile up. Reference books, magazines, and newspapers should be available and easily accessible.

Positive family discussions can lead to the discovery of the best study conditions for each child. Children's needs and priorities can be outlined. Best times for study may be clarified and changed depending upon season and other conditions. Some children work best during certain times of day, and the amount of study time depends upon attention span. Different ways of taking short breaks (exercise, rest, listen to music, etc.) can be specified. Family discussion might lead to options that could help some children. Reading can be aloud or to others. Sometimes, peer or sibling study groups can be arranged. It might emerge that brief professional tutoring can help one of the children overcome some learning obstacle.

For some children, favorable conditions might be rewards (and penalties) if necessary. Most parents understand the use of positive reinforcers such as watching television or staying up later as a treat for studying and being productive for a relatively long period of time. With teen-agers, the family car might be made available only if certain conditions (study time and productivity) have been met. Daily or weekly notes from the teacher may be invaluable as feedback for parents about their child's school study performance or adequacy of homework assignments.

Highly preferred activities can be arranged to follow non-preferred activities, thereby strengthening the frequency of the nonpreferred activity (studying). For example, playing basketball, Frisbee, or just having free time should take place *immediately after* studying. Inadvertently, children and teen-agers weaken the study habit by frequently studying only after fun activities.

Stress Mastery, Achievement, and Independence. From earliest childhood, a feeling of mastery should be promoted. Young children experience a sense of personal power by being able to influence their environment. Every opportunity can be used to enable the child to achieve even the simplest goal. Mobiles and textured toys are grasped and played with by the infant. This is a very early beginning of being able to touch objects and cause something to happen. The toddler should be given many opportunities to use self-discipline to attain a goal. Building a tower of four, then five, and then six blocks requires coordination, practice, and determination. Encouragement and praise by adults are the ingredients that aid the child to keep trying until success is reached. The focus is always on helping children feel that they can achieve things efficiently and by themselves.

By the teen years and throughout adult life, achievement motivation should operate. This is the degree to which an individual experiences the wish to set goals and engage in the behavior necessary to achieve them. Successful professionals, business people, artisans, etc., have high achievement motivation. The key ages are between 6 and 8 years: Training in mastery and independence at this age sets the stage for later productivity. The drive to achieve is one of the strongest influences on study habits and good general performance in school. A useful summary is that "nothing succeeds like success." Assuring successful achievement at an early age is an excellent preventative for later negative attitudes toward achievement. In our society, study is an essential ingredient for achievement. Tasks such as looking facts up, collecting information, arranging things in order, etc., can be satisfying to children. This leads them to feel like "winners" by being able to successfully prepare for and complete tasks.

Demonstrate a Positive Attitude Toward Learning and Study. The best situation is for parents to be proud of their own achievements and interested in their child's achievement. Therefore, parents should serve as models who prepare, organize, study, and are productive. Negative or critical comments to children are to be avoided. Statements such as "You can't study this simple stuff?" or "When will anything sink into your head?" are insulting. An understanding of children's feelings should be clearly communicated—"It looks like a lot of work" or "It can be discouraging to have so much to do." This then should be followed by a basically positive and optimistic attitude: "After you've studied, we'll review it together." The expectation is that children can study and learn to the best of their ability. Too much help is not appropriate, since it does not promote independence and may well reinforce a feeling of helplessness. When help is requested, assistance is given in the form of guidelines and how to overcome obstacles. Children should not be nagged or reminded to do homework.

From an early age, learning and discovering new things can be encouraged. Educational toys, children's periodical magazines, and books should be available. Spontaneous interest in topics should always be fostered. If children express an interest in stars and planets, they could be taken to a museum to see a show on astronomy. The family can go to a library, skim through books on astronomy, take some out, and discuss the information at home. This is a direct way of demonstrating the excitement of study to discover answers to interesting questions. Similarly, adult enthusiasm over reading and knowledge should be openly displayed. Young children can observe how study and learning are necessary and a natural way of life. Children should watch the steps of adults reading assembly instructions, putting objects together, and then reading the operating instructions aloud. Mathematics is used to figure out cost of items, distance to some location, etc. Invaluable is the lesson observed when an adult says, "I don't know the answer" or "I wonder how this works" and then looks the answer up in a book.

You should read aloud to toddlers. Picture books should be plentiful and available. When children learn to read, they ought to read aloud to the family. Reading answers questions, and children can choose their own books from a library. Discussion of books and current events should be a family custom. The key is to stimulate children's curiosity and expose them to many different things and ideas. Their interests should be encouraged. Art materials could be given as presents and productions proudly displayed. Much effort and good work could be rewarded with special events. Similarly, progress in school may be kept on a chart at home and good schoolwork displayed on a bulletin board.

What to Do

Provide Better Study Methods and Conditions. If children or teen-agers are at all motivated to do better, you can help them by showing them more effective *self-control.* They should monitor their work by recording when and the amount of time actually spent studying. A stop watch is invaluable. Self-observation often serves to sensitize individuals and help them to be more aware of their own behavior. Frequently, the process of recording by itself leads to improved use of time. A typical report is research[4] done in a history class. A girl observed and recorded her history study time. In 1 week she increased her study time by 50 percent. After she stopped recording, the study time continued at the improved level.

When necessary, change of habits can be constructively discussed, based upon the feedback obtained by self-observation. Various plans may be used. Tasks can be alternated so the work is less tiring and more interesting. Rest breaks should be planned. Resting, taking a walk, or listening to music for 10 minutes can prevent fatigue. A good strategy is to take breaks when a subtask is completed or after a specified number of pages. Also useful is only studying in one place under the correct conditions (called "stimulus control" or "cue regulation"). If daydreaming or any behavior incompatible with learning occurs, the individual is to leave the study area. *Only* efficient study takes place in the work area.

Pertinent questions should be asked, such as "Where do you start on this project?" If children draw a blank, it is helpful to figure out solutions together. Issues should be clarified and obstacles removed. Not helpful is "Do it yourself," "Leave me alone," or "Let me do it for you; it's easier that way." Tasks should be broken down into steps and the first step taken (like the proverb, "Every journey begins with a single step"). When a task is set, it should be completed. The trick is to set doable tasks, so children do not give up, jump around, and never finish anything. Impulsive children can be helped to be more reflective. You can suggest that they say, "Stop and think," to themselves. This form of self-instruction can be very useful in the process of verbalizing the problem and looking for solutions. Very poor writers might dictate or learn to type.

Homework time should be agreed upon and adhered to. Efforts should be praised and mistakes matter-of-factly pointed out. At times a "study-buddy" system with a good student may illustrate good study habits by a peer. Additionally, the peer may help keep the child on the right track. When arranged properly, the child might help remind his friend to write down assignments, keep track of due dates, etc. Study groups are very helpful to some children.

One most direct method is to show children *how* to study, rather than helping them with the content. A straightforward, effective, and researched method is called SQ3R (survey, question, read, review, recite).[5,6] The survey provides an overview, where headings and summaries are skimmed. The headings and topics are turned into questions, and the material is read to answer the questions. Key issues are reviewed and recited aloud. One-page chapter outlines are very useful. High school students[7] were taught a combination of SQ3R, self-monitoring, self-reward, and planning strategies. This combination was very effective in dramatically improving study skills. Planning involves breaking down tasks into small, manageable parts. Study time was scheduled and cramming avoided. When, where, and how much studying was structured. Self-rewards were given for successfully completing the planned tasks. Another study[1] with high school students used the SQ3R method combined with other approaches. Students became more aware of their own study habits. They learned the reasons for, and consequences of, studying and what to expect if their studying improved. Studying was only done in one place (stimulus control). Longer study time and longer goals were rewarded. Underlining and taking notes enhanced recall, and work was organized for the whole semester.

Parts of the SQ3R method should be used for listening to lectures and preparing for exams. In class, notes should be taken concerning key points and significant material. Verbatim notes are not useful. Notes should be revised, reorganized, and clarified on the same day. Exam questions should be predicted and practiced for. Important concepts should be reviewed and recited. Performance expected on tests should be *rehearsed*. While rehearsing, relaxation should be practiced to combat test anxiety.

Make Study and Homework More Rewarding. Most children complain about the amount or difficulty of their homework. These complaints should be listened to, acknowledged, but not argued about. Rather than criticism, complaints should be met with serious concern and positive expectations—"I see it really looks difficult to you. You'll get it by using your head." Ranting and raving by parent or child doesn't help but instead usually leads to less work. Continued pressure doesn't lead to independent study habits. You should tell children that it is their responsibility to study and that if they don't, they will fail. Often, children will begin to study effectively when you stick to your resolve of noninterference. Planning help is provided only if requested. For example, some children may work better in the morning and do a half-hour or hour of homework after an early breakfast. Progress and meeting of deadlines are to be praised! With many children a point reward system[8] is very effective. Good study habits and academic performance earn points which are exchanged for activities, goods, or privileges. Put simply, attending to the task of homework should result in some positive reinforcement. Children must clearly understand their assignment, have all necessary materials available, and be able to work in a conducive quiet atmosphere with no distractions.

Rewards or penalties must be *objectively* administered. Excuse making or any behavior interfering with study is never rewarded. Paying attention and sticking to the task for longer and longer periods are rewarded in gradual steps. With teen-agers, behavioral contracts are often good motivators. The signed contracts specify what rewarding events will follow the successful completion of specific studying and performance. For example, 1 month of satisfactory completion of homework assignments will lead to the receiving of three phonograph albums of the teen-ager's choice. Short- and long-term goals may be charted and progress recorded (30 pages read by 10/15, 90 pages read by 10/25, outline prepared by 11/1, and report finished by 11/15). With or without contracts, communication must be clear, not vague. Agreements are to be consistently followed through with no exceptions. It is helpful to write down what kind of study behavior is expected and what usually precedes or follows that behavior. This has been called parental *ABC's*, where the *A*ntecedents of *B*ehavior and its *C*onsequences are specified. By altering either antecedents or consequences, study behavior can be influenced. For example, snacks might be arranged to follow successful completion of 1 half-hour of homework. In the same vein, children may be taught *self-reinforcement*. They administer positive consequences for themselves after goals are accomplished. In some cases self-punishment has helped. When daydreams or other distracting behavior takes place, a rubberband around the wrist is snapped in a stinging fashion. Or teen-agers may deprive themselves of some pleasure if a sufficient amount of study is not accomplished on a given day.

A useful notion is that what children say to themselves may be more important than actual events. They can be helped to use positive self-talk which is more adaptive than pessimistic ideas. For example, "I'll do a little at a time and I'll make progress" is much better than thinking that "I have so much to do, it will never get done." Children can be shown that assignments might be exciting if they think creatively. For example, a report may be due concerning special events in a city. Asking "How can I make this more fun?" can lead children to be creative. They might draw a map to designate what will take place and where. They might visit the location or even watch construction and setting up for the event and describe the process.

Professional Methods. The most direct way of improving study habits is to hire a professional person to help your child develop effective skills and unlearn bad habits. In the past, tutors who were experts in a particular academic subject were usually hired. Recently tutors have been hired specifically to teach study skills. It is quite feasible that a regular classroom teacher would have the ability to analyze a child's study problems and teach appropriate habits. However, there are many teachers trained in special education who have developed special skills in teaching good study habits. Specifically, teachers trained to work with children with learning disabilities have been very effective tutors. This occurs since they have training and experience in pinpointing learning strengths and weaknesses. Similarly, there are psychologists who are experts in learning who can provide psychoeducational testing and appropriate remediation. A psychologist's services would be clearly indicated if the cause of poor study skills was primarily psychological in nature.

Another method used by mental health professionals is hypnosis. This will be briefly described here for your information. However, it should be clear that parts of the technique involve the use of "suggestion" and could be partially adapted by parents. Many of the techniques described have been used successfully without hypnotic induction. If there is some desire to improve, positive hypnotic suggestions can improve schoolwork. Hypnosis does not work when the suggested behavior is against someone's will. A prevailing belief is that hypnosis aids relaxation and enables children to focus better. Typically, concentration is taught and distractions are to be disregarded. Under hypnosis, the suggestion is to think only about what is being studied. The individual is told to breathe deeply, feel calm, relax, and only pay attention to the material. "You will study longer and remember more." Suggestions are also made about feeling good when you read, and that it is okay to make mistakes. The focus is always on wanting to study and enjoying the process. Students are often told to outline work and study efficiently. They will only be interested in their work. They are told that they will quickly understand and will remember since the material will leave a lasting impression. The suggestion is that individuals will be totally absorbed in study and not want to interact with anyone. Before studying, they are often told to relax for a few minutes. They will develop the habit of studying for at least 2 hours every day.

Important to mention here is the use of hypnosis for test anxiety. This follows logically since one significant goal of study is to do well on examinations. Under hypnosis, students are told to read test questions carefully and answer them fully. They are often told to concentrate on passing rather than on getting high grades. This frequently leads to a more relaxed test taking attitude. They are told to read all of the questions and start, that "the information will come to you." The suggestion is also made that they will complete the test and feel very good. A common theme is to not try to force memory, but to focus, relax, and let the recall emerge.

Case Report

A 14-year-old boy, who had been in high school for 4 months, was unable to study effectively. He lost his concentration quickly, forgot much of the material, and felt very tense and inadequate. Six therapy sessions were sufficient to change the vicious cycle of poor study and increasing feelings of inadequacy and worry. Simple muscle relaxation was taught. He practiced relaxing at home and was told to lie down and relax for 3 minutes before studying. Study was to take place only at his desk. If he became distracted or couldn't study, he was to briefly leave and then come back. He recorded the amount of time studied by using a stop watch. The watch was stopped if he left his desk for any reason, and then restarted upon his return. He liked the idea of self-reward as his study time and effectiveness improved. His desired feelings of independence were boosted by letting him decide what the rewards would be and when they would take place. For example, he decided to watch television only on those evenings when he had reached the goal he set for himself.

He was very responsive to the explanation of the SQ3R method of study. He wrote down the key concepts of survey, question, read, review, and recite. He had been reading his assignments with no note taking, underlining, or asking key questions. Particularly helpful to him was the skimming of material and reading to answer key questions which he posed (from headings and topics he or the teacher deemed significant).

Books for Parents about Poor Study Habits

Cahoon, Owen W., Price, Alvin H., and Scoresby, A. Lynn.: *Parents and the Achieving Child.* Brigham Young University Press, Provo, Utah (1979).

McWhirter, J.J.: *The Learning Disabled Child: A School and Family Concern.* Research Press, Champaign, IL (1977).

Robinson, F.: *Effective Study.* Harper & Row, New York (1970).

Strong, Ruth: *Guided Study and Homework.* National Education Association, Washington, D.C. (1968).

Voeks, Virginia: *On Becoming an Educated Person.* W.B. Saunders, Philadelphia (1970).

Zifferblatt, Steven M.: *Improving Study and Homework Behaviors*. Research Press, Champaign, IL (1970).

Books for Children about Poor Study Habits

Cleary, Beverly Bunn: *Mitch and Amy*. William Morrow, West Caldwell, NJ (1967). Ages 9–11.

Nine-year-old twins both have school difficulties. Amy does poorly in arithmetic and Mitch has reading problems. Amy discovers a book which engages Mitch's interest. Both improve their problems while in fourth grade.

Staton, Thomas F.: 1) *How to Study.* 2) *Programmed Study Technique*. American Guidance Service, Circle Pines, MN (1964). Teen-agers.

Students in grades 7 to 12 are helped to develop more effective study habits.

References

1. Harris, Mary B. and Ream, Fred: "A program to improve study habits of high-school students." *Psychology in the Schools* 9: (1972), pp. 325–330.
2. National Assessment of Educational Progress. *Newsletter* 11: (1978), pp. 1–3.
3. Millman, Howard L.: "Psychoneurological learning and behavior problems: The importance of treatment coordination." *Journal of Clinical Child Psychology* 3: (1974), pp. 26–30.
4. Broden, M., Hall, R.V., and Mitts, B.: "The effect of self-recording on the classroom behavior of two eighth grade students." *Journal of Applied Behavior Analysis* 4: (1971), pp. 191–200.
5. Robinson, F.P.: *Effective Study.* Harper & Row, New York (1970).
6. Beneke, William M. and Harris, Mary B.: "Teaching self-control of study behavior." *Behavior Research and Therapy* 10: (1972), pp. 35 –41.
7. Greiner, Jerry M. and Karoly, Paul: "Effects of self-control training on study activity and academic performance: An analysis of self-monitoring, self-reward, and systematic-plan-

ning components.'' *Journal of Counseling Psychology* 23: (1976), pp. 495–502.

8. Ayllon, Teodoro and Roberts, Michael D.: ''Eliminating discipline problems by strengthening academic performance.'' *Journal of Applied Behavior Analysis* 7: (1974), pp.71–76.

Index

⊘ **SIGNET** (0451)

BRINGING UP BABY

☐ **HOW TO DISCIPLINE WITH LOVE: From Crib to College by Dr. Fitzhugh Dodson.** A leading authority on child-rearing offers parents a flexible program of positive reinforcement for teaching children desirable behavior at every stage of development. (153421—$4.50)

☐ **HOW TO FATHER by Dr. Fitzhugh Dodson.** An authority on child care guides the new father through all stages of child's growth—from infancy through adolescence—instructing him on discipline, teaching, affecting his child's moods, developing his interests, and forming a loving and positive child-father relationship. Appendices, illustrations and index included. (154363—$4.95)

☐ **HOW TO PARENT by Dr. Fitzhugh Dodson.** Based on a common sense combination of love and discipline, Dr. Dodson's approach to child-raising offers a creative, complete, and mutually enjoyable program for helping parents guide their children through the all-important years from birth to five. (119088—$3.95)

☐ **HOW TO REALLY LOVE YOUR CHILD by Ross Campbell, M.D.** This famed psychiatrist who has helped countless parents with "problem children" tells how to successfully communicate your love for your child even in times of stress and when discipline is necessary. Clearly written, with a wealth of case histories. (153464—$3.50)

☐ **DR. MOM: A Guide to Baby and Child Care by Marianne Neifert, M.D., with Anne Price and Nancy Dana.** Move over Dr. Spock! Here comes Dr. Mom—the up-and-coming authority on child rearing! This indispensible reference covers every aspect of parenting from conception to age five, including: understanding medical symptoms, discipline, daycare, non-sexist child rearing and much more! (148509—$4.95)

*Price slightly higher in Canada

**Buy them at your local
bookstore or use coupon
on next page for ordering.**

⊘ **SIGNET**   ⊜ **ONYX**   ⊕ **MENTOR**

EXPLORING THE MIND

(0451)

☐ **THE AUTOBIOGRAPHY OF A SCHIZOPHRENIC GIRL, With An Analytic Interpretation By Marguerite Sechehaye.** In perfect, almost painfully vivid language, a schizophrenic known only as "Renee" recreates her journey into the depths of mental illness, and her step-by-step return to sanity. A magnificent example of human survival and triumph. Foreword by Frank Conroy.   (136217—$3.95)*

☐ **VIVIENNE: THE LIFE AND SUICIDE OF AN ADOLESCENT GIRL by John E. Mack and Holly Hickler.** In her own words and the words of those who loved her—the searingly true story of a girl who might have been saved.... "Moving sensitive, insightful."—*Washington Post*. A *New York Times* Notable Book.   (624335—$3.95)*

☐ **THIS STRANGER MY SON by Louise Wilson.** A mother's moving, harrowing story of her struggle to save her deeply disturbed child. "Mrs. Wilson's account transcends the noisome details, cuts through the outer garments to the struggling spirit of the youngster beneath.—Thomas Lask, *The New York Times*   (113012—$2.50)

*Prices slightly higher in Canada

Buy them at your local bookstore or use this convenient coupon for ordering.

NEW AMERICAN LIBRARY,
P.O. Box 999, Bergenfield, New Jersey 07621

Please send me the books I have checked above. I am enclosing $_____ (please add $1.00 to this order to cover postage and handling). Send check or money order—no cash or C.O.D.'s. Prices and numbers are subject to change without notice.

Name_____

Address_____

City_____State_____Zip Code_____
Allow 4-6 weeks for delivery.
This offer is subject to withdrawal without notice.

⊘ SIGNET   ⊕ MENTOR

HELPFUL GUIDES

(0451)

☐ **FEELING GOOD: The New Mood Therapy by David Burns, M.D.** This one-of-a-kind integrated approach to depression introduces the principles of Cognitive Therapy, which illustrate that by changing the way we think we can alter our moods and get rid of depression. (146905—$4.95)

☐ **INTIMATE CONNECTIONS by David D. Burns, M.D.** In this breakthrough book, Dr. David Burns, author of the bestselling *Feeling Good*, applies the proven principles of Cognitive Therapy to eliminating the negative thinking and low self-esteem that cause loneliness and shyness, and shows you how to make close friends and find a loving partner.

(148452—$4.95)*

☐ **BORN TO WIN: Transactional Analysis with Gestalt Experiments by Muriel James and Dorothy Jongeward.** This landmark bestseller has convinced millions of readers that they were **Born to Win!** "Enriching, stimulating, rewarding . . . for anyone interested in understanding himself, his relationships with others and his goals."—*Kansas City Times*

(141954—$4.50)*

☐ **UNDERSTANDING YOURSELF by Dr. Christopher Evans.** An interesting collection of questionnaires, tests, quizzes and games, scientifically designed by a team of psychologists to offer a greater self-awareness. Photographs and illustrations included. (134532—$4.95)

☐ **OVERCOMING PROCRASTINATION by Albert Ellis, Ph.D. and William J. Knaus, Ed.D.** The scientifically proven techniques of Rational-Motive Therapy are applied to procrastination (delaying tactics, frustration, and self-disgust). Examines the causes of procrastination, and the links between procrastination and obesity, drugs, depression, and sexual dysfunction, and other personality and health problems.

(152085—$3.95)

*Prices slightly higher in Canada

**Buy them at your local
bookstore or use coupon
on next page for ordering.**

⊘ SIGNET (0451)

BABY CARE

☐ **YOU AND YOUR BABY: A Guide to Pregnancy, Birth and the First Year by Dr. Frederick W. Rutherford.** A practical hand-book for new parents on pregnancy, preparation for the baby, and the infant's emotional and physical development during the first year. (152905—$4.95)

☐ **THE MOTHERS' AND FATHERS' MEDICAL ENCYCLOPEDIA by Virginia E. Pomeranz, M.D., and Dodi Schultz.** From infancy through adolescence, an all-inclusive reference book designed to give you fast, accurate, and vital information when you need it most. Fully illustrated. (255376—$9.95)

☐ **POSITIVE PARENTING: HOW TO RAISE A HEALTHIER AND HAPPIER CHILD (from birth to three years) by Alvin N. Eden, M.D.** This book by a famous pediatrician tells you in words you can understand all that you can expect from your child during these key years—and all that your child can expect from you. (146409—$3.95)*

☐ **PREGNANCY, BIRTH AND FAMILY PLANNING by Alan F. Gutamacher, M.D.,** The most comprehensive, comforting, and fact-filled guide ever published—newly revised and updated for today's expectant parents. (147626—$4.95)*

*Price slightly higher in Canada

Buy them at your local bookstore or use this convenient coupon for ordering.

NEW AMERICAN LIBRARY,
P.O. Box 999, Bergenfield, New Jersey 07621

Please send me the books I have checked above. I am enclosing $_____ (please add $1.00 to this order to cover postage and handling). Send check or money order—no cash or C.O.D.'s. Prices and numbers are subject to change without notice.

Name_____

Address_____

City_____State_____Zip Code_____

Allow 4-6 weeks for delivery.
This offer is subject to withdrawal without notice.

There's an epidemic with 27 million victims. And no visible symptoms.

It's an epidemic of people who can't read.

Believe it or not, 27 million Americans are functionally illiterate, about one adult in five.

The solution to this problem is you... when you join the fight against illiteracy. So call the Coalition for Literacy at toll-free 1-800-228-8813 and volunteer.

Volunteer Against Illiteracy. The only degree you need is a degree of caring.

THIS AD PRODUCED BY MARTIN LITHOGRAPHERS
A MARTIN COMMUNICATIONS COMPANY